FREEDOM WITH RESPONSIBILITY

The Social Market Economy in Germany, 1918–1963

Freedom
with Responsibility

The Social Market Economy in Germany,
1918–1963

A. J. Nicholls

CLARENDON PRESS · OXFORD

*This book has been printed digitally and produced in a standard specification
in order to ensure its continuing availability*

OXFORD
UNIVERSITY PRESS

Great Clarendon Street, Oxford OX2 6DP

Oxford University Press is a department of the University of Oxford.
It furthers the University's objective of excellence in research, scholarship,
and education by publishing world-wide in

Oxford New York

Auckland Bangkok Buenos Aires Cape Town Chennai
Dar es Salaam Delhi Hong Kong Istanbul Karachi Kolkata
Kuala Lumpur Madrid Melbourne Mexico City Mumbai Nairobi
São Paulo Shanghai Taipei Tokyo Toronto

Oxford is a registered trade mark of Oxford University Press
in the UK and in certain other countries

Published in the United States
by Oxford University Press Inc., New York

ISBN 0-19-820852-9

Antony Rowe Ltd., Eastbourne

For
Alex, Caroline,
and Isabel

Preface for the Paperback Edition

This book was first published in the early years of a newly united Germany. Its theme, however, has not become less relevant during the period since 1994. Concern over Germany's apparently faltering economic performance, especially in relation to unemployment and public indebtedness, is often expressed as criticism of the 'social market economy'. I hope my book will demonstrate that the real social market economy of Ludwig Erhard was not an uneasy mixture of laissez-faire and a welfare state. It was an attempt to maximize enterprise and competition whilst retaining the state's responsibility for the creation of a decent society. Not only Germany, but Europe in general could learn a lot from the concepts of Ludwig Erhard, and it is hoped that this book will help to draw the attention of a new generation to the views he expressed and implemented successfully between 1948 and 1963.

A. J. Nicholls
Oxford, June 1999

Acknowledgements

IT is my pleasant duty to acknowledge the help I have received when writing this book from a number of individuals and institutions. The Social Science Research Council (now the Economic and Social Research Council), the British Academy, and the Modern History Faculty of Oxford University assisted me to make a number of visits to archives in Germany. I have been given unstinting help by the directors and staff of many research institutions. First and foremost I should mention Dr Karl Hohmann, director of the Ludwig-Erhard-Stiftung, Bonn, whose assistance, with that of his colleagues, was invaluable. The Konrad-Adenauer-Stiftung in St Augustin, the Friedrich-Ebert Stiftung in Bonn, the Bundesarchiv in Koblenz, the *Zwischenarchiv* in Hangelar, the Walter-Eucken-Institut in Freiburg im Breisgau, the Institut für Zeitgeschichte in Munich, the Theodor-Heuss-Akademie in Gummersbach, and the university archives in Münster have all been exceedingly helpful, and I should not neglect to thank the staff at the Public Record Office in London.

I have received wise advice and encouragement from many scholars whose expertise far outreaches my own: Dieter Grosser, Hans-Peter Schwarz, Carl-Christoph Schweitzer, and Christian Watrin have been particularly helpful and I thank them most warmly, although they will probably not agree with everything I have to say in this book. I should also like to say a special word of thanks to Hans Joachim Voth for his helpful suggestions and comments. Like all others mentioned, he bears no responsibility for any faults this book may contain.

Lastly, I am happy to acknowledge my enormous debt to the Warden and Fellows of St Antony's College, who have supported me through the lengthy gestation of this book, and I thank my family for their forbearance and encouragement.

A.J.N.

Contents

List of Tables

Abbreviations

ASM	Aktionsgemeinschaft Soziale Marktwirtschaft (Action Group for the Realization of the Social Market Economy)
ASU	Arbeitsgemeinschaft Selbstständiger Unternehmer (Working Association of Independent Businessmen)
BA	Bundesarchiv (Federal German Archives, Koblenz)
BAZA	Bundesarchiv: Zwischenarchiv (Federal German Archives, Hangelar)
BDA	Bundesvereinigung der Deutschen Arbeitgeberverbände (Federation of German Employers' Associations)
BDI	Bundesverband der Deutschen Industrie (Federal Association of German Industry)
BHE	Bund der Heimatvertriebenen und Entrechteten (Refugees' Party)
BICO	Bipartite Control Office
CDU	Christlich-Demokratische Union (Christian Democratic Union)
CSU	Christlich-Soziale Union (Christian Social Union)
DDP	Deutsche Demokratische Partei (German Democratic Party)
DGB	Deutscher Gewerkschaftsbund (German Trade Union Federation)
DIHT	Deutscher Industrie- und Handelstag (German Association of Industry and Commerce)
DVP	Deutsche Volkspartei (German People's Party)
ECA	Economic Co-operation Agency
ECSC	European Coal and Steel Community
EEC	European Economic Community
EPU	European Payments Union
FATM	Forschungsstelle für allgemeine und textile Marktwirtschaft an der Universität Münster (Research Unit for General and Textile Market Economy at the University of Münster)
FDP	Freie Demokratische Partei (Free Democratic Party)
FES	Friedrich-Ebert-Stiftung
FOSIWO	Forschungsinstitut für Siedlungs- und Wohnungswesen der Westfälischen Universität zu Münster (Research Institute for Settlement and Housing Policy, University of Münster)
FRG	Federal Republic of Germany
GATT	General Agreement on Tariffs and Trade
GDR	German Democratic Republic

IAR	International Authority for the Ruhr
IfZG	Institut für Zeitgeschichte
JEIA	Joint Export Import Agency
KAS	Konrad-Adenauer-Stiftung (Konrad Adenauer Foundation)
KPD	Kommunistische Partei Deutschlands (Communist Party of Germany)
LES	Ludwig-Erhard-Stiftung
NL	Nachlaß (personal papers)
NSDAP	Nationalsozialistische Deutsche Arbeiterpartei (National Socialist German Workers' Party)
OECD	Organization for European Co-operation and Development
OEEC	Organization for European Economic Co-operation
PRO	Public Record Office, Kew
PV	Parteivorstand (Party Executive [of SPD])
SED	Sozialistische Einheitspartei Deutschlands (Socialist Unity Party of Germany)
SPD	Sozialdemokratische Partei Deutschlands (Social Democratic Party of Germany)
THA	Theodor-Heuss-Akademie
VfW	Verwaltung für Wirtschaft (the Economics Administration of Bizone, the forerunner of the Federal Economics Ministry)
Waage	The title given to the Gemeinschaft zur Förderung des sozialen Ausgleiches (Association for the Furtherance of Social Compromise). The title refers to 'scales' representing the concept of balance.
WEI	Walter-Eucken-Institut Archive
Wipo	Wirtschaftspolitischer Auschuß (Economic Policy Subcommittee [of SPD])

Introduction

WHEN I began to work on this book in the 1980s, the social market economy was a topic of almost antiquarian interest. The search for a 'middle way' between *laissez-faire* capitalism and collectivist economic systems no longer seemed necessary. On the left, post-Keynesian forms of *dirigisme* were still popular; on the right the doctrines of Friedrich von Hayek were discrediting the concepts of social justice and market regulation. In studying the social market I was therefore concerned with a particular phase in West German history, a phase which seemed to me to be of crucial importance in shaping the political culture of the Federal Republic.

There were, to be sure, many controversial features even in this historical story. How important was Ludwig Erhard's social market economy to Germany's economic recovery after the war? How sincere were the social market economists, either in their support for unfettered competition or in their concern to avoid the social evils associated with nineteenth-century economic liberalism? These questions seemed quite enough to justify a scholarly inquiry into the history of a concept which has all too often been either ignored or misrepresented in Anglo-Saxon countries.

Since November 1989, however, discussion of the social market economy has become a matter of contemporary relevance. With the collapse of Communism in the former Soviet bloc, newly liberated peoples have been seeking an economic formula to lead them from their dispiriting present into a bright new free-enterprise future. On the other hand, many of them have been unhappy to jettison the comforting features of Communism—above all, security of employment and low-priced, if substandard, living accommodation—in order to plunge unprepared into the icy waters of Western-style competition.

In Moscow and other former Communist capitals there has been a struggle between those who advocate a rush into market freedom and the virtual jettisoning of public enterprises, including public services, and those who wish to proceed more slowly.

Idealistic reformers within the socialist system sometimes hankered after a form of liberalized collectivism—'socialism with a human face'. Such a concept is certainly incompatible with the social market economy as it is described in this book. It would be nearer to what Wilhelm Röpke contemptuously described during the Second World War as an 'alcohol-free cocktail'—a bogus market without real competition.[1]

Nevertheless, it is not at all clear that what is actually happening in former Communist countries can really be described as a social market. To take the most obvious example, it was assumed in West Germany in 1990 that the former German Democratic Republic could be incorporated into the Federal Republic with comparative ease. The scenario would be similar to that in West Germany in 1948, when a combination of currency reform and Erhard's economic liberalization produced the famous 'economic miracle'—a journalistic term which Erhard himself always disliked.

There was indeed a currency reform in July 1990, when the Western D-Mark was introduced into what was then still the GDR. Privatization was briskly implemented. East German state enterprises were sold off in large numbers by the rather ominously named Treuhand. Between 1990 and 1992 it disposed of thousands of state undertakings. But the results have not been the same as those experienced in the years 1948–50. Then, West Germany had a huge industrial potential lying underused as the result of an irrational war economy. The infrastructure of a capitalist economy—joint-stock companies, banks, insurance firms, wholesalers and retailers—had all survived the Third Reich, even if some of them were a trifle reluctant to re-enter the hurly-burly of market competition. Above all, there was a fully developed system of commercial law, and enough expertise to operate it effectively. None of these things was true about East Germany, let alone the former Soviet Union, in the early 1990s.

The rapid introduction of free-market capitalism into such a system has led to very serious social problems. To quote an East German jibe, real existing socialism has been replaced by real existing unemployment. Nor do the opportunities presented by a supposedly free market seem very convincing to many East Germans. One British observer of the changes in the former GDR wrote that: 'The old state monopoly looks to the average unemployable East German as being simply replaced by large-scale private monopolies.'[2]

Erhard, whose views on policies to be adopted in the event of German reunification are on record,[3] would certainly have approved

---

[1] Röpke to Eucken, 23 Feb. 1942, BA Rüstow NL, no. 3.

[2] N. Hope, 'The Integration of the DDR and the BRD: The Process So Far', in B. Ashbook and P. P. Hasler, *The New Germany*, i: *Divided or United by a Common European Culture?* (Glasgow, 1992), 39.

[3] See Erhard's article 'Wirtschaftliche Probleme der Wiedervereinigung' of 12 Sept. 1953, referring to hopes for a rapid reunification of Germany at that time. This is repr. in L. Erhard, *Deutsche Wirtschaftspolitik: Der Weg der sozialen Marktwirtschaft* (Düsseldorf, 1962), 225–30.

social market policies lead to initial unemploy.

of a rapid currency reform in East Germany, and of the reintroduction of the free-market mechanism as quickly as possible. It is unlikely that he would have been too worried about unemployment, since in a socialist state, unemployment is camouflaged by the inefficiencies of a command economy, and the period of adjustment is bound to be a painful one.

One might argue that the situation in East Germany in the early 1990s is similar to that in the Federal Republic from 1948 to 1953, when unemployment was high and many complaints were heard about social injustice. It is as well to remember that, as I describe below, the popularity of Erhard himself waned sharply in West Germany in the years following the initial liberalization of the economy. Whereas, in 1949, his social-market slogan helped Adenauer to victory in the first Bundestag elections, by the winter of 1950–1 Erhard's policies had become unpopular, and there was a clamour for a return to the old forms of resource allocation. One purpose of this book is to demonstrate that the victory of the free market in West Germany was by no means a foregone conclusion in the years after currency reform in 1948, and that without Erhard's determination, buttressed by vocal members of the German economics profession, the 'economic miracle' might have faded earlier than it actually did. Yet it was that economic expansion which helped generate growth throughout Western Europe, making the Federal Republic the economic 'locomotive' for Western recovery.

Nevertheless, at the time of writing, the crisis in the former German Democratic Republic appears deeper than that in West Germany after 1948, and it is not clear that the principles of the social market have been implemented there consistently. Erhard himself would probably not have approved of a currency reform which was generous to consumers and crippling in its impact on industrial enterprises. He would have advocated tax concessions for undertakings operating in East Germany.[4] He would also have expected a clear-cut settlement of property rights, without which no free-market system can function effectively, and he would have wanted to give East Germans access to the market and opportunities to compete effectively in it. In West Germany after 1948 the inhabitants had the chance to involve themselves in the competitive economy. The enterprises were up and running, the markets were available, especially after the European Payments Union went into operation and the Korean War increased global demand for German products. Today, it seems much more difficult for

involvement in eco

---

[4] Ibid. 229.

East Germans to gain access to employment. They are being blamed for lack of initiative in a situation where the rules of the game seem designed to obstruct their progress.

In the German case, the wealth of the Federal Republic can doubtless be some guarantee of a decent living-standard, even for those whose jobs have vanished. We can be reasonably hopeful that in a few years the problems of the former GDR will be only a memory. But in other Soviet-bloc countries, and particularly in the former Soviet Union, a return to *laissez-faire* seems to mean the appearance of social evils, such as destitution and homelessness, on a scale unseen in Europe since the nineteenth century. How far is that compatible with the 'social market economy' described in this book?

The key to this question is the weight to be placed on the word 'social' in the social-market-economy formula. It is interesting to note that in Britain there has been relatively little interest in the term, and that politicians who have used it seem vague about its meaning. For Conservatives it has usually meant a justification of *laissez-faire*, with the market itself being regarded as social. By the same token, socialists in Britain, of whom the late Lord Balogh was an early example, took their cue from German social democratic critics of Erhard in the late 1940s, and dismissed the term 'social' as a cosmetic device designed to sweeten the pill of a restored capitalist economy.[5]

Curiously enough, the latter view now seems to be rather widespread in Germany itself. On 18 February 1992, the vice-president of the Bundesbank, Dr Hans Tietmeyer, delivered the Ludwig Erhard Memorial Lecture in the London School of Economics and began by warning his listeners that:

There is hardly any term used to mean so many different things in public discussions as that of the social market economy. All the same, the social market economy is believed by many today to be *the* model *per se* for an economic and social order. It is therefore not surprising that the term is widely misused as a 'Trojan Horse', concealing what are often decidedly interventionist ideas which actually go against the grain of the concept.[6]

Tietmeyer pointed out that Friedrich von Hayek actually regretted that the term 'social market economy' had ever been coined. He apparently

---

[5] T. Balogh, *Germany: An Experiment in 'Planning' by the 'Free' Price Mechanism* (Oxford, 1950). For German social-democratic views on the social market economy, see below, Ch. 12.

[6] H. Tietmeyer, *Economic and Monetary Union: A German Perspective* (European Institute, London School of Economics, and Konrad Adenauer Foundation; London, 1992), 1–2.

saw its value only in the fact that it could be used in post-war Germany to 'make palatable to wider circles the sort of social order for which I am pleading'.[7]

It should be recorded that Dr Tietmeyer then went on to make a number of very sound observations about the social market economy, but the tendency to regard it largely as a public-relations device is widespread in German academic circles. In April 1990, for example, the Ludwig Erhard Foundation organized a conference at the Karl Marx University in Leipzig to spread the word of Erhard's teachings in what was then still the German Democratic Republic. One West German historian, Professor Werner Kaltefleiter, warned his audience that international comparisons had shown that, the more social policy there was, the less economic growth. He went further, and distanced himself from the whole notion of a social market, claiming that the concept had, at most, a propaganda meaning which had been useful in 1948, when the desperate condition of so many Germans had created severe social tensions.[8]

Yet if the term 'social' is just a cosmetic addition to what otherwise is a policy of free enterprise, we should cease to use it altogether. It is a major purpose of this book to demonstrate that the authors of the concept, and those who struggled hard to put it into practice, took the word 'social' seriously, and that the success of West Germany's economy after the catastrophe of the Second World War was due to a happy combination of market freedom and social responsibility.

Furthermore, the market itself was not something which miraculously appeared through a process of benign neglect. It needed a clear legal framework supported by a powerful state to protect it from malpractice and distortion. At the same time it was recognized that public policy was bound to have important effects on the economy, and that governments should tailor their fiscal and monetary policies to assist stability and growth rather than to generate uncertainty and stagnation.

It was one of the stabilizing factors in the political system of the Federal Republic that these principles were accepted by all the major parties by the end of the 1950s. In particular, the Social Democratic Party, which led West Germany's coalition governments in the 1970s and early 1980s, had jettisoned its commitment to socialist economic doctrines, and thereby transformed its political fortunes. From a British

---

[7] Ibid. 2, citing F. A. von Hayek, *Law, Legislation and Liberty*, ii: *The Mirage of Social Justice* (Chicago, 1976), 180. It is worth remembering that von Hayek was consistently critical of the concept of the social market economy.

[8] 'Soziale Marktwirtschaft. Symposion von Ludwig-Erhard-Stiftung und *FAZ* in Leipzig', *Orientierungen zur Wirtschafts- und Gesellschaftspolitik*, 44 (Bonn, June 1990), 75.

perspective, one notes that no such transformation appears to have occurred in the Labour Party, which has rather undertaken a series of tactical retreats without redefining its fundamental values.

This does not mean that the economists described in this book regarded themselves as socialists. But many of them did accept that the socialist critique of capitalism, as it had emerged from the nineteenth century, required an answer which addressed itself to the social problems all too evident in industrial society. Opposed to tyranny and dogmatism of any kind, they persuaded their fellow-countrymen that common sense and respect for the rights of others were the most important attributes of a just society. In doing so, they achieved an economic and political triumph in West Germany, and their example should not be forgotten now that even more daunting tasks of reconstruction face us all—in Europe and elsewhere.

For that reason, I consider that the socio-economic theories discussed below are also of interest to those of us who are fortunate enough to live in Western, 'developed' societies. The arguments in which neo-liberal economists were involved in the 1930s certainly seem relevant, for example, to the contemporary situation in Britain. The problems of mass unemployment and working-class alienation are with us today just as they were during the Great Depression. The fact that terms like 'working class' are no longer fashionable does not alter the social realities created by our economic malaise, as a glance at rising crime-rates will indicate. Indeed, it is depressing that in the 1990s no such fundamental discussion about the nature of the economic system, or ways in which it might be improved, appears to be taking place. Instead, there is a fatalistic acceptance of unemployment and impoverishment as inevitable consequences of an 'efficient' economy. Fatalism of this kind can be extremely dangerous, as the experience of the Weimar Republic showed.

The architects of the social market economy were, of course, mainly concerned to oppose a collectivist—i.e. a Fascist or Marxist—solution to the problem. The latter of these is now comprehensively discredited; there seems some danger that the former may be reappearing. Passivity in the face of social misery was one fault of which the social-market protagonists could not be accused, and for that reason also their careers are of considerable contemporary interest.

Finally, there is one problem of definition which should be mentioned before the narrative begins. This concerns the complicated issue of corporatism. 'Corporatism' is a term used with caution in this book; it has tended to have rather different meanings in different contexts. In general, it refers to any economic system in which corporations of producers collude with the government at the expense of the consumer. It could be objected that this happens in all modern societies. Certainly historians have seen corporatism at work in the Weimar Republic and in the German economy after 1949.[9] Some British Conservative politicians in the 1990s appear to regard any form of consultation between government, employers, and trade unions as a form of corporatism.

It should be pointed out that in Germany before 1945 corporatism had a rather more specific and sinister meaning. It was associated with restrictions on freedom of commerce, guild limitations on individual craftsmen, and the rejection of free trade. The anarchy of individualism was to be eliminated in both the political and the economic sphere. Corporatism tended to be popular with those sections of German society which felt themselves to have lost status or influence as the result of the economic liberalization which had occurred between the period of Napoleonic conquest and German unification in 1871. The concept was that the 'organic' elements in society—the *Stände* or corporations—should come together to represent their legitimate interests and thus eliminate the need for divisive party politics, which were based on greedy individualism.

It is no surprise that Bismarck was enthusiastic about the concept—it offered him a means of marginalizing the Reichstag and weakening the forces of German liberalism, which he despised. He advocated a form of corporate representation of Germany's economic interests—the Economic Council (*Wirtschaftsrat*)—which he hoped could become as important as parliament in decision-making. It would obviously be weighted towards the propertied and established sections of society— the landowners, factory owners, master craftsmen, and merchants— and although labour might have some voice, it would be a feeble one. From an economic point of view, such a body was likely to favour the cosy protection of the status quo rather than free trade and vigorous competition.

Bismarck was unable to achieve his ideal because the parliamentary parties in Germany defended their position too tenaciously,[10] but corporatist ideas continued to flourish on the right in Germany, Austria,

---

[9] There is no space to go into the lengthy historical debate on corporatism. W. Abelshauser's article, 'The First Post-liberal Nation: Stages in the Development of Modern Corporatism in Germany', *European History Quarterly*, 14/3 (July 1984), 285–317, is a helpful introduction to the problem. There are valuable comments about the situation in the early years of the Weimar Republic in C. S. Maier, *Recasting Bourgeois Europe: Stabilization in France, Germany and Italy in the Decade after World War I* (Princeton, NJ, 1988), ch. 1 and pp. 581–92.

[10] Abelshauser, 'The First Post-liberal Nation', 285–95.

and Italy. During the inter-war period they became the main social theory underpinning Fascism. Corporations, it was believed, would knit the community together, whereas parliamentary liberalism divided it. The ultimate disaster to which that form of liberalism would lead was Marxism, with its vision of international class war. Corporatism would overcome such a danger by reconciling workers with their natural leaders—the entrepreneurs, farmers, and craftsmen. By organizing industrial and agricultural production through a system of corporations, unhealthy competition could be avoided, the workers could be given status without responsibility, and the economy could be harnessed to the national interest—an interest usually, but not always, associated with some form of aggressive foreign policy. In Germany and Italy this form of economic organization was to perish in the Second World War. In Franco's Spain it survived until the 1970s.

The neo-liberal theories adumbrated in this book were strongly opposed to any such system. They sought to divorce the state from pressure groups of any kind, whether they represented capital or labour. The task of the state was to set out the rules for market operation and to resist benefits being granted to any vested interests, however politically powerful they might be. But that does not mean that in the real world businessmen and union leaders were expected to behave with Olympian impartiality. Social market economists accepted that individuals and groups would always be seeking special privileges; they simply wanted to set up a system which made this quest more difficult. In their view the law and administration of Germany had been weighted for too long in favour of powerful producers against their less influential competitors—not to mention the consumer.

Doubtless the Germans have not always succeeded in creating such an ideal system—even after 1949. Critics of the Federal Republic's economy today claim that it is still more resistant to foreign penetration than that of many other Western countries.[11] Nevertheless, I do not believe that the West German economy as it emerged in the 1960s could be described as corporatist. One political scientist has defined corporatism thus:

a system of interest representation in which the constituent units are organized into a limited number of singular, compulsory, non-competitive, hierarchically

[11] See, e.g., R. Dahrendorf, 'Was jetzt kommt wird sehr weh tun', in *Die Zeit*, 15 May 1992: 'Anybody who goes out into the world and talks to [foreign] businessmen always hears the same: "Germany? You can't get in there." The corporative network of government, big banks, and big firms is reckoned to be impenetrable.' Perhaps foreign businessmen are right, but we should remember that success always has its critics, especially amongst those whose economic performance has been less than outstanding.

ordered and functionally differentiated categories, recognized and licensed (if not created) by the state and granted deliberate representative monopoly within their respective categories in exchange for observing certain controls on the selection of leaders and articulation of demands and supports.[12]

I cannot see how this definition can be applied to the Federal Republic. Germany's banks may adopt a more benevolent attitude towards long-term investment than do Anglo-Saxon ones; some of the West German *Länder* may have supported firms like BMW in times of crisis,[13] but the pressures of competition have remained. Germany's export-orientated industries have consistently held their own against the tough competition to be found in world markets, and the fact that West Germany developed a political culture more akin to the American model than that of the Wilhelmine Empire or the Weimar Republic has surely not been unimportant in helping the Federal Republic to achieve this success. That political culture owes a good deal to the social market economy.

[12] P. C. Schmitter, 'Still the Century of Corporatism?', *Review of Politics*, 36/1 (Notre Dame, Ind., Jan. 1974), 93–4. This is also cited in S. Reich, *The Fruits of Fascism: Postwar Prosperity in Historical Perspective* (Ithaca, NY, 1990), 46. Reich argues that the West Germans have supported national 'product champions' in the automobile industry to the detriment of American multinationals. It is a fascinating thesis, but one I do not find convincing, since all governments have industrial policies but some of them, like the British, are much less successful than others.

[13] For the salvation of BMW in 1959, see Reich, *Fruits of Fascism*, 254–5.

Prologue

Neo-Liberalism and the Social Market

ON 29 August 1948 Ludwig Erhard told the assembled delegates to the Recklinghausen conference of the Christian Democratic Union (CDU) that he stood for a 'socially committed market economy'.[1] A year later the CDU fought the first elections to the German Bundestag on an economic platform described as the social market economy. This programme was enshrined in the 'Düsseldorf Principles', adopted by the party on 16 July 1949. It sharply rejected state planning and bureaucratic controls, but also opposed the 'free economy' associated with traditional *laissez-faire* liberalism.[2] Conflicts over economic policy played a large part in the election campaign. Erhard's supporters argued that he was liberating the West German people from a straitjacket of controls; their leading socialist opponent denounced Erhard's policy as: 'The fat propaganda balloon of private enterprise filled with the putrid gases of decaying liberalism.'[3]

Politically, at least, Erhard won the argument. He remained in charge of the West German economy until 1963, when he became Federal Chancellor. His period in office was marked by steady economic growth and an impressive rise in per capita income. Yet the programme for which he stood has not always been clearly comprehended by his own countrymen, let alone by outside observers.[4] All too often it has been

---

[1] Konrad-Adenauer-Stiftung/H. Putz (ed.), *Konrad Adenauer und die CDU der britischen Besatzungszone, 1946–1949. Dokumente zur Gründungsgeschichte der CDU Deutschlands* (Bonn, 1975), 658.

[2] Ibid. 866 ff. The German for 'Düsseldorf Principles' is *Düsseldorfer Leitsätze*, which literally translates as 'Düsseldorf Guide-lines'. The real meaning is better conveyed by 'principles' in this context.

[3] P. Weymar, *Konrad Adenauer: The Authorized Biography* (London, 1957), 250.

[4] Although the economic achievements of West Germany have often been described, the intellectual background to them has been less well served. Readers' attention is drawn to the historical sections of the excellent study by D. Grosser, T. Lange, A. Müller-Armack, and B. Neuss, *Soziale Marktwirtschaft: Geschichte, Konzept, Leistung* (2nd edn.; Stuttgart, 1990). Other important works include: G. Ambrosius, *Die Durchsetzung der sozialen Marktwirtschaft in Westdeutschland 1945–49* (Stuttgart, 1977); C. Heusgen, *Ludwig Erhards Lehre von der sozialen Marktwirtschaft: Ursprünge, Kerngehalt, Wandlungen* (Bern, 1981); H. F. Wünsche, *Ludwig Erhards Gesellschafts- und Wirtschaftskonzeption: Soziale Marktwirtschaft als politische Ökonomie* (Stuttgart, 1986). Carlo Motteli, *Licht und Schatten der sozialen Marktwirtschaft: Leitbild und Wirklichkeit der Bundesrepublik Deutschland* (Zurich, 1961) contains useful definitions of the social market economy. See esp. pp. 45–6. For hostile views of the social market economy, see R. Blum, *Soziale Marktwirtschaft: Wirt-*

assumed that Erhard was simply a champion of *laissez-faire*. It is this
aspect of West German economic policies which has appealed to conservative economists and politicians in Anglo-Saxon countries. On the
other hand, Erhard's socialist critics have given little weight to the
'social' aspect of his policies.

Yet the social market economy was not just a slogan cobbled up for
an election campaign. It was a serious attempt by political economists
and others to overcome what they saw as the twin evils of collectivism
and unrestrained *laissez-faire*. It had its roots in controversies which
had burst forth in the inter-war period. Its protagonists were men of
vision and not inconsiderable influence. The purpose of this book is
to explain what the theory of the social market economy was, to examine its intellectual origins, and to estimate its practical influence on
Germany's political culture.

The term 'social market economy' did not actually appear until after
1945. Before then, the intellectual tendency it reflected was sometimes
described by the inelegant term 'neo-liberalism'.[5] Later the expression
'ordo-liberal' was coined to define a particular shade of opinion within
the liberal camp. Liberals are not known for their conformity. Economists rarely agree with one another for very long. It is not surprising,
therefore, that differences of emphasis, and even conflicts of opinion,
are to be found amongst the adherents of the social market economy.
All of those who were still alive in 1948, however, were united in their

schaftspolitik zwischen Neoliberalismus und Ordoliberalismus (Tübingen, 1969) and E. E.
Nawroth, *Die Sozial- und Wirtschaftsphilosophie des Neoliberalismus* (Heidelberg, 1962).

In English, apart from the able study by H. C. Wallich, *Mainsprings of the German
Revival* (New Haven, Conn., 1955), 113–25, which is mainly an attempt to analyse the
development of the German economy, writings on this subject have usually been partisan
or unbalanced. One of the best introductions to the subject in English is C. Watrin, 'The
Principles of the Social Market Economy: Its Origins and Early History', in R. Richter
(ed.), *A Symposium: Currency and Economic Reform. West Germany After World War II*
(*Zeitschrift für die gesamte Staatswissenschaft*, Sonderheft, 135; Tübingen, 1979), 405–25. A
helpful, if somewhat uneven, collection of essays—which includes translations of articles
by architects of the social market economy as well as more recent commentaries—is
presented in two volumes edited by A. Peacock and H. Willgerodt, *Germany's Social
Market Economy: Origins and Evolution*, and *German Neoliberals and the Social Market Economy*
(London, 1989).

[5] Attempts have been made to draw fine distinctions between 'neo-liberalism' or
'ordo-liberalism' and the social market economy. For the former, the overriding objective
was perfect competition protected by the state. This would itself take care of social
needs. Adherents of the social market economy argued that free competition, though
indispensable, was not enough. A decent society required positive measures to enable
individuals to develop their talents and retain their moral integrity. However, these are
nuances of meaning which were not always consistently adhered to, and in this book I
shall use the term 'neo-liberal' to describe all supporters of the social market economy.

support for Ludwig Erhard, and many of them played an active role in trying to implement his views.[6]

Who were the social market economists? Why did they come to think as they did? What efforts did they make to implement their theories?

Most of them formed their opinions in the Weimar Republic, under the impact of two traumatic experiences. The first was the rampant inflation which destroyed Germany's currency in the period between 1918 and 1923, and the second was the Great Depression, which brought with it widespread economic ruin, and victory for Adolf Hitler.

From the point of view of academic economists, these disasters had been due to government policies which had shown either an ignorance of, or a capacity to ignore, the principles upon which sound economies should be based. In the first case—that of inflation—the government had refused to take measures to stabilize the mark until the currency had become completely worthless, despite the fact that the evils of inflation had been clearly apparent for several years and were themselves the legacy of policies adopted during the First World War. So far as the Great Depression was concerned, the obsession with deflationary measures, coupled with nationalist hopes that German austerity would force France and Britain to abolish reparations and countenance German rearmament, had greatly exacerbated the contraction in business activity, thereby increasing unemployment, bankruptcies, and social unrest. Why had German economists been unable to foresee these disasters and propose measures to prevent them?

This was just the question put by the former Prussian Finance Minister in the Weimar Republic, Hermann Höpker-Aschoff, to the Professor of Economics in Münster, Alfred Müller-Armack, when they were walking through the war-damaged Westphalian city in the grey austerity of 1946.[7] Höpker-Aschoff complained that German social science had let the politicians down during the slump and that: 'if only we had had a Keynes at that time, everything would have been different'.

Müller-Armack felt that such charges were unjust because there were indeed German economists who had seen the wrong-headedness of

---

[6] The extent to which social market economic theories were applied in practice, and the importance of their impact on the German economy, is a very controversial subject. It is discussed at length in chapters below. An important survey of Germany's market economy since 1948 is given in H. Giersch, K.-H. Paqué, and H. Schmieding, *The Fading Miracle: Four Decades of Market Economy in Germany* (Cambridge, 1992).

[7] A. Müller-Armack, *Auf dem Weg nach Europa: Erinnerungen und Ausblicke* (Tübingen, 1971), 14–16.

government policies.[8] Yet he had himself experienced the frustration of seeing sound economic practice overridden by 'experts' whose views smacked more of political expediency than scientific principle. In particular his generation of young economists in the 1920s had 'regarded it as a wretched failure on the part of our profession that, influenced by the historicist school of thought, it showed so little capacity to analyse correctly the phenomenon of galloping inflation after 1918'.[9]

It is with the ideas and intellectual development of this generation that this book is concerned, and with their impact on the politics of West Germany after 1945.

---

[8] This view was reinforced by W. Grottkopp in his book *Die Große Krise: Lehren aus der Überwindung der Wirtschaftskrise, 1929/1932* (Düsseldorf, 1964) in which he argued that the theoretical concepts necessary to overcome the economic depression already existed in Germany before 1930 and that when Keynes published his proposals a few years later they were just 'eine neue Form für eine alte Sache'. Müller-Armack refers to this himself in 'Wissenschaft und Wirtschaftspolitik—Erfahrungen im Laufe ihrer Zusammenarbeit' in A. Müller-Armack and H. B. Schmidt (eds.), *Wirtschafts- und Finanzpolitik im Zeichen der sozialen Marktwirtschaft. Festgabe für Franz Etzel* (Stuttgart-Degerloch, 1967), 73. In the 1980s some German economic historians have argued that no effective measures could have been taken to ameliorate the slump anyway, but that was not the view of social market economists. See below, Ch. 2.

[9] Müller-Armack, *Auf dem Wegnach Europa*, 12, and 14–16. See also id., 'Wirtschaftspolitik als Beruf', *Wirtschaftspolitische Chronik*, 1 (Cologne, 1969), 9.

1

Liberal Economics in Crisis: The Weimar Period

'ECONOMIC thought is a political force. It determines and orientates economic and political action.' These words were delivered at the London School of Economics in March 1950 by Walter Eucken, the doyen of German economists.[1] They were among his last public utterances, for he died in his London hotel on 20 March. The statement encapsulates Eucken's unshakeable belief in the importance of his chosen academic subject, and his critical attitude towards many of his German forerunners, who had, in his view, allowed themselves to be intimidated by nationalist politicians and self-interested 'practical' men to such an extent that their discipline had lost its rightful place among the social sciences.

The reasons for this development were, he believed, to be sought in Germany's history. As in most other parts of Europe, traditions of price-fixing and private monopoly were powerful among the Germans. In the late fifteenth and early sixteenth centuries German emperors were dependent on great merchants, like the Fuggers, Welsers, and Hochstetters, for their capital needs, and granted them trading privileges as a reward for cash. Opposition to such monopolistic activities caused the Emperor Charles V to issue an edict at Madrid in 1525 abolishing monopolies and similar restraints on trade, but he evidently took this measure with reluctance and soon ignored it in practice.[2] In the early modern period, economic activity was hedged about with legal restraints and privileges for vested interests. It was only under the influence of reforming administrations in the eighteenth century, the age in which Adam Smith's classical economic theory was developed, that these barriers began to be torn down.

The French Revolution hastened this process throughout Europe. Liberal economists of Eucken's generation may have had reservations

---

[1] W. Eucken, *This Unsuccessful Age (or The Pains of Economic Progress)* (London, 1951), 83.

[2] C. E. Fischer, 'Die Geschichte der deutschen Versuche zur Lösung des Kartell- und Monopol-Problems', *Zeitschrift für die gesamte Staatswissenschaft*, 110 (1954), 431–2.

about political democracy, but they regarded the achievement of free-dom for industrial and commercial enterprises (*Gewerbefreiheit*) as an unmitigated benefit brought by the French Revolution. In the first half of the nineteenth century German liberals had hoped that the unification of their country would be accompanied by the abolition of restraints on industry and trade. To a large extent, this proved to be true. By the time the second German Reich was established, in 1871, the laws of most German states had already been altered to eliminate guild restrictions, limitations on usury, and most restraints on the movement of labour.[3]

This development was not, of course, confined to Germany. The Habsburg monarchy, that curious mixture of dynastic privilege and rational administration, often took the lead in promulgating measures against monopolies, guilds, and cartels. Economic theories stressing the need for strong competition in a free economy remained powerful in Austria after they had tended to fall out of favour in Germany. Some historians have even attributed American antitrust legislation, such as the Sherman Act of 1890, to the influence of Austrian economists.[4]

In Germany, however, a combination of economic difficulties and Bismarck's political skulduggery soon weakened the liberal movement. The collapse of the feverish boom which marked the foundation of the German Empire threatened the existence of many business enterprises after 1873. Nor was this the only reason why the negative aspects of *laissez-faire* capitalism were appreciated at an early stage in Germany. The mushroom growth of heavy industry in areas such as the Ruhr and the Rhineland had produced severe social problems. Industrial-ization seemed to strengthen political movements, such as the Catholic Centre Party or atheist social democracy, which were feared to be subversive of national interests. Furthermore, state paternalism had always been stronger in Germany than in Anglo-Saxon countries. Since German capitalism had to fight for its existence against strongly established competition, especially from Britain, businessmen were much more inclined to seek government protection. The invigorating winds of free trade, so beloved of economic theorists, did not prove so

---

[3] For a general discussion of the liberalization of finance, trade, and industry in the mid-nineteenth cent., see T. S. Hamerow, *The Social Foundations of German Unification: Struggles and Accomplishments* (Princeton, NJ, 1972). See also H. Böhme, *Deutschlands Weg zur Großmacht* (Cologne, 1966) for an excellent account of the relationship between national unification and economic nationalism. For a discussion of the regression towards illiberal and 'corporatist' practices after 1870, including Bismarck's abortive attempts to marginalize the Reichstag by establishing a *Wirtschaftsrat*, a council of corporate bodies, see Abelshauser, 'The First Post-liberal Nation', 285–95.

[4] C. E. Fischer, 'Kartell- und Monopol-Problem', 440.

attractive to those struggling against bankruptcy in the market-place. The defenders of liberal economic doctrines began to be seen as Anglophil academics unversed in the realities of the business world.

The year 1879 saw German commercial policy switch—albeit in a fairly mild manner—from free trade to protection, with duties on grain and iron imports. This was done partly to help Bismarck split the liberals in the Reichstag and partly because it gave him a source of customs revenue virtually free from parliamentary control. Nevertheless, its economic implications were of an illiberal character.

This was summed up by one of Eucken's collaborators in a letter to him on 25 January 1933—less than a week before Hitler took over power in Germany. As the writer put it, Bismarck had

lured the wild beasts of pluralistic economic egoism out of their cage so that they could tear to pieces the liberal parties which were at that moment obstructing him, and which he disliked fundamentally for their positive, idealistic qualities. He succeeded in his intention, and this disaster is still affecting us. The complete collapse of the middle-class parties, which we are experiencing today, is ultimately the dismal consequence of Bismarck's actions at that time.[5]

Hence it was the betrayal of liberal ideals in the economic sphere which ultimately led to the destruction of political liberties—the process was possibly slow, but inevitable. The notion that economic freedom was necessary for political freedom was to be a central theme of neo-liberal arguments after the Second World War.

Protectionism is, as its liberal critics never tire of arguing, like drug addiction: once the first dose has been taken, ever heavier doses are needed to satisfy the patient. In the German case the 'first dose', administered in 1879, looked harmless enough, a duty of only one mark per hundred kilos of wheat or rye. By 1890 this had more than trebled and by 1906 it had doubled again. Heavy industry also enjoyed protection as the result of what free traders regarded as an unholy alliance between big business and so-called *Junker* landowners in eastern Prussia.

At the same time competition was being restricted by the growth of cartels. In a period of economic downturn these were formed amongst manufacturers to keep prices from collapsing. They were justified as 'children of necessity' in a time of crisis.[6] Cartel members bound themselves to sell their products only at artificially fixed prices, and market shares were divided up between them. Such arrangements seemed to

---

[5] A. Rüstow to Eucken, 25 Jan. 1933, BA Rüstow NL, no. 210.
[6] C. E. Fischer, 'Kartell- und Monopol-Problem', 441.

violate the liberal regulations governing trade and industry first issued in 1869, but when the matter was tested at law, the German supreme court, or *Reichsgericht*, adjudged cartel contracts to be legal.

Defenders of economic liberalism subsequently came to see this important decision, handed down on 4 February 1897, as a major disaster for their cause,[7] and certainly cartelization went ahead rapidly in the years which followed. From the 1890s, the academic establishment in the German economics profession—headed by the august figure of Gustav von Schmoller—actually came to favour cartels, despite their obvious incompatibility with the rules of free competition. Schmoller even claimed that cartels were the bearers of economic progress because 'aside from their direct purpose of regulating prices and creating monopolies... and high profits, cartels have created laboratories, libraries, news agencies... which further technical progress'.[8]

Even academics whose views reflected their grounding in classical economics came to believe that cartels, and even monopolies, were the logical outcome of free competition, and could not therefore be harmful. One of the most influential textbooks in the 1930s—Alfred Weber's *Allgemeine Volkswirtschaftslehre*—described cartels as organizations which limited the losses caused by competition and business fluctuations. Exponents of *laissez-faire* pointed out that they were based on an individual's freedom of contract. Nationalists liked them because they symbolized the victory of the strong over the weak.

The extent to which cartels and the relatively mild measures of tariff protection before 1914 really affected the German economy is a matter of enduring controversy. There is no doubt, however, that the climate of national protectionism and the retreat from free-market competition demoralized liberal economists. This was all part of a change in the intellectual climate after 1848. The failure of the liberal revolution in that year and the subsequent victory of Bismarck's cynical *Realpolitik* encouraged an amoral political relativism to creep into intellectual life, particularly at universities. It was associated with the concept of 'historicism', a view according to which events had to be judged in the light of their historical background rather than be measured against fixed moral, political, or economic principles. This theory enabled

---

[7] See, e.g., F. Böhm, 'Das Reichsgericht und die Kartelle', *ORDO: Jahrbuch für die Ordnung von Wirtschaft und Gesellschaft*, 1 (1948), 197 ff.

[8] G. Schmoller, *Grundriß der allgemeinen Volkslehre*, pt. 1 (Leipzig, 1900), 451, cited in F. Blaich, *Kartell- und Monopolpolitik im kaiserlichen Deutschland: Das Problem der Marktmacht im deutschen Reichstag zwischen 1879 und 1914* (Düsseldorf, 1973), 28.

German philosophers, historians, and even classical scholars[9] to enthuse over the triumphs of Bismarck and Moltke without thinking too much about the negative features of a system created by 'blood and iron'. Similarly, economists began to think in terms of national expediency rather than classical economic theory. They tended to take a pessimistic view of the international trading-system, urging the creation of protected markets and sources of supply.

Political parties reflected contemporary attitudes. Those which might have been expected to champion free trade and free competition were the liberal parties. Yet, as Rüstow noted in his remark quoted above, the liberals were ambivalent on this issue. The development of German liberalism had been so confused by nationalist ambitions and social fears that a clear-cut policy on economic matters was difficult to achieve. On the one hand, there were the National Liberals, who put loyalty to a powerful German state before their desire for responsible parliamentary government and even before their quite genuine concern about civil liberties. On the other was a dwindling band of left liberals or 'Progressives', who clove to the notion of individual freedom and minimal government. Even the latter group, whose most prominent representative in the latter part of the nineteenth century was Eugen Richter, were as concerned to protect middle-class property from the encroachments of socialism as they were to protect competition in the domestic market and free trade with the outside world.

This political divide was exacerbated by economic pressures. Free trade had been a staple of liberal thought ever since the writings of Adam Smith had made a powerful impact on intellectual and official circles in Germany towards the end of the eighteenth century. However, it did not suit many important regional groups upon whom the liberals had to rely for their political support. Small and middling farmers in southern and western Germany, for example, had no wish to see their markets swamped by cheap imports. The same objections were shared by businessmen in provincial towns. Such opposition to what was contemptuously called 'Manchesterism' became stronger as the Empire matured.

Certainly the liberal parties were operating in a very much less favourable environment than their counterparts in Britain. There, the triumph of free trade, spearheaded by the Anti-Corn Law League, had preceded a period of boom and tranquillity which anchored the

---

[9] On the development of classical scholarship in Germany in the 19th cent., see the interesting chapter by Walter Jens, 'The Classical Tradition in Germany: Grandeur and Decay', in E. J. Feuchtwanger (ed.), *Upheaval and Continuity: A Century of German History* (London, 1973), 73–6.

concept of cheap food in the popular imagination. Nor were British liberals troubled by the existence of a democratic franchise, because such a thing did not appear in the United Kingdom until after the First World War. In Germany, on the other hand, Reichstag elections were fought on manhood suffrage. This gave votes to masses of people unlikely to appreciate middle-class intellectuals' enthusiasm for the invigorating effect of market forces on incompetent producers and unproductive workers. Whereas in Britain in 1914 the Labour Party was a trade-union pressure-group dependent for its influence on the existence of a Liberal government, in Germany the 1912 Reichstag elections confirmed that the apparently revolutionary Social Democrats (SPD) were the largest party in the Reich. The Roman Catholic Centre came in second place, and the National Liberals were an unconvincing third. It was small wonder that they did not see it as their task to proselytize for free trade and unhampered competition, especially since few of their leaders actually believed in them. 'The Economy' was a matter for hard-headed businessmen who knew what they were doing.

As for the left or progressive liberals, they were even smaller in numbers than their more nationalist counterparts. If there was to be a left-wing alliance in Germany, the progressive liberals would have to be junior partners to Social Democracy. It was not surprising that liberals who felt concern about the social evils accompanying rapid industrialization should think in terms of seeking compromise with reformist socialists. One strident, though not always consistent, voice urging an opening to the left for German liberalism belonged to Friedrich Naumann. He developed views which were described as 'social liberalism', although in truth they were more nearly a form of nationalist, Protestant paternalism. Humane working-conditions and worker participation would lead to a compromise between industrial workers and capital. But he did not envisage that improving the market mechanism or increasing competition might in themselves bring social benefits. Instead, the proletariat and the entrepreneurs would be united by their nationalism in a common enterprise. Their combined power would supplant that of aristocrats and Prussian landowners.[10]

One area where this new attitude was most marked was in the liberal attitude towards competition and restraints on trade. Although

[10] For a good account of Naumann's ideas, see P. Theiner, *Sozialer Liberalismus und deutsche Weltpolitik: Friedrich Naumann im Wilhelminischen Deutschland* (Baden-Baden, 1983), esp. sect. 3. See also P. G. Beckerath and A. Gröppler, 'Der Begriff der sozialen Verantwortung bei Friedrich Naumann', *Preisschriften und Abhandlungen der Friedrich-Naumann-Stiftung*, 1 (Bonn, 1962), 35–6.

some liberals were ready to control monopoly enterprises, relatively few of them seemed particularly worried about cartels, which were accepted as 'a fact of economic life'.[11] Many on the left of the liberal movement were impressed by the shift away from Adam Smith's view of open markets towards a form of 'organized' capitalism.

Lujo Brentano, a respected liberal economist and a warm admirer of Naumann, said in 1904: 'We still speak as though we live in an age of economic freedom [*Gewerbefreiheit*] and competition. This is an example of how our past experiences hinder our perception and judgment of the world around us. Today, economic freedom and competition belong to the past. We live in an age of increasingly expanding monopoly.'[12]

Businessmen, too, often preferred to seek help from the state rather than rely on their own competitive ability. There was, of course, no unanimity of view in the business world in Germany. Even industry was divided over tariff policies. Large firms often tried to obtain advantages from the state through direct official contacts or through the lobbying of their powerful trade-associations. Although entrepreneurs resented interference in their own businesses, there was little of the gut rejection of state action common among Anglo-Saxon businessmen.

To take two prominent examples, Hugo Stinnes, the Ruhr coal and steel magnate, and Walther Rathenau, the head of the major electrical company, Allgemeine Elektrizitäts-Gesellschaft (AEG), had no love lost for each other, and their enterprises exemplified different economic interests—Stinnes the old-established 'smoke-stack' industries and Rathenau the newer, export-orientated, scientifically based enterprises in which Germany had established a commanding position. Yet neither of these men wished to see a genuinely open market. Stinnes and other Ruhr magnates looked to protective tariffs and price-fixing through cartels; Rathenau seems to have preferred a market organized by the state for businessmen's benefit. Neither was advocating the sovereignty of the consumer.

These tendencies were greatly strengthened by the experience of the First World War, in which the economy was partly militarized. Measures of economic mobilization were carried out with scant regard for market forces. The expansion of the fiduciary issue and government debt paved the way for post-war inflation. The Reich Economics Office was influenced by Rathenau's concepts of a type of managed capitalism (*Gemeinwirtschaft*) in which state officials would work with industrialists to control the economy. Industrial production boards established in

---

[11] J. J. Sheehan, *German Liberalism in the Nineteenth Century* (Chicago, 1978), 257.
[12] Ibid. 257.

war industries seemed to foreshadow a kind of corporatist management of the economy, in which industrialists and trade-union representatives would be able to arrange matters at the expense of the consumer. In fact, German trade unions were much weaker than their British counterparts, even though they had gained in membership during the later stages of the war. As for the employers, most of them disliked state interference and wanted to be free of it.

When, in the autumn of 1918, it became clear that the war was lost and that Germany was threatened with revolution, the leaders of heavy industry struck a bargain with the trade unions, the so-called Stinnes-Legien agreement, signed on 15 November 1918. The unions achieved recognition as bargaining partners, and the employers conceded the eight-hour working day. On the other hand, by accepting the agreement, the unions effectively conceded that the ownership and management of industry should not be the object of revolutionary experiments.

The November Revolution of 1918 ushered in a short period of political democracy in Germany, but there was no liberalization of the German economy. On the contrary, the revolutionary period produced various abortive schemes for the socialization of industry. Of more lasting significance was the establishment of the Reich Ministry of Economics, an institution with *dirigiste* tendencies which were encouraged in the early 1920s by both trade unions and big business. A Central Working Association (*Zentralarbeitsgemeinschaft* or ZAG) was set up, representing the industrial employers' associations and trade unions.[13]

The operations of the ZAG were largely futile, and it brought the trade unions no lasting benefits. It fell apart in 1924. However, it did add weight to the clamour of producer interests which hamstrung the policies of weak Republican coalitions in the early 1920s. Since both

---

[13] For a discussion of the relationship between different sections of industry in the first decades of the 20th cent., see H. Pogge von Strandmann, 'Widersprüche im Modernisierungsprozeß Deutschlands: Der Kampf der verarbeitenden Industrie gegen die Schwerindustrie', in D. Stegmann, B.-J. Wendt, P.-C. Witt (eds.), *Industrielle Gesellschaft und politisches System: Beiträge zur politischen Sozialgeschichte. Festschrift für Fritz Fischer* (Bonn, 1978), 225–40. For the foundation of ZAG, see H.-A. Winkler, *Von der Revolution zur Stabilisierung: Arbeiter und Arbeiterbewegung in der Weimarer Republik, 1918 bis 1924* (Berlin, 1984), 75–9. The Reich Economics Ministry did try, with some success, to improve the statistical information available relating to the German economy, and its support for public-expenditure projects may have been helpful in easing the problems of the demobilization period. See P.-C. Witt, 'Bemerkungen zur Wirtschaftspolitik in der "Übergangswirtschaft" 1918–1919: Zur Entwicklung von Konjunkturbeobachtung und Konjunktursteuerung in Deutschland', in Stegmann et al. (eds.), *Industrielle Gesellschaft*, 79–96.

sides of industry would benefit from expansion and increased employment, they accepted the inflation of the money supply. Employers were able to pay higher nominal wages, even though their real value was immediately eroded by rising prices.

All this contributed to the growth of inflation, although it was by no means its sole cause. It had first been fostered by the policies of the imperial government when funding the war. The Weimar Republic took over a hugely swollen public debt, which was then exacerbated by the need to support war pensioners and by the reparations demands of the Allies. Serious attempts at tax reform by the Reich Finance Minister, Matthias Erzberger, were undermined by tax evasion and a virulently hostile nationalist opposition. Erzberger was forced to resign in 1920 and was murdered the following year.

From then on, public finances were effectively propped up by the printing-presses of the Reichsbank, which poured forth increasing numbers of marks. The bank was independent of government control, and refused to commit its own gold reserves to support a programme of stabilization. In this it had the backing of industrialists' associations, using the argument that, without a reduction in Allied reparations demands, no solution to Germany's economic problems would be possible. Inflation was blamed on the unfavourable trade-balance supposedly caused by reparations. Needless to say, this was a gross oversimplification.[14]

After the Franco-Belgian occupation of the Ruhr in January 1923, and the disastrous attempt to fund passive resistance, the mark collapsed completely and money became worthless. By the summer of that year there was a serious shortage of liquidity, the economy was beginning to seize up, and the political system faced threats from the left and the right. The Communists were planning a revolution and in November 1923 Hitler carried out his abortive beer-hall Putsch in Munich. The Republic survived, however. A great coalition under Gustav Stresemann initiated measures which eventually led to stabilization, and 1924 saw the introduction of a new currency, the Reichsmark.

It should be noted, however, that this victory over inflation did not generate a wave of enthusiasm for the Republican regime. Rather the inflation itself was blamed on the new Republic. As for the free-market mechanism, that had been operating even at the time of hyperinflation in the summer of 1923, so there was no sense of liberation when the new currency was introduced. On the contrary, stabilization brought drastic cuts in public spending and large-scale unemployment. Nor did

[14] Maier, *Recasting Bourgeois Europe*, 296–300.

it do anything to restore the savings wiped out in the previous decade. Relief over the reappearance of a stable currency was soured by resentment at reparations payments accepted under the Dawes Plan, and by a belief that particular sections of society had benefited from war and inflation, whereas the most deserving citizens had been ruined. Hence the new currency, the Reichsmark, did not become a symbol of hope and optimism like the D-Mark in West Germany after June 1948.

After the stabilization of the currency, the tendency towards cartelization in German industry, designed to shield established firms from competition, was intensified. In 1924 the organization representing the interests of heavy industry was able to come to an agreement with its counterpart in the consumer-goods sector. The result was the acceptance by the latter of even more comprehensive cartel arrangements, some of which extended beyond Germany's frontiers.[15] Protectionism was a knee-jerk reaction in business circles.

The humiliating terms imposed on Germany by the Versailles Treaty in June 1919 stimulated politicians, and even economists, to look at the country's financial and economic problems from a nationalistic rather than a purely professional viewpoint. It is true that protectionist trade-policies had to be temporarily abandoned when the treaty forbade Germany to erect tariff barriers against her former enemies, but that was hardly calculated to win friends for free trade in Germany. When, in 1925, the treaty restraints lapsed, protectionism was once again on the agenda. Among the Left and the Right in Germany, therefore, there was a tendency to dismiss or ignore the teachings of the classical economists, and seek solutions either in the prescriptions of Marxist class-war and millenarian socialism or in those of economic nationalism.

Tariffs were not the only form of state support sought by business interests in the Weimar period. The upheavals of war and revolution, including losses of German territory, most particularly to Poland, did cause genuine problems for many German firms, especially those of medium size. They asked for, and often received, state subsidies to help them survive. Even after the post-war difficulties had subsided, many businesses still claimed state help, either in the form of subsidies or, after a Reichstag decision against them in 1927, state guarantees for private loans. The larger German states, like Prussia, and the municipalities also subsidized some private businesses which seemed vital to local employment.

---

[15] For the 'AVI' agreement between the industrialists' associations, see U. Nocken, 'Corporatism and Pluralism in Modern German History', in Stegmann *et al.* (eds.), *Industrielle Gesellschaft*, 49. 'AVI' stood for *Arbeitsgemeinschaft der Eisenverarbeitenden Industrie*— the association representing the interests of the metal-working industry.

The eastern regions of Prussia—economically the most unhelpful environment for industrial development—were often targets for subsidies. Ship-building, motor-car production, and railway workshops were among the most favoured candidates for state help. As a result, German motor-car manufacturing lagged behind that of the USA in production techniques, while good money was spent propping up inefficient enterprises. One automobile firm in Elbing in East Prussia was supported by grants and government contracts to the tune of millions of marks before the slump of 1930 put a stop to further efforts on its behalf. Even the industrial employers' association, the *Reichsverband der deutschen Industrie* (RDI), complained about the high level of government subsidies, referring to it as 'cold socialization'. Nevertheless, industry still sought government help whenever it could get it, and political influence was exerted to that end.[16]

Indeed, the revolution of November 1918 which overthrew the Wilhelmine Empire did not improve matters so far as liberal economists were concerned. It was true that a new and apparently much larger successor to the left-wing progressives appeared in the shape of the Democratic Party or DDP. On the other hand, aspirations towards a united German liberal movement failed when the former National Liberal leader, Gustav Stresemann, formed his own German People's Party, or DVP.

The Democratic Party performed well in the elections to the German National Assembly in January 1919. Nevertheless, it did not feel able to espouse a confident and consumer-orientated liberal economic policy. The influence of business pressure-groups within the party structure was too great for that,[17] as was the overriding influence of nationalism. Since, under the Versailles Treaty, Germany was temporarily forbidden to protect her markets, the restoration of tariff barriers became a symbol of national sovereignty.

Naumann's influence on the DDP in its early days can be gauged by the fact that he was elected its chairman by the DDP congress in July 1919, defeating the candidate of the party's professional caucus, a follower of Eugen Richter. Naumann's socio-economic ideas—'far removed from Manchesterism'—were certainly reflected in the Demo-

---

[16] F. Blaich, ' "Garantierter Kapitalismus": Subventionspolitik und Wirtschaftsordnung in Deutschland zwischen 1925 und 1932', *Zeitschrift für Unternehmensgeschichte*, 22/1 (Wiesbaden, 1977), 50–70. See also H. James, 'Economic Reasons for the Collapse of the Weimar Republic', in I. Kershaw (ed.), *Weimar: Why Did German Democracy Fail* (London, 1990), 30–57.

[17] L. Albertin, *Liberalismus und Demokratie am Anfang der Weimarer Republik: Eine vergleichende Analyse der Deutschen Demokratischen Partei und der Deutschen Volkspartei* (Düsseldorf, 1972), esp. ch. 3.

cratic Party's programme, even though he himself was dead by the time it was promulgated. Greater Germany and colonial possessions were as important in this context as the control of overmighty economic subjects, and much more important than free trade.[18]

From the outset, the ambivalence of the Democratic Party's economic programme confused its supporters. Adopted in December 1919, it certainly rejected socialism by claiming that 'general nationalization [*Verstaatlichung*] would mean a deadly bureacratization of the economy and a fateful reduction in its output'.[19] It supported private property and praised the initiative of the entrepreneur, but it made no mention of competition, the free-market mechanism, or free trade. Quite apart from the fact that liberals at this time preferred to stress Germany's nationalist aspirations and blamed economic problems on the war or the Treaty of Versailles, their own perceived constituency was such that no consensus could be achieved except on the basis of negative preferences.

The left wing wished to combine social with political democracy, even though they denied espousing socialism. They seemed to favour some sort of controlled economy, and certainly supported co-determination in industry, and state arbitration in labour disputes. On the other hand, more conventional liberals pressed for a return to market forces and were unsympathetic to trade unions. Early in 1919 the main threat had apparently come from socialism; later, in the 1920s, the power of industrial capital seemed more menacing.

In 1927 one of the DDP's leading economic spokesmen, Hermann Fischer of the *Hansabund*, advised that the party should avoid trying to work out a clearer programme, because it would simply arouse difficulties and not achieve anything practical.[20] When, two years later, Gustav Stolper delivered a ringing encomium for the benefits of capitalism and the sovereignty of the consumer, delegates at the Democratic Party congress cheered enthusiastically. Nevertheless, his proposals for the economy were shelved after objections from white-collar unions and the Democratic Party's youth organization.[21]

[18] W. Stephan, *Aufstieg und Verfall des Linksliberalismus 1918–1933: Geschichte der Deutschen Demokratischen Partei* (Göttingen, 1973), 18 and 143–52. It is noteworthy that academic economists played no part in drafting the economic sections of the DDP's programme. The main economic spokesmen in the party were journalists like Arthur Feiler of the *Frankfurter Zeitung* and Gustav Stolper, editor of the *Volkswirt*, or pressure-group representatives like Hermann Fischer of the *Hansabund*.

[19] W. Treue, *Deutsche Parteiprogramme, 1861–1954* (Frankfurt/M., 1954), 125.

[20] W. Schneider, *Die Deutsche Demokratische Partei in der Weimarer Republik, 1924–1930* (Munich, 1978), 163–4.

[21] Ibid. 171–4.

For most of its career, therefore, the DDP was struggling to face both ways, warding off enemies on the left and the right. It had to pursue a policy of steering between Scylla and Charybdis in economic matters which crippled its ability to offer clear-cut, intellectually satisfying alternatives to its Marxist or nationalist rivals.[22]

As for the Democratic ministers in Reich governments, their policy showed even less consistency than that of the party itself. The major figure in economic affairs during the early twenties who stood close to the DDP was Walther Rathenau. As we have seen, he was not an enthusiastic free-trade liberal, but seemed to prefer a form of directed economy worked out as the result of consultation between big business and trade unions.

A more orthodox liberal position was that adopted by Eduard Hamm, a brave and respectable, if not very inspiring, Bavarian Democrat who became Reich Economics Minister, 1923–5. Preoccupied with problems arising from currency stabilization and the need to cut public expenditure, he was certainly not able to couple revaluation of the mark with a stirring popular appeal to consumers as Ludwig Erhard was to do in 1948.

Lastly, Hermann Dietrich, DDP Minister of Agriculture, 1928–30, and then Minister of Economics and Finance, 1930–2, showed little concern for free trade. In March 1929 he told the Reichstag:

The time in which free trade had any meaning is completely past, as is evidenced by the attitude of all states in the world, right down to the smallest. There is no point any more in talking about these things, and today there is not a single free-trader in the Democratic parliamentary delegation [*Fraktion*].

This statement was greeted with approval by his supporters on the DDP benches.[23]

Dietrich was responsible for setting up a rye cartel with Poland, and then established a national rye-purchasing agency, with the aim of artificially sustaining the price of rye. Since he simultaneously wished to cut production, one can only sympathize with the view that his policy was 'unsystematic and inconsistent' and lacked a 'theoretically based economic concept'.[24]

Certainly it did nothing for the DDP, many of whose voters were small farmers, dependent on cheap fodder for their livestock. As the

---

[22] E. Portner, *Die Verfassungspolitik der Liberalen—1919—Ein Beitrag zur Deutung der Weimarer Verfassung* (Bonn, 1973), 188–9; see also Maier, *Recasting Bourgeois Europe*, 444 and 457.

[23] *Verhandlungen des Reichstages IV, Wahlperiode 1928. Stenographische Berichte*, p. 1494.

[24] Schneider, *Die Deutsche Demokratische Partei*, 197–8.

parliamentary leader of the Democrats, Erich Koch-Weser, remarked: 'Dietrich's food policy is a fiasco. It alienates us from the consumers without winning us the vote of a single farmer.'[25]

It was small wonder that in 1930 the party was in such dire straits that many of its leaders decided to merge with the nationalist Jungdeutscher Orden to form the new Staatspartei, the main aim of which was a stronger and more centralized state. On economic matters it claimed to stand for a type of 'social capitalism' which would encourage small businessmen and at the same time not obstruct the national state (*Volksstaat*). Cartels and trusts should be subject to controls which would prevent them from suppressing independent initiative or imposing uneconomic prices on others. But there was no clear commitment to competition, let alone free trade.

So far as the more conservative liberals in Stresemann's German People's Party (DVP) were concerned, the DVP's economic programme rested on the defence of private property and a commitment to aid various special interests such as the shipping industry or the free professions.[26] There was a marked lack of any clear-cut economic strategy.

The DDP and the DVP, therefore, tolerated cartels, economic concentration, and monopolies. They willingly yielded to pressure-group demands to help business. As one historian has pointed out, their need for financial support from business circles led them to adopt socio-economic policies which were 'anti-liberal'.[27] Certainly they advocated cuts in public spending and attacked trade unions, but price rings and trusts were regarded as economic necessities. So, quite apart from the weakness of German liberal political parties, which declined catastrophically in popular support from 1928 onwards,[28] neither of them was ideologically consistent in its attitude to economic policy. To a great extent this was due to the narrowness of these parties' electoral support, since theories which might appeal to the mass of consumers were unlikely to be accepted by the interest groups—whether of steel barons or senior civil servants—whose financial commitment was needed to keep the parties afloat at all. A similar problem was to beset the liberal Free Democratic Party in the post-1945 period.[29]

---

[25] Ibid. 199.

[26] Treue, *Parteiprogramme*, 152 (Staatspartei) and 118–22 (DVP).

[27] L. Dohn, 'Wirtschafts- und Sozialpolitik der Deutschen Demokratischen Partei und Deutschen Volkspartei', in K. Holl, G. Trautmann, and H. Vorländer (eds.), *Sozialer Liberalismus* (Göttingen, 1986), 85 and 105, n. 3.

[28] The DPP's decline really set in as early as 1920. The demise of the liberal parties is well described in L. E. Jones, *German Liberalism and the Dissolution of the Weimar Party System, 1918–1933* (Chapel Hill, 1988), 67–80, 309–91, et passim. For Liberal attitudes to cartels, see Sheehan, *German Liberalism*, 256–7.

[29] See below, Ch. 6.

What was needed, but what did not exist, was a popular liberal party, drawing support from both confessions and most social strata in Germany. Such an ideal would have seemed utopian in the early 1930s.

Despite these unfortunate political circumstances, there were, of course, still voices to be heard in the economics profession which defended the old canons of *laissez-faire* liberalism. One of the most powerful of these was Ludwig Mises, an Austrian economist who clung with almost puritanical fervour to the principles of Gladstonian finance. In particular, he regarded any interference with gold-backed currency as a monstrous dereliction, which would be punished by the workings of inexorable market forces. He expounded such views in his *Theory of Money*, first published in 1911. Thirteen years later he was able to produce a revised edition which castigated the *étatisme* of wartime and post-war governments. He pointed to catastrophic inflations as the result of their attempts to interfere with the iron laws of supply and demand, and particularly their manipulation of national currencies. The only way to cope with inflation was to reduce the money supply.

Mises was effective as an aggressive polemicist against nationalist neo-mercantilism and Marxism. He argued that the laws of economics were being ignored by the proponents of *étatiste* theory.[30] Socialism, nationalism, and militarism were all lumped together as heresies in Mises' writings, and in this he certainly exemplified pure liberal views.

On the other hand, Mises and other exponents of fundamentalist liberalism at this time showed themselves lacking in political sense or even common humanity. When expounding, with engaging simplicity, the workings of the price mechanism and its superiority over state rationing, for example, Mises chose to overlook the fact that the logic of his theories might involve many people starving for lack of food. His views can be compared to those of utilitarian British administrators in the 1840s, who, when faced with the Irish famine, refused to give aid on the grounds that it would reduce the 'self-reliance' of the starving peasantry.[31]

Similarly, when he came to explain the causes of the economic depression which struck Germany with peculiar force after 1929, he

[30] L. von Mises, *Theorie des Geldes und der Umlaufsmittel* (2nd edn.; Munich, 1924), 227. He mentions particularly the views of the prominent German economists Georg Friedrich Knapp and Adolf Wagner. In the 1920s Mises published work as Ludwig Mises. Later on, he adopted the form 'von Mises'. For the sake of consistency, his name will be given as 'von Mises' in bibliographical references.

[31] Cf. C. B. Woodham-Smith, *The Great Hunger: Ireland 1845–1849* (6th edn.; London, 1980), e.g. 143–64.

attacked all forms of government intervention, including unemployment benefit. He saw the latter as a disastrous distortion of the mechanism of supply and demand in the labour market. Mises explained economic crises as resulting from artificially low interest-rates, which generated inflation, artificially high wages, which were caused by trade-union pressure, and unemployment pay, which priced the workless out of jobs. Unemployment benefit was not, as public opinion had been erroneously led to believe, a measure to ease privation caused by slumps. On the contrary, it was 'a link in the chain of causes which have led to the creation of mass unemployment as a chronic condition'.[32] The solution was to restore the labour market in its pristine *laissez-faire* form, unencumbered by trade unions or the dole. Natural equilibrium would then be restored. Workers would price themselves back into jobs. Economically viable enterprises intent on satisfying consumer demand would once again flourish.

Mises does not seem to have asked himself what would happen in the meantime to the millions of people without means of subsistence. It was this blind spot when faced with massive human suffering which rendered *laissez-faire* economics—or 'paleo-liberalism', as its more moderate liberal critics came to describe it—unpalatable to most Germans. It was hardly surprising that many of them preferred the interventionist populism of Adolf Hitler, who, in his first speech to the Reichstag as German Chancellor, told the assembled deputies that: 'The people do not live for the economy [*die Wirtschaft*] and the economy does not exist for capital: rather capital should serve the economy and the economy [should serve] the people.'[33]

Mises was not by any means a Fascist himself. In 1927 he published a book warning liberals against Mussolini, whose apparent defence of bourgeois values against Bolshevism would in fact lead to another kind of collectivist tyranny.[34] Mises and other Austrian liberals also subjected

---

[32] L. von Mises, *Die Ursachen der Wirtschaftskrise* (Tübingen, 1931), 18.

[33] *Hitler: Reden 1932 bis 1945*, ed. M. Domarus (4 vols.; Wiesbaden, 1973), i. 233. It should be pointed out that Hitler was careful to make qualifying remarks in his speech which seemed to imply that he was not proposing radical departures from accepted fiscal or economic practice. Nazi *dirigisme* was imposed in a haphazard and relatively cautious fashion.

[34] *Liberalismus* (Jena, 1927), 34–7, 164–5. It is curious that C.-D. Krohn in his *Wirtschaftstheorie als politische Interessen: Die akademische Nationalökonomie in Deutschland 1918–1933* (Frankfurt/M., 1981), 37–8, should represent Mises' views in this book by an accurate but misleadingly incomplete quotation which seems to suggest that Mises supported Italian Fascism. A fair-minded reading of the book must come to the opposite conclusion, even though Mises appreciated the fact that that Fascism had blocked Bolshevism in Italy. Similarly Krohn's contention that Eucken was sympathetic to Nazism in the early 1930s, and that there was a common front between liberal economists and

contemporary nationalist economic views to a stringent critique, stressing their lack of theoretical consistency and their vulnerability to manipulation by vested interests. One of Mises' strengths was his relentless insistence that, in any properly functioning economy, the consumer had to be put at the centre of the economic process. It was consumer demand which regulated the system and which brought order out of chaos. Furthermore, this was a truly democratic system, because the capitalist was bound to tailor his activities to the needs of the mass market. 'For the economy the decisive element of consumption is that of the masses.'[35] An economy geared to the needs of producers would inevitably lose its competitiveness and efficiency. He instanced the folly of trying to prop up European grain producers against American competition, and pointed to the success Danish and Dutch farmers were having in responding to consumer needs.[36]

His stress on protecting the value of the currency also reflected a fundamental principle of economic liberalism unpalatable to nationalist dictators and socialist theorists alike. Sound money was a way of protecting liberty, the pursuit of which was a unique feature of Western civilization. It was 'a concern', he informed his Anglo-Saxon readers after the Second World War, 'unknown to Orientals'. Sound money was essential to this enterprise: 'Ideologically it belongs in the same class with political constitutions and bills of rights'.[37]

For many of Mises' liberal contemporaries the major problem seemed to be to retain the advantages of the consumer-orientated economic system whilst overcoming the distortions and privations which a crude policy of *laissez-faire* had indisputably brought with it.

Nazis against social democracy does not seem to me to be demonstrated by the sources. On the contrary, nationalist economists like Sombart tended to go over to Nazism, whereas classical liberals remained aloof—which does not mean that they sympathized with socialism either. See also C.-D. Krohn, 'Autoritärer Kapitalismus: Wirtschaftskonzeptionen im Übergang von der Weimarer Republik zum Nationalsozialismus', in Stegmann *et al.* (eds.), *Industrielle Gesellschaft*, 113–29.

[35] von Mises, *Ursachen der Wirtschaftskrise*, 10.
[36] Ibid. 26.
[37] See the epilogue to the English trans. of his *Theorie des Geldes—The Theory of Money and Credit* (tr. H. E. Bateson; Yale, 1953), 413–14.

2

The Origins of Neo-liberalism: Depression and Dictatorship

IN Germany there were several gifted young scholars who were trying to defend the tradition of classical liberal economic theory against nationalist and Marxist heresies. One of them was Walter Eucken himself. He came from a distinguished academic family; his father, Rudolf, was a professor of philosophy at Jena and his brother was a physical chemist. In 1908 Rudolf was awarded the Nobel prize for his work, which was a development of Kantian ethical theory. He believed that ideal values had to be defended, and stressed that there were natural laws which man must respect, even if he was blessed with free will. He disliked utilitarianism and positivism, which he regarded as being fundamentally un-German. 'It is no matter of chance', he wrote, 'that great positivists have arisen in France and England but not in Germany.'

He urged men to eschew materialism and build up an inner, spiritual life, although the exact nature of this spirituality was left rather vague. His voluminous writings enjoyed wide popularity, and his book *Der Sinn und Wert des Lebens* (The Sense and Value of Life) became a best-seller. Unfortunately, Rudolf Eucken's idealism was of a rather parochial kind, which shaded without difficulty into nationalism. During the First World War he opposed attempts to encourage a negotiated peace, and attributed Germany's defeat to a failure of will. He reacted strongly against the November Revolution of 1918, attacking socialism as a doctrine which would produce dreary equality and stunt the individual's inner life at a time when what was needed was a spiritual regeneration.[1]

Rudolf Eucken was certainly a defender of individual responsibility and liberty against mindless state-worship. He was also an élitist. His

---

[1] For Rudolf Eucken's views on positivism, see R. Eucken, *Rudolf Eucken: His Life, Work and Travels—by Himself* (trans. J. McCabe; London, 1921), 126; see H. Lübbe, *Politische Philosophie in Deutschland: Studien zu ihrer Geschichte* (Munich, 1974), 176–7; for his critique of socialism, see R. Eucken, *Socialism: An Analysis* (trans. J. McCabe; London, 1921), 186 *et passim*. See also F. Bilger, *La Pensée économique libérale dans l'Allemagne contemporaine* (Paris, 1964), 40–2.

son Walter seems to have taken over both his father's distrust of the masses and his individualism, but he was less vulnerable to nationalist prejudices than his father had been. Possibly the fact that Walter's childhood was spent in a more cosmopolitan university atmosphere than that which his father had experienced in mid-nineteenth century East Friesland may explain his broader outlook.

In many respects the young Walter Eucken seemed the epitome of the German educated middle class, the *Bildungsbürgertum*. Tall, slim, and hawk-like of features, and with a high forehead, he attracted the attention of an artist-friend of the family, Ferdinand Hodler, who used him as a model for the principal figure in an epic painting depicting the students of Jena departing for the war of liberation against Napoleon. At the time of writing, this picture still hangs in the main hall of Jena University. Eucken was typical of the liberal intelligentsia also in that his family was Protestant and some of his near relatives were pastors in the Lutheran Church. His own academic career followed a predictable pattern; he studied economics at Kiel University and then moved on to Bonn to complete his studies—the outcome of which was a doctorate in 1913 on the subject of the mercantile marine. However, Eucken's move to Bonn had not simply been part of the normal wanderlust associated with well-to-do German students in the Wilhelmine Empire. He had gone there deliberately to study under Heinrich Dietzel, one of the few academics who still adhered to the classical liberal tradition according to which the aim of economics should be to develop theories of economic processes on the basis of deductive reasoning.[2] This was in contrast to the 'historical school' of economists associated with Gustav von Schmoller, whose main object was to explain existing economic activities using 'scientific' methods of analysis. Eucken's own doctorate proved he could perform such exercises, but he set his sights on higher targets in his own scientific investigations.

During the First World War Eucken served with the colours for four years and then took up a junior post at the University of Berlin, where he met his future wife. Having settled to write his second doctorate, on providing for the world's requirements of nitrogen, he seemed to be heading for a comfortable, if unremarkable, professional future. However, the desperate experience of the great inflation which wracked Germany in the early 1920s provoked Eucken into writing a critique of German monetary policy. This proved to be his first important polemical work, *Kritische Betrachtungen zum deutschen Geldproblem* (Criti-

---

[2] Bilger, *La Pensée économique libérale*, 42–3. The title of Eucken's thesis was *Verbandsbildung in der Schiffahrt* (Munich, 1914).

cal Observations on Germany's Monetary Problem). In it he argued that during the First World War some quite naïve and wrong-headed opinions had appeared, based on the notion that inflation was caused by a balance-of-payments deficit due to shortages of goods, an excess of imports over exports, and speculation in currency. Eucken argued that the whole idea of a negative balance of payments was erroneous, because unless the importers had something with which to balance their payments, they would not obtain goods. He put the blame for inflation on governments' budget deficits and the artificially low rates of interest being charged by the Reichsbank. Hence the cure for inflation was a drastic reduction in government spending, coupled with interest rates set at an economically realistic level. According to his account, in July 1923 the Reichsbank was charging interest of only 18 per cent, whereas unofficial interest-rates were 360 per cent per day.[3] After raising the interest rates and cutting public expenditure, the government should prevent further inflation by introducing a gold-backed currency to control the money supply. When, at a conference in Stuttgart in 1924, the prestigious German Association for Social Policy (*Verein für Socialpolitik*) discussed the causes of inflation, Eucken sided with Mises in a group of economists who spoke up against the fashionable balance-of-payments explanation, and stressed the importance of domestic control over credit and the money supply.[4]

Eucken's proposals to combat inflation may themselves have been naïve, since they would have led to massive unemployment and, under the turbulent circumstances of the Weimar Republic in the early 1920s, possibly even a revolution. Nevertheless, when the German currency finally did collapse altogether, in the late summer of 1923, the Stresemann and Luther Governments had to force their countrymen to take economic medicine of a type very similar to that which Eucken prescribed, and his analysis of the causes of the inflation would be accepted today as more convincing than those of the 'balance-of-payments' school.[5]

---

[3] W. Eucken, *Kritische Betrachtungen zum deutschen Geldproblem* (Jena, 1923), 61. For the continuing importance of sound money and a consistent control of the money supply in Eucken's concept of an optimal economic system, see W. J. Folz, *Das geldtheoretische und geldpolitische Werk Walter Euckens* (Berlin, 1970), 197–206.

[4] W. Eucken, *Kritische Betrachtungen*, 80. See also Eucken's contribution to the 1924 Stuttgart conference in *Verhandlungen des Vereins für Socialpolitik* (Munich, 1925), 296. I am grateful to Joachim Voth for drawing this to my attention.

[5] Cf. C. Bresciani-Turroni, *The Economics of Inflation: A Study of Currency Depreciation in Post-war Germany, 1914–1923*, (London, 1968; 1st edn. 1937); G. D. Feldman, C.-L. Holtfrerich, G. A. Ritter, and P.-C. Witt (eds.), *Die deutsche Inflation. Eine Zwischenbilanz: Beiträge zu Inflation und Wiederaufbau in Deutschland und Europa 1914–1924* (Berlin, 1982);

The inflation which culminated in the ruin of the German currency in 1923 had traumatic effects on the country's economy and society. The loss of savings and general uncertainty created by the inflation were themselves seriously damaging to Germany's political stability. Frictions between classes and interest groups were sharpened by the belief that others had gained unfairly through the collapse of the currency. Stock-exchange speculators and big capitalists were supposed to have made large profits at the expense of the ordinary, hard-working citizen. Middle-class Germans believed that inflation had shifted wealth from their pockets to those of unionized workers. Those respectable people who had capital in the form of savings accounts or insurance policies had certainly been badly hit by the destruction of the old currency and its replacement by the new Reichsmark. The issue of debt revaluation was a highly contentious one in the years which followed, and divided liberal supporters between debtors and creditors.[6]

This situation was exacerbated by the harsh measures needed to overcome inflation—the abolition of the old mark and its replacement with a new currency, drastic cuts in public expenditure, and high interest-rates to curb borrowing. The result was an increase in unemployment and a severe squeeze on commercial undertakings—small businesses and farmers being particularly hard hit. Once again, social friction was caused by economic hardship.

It is fashionable nowadays to describe the economic position of Weimar in the late 1920s as being virtually hopeless. High public spending, high taxes, high nominal wages, low rates of profit, and cumbersome labour-relations procedures are supposed to have held back Germany's industrial progress even during the period 1926–9, when the Republic seemed to be enjoying something of a recovery. That period is now sometimes referred to as 'the crisis before the crisis'. Such an interpretation leads to the conclusion that when the American stock-market crash of 1929 hit Germany, it could not recover without experiencing a drastic reduction in economic activity and massive unemployment—an experience needed to 'purge' the errors of the profligate 1920s.[7]

G. D. Feldman (ed.), *Die Nachwirkungen der Inflation auf die deutsche Geschichte* (Berlin, 1985). For a more positive view of inflation, see C.-L. Holtfrerich, *Die deutsche Inflation 1914–1923: Ursachen und Folgen in internationaler Perspektive* (Berlin 1980). Holtfrerich would not, however, reject the analysis of the *causes* of inflation given by Eucken, only the conclusion that it was necessarily bad for the economy.

[6] Jones, *German Liberalism and the Dissolution of the Weimar Party System*, 235–7 and 258–65.

[7] This argument is sometimes referred to as the 'Borchardt thesis', after the distinguished German economic historian Knut Borchardt. For a statement of it in English,

Seductive though this theory is, it remains highly contentious. A contrary argument might be that Germany's economic performance during the period 1926–9 was remarkably impressive, and that German export industries, in particular, were staging a recovery.[8] In that case the necessity for a 'purge' of the German economy appears less convincing. Whatever the outcome of this academic controversy in our own time, it should be borne in mind that the same issues were being fiercely debated in the 1920s themselves. Economists and politicians, as well as businessmen and trade unionists, were deeply divided over them.

One of the difficulties faced by economists in the 1920s in Germany was that resentment against the provisions of the Versailles Treaty clouded the judgement of even relatively hard-headed financial and economic specialists, and remained uppermost in the minds of politicians. Thus it had been impossible to take effective action against inflation in the early 1920s because measures of retrenchment would have been condemned as bowing the knee to Allied pressure for reparations. After the Dawes Plan of 1924 had modified the schedule of reparations payments in Germany's favour, and even after the Young Plan had presented a long-term scheme for the total repayment of reparations, neither the political leadership nor the economic establishment in Germany was willing to concede that the reparations issue should be regarded as settled.

Other complaints concerned the loss of Upper Silesia's industrial area to Poland, the occupation of the Saar basin by France, and the loss of Germany's colonies. The latter was an extraordinary issue to give concern to economically trained minds, since Germany's colonies had been of little commercial value and cost the country more than they contributed to it. Yet even Hjalmar Schacht—a liberal banker who later collaborated with the Nazis and helped Hitler into power—seems to have genuinely believed that the return of Germany's colonial possessions was essential for her economic well-being.[9]

Therefore discussions about German economic policy were often overshadowed by nationalist considerations which made rational policy-choices difficult. There was also an atmosphere of political and cultural

see J. von Kruedener (ed.), *Economic Crisis and Political Collapse: The Weimar Republic, 1924–1933* (Oxford, 1990), pp. xi–xxx and 99–151.

[8] J. Lee, 'Policy and Performance in the German Economy, 1925–35. A Comment on the Borchardt Thesis', in M. Laffan (ed.), *The Burden of German History, 1939–1945* (London, 1988), 132–5.

[9] For Schacht's fundamentally mercantilist ideas, see H. Schacht, *My First 76 Years: The Autobiography of Hjalmar Schacht* (London, 1955), 378–80.

which appeared to be statesmanlike calls for public thrift but which actually concealed an *étatiste* desire to control the economy.

Hence in January 1928 he publicly attacked Schacht, who, as we have seen, was complaining about the extent of German borrowing from abroad. Schacht claimed that such loans created unjustified consumption in Germany and warned that the country could not go on living on credit for ever. It was not a 'colonial development area' and should be able to rely on its own resources of production. This was a line of argument which foreshadowed his later excursions into autarky during the Third Reich. Eucken decribed Schacht's view as reflecting an 'astonishing radicalism' and pointed out that it was perfectly justifiable for German manufacturers to borrow money more cheaply in America than they could at home in order to equip their factories with more efficient plant. By doing so, they would be able to increase productivity and thus help Germany pay her way. Thrift and self-denial were not enough if capital was needed.[12]

Puritanical deflation for its own sake was not at all compatible with liberal theory, and Eucken resisted it. On the other hand, he was quite willing to accept the deflationary consequences of the market mechanism if these would result in re-establishing an equilibrium upset by earlier political distortions.

In comments on Germany's reparations problem, for example, he denied the common nationalistic view that the country could not afford reparations until it had achieved a positive balance of payments. Writing in 1925, he described how the reparations agent established as part of the Dawes Plan could use German marks to buy foreign currency so long as the Reichsbank kept up the value of the mark by high interest-rates and public-expenditure restrictions. This would reduce home consumption and force German industrialists to export their products, and that in turn would solve the balance-of-payments problem, enabling interest rates eventually to return to a more 'normal' level. He accepted that such measures might have deflationary effects and cause unemployment, but he regarded that as a temporary disadvantage to be accepted.[13] He pointed to the world-wide tendency to return to the discipline of the gold standard, which he also welcomed, despite the warnings about deflation being voiced by Keynes, with whose writings Eucken was acquainted from an early stage.[14]

---

[12] W. Eucken, 'Auslandsleihen', *Magazin der Wirtschaft*, 4/4 (26 Jan. 1928), 120–23.

[13] Id., 'Das Übertragungsproblem: Ein Beitrag zur Theorie des internationalen Handels', *Jahrbücher für Nationalökonomie und Statistik*, 3rd. ser., 68 (1925), 145–64.

[14] Id., 'Das internationale Währungsproblem: Ein Überblick', *Schriften der Vereinigung für staatswissenschaftliche Fortbildung*, 1 (1925), 15.

Eucken certainly knew by 1928 that the deflationary effects of reparations transfers were being masked by loans from the USA, and that if US interest rates were to rise, this ameliorative flow of money might also dry up. He regarded it as necessary for Germany to experience deflation so as to reorientate her economy towards exports, but he was afraid of the disastrous consequences if this occurred as the result of a sudden loss of American funding, especially if that happened when industry was booming. In this respect Eucken can be seen to have appreciated the threat of an American slump at a time when others in Germany and America were in bullish mood.[15]

Although the spirit of the times was against him, Eucken was not alone in trying to champion a return to the liberal values of an earlier age, tempered by the experience of rapid industrialization and the trials of boom and slump. Among the brothers-in-arms who did step forward to champion the free market in the crisis years before Hitler's accession to power were Wilhelm Röpke and Alexander Rüstow.

Röpke was a rising star in the economics firmament, one might almost describe him as a prodigy. Born the son of a country doctor in Scharmstedt on the Lüneburg Heath in Protestant North Germany, Röpke would have been an ideal model for an Aryan German as envisaged in the fantasies of Alfred Rosenberg or other Nazi ideologues. Vigorous, brave, blond, and blue-eyed, he had served as an eighteen-year-old in the First World War. Unfortunately for those same ideologues, however, Röpke was anything but a Nazi. He remained staunchly liberal in his views on politics and economic matters, and was not afraid to enter the lists against the reactionary nationalism which threatened to destroy Weimar democracy.

After the war ended he trained as an economist at Marburg University, where he resisted the violently reactionary attitudes which manifested themselves amongst fellow students and staff. He was taught by Professor Walter Troeltsch and produced a thesis on productivity in the German potash-mining industry. It is noteworthy that in this book, which was published in 1922, he expressed approval of works councils (*Betriebsräte*) to represent the employees, on the grounds that a more democratic atmosphere at work improved labour relations. He also confirmed that low wages caused poor productivity, whereas higher wages would lead to higher productivity and lower labour-costs, a radical position for a middle-class economist to adopt at that time. On

[15] See Eucken's contribution to the conference of the *Friedrich-List-Gesellschaft* at Pyrmont, 5–6 June 1928: 'Der grundsätzliche Zusammenhang zwischen Aufbringung und Übertragung von Reparationszahlungen' (Sonderdruck, n.d.), WEI Eucken NL.

the other hand, he came down firmly against socialization of the potash industry, a solution to its problems much in vogue on the left in the early 1920s.

Having spent a year with the German Foreign Office as an adviser on reparations questions, he turned to university teaching, taking up a junior post at Jena. There he published a book on business cycles and the nature of international commerce. In this he pointed to the growing interdependence of national economies and the division of labour on a world-wide scale. He spoke with evident approval of a capitalist spirit pervading the world—'anti-feudal, unheroic, and opposed to the brutal use of force'. Like Eucken, Röpke was contemptuous of those who wanted to throttle back foreign investment by imposing import bans or credit restrictions. Such a policy would be 'the summit of short-sightedness' (*der Gipfel der Verblendung*).[16]

Peaceful world trade was indispensable, and the penalty for its neglect would be the collapse of Western civilization. Röpke certainly believed in the benefits of free-enterprise capitalism, but he also appreciated that cyclical fluctuations could have damaging results. Governments could play a role in maintaining confidence by initiating moderate programmes of investment to counter slumps. Ground rules laid down by the government to prevent sudden plant-closures or to encourage future trading on stock exchanges could also help to smooth over the peaks and troughs of the trade cycle.[17] Like most liberal economists, Röpke believed that the effects of cyclical fluctuations could best be coped with if competition was allowed free rein, and governments pursued sensible monetary policies designed to help the operation of market forces rather than to obstruct them. Nevertheless, he did not accept the view that governments should simply do nothing when faced with economic crises.

In 1927 Röpke won a Rockefeller Foundation fellowship to the USA and spent a year there studying American agricultural problems. This experience does not seem to have left him with a great admiration for

---

[16] W. Röpke, *Die Konjunktur: Ein systematischer Versuch als Beitrag zur Morphologie der Verkehrswirtschaft* (Jena, 1922), 132. See also id., 'Auslandskredite und Konjunktur', in K. Diehl (ed.), *Schriften des Vereins für Socialpolitik*, clxxiii: *Beiträge zur Wirtschaftstheorie, Konjunturforschung und Konjunkturtheorie* (Munich, 1928), 244–5. His views are set out more generally in W. Röpke, *Geld und Außenhandel* (Jena, 1925). For his description of the potash industry, id., *Die Arbeitsleistung im deutschen Kalibergbau unter besonderer Berücksichtigung des hannoverschen Kalibergbaus* (Berlin, 1922), esp. 69–70. For Röpke's opposition to brutal nationalist tendencies in Marburg, see id., *The German Question* (trans. E. W. Dickes; London, 1946), 68–9.

[17] Röpke, *Die Konjunktur*, 74–5 and 126–7.

the Americans,[18] but he was able to observe the world's largest market economy in operation at first hand. The following year, whilst still not 30 years of age, he became a full professor of economics at Graz, and in 1929 was called to a chair at the University of Marburg.

Alexander Rüstow, on the other hand, was a man whose career combined practical experience of business administration with professional academic training and broad cultural interests. He had been educated in classical philosophy and mathematical logic and, before the First World War, had seemed destined for a career as a philosopher. At the University of Göttingen he was a pupil of the neo-Kantian idealist Leonhard Nelson, a passionate believer in social justice, whose élitist views were incompatible with democracy, but whose pupils included ethical socialists as well as socially concerned liberals.[19]

Rüstow himself had been associated with avant-garde trends in art and psychology; his first wife was the painter Mathilde Herberger. He served throughout the First World War in the artillery, and by the end of that appalling conflict he had become a socialist, welcoming the November Revolution which overthrew the Kaiser's empire, and even participating in it. The new leadership in Germany was short of academically trained personnel, and Rüstow was appointed to the section of the Reich Economics Ministry dealing with the proposed nationalization of the coal industry. This experience helped to disillusion him with socialist planning. Instead of dynamic schemes to reform society, he found progress blocked by a welter of vested interests, not to mention bureaucratic red tape.

In 1924 he became director of economic and political research at the Association of German Engineering Manufacturers (*Verein deutscher Maschinenbauanstalten*—VDMA) in Berlin. Here his task was to protect the interests of a branch of industry which suffered at the hands of both interfering bureaucrats and price-fixing cartels in the coal and

[18] See Röpke's comments in letters to Rüstow when he was thinking of taking a chair in Tennessee (7 May 1940) and his belief that the USA would collapse internally if Britain gave in (18 July 1940), BA Rüstow NL, no. 7.

[19] See the biographical sketch by his son Dankwart A. Rustow in A. Rüstow, *Freedom and Domination: A Historical Critique of Civilization* (Princeton, NJ, 1980), pp. xiii ff. Also G. Eisermann (ed.), *Wirtschaft und Kultursystem. Festschrift für Alexander Rüstow* (Elben-Zurich). Ch. by W. Röpke, 15–16. For Nelson's views, see L. Nelson, *Politics and Education* (trans. W. Lonsdale; London, 1928), esp. 244–7, and P. Schröder (ed.), *Vernunft, Erkenntnis, Sittlichkeit: Internationales philosophisches Symposion Göttingen vom 27.–29. Oktober 1977 aus Anlaß des 50. Todestages von Leonhard Nelson* (Hamburg, 1979), 151–61. For Nelson's influence on ethical socialism, see below, Ch. 3. For Rüstow's conversion from socialism and his links with Heimann, see K. Meier-Rust, 'Der neue Liberalismus nach Alexander Rüstow', *Orientierungen zur Wirtschafts- und Gesellschaftspolitik*, 56 (June, 1993), 10–14.

steel sectors. The 'free market' turned out to be nothing like as free as liberal theories postulated. Coal and steel firms, upon whom the engineering industry depended for its supplies, were past masters at cartelization and price-fixing. German steel prices were far higher at home than they were abroad. The influence of heavy industry—especially in the Ruhr-Rhine complex—was certainly much greater in the German system than that of consumer industries—even if the power of the coal and steel producers was sometimes exaggerated.[20] Furthermore, the manufacturers represented in the VDMA had to contend with state policies which put burdens on them for the benefit of large landowners in eastern Prussia, popularly, if somewhat inaccurately, known as *Junker*. These conservative interests had been protected by tariffs in imperial Germany. Curiously enough, the Weimar Republic extended them government aid as well, despite their openly reactionary political character. Direct subventions and, later on, import duties on grain helped to push up wage costs in German industry. It was Rüstow's task to analyse these developments and do what he could to resist them.

It was small wonder that he reacted strongly against the weak and vacillating economic policies of the Weimar Republic, whose political system made it easy for pressure groups to win concessions from the state at the expense of the common good. Like Eucken, Rüstow despised those economists who provided theoretical justifications for such pusillanimous behaviour. In January 1941, when the cause of liberalism seemed hopelessly lost, and Rüstow himself was in exile in Turkey, he wrote to Wilhelm Röpke giving the following quotation from Ricardo:

There are so many combinations and so many operating causes in political economy that there is a great danger of appealing to experience in favour of a particular doctrine, unless we are sure that all the causes of the variations are seen and their effects duly estimated.[21]

Rüstow added the comment that 'This sentence disposes of whole libraries of economic literature and much in other disciplines as well.'

In the Weimar Republic economic problems were so pressing that such lofty considerations of principle seemed something of a luxury. During the 1920s liberal economists put more stress on resisting high

---

[20] For excellent scholarly discussions of this problem the reader's attention is drawn to G. D. Feldman, *Iron and Steel in the German Inflation, 1916–1923* (Princeton, NJ, 1977) and B. Weissbrod, *Schwerindustrie in der Weimarer Republik: Interessenpolitik zwischen Stabilisierung und Krise* (Wuppertal, 1978).

[21] Rüstow to Röpke, 9 Jan. 1941, BA Rüstow NL, no. 7, p. 725. The quotation is from a letter from Ricardo to Malthus.

taxation and socialist moves towards public ownership. Gustav Stolper, in his journal, *Der deutsche Volkswirt*, argued that 50 per cent of Germany's national income was in some way or other in the public sector. This had to be drastically reduced. Redistributive taxation had to be opposed.[22]

Similar opinions were to he heard at a conference organized by the prestigious Friedrich List Society, held at Eilsen on 26–8 October 1929. The aim of the conference was to investigate the possibility of reforming Germany's tax system in view of a potential reduction in the reparations burden to be expected under the Young Plan. One of the themes strongly represented among the audience was the belief that inequality of wealth was necessary to promote capital formation, and that this inequality had been undermined by a combination of inflation and redistributive taxation. Johannes Popitz, another financial specialist who was to help pave the way for Hitler three years later, waxed eloquent on the sufferings of the wealthy in Weimar, and impressed upon his listeners the necessity of giving the upper classes economic security. The former Reich Chancellor Hans Luther used the conference as a platform for his favourite hobby-horse—the need to rationalize the state. This was a euphemistic description for centralization under authoritarian, bureaucratic control.

Eucken, Röpke, and Rüstow were all present at this meeting, and the two latter made important contributions. Röpke gently presented himself as an *advocatus diaboli* against the view that unequal wealth-distribution was peculiarly helpful for capital formation. The doctrine that the poor made no contribution to capital formation was wrong because it was based on an outmoded Malthusian concept according to which the poor always had far more children than the rich and could therefore generate no savings. In Weimar Germany this had clearly become untrue—the lower classes were exercising more discipline and having fewer children. Small savings were very important to the capital market through the investments of savings banks. Studies had shown

---

[22] T. Stolper, *Ein Leben in Brennpunkten unserer Zeit: Gustav Stolper, 1888–1947* (Stuttgart, 1979), 225–7. It has been claimed that Gustav Stolper presaged the social market economy in his journal *Der deutsche Volkswirt*. Certainly he was in favour of overcoming class resentments, which he saw as damaging to the economy. However, his stress on entrepreneurial independence or 'leadership' and his advocacy of better social-insurance systems do not add up to a theory of the social market. The fact that he advocated state intervention to set 'just wages' is incompatible with neo-liberal theories of market freedom, and the state protection of competition does not seem to have loomed very large in his conception of an economic system. See W. F. Stolper, 'Gustav Stolper und "Der deutsche Volkswirt", 1926 bis 1933', in H. Froels and H. Sufils (eds.), *Querschnitt 60 Jahre deutscher Wirtschaftsgeschichte* (Verlag der Wirtschaftswerke, 1986) (unpaginated and with no place of publication).

that in Britain and the USA the savings of the lower classes were more stable than those of the wealthier classes. Röpke was also willing to consider, though not to accept without question, the view that mass consumption created by a more even distribution of wealth helped to expand the market for mass production.[23]

He stressed the importance of lower-middle-class savings and pointed to the extraordinarily rapid recovery of the savings level after the stabilization of the mark. If these facts were accepted, then a policy of reducing taxes on the wealthy at the expense of the mass of the population would not seem to be the optimum method of encouraging capital formation, although he agreed that redistributive taxation might encourage capital flight abroad. He stressed that the type of taxation favoured was very important—inheritance taxes, despite their bad reputation, were actually less damaging than others. At the same conference Rüstow urged that industrial enterprises should be helped to maintain their profit levels even at a time of rising wages. This should be done by cuts in corporation tax.[24] The partiality of this argument—coming as it did from a representative of an industrial pressure-group—was painfully obvious, especially as Rüstow coupled it with the rather illogical claim that taxes on farmers were *not* damaging, but rather encouraged efficiency. Perhaps it was fortunate that there do not seem to have been many farmers at the meeting, or at least none of those already threatened with bankruptcy by falling prices and rising costs.

Nevertheless, these contributions did reveal certain elements in what was subsequently to become neo-liberal thought. First, there was an absence of parochial nationalism—open markets were preferred to protection. Secondly, there was a willingness to accept that the interests of the mass of the population were important, and that government policy should take those interests into account. It was not enough just to regard economics as a form of advocacy on behalf of the rich. Thirdly, there was the belief that the spreading of wealth among hard-working people could only have a beneficial economic effect. Lastly, there was the view that taxation policy could be targeted to help dynamic parts of the economy to help themselves. This was a policy which was to be implemented in 1948 and thereafter.

Taxation and public expenditure were not the only threats to an effective market economy in the 1920s. Another was cartelization, about

---

[23] G. Colm and H. Neisser (eds.), *Kapitalbildung und Steuersystem. Verhandlungen und Gutachten der Konferenz von Eilsen vom 26. bis 28. Oktober 1929* (2 vols.; Berlin, 1930), i. 68–70.
[24] Ibid. 473–4.

which Eucken and Rüstow were deeply concerned. Eucken had been influenced in his thinking on this subject by developments in his own career.

After a period teaching as a lecturer at Tübingen University, he was called to a chair at Freiburg im Breisgau in 1927. There, he met a number of intellectuals who were to influence his work in subsequent years. It is significant that several of these were not professional economists. Husserl was a logical philosopher who stimulated Eucken's desire to link economic studies to other theories of human behaviour. Of even greater importance in their effect on Eucken's thought were two legal specialists, Hans Grossmann-Doerth, who had been a professor of civil law in Prague before going to Freiburg in 1932, and Franz Böhm. Böhm was an official in the department of the Reich Economics Ministry dealing with the regulation of cartels. He came to regard them with great distaste as a pernicious influence on the German economy. Both he and Grossmann-Doerth drew Eucken's attention to the vital role played by the law in the economic process. The law was not just a formal recognition of economic tendencies, as German economists often assumed. There was a serious danger that economic practices—such as cartelization or monopolistic restraints on competition, would become legal practice by default, whereas a strong legal code could defend competition and thus help the economy to work efficiently.[25]

Böhm decided to write a second thesis, or *Habilitationsschrift*, at Freiburg. It was this which became his famous attack on cartels and monopolies, *Wettbewerb und Monopolkampf* (Competition and the Struggle against Monopoly), published in 1933. A prescription for the eradication of obstructions to competition by means of reforming the law, it helped to establish one of the central planks of the neo-liberal programme as it was to emerge after the Second World War.

Böhm did not shrink from recommending legal protection for competition, and his insistence on state action in this sphere encouraged Eucken's own growing willingness to reject *laissez-faire* as a reasonable prescription for twentieth-century economic life. Böhm argued that in Germany there was an expectation that the law should simply reflect the current practices of the business world, even if these violated the principles of the free market by stifling competition. He took issue with one legal expert, Nipperdey, who had told a conference of German jurists that: 'Civil law does not exist to obstruct the development of the economy, to implement pure ethics, or to make life soft for the weak.'

---

[25] Cf. Bilger, *La Pensée économique libérale*, 47–8.

Böhm saw this as dangerous relativism. Business had become so used to treating law as a handmaiden, which would legitimize the actions of powerful vested interests, that it was in danger of losing its respect for the sovereign importance of law in the regulation of competition. This had to stop. If competition was to fulfil its economic purpose, it must be protected from special-interest groups and monopolies: 'Where the rules of competition are called in question, law is the master, not the servant of economic interests.'[26]

Here it should be noted that the process of cartelization, like other protective practices, had not ceased or even diminished with the establishment of the Weimar Republic. The new Republican government, dominated by Marxist social democrats and Roman Catholic Centre Party politicians, was not inclined temperamentally to leave economic matters to the free play of market forces.

In November 1923 a law was passed placing cartels under state control in order to ensure that they were not abused to damage the national interest. At first the cartel organizers were uneasy about this arrangement, but they soon found that in practice their position was strengthened by state authority and trade-union support. The numbers of cartels mushroomed, and by 1925 there were 2,500 of them. As Eucken wrote for his London lecture audience in 1950, this demonstrated the truth of the claim that: 'Economic policy, therefore, should not direct itself against abuse of power by existing monopolies, but rather against their very existence.'[27]

What Eucken and other liberals thought was a self-operating mechanism would not require a bureaucratic apparatus to operate and would be immune to the special pleadings of organized lobbies. In the 1920s, however, there seemed to be no chance of achieving such a happy arrangement. Industrial and agricultural pressure-groups became used to a situation in which they were constantly trying to dun the state for subventions from the taxpayer or protective measures against competition. The price of commodities on the domestic market grew away from those in the world outside. One business journal estimated that between 1925 and 1929 monopolies and protection cost the German economy about 1.5 billion marks.[28] In July 1933 the domestic cost of steel was double the export price, and even privileged

---

[26] F. Böhm, *Wettbewerb und Monopolkampf: Eine Untersuchung zur Frage des wirtschaftlichen Kampfrechts und zur Frage der rechtlichen Struktur der geltenden Wirtschaftsordnung* (Berlin, 1933; facsimile repr. with preface by Böhm, 1964), 323.

[27] W. Eucken, *This Unsuccessful Age*, 35.

[28] Over £1.5 billion at 1990 values. ('Billion' is used throughout the present book in the American sense, i.e. to mean one thousand million.)

German customers had to pay about 25 per cent more than foreigners.[29] During the Third Reich, of course, cartelization was institutionalized throughout industry and put under Nazi control. As time went on, however, some of the more far-sighted entrepreneurs began to realize that it was reducing both their independence and their economic efficiency.

During the Weimar Republic Eucken was in many ways a typical liberal, who accepted the *laissez-faire* approach to the economy we have seen adumbrated above by Ludwig Mises. In common with other liberals in Germany at this time, he was uneasy about democracy, regarding the influence of the masses as dangerous. It was in order to bribe those ignorant masses that wise diplomacy had given way to nationalist demagogy—and the Versailles Treaty had been the result.[30] Similarly, it was to appease mass demands that governments had devalued their currencies and dabbled in economic planning. The result of such actions was economic stagnation, leading to crisis. A state which interfered with the free-price mechanism was bound to weaken, not to strengthen, its own authority. Every intervention was a concession to vested interests. In October 1932, writing of the developed economies in the Western world, Eucken argued that:

If the state . . . recognizes what great dangers have arisen for it as the result of its involvement in the economy and if it can find the strength to free itself from the influence of the masses and once again to distance itself in one way or another from the economic process . . . then the way will have been cleared . . . for a further powerful development of capitalism in a new form.[31]

The concept of a strong state standing above the economic struggle was central to liberal economic theories in Germany and found expression in a famous lecture to the German Association for Social Policy (*Verein für Socialpolitik*) delivered in Dresden on 28 September 1932 by Alexander Rüstow. Rüstow ended his speech by rejecting the old smear against Manchester liberalism that it only wanted to weaken the state. Liberalism had not demanded weakness from the state, but only freedom for economic development under state protection. 'In any case, the new liberalism . . . which I stand for with my friends, de-

---

[29] W. Röpke, *German Commercial Policy* (London, 1934), 30–1. For a discussion of the impact of cartels in Weimar, see H. James, *The German Slump: Politics and Economics, 1924–1936* (Oxford, 1986), 154–60 and 173–4. James doubts that price 'stickiness' in Germany could be attributed mainly to cartels, but he accepts that they were a factor in creating price rigidity.

[30] W. Eucken 'Staatliche Strukturwandlungen und die Krisis des Kapitalismus', *Weltwirtschaftliches Archiv*, 36/2 (Oct. 1932), 318–19.

[31] Ibid. 318.

mands a strong state, a state standing where it belongs, above the economy and above the interest groups.'[32]

This in itself was not really very new, and could apparently have been compatible with the kind of *laissez-faire* liberalism exemplified by Herbert Spencer's notorious tract, *The Man versus the State*.[33] But Rüstow specifically denied that the state he was advocating would be a passive 'night-watchman'. It should be prepared to intervene decisively, not to prop up ailing industries or obstruct market forces but, on the contrary, to protect competition and help the economy to adapt itself as quickly as possible to changed market conditions.[34] In this respect the speech heralded the concept of the 'third way' which was to become the goal of many younger German liberal economists, and which had been germinating during the 1920s. It has been seen as a landmark in the prehistory of the social market economy. Rüstow's words certainly made a great impression on his listeners, among whom was at least one future Minister of Economics in the Federal Republic of Germany.[35]

The depth of the economic crisis lent weight to the view that *laissez-faire*—'Manchester Liberalism', as it was contemptuously referred to in Germany—could not provide an answer to the problems of advanced industrial economies. At the same time, neither nationally orientated pragmatic protectionism nor socialist planning seemed to have fared any better. Rüstow, like others of his generation, sought to develop a new economic system which would retain the advantages of the free market, with its built-in equilibrium and its self-operating mechanisms, whilst eliminating the tragic social consequences associated with boom and slump. In this respect he was ahead of Eucken, who had not been swayed by revolutionary fervour and who had retained the conventional attitudes of nineteenth-century German liberalism. It was typical that, when Rüstow read Eucken's attack on the masses in October 1932, he should write to his colleague pointing out that the real culprits were not the masses but vested interests (*Interessenten*) and that the masses had actually done badly during the war and inflation, only

[32] A. Rüstow, 'Die staatspolitischen Voraussetzungen des wirtschaftspolitischen Liberalismus', in *Alexander Rüstow, Rede und Antwort: 21 Reden und viele Diskussionsbeiträge aus den Jahren 1932–62*, ed. W. Hoch (Ludwigsberg, 1963), 258.

[33] Herbert Spencer, *The Man versus the State* (London, 1884, with numerous reprints). Spencer combined an unpleasant form of Social Darwinism with orthodox *laissez-faire* theories. For a good recent study of his thought, see M. W. Taylor, *Men versus the State: Herbert Spencer and Late Victorian Individualism* (Oxford, 1992).

[34] A. Rüstow, *Rede und Antwort*, 252–4.

[35] Karl Schiller. Dr Schiller mentioned this in a conversation with the author on 15 July 1983.

recouping something of their losses in the high wage-settlements of 1927/8. Rüstow did not deny that mass influence on foreign policy was damaging, but he seemed much more inclined to blame Germany's troubles on the cynical policies of Bismarck, who had deliberately destroyed the old liberal parties for his own ends by releasing the 'wild beasts of pluralistic economic egoism'.[36]

'Pluralism' in Rüstow's eyes was an anarchic condition of conflict between powerful pressure-groups in which the public interest was bound to be sacrificed. As a consequence of his own practical experiences and political inclinations, he saw the chief bastions of this pluralism in vested interests such as cartels, monopolies, and landowners' associations. Trade unions could also have a pernicious influence, but he felt more sympathy with them because they were essentially defence mechanisms of the poor. If liberalism were to re-emerge from the ashes of the slump, it would have to find ways of taming the interest groups and creating a free economy in which the rights of all consumers—especially the poorest—were effectively protected.

Eucken and Rüstow certainly shared the same views about both the conduct of economic affairs and the inadequacies of German professional economists. In the spring of 1929, for example, they corresponded about the failings of the *Verein für Socialpolitik*, the most distinguished association of German social scientists. Eucken pointed out that it was very difficult to achieve any sort of consensus because, besides liberally minded economists like himself, there were many who inclined towards a socialist-type planned economy. Only careful analysis of specific problems could dispose effectively of 'fact-grubbers' (*Stoffhuber*) and vulgar economists on the one hand, and theoreticians detached from reality on the other.[37] He went on to say that it should be their task to bring forth at least the same sort of transformation in economics which Galileo and Kepler had achieved in the natural sciences. No such transformation proved possible, however, before Hitler overthrew German democracy in 1933.

Both Eucken and Rüstow were involved in the executive committee of the German League for Free Economic Policy (*Deutscher Bund für freie Wirtschaftspolitik*), an association of businessmen and economists dedicated to the furtherance of the free market.[38] In the early thirties it was swimming against a powerful tide of interventionism, but it organized

---

[36] Rüstow to Eucken, 25 Jan. 1933, BA Rüstow NL, no. 210.
[37] Eucken to Rüstow, 27 Mar. 1929, ibid., no. 2.
[38] The chairman was the mayor of Hamburg, Dr Carl Petersen. Other members of the *Vorstand* included Wilhelm Vogele, Wilhelm Röpke, and Adolf Weber.

public discussions and stimulated publications, such as a broadside against quota systems and in favour of free trade, which appeared in 1932.[39]

Rüstow and his colleagues did not content themselves with academic matters. They also tried to influence the actions of the government. In February 1930 Rüstow was writing to Eucken complaining about the incapacity of the Müller Cabinet, in which the influence of economic liberalism desperately needed strengthening. He complained of the outrageous demands of the agricultural lobby—the so-called 'green front'—abetted by social democrats. A key role would be played by the tariff commission of the Reich Economic Council, an expert body which advised the Reichstag. About ninety demands for increased industrial duties were already on the table and Rüstow was concerned to mobilize support for free-trade principles. Rapid steps had to be taken to present the commission with expert arguments and supporting material. 'We shall, of course, do all we can here,' he wrote to Eucken, 'but we urgently need brothers-in-arms.' He chaffed Eucken for sitting peacefully behind the lines in Freiburg, and begged him to consider whether he could not do something effective, such as writing a popular account of the elementary principles of foreign trade, so that the public would at least start to grasp the problem.[40]

This particular issue dwindled in importance as the crisis deepened. Unemployment and bankruptcy were the twin spectres haunting the German economy. Both Eucken and Rüstow believed that wages in Germany were too high and would have to be reduced before growth could start again. But Rüstow saw that a simple reduction in wages was neither politically defensible nor economically sufficient to overcome the crisis. He wrote sharply to Eucken in June 1930 that Germany's industrialists had called wolf so often about wage increases—even at times when they had no justification for doing so—that they were not taken seriously when the wolf had them in its jaws.[41] Rüstow made it clear that he did not share a class-based attitude towards unemployment insurance or arbitration in labour disputes, and claimed that it was precisely the element of social hostility involved in such arguments which made it difficult for more reasonable criticism to gain public support.

As the political and economic situation worsened in the early 1930s, Röpke, too, tried to resist calls for authoritarian measures which became fashionable on the right. In particular, he attacked the anti-democratic,

---

[39] *Kontingente, was sie sind und wie sie wirken* (Berlin, 1932) (BA Rüstow NL).
[40] Rüstow to Eucken, 4 Feb. 1930, BA Rüstow NL, no. 3.
[41] Rüstow to Eucken, 2 June 1930, ibid.

nationalist journal *Die Tat*, which was hostile to parliamentary democracy. One of its leading writers was named Ferdinand Fried, and Röpke published his own ripostes under the pseudonym 'Ulrich Unfried'— *Unfried* being the German word for discord.[42] Röpke's commitment to liberal causes did not go unnoticed by the Nazis and their right-wing allies.

In the winter of 1930–1 Röpke was asked to serve on a government-initiated commission of inquiry into measures which might be taken to alleviate unemployment. This was chaired by the former Minister of Labour, Heinrich Brauns, who—to Röpke's dismay—began by ruling out all consideration of the causes of unemployment from the commission's terms of reference.[43] Röpke felt that the slump had its roots in the preceding boom, which had been characterized by profligate expansion and a willingness to treat short-term loans as though they were long-term credits. As a student of business cycles, he did not believe the depression could or should be arrested by what he termed artificial means, but nor should it simply be allowed to run its course without any measures being taken to speed up eventual recovery.

He and the commission were generally unimpressed by suggestions that hours of work should be cut to spread unemployment, or that married women should be forced to give up their jobs.[44] The commission rejected fears of overproduction as nonsense, but stressed the need to create a willingness on the part of capitalists to invest. Something had to be done to get the economy moving again, and, in particular, two steps were necessary: the first was to attract long-term loans to Germany from abroad; the second was for the government to intervene on its own account so as to set the ball rolling and stimulate an upward cycle of investment. Röpke and the commission recommended a number of infrastructural public investment targets, such as improvements to the road network (though *not* autobahns), agricultural improvement schemes, investment in power stations and support for the building industry in the construction of private dwellings. Röpke described this as an *Initialzündung* (starting impulse or kick-start), a term for which he could claim paternity.[45]

[42] F. Neumark, 'Erinnerungen an Wilhelm Röpke' in Ludwig-Erhard-Stiftung, Bonn (ed.), *Wilhelm Röpke: Beiträge zu seinem Leben und Werk* (Stuttgart, 1980), 7–8.
[43] W. Röpke, 'Praktische Konjunkturpolitik: Die Arbeit der Braunskommission', *Weltwirtschaftliches Archiv*, 34/2 (1931), 435–40.
[44] Ibid.
[45] 'Gutachten zur Arbeitslosenfrage. Erstattet von der Gutachterkommission zur Arbeitslosenfrage', *Sonderveröffentlichung des Reichsarbeitsblattes* (Berlin, 1931), pt. 2, pp. 4–5. For Röpke's views, see W. Röpke 'Trends in German Business Cycle Policy', *Economic Journal*, 43 (1933), 430–1.

Röpke correctly commented that, if the government went on sitting with folded arms and allowing the crisis to deepen, the number of victims would be so great and the anti-capitalist feeling so intense that 'Liberalism—or the remnants of it which still exist—will disappear into the museum.'[46]

If things were so bad that private investment was insufficient to get things moving upwards, then the public purse should be used to ensure that the first steps were taken in the right direction.

On the other hand, he and the Brauns Commission set their faces firmly against measures which might have an inflationary character. In his own commentary on the report issued by the commission, he stated that 'a permanent condition of economic boom (*Hochkonjunktur*) is a total impossibility'.[47] He believed in the trade cycle as both inevitable and necessary, but thought that government policies should be adapted to exploit its beneficial and alleviate its malevolent effects.

This report helps to illustrate certain embryonic features of neo-liberal thinking, and explains the anger which many economists felt at what they saw as the ignorance of politicians. In particular, it exemplifies the insistence on working with market forces instead of against them, and the impossibility of creating an artificial system of government-controlled economic activity. Röpke respected the work of Keynes, for example, but he rapidly distanced himself from what he described as primitive Keynesianism, which sought to use measures to stimulate employment, not as a temporary expedient to overcome economic crisis, but as a permanent feature of economic policy. Nevertheless, it is important to underscore the differences between Röpke's position and that of rigid deflationists like Mises, who regarded wage cuts, abolition of unemployment benefits, and the enfeeblement of trade unions as the only path to salvation. Before the crisis had reached such desperate proportions, he had already pointed to the extent to which state action might influence the economy, given the size of the GNP controlled by the public sector. 'Individualism' and 'socialism' were both outmoded concepts. Nevertheless, he did not believe in the inevitable failure of capitalism; he had faith in its power to create prosperity so long as it was not 'jettisoned by political ignorance'.[48]

Like Rüstow, Röpke had no desire to be bracketed with those whom

---

[46] Röpke, 'Praktische Konjunkturpolitik', 450.

[47] Ibid. 449.

[48] L. A. Bentin, *Johannes Popitz und Carl Schmitt: Zur wirtschaftlichen Theorie des totalen Staates in Deutschland* (Munich, 1972), 145, citing Röpke 'Staatsinterventionismus' in L. Elster (ed.), *Handwörterbuch der Staatswissenschaften* (supp. vol.) (Jena, 1929), 861–82.

he regarded as socially reactionary, even if he felt it his duty to combat socialist errors in the economic field.

The willingness of men like Röpke and Rüstow to take action to solve the economic crisis, rather than sitting idly by, watching the deflationary policies of Brüning wreck the economy, was of course shared by a number of economists in Weimar Germany. It is not true to suggest, as was done after the Second World War, that no economists in Germany had alternative policies to offer. What is true, however, is that the confused and divided nature of the economics profession gave the bankers—in this case successive Reichsbank presidents in the shape of Hjalmar Schacht and Hans Luther—and the politicians an easy opportunity to impose their own view of orthodoxy on the situation. It must also be said that the rapid deterioration on both the economic and political fronts in 1931 made a coherent economic strategy very difficult to establish. This was especially true for a government, like that of Chancellor Heinrich Brüning, which did not enjoy a majority in the Reichstag, but was dependent on the goodwill of an octogenarian field-marshal in the shape of President Hindenburg.

Among those who sought economic alternatives during the crisis were officials in the Reich Economics Ministry; in particular Wilhelm Lautenbach and his assistant, Hanns-Joachim Rüstow, Alexander Rüstow's brother. Lautenbach, who had helped Röpke in his work for the Brauns Commission, was convinced that the slump had been caused by a reduction in the investment quotient as a result of falling profitability in business. He associated this with high interest-rates which—at a time of falling prices—deterred investment. In the summer of 1931 base interest-rates were in double figures and had only dropped to 7 per cent in January 1932, at a point when the money supply had fallen by over 25 per cent since 1930.

In the late spring and summer of 1931 the world economic crisis had taken a further series of catastrophic downward lurches, with a bank collapse in Austria which led to a banking crisis in Germany, culminating in an enforced 'holiday' in July to prevent a run on the banks. In Britain the pound came under pressure. The Labour government collapsed in a welter of recriminations, and on 27 August Ramsay Macdonald's National Coalition introduced a severe austerity-package in an attempt to balance the budget.

Even liberal economists were now beginning to fear that if the deflationary spiral was allowed to continue it would not merely 'cleanse' the economy of inefficient producers, but would destroy many normally healthy enterprises as well. Lautenbach produced a plan according to which the Reichsbank would guarantee credits to the German railways and public authorities to renovate the rail system and improve roads. This would involve a total expenditure of 1.5 billion marks. At the same time artificially high cartel-prices within Germany would be forced down, as would wage rates. This would enable employers to take on new workers, because at the same time they could reduce the wages of those already in employment. The concept was that such a scheme would stop the runaway increase in unemployment and create confidence among employers, thus reviving their willingness to invest.

These ideas were being taken seriously enough in the late summer of 1931 for the president of the Reichsbank, Hans Luther, to call a meeting of academics and other economic experts to discuss them. Formally, the meeting, which was held in secret, was under the auspices of the *Friedrich-List-Gesellschaft*. Both Eucken and Röpke were present at the meeting, which took place on 16–17 September 1931. It seems not unlikely that Luther was alarmed at the prospect of the Reichsbank being forced into a scheme which it would find irresponsibly inflationary, and hoped for support from an academic group which would enable him to torpedo the whole enterprise before it really got started. If this was his intention, he was successful, since by the end of the discussions he could claim that the sense of the meeting was that the scheme as it stood was too ambitious to be undertaken safely. Smaller versions of it, which did recommend themselves to many of those present, would not be enough, he claimed, to affect the overall situation and would fall within the parameters of existing Reichsbank policy.[49]

However, Luther glossed over the very striking emphasis placed by many speakers at the conference on the extreme dangers of doing nothing in the crisis. Indeed, only a very few of those present actually thought it best just to let the crisis burn itself out and rely on the self-healing mechanisms of the market. Among those who expressed qualified support for Lautenbach's scheme were Eucken and Röpke. Both stressed their commitment to market principles and denied any sort of desire to engage in planning or interventionism for its own sake. Röpke claimed that even to contemplate such measures as were

[49] For the version of the Lautenbach scheme presented to the conference, see K. Borchardt and H. O. Schötz (eds.), *Wirtschaftspolitik in der Krise: Die (Geheim-) Konferenz der Friedrich-List-Gesellschaft im September 1931 über die Möglichkeiten und Folgen einer Kreditausweitung* (Baden-Baden, 1991), 309–25. For Luther's summing up, see ibid. 300–4. The text of the proceedings is published in this book, together with a helpful introduction by Knut Borchardt. For a discussion of the issues involved, see also K. Borchardt, 'Wirtschaftliche Beratung in der Krise: Die Rolle der Wissenschaft', in H.-A. Winkler (ed.), *Die deutsche Staatskrise 1930–1933: Handlungsspielräume und Alternativen* (Munich, 1992).

before them was distasteful (*unbehaglich*) and Eucken stressed that the real problem which faced the German economy was rigidity in prices and wages. Both cartel-restrictions and burdensome wage-contracts would have to be abrogated if the price mechanism was to be able to carry out its economic function.

Nevertheless, Eucken went on to point out that, with all the dangers involved in the Lautenbach Plan, the dangers of doing nothing were greater: *nunquam periculum sine periculo vincitur*.[50] In a situation where there was a complete dearth of entrepreneurial initiative, it was up to the state to help capitalism by mobilizing the life forces of the private market economy. Once that had got under way, then the normal price-regulators, which were not working in the crisis, would take over again.

Röpke argued that the situation had now reached the point where the crisis had entered a secondary phase, which went beyond a simple rectification of errors made during the boom period. In this phase of secondary deflation the crisis fed upon itself and the normal processes of self-correction would not work. Röpke was aware how difficult it would be to turn this situation around. The events of the summer had made hopes of a foreign loan remote, and Germany could not restart the world economy on her own. He made it clear he would much prefer an international action to a German one, but felt that something would have to be done to stop the disastrous process of contraction. Although he was cautious about claiming that they could achieve *Initialzündung*, a term for which he showed no particular enthusiasm, he was clearly in favour of risking the Lautenbach scheme, even though he thought it should be carried out cautiously, step by step, to avoid damaging Germany's standing abroad. Pre-empting one of Luther's arguments, he denied that the alternatives were 'all or nothing'. The most important consideration was to set in motion a positive chain of events to counteract the cumulative process of depression which had Germany in its grip.[51]

Eucken and Röpke were not the only experts who, however cautiously, supported Lautenbach in this discussion. The reformist Social Democrat Eduard Heimann saw merit in the scheme, although he rightly pointed out that it would be difficult to restore economic confidence without first establishing political stability. Heinrich Rittershausen, a specialist in finance and banking who had recently spent periods of research in Paris and at the London School of Economics, was

---

[50] Borchardt and Schötz (eds.), *Wirtschaftspolitik in der Krise*, 148.
[51] Ibid. 284–8.

optimistic about the possibilities of expanding credit by government initiative, and critical of the high interest-rates being charged by the Reichsbank. He, like Eucken and Röpke, referred to contemporary works of Keynes, though without treating these in any sense as holy writ. Rittershausen would find himself in a similarly lively discussion over economic policy with Eucken in January 1948, and on that occasion the outcome was much more satisfactory for both of them.[52]

At this juncture however, the Reichsbank and the government remained wedded to their deflationary course. They were reinforced in this the following weekend, when the British government decided to go off the gold standard, thus devaluing the pound. Whether the German position in its response to this was entirely logical is a matter open to debate.[53] Certainly the negative consequences of allowing the crisis to burn itself out without taking corrective measures, consequences about which Röpke and Eucken had presented such dire warnings in the *List-Gesellschaft* meeting, were not slow to arrive. Unemployment was over 6 million in the winter of 1931–2, and the unpopularity of the Brüning Government plumbed new depths. The beneficiary was Hitler.

It is easy to be wise after events. The economic situation facing Germany in 1931–2 was extremely hazardous, and was not helped by the difficulties faced by other countries, such as Britain and the USA. Nevertheless, the question still remains whether Chancellor Brüning really paid enough attention to the negative domestic effects of his government's deflationary policies, and whether his main aim was to ameliorate hardship, or whether he was not rather concentrating on foreign-policy objectives such as 'breaking the chains of Versailles'.

Röpke remained highly critical of Brüning, describing him after the Second World War as a 'stubborn Westphalian imbued with reserve-officer and front-soldier complexes which sometimes produced comic results. His economic policy at that time [1931–2] was a copy-book example of how not to try to overcome such a crisis.'[54]

---

[52] See below, Ch. 9. For Rittershausen's contributions to the discussion, see Borchardt and Schötz (eds.), *Wirtschaftspolitik in der Krise*, 149–56 and 177–84.

[53] For Borchardt's views, see Borchardt and Schötz (eds.), *Wirtschaftspolitik in der Krise*, 46–50, and Borchardt, 'Wirtschaftspolitische Beratung in der Krise', *passim*. For other views, see C.-L. Holtfrerich, 'Vernachlässigte Perspektiven der wirtschaftlichen Probleme der Weimarer Republik', in Winkler (ed.), *Die deutsche Staatskrise*, 133–50, and the brief comment by H. Mommsen, ibid. 152. There is a very judicious contribution to the debate in G. D. Feldman, 'Industrialists, Bankers and the Problem of Unemployment in the Weimar Republic', *Central European History*, 25/1 (1992) (Atlantic Highlands, NJ, 1993), 76–96.

[54] Letter from Röpke to Pechel, 7 Feb. 1947, publ. in *Wilhelm Röpke, Briefe: Der Innere Kompaß, 1934–1966*, ed. E. Röpke (Erlenbach-Zurich, 1976), 93.

Brüning certainly seems to have set his face against any attempt to remedy the hardships of the slump by reflationary policies, even when mild protests were made to him by such people as Luther, or by the state secretary in the Finance Ministry, Hans Schäffer. To the latter, Brüning sneeringly remarked that the German people always collapsed just before they were about to win a victory, a reference to his own obsession with the shame of Germany's defeat in November 1918.[55]

Lautenbach's scheme was dropped, though it did bear some relationship to the measures actually put into effect by the Papen Government about a year later. Alexander Rüstow himself subsequently denied that he had been consulted about Papen's policy.[56]

Although Röpke had been in contact with Rüstow for several years, and both of them were involved in the *Deutscher Bund für freie Wirtschaftspolitik*,[57] they do not seem to have been close friends. However, political events in Germany were soon to throw them together in a dramatic and unexpected manner. Hitler's accession to power in January 1933 and the Nazi 'revolution', which destroyed democracy in the months which followed, boded ill for academic freedom at German universities. As dean of his faculty at Marburg University, it fell to Röpke to deliver a valedictory speech in honour of his former teacher and deceased colleague, Professor Walter Troeltsch. In the course of this address Röpke remarked that Troeltsch would not have fitted well into the contemporary scene because he was a 'gardener' of culture, whereas the current fashion was to uproot that cultural garden and transform it into primeval forest (*Urwald*). Such comments could not pass unpunished in the Third Reich. It therefore came as no surprise when Röpke was one of the first casualties of the Nazi Law to Restore the Professional Civil Service, which was actually a political purge of the bureaucracy, including the university teaching profession.[58] Friends

---

[55] H.-J. Rüstow, 'Entstehung und Überwindung der Wirtschaftskrise', 140. See also D. Hertz-Eichenrode, *Wirtschaftskrise und Arbeitsbeschaffung: Konjunkturpolitik 1925/6 und die Grundlagen der Krisenpolitik Brünings* (Frankfurt, 1982), 136–4; U. Büttner, 'Politische Alternativen zum Brüningschen Deflationskurs: Ein Beitrag zur Diskussion über "ökonomische Zwangslagen" in der Endphase von Weimar', *Vierteljahrshefte für Zeitgeschichte*, 36/2 (Apr. 1989), 216. Also G. Schulz 'Inflationstrauma, Finanzpolitik und Krisenbekämpfung in den Jahren der Wirtschaftskrise, 1930–1933', in Feldman (ed.), *Die Nachwirkungen der Inflation*, 263–6.

[56] See the exchange of letters, 27 Oct. and 2 Nov. 1932, between Rüstow and W. Köhler, the director of the Goebel AG in Darmstadt. Köhler was highly critical of Papen's plans and accused Rüstow of being responsible for them. BA Rüstow NL, no. 26.

[57] See letter of 26 Apr. 1932, Röpke to Rüstow, over the waiver of Röpke's subscription to the association. Ibid., no. 27.

[58] Neumark, 'Erinnerungen an Wilhelm Röpke', 9–13. The law came into effect on 7 Apr. 1933.

urged Röpke to compromise with the new regime in order to regain his position. Since he was neither Jewish nor a Marxist it might well have been possible for him to work his passage in this way, but he refused to bow the knee to National Socialism and had little time for those who did. The alternatives were impotence or exile. Röpke chose the latter. The opportunity arose to migrate to Turkey. In the autumn of 1932 Atatürk, the Turkish dictator, had instructed a professor of education in Geneva, Albert Malche, to plan the reform of Turkish universities along modern lines. When the Nazi purges began, Malche saw the opportunity of providing help for their victims, and together with a Frankfurt pathologist, Philipp Schwartz, he started to organize a group of German scholars and clinicians to migrate to Turkey. Röpke accepted their invitation and himself became active in the Emergency Association of German Academics Abroad, which continued its work in Switzerland and recruited more scholars for Turkish universities.

One of those whom he helped to leave was Alexander Rüstow. As an employee of an industrialists' association, Rüstow was not in quite such a vulnerable position as Röpke, but he had made no secret of his hostility to National Socialism, and his efforts to persuade governments to take firm action against interest groups in 1932 was evidently seen as an indication that he favoured the regime of General von Schleicher, whom Hitler replaced as Chancellor. In March 1933 his home was searched by the Gestapo, who confiscated a starting-pistol and a card-index file marked 'SS'. This did not prove as exciting for them as it looked because it related to Rüstow's thoughts on 'Selige Sehnsucht', a poem by Goethe.[59] Rüstow was not immediately subjected to further harassment but his position was evidently insecure. Had he been in Germany on 30 June 1934 he might well have died during the 'night of the long knives', in which Röhm, Schleicher, and others who had fallen foul of the regime were murdered. As it was, he was safe in Turkey, established in Kadiköy, a suburb of Istanbul overlooking the Sea of Marmara. Röpke himself lived within hailing distance, as did another German economist, Alfred Isaac.[60] The exiles tried to put a brave face on their changed circumstances, but this new life was very different from that to which they were accustomed. Grappling with the Turkish language, in which they were ultimately supposed to instruct their pupils, was not easy.[61] Although in one

---

[59] D. A. Rustow in A. Rüstow, *Freedom and Domination*, p. xvii.

[60] Neumark, 'Erinnerungen an Wilhelm Röpke', 13.

[61] For Rüstow's comments on life in Turkey, see his letter to Eucken of 5 Jan. 1936, in which he describes his teaching commitments as 'unpleasant' but 'bearable'. Since he was able to concentrate them all in two days a week and spend the rest of his time on his own work, this was hardly surprising. He also bemoaned the lack of libraries, but

sense political refugees, they had not been formally declared enemies of the state by the Nazis and they retained their German nationality. They had to beware of attempts by the German government to manipulate them for political purposes. Nevertheless, Rüstow maintained contact with men of independent mind in Germany, including Eucken, with whom he kept up a lively correspondence.

For all the neo-liberals, the phenomenon of the Third Reich, whether viewed from abroad or experienced at home, was to affect their way of thinking about the nature of human society. On the one hand, it strengthened their aversion to violence, national egoism, and power-worship. On the other, it tended to weaken their fastidious attitude towards the masses and political democracy, since it was the supposedly superior élites who had helped Hitler into power. They were therefore impelled to seek a way of combining liberal values with social justice.

claimed to have made this good by extensive second-hand purchases. Rüstow to Eucken, 5 Jan. 1936, BA Rüstow NL, no. 3, pp. 458–9.

3

Neo-liberalism and its Enemies: National Socialism and Social Democracy

HITLER'S accession to power in January 1933 seemed to underline the impotence of the economics profession in the face of the world economic crisis. As a British historian of the German slump has written: 'Most economists, then, were in practice useless in the sense that they could offer interesting diagnoses, but no cures. Many Germans in the 1930's, however, clearly wanted a cure, and wanted it very urgently.'[1]

As we have seen, Röpke, at least, had proposed a 'cure', as had the Rüstow brothers, and they were not alone. Nevertheless, in the public mind economists seemed to have failed Germany, and this sense of failure was damaging to the confidence of the profession as a whole. The self-esteem of German economists *vis-à-vis* state officials and 'men of business' had, in any case, never been very great.

After Walter Eucken's untimely death in 1950, Leonhard Miksch remarked in an obituary that, when Eucken began his career, the German economics profession was not in a healthy state: 'Classical economic theory of Anglo-Saxon origin', he wrote, '. . . was only half-heartedly accepted in Germany. It was derided as being ideologically flabby and lacking in historical understanding.'[2]

Eucken and his sympathizers were determined to change this un-favourable intellectual climate, even though they were swimming against a powerful collectivist tide. Most of their contemporaries were willing to see economics used as the handmaiden of nationalist politics, the aim of which was to restore Germany to her former status as a leading European power. As we have seen, Heinrich Brüning, the last respectable politician to lead Germany before 1949, firmly rejected possible alternatives to his policy of deflation because they might help Germany's former enemies, particularly the French. After Brüning fell,

---

[1] James, *The German Slump*, 342.
[2] L. Miksch, 'Walter Eucken', *Kyklos: Internationale Zeitschrift für Sozialwissenschaft*, 4/fasc. 4 (1950), 282.

in May 1932, Franz von Papen seemed more flexible, but both he and his military successor, General von Schleicher, put nationalist objectives such as rearmament before attempts to improve international co-operation. Nor were they encouraged from abroad to do otherwise. As the depression deepened, so a devil-take-the-hindmost attitude developed in Western countries, weakening further the recuperative powers of the world economy.

Once Hitler had taken over, on 30 January 1933, the outlook became entirely bleak from the liberal viewpoint. Although Nazi economic policy was soon run by the apparently 'respectable' Hjalmar Schacht, it involved increased cartel regulation in the domestic market and stringent controls over foreign trade. 'Autarky' became a fashionable objective, even if Schacht himself was too sophisticated to take it very seriously.

Hitler's own economic views are best summed up in his notorious memorandum on the Four Year Plan in 1936: 'The nation does not live for the economy, for economic leaders, or for economic and financial theories: on the contrary, it is finance and the economy, economic leaders and theories, which all owe an unqualified service in this struggle for the self-assertion of our nation.'[3]

The triumph of such primitive notions was in one sense a justification of the position adopted by Eucken, Rüstow, Röpke, Böhm, and others of their persuasion during the early 1930s. By abdicating responsibility for economic policy, the economics profession had left the way open for simplistic collectivism. Far from strengthening any commitment to liberal economics, the experience of the slump served to alienate the public from it still further. 'Capitalism' and the 'anarchy' of the market were blamed for the depression. Economic stagnation in capitalist countries could be contrasted with the 'achievements' of the Five Year Plans in Soviet Russia. Roosevelt's 'New Deal', admirable though its intentions were, implied an interventionist philosophy on the part of government, and even in Britain the old commitment to free trade had been supplanted by a system of imperial preference. In salons and universities, Marxist and Fascist intellectuals were able to agree with each other on one point at least, economic liberalism was 'dead' and could not solve the problems of the mass age.

It is in their moment of greatest triumph, however, that intellectual orthodoxies are most vulnerable. The more the free-price mechanism

---

[3] Quoted and trans. in J. Noakes and G. Pridham (eds.), *Documents on Nazism* (1st edn.; London, 1974), 403.

and the laws of supply and demand were repressed by planners, controls, cartels, and tariffs, the more glaring were the failings of systems which tried to operate without them. Nevertheless, failures alone cannot activate opposition. Commitment and determination are needed if an alternative view is to make headway.

This was especially true under the circumstances in Germany after 30 January 1933. Political history can easily be slotted into periods bounded by the outbreak of wars, the collapse of ministries, the triumph of revolution or counter-revolution. Intellectual and economic trends are more difficult to treat in this way. Life in German universities did not cease because Hitler came to power. It became less pleasant and more sinister. Many opponents of the regime, including liberals like Röpke and Rüstow, but in more cases social democrats, Communists, and Jews, were forced to flee the country. Otherwise, work had to go on. Some economists threw in their lot with the regime and supported the 'national awakening'. For those who regarded economics simply as a handmaiden of national power-politics, such a transition was easy. Some of a more liberal disposition might also be attracted by the dynamism of Hitler's regime, and the new start it apparently offered after years of depression. They might hope their expertise would temper the crude nationalism of their Nazi masters—a vain aspiration as things turned out.

Others, however, stuck to their academic task without openly defying Nazi domination, but also without accepting Nazi ideology. Amongst them were to be found Walter Eucken and his colleagues at Freiburg. The record of the Freiburg school of economists was exemplary in the distance it managed to maintain from the Nazi regime. This was due in large part to the courage and determination of Eucken himself, who refused to allow the malignant pressures on university life in the Third Reich to deflect his colleagues from their academic pursuits. These pressures were indeed very strong. At Freiburg University, as elsewhere, the process euphemistically described as 'co-ordination', or *Gleichschaltung*, threatened the fundamental values of education. The nationalist philosopher Martin Heidegger became vice-chancellor (*Rektor*) of the university, and on 19 July 1933 he told the student body: 'Academic freedom, about which so much fuss is made, is being driven out of German universities because this freedom, being only negative in character, was not genuine . . . The concept of freedom for the German student can now recover its true nature.'[4]

---

[4] H. Michaelis and E. Schraepler (eds.), *Ursachen und Folgen vom deutschen Zusammenbruch 1918 und 1945 bis zur staatlichen Neuordnung Deutschlands in der Gegenwart* (26 vols.; Berlin, n.d.), ix. 460–1.

The sort of 'true' freedom envisaged by Heidegger can be divined from references in the same speech to the folk community, national honour, and the spiritual task of the German people. The latter was described in such woolly terms as to be incomprehensible, but led on to talk of 'knowledge service' (*Wissensdienst*), which should have the same status as labour service or military service. In the autumn of the same year, Heidegger joined with some other high-ranking academic figures in a public declaration of support for Hitler.

Röpke later looked back on the deportment of academics in the Nazi era with anger and contempt: 'the representatives of learning in general behaved with what can be described only as cowardice or cynical opportunism or mental and moral perversion . . . It was a scene of prostitution that has stained the honourable history of German learning, and represents one of the worst and most fateful examples of group responsibility.'[5]

The number of students at German universities declined, but even more damaging was the effect on their reputation in the outside world. Whilst universities in Britain and the USA received a welcome injection of professional expertise as independent-minded or persecuted staff-members emigrated, the pre-eminent position of German scholarship was sacrificed.

Despite all this, Eucken did not allow the work of his economics department to be compromised by the new situation. His researches remained free from Nazi taint, and he maintained links with colleagues abroad, even if they were *personae non gratae* with the regime.

His own position in relation to Nazi doctrines was not in doubt. In October 1933, at a time when Heidegger and his sympathizers were committing German academic life to the Führer, Eucken published an article under the title 'What is the Point of Thought' ('Denken— Warum?'). In this he contrasted the respect for reason and common sense shown by the political theorists of the eighteenth century with the fear of reason, contempt for thought, and confidence in irrational forces which characterized the modern epoch. Romanticism had begun the flight from reason; Schopenhauer and Nietzsche had decisively furthered it. The anti-rational views of a narrow intellectual stratum had penetrated into the broader public and now dominated contemporary thinking. To act had become more important than to think. Thought was condemned as 'liberal'—in itself a term of abuse. Fashionable social scientists sneered at Kant's firm belief in an unchanging, unalterable logical structure of human reason. They claimed that advances

[5] The comments by Röpke are from Röpke, *The German Question*, 73 *et passim*.

in anthropology had proved this to be untrue. So why should one continue to think?

Eucken gave a fearless answer. The course of history does not deny the laws of logic; it confirms them. The formulations based on logical thought constantly prove themselves to be true when the facts are examined. This holds good for daily life, in scientific research, and even at the more rarefied levels of diplomacy, since Bismarck's policies were formulated on the basis of sound information logically deployed. He poured scorn on the notion that reason is something relative and subjective. It did not matter if anthropologists believed that the thought of the Hottentots was different from that of the Germans, or that the average German did not think like Leibniz; the validity of conclusions arrived at by the process of logic was in no way diminished by such claims. It was all very well to demand strong wills and healthy bodies, but the age was showing an unhealthy commitment to a barren and arbitrary irrationalism, an uncritical wallowing in emotions. By rejecting the creative power of rational thought, society was damaging itself.

To publish this at a time when Hitler had established his one-party regime and many opponents were already suffering persecution was the action of a brave man. It clearly put Eucken at the opposite end of the intellectual spectrum to Heidegger, and made him a *bête noire* for Nazi students.[6]

Certainly German universities were grievously damaged by the Nazis. Many staff were either dismissed or felt themselves forced to leave. The professional bodies representing staff and the student organizations were put under Nazi control. Philistine pressures brought to bear on the academic community included the ritual burning of books and such pinpricks against independent minds as the withdrawal of Thomas Mann's honorary doctorate by the University of Bonn. The humiliation of higher learning under Hitler is perhaps best illustrated by Gauleiter Julius Streicher's notorious speech in Berlin in 1938, when he declaimed: 'If you put the brains of all university professors into one side of a pair of scales and the brain of the Führer into the other, which side do you think would sink?'[7]

Eucken refused to be intimidated. In 1934 and 1935 his assistant, Paul Hensel, organized academic discussion-groups in the Black Forest, so

---

[6] W. Eucken, 'Denken—Warum?' in *Tatwelt*, Oct. 1933, 148–52. I am grateful to Hans Joachim Voth for drawing my attention to this article.

[7] Noakes and Pridham (eds.), *Documents on Nazism*, 350. I have taken the liberty of changing the second word from 'one' to 'you', since I think it is more in keeping with Streicher's style. On university life in Germany under the Nazis—with special reference to the University of Hamburg—see J. Giles, *Students and National Socialism in Germany* (Princeton, NJ, 1985), esp. 101–29 and 151–62.

as to counteract the influence of some Nazi lecturers.[8] Eucken's lack of timidity can be illustrated by his invitation to a well-known social democratic economist, Gerhard Weisser, to address his seminar. Weisser was a reformist socialist—formerly a pupil of Leonhard Nelson—who believed that the market principle was compatible with a planned economy which would include the widest possible range of economic enterprises. It was a tribute to Eucken's students and his own authority within his department that no repercussions arose from these and similar discussions, which would have been strongly disapproved of by committed Nazis.[9] One advantage economists did possess in their dealings with the regime was that their subject was somewhat too technical for most Nazi functionaries to understand, so that the incompatibility between economic theories and Nazi ideology was not always apparent.

Eucken certainly saw no reason to alter his intention to rehabilitate classical economic theory and promote its practical application within the German economics profession. His writings, both before and after Hitler came to power, were bent towards that end. He saw liberal economics as a true science, which had to be defended against ignorant barbarism. Galileo and Kepler had been mocked and reviled, but their ideas eventually displaced those of their enemies. As Eucken himself put it:

However stridently and belligerently their opponents might behave, and however much they might predominate in numbers, they were ultimately forgotten, because their methods did not work. It will be just as impossible for the anti-rational trend of today to root out the rationally based school of economics. It is to this school that the future belongs, because it can solve the problems presented by the real world of economic life . . .[10]

Eucken wrote these words in 1934 as part of an introduction to a series of publications dealing with problems of theoretical economics. They illustrated his particular concern that economics should be accepted as a scientific discipline, based on coherent and defensible theories. He felt that the legacy of classical economists such as Adam Smith had been neglected, or even betrayed, by the German 'historical' school, which downgraded economics to make it a tool of vested interests. Such an approach was particularly associated with Gustav

---

[8] E.-W. Dürr, *Wesen und Ziele des Ordoliberalismus* (Winterthur, 1954), 9.

[9] The author was told of this occasion by Prof. Weisser himself, in an interview in Göttingen on 21 July 1984. For Weisser's views on democratic socialism see below, Chs. 14 and 16.

[10] W. Eucken, *Kapitaltheoretische Untersuchungen* (2nd edn.; Tübingen, 1954), 51. For information about the first edition, see the postscript by F. W. Meyer, 333–6.

von Schmoller, the doyen of German political economy in the second
half of the nineteenth century. In 1880 Schmoller had described the
function of his profession thus: 'Like the chorus of a Greek tragedy, it
should not itself participate in the action but, separated from the stage
on which practical men are acting, accompany their work with a commentary and assess it according to the highest ideals of the age.'[11]

In Eucken's view it was precisely this willingness on the part of
German economists to allow their profession to be reduced to such a
humble role which had lost them so much public esteem. Eucken's
critique of this peculiarly 'historicist' approach to economics was illustrated very clearly in an article he published in *Schmollers Jahrbuch* for
1938.[12] He pointed out that, since the 1880s, there had been a tendency
among historians and social scientists in Germany to assume that all
truth was relative to its historical context. This implied that no firm
principles of economics could be worked out which would apply to all
economic systems. As a result, he claimed, German economists had
lost confidence in themselves as far as general theories were concerned,
and devoted their attention to specific areas of the economic process
at specific periods of time. 'Thus', he claimed 'there spread among
German economists a pedantic attention to detailed facts' (*ein punktuelles
Denken*).[13]

Eucken argued that this was to betray the discipline of economics.
Adam Smith had worked out his theories against a background of
eighteenth-century mercantilism, but they were of general validity, and
could be applied just as well to economic situations far removed from
Hanoverian Britain. Eucken drew a parallel with theories in natural
science, which remained true no matter what form of national development was occurring around them. If economists allowed economic
truths to be relativized, they opened the way for all kinds of special
pleading by vested interests. Theories of economics were not dogmas
or doctrines which could change with changing circumstances. They
were perceived truths about economic behaviour which held good
wherever the economic process operated.[14]

In the same year he produced a short and clearly written book
entitled 'What is the Point of Economics?' (*Nationalökonomie: Wozu?*).
In this he argued against the popular view that economists were of no
value to those who had to deal with practical affairs, and that in

[11] Id., *Nationalökonomie: Wozu?* (Leipzig, 1938), 44.
[12] Id., 'Die Überwindung des Historismus', *Schmollers Jahrbuch*, 62/2 (Munich, 1938),
63–86.
[13] Ibid. 69–70. 'Der Kultus des Faktischen', he wrote, 'breitet sich aus.'
[14] Ibid. 77–8, 81–2.

any case they were all divided against each other. He pointed out that in daily life practical people—whether they be businessmen or housewives—could not have a comprehensive view of the whole economy. He instanced the case of the Great Depression in the early 1930s, when employers had argued that wages were too high and thus caused unemployment, whereas trade unions argued that wages were too low and had restricted consumption. Who was right? Only scientific investigation and construction of valid general theories could answer that.

The greatest achievements of economic science had come in the first half of the nineteenth century, when, basing their actions on the theories of classical economists, statesmen had freed economic enterprise from mercantilist restrictions and feudal limitations on labour or trade. But, able as the classical authorities had been, they had not foreseen the complexities of historical development in modern states. Political forces had emerged which tended to thrust economic theorists on to the sidelines. Eucken pointed to the dangers of this situation, given the need felt by governments everywhere to adopt dynamic economic policies. A policy of stimulating business activity (*Konjunkturpolitik*) could be successful only if it was based on a scientific understanding of business cycles.

State intervention of various kinds in the economy was growing all the time, but without adequate realization of its impact on the overall market mechanism. For example, to hold coffee-prices at an artificially high level to cope with overproduction had simply led to even greater overproduction. Similarly, the belief that competition created 'chaos', and should be regulated, ignored the fact that there were different types of competition, some of which were necessary in a healthy economy. Only economic science could clarify these problems, explain the various different categories of economic activity, and set out the rules according to which a coherent economic order (*Wirtschaftsverfassung*) could be created.[15]

One of the difficulties faced by Eucken and his colleagues in Freiburg was that they were having to deal with economic issues in isolation from political ones. As we have seen, Eucken himself was no great enthusiast for mass politics, but nor did he relish a nationalist dictatorship contemptuous of the rule of law. It was therefore hard to enunciate 'correct' theories about economic processes if the political situation made it less and less likely they would ever be heeded. It was hardly surprising that some economists hoped that their expertise might be of

---

[15] W. Eucken, *Nationalökonomie: Wozu?*, 53–5.

use within the new and apparently dynamic regime led by Hitler, and that the Nazis might be persuaded to accept sound economic policies, more especially since their own ideas on the subject seemed either ambivalent or hopelessly naïve.[16]

Rüstow's call for a strong state in 1932 could have been seen as an appeal for authoritarian rule, although he himself clearly opposed the Nazis.[17] Economic liberals who chose to stay in Germany could therefore try to stress those features of the new regime with which they did have some sympathy in order to limit the damage Nazi attitudes would otherwise inflict on the national economy.

One interesting example of this dilemma occurs in the preface to Franz Böhm's treatise on the protection of competition against monopolies and cartels, which was published in 1933. Böhm pointed out that all the fulminations of politicians had not succeeded in altering the economic facts of life. Attempts to overcome economic difficulties by giving privileges to one interest-group or another had proved counterproductive. Now the Nazis were talking of a corporate state. Politically, Böhm implied, this might be a good thing, overcoming the class conflict and party strife of the Weimar Republic. The real danger was that, in the economic sphere, cartels and other special-interest groups would use this corporate form of organization to stifle competition, eliminate consumer choice, and undermine the market.[18] 'The experience of the last decades', he wrote, 'has shown that business associations and interest groups have mastered the art of turning every politically influential ideology to their own purposes in a most effective manner.'[19]

Whether sailing under the flag of entrepreneurial independence, exploiting the chances offered by a planned economy, or adapting themselves to the concept of economic democracy, they constantly pressed their own special interests. It was greatly to be feared that monopolists and cartel lobbies would seek to obtain from the corporate state those privileges denied to them by earlier systems of government. Böhm argued that the whole intention of the new corporatist theories, which had caught the imagination of the public, was to organize the nation politically so that conflicts between classes, parties, and economic interests would cease. The individual would be satisfied to follow his own calling, appreciating that, far from being at odds with

---

[16] For an interesting discussion of the ambivalence of the Nazi leadership towards capitalism, see H. A. Turner, *German Big Business and the Rise of Hitler* (Oxford, 1985), 60–82 and 181–91.

[17] See above, Ch. 2.

[18] Böhm, *Wettbewerb und Monopolkampf*, pp. vi–xiv.

[19] Ibid., p. xi.

those in other walks of life, his relationship with them was naturally harmonious. It was clear, however, that such harmony would soon be disrupted if certain trades or professions were given the right to dominate their own market at the expense of consumers. If that happened the political concept of the corporate state would be overwhelmed by the economic egoism of special-interest groups. The resulting conflict would be even more destructive of the community interest than the old party system had been.[20]

How far Böhm really thought that corporatism was a valid idea is open to question. His own career does not suggest any tendency to bow the knee to National Socialism. He had left the Ministry of Economics to take up academic work at Freiburg University in 1933, and stayed on there as a lecturer in the law faculty. In 1938 he obtained a post at a college of commerce (*Handelshochschule*) in Leipzig, but was soon suspended for outspoken criticism of anti-Semitism, his own wife being Jewish. Although it was suggested to him that he might find employment in part of the Nazi empire, such as Göring's Four Year Plan office, he refused to compromise. In 1940 he had his right to lecture taken away from him, and was also removed from the list of active state lawyers.[21]

Certainly Böhm's concern to protect the individual's economic rights by establishing a legal framework designed to further competition could hardly have been more alien to the power-worshippers in the Nazi party. Nevertheless, his comments reveal the problems facing men of intelligence and good will at the beginning of the Third Reich. Many of them had not been enthusiastic about the form democracy had taken under the Weimar Republic. Most of them accepted that Germany had been harshly treated by the peace settlement in 1919. They could not be sure how long the Nazi domination of Germany would last, or what sort of system would replace it if it were to fall. So long as bourgeois life in Germany was not greatly disturbed by Hitler's regime, it seemed reasonable to make the best of a bad job by trying to influence government policies in the direction of market economics.

On the other hand, it should not be forgotten that, within a few months of Hitler's accession to power, the individual rights which liberals sought to protect had been widely violated. In particular, free speech had been crushed by intimidation and the Goebbels propaganda machine. Books and articles, however scholarly, had to be carefully

---

[20] Ibid., p. xiv.
[21] For biographical details, see the curriculum vitae in KAS Böhm NL.

phrased if the author and his publisher were not to run the risk of official disapproval. Although, before 1939, Nazi repression was not as pervasive as Stalin's terror in Russia, criticism of the regime could be taken as a pretext for imprisonment or removal of career prospects. In assessing the work of neo-liberals in Germany during the Third Reich, one has to bear in mind that it was not a friendly environment in which to campaign for the rule of law and free competition. If even such a clear-headed and personally courageous figure as Franz Böhm tried at first to enlist the support of Hitler's authoritarian regime in his battle against greedy pressure-groups, it is not surprising that other conventionally trained economists might feel tempted to work with the Nazis. Protestant intellectuals, in particular, were bereft of a political base by the end of the Weimar period. German liberalism had fallen to pieces as a political movement. There was some reason to hope that the Nazis, whose economic notions seemed superficial and contradictory, might be open to wise professional advice once they assumed the responsibility of power. The fact that Hjalmar Schacht, the former head of the Reichsbank who had been associated with the stabilization of the mark in 1924, was willing to resume office under the Nazis and even to become Economics Minister, gave some credence to this view.

The heady enthusiasm created by a new, nationalistic government bursting with confidence should also not be underestimated. After a grim period of hopelessness and economic contraction, Germany's industrial life began to move again. Within three years the economy was booming, and by the end of 1936 unemployment figures of 6 million had dwindled to such an extent that labour shortages began to be more of a problem than labour surplus. The impact of these events, and the political climate they created, was felt by all classes of the population, including members of the learned professions. Those who were not crystal clear in their commitment to parliamentary democracy were willing to compromise with the new regime if it met some of their own academic and personal needs.

Many individuals faced an awkward moral choice between acceptance of a regime which they found distasteful, but with the objectives of which they sympathized, and the uncertain fate awaiting those who rejected the new system. The latter would at best lose hope of promotion and at worst find themselves unemployed or physically persecuted. It is easy for critics who have never been in such a dilemma to take a lofty view of those who chose discretion rather than valour.

It is, of course, also true that many 'nationally minded' academics were delighted with Hitler's success in breaking the shackles of Versailles. Conventionally trained economists regarded the destruction of trade unions with approval, and were relieved by the apparent willingness of the Nazi regime to allow the capitalist system to survive. For those who had already accepted Schmoller's role of a Greek chorus, the effectiveness of Nazi programmes seemed to justify the methods employed.

One market economist who did succumb, albeit temporarily, to Nazi dynamism was Alfred Müller-Armack.[22] Of all the major architects of the social market economy, Müller-Armack was the only one actually to become a member of the Nazi Party. Two years younger than Röpke, he had made an average rather than a brilliant start to his career, having gained his doctorate at Cologne in 1923 and qualified as a university lecturer at the same university in 1926. His academic supervisor, Leopold von Weise, had also worked on the concept of 'social liberalism', and Müller-Armack developed an early interest in social questions.

Like many other economists, he was concerned about the extent to which an interventionist policy had been allowed to develop in Germany on a hand-to-mouth basis, without the development of an appropriate theory or economic system to regulate it. Parliament and administration had yielded piecemeal to demands for help from various quarters; the national interest had suffered thereby. Dismissing determinist theories of economic development, and particularly Marxism, Müller-Armack urged the need to understand the workings of the capitalist system and to develop a coherent policy towards interventionism which would preserve individual initiative whilst accepting the political facts and the necessities created by historical situations.

Such views did not cause him to espouse classical liberal solutions to Germany's economic problems. On the contrary, they led him into an admiration for Italian Fascism. He regarded liberalism and Marxism as products of an outmoded system of thought which had been created in the age of enlightenment, but which had now been superseded by the German historical school. He was particularly dismissive of natural law and individual rights based on concepts of reason. Parliamentary government should be replaced by a dynamic leadership responsive to the national will. Free trade was an exploded concept, and the depression was demonstrating how each nation had to look to its own interests. Marxists were wrong to want to abolish private enterprise,

[22] Before 1945 he was sometimes referred to simply as Müller.

but private business should be harnessed to the historic tasks of the state. There was little in all this with which Hitler could not have agreed.

Before 1933 Müller-Armack's ideas were expressed in rather vague terms, although he displayed a distaste for uncontrolled cartels and a belief in a regulated market. In 1933, however, he published *Staatsidee und Wirtschaftsordnung im neuen Reich*, in which he enthusiastically recommended a form of corporatist economic system. He did, nevertheless, admit that ethical considerations remained important in human affairs, and stressed the need for economic policy to have a social component.[23]

It is possible that he overstated his commitment to the new order for career reasons. His decision to join the Nazi Party in May 1933 seems to have been conditioned by a mixture of concern for his professional position, which was at that time still insecure, and the hope that the dynamic new Nazi government might be persuaded to take measures to pull Germany out of the depression.[24]

At this time Müller-Armack was neither well known to, nor highly regarded by, the neo-liberal school of economists. Even during the Second World War Rüstow wrote to Eucken asking who he was, and expressing some doubts about the quality of his work. Eucken replied that he had met him only once, but that he seemed more interested in administration than scholarly matters and was the sort of person who might have been a railway official rather than a professor. In any case, it would be difficult to have an academic discussion with him.[25]

Nevertheless, Müller-Armack was a serious-minded and energetic man, even if he lacked the heroic qualities of his socially rather more elevated colleagues in the Freiburg School. Despite his membership of the NSDAP, he remained a committed Christian. The incompatibility of Hitler's behaviour with Christian moral principles became glaringly

---

[23] For Müller-Armack's social commitment, see the obituary address by Christian Watrin, 25 June 1979, C. Watrin, *Alfred Müller-Armack* (Krefeld, 1980), 17. His economic views in the early 1930s were set out in A. Müller-Armack, *Entwicklungsgesetze des Kapitalismus: Ökonomische, geschichtstheoretische und soziologische Studien zur modernen Wirtschaftsverfassung* (Berlin, 1932), esp. 104–17 and 215–17. For his espousal of Fascist corporatism, see A. Müller-Armack, *Staatsidee und Wirtschaftsordnung im neuen Reich* (Berlin, 1933), esp. 7–11, 25–8, 33–5, 53–62. His comment that ethical questions remained of undiminished importance when making political decisions is on p. 27. It is one of the few redeeming features of a generally wretched book.

[24] It is, of course, impossible to be sure of any individual's motives in joining the NSDAP in this period. It is unlikely that Müller-Armack remained an enthusiastic Nazi for very long. See correspondence relating to his denazification, 1946–7, in Müller-Armack NL, KAS I-236-030.

[25] Eucken to Rüstow, 27 Sept. 1942, BA Rüstow NL, no. 3, pp. 256–9.

obvious at the time of the 'Röhm purge' in June 1934. After the inception of the Four Year Plan in 1936, Müller-Armack was confronted with *dirigiste* policies incompatible with his own commitment to the market economy. He turned somewhat aside from his work on economic theory and began researching the connections between religious denominations and economic development in various parts of Europe.

For all the neo-liberals, whether at home or abroad, the Third Reich was a phenomenon which was to affect their way of thinking about the nature of human society. On the one hand, it strengthened their aversion to violence, national egoism, and power-worship. On the other, it tended to weaken their fastidious attitude towards the masses, forcing them to seek a method of combining market economics with social justice. Operating under very different circumstances and sometimes in isolation from one another, neo-liberal intellectuals continued to seek their 'middle way' between *laissez-faire* and collectivism, despite the pressures put upon them by Hitler's increasingly repressive regime.

The last, but in many ways the most influential, figure associated with the social market economy has yet to make his appearance in this narrative. This is not fortuitous. Before the Second World War he had not attained much prominence. Like Müller-Armack, he was not from a privileged and intellectual middle-class background, and had not made quite the same dazzling start to his career as Eucken or the precocious Röpke. Nor had he obtained a university chair.

Ludwig Erhard was the son of a shopkeeper in Fürth in northern Bavaria. Having been severely wounded in the First World War, he was not considered fit enough to enter the family drapery business. Instead he enrolled for a diploma course at the new college of commerce (*Handelshochschule*) which had just been established in Nuremberg.

His mentor there was Wilhelm Rieger, a believer in the strict application of market principles to the problems of micro-economics. Rieger rejected the ideas of a 'just price' or a 'reasonable profit' which were widespread amongst small businessmen at that time. The only 'just' price was the market price. He was a firm believer in sound money and was one of those demanding tough measures to stabilize the mark in 1923. As he put it, 'Inflation cannot give or distribute more than we have produced. We must confine ourselves to that which our economy produces.'[26]

Erhard did not rest content with his diploma but went on to work

---

[26] Heusgen, *Ludwig Erhards Lehre*, 52 and 66, citing W. Rieger *Einführung in die Privatwirtschaftslehre* (Nuremberg, 1928), 52. See also W. Rieger, 'Die Wiederherstellung einer stabilen Rechnungseinheit', in *Wilhelm Rieger: Erinnerungen und Dokumente aus 50 Jahren seines Wirkens*, ed. J. Fettel (Nuremberg, 1968), 165.

for a doctorate under Franz Oppenheimer, another academic with an original turn of mind. Oppenheimer was a professor of sociology and theoretical economics at Frankfurt University. The combination of disciplines is not without interest, for it illustrates a tendency among neoliberal thinkers to combine concern for healthy social relationships with their commitment to the free market.

Oppenheimer developed his own, rather idiosyncratic, views into a concept of what he called 'liberal socialism'. This involved a rejection of both *laissez-faire* capitalism and Marxism, and the establishment of a just social order within which free competition would be protected by the state. Before that could be done, however, there would have to be an assault on the unjust distribution of landed property, which Oppenheimer saw as the main cause of economic distress. The market could operate properly only if men enjoyed a fundamental equality which was incompatible with the existence of overmighty landowners. 'What is the cause of social deprivation?' he asked rhetorically, '. . . for three centuries there has always come the same answer: "Monopoly."'

Once ground rents and land speculation had been abolished, the economy would blossom in untrammelled competition. This was what distinguished liberal socialism from the collectivist variety espoused by Marx. Nobody could claim that to make such a system work men would have to become angels. They would be following their natural impulses. It will be noticed that Oppenheimer did not approach his discipline from the classical liberal standpoint. He seems to have based his prescriptions as much on the labour theory of value as on supply-and-demand. Without accepting Marx's class-war analysis, he was concerned to ensure that labour received its just rewards, as it would in a competitive economy from which landlordism had been banished by legal rather than confiscatory measures.[27]

Oppenheimer's teaching impressed economists of varied political persuasions. Some reformist social democrats, like Eduard Heimann and Adolf Löwe, were among them, as was Erik Nölting, a leading

---

[27] F. Oppenheimer, *Die soziale Frage und der Sozialismus: Eine kritische Auseinandersetzung mit der marxistischen Theorie* (Jena, 1925). See, e.g., remarks on the evils of monopoly, 3–4; and on human behaviour, 103–4. See also H. F. Wünsche, *Ludwig Erhards Gesellschafts- und Wirtschaftskonzeption: Soziale Marktwirtschaft als politische Ökonomie* (Stuttgart, 1986), 74–81. Horst Wünsche makes out a most interesting case for regarding Erhard's economic and social conceptions as quite distinct from those of neo-liberals and other architects of the social market economy, and claims for him a consistency of approach to economic problems which puts him in a different category from others tackling the same problems. I have found a great deal of value in Wünsche's account, especially in the light he sheds on Erhard's early writings and the evidence of his reading habits provided by his library. Nevertheless, I still regard Erhard as a man whose major strengths lay in the fields of public relations and politics rather than theory.

exponent of socialist planning after the Second World War. Others were free-marketeers or even showed sympathy with the Nazis.[28]

Erhard did not accept all of Oppenheimer's notions, but he did regard him as the most influential of all his teachers. He took from him a commitment to free competition, a belief in the need to ensure that as many people as possible could participate in the market process, and the conviction that the competitive system could function best if property was widely distributed. Later on, when he was Chancellor of the Federal Republic, Erhard was to comment that he—and his friend Röpke—had reversed the adjective and the noun in 'liberal socialism', so that it became 'social liberalism'. Nevertheless, he had remained true to the spirit of his master's teaching.[29] Oppenheimer certainly reinforced Erhard's own conviction that social responsibility was an essential aspect of the economist's profession. It will be noticed that many of these ideas were very similiar to those being advocated by Rüstow, although Erhard arrived at them from the starting-point of economic theory rather than philosophical speculation.

One seminal influence which Erhard *did* share with other younger liberal economists was the experience of the inflation in the early 1920s. Partly as a result of it, he became fascinated with the problem of currency stability and wrote his doctoral thesis on the nature of money.[30] It should not be thought, however, that Erhard made a fetish of 'monetarism'. He took from Oppenheimer and his other teachers the view that money was simply a substitute for barter and had no intrinsic value:

It is a fallacy to believe that money is something apparently eternally present in the economy. In truth it is created daily by production [*Leistung*] and is dissipated in consumption, just as the illusion of lasting brilliance experienced at a great firework-display is actually caused by thousands of rockets which rise, one after the other, and then fall back again into the void.[31]

Erhard believed that it was the production and consumption of goods which was crucial to the creation of stable and prosperous economic conditions, not the manipulation of money. On the other

[28] Wünsche, *Erhards Gesellschaftskonzeption*, 59. For the flavour of some of their views, see G. Schmölders, *Der Wettbewerb als Mittel volkswirtschaftlicher Leistungssteigerung und Leistungsauslese* (Berlin, 1942), 196–208.

[29] In introd. to F. Oppenheimer, *Erlebtes, Erstrebtes, Erreichtes: Lebenserinnerungen* (Düsseldorf, 1964), 5. See also K. Hohmann, *Fränkische Lebensbilder*, ii: *Ludwig Erhard (1897–1977)* (Neustadt-Aisch 1984), 7–8. See also the same author's 'Aus dem Leben Ludwig Erhards: Die Jahre bis 1945', *Orientierungen zur Wirtschafts- und Gesellschaftspolitik*, 11 (Apr. 1982), 50 ff.

[30] L. Erhard, *Wesen und Inhalt der Werteinheit* (Frankfurt/M., n.d. [1924]).

[31] Wünsche *Erhards Gesellschaftskonzeption*, 157.

hand, he certainly favoured balanced budgets and the limitation of public debt.[32] His views were those of a liberally minded 'small man' from a shopkeeping background, a fact which may ultimately have given him an advantage over the sons of the intelligentsia, like Eucken or Röpke, whose minds were set on loftier abstractions.

In 1928 he took up employment in an institute founded at the Nuremberg Commercial College by Wilhelm Vershofen, a German pioneer in the field of market research. Vershofen looked to the USA as the inspiration for his organization; he wanted to collect empirical data on consumption and marketing which could be used in a scientific fashion to help avoid overproduction and mass unemployment.[33] Vershofen strengthened Erhard's existing inclination to stress the importance of the consumer in the economic process. He was also a strong believer in open international trade and flexible exchange-rates—a position which was to become very unfashionable in the years which followed.[34]

Erhard himself worked at the institute until 1942, although he does not seem to have got on too well with Vershofen, who was not the easiest of masters to serve. Erhard was responsible for many of the institute's publications, which were largely concerned with market research into consumer-goods industries—an economic sector less highly organized than those like coal, steel, and heavy engineering, and which benefited less from government protection. The institute also conducted surveys of production costs in consumer-goods industries. It was important to cultivate good personal relations with industrialists in the consumer-goods sector and with the officials who ran their trade organizations. Neither Vershofen nor his deputy relished this task, and it fell to Erhard to develop such contacts.[35] He thereby gained considerable knowledge about the actual operation of industrial concerns.

During his early years at the institute, Erhard visited the headquarters of the *Verein deutscher Maschinenbauanstalten*, where the head of the economics department was, of course, Alexander Rüstow. Rüstow had a soft spot for Vershofen, despite differences of opinion about some matters, and he evidently got on well with his new assistant. It is also clear that Erhard was aware of Wilhelm Röpke and his work.[36]

[32] Ibid. 153.
[33] Hohmann, *Fränkische Lebensbilder*, 211–18.
[34] Heusgen, *Ludwig Erhards Lehre*, 78–84.
[35] Wünsche, *Erhards Gesellschaftskonzeption*, 90 n. 1.
[36] T. Eschenburg, 'Aus persönlichem Erleben: Zur Kurzfassung der Denkschrift 1943/44', in L. Erhard, *Kriegsfinanzierung und Schuldenkonsolidierung Faksimiledruck der Denkschrift von 1943/44* (with introd. comments by Erhard, Eschenburg, and G. Schmölders) (Frankfurt/M., 1977), p. xv.

Certainly he cannot be regarded at this stage as part of a neo-liberal 'school'. His views on the economic crisis in the early 1930s were fairly radical, as might have been expected from a student of Oppenheimer. He shared his old teacher's view that the maldistribution of landed property should be rectified. He also believed that private profit and community interests were by no means naturally identical, but that the state must on occasion intervene to restrain private activities for the benefit of the economy as a whole. This should not involve a 'radical rupture in economic development' or 'economic experiments' but should rather stimulate demand for consumer goods and discourage the hoarding of capital. Erhard consistently favoured state intervention in the form of a policy of easier credit, which would reactivate consumer industries. He regarded such action as far more promising than financial help for production industry, which was unlikely to lead to a rapid rise in economic activity.[37]

Erhard was highly critical of nationalist economists like Hjalmar Schacht, and publicly attacked the views of the 'Harzburg Front'. As a result he could not hope for promotion to a university chair when the Nazis came to power, and he settled down to his work in the institute, which was expanding its activities, thanks not least to his energetic pursuit of contacts with industry.[38]

Despite his fundamentally liberal approach to politics, Erhard seems to have had some hopes that the proclaimed corporatism of the Nazis might enable the relatively weak consumer-goods industry to be defended against the excessive power of the coal and steel barons. In practice this hope proved vain; Nazi policies did not favour consumer production.[39]

On 15 July 1933, Hitler's government introduced the compulsory cartelization of German industry. In his writings on the subject in the 1930s Erhard was only cautiously critical. As befitted a market researcher concerned mainly with consumer goods, he ingeniously drew a distinction between price-fixing cartels in basic industries like coal and steel and those in industries producing finished goods. The former would damage the market and cripple competition by creating rigid (*starr*) prices, whereas in the latter case there would be so much

---

[37] See Erhard's article, 'Wirtschaftsbelebung von der Verbraucherseite', *Der deutsche Ökonomist*, 7 Oct. 1932, in *Ludwig Erhard, Gedanken aus fünf Jahrzehnten: Reden und Schriften*, ed. K. Hohmann (Düsseldorf, 1988), 37–42. See also V. Laitenberger, *Ludwig Erhard: Der Nationalökonom als Politiker* (Göttingen, 1986), 21–3, citing an unpublished manuscript by Erhard, 'Die Überwindung der Wirtschaftkrise durch wirtschaftspolitische Beeinflussungen'.

[38] Laitenberger, *Ludwig Erhard*, 25.

[39] Ibid. 27.

room for variations in quality and production types that competition could continue to operate. Price-fixing could then exert a beneficial effect by preventing ruinous dumping-techniques from driving perfectly respectable businesses into bankruptcy. The damage wrought by suicidal price-cutting was a problem which exercised many economists and businessmen in the traumatic years of the Great Depression.

As Erhard put it in 1936

A cartel is not actually damaging to the community if it devotes its energies to recovering the cost of production plus a reasonable profit, and if there are indeed situations in which such an objective is temporarily impossible, nobody can deny that they [cartels] can fundamentally be justified.[40]

This remark can hardly be taken as a ringing encomium for cartels, and it is clear throughout that Erhard preferred competition to restraints on entrepreneurial freedom. He did, however, show an early appreciation of the fact that a free market might be politically unpopular, and that prices approved by a state authority would be seen to be more 'just'. Society lacked the confidence in its own judgement to let prices be set without interference. Unless clear guide-lines existed, people would prefer to leave matters in the 'hands of persons . . . who could guarantee "just" decisions'.[41] Such supervision could be defended only if it tended towards what the market price was likely in practice to be. Erhard approved of Carl Goerdeler, the first Price Commissioner in the Third Reich, precisely because he took a liberal view of his functions. By 1936, when Goerdeler was replaced by a far more *dirigiste* and loyal Nazi, Erhard was already warning against exaggerated hopes being pinned on pricing policies. The real hope for the future lay in increased production.[42]

Erhard remained in touch with Goerdeler and seems to have influenced his thinking on economic matters. Goerdeler, who started out from a conservative, corporatist standpoint, had the intention of writing a popular handbook which would explain the principles of political economy to the man in the street. His draft of this shows the impact of Erhard's advice, stressing as it does the need for economic freedom, equality before the law, stable currency and balanced budgets, limitation of bureaucratic interference in the economy, prevention of unhealthy concentrations of economic power, and prohibition of cartels or other forms of price-fixing.[43]

---

[40] Wünsche, *Erhards Gesellschaftskonzeption*, 138–9.
[41] Ibid. 105.
[42] Ibid. 117.
[43] V. Laitenberger, 'Zur Programmatik und zur Politik Ludwig Erhards in der Vor- und Frühgeschichte der Bundesrepublik Deutschland', *Orientierungen zur Wirtschafts- und Gesellschaftspolitik*, 3 (1980), 20.

However pragmatic Erhard may have been on the cartel question, his commitment to market prices, his hostility to monopolies, and his interest in consumer industries put him into a category of professional economists unsympathetic to the prevailing mood in Germany during the 1930s, when cartelization, corporatism, and planning for nationalist purposes were very high on the agenda. It is interesting to note Erhard's later judgement on the failure of the Weimar Republic, which he had witnessed from his institute in Nuremberg. It was due, he claimed, not just to a lack of enthusiasm for democracy, but also to the Republic's 'impossible economic system, which was a fateful mixture of socialism, cartelization, and old-fashioned capitalism'.[44]

Erhard never ceased to be influenced by his dislike for these three evils: collectivism, market distortion, and *laissez-faire*. It was an attitude of mind which naturally led on to the social market economy. Certainly it was far removed from Marxism, which still coloured the views of the major democratic party in Germany, the SPD.

Implicit in neo-liberal thought was a rejection of socialism. The Weimar Republic had been dominated by the two parties which favoured a social, if not a socialist, approach. The Roman Catholic Centre Party was ill at ease with liberal individualism and, even though it accepted the sanctity of property, it regarded the market mechanism with distrust. But the real enemy was Marxism, represented by both the Communists and the Social Democratic Party, the SPD. The Communists could not conceivably compromise with liberal economic theories. However, it is important to notice that, just as there were those in the liberal camp ready to modify classical liberal doctrines about state interference in the light of historical experience, so there was an embryonic movement within the SPD to reassess the value of the free-market mechanism.

Once the new and fully democratic republic had been established in 1919, it was obvious to many in the SPD that it would be necessary for their party to attract voters who did not regard themselves as 'working class' let alone 'proletarian'. The SPD would have to turn itself into a genuine 'people's party', appealing to white-collar and professional people as well as rural voters, if it wished to expand its electoral base.[45] For the same reasons, the Centre Party needed to break out of its Roman

[44] J. M. Lukomski, *Ludwig Erhard, der Mensch und der Politiker* (2nd edn.; Düsseldorf, 1965), 45. The quotation is not taken verbatim from Erhard, but represents his views exactly.
[45] For the strength of the feeling in the majority SPD that such a broadening of the party's appeal was necessary, see H.-A. Winkler, *Von der Revolution zur Stabilisierung: Arbeiter und Arbeiterbewegung in der Weimarer Republik, 1918 bis 1924* (Berlin, 1984), 434–5.

Catholic ghetto and appeal to other denominations of the Christian faith.

It soon became obvious that neither party could succeed in this endeavour. The Centre continued to represent the Roman Catholic minority in Germany, and the SPD remained predominantly an *Arbeiter-partei*, or workers' party, even if some white-collar and rural workers supported it. It was not until after the Second World War that the SPD and the new Christian Democratic parties began to broaden their support to the point where they became genuine 'people's parties'.

For the Social Democrats to widen their appeal, they would have to reconsider their programme and stated objectives, deeply influenced as these were by the doctrines of class war and dialectical materialism. Although German social democracy was developed independently of Marx and would have existed without him, the influence of Marxist doctrine had been very important in helping to formulate policies at the time of the SPD's rebirth, after its emergence from Bismarckian illegality in 1890. Not surprisingly, the Prussian party, in particular, was embittered by its experiences and inclined to distrust any form of collaboration with 'bourgeois' politicians. The 1891 Erfurt Programme, which was for many years the ark of the covenant of German social democracy, looked forward to the expropriation of capitalist property and the victory of the proletariat, although its immediate aims were more modest, and concentrated on a thoroughgoing democratization of the German Empire.

In 1917 the Social Democrats had split over SPD support for the imperial war effort. The majority party (MSPD) was considerably less radical in its attitudes than the self-consciously revolutionary Independent Social Democratic Party (USPD), which had the Erfurt Programme printed in its membership books. The MSPD, led by Ebert, Scheidemann, Braun, and other pragmatic working-class politicians, was inclined to modify its economic policies in order to attract votes outside the limitations of the industrial proletariat. At its Kassel party congress in October 1920, a commission was set up to redraft the Erfurt Programme along more modern lines, and it was symptomatic of the mood in the party that the famous author of 'revisionism' in the SPD, Eduard Bernstein, was elected a member of this commission, against the original intentions of the party leadership.[46]

On 17 July 1921 a draft text was published which was a victory for moderation. There was no mention of class war. Proletarianization was described, not as the result of ineluctable historical forces, but as the

[46] Ibid. 437.

outcome of war and industrial concentration. Socialization of major industrial enterprises should take place when power concentrations made private ownership unjustifiable. It is true that when this was put to the Görlitz party congress in September 1921 some class-war rhetoric crept back into it. There was still talk of socializing large combines and transforming the capitalist system into a socialist one which would serve the common good. Nevertheless, the impression of the congress given by those who enthused over its work was that it had moved the party away from an association with a particular social class and had given it the character of a mass party committed to democracy.[47]

However, this opportunity was not followed up. The ill-fated USPD itself split over its relationship to Lenin's Communist International. Some members joined the newly formed Communist Party. Most of the others found their way to the majority SPD, the leadership of which yielded to the understandable temptation to make compromises in order to win the prodigals back into the fold. The result was a shift backwards—at least in rhetoric—to the old Marxist clichés. In 1925 the party did promulgate a new programme at its conference in Heidelberg. This document had to balance the pragmatism of the Görlitz document with the revolutionary expectations of former Independent Social Democrats, and even ex-Communists, who were now once again within the party. The chief author of the programme was Rudolf Hilferding, formerly a leading member of the USPD, and the man who was to dominate social democratic economic policy discussions in the second half of the 1920s. His handiwork at Heidelberg is described by the historian of the SPD in Weimar as 'the ideological price which the Majority Social Democrats had to pay for reunification with the SPD'.[48]

Certainly the tone of the Heidelberg Programme was unlikely to appeal to moderate opinion. It blamed capitalism for the declining living standards of the population and went on to assert that:

The aim of the working class can be achieved only through the transformation of capitalist private ownership of the means of production into community property. The transformation of capitalist production into socialist production, which is conducted by and on behalf of the community as a whole, will have the effect of allowing productive forces to develop and grow so that they become the source of the most wide-ranging welfare and fulfilment for all.[49]

---

[47] Ibid. 440–8.

[48] H.-A. Winkler, *Der Schein der Normalität: Arbeiter und Arbeiterbewegung in der Weimarer Republik, 1924 bis 1930*, (Berlin, 1985), 326.

[49] 'Das Parteiprogramm der Sozialdemokratischen Partei Deutschlands', in *Sozialdemokratischer Parteitag 1925 in Heidelberg, Protokoll mit dem Bericht der Frauenkonferenz* (repr. Berlin, 1974), 5.

This echoed the preamble to the Erfurt Programme, which had talked of the transformation of capitalist ownership of the means of production into social production, and claimed that this was the only way in which

large-scale production and the constantly growing productive capacities of the community can be changed, for the classes which have until now been exploited, from a source of misery and repression into a source of supreme welfare and universal self-fulfilment.[50]

It was, however, nothing new for the rhetoric of the party to be somewhat different from its practice. Before the First World War the chairman of the SPD, August Bebel, had been a humane and far-sighted politician, not a power-hungry revolutionary consumed with class resentments. His real goals had been democracy and a decent way of life for German workers. In the Weimar period social democratic leaders like the President of the Republic, Friedrich Ebert, or the Prime Minister of Prussia, Otto Braun, followed pragmatic and cautious policies of social reform. Their intention was to root democracy in the stony ground of a nation still smarting from defeat and disturbed by revolution. It was not their fault that they failed.

As for the Heidelberg Programme, those who bothered to read as far as its—relatively brief—section on economic policy found a blueprint for socialization which was not quite as comprehensive as the preamble would have suggested. Land and natural resources were to be removed from private ownership and put at the service of the community. The councils of workers in factories (*Betriebsräte*) established during the revolutionary period were to be developed into a system of workers' co-determination in the economy. There should also be government control over cartels and trusts. State and communal enterprises should be expanded, although 'bureaucratization' must be avoided. Co-operatives should also be supported. Otherwise such demands as the reduction of external tariffs by long-term trade-agreements with foreign countries, or the furtherance of high productivity in industry and agriculture, would hardly have been controversial among liberal economists.

The fact was that in the SPD, as in other labour movements, many different strands of working-class politics came together, and some of them owed little to Marx. Guild socialism, British Fabianism, and the co-operative movement had all made their mark. The experiences of the November Revolution 1918/19 had also caused some members of the party to revise their views about 'socialization' and a totally planned

---

[50] *Erfurt Programm 1891* (repr. Berlin, 1978), 4.

economy. The example of Russia, where Red revolution had led to party dictatorship and economic stagnation, was not encouraging. The view began to be expressed that class war and the socialization of the entire economic process was less important than social justice and freedom in the broadest sense. Social democrats who thought along these lines often sought the roots of the working-class movement elsewhere than in *Das Kapital*—in the beliefs of earlier 'utopian' socialists, for example, or even in the Christian message of the Sermon on the Mount.

It was noteworthy—if hardly surprising—that many of the unconventional attitudes towards social democratic doctrine emanated from within the socialist youth movement. Criticism of old orthodoxies came from different ideological directions, but their common denominator was the rejection of historical determinism, crude materialism, and the concept of international class war. At Easter 1923, for example, a group of young socialists responded to the French occupation of the Ruhr by a demonstrative rally at Hofgeismar near Kassel to bear witness to their commitment to the German national state—albeit in a classless and socialist form. Among those present was Heinrich Deist, who spoke of the importance of irrational impulses in human life, and Eduard Heimann, who also stressed the spiritual aspects of socialism. 'Hofgeismar' became a label for a reformist spirit on the right of the German Youth movement.[51]

Eduard Heimann himself was an interesting example of a socialist intellectual who followed a similar line of thought. Although Heimann came from a middle-class Jewish family, his father was a convinced socialist and was an SPD Reichstag deputy until 1932. Heimann himself was very attracted by the idealism of the German Youth movement, but he followed the SPD in the November Revolution of 1918. In the early months of 1919 he became the general secretary of the Socialization Commission set up by the provisional government in Berlin. Trained as an academic economist—he was a student of Franz Oppenheimer and Alfred Weber—he could appreciate the unwisdom of some of the socialization schemes being bruited about in the early days of the revolution. His experiences in the commission reinforced existing doubts about Marxist teachings relating to the 'expropriation of the expropriators' and the necessity of eliminating the market mechanism in a socialist society.

---

[51] Winkler, *Der Schein der Normalität*, 367–9. Winkler claims that 'the Godesberg Programme of German Social Democracy of 1959 is, so far as its spiritual position is concerned, far nearer to Hofgeismar than to Heidelberg', ibid. 378.

Heimann and others of like mind were also very interested in the ethical aspects of socialism, feeling that it was necessary to formulate clearly the fundamental values for which social democrats ought to be struggling. He was a friend of the theologian Paul Tillich and founded with him an ethical socialist circle which set itself the task of formulating plans for social reform. Heimann and Tillich published a monthly journal, *Neue Blätter für den Sozialismus*, to help broaden the discussion of such issues, and in 1929, at a conference of socialist intellectuals at Heppenheim, Heimann presented his views in challenging form. He stressed the compatibility of market economics with a future socialist system.[52] Capitalism had fulfilled its historic task of freeing man from feudalism, but it needed to be protected from its own inherent distortions by a strong state with a firm social policy.

In an article he published in 1930, Heimann argued that destruction of the market mechanism in the Soviet Union had been a catastrophe.

The Market is the motor force of the modern economy. Its destruction would be a leap into the void . . . It is the historical task of socialism to abolish the anti-social tyranny of capitalism and to consolidate the economic achievements of capitalism. The foundation of all this, however, is the market relationship. The market is certainly not identical with capitalism. It would be just as silly to blame the field for becoming choked with weeds, if one had not taken steps to avoid that happening, as it is to hold the market principle responsible for the fact that a market left unregulated will become overgrown by capitalism . . .[53]

Heimann argued that capitalists had every reason to confuse the market economy with capitalism in order to blur the distinction between them. The alternative for Heimann was a socialist form of economic organization which retained the market mechanism. Heimann himself was certainly not a powerful figure in the SPD, but he enjoyed friendly relations with many social democratic economists. Among these was Adolf Löwe, a distinguished academic of liberal background who was a professor of economic theory in Kiel and who later took over the chair of political economy at Frankfurt, and another economist at the Institute of World Economics at Kiel, Günter Keiser. Both these men were on the editorial board of the *Neue Blätter*. Gerhard Weisser, an academically trained economist who became SPD finance director in the city of Madgeburg, was also impressed with Heimann's views.[54] As we shall

---

[52] H.-D. Ortlieb (ed.), *Eduard Heimann: Sozialismus im Wandel der modernen Gesellschaft. Aufsätze zur Theorie und Praxis, Ein Erinnerungsband* (Berlin, 1975), 1–6.

[53] E. Heimann, 'Sozialisierung', in *Neue Blätter für den Sozialismus, Zeitschrift für geistige und politische Gestaltung*, 1 (1930), repr. in Ortlieb (ed.), *Sozialismus im Wandel*, 43.

[54] For the editorial board of *Neue Blätter*, see Ortlieb (ed.), *Sozialismus im Wandel*, 11. For Weisser's admiration of Heimann, see G. Weisser, *Sozialisierung bei freisozialistischer*

see below, the latter economists played an important role in the economic administration of the British zone in Germany after 1945, and Weisser was at the centre of discussions about economic policy within the SPD from 1948 onwards. For his part, Löwe was a determined opponent of cartels and monopolies, and scorned the idea that socialism would emerge from a progressive increase in the power of private monopolies.

Weisser, like Heimann, had been a member of the middle-class romantic German Youth movement before the First World War, although both had adhered to it for idealistic reasons and completely rejected the nationalist racialism which became noticeable later on.[55]

The intellectual background of such men is not without interest, because it exhibits considerable similarities with the sort of ambience in which many neo-liberal thinkers had also grown up. Heimann was a pupil of Franz Oppenheimer, who was well known—if not widely accepted—in neo-liberal circles and who had, of course, been the teacher of Ludwig Erhard.[56] Weisser had studied philosophy under the neo-Kantian moral philosopher Leonhard Nelson, who had also been a teacher of Alexander Rüstow. Nelson was himself no great friend of democracy—if anything he was a Platonic élitist—but he did believe in certain human values such as a sense of justice.

Nelson's circle of students and disciples in the Weimar Republic included Willi Eichler, a young man of limited means who became his private secretary, and two gifted academic women, Grete Henry-Hermann, later a professor of philosophy, and Suzanne Miller, who would become a distinguished historian of the labour movement in Germany. All three joined the SPD, although Eichler had a somewhat stormy career as the organizer of a radical youth group, the International Socialist Fighting League (ISK), which at one point got him ejected from the party.[57] After working in socialist journalism, he emigrated to

Wirtschaftsverfassung (Hamburg, 1947). This was a lecture delivered by Weisser in Hamburg on 28 Feb. 1947. Also private information given to the author in an interview with Prof. Weisser, 21 July 1984. For Löwe's friendship with Heimann, see G. Könke, 'Planwirtschaft oder Marktwirtschaft? Ordnungspolitische Vorstellungen sozialdemokratischer Nationalökonomen in der Weimarer Republik', in *Vierteljahrsschrift für Sozial- und Wirtschaftsgeschichte*, 77/4 (1990), 478.

[55] Heimann was not, in any case, an 'Aryan'. See Ortlieb (ed.), *Sozialismus im Wandel*, 1 and interview with Weisser, 21 July 1984.

[56] See above, pp. 74–5.

[57] Eichler and others in the Nelson group—originally the *Internationale Sozialistische Jugend* (ISJ)—came to the Social Democrats from the radical USPD, and some had even been members of the Communist Party before their élitist ethical views caused them to be ejected. Eichler's problems with the SPD occurred in 1925, when he and his colleagues refused to support the Centre Party candidate against Hindenburg in the presidential elections. Winkler, *Der Schein der Normalität*, 374.

Paris in 1933 and went on to London six years later. After the Second World War, he and his women colleagues were to be deeply involved in the struggle to alter the fundamental programme of the SPD.

One should, of course, avoid the suggestion that personal links can explain intellectual developments. In general, the neo-liberal economists had little sympathy with the SPD, which they regarded as 'collectivist' and closely bound up with overmighty pressure-groups—the trade unions. Röpke referred with contempt to the 'alcohol-free cocktail' of liberal socialism which people like Heimann were trying to serve up.

Nevertheless, the discussions in the 1920s, and the practice of the SPD when it held the reins of power, could give rise to some optimism about the possibility of bridging the gap between the two positions.

For one thing, both tendencies—the reformist or 'democratic' socialist, and the neo-liberal—opposed strict central direction of the economy and bureaucratization. Heimann warned against what he saw as the false belief that the concentration of economic power in capitalist monopolies would carry society down the road towards socialism. It was wrong to think that all socialists had to do was to encourage the development of larger and larger enterprises until eventually only a small number of gigantic firms could easily be taken into public ownership. This 'public' ownership, however, would be, not a 'people's economy', but an officials' economy.[58] That would simply be to exchange one set of tyrants for another.

Marx himself had not wanted that type of system, and had indeed looked forward to the withering-away of the state. But the fact that Marx had made an elementary mistake in thinking that the capitalist system was so simple it could be managed collectively once the ownership of the means of production had passed to the people was no excuse for contemporary socialists to take the easy way out and opt for a state-run economy. What was needed was recognition that the consumer-orientated price-mechanism could and must operate perfectly well without capitalist domination.

Heimann's arguments revealed a distaste for large, impersonal businesses and a concern to improve the quality of life at work, which he rightly saw would not be achieved by creating mammoth state monopolies. In this he was aiming for the same goals as men like Rüstow and Röpke, but choosing a different path to attain them.

---

[58] Heimann, 'Sozialisierung', 37–42. For Heimann's hostility to bureaucracy, see Könke, 'Planwirtschaft oder Marktwirtschaft?', 473. Röpke's 'alchohol-free cocktail' remark was made in a letter to Eucken, 23 Feb. 1940. Copy in BA Rüstow NL, no. 3.

Both groups also opposed the tendency towards cartels and mono-polies which was being actively encouraged by governments and orthodox economic theorists. Both wanted a strong state to ensure a decent share of the social product for the mass of the population, and both opposed *laissez-faire*. For both, the market mechanism was an essential tool in achieving economic prosperity.

From the early 1930s onwards one could say the neo-liberal and democratic socialist thought had the following in common:

1. Protection of competition against cartels and concentrations of economic power.
2. Improvement of the lot of the employee at his place of work.
3. Social justice, at least for children and those incapable of competing in the economic struggle. Some sort of measures to ensure a fair chance at the start of a person's career.
4. A willingness to contemplate state intervention to cope with the effects of the trade cycle, so long as it was compatible with market forces.

Heimann himself argued that the capitalist system had produced many means by which the market could be influenced in a socially desirable direction without the necessity of central planning *à la* Soviet Russia. He rather naïvely praised the American government's use of its monopoly of the fiduciary issue to influence the general course of business activity and create an 'ordered capitalist freedom' (*geordnete kapitalistische Freiheit*), which had been very successful for many years. He also admired US antitrust policy, and contrasted it with planning in Russia, which was lurching from one crisis to another.[59] Here again, a similarity existed between neo-liberals and socialist reformers in that both eschewed direct management of the economy by officials and preferred indirect steerage though taxation, monetary, and trade policies.

It is, of course, important not to run away with the idea that demo-cratic socialism and the social market economy were fundamentally the same. For Heimann, and others like him, the main point was to retain the market principle in a socialist system. How this was to be done whilst eliminating the power of capitalism was not quite clear. For

---

[59] Heimann, 'Sozialisierung', 44–5. Heimann (who was writing early in 1930) opti-mistically claimed that, despite the recent stock-market crisis, production in America seemed unaffected. Events rapidly demolished this positive view. It was not the least of the problems facing both neo-liberal and social democratic reformers that the slump in the early 1930s seemed to fulfil Marxist prophecies of an ultimate crisis in capitalism, whereas Stalin's five-year plans, criminal and wasteful though their execution was, appeared at the time to be achieving their goals.

the neo-liberals no such attack on the capitalist system was intended, simply a restoration of the market which they felt had been distorted by cartels and monopolies.

In any case, the official SPD line remained very inhospitable to a free-market mechanism. Rudolf Hilferding, who had become the SPD's leading economic theorist after 1925, was much taken with the concept of 'organized capitalism', according to which the capitalist system itself was moving away from free competition and towards corporate planning. He told the 1927 congress of the SPD, held in Kiel, that it should be the aim of Social Democrats to encourage this development, which would culminate in the victory of the socialist principle of planned production.[60]

After 1929, however, the Great Depression revealed how unplanned—and indeed chaotic—Germany's capitalist system was. The SPD had to try to present credible alternative policies to the deflationary programme espoused by Brüning. This involved stimulating a capitalist economy rather than waiting for it to develop into socialism of its own accord. No very coherent set of proposals emerged, and the party could not be said to have answered the economic questions posed by the slump with any real conviction. Nevertheless, there were voices within German Social Democracy demanding a more positive attitude to the market. One of the most interesting schemes to combat the slump was that of W. Woytinsky, who in 1931 proposed an 'action programme' including price increases and measures to ginger up the economy by government credits. Woytinsky expressly linked his ideas to those of J. M. Keynes in Britain, whose proposals for demand stimulation were aimed at saving Western capitalism rather than destroying it.

As we have seen in the previous chapter, Heimann himself pressed for action and gave at least qualified support to the reflationary Lautenbach Plan at the meeting of the *Friedrich-List-Gesellschaft* in September 1931. Other SPD economic specialists, such as E. Lederer and F. Tarnow, began to support efforts to enliven, rather than to eliminate, the market—even if they stressed the need for state intervention to achieve that end.[61]

After the collapse of Weimar in 1933, however, there was a tendency to relapse into class-war attitudes. For the first few years of the Nazi

---

[60] M. Held, *Sozialdemokratie und Keynesianismus: Von der Weltwirtschaftskrise bis zum Godesberger Programm* (Frankfurt/M., 1982), 108.

[61] For Heimann's contributions to the debate on the Lautenbach proposals, see Borchardt and Schötz (eds.), *Wirtschaftspolitik in der Krise*, 119–22 and 218. For other social democratic views, Held, *Sozialdemokratie und Keynesianismus*, 112–14.

regime most of the German 'establishment' seemed to welcome the Third Reich, despite its arbitrary repression of democratic political parties like the SPD. Resentment over the part played by conservative social circles in helping the rise of Hitler embittered even moderate Social Democrats. In the Prague manifesto of the exiled SPD leadership, published in 1934, Hilferding went back to Marxist certainties with a section headed 'Revolution and Economy', demanding the establishment of socialist planning to supplant the striving for profit under capitalism. The socialization of heavy industry, banks and, large landholdings would be just the beginning of the transformation process leading to a fully socialist system.[62] The door seemed closed to any acceptance of the market economy by Germany's labour movement.

[62] Held, *Sozialdemokratie und Keynesianismus*, 171–2.

4

The Struggle against Collectivism, 1933–1945

IF life was difficult for liberal economists within Germany after Hitler had come to power, for those in exile the situation was not much easier. They had to try to keep abreast of scholarly developments in their home country; by no means an easy task when one was cast out in Turkey, for example. Rüstow certainly found it hard to maintain his library to the standard he felt necessary, as his voluminous correspondence with Eucken and Röpke illustrates. Nevertheless, despite the academic and emotional handicaps of life on the Bosphorus, Rüstow set about researching a monumental study of the human condition, drawing on his knowledge of philosophy, history, sociology, and economics.[1]

For his part, Röpke, who already enjoyed an international reputation as an economist, and whose command of English gave him an advantage over some other exiles, was able to leave Turkey in the mid-1930s and go to Geneva, where he obtained a special Rockefeller-funded research professorship at the Institut des Études Internationales. There he produced a steady stream of monographs—some of them in English—and high-quality journalism in the Swiss press. He castigated not only collectivist socialism but also German and Italian Fascism in a fashion which illustrated his intellectual consistency and his fearlessness. Switzerland cannot have seemed an entirely safe haven for anti-Nazi exiles, especially by the summer of 1940, when the Nazis had overrun much of central and western Europe. Röpke did consider leaving for America but thought better of it.[2]

One of the early fruits of Röpke's period of exile in Turkey was *German Commercial Policy*, a book published in London and New York under the auspices of the Geneva institute. This was a critique of the policies of trade controls imposed by Schacht and his immediate predecessors, combined with a warning to Anglo-Saxon readers

[1] *Ortsbestimmung der Gegenwart*, trans. as *Freedom and Domination: A Historical Critique of Civilization* (abr. and trans. S. Attansio; ed. D. A. Rustow; Princeton, NJ, 1980).
[2] See Röpke to Rüstow, 7 May 1940, BA Rüstow NL, no. 7. Röpke was offered a chair at Vanderbilt University, Tennessee.

against the dangers of the interventionism and national egoism which threatened the world trading-system. Writing in 1934, he looked back to the situation in Germany a century earlier. New Year's Eve 1833–4 had witnessed the end of petty protectionism throughout much of Germany under the new regime of the *Zollverein*. As the customs barriers and turnpikes came down, so German consumers could rejoice. The only sufferers were the smugglers, whose livelihood had disappeared. 1934 provided a dismal contrast. Röpke pointed to the

miserable reality of ever-growing customs barriers and all the new-fangled devices such as quota systems, exchange control systems, import trading boards, currency tampering, and so on, which are threatening to break up that densely woven net once bearing the proud name of world economy into small fragments . . .[3]

Röpke was very harshly disposed towards those who used the rhetoric of patriotism when justifying protection. Commerce was not like war. The real differences lay not between one nation and another but between those producers who were protected, on the one hand, and the consumers and rival producers on the other. Thus he was very critical of ideas of autarky, pointing out how ludicrous it was for countries which could very well import raw materials from abroad to manufacture them at home at exorbitant cost. Most people would understand that to grow oranges in Scotland—technically possible though it might be—would mean 'self-inflicted impoverishment'. Yet if one took some more complicated industrial process, such as the production of synthetic petrol, the public was more likely to be gulled by 'incomprehensible and scholarly thinking' and claims that the national interest was involved. The result was that 'the commonsense view of the matter' would be overridden.[4]

This was, of course, a very topical issue in Germany at that time, since the prophets of autarky were loudly proclaiming the need for self-sufficiency in such things as food, petrol, and rubber. In the latter cases the immensely costly but technically brilliant industrial processes involved were supported by powerful pressure-groups which enjoyed government support. The economic folly against which Röpke was warning reached a new peak in 1936 with the announcement of Hitler's Four Year Plan, a scheme of autarky so extreme and economically irresponsible that even Schacht could not be trusted to support it. Hermann Göring supplanted him as the driving force behind German economic policy.

[3] W. Röpke, *German Commercial Policy* (London, 1934), 1–2.   [4] Ibid. 30–1.

Röpke's book presented the history of German commercial policy in the nineteenth and twentieth centuries as a struggle between the beneficial doctrine of free trade and the lurking menace of protection. In support of the latter the agricultural lobby, and especially the great landowners of eastern Prussia, had played a particularly damaging role. By insisting on high tariffs, subsequently reinforced by government purchasing arrangements and export bounties for grain, they had distorted the whole market in foodstuffs, increasing costs for the consumer and damaging the interests of small mixed farmers in central and western Germany. This had prevented what Röpke called the 'Danization' of agriculture—diversifying out of cereals to cater for an expanding European market, as the farmers of Denmark and Holland had done. Instead, even the Republican governments of Weimar Germany, headed by social democrats and liberals, had gone on using tariffs, subsidies, and preferential marketing-arrangements to prop up the *Junker* grain producers, despite the fact that they were among the Republic's worst enemies.

The falling prices of agricultural products in 1928/9 had faced the German government with a choice: either they could try to reform agriculture along 'Danish' lines or they could carry protectionism to extremes. Röpke made it clear that he would have favoured land reform in eastern Germany, to weaken conservative elements there and create more independent farmers. The government, however, chose to appease the *Junker*,

blind to the fact that it was now embarking on a policy which was eventually to shake the total economic structure of Germany to its foundations. Since the traditional methods of tariff protection seemed no longer to suffice, a new and powerful machinery of protective intervention was built up to deal with the new situation, the old story of interventionism being repeated that one step in this direction is always liable to lead to other and still bolder steps until, in the end, a maze is created in which only a few experts can find their way, with the greater part of the public groping its way in the dark, not knowing what it is all about.[5]

This was all sturdy liberal stuff, but it did not mean that Röpke was committed to *laissez-faire*. He accepted that agriculture was in some sense a special case, since it was not just an ordinary business, and that some measures were needed to maintain a nation's farmers. A plausible case could be made for the argument that 'some kind of state intervention, if carefully and rationally conducted, might do more good than evil', provided that it did not try to prop up an untenable position but was aimed at 'smoothing the way for that new equilibrium which

[5] Ibid. 57 and 42–6.

the natural tendencies are working to bring about'.[6] He went on to make the following significant statement:

I believe it to be a great mistake to say that we are sinning against the spirit of liberalism by admitting that there are kinds of state intervention which are rational and useful, and I believe further that that is just the mistake which has discredited economic liberalism so much in these days.

Interventionism in general should be denounced, but a set of principles should be worked out for use in exceptional cases to ensure that intervention would not then just be 'sand thrown into the complicated machinery of our economic system'.[7] He suggested that this should be called 'liberal interventionism', a term he claimed to have borrowed from Rüstow's contribution to the proceedings of the *Verein für Socialpolitik* in 1932. The cardinal principle of this liberal interventionism should be that state action must never be conducted against the natural tendencies of economic development, but only in harmony with them. State measures should always be compatible with the market (*marktgerecht*, as the Germans put it).

Certainly he was very clear that the policies which Brüning, Papen, and Schacht had been following in Germany since 1930 were anything but *marktgerecht*. He was particularly critical of the exchange-control regulations established in 1931 and made more stringent under the Third Reich. Blocked accounts which could only be used by the importers of German goods were clearly a form of export subsidy and incompatible with free-market principles. Schacht had introduced even more complicated and ingenious procedures. 'It would require a special study to ascertain exactly the gains and losses all round', but from this experience 'at least one thing could be learnt: that you get deeper and deeper into the jungle once you have left the golden road of economic liberalism'.[8]

To demonstrate the superiority of this 'golden road' over its rivals. Röpke set to work on a general explanation of economic processes, a superior kind of textbook called 'What Economics Teaches Us' (*Die Lehre von der Wirtschaft*)—perhaps better translated as 'What We Can Learn from the Economy'. Published in the still-independent state of Austria in 1937, it was a defence of the free market against collectivist alternatives. He began with a lyrical description of the benefits of the division of labour, echoing a famous passage in Adam Smith's *Wealth of Nations*, but updating it with reference to copper from the Congo, silk from Japan, tea from Java, sheep from New Zealand, and lenses

---

[6] Ibid. 48–51.   [7] Ibid.   [8] Ibid. 75.

from Germany. Millions had their needs satisfied by the market, and the beauty of it was that it was a self-operating mechanism: 'But who arranges everything and thereby ensures the orderly functioning of the process? Nobody. There is no dictator, who, with a view of the whole [system] orders the people to their individual occupations'.[9]

Instead there was a 'spontaneous harmony' (*Ordnung*), which was far superior to a commanded harmony, even if it might have its faults. He described the laws of supply and demand and claimed that the lessons drawn from economics were nothing more than the study of alternatives.[10] Individual human choices lay at the root of the market and ensured its success.

Röpke was careful to rebut many of the criticisms of liberal economics current among Marxists and Fascists in the 1930s. There was, for example, a complete distinction between trade and plunder or piracy. He deplored rhetoric about the 'conquest of markets' or 'imperialist exploitation' of foreign countries. The idea that an industrialist was the 'exploiter' of his workers fell into that category. On the other hand, it was also absurd for the businessman to use terminology which implied that he was a public benefactor—a sort of Francis of Assisi of trade and industry. American advertising techniques were a peculiar perversion in this respect.

He also considered other forms of distribution than that presented by the price mechanism. There was the possibility of free provision for everybody; he termed this the 'mass buffet' and cited the free Soviet transport system as an example of it.[11] This would lead to an excess of demand and shortages, culminating in grave injustices. The next possibility was rationing. That was cumbersome and encouraged crime, and the same objection applied to mixed systems of rationing and free prices. Only the free-price mechanism worked perfectly. Even with that, however, there were drawbacks, because some social needs could not be met by private self-interest. These included major areas of policy, such as security against internal subversion and foreign attack, and public health, as well as specific amenities such as street lighting.

If the market and the price mechanism were to function effectively, there had to be a stable means of exchange, and—like Mises or other hard-line liberals—Röpke favoured gold. All other forms of currency were bound to lose their value.[12] It was important to stop governments

[9] W. Röpke, *Die Lehre von der Wirtschaft* (Vienna, 1937), 3–4.

[10] Ibid. 13.

[11] Ibid. 25–40. Whether such a transport system actually existed is a matter of some doubt.

[12] Ibid. 90.

interfering with prices, since their intervention was always disastrous. Here he was moved to cite the case greatly beloved of liberal economists, the Brazilian coffee-purchasing scheme. In order to keep the price of coffee high, the Brazilian government had bought up and stored large quantities of it. The result was that growers, instead of adjusting their production to the level of real demand, simply grew more and more coffee, assuming that the government would buy it. Eventually the whole scheme collapsed, leaving behind it very large public debts and unsaleable stocks of coffee, much of which had to be tipped into the sea.[13] At this time, of course, Röpke had no notion of the enormous grain-mountains and wine lakes of the EEC. His comments on them would have been equally devastating.[14] In both cases the problem was not the workings of the capitalist system, but its perversion through state intervention.

Another issue which had been obsessing men for thousands of years was the contrast between rich and poor. Yet there was no use imagining that arbitrary measures could alter this situation. Raising wages at the expense of capital would soon damage workers' interests by reducing investment and destroying jobs. Wage rises would also cause inflation. Similarly, rent and interest rates fulfilled economic functions by defining the scarcity of land and money. Nevertheless, he did not argue that grossly unequal distribution of wealth had to be tolerated. He advocated a high level of capitalization, low government expenditure, low birth-rates, and a pacific foreign policy. This would result in higher wages, a broadening of the capital base, and an expansion of individual savings. That, in turn, would help to eradicate the phenomenon of proletarianization, which Röpke saw as the most pressing threat to human civilization.[15]

Röpke rejected many of the criticisms levelled at market economics which held it responsible for the depression, for poverty, and for the miseries of industrialization. Without the industrial expansion associated with market forces, the enormous growth of populations in developed countries could not have been sustained. Romantic notions about a pre-industrial past were largely absurd. Even if we could live like Goethe, Schiller, or Byron, most of us would shrink from an existence among stinking dark streets, without comfort, hygiene, or modern medical treatment.[16] As for boom and slump, a lot of the recent difficulties had resulted from the First World War, not market

[13] Ibid. 120.
[14] Indeed, he was to be a harsh critic of the EEC. See below, Ch. 15.
[15] W. Röpke, *Lehre*, 166–70.
[16] Ibid. 194–5.

economics: 'we ought not to make our economic system the whipping-boy for the sins of the politicians'.[17]

He accepted that the market was not perfect. This did not mean it should be replaced by a communist system. What was needed was the 'third way', between *laissez-faire* and collectivism. To achieve this it was necessary for the state to protect the market to ensure genuinely free competition and resist monopolies, corruption, and other distortions. The economic crisis had made many people feel that human needs and values—like the family, the profession, the community, and the nation—were more important than capitalist success. For all the respect that was due to capitalist theorists, one had to agree that: 'The capitalist impregnation of all sectors of life in our society is a curse which we must banish, and the free expansion of the economy must not lead to the perversion of genuine human values.'[18]

The worst and most unnatural feature of contemporary life was the existence of the proletariat. Sooner or later society would be faced with the choice, overcome the proletarian problem or go under to Communism. Röpke's method of dealing with this problem was to demand measures which would encourage 'small and medium-sized property-holdings, give support to independent farmers, break up industrial cities, revive pride in work and in professional standards, and combat the feeling of human rootlessness' apparent in modern society. He warned against the contemporary obsession with size for its own sake. Referring to a 'pseudo-ideal' of 'the bigger the better', he said people should free themselves from centralization, over-organization, and mammoth organizations, and go back to the 'natural, the humane, the spontaneous, the differentiated, and the individualistic'.[19] Even from the purely economic viewpoint, what Röpke called the 'skyscraper principle' had not proved effective. The business advantages of bigness were less than was supposed.

Despite all their disadvantages in exile, Rüstow and Röpke hammered away at these neo-liberal themes, extolling the virtues of the 'third way' and stressing its superiority to *laissez-faire* liberalism or collectivism.

In 1938 they were both present at a colloquium organized at the Palais Royal in Paris to honour Walter Lippmann, whose book *The Good Society* had just been published. Rüstow, in particular, stressed the limitations of *laissez-faire* liberalism, set out the causes of its decline, and urged the necessity of a constructive alternative which would overcome social injustice. He was supported by Lippmann. It was at

---

[17] Ibid. 188.   [18] Ibid. 190.   [19] Ibid. 190–2.

this colloquium that the cumbersome term 'neo-liberal'—never popular with those whom it described—was born.[20]

Some support for the neo-liberal position came from non-German sympathizers. Apart from Walter Lippmann, there was interest from Italian and French economists. Costantino Bresciani-Turroni, the historian of Germany's inflation in the Weimar period,[21] Luigi Einaudi, and Jacques Rueff were among those who contributed ideas and encouragement.[22] There seemed little chance of achieving anything while Hitler's regime survived, but the exiles tried to keep the anti-collectivist banner flying.

In September 1939 Röpke organized an international conference at his institute in Geneva to which he invited a number of academic experts to discuss the disintegration of the international economic system. Unfortunately the only speaker from outside Switzerland who was able to reach Geneva was Rüstow himself—from Istanbul. The other participants were thwarted by the outbreak of war. Nevertheless, the two neo-liberals were not daunted by this set-back. Röpke published an extended account of his views in the book *International Economic Disintegration*, which appeared in London and New York in 1942 and which included Rüstow's intended lecture as an epilogue.[23] Rüstow himself expanded on this back in Turkey and at the end of the war produced it as a book, *Das Versagen des Wirtschaftsliberalismus* (The Failure of Economic Liberalism), which, despite its title, was every bit as devastating about socialist societies as about the catastrophic effects of *laissez-faire*.[24]

The same themes were tackled by Röpke with even greater vigour in his book *Die Gesellschaftskrise der Gegenwart* (The Contemporary Crisis of Society), in which he described the proper direction for the future as the 'third way', which would have to 'overcome the problems of proletarianization, mammoth industries, monopolies, the multifarious

---

[20] Eisermann (ed.), *Wirtschaft und Kultursystem*, 20.

[21] The first edition of Bresciani-Turroni's *Economics of Inflation* was published in 1937. It exploded many of the myths about the German inflation but was ignored or only superficially referred to by historians until relatively recently, when the soundness of its judgements came to be recognized. The author had been a member of the Italian reparations commission after the First World War.

[22] F. Greiss and F. W. Meyer (eds.), *Wirtschaft, Gesellschaft und Kultur. Festgabe für Müller-Armack* (Berlin, 1961), 4–5.

[23] W. Röpke, *International Economic Disintegration* (London, 1942). This book contains an epilogue written after the outbreak of the Second World War entitled 'The Age of Tyranny'. It also has an appendix provided by Alexander Rüstow: 'General Sociological Causes of the Economic Disintegration and Possibilities of Reconstruction', 267 ff.

[24] A. Rüstow, *Das Versagen des Wirtschaftsliberalismus* (2nd edn.; n.p., 1950). For introductory remarks, see pp. iii–iv.

types of exploitation, and the mechanizing effects of capitalistic mass civilization'.[25]

The key to a free society was the existence of the broadest possible class of people with economic independence. The more farmers, artisans, professional people, and small businessmen in a society, the better it was likely to be.

To attain this admirable goal, a return to *laissez-faire* was not enough— indeed it would just lead to a return of the evils he was trying to eliminate. The state would have to protect 'fair play' in the market, encourage decentralization, and support artisan labour. In addition, and this was a new emphasis for Röpke, there should be a part of the economy reserved for the public sector. One should not speak of 'chemical purity' in relation to the market economy any more than when talking of democracy. Essential monopolies such as electricity supply or similar utilities should be public and not private enterprises. 'Fanaticism', he warned his liberal readers, 'must be avoided by us just as carefully as that soggy lack of principle to which the world has surrendered itself in the last twenty years.'[26]

On the whole, however, competition itself could be relied upon to prevent the creation of great and lasting imbalances in property ownership, so long as the twin evils of feudalism and monopoly were banished.

Röpke stressed that state intervention was necessary to lay down the ground rules of competition and prevent abuses. He cited the well-known metaphor of the traffic regulations on public roads. If there were no rules, there would be chaos and injustice. If, on the other hand, every motor car had its journey planned by the traffic authorities, the system would soon choke up. In fact there was a set of rules understood by everybody and enforced by the police. The initiative was left with the individual motorist, but he had to operate within the framework of regulations set out for him. The same should apply to the economy.[27]

Underlying the critique of modern industrial society presented by both Röpke and Rüstow was a deep-seated distaste for its uglier features, and in particular for the depersonalizing effects of large-scale, 'rationalized' enterprises on the workers involved in them. Röpke loathed collectivism precisely because he saw it as involving 'liberty

[25] W. Röpke, *Die Gesellschaftskrise der Gegenwart* (4th. rev. edn.; Zurich, 1942) (trans. A. and P. Jacobsohn as *The Social Crisis of Our Time* (London, 1950)), 286.

[26] Ibid. *Gesellschaftskrise*, 292.

[27] Ibid. 300.

and privacy being wiped out; mechanization and proletarianization driven to the extreme; society crushed into an amorphous mass'.

Yet collectivist society was not entirely new or revolutionary. 'It is rather the last stage and consequence of a long *pre-collectivist* development characterized by increasing mechanization and proletarianization, by ever-greater concentration and centralization, by the growing domination of men by the "apparatus", by the spread of monopolist octopuses, by the continuous decrease of independent modest existences and of vitally satisfactory forms of life and work, by more and more regimentation and organization.'[28] This would erode the cultural resources of the Western world until ultimately it would be turned into a social dust-bowl.

It was no use imagining that this would be put right just by a return to economic freedom. That would indeed destroy collectivism but not the other symptoms of the disease.

Would a country having scarcely any peasant proprietors, artisans or urban middle class elements get them by economic liberty? Would the proletariat disappear? Would society become stable economically and socially? Would work and life recapture more sense and dignity? If not how could economic liberty be expected to arouse enthusiasm?[29]

Röpke answered this question in the negative. What was needed was an opposite pole to collectivism and that was a society in which the 'greatest possible numbers of men are leading a life based on private property, the sort of life which, providing real independence, enables men to be trouble-free and to regard economic liberty as a matter of course'.[30]

In the 1990s, many reformers in Eastern Europe are bemoaning the lack of precisely that social group in former Communist countries, particularly the Soviet Union. Röpke's view was not just an exercise in nostalgia, but a statement of socio-economic truths which have lasting importance.

A particular area of difficulty for the neo-liberals was provided by agriculture. In Germany there was a very widespread belief that the independent farmer—the yeoman on his own soil—represented a form of life superior to that represented by the city dweller. This view was shared by many neo-liberal theorists, even though it must be said that few of them had any direct experience of farming or the hardships of rural life. What attracted Röpke and Rüstow to the small farmer was precisely his independence and individuality.

---

[28] Röpke, *Economic Disintegration*, 262.   [29] Ibid. 263.   [30] Ibid. 264.

It is important not to confuse this attitude towards agriculture with that of the authoritarian Right in Germany—the conservatives, anti-Semites, and Nazis. They certainly idealized the closed world of the medieval community, with its guilds and peasant households. During the Weimar Republic they had consciously appealed to the anxieties of farmers, small businessmen, and craftsmen, who were faced with the threat of proletarianization in an expanding industrial society. Yet Fascist solutions to this problem, which was by no means unique to Germany, were very different from those of the neo-liberals. Nazi *Mittelstandpolitik*[31] required that farmers be shielded from competition, protected by tariffs and trade barriers, and rigorously controlled in the exercise of their occupations. Under the Third Reich the farmer was given security and status within the smothering embrace of Richard Darré's *Reichsnährstand*, the Nazi agricultural organization. In some ways its price-fixing techniques were similar to the disastrous Common Agricultural Policy of the European Community in our own time. In the short term it saved the small German farmer from bankruptcy and ensured him higher prices for his produce. In the long term it con-tributed to an increased flight from the land, a chronic shortage of agricultural capital, and the progressive demoralization of German farming communities.

For the neo-liberals the plight of agriculture was also a matter of vital importance, but their solutions were radically different. They did not believe in flying in the face of world economic trends. Farmers should be encouraged to adapt themselves to the market and to profit from it; they should not seek suspended animation in a semi-feudal past.

If overproduction occurred, farmers should be given encouragement to reduce unprofitable crops and switch into more promising markets. The state could help them with credits and advice, thus smoothing the path of transition to effectively competitive agriculture. As we have seen, Röpke, especially, admired the way in which Danish and Dutch farmers had prospered by adapting themselves to the market. He urged German farmers to follow suit.[32] For those farmers who were simply not in a position to adapt to the market, the state should provide help with retraining to enable them to leave agriculture for some more promising activity. In his famous speech to the *Verein für Socialpolitik* in Dresden on 28 September 1932, Rüstow had spoken of the need to replace subventions for unsuccessful economic under-

---

[31] Literally 'middle-class policy', but one should remember that 'middle class' is here used emotively to mean the 'small men' who were the backbone of society.
[32] Röpke, *Gesellschaftskrise*, 330–4.

takings with state help which was compatible with market forces. This would cost far less and be far more effective.[33] It was just this sort of help which he and Röpke envisaged for struggling farmers.

If the 'third way' differed markedly from conservative formulations over agriculture, it also had potentially unpalatable implications for the social sphere. The concern over proletarianization and *Vermassung* led, as we have seen, to a demand for a broad distribution of wealth and property. At first sight this might seem to be a socialist demand, and Rüstow himself admitted that socialists were right to be angry over the maldistribution of wealth. Where they had gone wrong, however, was to attribute this problem to the workings of the market, whereas it was in the sphere of free competition that the solution to social injustice was to be found.

Nevertheless, the market, however well protected from *laissez-faire* distortions, could not by itself ensure the sort of social harmony which a broad distribution of property would achieve. Rüstow was quite prepared to advocate taxation policies which would militate against excessive concentrations of wealth. The inequalities created by the inheritance of property might also be a proper target for action by the state.

Most unjust of all are those inequalities in the conditions existing at the start of economic life, derived in part from unequal inheritances, which depend on how carefully one chooses one's parents. This being the case we are led to demand equal opportunity and just initial conditions for all.[34]

He regarded unlimited right of inheritance as a 'feudal element' which gave a 'semi-feudal, plutocratic' character to capitalism. This explained 'the bad conscience . . . so typical of latter-day liberalism in the face of the indisputably reasonable demands for justice made by the socialists'. Rüstow was able to cite the authority of John Stuart Mill and other saints in the canon of economic liberalism when he made this controversial claim. He pointed out that in the *Principles of Political Economy* Mill said he saw nothing objectionable in 'fixing a limit to what any one may acquire by the mere favour of others, without the exercise of his faculties, and in requiring that if he desires any further accessions to fortune, he shall work for it'.[35]

Rüstow did indeed begin to see the question of equal opportunities as one of the real keys to the creation of a society which combined

---

[33] A. Rüstow, 'Die staatspolitischen Voraussetzungen des wirtschaftspolitischen Liberalismus', 253.

[34] Id., app. to Röpke, *Economic Disintegration*, 281.

[35] A. Rüstow, *Versagen des Wirtschaftsliberalismus*, 98n. 6.

economic efficiency with social justice. In a letter to Eucken on 25 July 1941 he wrote:

Equality at the start of life, or justice at the start [*Startgleichheit bzw. Startgerechtigkeit*] is becoming more and more important for me . . . The complete neglect of this seems to me to be the really justifiable core of the social accusations which socialism has levelled against the market economy in its original form. This does not, however, relate to private property but to inheritance laws. If nobody can inherit more than a plot of land [*eine Hufe*] and every person reaching the age of majority has the right to such a 'plot', then economic justice will have been completely satisfied.[36]

Returning to the same theme the following year, he told Eucken that 'it becomes less and less possible to avoid making the choice; either everybody must have property or nobody must have it. One will also have fewer reservations about giving more authority to the state if this counterweight [widespread ownership of property] is present.'[37]

Not all neo-liberals went as far in this direction as Rüstow, who had retained something of the fiery radicalism of his youth and had little sympathy with what he regarded as the social prejudices of some *laissez-faire* enthusiasts, with their hatred of trade unions and their willingness to take hard economic decisions at the expense of the working population. He often employed the term 'paleo-liberal' to describe such attitudes. Writing to Röpke on 13 July 1946, he described Ludwig Mises as 'an old liberal ultra . . . who belongs behind glass in a museum. Hayek too . . . has never been quite transparent to me.'[38]

Other supporters of the competitive but state-protected market economy did not exhibit Rüstow's zeal for social reform—Eucken, for example, was more concerned with the restoration of the price mechanism than with social engineering. Yet the concept of equal opportunities (*Startgleichheit*) was an essential feature of the theory of the social market economy as it emerged after the war. It was one of the aspects of that theory which proved most attractive to those, including many social democrats, who were otherwise disposed to be highly critical of capitalism. It should, of course, be stressed that this was not a primitive socialist view of equality, but rather the ideal of a career open to talent which had been traditionally held by democrats since the end of the eighteenth century.

The exponents of the free market living in exile may have felt impotent and indignant, but they were at least able to conduct a public

[36] Rüstow to Eucken, 25 July 1941, BA Rüstow NL, no. 3, fo. 327.
[37] Rüstow to Eucken, 9 Feb. 1943, ibid., no. 3.
[38] Rüstow to Röpke, 13 July 1943, ibid., no. 7, p. 52. Rüstow seems to have felt that von Hayek harboured social prejudices which coloured his judgement.

campaign against collectivism. Those economists of liberal persuasion left in the Third Reich faced different and even less tractable problems. For one thing, Hitler's economic policy, if such it could be called, had apparently succeeded. Since 1936, when full employment had effectively been achieved, the economy had gone ahead at full steam, with heavy industry, engineering, and chemicals prospering mightily. If 1928 is taken as the base year, the index of industrial production rose from 61.2 in 1932 to 116.7 in 1938. Even some academically trained economists were impressed by this. In 1939 Günter Keiser, who was to become an important expert in the planning staff in the British zone of occupation after the war, wrote an analysis of what he called the German 'economic miracle', which he attributed to a combination of expansionist government expenditure and state-controlled prices.[39]

For liberal economists, the dangers of Nazi measures—and especially their inflationary aspect—were obvious. But the totalitarian character of Hitler's regime was growing more menacing towards the end of the 1930s, and even academic opposition became dangerous.

In practical terms, the overheating of the German economy caused by excessive public spending—especially in the armed forces—meant more and more direct interference by state authorities of one kind or another. If any entrepreneurs had been foolish enough to think that National Socialism would just destroy the trade unions and leave businessmen to their own devices, they now discovered their mistake. For many of them, no doubt, secure profits from lucrative government contracts seemed a more than adequate substitute for the uncertainties of a competitive market. But the more far-sighted began to worry about the possibility of a cut-back in defence expenditure once the government had achieved its goals. One beneficiary of such concerns was Alfred Müller-Armack.

For a man like Alfred Müller-Armack, who had welcomed the Third Reich in 1933, the development of National Socialist policies provided an important learning process which decisively influenced his later beliefs. Although Müller-Armack was probably never a very enthusiastic Nazi, his party membership certainly had its advantages. In 1938, despite later claims that he was *persona non grata* with the Reich Education Ministry,[40] he was called to a chair in economics at the University of Münster in Westphalia.

---

[39] It was perhaps just as well that the book was never published. The typescript is in the Institut für Zeitgeschichte in Munich. I am grateful to Dr Christoph Buchheim for drawing it to my attention.

[40] Müller-Armack papers, correspondence relating to denazification, Müller-Armack NL, KAS I-236-030.

Apart from academic preferment, this move also brought him good fortune in the shape of a dynamic and ebullient industrialist by the name of Ernst Hellmuth Vits, who ran a synthetic-fibre plant in Wuppertal, the Vereinigte Glanzstoff-Fabrik. Under the Nazis, industry was organized into corporate groups, or *Wirtschaftsgruppen*, and Vits led the textile group in Westphalia. He and his colleagues were concerned about the future of their industry, because by the late 1930s synthetic-fibre production had been greatly increased to meet government demand. Gratifying though this was, it did pose the question as to what would happen when the rush of state contracts dried up. Even greater uncertainty was created by the early course of the war, since, on the one hand, Germany was cut off from her main sources of cotton supply, whilst on the other, she came to control vast areas of central and eastern Europe, the textile resources of which were supposed to be mobilized. Vits was able to convince his economic group that there was an urgent need for consumer research if the industry was to carry on into a prosperous future. At the same time, civilian and military authorities wanted information about textile resources in Europe.

It was agreed that a research centre should be set up, attached to a university, and, since Vits had been a student at Münster, he persuaded his colleagues that it should go there. The senior economics professor showed no interest in such an institution, and so Müller-Armack was asked to become its first director. He insisted that it should not confine itself to the narrow problems of the textile industry, but should adopt a broader and more theoretical approach to the whole question of the market economy. The centre was thus established, in April 1931, as a Research Unit for General and Textile Market Economy. Erhard, working in a similar field, evidently had contacts with it, and Müller-Armack's acquaintance with him seems to have dated from that time.[41] The institute was supported financially by an association of textile

[41] *Forschungsstelle für allgemeine und textile Marktwirtschaft an der Universität Münster* (FATM). See T. Mandt, '25 Jahre textilwirtschaftliche Forschung in Münster', *Textildienst*, 9/10 (Münster, 1965), 353–73, and *25 Jahre Forschungsstelle für allgemeine und textile Marktwirtschaft an der Universität Münster, 1946–1966* (n.p., n.d.), esp. the contribution by Vits: 'Zur Geschichte der Forschungsstelle'. According to Müller-Armack, after the war, Ludwig Erhard had advised him about the name of the unit, and the two had met at its opening ceremony. Certainly they did exchange ideas on consumer research, although the extent to which Müller-Armack appreciated the work done in the Nuremberg institute seems doubtful. I am grateful to Dr Mandt for giving me his views on this subject. For Müller-Armack's version, A. Müller-Armack, 'Wirtschaftspolitik zwischen Wissenschaft und Politik', in G. Schröder, A. Müller-Armack, K. Hohmann, J. Gross, and R. Altmann (eds.), *Ludwig Erhard: Beiträge zu seiner politischen Biographie. Festschrift zum fünfundsiebzigsten Geburtstag* (Frankfurt/M., 1971), 473–4.

firms established for this purpose in October of the same year.[42] By the end of 1943 it had a staff of thirty, including four translators to help monitor foreign textile-markets. Numerous reports were prepared on textile supplies and consumption throughout Nazi-occupied Europe. Many of these were commissioned by the Reich Economics Ministry or the Wehrmacht.[43]

This was not the first specialized institute for which Müller-Armack had found himself having to take responsibility. In October 1939 he had assumed the directorship of a university research unit for the study of urban settlement and housing policy, the *Forschungsstelle für Siedlungsund Wohnungswesen* (FOSIWO). This had been established in 1929 by Professor Werner F. Bruck.[44] Bruck had been *persona non grata* with the Nazis and was forced into exile in Britain in 1933. That particular crisis had been overcome by the time Müller-Armack took over the unit, but circumstances remained difficult, especially because his period of office coincided with grandiose Nazi schemes for population resettlement and the control of the building industry. Indeed, both the research units which he headed brought Müller-Armack up against the consequences of a directed economy. In both he was forced to listen to—and sometimes even to publish—crude attacks on liberal economic principles.

To take the example of housing policy first, the FOSIWO found itself affected by drastic measures designed to build between 5 and 6 million new homes in ten years—homes which would, furthermore, be suited to the fertile Aryan families so beloved of Nazi fanatics. The two-bedroomed flat was to be a thing of the past. On 15 November 1940, Hitler issued a decree, or *Führererlaß*, initiating the scheme, which was to be financed by the Reich and backed up by compulsory-purchase orders, fixed land-prices, and controlled rents. Dr Robert Ley, the leader of the German Labour Front, was made Reich Housing Commissar, and Nazi Gauleiters were given wide-ranging powers to implement the plan in their areas. The whole scheme was a negation of economic liberalism, as its enthusiasts cheerfully admitted.

---

[42] The institute's offices were provided by the university; most staff costs and other expenses by the sponsoring body. Müller-Armack NL, KAS I-236-024. See the report of the first meeting of the association of firms supporting the research centre, 23 Oct. 1941, in *Westfälische Wirtschaft. Amtliches Organ der Wirtschaftskammer Westfalen und Lippe*, 31 Oct. 1943. Also Mandt, '25 Jahre Forschungsstelle', 242–71.

[43] Mandt. '25 Jahre textilwirtschaftliche Forschung in Münster', 363; Müller-Armack wrote a report on textile rationing in Hungary, Rumania, and Bulgaria. Müller-Armack NL, KAS I-236-024.

[44] H.-J. Seraphim, *25 Jahre Institut für Siedlungs- und Wohnungswesen der Westfälischen Wilhelm-Universität zu Münster* (Münster, 1964), 16–18.

In November 1940, the Gauleiter of southern Westphalia insisted that Müller-Armack publish a lecture by a Nazi official who boasted that the Führer had now given Germany the chance of decent housing for all. He had shown that this could be done by ending the speculation in land caused by the old *laissez-faire* economy. The lecturer blamed the sharp rise in the price of land since the end of the nineteenth century on an economic system which allowed prices to be set without any official restraint and according to the 'liberalistic principle of supply and demand'. He poured scorn on this 'old liberalistic era', when private persons were allowed to profit from land shortage to the detriment of the common good.[45]

A similar attitude was reflected in the first report of the new textile research unit in October 1941. The leader of the *Wirtschaftsgruppe* for the textile industry, Hans Croon, began an article on the relationship of the institute to industry with a contemptuous attack on liberal market theories. He claimed that after the war economic control (*Wirtschaftslenkung*) would have to continue because

we judge its advantages to be far greater than those of an apparent economic freedom, as we have known it before 1933 in the shape of irregular business-cycles and constantly recurring crises. The liberal theory that economic crisis is a stimulus to achievement and the best way of furthering increased productivity will not be able to find many adherents in Germany.[46]

He went on to claim that the whole concept of a market conditioned by the wishes of millions of consumers was a fiction, because such needs were mediated through—and often created by—merchants and middlemen. In the future, Germans would rely on planning from above (*von oben her*). Market research was needed precisely because the old free-market response to consumers' needs was no longer going to operate.

Müller-Armack himself accepted this point in his own contribution to the working report. It was necessary, he argued, to develop criteria for market diagnosis which would also be valid in a command economy. It was therefore no use simply building up data about market prices, as they were doing at Harvard, for example.[47] Nevertheless, he insisted that it would be wrong to imagine that classical economic theories

---

[45] J. Laubahn, 'Bauland/Mietwohnung Heimstätte: Die Verwürzelung unseres Volkes mit seinem Boden', FOSIWO, *Materiellensammlung*, xxxix, ed. A. Müller (Jena, 1941), 11 and 18–19. The word 'liberalistisch' was a common term of abuse at this time. Müller-Armack's short preface was as unenthusiastic as was possible under the circumstances.
[46] H. Croon, 'Das Verhältnis der Textilindustrie zur Forschungsstelle für allgemeine und textile Wirtschaft' in FATM, *Arbeitsberichte zur Marktforschung* (Münster, 1941), no. 1, pp. 1–2.
[47] A. Müller (Armack) 'Die Marktforschung in der gelenkten Wirtschaft', ibid. 12–13.

could be relevant only to the environment of economic liberalism in which they were first developed. This body of theory had long since escaped from its original preconceptions, and had become an intellectual tool suited to different forms of economic system. It was not a very convincing argument, and it illustrates the defensive posture into which classically trained economists had been forced by 1941. This can be seen as producing two effects: on the one hand, the crudity of Nazi views on the economy and the obvious inefficiencies of their system sharpened the critical faculties of those already influenced by traditional economic theory. On the other, the strength of the case against *laissez-faire* liberalism seemed proven. That, indeed, was a cause which seemed impossible to defend, even if individual economists might still hanker after it. If economic liberalism was going to revive, it would need a special component capable of rebutting the charge that it was simply a rich man's doctrine, designed to justify the exploitation of the weak by the strong.

Müller-Armack had certainly been successful in insisting that his new textile research unit should adopt a strictly academic attitude to market research, and should not just act as an empirical collector of information for industrialists. In an address to the first meeting of the industrialists' association supporting the unit, he said that scholarship might certainly frame its investigations under the influence of industrial practice, but that 'the core of all scholarly effort remains the pursuit of knowledge'.[48]

He pointed to the field of cost theory, where the work of Cournot, Marshall, and others had been developed—above all by Schmalenbach—into a theory of business management (*Betriebswirtschaft*). The rationalization of costing and industrial organization would not have been possible without such theories.[49] He was also eager to stress that individual branches of the economy must be related to the whole corpus of economic theory and not just treated in isolation. In a later article, he warned that, just as there was no economic theory which applied especially to transport or insurance, neither could there be any such thing for textiles: 'Economics presents us instead with a homogenous intellectual apparatus, which can be then applied in the various special branches of the economy.'[50]

[48] A. Müller-Armack, 'Wissenschaft und Wirtschaftspraxis', lecture delivered to the Förderergesellschaft der Forschungsstelle on 23 Oct. 1941. FATM, *Arbeitsberichte zur Marktforschung* (Münster, 1941), no. 3, p. 70.

[49] Ibid. 71.

[50] A. Müller-Armack, 'Zur volkswirtschaftlichen Problematik des Textilmarktes', in FATM, *Arbeitsberichte zur Marktforschung'* (Münster, 1943), no. 6, p. 161.

Müller-Armack evidently did good work in organizing the institute into its various departments, so that it did indeed become effective both as an academic research unit and as a collection centre for valuable information. What is more in doubt is his own intellectual attitude to its work. The historian of the unit believes he was not particularly interested in applied economics, but was happy to use the unit's facilities to pursue his own studies, which concerned the relationship between religious affiliation and economic activity.[51] The tough-minded entrepreneurs who supported the unit may indeed have been mildly surprised to be lectured at on the importance of the Huguenots in the development of the textile industry.[52]

Despite this, Müller-Armack undoubtedly gained important insights into actual business practice which would come in useful in the post-war period. One is also tempted to speculate on the effect of such contacts with applied economics on his own intellectual development. The crude *dirigiste* notions of some entrepreneurs, not to mention the Nazis, made him eager to salvage as much from classical economic theory as was possible within the framework of a directed economy. He himself may, at this stage, have believed that the free market was a thing of the past. But the experience of the Third Reich showed him how popular resentment against the effects of an unregulated market economy could be harnessed to a totalitarian system which treated the realities of economic life as if they were of no account. It is not altogether fanciful to link his reaction to this to his later stress on the social aspect of the social market economy and its incompatibility with *laissez-faire*. Only by reforming the liberal alternative to totalitarianism could it be made secure against collectivism.

The directorship of the textile research institute was certainly valuable to Müller-Armack in another, more material sense. He was permitted, quite exceptionally, to receive that admirable Swiss newspaper, the *Neue Zürcher Zeitung*. This had to be kept in his office and locked in his safe. Only such articles as were directly relevant to the textile market were to be cut out and shown to the other members of the staff. Müller-Armack himself, however, could read the news from the Western world, including the truth about the progress of the war. He was therefore able to assess at an early stage the likelihood of Nazi defeat.[53] It should also be mentioned that the research unit possessed

---

[51] Conversation with Dr T. Mandt, May 1983.
[52] Müller-Armack, 'Wissenschaft und Wirtschaftspraxis', 67.
[53] I am grateful to Dr Mandt for this information. See fn. 51.

its own duplicating and printing apparatus, which was to prove very useful in the years immediately after the war.[54]

Nevertheless, Müller-Armack's own interests remained on a wider and perhaps more elevated plane. During the late 1930s he began research into the connections between religious denomination and economic development in various parts of Europe. He concluded that religious beliefs were more important influences on the economic activity of human beings than cultural traditions or racial characteristics. The lack of a clear concept of social organization in German religious thought—and he especially picked out Lutheranism in this respect—had, he believed, left Germany vulnerable to despotism, whereas in England Christianity had taken a form which had been able to resist it. Although 'Marxism' was the despotic bogey referred to in the book on the subject he published during the Second World War, it is clear that his message was equally inimical to Nazi racialism.[55]

In conducting research for this book, his position as director of the textile institute came in very useful. He was commissioned to write a report on textile marketing in south-eastern Europe, and in May 1943 went to Budapest and Sofia. He travelled with a delegation of textile manufacturers hoping to negotiate supplies from Hungary. They were treated with great ceremony, being put up at the Ritz in Budapest. Müller-Armack later described the enthusiasm with which the German visitors—ostensibly representing the *Herrenvolk* in Hitler's European fortress—threw themselves into the delights of the elegant Hungarian capital, blessed as it still was with a relatively free market. Although the German delegation had an impossible task, since it was trying to trade off worthless credits against tangible Hungarian exports, its members did not hurry to return to the Third Reich. They found life in Hungary too attractive, even though German currency regulations had prevented Müller-Armack himself taking more than ten Reichsmarks out of the country. This became a serious problem as he travelled further east, and eventually he came back from Sofia with no money at all, having kept himself going on the train by illegally bartering a gift of Bulgarian tobacco for some mineral water. It was an experience which strengthened his antipathy towards planned economies and added force to his later observation that controlled bilateral trade-arrangements always proved unsatisfactory, because one partner was bound to build

---

[54] Mandt, '25 Jahre textilwirtschaftliche Forschung in Münster', 362.

[55] A. Müller-Armack, *Genealogie der Wirtschaftsstile: Die geistesgeschichtlichen Ursprünge der Staats- und Wirtschaftsformen bis zum Ausgang des 18. Jahrhunderts* (3rd edn.; Münster, 1944), 268.

up surpluses at the expense of the other, ultimately damaging the interests of both parties.[56]

For Müller-Armack, the war was part of a learning process, instilling into him an aversion against authoritarian corporatism, a system he had been inclined to welcome in 1933. In the case of Walter Eucken and his Freiburg colleagues, the Nazi period was a nightmare to be endured and a challenge to produce a rational alternative to Hitler's command economy.

For members of the Freiburg group and their associates, the experience of life under National Socialism simply reinforced their existing hostility to collectivism. Their problem was largely one of survival.

Despite the difficulties facing them, the academic adherents of the free market did try to retain their integrity and to keep their principles alive, albeit in a camouflaged and apparently harmless form. Walter Eucken and his colleagues, including Franz Böhm, Leonhard Miksch, and Erwin von Beckerath, discreetly continued to produce theoretical works favouring the reactivation of the market economy.

In 1939 Eucken published his *Grundlagen der Nationalökonomie* (Foundations of Economics), which was quickly reprinted and had reached a fourth edition by 1944. At first glance this seemed a fairly opaque academic book, critical of Keynes and of empirical approaches to academic problems. It is unlikely that the average Nazi Gauleiter would have bothered to read past the first chapter, and even if he had done so, it would have been difficult for him to find much in the book that was objectionable or subversive. Nevertheless, it contained many fundamental tenets of neo-liberal theory.

Eucken argued that in any phase of human development a reasoned analysis ought to be able to detect an economic system. This could only be done if the total economy was thereby encompassed, so that the principles underlying the entire process—*die Gesamtordnung*—could be understood. It should be the aim of economic theory to work out a comprehensive picture of how the national and international system operated and what its ground rules were.[57]

Eucken was obviously not able to be too specific about the nature of his preferred *Gesamtordnung*, but his implied criticism of directed economies, his description of the workings of the market economy,[58] and his contrast between competitive and monopoly-fixed prices[59] leave

---

[56] Id., *Auf dem Weg nach Europa*, 23–35, gives details of the Hungarian visit and Müller-Armack's views about it.

[57] W. Eucken, *Die Grundlagen der Nationalökonomie* (8th edn.; New York, 1965), 240.

[58] Ibid. 78–86.   [59] Ibid. 241–2.

little room for doubt where his sympathies lay. The system to which his theories lent support was a consumer-dominated market economy in which the state lays down the rules of operation but refrains from direct interference. This was an ideal quite at variance, not only with Marxist theories, but also with the production-orientated, power-seeking eclecticism of Nazi economic policy. Eucken made contemptuous reference to ideologies and doctrines which by implication were incompatible with sound economic principles.[60] Once again, however, there was no suggestion of a return to *laissez-faire*: 'The history of the last century has emphatically taught us that the problem will not solve itself. Premeditated organization of the system is necessary.'[61]

During the war muted discussions took place among German economists about the nature of the system which would follow the ending of hostilities. Since the financial policies—if such they could be called—of the Nazi government were evidently going to be unsuccessful, some form of post-war planning had to take place, despite the displeasure of the authorities. In May 1943 the inflationary trends in the economy were so obvious that Goebbels had to intervene to prevent discussion in the press of ways to stop money losing its value. Attempts by the Economics Minister, Funk, to increase taxes and curb excessive purchasing-power were blocked by Hitler himself. In this deadlock, experts were able to exchange views in the context of apparently harmless discussions about monetary theory.[62]

In November 1941 Eucken told a meeting of a group called the *Arbeitsgemeinschaft Preispolitik* that the current economic system could only be an interim phase, and urged a return to market prices and competition.[63] Another important group, which met mainly in Freiburg and in which Eucken and Franz Böhm were active participants, was one known as the *Arbeitsgemeinschaft Erwin von Beckerath*. Erwin von Beckerath was an economist in Bonn who had been appointed by the Nazi Academy of German Law to set up an inquiry into the German economy. He gathered a number of distinguished economists to help in this enterprise, many of whom were of doubtful loyalty to the Nazi system. In November 1940 the first meeting of this group busied itself with a discussion of Eucken's *Grundlagen*, which was generally well

---

[60] Ibid. 241.
[61] 'Denkende Gestaltung der Ordnung ist nötig'. Ibid. 240.
[62] L. Herbst, 'Krisenüberwindung und Wirtschaftsneuordnung: Ludwig Erhards Beteiligung an den Nachkriegsplanungen am Ende des zweiten Weltkrieges', *Vierteljahrshefte für Zeitgeschichte*, 25/3 (July 1977), 308–9.
[63] Ibid. 312.

received.[64] In spring the following year a subcommittee was established, chaired by Adolf Lampe in Freiburg. Eucken was a member of this also. Its unofficial aim was to consider the effects of total war on national economies and what measures should be taken after the war. Although the Academy of German Law was closed in March 1943, von Beckerath carried on his work privately, meetings taking place in Freiburg, where Lampe and Eucken acted as hosts.[65]

A number of neo-liberal concepts can be detected in the memorandum drawn up by the *Arbeitsgemeinschaft* in September 1943. This argued that it would be up to each national economy after the war to overcome hardships by its own efforts, a view scarcely compatible with Nazi bombast about the spoils of victory. Furthermore, it recommended that 'pseudo-social' experiments be avoided. The planned economy of wartime would have to be dismantled as quickly as possible and the laws of supply and demand should be allowed to operate: 'The peacetime economy will witness the reinstatement of the dethroned consumer in his sovereign rights.' Competition would have to be protected, cartels and monopolies abolished. There would have to be a fall in real wages, but compensatory measures might be taken through taxation, and there must be a major effort to overcome the housing shortage.[66]

The meetings of the Freiburg group were characterized by wide-ranging and astonishingly frank discussions about the needs of the post-war economy, both in Germany and in the world at large. As early as November 1942, Lampe was drafting a memorandum in which he claimed that the wartime directed economy was unsuitable for peacetime and that the free market was much better than the reputation it

---

[64] C. Blumenberg-Lampe, *Das wirtschaftspolitische Programm der 'Freiburger Kreise': Entwurf einer freiheitlich-sozialen Nachkriegswirtschaft. Nationalökonomen gegen den Nationalsozialismus* (Berlin, 1973), 30–42. See also L. Herbst, *Der totale Krieg und die Ordnung der Wirtschaft: Der Kriegswirtschaft im Spannungsfeld von Politik, Ideologie und Propaganda, 1939–1945* (Stuttgart, 1982), 148–50. Herbst points to the attractiveness of neo-liberalism for the Nazis because it was a serious economic theory which negated *laissez-faire*. However, he also admits that neo-liberal contributions to the debate in the war years occasionally went 'far beyond what was conceivable for the economic policy of the Third Reich', ibid. 149.

[65] Ibid.

[66] *Arbeitsgemeinschaft E. von Beckerath*, 'Wichtigste Probleme des Wiederaufbaus der Friedenswirtschaft und ihre Lösung durch primär marktwirtschaftliche Wirtschaftsordunung', 24/25 Sept. 1943. This document is listed in app. 3 of Blumenberg-Lampe, *Das wirtschaftspolitische Programm*, 160, where it is numbered 14a. The author was allowed to consult a transcript of the original document being prepared for publication from the Lampe Papers in the Konrad-Adenauer-Stiftung. The document numbers cited hereafter are from that source. I am very grateful to Dr Blumenberg-Lampe and the Konrad-Adenauer-Stiftung for permission to read these documents.

enjoyed among the public at large. However, it would be no good just leaving everything to work itself out in a completely disorganized economy. First of all, it would be necessary to dispose of the excess money, or 'purchasing-power overhang', as the Germans picturesquely called it, created by the command economy. That would have to be done by transforming all war debts into bonds which would be very difficult to convert into currency.[67]

At a meeting of the group in Freiburg, 24–6 July 1943, Eucken presented a paper in which he described his view of the change-over from war to peace. This should go through two stages—a preliminary stage and a 'stage of actual transition'. In the preliminary stage the system of fixed prices and wages should remain, but the government should order the production of as many consumer goods as possible, relying on information from the retail trade to decide what items should be chosen. The budget had to be balanced and the excess of purchasing power destroyed. If necessary, there would have to be a complete reform of the currency, replacing the old money with a new and stable unit of exchange. Interest rates would probably have to rise. There would then come the second and actual phase of transformation, in which prices would run free and the disciplines of the market would once again impose themselves.[68]

Although Eucken was not recommending the abolition of the Reichsmark, he was ready to contemplate it, and it is not without interest that, in the early summer of 1943, he outlined a course of action very similar to that which actually occurred over the next five years. In practice, of course, it took far longer and was carried out under much more difficult circumstances than even he envisaged. From then until the summer of 1944, Lampe, Eucken, and their colleagues discussed ways of stabilizing the German currency, and by September 1944 Lampe was again proposing currency reform as a means of liquidating excessive purchasing-power. Three years later he was pressing the same sort of solution on the Allied occupation authorities in Baden.[69]

As befitted liberal economists, the members of the group were eager to re-establish the world trading-system and to stabilize international exchange arrangements. They studied with interest the ideas being propounded by Keynes, as he laid the foundations for what was to become the Bretton Woods system of international currency regu-

---

[67] KAS Lampe NL, doc. 1, pp. 6–7.
[68] Ibid., doc. 12, pp. 1–3.
[69] Ibid., doc. 47, pp. 1–4. This document is not listed in Blumenberg-Lampe, *Das wirtschaftspolitische Programm*, because it falls outside the scope of the book.

lations. At a group conference held in late November 1943, Eucken commented in detail on Keynes's plans.

He described with approval Keynes's suggestions for an International Clearing Union (ICU), based on an international unit of exchange linked to the gold price, but not being in itself a gold-backed currency. This would enable the organization to iron out balance-of-payments problems. Each nation would have a credit limit with the International Clearing Union, and long before that limit was reached, the organization would act to persuade the country concerned to correct its balance of payments by restricting its money supply.

Eucken welcomed these suggestions because he accepted the primacy of currency policy for the expansion of world trade. In words which have relevance to our contemporary situation, he stressed that: 'Without the avoidance of currency fluctuations caused by devaluation etc. it will be impossible to build up the world economy in the grand style.'[70]

It is difficult to imagine what he and his colleagues would have thought of the unstable conditions faced by businessmen in the money markets of the 1980s and 1990s.

Eucken was much less happy about some of Keynes's broader concepts for a world economic system which would try to even out price fluctuations by setting up pools of raw materials and food, and would promote mass employment by centrally stimulated credit-measures. Although Keynes's system would operate in the form of a market system, the most important elements in that system would be effectively monopolized and put under central control. Eucken feared that the result would be a form of directed economy on a world scale: 'The attempt to create such a type of world order and to carry out such a comprehensive direction of economic policy [*Konjunkturpolitik*] is highly objectionable.'[71]

Here we can detect the underlying principle of neo-liberalism: state intervention to create proper conditions for free competition was to be encouraged; state intervention in the economic process, let alone supranational direction of it, was to be avoided.

Franz Böhm wasted no opportunity to press for state intervention to protect competition against monopolies and cartels—not by bureaucratic restraints but by alterations in the law which would give private price-fixing no contractual validity. In May 1944 he presented a meeting of the group, attended by both von Beckerath and Eucken, with a paper on economic concentration in which he pointed to the dangers created by very large businesses, pressure on small businesses from

---

[70] Ibid., doc. 23, pp. 6–7.   [71] Ibid., doc. 23, p. 8.

mightier competitors, and, above all, price-fixing cartels. The latter were incompatible with the market economy (*systemwidrig*). Any kind of legal protection should be withdrawn from businessmen who attempted to impose alien market-forms on the system by price-fixing deals or by the use of business methods designed to inhibit competition.[72] Not all of the economic experts present accepted Böhm's radical formula. Nevertheless, the belief that competition must be protected and cartels controlled, if not abolished, does not seem to have been seriously challenged.

Labour relations were also the subject of discussion at Freiburg. One of those involved in the *Arbeitsgemeinschaft*, Albrecht, told the group in March 1944 that socialization would be of no benefit to the workers. Under a free-market system, they should have representation in the factories, but unlike the situation in the Nazi Labour Front, they should possess enough independence to present themselves in their workplace as free contractual partners. They also ought to have a say in wage settlements, although he appreciated the dangers inherent in such a policy. Trade unions ought not to be able to fix wages for whole industries, because this would lead to excessively high wages and unemployment. Plant negotiations should be the order of the day. Nevertheless, free collective bargaining by trade unions was his suggestion. It certainly did not convince all his listeners; Lampe wanted strikes to be illegal, for example, and another participant, von Dietze, claimed that workers could organize if they wanted, but should 'just keep their fingers from meddling with wage policy'.[73] What is clear is that the proposals were not simply a receipt for a return to *laissez-faire* labour relations of the pre-1914 type. Employees could expect some organized protection in their work-place and would participate in matters concerning labour welfare, including the welfare of the unemployed.[74] Workers should be given maximum information about the labour market, and transport improvements should be encouraged in order to increase labour mobility.

Generally speaking, the Freiburg circle was moving towards neo-liberal solutions for Germany's economic problems: a market economy in which competition was protected, with a stable currency and a certain amount of help from the state in the early stages to assist the market to function again. At the same time, indirect influences such as tax policy might be used to push the system in socially desirable directions. It was also made clear that housing would be an area of

---

[72] Ibid., doc. 31, p. 5.   [73] Ibid., doc. 27, p. 4ff.   [74] Ibid., doc. 29, pp. 11–13.

especial concern in the post-war era, and that rents might have to be controlled.[75]

This does not mean that there was a uniform concept of a post-war recovery programme. Divisions of view certainly existed about the role of the state in the economy, even after the immediate crisis had passed. In the summer of 1944 Erich Preiser submitted a paper on control of the business cycle designed to prevent boom and slump, underconsumption, and underemployment. He argued that a balanced economy could not be achieved through the spontaneous forces within the market. After the war 'the free market economy of the liberal type will not be possible for any nation on earth'.[76] The market would have to be regulated in two ways: first, real competition would have to be protected from the abuse of economic power, and secondly, a stable level of business activity would have to be maintained through government action. To help achieve this he proposed an integrated European economy which would involve a great deal of international co-operation. A mere customs union would not suffice, because 'wealth does not depend on market size but on the continuing stability of economic activity'. Preiser's proposals are all the more remarkable when one remembers they were drawn up during some of the bitterest fighting of the Second World War. They illustrated a dilemma facing many neo-liberals at that time. What was the role of the state in the economy to be? Was there to be a market economy limited by general rules or a planned economy with market elements in it? Eucken and his colleagues firmly supported the former, but the outcome of the debate was by no means clear in 1945.

One person who had few doubts on the subject was Ludwig Erhard. In 1942 he had left Vershoven's Nuremberg institute. This may have been due to his refusal to join the Nazi Labour Front; it could also have been caused by personal friction with his chief, since by this time the two men were evidently not finding collaboration too easy. Vershofen was a prickly customer, and doubtless Erhard was tired of playing a subordinate role.

Erhard set up his own institute for industrial research, supported by funds from various industrial enterprises including Mannesmann and the cigarette firm of Reemstma. This 'institute' actually consisted of

---

[75] Ibid., doc. 13. This was a paper by Lampe entitled 'Entwurf, Umrisse eines Systems wirtschaftspolitischer Wiederaufbaumaßnahmen nach dem Kriege', which was discussed at a meeting of the *Arbeitsgemeinschaft*, 23–6 Sep. 1943.

[76] Ibid., doc. 36, pp. 4–5. This paper was not drawn up specifically for the group but was sent to them by Preiser for discussion. It is numbered doc. 28 in Blumenberg-Lampe, *Das wirtschaftspolitische Programm*, 162.

himself and a secretary, and its real purpose was to draw up proposals for a post-war economy. In summer 1944 Erhard circulated a memorandum to various important industrialists and bankers, among whom were the representatives of IG Farben, Flick, Siemens, the Dresdener Bank, and the Deutsche Bank.[77]

The wording of the document was cautious and obviously affected by the constraints of life in Nazi Germany. Its author also had to pay attention to the limitations imposed on economic policy by the exigencies of war. Erhard could not, therefore, expound a blueprint for a social market economy in 1944. Nevertheless, his memorandum was remarkable for its frankness, and for its restatement of several principles central to the neo-liberal viewpoint.[78]

Although Erhard did not say in so many words that Germany had lost the war, he painted a gloomy picture of the post-war era as one of dislocation and shortages. He glossed over the possibility of foreign support for the German economy and even assumed that expatriate workers would go home after the war.[79] There was no echo of Nazi propaganda in his arguments.

Erhard's aim was to make sure that the peacetime economy would be regulated according to sound economic principles. It is evident that he and the interest groups for whom he was writing were afraid that the end of hostilities might bring with it a repudiation of the national debt and a massive inflation, either open, as in the years 1918–23, or camouflaged by government price-controls. The upshot would be more state interference and the ultimate socialization of industry.

Erhard pointed out that inflation was masked under the Nazi system by draconian price-controls. There had been an invisible or 'noiseless' expansion of the money supply, creating the dangerous *Kaufkraftüberhang*—excess purchasing-power. He argued that only drastic, but carefully timed, measures could restore the country to economic health. He was opposed to a controlled or staged inflation (*dosierte Inflation*) which would gradually raise the price level, thereby maintaining employment and mopping up surplus money. This would

---

[77] Erhard, *Kriegsfinanzierung*. See also, Herbst, 'Krisenüberwindung', 321–30, and id., *Der totale Krieg*, 383–7.

[78] Ludolf Herbst stresses the extent to which Erhard seemed to accept the *dirigisme* of the Third Reich. He claims that the memorandum 'does not belong to the early history (*Vorfeld*) of the social market economy but is a typical document of the transition phase from war to peace economy'. See 'Erhards Beteiligung', 340. This does not seem to me to do justice to the text of the memorandum, especially when the circumstances under which it was written are taken into account.

[79] Erhard, *Kriegsfinanzierung*, 263. He does make vague references to external inputs, but this question was relegated to an appendix which was never written: ibid., 58–9.

be indiscriminately damaging in its effects and would undermine public confidence.[80] Erhard approached the problem as if Germany were a bankrupt concern, which it effectively was, although he was wise enough not to say so. There should be a rescheduling or scaling-down of public debt and a sharp reduction in purchasing power, but certain categories of creditors should be given priority according to the most urgent social needs.

He certainly did not demand the immediate removal of state controls, which he accepted as being essential for the transition from war to peace. There was not to be an immediate rush into currency reform, debt consolidation, and cuts in the money supply. First of all, there had to be a comprehensive demobilization of labour and reorientation of the economy towards peacetime production. Until that happened, the old forms of artificial credit-creation used during the war would be maintained. But, once this period of transition was over, there would come the critical moment when excess purchasing-power would have to be mopped up, the money supply drastically curtailed, and the state's budget balanced. The government should establish preconditions for the reintroduction of market forces and then ensure that such forces would be able to operate freely.

Erhard accepted that much would have to be done to readjust to the peacetime economy, and gave a high priority to housing the homeless, an obvious need in a country already devastated by bombing. Yet debt conversion and sound money remained at the heart of his programme. In answer to the criticism that this would simply lead to deflation and stagnation, he claimed that such results would only transpire if old-fashioned *laissez-faire* policies were pursued. Credit facilities would have to be provided to stimulate production. Democratic governments before 1933 had appreciated this, but had been too half-hearted about it. The Nazis had been more decisive, but because of their stress on heavy industry and arms production they had been forced to impose severe economic controls and to tolerate hidden inflation. What had never been tried, and what was needed, was a determined boost for consumer industries. They would themselves generate both production and demand, enabling the economy to revive as the result of its own strengths.[81] The only way to overcome social tensions after the war would be by increased production. This could not be achieved by state direction. After the demobilization period the state should confine

[80] For Erhard's critique of *dosierte Inflation,* which he evidently saw as a serious threat to the market economy, see ibid. 105 ff., 137–8, 154–6. For Erhard's summary of his own policy, see ibid. 260–1.

[81] Ibid. 232–44, 258.

itself to the regulation of finances and credit, and avoid directing production: 'The most sought-after objective remains in each case the free market economy based on true competition—with the inherent regulative mechanism which that system contains.'[82]

Lest this should be misunderstood, however, he stressed that: 'certainly the state will never again be pushed back into the role of a night-watchman, because even the freest market economy, and especially this one, needs an instrument to draw up the rules and supervise their implementation'.[83] His aim was 'a peacetime economy serving human welfare'.

Erhard himself found a positive reception for his ideas, not only in industry but even in the Reich Ministry of Economics, with which he maintained discreet contact during the latter months of 1944.[84] This did not, of course, mean that his views were compatible with those of the Nazis. Indeed, the extent to which his memorandum ran counter to the aims of National Socialism can be illustrated by the fact that a copy of it was sent to the resistance leader, Carl Goerdeler, just as he was about to embark on the attempt to overthrow Hitler on 20 July 1944. Goerdeler, who was, of course, no stranger to Erhard, seems to have approved of Erhard's proposals for dealing with the national debt.[85]

This was by no means the only link between neo-liberalism and anti-Nazi resistance. As we have seen, Franz Böhm had sacrificed his official career by his outspoken comments on Nazi racial policies in 1938. He had been forced to give up a lectureship at Jena and had then been suspended from another post at the Commercial University in Leipzig. Spurning the opportunity to take service under Göring in the organization of the Nazi Four Year Plan, he was finally deprived of his right to teach at universities in 1940. He became involved in Bonhoeffer's circle of anti-Nazi Christians and was one of the authors of a memorandum drawn up in Freiburg envisaging the political shape of a new German society after Hitler's fall. He also had meetings with Goerdeler in the latter's flat in Leipzig where they discussed the prospects for a coup against the regime.[86] Lampe, too, had contacts with

---

[82] Ibid. 264.

[83] Ibid. 26.

[84] Herbst, 'Krisenüberwindung', 335, and Herbst, *Der totaler Krieg*, 387–96. Erhard's memorandum—or at least a shortened version of it—was shown to senior officials in the Economics Ministry. This is proved by a letter from Rudolf Stahl to Ministerialdirektor and SS-Gruppenführer Ohlendorff dated 14 Nov. 1944, which explains the activities of Erhard's institute. BA R7 2131.

[85] Erhard, *Kriegsfinanzierung*, p. xii.

[86] See Böhm NL, KAS 001-004. Also Franz Böhm, *Reden und Schriften* (Karlsruhe, 1960) 281.

Goerdeler's group, and was arrested for a time after the failure of the coup in the summer of 1944. His experiences in custody undoubtedly hastened his untimely death in 1948.[87]

By this time Müller-Armack was also considering the future of the German economy after the war. As early as May 1944 he drafted a strong critique of the command economy under the title 'The Testing-Time of Economic Planning'.[88] In this document he cautiously pointed to the failings of the centrally directed war-economy—particularly its inflexibility in response to consumer requirements and its inability to stimulate production. He denied that such a system would be the best means of meeting Germany's economic needs after the war. The free market ought not to be consigned to the intellectual scrap-heap; it had much more elasticity than planned economies, quite apart from the fact that individual freedom could not be preserved if economic activity was centrally directed.[89]

Müller-Armack stressed that he did not advocate a sudden abolition of controls. Nor was he supporting a return to the unrestrained *laissez-faire* of the previous century. Economic liberalism had been proved wrong when it fostered a belief in the price mechanism as a fully automatic machine which could be left to function by itself. Like any other machine, however good, it required sensible direction. The answer lay in a 'guided market economy' (*gesteuerte Marktwirtschaft*). Such an economy would not:

leave the machine to run itself at full blast, as liberalism does, nor would it see it as opportune to shut down all the valves and tie up all the levers, as the command economy does, but rather it attempts to operate the machine by a sensible technique of impulses and safeguards, thereby achieving a desired result.[90]

Here was the basis of Müller-Armack's blueprint for a social market economy, the first part of which was published in Hamburg two years later.[91] None of this activity was able to influence Nazi economic policy, nor did it lead to successful acts of resistance. It did mean,

---

[87] See below, Ch. 9.
[88] 'Die Bewährungsprobe der Wirtschaftslenkung', Müller-Armack NL, KAS I-236-074.
[89] Ibid., p. 86.
[90] Ibid., p. 87.
[91] The typescript in the Müller-Armack Papers bears the handwritten date 'May 44'. It contains references which make it evident that it was written during the war. e.g. it refers to the autarkical economy in Hitler's Europe (*Großraumwirtschaft*) which 'is today a reality' (p. 46). In the version published in 1946 this became 'was a reality during the war'. See A. Müller-Armack, *Wirtschaftsordnung und Wirtschaftspolitik: Studien und Konzepte zur sozialen Marktwirtschaft und zur europäischen Integration* (2nd edn.; Bern, 1976), 60.

however, that both inside and outside Germany an economic alternative existed to those collectivist views which otherwise seemed dominant. There were, of course, different shades of opinion within the anti-collectivist camp. Eucken and Böhm emphasized the need for a free-price mechanism and open competition protected by the state, Röpke and Rüstow stressed the advantages of small-scale producers and equal opportunities, Erhard was willing to consider credits for consumer industries, and Müller-Armack was probably still the most *dirigiste* of all, advocating government action to influence the market, even though the price mechanism as such was to operate freely. Nevertheless, the common ground between these men meant that after the war they could join forces to restore the open market and consumer-orientated competition.

Most of those involved in these wartime speculations later emerged as advocates of the social market economy. Müller-Armack could claim to have invented the term. Erhard himself implemented the policy. Eucken, Böhm, Lampe, and von Beckerath were all members of the advisory council set up by the Economics Administration in Frankfurt in 1948 and were thereby able to strengthen Erhard's hand against his critics.[92] Böhm chaired the council in 1948, and von Beckerath took over as chairman from June 1950 until his death in 1964. In this way one can detect a line of continuity between neo-liberal efforts during the war and the social market economy as it appeared in the early years of the Federal Republic.

[92] See below, Ch. 9. See also Blumenberg-Lampe, *Das wirtschaftspolitische Programm,* 152–3.

5

West Germany in Ruins:
The Aftermath of Defeat

IN 1945 West Germany presented a scene of apparently irreparable devastation. Most of the major cities had been pulverized by bombing, and in the Ruhr area—or more properly in the Rhineland-Westphalian industrial complex—the results of the Allied bombing campaign were particularly spectacular. To this had been added destruction connected with ground fighting, including deliberate sabotage by retreating Nazi forces. Transport was particularly badly hit, bridges and railway junctions having been favourite targets of attack. Private dwellings and shops had also been destroyed in large numbers. The problems of homelessness were exacerbated by refugees fleeing from Soviet armies in the east, and by wartime evacuees who wanted to return to their homes. By 1950 the western, and in particular the Anglo-American, zones of occupation had been forced to take in 7.5 million Germans previously domiciled in the eastern regions of Germany or in other parts of the Nazi empire such as the Sudetenland.[1] Owing to the shortage of housing in cities, the majority of these people were billeted in the countryside or kept in refugee camps, so that they did not have easy access to industrial centres—even if there had been work for them in such places.

Added to these physical problems were the attitudes of Germany's occupiers. It would be wrong to suggest, as some German historians have done,[2] that up to 1948 the Western Allies pursued a policy of deliberately weakening the German economy. The fantasy of 'agrarianizing' Germany which had surfaced in the Morgenthau Plan of 1944 had quickly been dropped, although not before it had played a valuable part in Goebbels's propaganda. None the less, the bitterness

---

[1] W. Benz, *Von der Besatzungsherrschaft zur Bundesrepublik: Stationen einer Staatsgründung, 1946–1949* (Frankfurt/M., 1984), 33.

[2] See, e.g., the contributions by F. Pingel and W. Plumpe in D. Petzina and W. Euchner (eds.), *Wirtschaftspolitik im britischen Besatzungsgebiet, 1945–49* (Düsseldorf, 1984). For a balanced and convincing revision of the 'British exploitation' view, see I. D. Turner, 'British Policy towards German Industry, 1945–9: Reconstruction, Restriction or Exploitation?', in id. (ed.), *Reconstruction in Post-war Germany: British Occupation Policy and the Western Zones, 1945–1955* (Oxford, 1989), esp. 85–91.

engendered by Nazi aggression and so many years of desperate fighting meant that Germany's occupiers took a stern and suspicious view of the native population. The Germans would have to pay for the war they had unleashed and to this end reparations totalling some $20 billion were to be squeezed out of them, half of which was to go to the Soviet Union.

Although the Russians did indeed manage to extract most of what they demanded from the Soviet zone of Germany,[3] the Western Powers were more confused about their attitude to reparations. Some factories were dismantled and sent to the Soviet authorities, who, it was assumed, would deliver food from their zone as a quid pro quo, especially because the eastern parts of the country had been its main grain-producing region. This assumption soon proved false, both because the agricultural lands east of the Oder–Neisse line were occupied by the Poles, and because conditions in the Soviet zone were themselves so difficult that a food surplus was hardly to be expected. The British zone of occupation had to be fed by grain imported from North America and purchased by the British, using a rapidly dwindling supply of dollars. Even so, the food rations were very low in the years 1945–8, a period which has been retained in the German folk-memory as one of hunger and privation.

The ambivalence of the Western Allies certainly did not help reconstruction in their zones. On the one hand, there was a natural and pragmatic tendency of the men on the spot to get things working again as soon as possible. On the other, there was fear of German military resurgence and a belief that German industrial power, in particular, had to be prevented from reappearing in a form which would threaten the country's neighbours. Both the British and the Americans wanted to see large German industrial concerns broken up into smaller units. The British government was inclined towards encouraging the public ownership of major industries, although that would obviously bring with it the question of what state authorities should control such enterprises. One way of ensuring that they remained devoted to peaceful use was to involve the trade unions in a form of co-partnership in running them, and the British did indeed encourage the German unions to think along these lines.[4] For their part, the US authorities

---

[3] A. Cairncross, *The Price of War: British Policy on German Reparations, 1941–1949* (Oxford, 1986), 207–18.

[4] The British authorities had no overall plan for industry in their zone when they took over, and their attitude towards trade unions was cautious. They and the trade unions, however, shared a desire to weaken the old concentrations of capitalist power in the Ruhr. See P. Hubsch, 'DGB Economic Policy with Particular Reference to the British

were not at all enthusiastic about 'socialization', but they did believe in deconcentration and, above all, in decartelization, which fitted in with their own antitrust legislation.[5]

All this seemed to add up to a very gloomy economic outlook for the Germans. However, there was another side to the picture, and one which has been stressed by economic historians. The first point to remember is that, although in 1945 the German Reich seemed to have been effectively smashed as a social entity and Germans later spoke of that year as the 'hour zero' (*Stunde Null*), from which they had to begin again from nothing, the country did possess some potential advantages. Since 1936 Germany's economy had been in a state of strong industrial expansion. This was particularly true in the field of capital-goods industries. Machine-tool production had been greatly stimulated by the policies of Hitler and his satraps, even if those policies had flown in the face of market economics. Between 1938 and 1943 the stock of machine tools in Germany increased by 75 per cent, and it has been claimed that at that point the number of such machine-making machines in the Third Reich exceeded those in the USA. Even if this is an exaggerated claim, the point has to be taken that the Germans had available to them very large stocks of capital equipment. The fact that most of this was being devoted to the warlike purposes of the Nazis did not alter its potential value for peacetime production. To take a specific, and emotive, example of Nazi investment which was to prove its worth in a quite different context, the Volkswagen plant at Wolfsburg in Lower Saxony had been set up to meet the ideological objectives of the Third Reich, and its output had been devoted to war purposes from 1939. Yet in the 1950s the 'beetle' car was to be the symbol of West Germany's success in her export drive.

Despite appearances, the war had not seriously reduced Germany's industrial capacity. The devastation caused by bombing was spectacular and tragic. Yet it had not done so very much damage to the sinews of German industry, and in particular to the machine tools upon which an industrial recovery would depend. Area—or 'carpet'—bombing had been adopted by the Royal Air Force initially because the primitive navigation-equipment available to Bomber Command in the early 1940s

Zone, 1945–9', in I. D. Turner (ed.), *Reconstruction in Post-war Germany*, 271–4, and 295–7. Ernest Bevin was not enthusiastic about co-determination in German industry, despite his relatively benevolent attitude to German trade unions—as against contempt for the SPD; see A. Bullock, *Ernest Bevin, Foreign Secretary* (London, 1983), 373–4, and Hubsch, 'DGB Economic Policy', 295.

[5] V. R. Berghahn, *The Americanisation of West German Industry 1945–1973* (Leamington Spa, 1986), 26–39.

made it impossible to hit precise targets—especially at night. Even when more exact methods of bomber navigation such as 'Oboe' were introduced later in the war, the apparent success of massed bomber attacks on major cities made the RAF reluctant to switch to what Air Marshal Harris described as 'panacea targets' in German industry. During the closing stages of the conflict, air attacks were concentrated on communications centres—especially railway junctions—a justifiable decision from the military viewpoint, but one which did not put industrial plant particularly at risk.

For their part, the Germans had gone to great lengths to protect industry from aerial bombardment, dispersing it into safer regions and sometimes even putting it underground. It was easier to protect factories than apartment blocks against fire-bomb attacks and they were also more resistant to assault by high explosives. The result was that a relatively small proportion of West Germany's machine tools was destroyed during the war—one estimate puts the loss at 6.5 per cent. Since real gross investment had peaked in 1942 at nearly two and a half times the level of 1936—a year of full-capacity utilization—it can be seen how great had been the industrial expansion in the feverish years of National Socialist rule. Even the highly unpopular Allied policy of dismantling plant for reparations purposes cost West Germany only about 3.5 per cent of its gross capital stock and, added to the deterioration of plant in the years 1945–7, this meant an overall loss of less than 7 per cent.[6]

If the country had great potential as far as industrial plant was concerned, what of labour? Here again, things looked very bad but there was a silver lining. Many German men of working age were incarcerated in prisoner-of-war camps. Others were located as refugees in areas far from industrial opportunities. Nevertheless, the overheated Nazi economy had given a mass of workers experience of, and skill in, industrial employment. Many of the refugees from the eastern territories could be relied upon to work effectively, if they could be encouraged to move towards the opportunities industry had to offer

---

[6] R. Krengel, *Anlagevermögen, Produktion und Beschäftigung der Industrie im Gebiet der BRD von 1924–56* (Berlin, 1958), 94, and W. Carlin, 'Economic Reconstruction in Western Germany, 1945–1955: The Displacement of "Vegetative Control"', in I. D. Turner (ed.), *Reconstruction in Post-war Germany*, 40–1. Krengel's estimates have recently been questioned by Hans Otto Lenel, who argues that Krengel may have exaggerated the industrial capacity available in West Germany in 1948. This is evidently an area which needs more research. If Krengel's estimates are on the high side, the achievements of the West German economy after June 1948 become even more remarkable. See H. O. Lenel, 'Zum Historikerstreit über die Produktionskapazitäten 1948', *Orientierungen zur Wirtschafts- und Gesellschaftspolitik*, 54 (Dec. 1992), 72–7.

them. Looking back on the late 1940s, some historians have regarded the migration of millions of people into West Germany as a great advantage for the economy.[7]

Such a view would have seemed frivolous at the time. In a *Land* like Schleswig-Holstein, where millions of expellees and refugees from the east had congregated, the task of looking after the migrant population was rightly regarded as a burden beyond the capacity of the local authorities to bear.[8] To have described the migrants as an economic asset would have aroused derision. The fact is that the workers were in the wrong place at the wrong time.

As for the advantages created by Nazi expansion of industry, these were quite obscured by the destruction of workers' dwellings, the damage to power stations, and, above all, the wreckage of communications. For the military authorities and the German officials who worked for them, the only objective in 1945 was to get the economy back into some sort of production. In particular the bottle-necks caused by power shortage and the collapse of the railway network had to be overcome.

There was, however, an even greater problem, which was less visible but more pervasive. As Erhard had pointed out in his wartime memorandum,[9] Germany was suffering from a very serious excess of purchasing power caused by irresponsible Nazi policies of reckless public spending and ruthlessly enforced price controls. The result was that, although inflation seemed to have been kept under control, it was simply camouflaged. The Reichsmark was effectively worthless except as a means of purchasing the very limited amount of rationed food which could be obtained in the shops. Otherwise, cigarettes were more valuable than money in a commercial transaction. The black market flourished, and barter was rife.

The Allies continued the methods of rationing and control which had characterized the Nazi war-economy, and in truth it must be said that for the initial months of the occupation they had little choice. However, despite their harshness towards the German population, the

[7] W. Abelshauser, *Wirtschaft in Westdeutschland 1945–1948: Rekonstruktion und Wachstumsbedingungen in der amerikanischen und britischen Zone* (Stuttgart, 1975), 127–8. Abelshauser does point out that much immigrant labour was settled in the countryside rather than in industrial districts.

[8] For the difficulties faced by refugees once market forces had been re-established in Schleswig-Holstein, see I. Connor, 'The Refugees and the Currency Reform', in I. D. Turner (ed.), *Reconstruction in Post-war Germany*, 305–16. The Schleswig-Holstein authorities faced desperate financial difficulties in Sept. 1948: see the exchange of correspondence between the British finance officer in Kiel and the financial adviser to BAOR, Berlin, PRO/FO/046/683.

[9] See above, Ch. 4.

Allies could not match the brutality of the Gestapo. For their part, the Germans were not inclined to be too punctilious about regulations imposed on them by foreigners. The controlled economy, or *Zwangs-wirtschaft*, as it was known in Germany, became ineffectual as well as unpopular.

From an early stage in the occupation, the Western Allies and German economic specialists began to consider the possibility of replacing the Reichsmark with a new currency which would command respect. To do this, they would have to eliminate the excess purchasing-power in the economy, which could only be done by drastically reducing the nominal value of savings and possibly even wages. Discussions about this problem among the Western Allies made little progress.[10] Not the least of their problems was that they were supposed to be governing Germany as a unity through the four-power Control Council in Berlin. The Soviet Union would never agree to a currency reform unless it controlled the note-presses in its zone, a prospect which the Americans, in particular, found intolerable. This was by no means the only obstacle to a rapid introduction of a new currency. Fears that shortages of goods and economic dislocation would create such problems that the new money would go the same way as the Reichsmark also hindered brisk action.[11]

Without reform, the economy was bound to stagnate. Apart from the worthless currency, most economic activity was smothered in regulations and red tape. All the accounts we have of economic activity at this time stress the inefficiency of labour deployment, and the lack of incentive for Germans to work—at least in the official economy. Estimates of production in the British zone for 1946–7 were such that the inhabitants could expect to buy a suit only once every forty years, a shirt every ten years, and a toothbrush every five years.[12] The fact that

[10] In May 1946 American experts—Goldsmith, Colm, and Dodge—produced a scheme for currency reform which the American administration presented to the Allied Control Council in August. It was not, however, able to gain the agreement of the other occupying powers, especially the British, who feared it would be too deflationary. C. Buchheim, 'Die Währungsreform 1948 in Westdeutschland', *Vierteljahrshefte für Zeitgeschichte*, 36/2 (Apr. 1988), 202–6. See also I. D. Turner, 'Great Britain and the Post-war Currency Reform', *Historical Journal*, 30/3 (1987), 685 ff.; and W. Krieger, *General Lucius D. Clay und die amerikanische Deutschlandpolitik, 1945–1949* (Stuttgart, 1987), 375–7.

[11] This was the view of Paul Chambers, the head of the finance division in the British Control Commission: I. D. Turner, 'Britain and Currency Reform', 690.

[12] C. Watrin, 'The Social Market Economy: Its Significance for the Economic Development of the Federal Republic of Germany in the Early Years of the Konrad Adenauer Administration', in A. J. Nicholls (ed.), *Adenauer at Oxford: The Konrad Adenauer Memorial Lectures* (Oxford, 1983), 44.

these estimates may have hidden a different reality does not detract from the demoralizing situation to which they bear witness.

In order to keep themselves alive, Germans were forced to divert their energies into areas which were economically rational from the individual's point of view but which made no sense for the economy as a whole. To the average worker this meant spending only four or five days (instead of the normal six) at the conventional work-place in order to earn enough devalued currency to pay for the allowance of rationed goods—assuming that such things could be found for sale. The rest of the time would be devoted to cultivating vegetables—including even tobacco—in any available garden, allotment, or window-box, tramping into the countryside trying to bargain with farmers for food, hustling cigarettes from occupation forces or other privileged people, scavenging for coal on railway sidings, and all kinds of other stratagems to keep the family fed and warm. The situation was particularly difficult for women, many of whom were having to cope on their own following the death or capture of so many adult males. The heroism of German women at this time is perhaps best illustrated by the work of the *Trümmerfrauen*, the female labour-gangs who helped to clear the rubble from so many of Germany's devastated urban streets. But one should not forget the daily nightmare of finding enough food, clothing, and fuel to keep the family alive. It was the women in the family who came face to face with the inadequacies and unfairnesses of the rationing-system.[13]

At the level of industrial plant, the breakdown of the market was reflected in what was known as the *Kompensationsgeschäft*, or barter economy, which came to dominate the industrial scene as printed money lost its value. Since labour was cheap—if inefficient—in terms of productivity, and since profits measured in Reichsmarks were meaningless, business management was no longer concerned with profitability and cost-effectiveness in the conventional sense. The aim was to keep enterprises going with as large a staff and as large an inventory as possible—the reverse of normal practice. In order to obtain essential equipment or production materials, managers had to spend their time engaging in complicated barter-transactions. Thus a factory which required ball-bearings might try to swap rubber tyres for paint, paint for steel wire, and then, if it was fortunate, the steel wire for ball-bearings. Such activities were illegal as well as time-consuming, and

---

[13] M. Fulbrook, *The Divided Nation: A History of Germany, 1918–1990* (Oxford, 1992), 150–2. For the harshness of everyday life in this period, see A. Kramer, *The West German Economy, 1945–1955* (New York, 1991), 71–88. For the number of days per week worked in factories, see Buchheim, 'Währungsreform 1948', 192.

helped to breed contempt for the law. Conventionally trained economists regarded the barter economy as more damaging than the black market, since the latter did at least involve some sort of price mechanism, whereas the former was utterly inefficient and undermined rational calculation of profit and loss. In the spring of 1948, a German economic expert who had been advising the Allies on the subject of currency reform wrote the following: 'As the result of price-controlled inflation [*preisgestoppte Inflation*], our economy has degenerated from that of a modern industrial nation enjoying the benefits of the division of labour, and has reverted to the stage of a primitive medieval barter-system.'[14]

From the neo-liberal standpoint, two essential preconditions were required for German recovery. The first was a currency reform which would eliminate the excess purchasing-power to which Erhard, among others, had already drawn attention. In itself, however, a new or reformed[15] currency would not suffice. Much more important would be the freeing of prices and the liberation of the market. Only in that way would production be organized rationally and true incentives to increased production reappear.

Such a policy would obviously involve painful adjustments. Industry would shed labour instead of hoarding it, prices would be likely—at least initially—to rise sharply, and the poor might find themselves facing starvation. The complete breakdown of Germany's foreign trade, which, like all other aspects of the economy, was now under strict Allied control, made it impossible to meet German needs by imports, especially at a time when Germany's European neighbours—and former victims—were suffering serious privations. One of the weaknesses of the free-market position in the immediate post-war period was that abolition of controls seemed impossible without generous foreign credits. A defeated and occupied nation seemed unlikely to be able to attract them.

In any case, the general political atmosphere was not at all favourable to neo-liberal viewpoints. The experience of war had led to lesser or greater amounts of market restraint in all belligerent and occupied countries. So far as the Western Allies were concerned, Britain was an

---

[14] C. Fischer, *Entwurf eines Gesetzes zur Neuordnung des Geldwesens (Homberger Plan)* (Heidelberg, 1948), 61. For an account of the 'vegetative' condition of West Germany's economy at this time, see Carlin, 'Economic Reconstruction in Western Germany,' esp. 47–53.

[15] It would theoretically have been possible just to let prices rise to the levels at which they would have been covered by the old currency. This would have revealed the extent to which real inflation had been camouflaged by price controls, but it would have had a very damaging psychological effect. It would also have been ruinous for poorer people.

extreme example of a parliamentary democracy with a rationed and directed economy, but even the Americans had developed a New Deal philosophy which seemed favourable to government planning. The French were protectionist in their economic policies, and were determined to prevent the Germans recovering their pre-war economic strength. All the Allies believed that Germany had to be kept under control, and this necessarily involved official direction of economic affairs.

Foreign trade was dominated by the so-called 'dollar gap', or dollar shortage, which arose from the fact that European countries needed goods, and above all foodstuffs, from America but could not afford to pay for them. Free convertibility of currencies and freedom of trade had been replaced by bilateral trading-agreements, import and export quotas, and foreign-exchange controls. The United States government was pressing for the liberalization of this economically disastrous situation, but with little success in the immediate post-war period. German trade was controlled by the Allies, and German exports had to be paid for in dollars. This limited possibilities for German trade, since European trading partners could not afford to pay in dollars. On the other hand, it protected West Germany against demands from formerly occupied countries like Belgium, Holland, and Norway, which wanted to be able to import German goods and pay for them with the surpluses of worthless Reichsmarks the Nazis had forced them to build up during the war.[16]

One area in which the Germans felt particularly aggrieved was that of coal production, where the Allies insisted on what the Germans felt to be a high level of coal exports being sold at prices below world market levels.[17] In order to obtain this coal, the Allied authorities set priorities for German production, with the intention of stimulating coal output. The British, in particular, working with a staff of German planners at the zonal economic headquarters in Minden, tried to direct the development of German industry into channels they regarded as healthy. The results of their efforts were a source of controversy and will be treated in later chapters. Suffice it to say at this point that liberal economists—including Ludwig Erhard—regarded them as disastrous, and there is much to be said to commend that opinion.

[16] C. Buchheim, *Die Wiedereingliederung Westdeutschlands in die Weltwirtschaft, 1945–1958* (Munich, 1990), 11–12.

[17] Ibid. 93–5. Actually the Germans were not so badly off as they claimed, because the world price quoted was the price of American coal at the port of entry. European prices were lower. Nevertheless, from Jan. 1946 until Aug. 1947 the West Germans were forced to export 18.5 million tons of coal at approximately $5 a ton less than they would have fetched in the open market.

In general, however, German views on the future of the economy were no more favourable to the free market than those of the Allies. They were influenced by a generalized hostility to *laissez-faire* capitalism, which was seen by both Marxist and Christian critics to have provided the economic infrastructure upon which Hitler had built up his power. If one had looked at the political complexion of the various *Länder* in the first half of 1947, there would not have been any very good reason to expect that the next few years would see a triumph of the free market and the free-price mechanism. In the Soviet zone of occupation the socio-economic infrastructure was being systematically changed to facilitate a planned economy. In the British zone, and even in the American controlled *Land* of Hesse, *Land* governments were demanding the socialization of basic industries.

Political parties shared the general tendency towards collectivist solutions for economic problems. The Social Democrats, who had emerged strongly on the West German political scene after the war, certainly rejected Communism, but were enthusiasts for planning and the public control of major enterprises. In Christian Democratic circles it was widely agreed that capitalist excesses would need to be curbed. The Roman Catholic Centre Party had never been noteworthy for its commitment to free trade, and the trade-union wing of the new Christian Democratic party was suspicious of 'liberalistic' doctrines. In the British zone the well-known—if rapidly pigeon-holed—Ahlen Programme of February 1947 committed the CDU to public ownership of major enterprises and a form of planned economy.[18]

Even the liberal parties which appeared after the war—numerically unimpressive as they were—did not support the free market quite as whole-heartedly as might have been expected. As had been the case in the inter-war period, they were as noteworthy for their nationalism as for their commitment to the principles of economic freedom.

The national issue indeed was another obstacle to an objective analysis of Germany's economic situation. Few politicians wished to take steps which might compromise the objective of German unity, without which a healthy German economy seemed impossible. CDU leaders in Berlin, like Jakob Kaiser and Andreas Hermes, wanted their party's economic policies to be based on a Christian socialist compromise between Soviet and Western systems, so that Germany could act as a 'bridge' between East and West, thereby maintaining its unity. It was an idealistic but impracticable concept, which was treated with contempt by the Soviet authorities and jettisoned as soon as possible

[18] KAS/Pütz, (ed.), *Adenauer und die CDU*, 280–6.

by harder-headed Western leaders like Konrad Adenauer. Nevertheless, it illustrated the difficulty of divorcing German national interests from a consideration of economic policies after 1945.

This was a problem faced up to with characteristic courage by Wilhelm Röpke when, early in 1945, he wrote what was in many ways his most remarkable book.

This was *Die deutsche Frage* (The German Question), a work which aroused great interest and was rapidly reprinted.[19] At a time when most German politicians were concerned above all to preserve the unity of their Fatherland, Röpke advanced the sensational thesis that it would be healthy for Germany if Prussia, the dominant *Land* in the old Reich, were to be dismembered and if, for the time being at least, the western parts of Germany would build their own free confederation, with the lands east of the Elbe being left to their own devices—or rather Soviet devices, since they were in the Russian zone. Röpke began the book by pointing to the year 1866 as the fateful turning-point in German history, the year in which 'Germany ceased to exist and made way for greater Prussia'.[20]

He argued that Germans should be ready to accept that Prussian/German policy had been responsible for the catastrophe of the world war, although he saw no reason to ignore the part played by those outside Germany who had appeased Hitler. Furthermore, he denied that there was anything inherently brutal in the German character: 'it is National Socialism, not the German people, which showed its true face in its atrocities'.[21]

In Röpke's view a major cause of German participation in this totalitarian system had been the unnatural domination of 'the old German homeland' by 'colonial Germany' east of the Elbe. The Wilhelmine Empire had seen the culturally and politically more advanced parts of the Reich falling under the blighting influence of Prussia. In the Weimar Republic the absence of land reform and the power of Ruhr industrialists had helped to undermine democracy, whilst a healthy federal development had been prevented by the retention of an overlarge Prussian state. Röpke claimed that the solution for Germany's problems lay in three revolutionary courses of action, moral, political,

---

[19] *Die deutsche Frage* (Erlenbach-Zurich, 1945). I have used the second, expanded, edition, which includes an epilogue added after the Potsdam Conference of July/Aug. 1945. For helpful comments on the book and its significance, see H.-P. Schwarz, *Vom Reich zur Bundesrepublik: Deutschland im Widerstreit des außenpolitischen Konzeptionen in den Jahren der Besatzungsherrschaft, 1945–1949* (2nd edn.; Neuwied-Berlin, 1980), 393–401.

[20] Röpke, *Die deutsche Frage*, 10.

[21] Ibid. 63.

and economic. Morally the Germans must accept responsibility for
what had happened and try to make a fresh start: 'The collectivist
morality of Greater Prussia is every bit as devalued as the mark was in
November 1923. There is no alternative to the creation of a new set of
spiritual values.'[22]

Politically this would have to be accompanied by a dissolution of the
Bismarckian Reich, with Prussia being pressed back to the Elbe. A truly
decentralized German confederation would have to be established,
with the western provinces of Prussia—Schleswig-Holstein, the Rhineland, Westphalia, and Hanover, for example—receiving as much
autonomy as Prussia itself.

Lastly, there must be an economic revolution which would break the
power of the great East Elbian landowners and dissolve the old industrial cartels. Truly free competition would have to be established
and the forces of the market should be allowed to create economic
prosperity.

Röpke looked at the reality of the Allied occupation of Germany
and saw in it both a limitation and an opportunity. He accepted the
fact that the Soviet authorities would be unlikely to be able to work
harmoniously with their Western colleagues. Indeed he expected that
all four allies would act independently in their own zones when it
came to the business of administration,[23] an expectation which in
practice proved correct. Röpke felt that this could actually have beneficial effects, because it would encourage decentralization. It would
also imply that, when creating a new, federal Germany, based on
regional patriotism and the market economy, the Soviet zone of occupation east of the Elbe would be left out. The Elbe, the frontier of
Prussia as Röpke saw it, was the *limes* of the Western World: 'For the
present we must accept the hard reality implied by this *limes*. We
have to draw the conclusion that under the existing circumstances the
federative reconstruction of Germany must be confined for the time
being to the German heartland west of the Elbe'.[24]

This was, of course, a highly contentious proposal, which ran clean
counter to the professed views of German liberals, conservatives,
nationalists, social democrats, and Communists. It was also contrary
to the policy promulgated by the three major allies at the Potsdam
Conference, held in the summer of 1945. Röpke had written his book
in the spring of that year, before the Potsdam declaration that Germany
should be administered as a unity by the occupying powers. In an
epilogue to the second edition, published that autumn, he argued that

[22] Ibid. 224.   [23] Ibid. 249–50.   [24] Ibid. 250.

the Potsdam decisions were absurd. The best thing about them was that they were so impracticable that they would never work. He urged the Western Allies to give up the nonsensical idea of 'a Greater Prussia directed from Berlin' and concentrate on political reconstruction in their own zones. The West German economy should be integrated with that of the West. The necessary purge of former Nazis should be carried out as rapidly as possible, so that Germans could then settle down to enjoy once again the advantages of the rule of law.[25]

This book has been cited at some length because it does illustrate the extent to which neo-liberal views were compatible with the limitations and the opportunities facing Germany in 1945. By opposing collectivism and Prussian hegemony, by accepting the Elbe as Germany's frontier—at least for the time being—and by concentrating on rapid economic rehabilitation of a Western-orientated economy, Röpke was writing as a prophet of the Federal Republic of Germany. This was a remarkable achievement at a time when neither the Allies nor the emerging German political parties seemed likely to support such a notion.

Of course, too much should not be made of the neo-liberal contribution to the way in which the 'German question' achieved at least a temporary solution in 1949. The force of circumstances arising from the Cold War and the creation of the Christian Democratic party were more directly responsible for the foundation of the Federal Republic. Most of those who favoured a federal, anti-Prussian solution were, moreover, Christian Democrats or Bavarians. The influential *Rheinischer Merkur*, with which Adenauer enjoyed close links, was strongly anti-Prussian and federalist in its views.[26] Yet the neo-liberal propositions championed by Röpke were important because they offered a forward-looking and comprehensive vision of Germany's future, whereas more parochial expressions of local particularism might be written off as mere *Kleinstaaterei*, the nostalgic dreams of predominantly Roman Catholic Germans trying to recapture a world lost in 1866. Furthermore, the fact that the social market economy fitted so neatly into the pattern of West Germany as it emerged in 1949 made it easier for the Christian Democrats to accept an economic policy which they might otherwise have associated with nationalist liberalism of the pre-1933 era.

Röpke did his best to propagate his views in Germany, although he and other liberal economists living abroad faced problems with censorship. The Russians shut down a bookshop in Vienna because it

[25] Ibid. 255 ff.
[26] Schwarz, *Vom Reich zur Bundesrepublik*, 413–22, 433.

was selling *Die deutsche Frage*, and Röpke was told that von Hayek's *Road to Serfdom* was banned in all zones.[27] Röpke was able to have his views on the German question discussed at the founding conference of the Mont Pèlerin Society in April 1947. This international gathering of liberally minded academics, many of whom were more inclined to unrestrained *laissez-faire* than Röpke, was to become an important source of encouragement for supporters of the free market during the years which followed.[28]

Röpke was by now very pessimistic about the prospects for the future, both of Germany and of Western civilization. His rather detached position outside Germany seems to have created a melancholy and even slightly embittered cast of mind. Anti-Communism came to dominate his thinking above all else. Nevertheless, his appetite for work remained undiminished, and his newspaper articles in the Swiss and German press were an important source of inspiration for liberals in West Germany.

[27] See the letter to von Hayek on 11 Mar. 1947, printed in *Wilhelm Röpke, Briefe 1934–1936: Der innere Kompaß*, ed. E. Röpke (Erlenbach-Zurich, 1976), 95.
[28] Letter, Röpke to Rüstow, 24 Apr. 1947, ibid. 96–7.

6
Neo-liberalism in the Immediate Post-war Period

LOOKING back from the prosperity and success of the 1960s, Röpke remarked that until 1948 the proponents of the 'third way' could be likened to Henry V's army before Agincourt: 'We few, we happy few, we band of brothers'.[1] The difference was that, although few, their situation was anything but happy. For much of the time, indeed, they were not even sure that they had any brothers. After Hitler's death the circumstances in devastated Germany were such that the mere exchange of ideas—let alone the mobilization of public opinion—was extremely difficult. The country was controlled by military authorities whose attitudes towards native academics ranged from indifference to hostility. Travel within the Allied occupation zones was not easy; to cross zonal boundaries was even more laborious.

Rigid control by Allied occupiers, restrictions on travel, chronic shortages of newsprint, and the lack of foreign currency were grave obstacles to those trying to enlighten both their fellow-countrymen and their occupiers about the true causes of Germany's economic distress. Müller-Armack, for example, faced daunting obstacles when trying to disseminate his views. Newsprint was almost impossible to obtain, and a licence was needed even to print a visiting-card.

Müller-Armack's part of Germany—Westphalia—had felt the full brunt of aerial bombardment during the war. In the summer of 1943 his institute for textile market research had been evacuated from Münster to the relative security of a monastery at Vreden-Ellwick near the Dutch frontier. Despite severe financial difficulties which almost extinguished the institute after the war, Müller-Armack himself was able to use the facilities at Vreden when drawing up his arguments in favour of a socially just but market-orientated economic system. With the help of Dutch Protestant friends and a rotaprint machine, he was able to circulate his views to colleagues in Germany.[2]

---

[1] See Röpke's chapter in Greiss and Meyer (eds.), *Wirtschaft, Gesellschaft und Kultur*, 4.
[2] The institute itself was regarded with suspicion by Allied occupiers as having been associated with the Nazis. It was only due to the efforts of Vits and Müller-Armack that it was revived later with funds from private industry. See the report on the institute's

Politically, liberalism was weak and discredited in Germany after the war. A group of businessmen did try to set up a branch of the old German Democratic Party in Münster, and in the summer of 1945 they contacted Müller-Armack, who participated in discussions on the need for retrenchment and currency stabilization. However, he was nervous that such political activity might jeopardize his position as a university professor and withdrew from the group, concentrating instead on propagating his views through academic discussions or contacts with industry.[3]

On 25 September 1945 he delivered a lecture in Münster on 'Possibilities for a Market Economy Today'. He pointed to the failings of the controlled economy and argued that an urgent necessity was the 'reintroduction of market forces as the only mechanism to organize large masses of people into economically useful work on the basis of their own self-interest'.[4]

He stressed the damage done to the German economy by the Nazi destruction of the market, and urged that the free-price mechanism be reintroduced as soon as possible. However, he accepted that such a measure could not be taken until the excess purchasing-power in the economy had been soaked up or blocked by some kind of currency reform. Before implementing such a reform, there had to be a minimum level of raw materials, especially coal, available in the country. So at the start Müller-Armack only envisaged liberating prices for non-essentials. Other items would remain controlled until the free-price level had dropped to something near the controlled-price level. Only then would the currency reform take place. These ideas were in some respects similar to those adumbrated by Erhard in his wartime memorandum. But Müller-Armack's readiness to envisage a long period of extensive controls and gradual price-adjustments before the implementation of currency reform was at odds with Erhard's concept, since it would imply the step-by-step inflation (*dosierte Inflation*) which Erhard regarded as disastrous.[5] However, it was not long before Müller-

activities in Müller-Armack NL, KAS I-236-024, and the rather rosier account in *Textildienst*, 10/9 (Münster, 1965), 247–71. See also R. Löwenthal and H.-P. Schwarz (eds.), *Die Zweite Republik: 25 Jahre Bundesrepublik Deutschland—eine Bilanz* (Stuttgart-Degerloch 1974), 124; Müller-Armack, *Auf dem Weg nach Europa*, 50–1.

[3] Müller-Armack NL, KAS I-236-001.
[4] Thesen zum Vortrag 'Marktwirtschaftliche Möglichkeiten heute', ibid., KAS I-236-074.
[5] See above, Ch. 4. Müller-Armack's views were set out in a paper dated 15 Oct. 1945, 'Zur Frage der vordringlichsten wirtschaftspolitischen Maßnahmen', printed in facsimile in E. Helmstädter (ed.), *Müller-Armack: Beiträge zur wirtschaftspolitischen Diskussion in der Nachkriegszeit* (Münster, 1983), 1–10.

Armack too started to advocate a more radical approach to the issues of the market and currency reform.

He corresponded with chambers of commerce and industry in the British zone of occupation, encouraging them to press for currency reform and at least a limited amount of market freedom. He was strongly in favour of a two-tier system of marketing which would enable firms to buy and sell freely once they had fulfilled a limited quota of deliveries at controlled prices.[6]

This half-way house between planning and complete market freedom seems to have emerged from Müller-Armack's discussions with enthusiastic *dirigistes* in the British zone, where belief in controls was becoming almost a religion. It was especially pronounced in the sphere of food supplies, agriculturalists being ready to accept state paternalism inherited from the Nazi *Reichsnährstand*. The British-appointed director of the zonal office for agriculture, Hans Schlange-Schöningen, wrote to his masters in April 1946 that:

In my area of competence . . . it would seem to me to be politically impossible to allow a free play of capitalist and liberalistic [sic] forces. It is rather my view that in the foreseeable future the only way to overcome the present and future difficulties will be by committing ourselves without reservation to a controlled, planned economy.[7]

A number of other officials active in the British administration—with some noteworthy exceptions such as Leonhard Miksch—also favoured planning, although they were rather more sophisticated in their view of it than the official leadership of the SPD. One of the most important spokesmen on this matter was Gerhard Weisser, a Social Democratic politician who had been made Minister of Finance in Brunswick in 1945 and then became general secretary of the *Zonenbeirat*, the advisory council for the British zonal administration in which senior German officials participated. Weisser had been a reformist Social Democrat before the war, and believed in indirect, rather than direct, methods of planning, taking comfort from a socialist interpretation of Keynes's

---

[6] By Apr. 1947 he was corresponding with *Handelskammer* all over North Germany and even as far south as Frankfurt. At one point he advised on counter-proposals to suggestions from the economics ministry of North-Rhine-Westphalia that even more severely restrictive measures should be adopted in the distribution of raw materials and goods. The *Industrie und Handelskammer* of this area described their counter-proposals as a 'social market economy'. See draft drawn up in the Vreden institute, 17 Apr. 1947, Müller-Armack NL, KAS I-236-074.

[7] Cited in W. Abelshauser, 'Freiheitlicher Sozialismus oder soziale Marktwirtschaft? Die Gutachtertagung über Grundfragen der Wirtschaftsplanung und Wirtschaftslenkung am 21. und 22. Juni 1946', *Vierteljahrshefte für Zeitgeschichte*, 24/4 (Oct. 1976), 418. Schlange-Schöningen was to be no friend of Erhard's liberalization measures in the summer of 1948. For a sympathetic description of Schlange-Schöningen's policy, see J. E. Farquharson, *The Western Allies and the Politics of Food: Agrarian Management in Postwar Germany* (Leamington Spa, 1985), 208–21.

General Theory, as well as from his own experiences in the Weimar Republic and the Third Reich. He, like Rüstow, was a former pupil of Leonhard Nelson, and he was by no means unacquainted with neo-liberal doctrines. As we have seen, he had addressed Eucken's seminar in Freiburg during the Nazi period. He himself, however, was a strong critic of liberal economic theories.[8]

As the result of the decision taken by the British and the Americans in the summer of 1946 to fuse their zones of occupation into what became known as 'Bizone', a number of meetings between German officials in the Anglo-Saxon zones occurred, and Weisser took the opportunity to invite leading administrators and experts to a conference in Hamburg on 21 and 22 June 1946, with the purpose of discussing the economic policy to be adopted in the next few years. He himself opened the conference with a lecture on 'Finding a Scientific Basis for Directing the Economy and Relaxing its Style' ('Wissenschaftliche Fundierung der Wirtschaftslenkung und Lockerung ihres Stils').[9] This indeed was the main thrust of the discussion: how to maintain planning and controls but to implement them in an 'indirect' and unobtrusive manner.

Weisser had invited Müller-Armack to provide a counter-argument from the point of view of a market economist. He certainly did not adopt an aggressively neo-liberal stance at the meeting, describing himself as 'devil's advocate' and accepting from the start that some form of control—if only 'with a light hand'—would be adopted in future. Nevertheless, Müller-Armack's contribution was a searching critique of the directed economy. He pointed out that without a free-price mechanism it was impossible to make rational decisions about the allocation of resources. No amount of market research could replace 'the immediate choice made by the consumer when he spends his money'. Furthermore, the absence of market pressures would inhibit technical progress, because the producer would have little incentive for innovation. The evils of the black market and illicit barter-dealing could only be eradicated through a return to the market.[10]

Most of the other contributors to the discussion favoured retaining controls, although with more or less sophisticated techniques designed to increase competition without sacrificing central direction. One of the compromise proposals came from Professor Kromphardt, an advocate of the 'split market' system, which would involve a limited free market

---

[8] See above, Ch. 4. See also below, Chs. 14 and 16 for Weisser's views on democratic socialism.

[9] Abelshauser, 'Freiheitlicher Sozialismus', 428.

[10] Ibid. 422, 432–3.

operating side by side with rationing and planned production.[11] Müller-Armack himself adopted at least a modified version of this notion, although he stressed the market mechanism more than its original author.

In supporting this idea Müller-Armack was responding to his own concern over the damaging social consequences of a 'jump into the cold water' of the free market at a time of severe shortages, and to the practical difficulties he foresaw as the results of his own contacts with industry. He had never himself been a disciple of the 'Freiburg School', and his opposition to state interference in the economy was by no means total. Not being as rigorous a theoretician as Röpke or Eucken, he adopted a more pragmatic approach to economic problems, being willing to consider interventionist measures to stimulate demand or ensure that economic development was socially beneficial, so long as such measures were compatible with market forces.

In November 1946 he drew up a plan to overcome the catastrophic problems being created by the Allied control system, a system which even the Social Democrats' economic spokesman in the British zone, Viktor Agartz, admitted was not functioning properly.[12] This was to be the split-market system, in which producers would be required to provide a set allocation of rationed goods at fixed prices and any surplus production could be sold for whatever it could fetch. The advantages of this arrangement were that it would undermine the black market, since prices in the 'free' sector would be allowed to find their own level. It would also encourage increased production by offering the incentive of real profits which could be expected from the surplus sales.

Müller-Armack claimed that this system would fit in well with the different ideological positions of Germany's occupiers, securing as it did the two positions they represented—freedom and restriction (*Gebundenheit*). This contradiction did not just exist between East and West; even more important was the contrast between the British and the Americans, who themselves represented the two different economic conceptions.[13] Müller-Armack saw his scheme as bridging the gap.

He argued that it would be largely self-operating, because producers would be eager to fulfil their norms of rationed goods in order to

---

[11] Ibid. 436–7; Abelshauser's view that Kromphardt later adopted a 'decidedly liberal position' in the *Wissenschaftlicher Beirat* of the Economics Administration does not seem to me to be borne out by the records I have seen, ibid. 423. See also Ch. 9, for details of Kromphardt's schemes.

[12] Typescript 'Plan zur Überwindung unserer Marktkrise', Münster, 1 Nov. 1946. Müller-Armack NL, KAS I-236.

[13] Ibid. p. 4.

be able to get on and sell surpluses at much higher prices. Yet he overlooked Röpke's objections to such a mixed arrangement mentioned above,[14] namely that it would need a good deal of policing in practice and would almost certainly lead to corruption. There was also the problem of how planners would be able to set the allocations for rationed goods if they did not have market forces to guide them, a point which Müller-Armack himself had made in Hamburg.

Underlying much neo-liberal concern about this split-market proposition was the fear that it could be used to establish a permanent system of controls, made just about bearable by the feeble 'free market' appendage to it. Certainly this was the evident intention of some of the more enthusiastic adherents of such a scheme on the Social Democratic side.[15] For Müller-Armack, however, the reverse seems to have been true. He saw the scheme as a way of reintroducing the market principle into an economy choked with controls. It would, as he put it, simply be an 'interim solution' and would not preclude any future decisions on the form the economy might ultimately take. Rather it was a practical scheme for the Germans which coincided with their ideological position 'in the middle between freedom and controls'.[16]

This whole discussion illustrates the confusions characterizing the economic debate in the early post-war years, clouded as it was by the physical and moral aftermath of Nazi dictatorship and defeat. In the end the 'split market' was to be quietly buried, but the social problems associated with the market were not simply ignored or brushed under the carpet.

In a paper dated July 1946, Müller-Armack did make the good point that, although the physical devastation in Germany was very severe, it was less important than the commercial devastation caused by the collapse of the world market. He blamed the world-wide drop in production of many agricultural products and raw materials on nationalist and socialist interference with the free market. He compared Germany's situation with that of the Weimar Republic in the years 1919–23, when inflation took hold and nobody was prepared to cure it. Yet, when it had to be done, the stabilization of the mark had worked.

Pointing to the work of Eucken, Böhm, Lampe, Grossmann-Doerth, and Röpke, he said there was a widespread academic consensus for the reintroduction of free prices and market forces. Market forces had formed the basis of the economy in most civilizations—nineteenth-century Europe was unusual in that it consciously theorized about an

---

[14] See above, Ch. 4.   [15] See below, Ch. 9.
[16] Müller-Armack, 'Plan zur Überwindung', pp. 5 and 17.

already well-tried mechanism. He drew attention to the unfair and irrational nature of the black market and barter economies and argued that patience was not enough. Something had to be done. Tax policy should be changed to make it less rather than more burdensome. The currency had to be reformed to reduce purchasing power, and market forces had to be liberated. Müller-Armack drew on his knowledge of the Westphalian coal industry to stress the need to arouse workers' self-interest in production through market forces. As he pointed out, attempts to direct labour into the coal industry had been nearly useless. The need of the hour was currency reform and a restoration of the market—even if some articles would have to remain rationed.[17]

One of the most serious social needs was that of housing, and Müller-Armack had not forgotten his long-standing interest in this question. The lack of housing had become desperate in the immediate post-war period, when so many Germans were homeless. In November 1945 he drew up a sixteen-page memorandum on 'The Economic and Social Preconditions for the Restoration of Our Housing and Construction Market'.[18] A major—and highly controversial—recommendation was the abolition of rent control. Instead of fixed prices, people should receive direct subsidies to help them pay rents. This provision too was to become a part of what he came to describe as the social market economy.

In 1946 Müller-Armack published his first important post-war book, *Wirtschaftslenkung und Marktwirtschaft* (Planned Economy and Market Economy). In its first part, which—as we have seen—he drafted during the war,[19] he relentlessly exposed the failures of the government-controlled economy as it had developed since 1936. In his defence of the market economy he echoed the arguments of Röpke, Rüstow, and the Freiburg School in denying that the market should take the blame for distortions created during the inter-war period by government interference, trade barriers, and currency manipulation. He stressed particularly that idiotic phenomena such as the burning of coffee and tobacco were the result of state efforts to prop up prices rather than of any natural adjustments within the market itself.[20]

In the second part, he set out the alternative of a return to free competition, but with proper provision to protect the type of social

---

[17] Id., 'Das Grundproblem unserer Wirtschaftspolitik: Rückkehr zur Marktwirtschaft', 15 July 1946, in Helmstädter (ed.), *Müller-Armack: Beiträge zur wirtschaftspolitischen Diskussion*, 1–13 (pagination recommences with each article).
[18] 'Die wirtschaftspolitischen Vorbedingungen für den Neuaufbau unserer Wohnungs- und Bauwirtschaft', Müller-Armack NL, KAS I-236-078.
[19] See above, Ch. 4.
[20] Müller-Armack, *Wirtschaftsordnung und Wirtschaftspolitik*, 23.

structure necessary to produce a healthy life. He specifically denied that it was part of his purpose simply to advocate a return to the *laissez-faire* system of the nineteenth century.[21]

Nevertheless, he pointed to the inconsistency of those who prated about democracy whilst being only too willing to limit freedom in the face of the smallest political difficulty. He referred to von Hayek's *Road to Serfdom*, which had been translated by Eva Röpke in 1945, and which stressed the interrelationship between economic and political systems. A command economy put too much power into the hands of those directing it. 'It is impossible', he claimed, 'to choose an economic solution which contradicts the fundamental spiritual values to which one is committed.'[22]

This ruled out the choice of a command economy. The old-fashioned liberal market economy, on the other hand, was incompatible with contemporary values and could not simply be resurrected. What was needed was a new synthesis, and here he employed the term 'social market' economy. This would be a third form of economic system, replacing both *laissez-faire* and collectivist controls. It would not just be a liberal market economy left to function by itself, but should be deliberately steered in a socially acceptable direction. Nor would it be a mish-mash of the free market and socialism. Rather it involved a fundamentally free-market economy modified by those measures which could be taken in conformity with market principles.[23]

During the next two years Müller-Armack developed his concept of the social market economy, until, in May 1948, he was able to present a blueprint, outlining its objectives and the means by which it could be achieved. The first section of his treatise consisted of a series of demands to the Western powers, urging them to create a central state body capable of carrying out economic and financial policies on their own initiative, to give (West) Germany the right to enter into trade relations with other countries, to stop the dismantling of German industry, to reform the currency, and to clarify the arrangements for equalizing the financial burdens on individuals created by losses in the war.[24] A central German bank should be set up. There should be a reduction in taxes to stimulate the will to work, and a reduction in government expenditure, including occupation costs. Germany should not be prohibited from producing vital industrial goods and should be granted a billion dollar credit for raw materials.

There then followed specific recommendations for the creation of

---

[21] Ibid. 80.   [22] Ibid. 89.   [23] Ibid. 108–16.
[24] A. Müller-Armack, *Genealogie der sozialen Marktwirtschaft: Frühschriften und weiterführende Konzepte* (2nd edn.; Bern, 1981), 94–9.

the social market economy.[25] The collapsing system of government controls should be replaced by the free market. Consumer choice would thus have the power to establish real prices and encourage production. Social security should be achieved by the following measures: the creation of a system of work which treated the employees as human beings and gave them what was described as the 'social right to participate' in the organization of their work (*ein soziales Mitgestaltungsrecht*), without, however, reducing managerial initiative and the responsibility of the employer. There should be a legally protected system of competition designed to ensure that the energies of ambitious individuals would be channelled in a fashion beneficial to the common good. There should be a conscious policy of resistance to monopolies, to prevent the abuse of economic power. Full employment was to be attained by regulating the business cycle through credit—and even limited state subventions if necessary.

Unhealthy inequalities of wealth should be overcome by what Müller-Armack described as a 'market-economy income redistribution' (*marktwirtschaftlicher Einkommensausgleich*) achieved by taxation, family allowances, and rent assistance for the needy. A policy of settling urban workers on the land should be adopted. Small farmers and other small businesses should be encouraged by the state. Work structures should include chances for workers' advancement. Co-operative self-help—as in housing construction, for example—should be provided for in the rules of the market. Social security systems should be more widely developed. A policy of 'social housing' should be adopted and town planning should be established. There should be minimum wages, and individual pay-settlements should be secured as the result of freely negotiated contracts. The state must restrict itself to establishing the general principles of economic policy, leaving the individual entrepreneur, worker, farmer, merchant, or housewife to operate within the framework so provided. Prices,[26] wages, and the selection of one's place of work should be freed from interference.

Looked at from the vantage-point of the 1990s, this would seem to be an interventionist programme. By comparison with the controlled and directed economy of post-war Germany, it was remarkably liberal. Müller-Armack did not speak for any homogeneous group of political economists, and Erhard or Eucken, for example, might not have found all the items in his package entirely to their taste. But the fundamental principles of this social market economy formed the basis of Erhard's

[25] Ibid. 99 ff.
[26] With the temporary exception of bread, milk, and fat prices, and rents for the elderly.

policy from 1948 onwards and Müller-Armack himself was to become one of his most trusted lieutenants.

Certainly it was not a socialist programme. The element of worker participation was far more limited than that proposed by German trade unions, for example, but it was sincerely meant, as the intellectual background of the neo-liberals set out above has demonstrated. Enthusiasm for small farmers was doubtless misplaced; Germany continued to change rapidly in the direction of urbanization. But the view that farmers should be encouraged to adapt themselves to market conditions with government assistance was a sound one and has played some part in helping Germany's rural population achieve the greatest prosperity it has ever known. The determination that economic freedom should not imply a *laissez-faire* attitude to social problems was implemented in the fields of social security and housing.

Above all, there was the belief that the market had to be established within certain ground rules so that it should operate in the interests of society as a whole. As Müller-Armack himself wrote in 1946, the market was not a natural phenomenon but a man-made one.[27] The manner in which it was organized—the 'traffic regulations', as Röpke had called them—were a legitimate and indeed vital concern for government. Only under those conditions would individual self-interest contribute properly to a healthy society, in which spiritual as well as material values would be protected.

From the beginning, of course, the 'social market' was attacked by the Left and the Right. In the 1940s the loudest condemnation came from the socialist side, which denounced the word 'social' as a cosmetic device, a smoke-screen of bogus benevolence behind which the discredited forces of capitalism were seeking to make themselves respectable. Even colleagues in Müller-Armack's own profession derided it as merely an electoral slogan rather than a contribution to economic theory. On the right, supporters of what Rüstow would have described as 'paleo-liberalism' sneered at the social aspect of the market as a deviation from the pure doctrines of *laissez-faire* and another form of state-directed economy. Their voices were rather muted in 1948 and the main attack came from the Left.[28]

Neo-liberals consistently denied such charges and reiterated their view that nostalgia for the conditions of the nineteenth century was not enough to meet the needs of the post-war economy. In 1948 they founded a journal to propagate their ideas, edited by Walter Eucken and Franz Böhm. Röpke and Rüstow were members of its advisory

[27] Müller-Armack, *Wirtschaftsordnung und Wirtschaftspolitik*, 105.
[28] Id., *Auf dem Weg nach Europa*, 81.

board. This was *ORDO*, described as a year-book for the regulation (*Ordnung*) of the economy and society. In its first edition the editors announced it as their belief that only competition in as many branches of the economy as possible would solve the problems of the economic and social order: 'Competition does not tolerate the conservation of social stratification.'[29] They rejected any type of planned economy, but they were also united in their rejection of the 'free' economy which incorporated the principles of *laissez-faire*. On the one hand, planned economies made people the slaves of bureaucracy. On the other, 'unrestricted freedom of economic activity leads likewise to conflicts between the interests of individuals and those of the community, and to the concentration of private economic power, which is economically and socially no less damaging than state omnipotence'.[30]

Apart from generating a more lively debate within Western Germany, the free-marketeers also built up international contacts with liberal economists. An example of this was the 'Mont Pèlerin Society', named after its first meeting-place. Its president was Friedrich von Hayek of London University and later the University of Chicago. Although many of its non-German members did not really accept the neo-liberal critique of *laissez-faire* economics, they were, nevertheless, a source of comfort to those trying to keep the small flame of market competition burning in the wilderness of post-war collectivism.[31]

Neo-liberalism attempted, therefore, to be a genuine alternative to the opposing forces of unrestrained capitalism and state control. It was not just a soggy compromise between the two—a receipt for a 'mixed economy'. It sought to harness the dynamic forces of competition whilst ensuring that economic activity for private benefit should help to create a just and harmonious social order. In this it differed sharply from the theories of the 'Chicago School', currently fashionable in Britain, but it was also incompatible with what passes for British 'social democratic' thought. Ideologically it was particularly well-suited to post-war Germany, where the doctrines of collectivism had been discredited by Hitler and by a widespread fear of Communism, but where the need for social responsibility was strongly felt as the country faced the results of its military catastrophe.

The formulation of such a theory was one thing; its implementation quite another. How could Müller-Armack himself hope to win adherents for a viewpoint so out of touch with contemporary beliefs?

[29] Editorial foreword to *ORDO: Jahrbuch für die Ordnung von Wirtschaft und Gesellschaft* (Opladen), 1 (May 1948), p. ix. The advisory board also included Karl Brandt, Constantin von Dietze, F. A. von Hayek, and F. A. Lutz.
[30] Ibid., p. x.
[31] Müller-Armack, *Auf dem Weg Nach Europa*, 44–5.

Once again, he was helped by contacts with industry. A group of businessmen in Hamburg-Altona calling itself the *Volkswirtschaftliche Gesellschaft* made contact with him in June 1947 through Höpker-Aschoff. They were eager to broadcast his ideas. In October they issued an anonymous pamphlet which reflected many of his views on currency reform and liberating the economy.[32] He remained in fruitful contact with them, and in May 1948 they published his *Proposals to Implement the Social Market Economy*.[33]

Perhaps most important was the fact that this organization had close links with the Free Democrats (FDP), the united liberal party which had emerged, after some tribulations, in the Western zones after the war.[34] In common with the CDU, the FDP had not expressed itself with great clarity or conviction on the subject of economic liberalism in the early years of its existence. The one party which might have been expected to jump at neo-liberal ideas, it was apparently half-hearted about them. In the Soviet zone, Wilhelm Külz, chairman of the Liberal Party, bravely declared his commitment to a free market but 'not in the Manchester sense of the free economy', and he accepted that 'the German economy required a planned economy for a long time'.[35] In the British zone, one powerful group centred on Essen was highly critical of old-style capitalism and accepted that centralized planning would have to be an essential part of the future economy. In November 1945 this group, of which the future FDP leader, Franz Blücher, was a member, published a programme the economic section of which began with words reminiscent of Hitler: 'The economy is there for the people and not the people for the economy.'[36] It then went on to state that 'Central planning is indispensable in order to bring production and material needs into harmony with each other.'

These ideas certainly did not go unchallenged, and the programme of the British zone's FDP, adopted in January 1946, was a much more liberal document, arguing that planning should be used only as far as

[32] See text of anonymous article 'Zur Lage' in the Müller-Armack papers, KAS I-236-A 006-9.

[33] *Vorschläge zur Verwirklichung der sozialen Marktwirtschaft*, ed. and publ. Volkswirtschaftliche Gesellschaft e. V. (Hamburg, 1948).

[34] H.-J. Ungeheuer, *Die Wirtschaftsprogrammatik und Wirtschaftspolitik der liberalen Parteien Deutschlands unter besonderer Berücksichtigung der Entwicklung in der SBZ und in der britischen Zone* (MA thesis; Bonn, 1982), 184–5. There was also a liberal party in the Soviet zone, the Liberal Democratic Party, which tried to claim partnership with the FDP but which eventually became a tool in the hands of the Soviet administration.

[35] J. Roesler, 'The Rise and Fall of the Planned Economy', *German History*, 9/1 (Oxford, 1991), 47.

[36] Cited in Ungeheuer, *Wirtschaftsprogrammatik*, 134–5. See also K. Schröder, *Die FDP in der britischen Besatzungszone, 1946–1948: Ein Beitrag zur Organisationsstruktur der Liberalen im Nachkriegsdeutschland* (Düsseldorf, 1984), 157.

necessary and should not become an end in itself.[37] Particularly strong opponents of planning and socialization were Friedrich Middelhauve and E. Wilkening, who was himself from Hamburg. Yet enthusiasm for the market was by no means unbridled. Blücher's supporters continued to hanker for an economy controlled by some sort of corporation independent of state control.

The FDP was, at this time, as much concerned with national and religious issues as with economic ones. Furthermore, it had not yet overcome the baneful legacy, discussed in an earlier chapter, of Walther Rathenau, with his notions of planned capitalism, and Friedrich Naumann, whose commitment to social reform did not involve enthusiasm for a strongly competitive market economy.[38] Following in the footsteps of the Weimar liberal parties, the DDP and DVP, the Free Democrats tended to regard themselves as appealing to the interests of the business community, without having a very clear concept of what their own socio-economic principles ought to be. Thomas Dehler, a Bavarian FDP spokesman who later became a liberal leader at the federal level, expressed this attitude with somewhat cynical frankness when he said: 'The FDP stands for a policy which also interests business circles and for which the latter are therefore also ready to make a contribution. We should approach such circles.'[39]

The fact that the Liberals were not so numerous as the Social Democrats or the Christian Democrats meant that financial support from interest groups was of more crucial importance to them. This made the FDP a less than suitable vehicle for the propagation of the social market economy, since that policy involved measures—for the rejection of cartels, for example, and the implementation of redistributive taxation—which the Free Democrats' backers would not be likely to accept. Certainly the FDP did not seem very attractive to neo-liberal theorists; hardly any of them joined it, whereas several became Christian Democrats—most notably Franz Böhm.[40]

Nevertheless, in the crucial period between the establishment of bizonal organizations in the summer of 1947 and the currency reform the following year it was the question of the role of the market and

---

[37] Ungeheuer, *Wirtschaftsprogrammatik*, 138.

[38] See above, Ch. 1. Ungeheuer points out the attraction of Rathenau's thinking for post-war liberals, which was reflected in the Essen case by a commitment to creating 'an organ of democratic self-administration' to carry out planning measures, rather than the state. *Wirtschaftsprogrammatik*, 135.

[39] Cited by Hans Vorländer, 'Der soziale Liberalismus der FDP', in Holl *et al.* (eds.), *Sozialer Liberalismus*, 197.

[40] Max-Gustav Lange, 'Die FDP: Versuch einer Erneuerung des Liberalismus', *Studien zur Entwicklung der deutschen Parteien bis zur Bundestagswahl 1953* (Schriften des Instituts für Politische Wissenschaft; Stuttgart, 1955), 312–3. Lange could find only one of the contributors to *ORDO*, Hans Ilau, who joined the FDP, and even he had left it by 1955.

the free-price mechanism—rather than the anti-cartel or social welfare aspects of neo-liberalism—which lay at the heart of the struggle for the future of West Germany's economy. It proved of great importance, therefore, that at precisely this time the FDP gave up its early support for planning and committed itself whole-heartedly to the market.

In March 1947 controversy arose because the FDP in the important *Land* of North-Rhine-Westphalia supported proposals put forward by the CDU premier, Karl Arnold, for the public ownership of major heavy industries, which were to be run in co-partnership with trade unions. These plans, which also aroused fierce opposition from Adenauer, caused a storm in the FDP. Middelhauve described the whole scheme as the 'first step to socialization' and Blücher had to retract his original support.[41] From this time onwards the free-market aspect of FDP economic policy came to the fore much more aggressively.

Although it is not possible to trace many direct influences of neo-liberal theorists over FDP policy-making, there is no doubt that Röpke and Müller-Armack provided the free-marketeers in the party with ammunition in their battle. In June Middelhauve spoke in the North-Rhine-Westphalian *Landtag* using language reflecting Röpke's view that 'collective economy [*Gemeinwirtschaft*] is the first step to a state-run economy', and pointing out that trade unions ought not to confuse their roles as employees with that of employers.

In July and August 1947 several articles by Röpke which had originally appeared in the *Neue Zürcher Zeitung* were published in the FDP *Informationsdienst*. The party's spokesmen started enthusing about the 'competitive economy' and attacking 'collectivism' as incompatible with human freedom. By January 1948 Blücher and his colleagues in the British-zone FDP were willing to commit themselves more decisively to the free market. On the North Sea island of Wageroog they drew up an economic programme which began with the slogan 'Freedom is indivisible' and said that they expected from a (future) German government that it would restrict its interference with the economic process to what was 'necessary'. This was evidently going to be interpreted in a very restricted fashion, since the programme also called for 'the liberation of the economy from state direction'. The liberation of all creative forces in society was the precondition of any healthy economy. Socialization in any form prevented this liberation.[42]

Once again, it is difficult to equate this programme with a commitment to the principles of the social market economy as it was being

[41] Ungeheuer, *Wirtschaftsprogrammatik*, 162–3.
[42] For this section, see ibid. 165–7, and the copy of the Wangeroogprogramm in BA Blücher NL, 230. Also referred to in Ungeheuer, *Wirtschaftsprogrammatik*, 183–4, and K. Schröder, *Die FDP in der britischen Besatzungszone*, 182–3.

developed up to 1948. Historians of the FDP certainly regard the social element in the programme with scepticism. One describes Middelhauve's speech in June 1947 as 'characteristic for the future relationship of the FDP with neo-liberalism, in that neo-liberal theories were in no way taken over *en bloc* as party ideology but only in so far as they strengthened the case against socialist tendencies'.[43] This view is certainly reinforced by the marked disinclination to tackle the cartel question. The Wangeroog programme spoke piously of preventing the abuse of property and opposing monopolies, but specifically provided for market-regulation agreements so long as they were supervised, and claimed that a general ban on such agreements was 'untenable for economic reasons'.[44] A man like Middelhauve was as much a nationalist as an economic liberal, and in the early 1950s his willingness to recruit former Nazis into leading positions in the FDP of North-Rhine-Westphalia damaged his reputation.[45]

So far as the social aspect of neo-liberal thought was concerned, it may have impressed individual liberals, including Blücher, who read and evidently appreciated Müller-Armack's views on the social market economy,[46] but in general there seems to have been little real enthusiasm for confronting the evils of industrial society. It may be unfair to suggest that social policy was *terra incognita* for the FDP until the 1960s, but the party certainly did not make that issue a high priority and always put the interests of its rather narrow, middle-class electorate before general concepts of social responsibility.[47] For all that, the commitment of the FDP to the free market was to have highly important consequences. In particular, it affected the career of Ludwig Erhard, as we shall see below.

[43] Ungeheuer, *Wirtschaftsprogrammatik*, 165.

[44] Wangeroog Programme 'Wirtschaftsprogramm', BA Blücher NL, no. 230, pt. 5.

[45] Cf. W. Burbach, 'Friedrich Mittelhauve', in W. Först (ed.), *Beiderseits der Grenzen* (Cologne, 1987), 203–9.

[46] On 27 Mar. 1948 Blücher wrote to Müller-Armack thanking him for his book *Wirtschaftslenkung und Marktwirtschaft*, which had arrived on his birthday. He claimed that he had already started to read it three weeks earlier, at the suggestion of his colleague Theodor Blank: THA Blücher Collection, A3 Nachlaß Blücher, no. 14. fo. 113. There is little reason, however, to assume any very close personal relationship with Müller-Armack.

[47] The *terra incognita* suggestion is made by Hans Vorländer, 'Der soziale Liberalismus der FDP', 198, citing Rolf Zundel *Die Erben des Liberalismus* (Freudenstadt, 1971), 23. To ·be fair to Zundel, he seems to be talking about classical liberalism in the early 19th cent. rather than the policy of the FDP, but he too dismisses the party's policies in the 1950s as being just socially conservative. Cf. 163. On this question see A. J. Nicholls, 'Ludwig Erhard and German Liberalism—an Ambivalent Relationship', in K. H. Jarausch and L. E. Jones (eds.), *In Search of Liberal Germany: Studies in the History of German Liberalism from 1789 to the Present* (Providence RI 1990), pp. 404–7.

7

Ludwig Erhard and the Origins of the Social Market Economy

FOR Ludwig Erhard, the end of the war had brought a sharp and unexpected change of fortune. From the summer of 1944 until Hitler's defeat his prospects cannot have seemed particularly rosy. He had no official position; his 'institute' was really a business consultancy, dependent on the whims of entrepreneurs and enjoying an ambivalent relationship to the Nazi authorities. Northern Bavaria, where he had his headquarters, was scarcely the nerve-centre of Germany. Yet Erhard possessed great resilience and, above all, optimism, characteristics which were to stand him in good stead in the years which followed.

When the Americans liberated Fürth in April 1945, they were impressed by Erhard's enthusiasm and clean record. They asked him to take over the economic administration (*Wirtschaftsamt*) for the area. In September the new Social Democratic premier of Bavaria, Wilhelm Hoegner, was looking for a suitable person to fill the post of Economics Minister. The American authorities warmly recommended Erhard, who accepted the post. Hoegner later came to believe that Erhard had been pressed on him because the Americans were unhappy about the socialist characteristics of the draft constitution then being discussed by Bavarian politicians. They hoped that Erhard would act as a brake on such tendencies.[1] Be that as it may, Erhard described himself in later years as an 'American invention', and his career owed much to this American patronage.[2]

As Economics Minister in Munich he was faced with a multiplicity of problems, ranging from looting to demobilization, and also had to develop Bavaria's export capacity.[3] He faced strong criticism from rivals in the newly formed Christian Social Union (CSU). In December 1946, elections for the Bavarian *Landtag* undermined Hoegner's government and it was replaced by a coalition led by the CSU. Although Erhard continued in office, he was attacked by some of his new CSU

---

[1] W. Hoegner, 'Erhard als bayerischer Wirtschaftsminister', in G. Schröder *et al.* (eds.), *Ludwig Erhard, Beiträge*, 128. See also Laitenberger, *Ludwig Erhard*, 44–51.

[2] Hohmann, *Fränkische Lebensbilder*, 26–7.

[3] Hoegner, 'Erhard als bayerischer Wirtschaftsminister', 126–7.

colleagues and had to resign on 10 January 1947. His ministry was taken over by a Social Democrat. He was pursued by accusations of incompetence and even impropriety. A parliamentary committee of inquiry was set up, presided over by Alois Schloegl, a representative of farming interests, who was very hostile to Erhard. Despite his efforts, the committee could find nothing dishonourable in Erhard's conduct. Accusations of administrative incompetence continued to dog him, and help to explain his distaste for the CSU in later years. Nevertheless, the fact that he had run a ministry meant that he could not simply be written off as an unworldly academic, but could claim practical experience in economic reconstruction.

One issue of great importance for the future of West Germany had arisen when Erhard was Bavarian Economics Minister; namely the decision taken by the Anglo-Saxon allies in summer 1946 to merge the economies of the American and British zones. This caused some difficulties, not least because the political organization of the two zones was rather different. In the British zone there was, as we have seen, a zonal body for economic administration, advised by a German council called the *Zonenbeirat*. This enabled German political parties to have some influence on the British zone's economic administration, which was centralized at Minden. By far the most powerful force at this time in the British zone were the Social Democrats (SPD). The head of the German economics administration (*Zentralamt*) in Minden was a Social Democratic economic specialist, Viktor Agartz, who was an enthusiast for planning, state control, and centralization.

In the American zone, on the other hand, the Germans had been able to exercise more self-government as the result of the creation of *Land*, or state, governments. The three *Länder* in the American zone had their own economics ministries and were hostile to centralized control. They also tended to be more sympathetic to market forces than their colleagues in the British zone. The British economic administration at Minden was regarded with suspicion as the seat of a power-hungry bureaucracy. British proposals for a central economics committee under the leadership of Agartz aroused fears that it would dominate the *Länder* and were strongly resisted by the south German states, among which Bavaria was the largest and most insistent on its rights. Erhard himself contributed to the public debate and argued that the fusion of the zones did not have to mean centralization or a commitment to planning in the economy.[4]

To the dismay of the Minden officials, Agartz was not accepted

---

[4] Ambrosius, *Die Durchsetzung der sozialen Marktwirtschaft*, 57–9.

as head of the new inter-zonal committee. In September 1946 the Germans representing economic administrations in the two zones agreed, after tough negotiating tactics on the part of the south Germans, to nominate Rudolf Mueller, the Economics Minister of Hesse in the American zone. He was a well-respected, but moderately liberal figure. The Minden group was even more upset by the fear that the headquarters of the new bizonal economic organization would be in Frankfurt—also in the American zone—and not in Düsseldorf, as they would have preferred. The British, of course, could point to the larger population in their zone, and the importance of the Ruhr/Westphalian industrial complex. The south Germans argued for Frankfurt as a good communications centre, but their real strength lay in the economic power of the Americans, from whom the British desperately needed help. The decision for Mueller was rightly seen as a set-back for both centralization and socialization, even though the Social Democrats soon managed to oust him after a new round of parliamentary elections in the *Länder*. The federal structure of Germany had been confirmed in the bizonal arrangements, and it had become obvious that socialization would have to wait for national, or at least West German, elections before it could be implemented.[5]

After his fall from office, Erhard had remained in Munich, propagating his views in private debate and public discussion. He had retained the remnants of his old research institute as a form of economic consultancy, and had also cultivated links with the University of Munich, where Professor Adolf Weber ran the seminar for economics and public policy (*Staatswirtschaft*). Weber was a senior economist of fairly conventional views, who was nevertheless inclined to support market principles. He set up an 'economics working party for Bavaria' in which Erhard participated and which brought together academics, politicians, and businessmen to consider problems of reconstruction. Erhard, who had already made contact with the group before he left Fürth, was active in the section dealing with money and credit. The working party drew up draft legislation for the reform of the currency

---

[5] In fact, the administration remained at Minden. For the 'Minden view' of these events, see correspondence between Minden, Berlin, and London in Aug. and Sept. 1946, PRO/FO/1034/20. The British adviser on German organizations in Minden, Dr Friedmann, was very indignant over Agartz's rejection, but his superiors in the British Foreign Office and the military governor's HQ were less concerned. They regarded Mueller as respectable, and noted that he was acceptable to the Americans. Sir William Strang pointed out, on 2 Oct. 1946, that no 'far-reaching social reforms' could possibly be carried out by bizonal administrations, whatever their political complexion, if the German people had not had a chance to express a view on them. It was not, therefore, just the American occupiers who scotched premature attempts to socialize the German economy.

and for a consequential redistribution of financial burdens in the interests of social justice. The plan for currency reform had been presented to the Americans by Erhard himself in July 1945. It was to prove a helpful experience for a more serious confrontation with the currency issue nearly three years later. In November 1947 Erhard was given the title of professor in Adolf Weber's faculty at the University of Munich. This strengthened his academic credentials.[6]

Erhard was also active as a publicist. He published a number of articles in the *Neue Zeitung* in which he was at pains to deny that a market economy necessarily had to be associated with uninhibited exploitation of the kind characteristic of capitalism in its early phases. 'The real contradistinction', he wrote in October 1946, 'is not between free and planned economic systems, not between capitalist and socialist systems, but between a market economy with a free price level adjustment on the one hand and an authoritarian economy with state controls extending into the sphere of distribution on the other.'[7] State interference was actually necessary—but to protect free competition. In June 1947 he attacked the notion that socialists had to be in favour of a centrally directed, planned economy. As a liberal economist he blamed capitalism for betraying the basic principles of the market economy: 'namely competition and price freedom'.[8] 'Looking back,' he wrote, 'it was surely a tragic aberration on the part of the socialists to deprecate competition, thereby playing into the hands of the cartels and other economic monsters, instead of realising that competition was the very giant-killer they were looking for.' He went on to comment that 'if it is true that socialists work for fair distribution of the social product, then it is equally true that supporters of the market economy can wholly subscribe to the same aim, since this is implicit in the principle of order to which they are committed'.[9] This attempt to persuade socialists that social justice and the truly free market were compatible with one another was a recurrent theme in the arguments of social market economists.[10]

---

[6] Laitenberger, *Ludwig Erhard*, 54–6.

[7] *Die Neue Zeitung*, 14 Oct. 1946, cited in L. Erhard, *The Economics of Success* (London, 1963), 8.

[8] Erhard, *The Economics of Success*, 11–12, citing 'Sprachverwirrungen um die Wirtschaftsordnung', *Die Neue Zeitung*, 23 June 1947.

[9] Ibid. 15.

[10] A striking example of this was to be Rüstow's speech to the conference of the *Aktionsgemeinschaft Soziale Marktwirtschaft* (Action Group for the Realization of the Social Market Economy—ASM), 18/19 Nov. 1953 in Bad Godesberg. Johann Lang (ed.), *Wir fordern von Regierung und Bundestag die Vollendung der sozialen Marktwirtschaft* (Bad Nauheim, 1954), 20.

Nevertheless, it must be said that for Erhard justice was less important than production, without which no distribution system could offer anything to a hungry population. To achieve the satisfaction of need, the only effective mechanism was that of the market. He pointed out that in this respect a peacetime economy was quite different from one committed to the needs of war. 'From the economist's point of view,' he wrote in April 1947, 'nothing is simpler than a war economy, nothing on the other hand is more complicated than a strongly differentiated peacetime economy.'[11] For the latter, a free market was indispensable.

The free-price mechanism cannot be replaced by the expertise of an official or by any form of market research. Besides, it can easily be demonstrated that the free-price mechanism and a planned economy are mutually exclusive because the latter could not have the lie constantly being given to its predicted benefits by the facts of the price mechanism, and the planning authority could not give up its prepared plans without abolishing its *raison d'être*.[12]

Even here, however, Erhard distanced himself from *laissez-faire* economics. He commented that 'Today a social and economic policy faces the task of providing all individuals in the economic process with the greatest possible equality of opportunity (*Startbedingungen*).' It was also the duty of policy-makers to eliminate economic privilege and power-concentration, and to work against the proletarianization of the people by the conscious cultivation of craft industries and small businesses.[13]

Erhard himself was probably less concerned about the social aspects of the new economic liberalism than the productive advantages of the market economy. In 1961, looking back on his achievements during the early years of the Federal Republic, he told an audience in Vienna that he had not been much concerned with 'god-like justice' but with the elimination of poverty.

If you ask me whether over the past twelve years the social product has been justly distributed, there are various answers. According to strictly moral criteria, I shall have to say No! According to the given circumstances of the time and the tasks we faced, tasks which had to be successfully overcome, I answer Yes.[14]

Nevertheless, Erhard was certainly not a tool in the hands of big business. If anything, his was a small-town, populist ideal, harking

[11] Erhard, 'Freie Wirtschaft oder Planwirtschaft?', *Die Neue Zeitung*, 7 Apr. 1947.
[12] Ibid.
[13] Ibid.
[14] Speech in Vienna, 8 Feb. 1961, in L. Erhard, *Deutsche Wirtschaftspolitik: Der Weg der sozialen Marktwirtschaft* (Düsseldorf, 1962), 548.

back to the days of Eugen Richter and the progressive liberals who opposed Bismarck in the nineteenth century.[15]

This attitude had won him liberal friends in his native Bavaria, including the *Land* FDP-leader, Thomas Dehler, who was, like Erhard, from Franconia. Not for the last time, the Free Democrats were to play an important part in Erhard's career. In January 1947, Franz Blücher, the leader of the FDP in the British zone, had become chairman of the finance committee of the new Economic Council in Frankfurt. He became extremely concerned that the Allies should not introduce a currency reform into Germany without consulting the Germans and in such a way that it might compromise German national interests. He therefore persuaded the committee to establish a special bureau to study the question and on 23 July this was endorsed by the Economic Council.[16]

The question then arose of who should run this new bureau. One FDP member of the Economic Council—a businessman from Munich called Everhard Bungartz—suggested Erhard as somebody with a 'liberal conception of economics'.[17] In September 1947 Erhard was duly appointed to run the Special Bureau for Monetary and Currency Matters (*Sonderstelle Geld und Kredit*), with its headquarters in Bad Homburg. In the first half of October he presided over a number of meetings to discuss the necessary preconditions for currency reform and the method of dealing with Germany's excess purchasing-power. The issues raised were largely those to which Erhard had addressed himself in his wartime memorandum, although they were complicated by the zonal problem, since a fundamental decision would have to be taken about whether a reformed currency would be introduced throughout Germany or just in the Western zones.[18]

Erhard took the view that there should be as drastic a reduction in the money supply as possible, so that the population would have real incentives to produce more goods. He at once ran into opposition from Günter Keiser of the Economics Administration, who claimed that however radical the currency reform was, it would not enable them to

---

[15] This was the interesting view expressed to the author by one of Erhard's most loyal lieutenants, Rudiger Altmann. It should not, of course, be thought that Erhard's statements on planning were always entirely consistent. It has been pointed out that in Sept. 1946 he spoke of the 'necessity accepted on all sides of a socially directed (*planvoll*) economy', Heusgen, *Ludwig Erhards Lehre*, 132. See also Abelshauser, 'Freiheitlicher Sozialismus'. Despite this, I remain more impressed by Erhard's commitment to the free-price mechanism as the ultimate objective.

[16] BA Blücher NL, no. 352, fos. 104–5, notes by Köhler and Blücher.

[17] Ungeheuer, *Wirtschaftsprogrammatik*, 192–3.

[18] BA Blücher NL, no. 354, records of meetings of the *Sonderstelle Geld und Kredit*, 1–16 Oct. 1947.

dispense with controls (*Bewirtschaftung*). Keiser evidently feared the deflationary effects of a drastic cut in purchasing power, whereas Erhard and those who thought like him did not believe that such measures would lead to deflation.[19] This turned out to be a useful rehearsal of the sort of arguments Erhard would face when he took over the Economics Administration in Frankfurt the following March, although such a possibility could hardly have been in his mind during the discussions at Bad Homburg. Certainly it was important that the activities of the bureau brought him into close touch with Blücher and with the head of the Finance Administration at Frankfurt, Alfred Hartmann. Erhard's position on currency reform can only have strengthened their perception that he was a clear-headed exponent of liberal economic views. Erhard also consulted with other economic experts, including Walter Eucken.[20]

Once he had set the main lines of direction in which his bureau should operate, Erhard seems to have left day-to-day business to others.[21] The bureau's task was to draw up a blueprint for currency reform which would be presented to the Allies, and in April 1948 the 'Homburg Plan' was produced. The Allies—or more realistically, the Americans—took little notice of this document and went ahead with their own plans. However, experts involved in Erhard's Special Bureau were among those called to secret discussions with the Americans in April and May 1948, and their representations, reinforced by Erhard's own authority, do seem to have eased the impact of the currency reform on the German public.[22]

Politically, Erhard's reputation as an opponent of socialization, planning, and cheap money was to stand him in good stead. As we shall see below,[23] the Economics Administration at Frankfurt experienced a crisis in late January 1948 when its director, the CSU politician Johannes Semler, was removed from office for upsetting the Americans by critical remarks about food supplies to Germany. This coincided with one of several reorganizations in the Frankfurt administrative

[19] Ibid., protocol of 5th Meeting of Bureau, 16 Oct. 1947, p. 9.
[20] Ibid. Hartmann attended most of the meetings in early Oct. and their proceedings were reported to Blücher.
[21] Interview with Prof. Möller in Munich, Sept. 1985. In particular, Erwin Heilscher, formerly a senior official in the Bavarian Finance Ministry, ran the *Sonderstelle* efficiently on a day-to-day basis.
[22] By that time Erhard was director of the Economics Administration. See Hans Möller, 'Die westdeutsche Währungsreform von 1948' in Deutsche Bundesbank (ed.), *Währung und Wirtschaft in Westdeutschland, 1876–1975* (Frankfurt/M., 1976), 444–54. See also Laitenberger, *Ludwig Erhard*, 56–61.
[23] See below, Ch. 9.

arrangements so that the Economic Council had to elect not only a new director for economics but also an administrative director (*Oberdirektor*) to oversee the work of the entire administration.

As had been the case since 1947, the Economic Council was evenly split, with forty-four CDU/CSU members opposing forty-six Social Democrats and Communists. The eight FDP members held the balance, a position they were to enjoy so often in West Germany's post-war history. The Christian Democrats were deeply divided over the post of economics director. Erhard's name was proposed, but dropped at an early stage in their deliberations, probably as the result of CSU hostility. The Bavarian party was in any case very keen to insist on Semler's reinstatement, a proposal which would have led directly to conflict with the Allies. The trade-union wing of the CDU wanted a candidate more in sympathy with the *dirigiste* proposals of the Ahlen Programme. Eventually the Christian delegation agreed to propose Hermann Pünder, mayor of Cologne, as *Oberdirektor* and to avoid appointing an economics director, leaving that administration under the control of its senior civil servant, Walter Strauß. Given the critical economic situation of Bizone at this time, such a proposal can only be regarded as highly irresponsible. In any case, the FDP, whose votes were necessary if the anti-socialist parties were going to succeed in the elections, would have none of it. They proposed Hermann Dietrich as *Oberdirektor* and Erhard as economics director. After much wrangling and delay, none of which enhanced the public image of the Economic Council or German politicians, a compromise was struck whereby Christians and Free Democrats would support a slate of Pünder and Erhard.[24] Thus it was that Erhard entered into his kingdom as the director of economic policy in Bizone, and ultimately of West Germany itself. He now had the opportunity to put his theories into practice.

[24] Laitenberger, *Ludwig Erhard*, 62–3, Ungeheuer, *Wirtschaftsprogrammatik*, 198–200. Adenauer had no part in Erhard's election, although he wanted Pünder to be *Oberdirektor*. Nevertheless, Erhard's appointment suited him because it deepened the chasm between the Economics Administration and the Social Democrats. See H.-P. Schwarz, *Adenauer: Der Aufstieg, 1876–1952* (3rd edn.; Stuttgart, 1991), 573.

8

The Social Market and the Crisis in the German Economy, 1947–1948

BEFORE describing Erhard's policies as director of the bizonal Economics Administration, it is necessary to take a closer look at the situation in Germany, and indeed in Western Europe, in the years 1947–8. At that time, and in subsequent memoir accounts, the year 1947 was seen as one of deepening political and economic crisis. Hopes that the alliance between the Anglo-Saxon powers and the Soviet Union would survive the war—based not least on a mutual fear of Germany—proved vain. In the Near East and the Balkans, Western interests seemed threatened by Soviet, or at least Communist, pressure. Western demands for free elections in Poland and for independent, if pro-Soviet, governments in other Eastern European countries were treated with contempt. 'Stalinization', with all its sinister and brutal implications, began to be implemented in the European territories between the Bug and the Elbe. Europe was divided by the 'Iron Curtain', a concept popularized by Winston Churchill in his famous speech at Fulton, Missouri, on 5 March, 1946, but already established as a shocking reality by Stalin's forces and their local Communist supporters.

Nor was it at all clear that Communist ambitions would be limited to the gains made by Stalin at Tehran and Yalta. Yugoslavia had become one of the most radical Communist dictatorships despite having been regarded as a joint sphere of influence during the war,[1] and the Communist threat in Greece had certainly not been foreshadowed by inter-Allied discussions. Although the Russians had not interfered directly in the occupation of Italy or in the liberation of Western areas like France and the Low Countries, the existence of powerful Communist parties in Italy and France seemed to pose a growing threat to the future of parliamentary democracy there. In central Europe, the Soviet authorities in Austria were evidently bent on assimilating this jointly occupied—but theoretically 'liberated'—country into their 'socialist' Europe. Most worrying of all was the case of Czechoslovakia,

---

[1] J. W. Wheeler-Bennett and A. J. Nicholls, *The Semblance of Peace: The International Settlement after the Second World War* (London, 1972), 559–61.

a country whose government, steered by President Benes and by Jan Masyryk, had punctiliously fostered good relations with the Soviet Union and could not be suspected of anti-Russian or anti-socialist prejudices. It was the overthrow of Czech democracy by the Communists in February 1948 which, more than anything else, convinced public opinion that Stalin posed a serious threat to Western countries as well as to the unfortunate peoples of Eastern Europe.

Underlying this perception was the awareness that Europe's economic situation was parlous and seemed to be getting worse. Shortages of food and consumer goods were acute in all European countries with the exception of Switzerland and Sweden, and even they were affected by the breakdown in inter-European trade resulting from the war. The British, despite their status as a victorious ally, were forced to endure years of austerity which actually seemed to grow worse as peace wore on. Bread rationing, for example, which had never been needed in wartime, was introduced in 1946. At the root of this economic problem lay an imbalance between the USA and Europe which found expression in the 'dollar gap'.

Before the war the Western European countries had satisfied their economic needs to a considerable extent by trading with their immediate neighbours. Germany, in particular, was an important source of machinery and other manufactured goods. With Germany limited in its export capacity by physical destruction and Allied controls, and with most European countries needing to restock after the war, the USA became the only effective source of supply for many raw materials and even manufactures. In order to purchase these, Europeans needed dollars, but they had few means of earning them. Even the elements seemed against Western recovery. In the winter of 1946–7 shortages of food and fuel were exacerbated by one of the hardest and longest winters of the century. Post-war euphoria was turning to desperation in many parts of northern Europe.

In the immediate post-war period substantial assistance had come from the USA in various forms of relief and *ad hoc* loans. But by 1947 this latter form of help was running out. A mutinous US Congress was no longer willing to keep on putting piecemeal aid into the outstretched palms of European countries, especially those which seemed to be squandering the money on costly experiments in socialism. The US Secretary of State, George Marshall, perceived a real danger that Western European economies would collapse in chaos and hunger, leaving the whole area an easy prey for Communism. It was to combat the threat of economic disaster that in June 1947 he announced his commitment to a comprehensive rescue-package for the European economy, on the understanding that the recipient countries would get together and formulate a plan for European recovery. It was this proposal, swiftly taken up by Ernest Bevin in Britain, which was to go down in history as the Marshall Plan. It was seen by the Americans as a step towards European integration and as a means to save the West from the Communist threat. The economic boom which followed its inception was connected with it in the public mind. The resurgence of confidence in the West which helped to neutralize the perceived Soviet threat was also attributed to Marshall Aid.

Like all human achievements, the Marshall Plan has had its fair share of critics. At first it was claimed to be an exercise in American imperialism, or a capitalist manœuvre to undermine socialism. It was also blamed for exacerbating the Cold War. More recently, some economic historians have cast doubt on its significance by suggesting that it was not necessary in the first place, and that it had very little effect on European recovery anyhow. They argue that post-war Europe was bound to recover, just as Europe had done after the First World War, and that recovery would be bound to lead to a boom. The crisis in 1947 was more perceived than real. Shortages certainly existed, but they were caused by bottle-necks in production which were being systematically overcome, and which were exaggerated by the peculiar severity and unusual length of the freak winter mentioned above. If Marshall Aid had not been granted, the theory runs, Europeans could simply have tightened their belts a notch or two and survived.[2]

The argument also has a political side to it, for it has been claimed that the Soviet threat to Western Europe was more apparent than real, that Stalin had no intention of attacking the West, and that Communist parties in Italy, France, or—for that matter—West Germany could never have hoped to attain power unless the Red Army intervened to support them. The last of these assertions may well be true, but it is an oversimplification of the scenario feared by Marshall and others in 1947. If the economic situation declined sharply from an already low level, there seemed a real danger of demoralization and chaos in the West, and nobody could be sure how that would turn out or what opportunities might present themselves to anti-democratic forces, whether of the left or right. It should be remembered that, if the Marshall Plan had

---

[2] This is, e.g., the thrust of the first chapter of A. S. Milward, *The Reconstruction of Western Europe, 1945–51* (London, 1984), 15–43. Milward does make the good point that dashed expectations of a better life after the war were as important as actual privation— although in Germany the latter should not be underestimated. For an interesting comment on Milward's argument, see M. J. Hogan. *The Marshall Plan: America, Britain and the Reconstruction of Western Europe, 1947–1952* (Cambridge, 1987), 431.

The Social Market and Economic Crisis

TABLE 1. *Foreign Aid to West Germany, 1945–1952* ($ million)

	1945/6	1947	1948	1949	1950	1951	1952
From USA							
Civilian supplies (to 30.6.46)	195	—	—	—	—	—	—
GARIOA[a] funds	78	237	788	503	177	12	0
Marshall Plan	—	—	142	420	303	416	114
Working capital of JEIA	—	18	—	—	—	—	—
Superfluous military material	(31)	(31)	(93)	(62)	—	—	—
Debits: payments not directly beneficial to the West German economy			(−42)	(−42)	(−42)	(−42)	(−42)
From Britain							
UK contributions	264	317	90	32	1	—	—
Working capital of JEIA	—	94	10	—	—	—	—
From France							
Working capital of JEIA	—	—	16	—	—	—	—
Drawing rights							
Received	—	—	8	46	65	—	—
Approved	—	—	−17	−147	−53	—	—
TOTALS	568	697	1088	874	451	386	72

[a] Government and Relief in Occupied Areas. Includes a residue of $81 million to Civilian Supplies.

Source: C. Buchheim, *Die Wiedereingliederung Westdeutschlands in die Weltwirtschaft, 1945–1958* (Munich, 1990), 72.

not materialized, the previous *ad hoc* loans and grants would have run out, leaving Western Europe worse off financially than in 1945. Comparisons with the post-war era after 1918 are neither entirely apposite nor particularly encouraging. On the one hand, the devastation wrought by the Second World War and the damage done to the international trading-system was far worse than that arising from the First World War. On the other, the dismal history of central and eastern Europe in the 1920s does not suggest that Europe's natural powers of recuperation would by themselves have proved sufficient to launch the Western world into its most prosperous epoch. Even if, in total, the amount of Marshall Aid to Europe was relatively small, it can be seen to have provided that 'crucial margin' necessary for successful recovery[3] (See Table 1).

It is also most important to notice that the Marshall Plan was linked to other American aims which have been subjects of controversy—the liberalization of world trade and the integration of Western Europe. Throughout the war the major economic objective of the USA had been

[3] A phrase used by Stephen A. Shuker, cited in Hogan, *The Marshall Plan*, 432.

the abolition of obstacles to international trade. Yet in the post-war world, trade was more hobbled than at any time in the twentieth century. Command economies controlled the trade of Eastern and much of Central Europe. Elsewhere, free markets and convertible currencies had been replaced by export and import quotas, bilateral trade-deals, trade embargoes, and foreign-exchange controls. In the case of countries like Britain and France, imperial preferences were another obstacle to commercial freedom. Colonialism, nationalism, and socialist controls formed a web of restrictions choking trade and stunting growth. The US government hoped that it could use the carrot of aid to induce European countries to work together in a multilateral sense to overcome trade barriers and eliminate petty national jealousies. Hence its insistence on a co-ordinated scheme to ensure that the aid itself was used to the best advantage and would set Europe on its own feet, so that further loans would be unnecessary.

Initially this seemed to imply that the European Recovery Programme (ERP), as Marshall Aid was officially called, would itself require central planning, and this was indeed seized upon by bureaucrats as an excuse for yet more controls. But the more American support was accepted, the more the Americans could exert pressure for the abandonment of bilateralism and protection. The constitution of the Organization of European Economic Co-operation (OEEC)—largely determined by the Americans—included a commitment to liberalize trade by the maximum possible interchange of goods and services, which should lead to attaining the object of abolishing as soon as possible the 'abnormal restrictions' which were then hampering trade. The more prosperity began to return to Western Europe, the less excuse there would be for the austere measures of a command economy.

In Germany all these issues were presented in an extreme form. Politically the country's future was entirely unclear. In the Soviet zone the forced union of the Social Democrats with the Communists had created a pro-Soviet Socialist Unity Party under Communist control. Other 'anti-Fascist' political parties, including the Liberals and the CDU, were rapidly being forced to toe a Stalinist line. It seemed likely that the Communists, who were also established as a political party in the Western zones, would try to exert influence over the whole country if it were administered as a national unit. The fact that Berlin lay within the Soviet zone and was vulnerable to Soviet pressure meant that the prospect of a Communist-controlled Germany was not entirely fanciful. In the Western zones the Allies had not so far given a clear lead to the Germans about their political future, and it was not until the collapse of four-power negotiations at the end of 1947 that Anglo-American policy finally hardened in favour of a West German option. Whereas in the immediate aftermath of the war many Germans were relieved to see the end of the Hitler dictatorship, two years of Allied occupation led to disillusionment and hostility, particularly towards the British, whose populous and devastated zone presented the most problems. Even the Americans, however, had angered Germans by their clumsy handling of the denazification issue, and by their apparent inconsistencies of policy.

Meanwhile, the conditions of life in the Western zones, and especially that administered by the British, continued to be extremely harsh, and food supplies in particular were a cause of increasing discontent. Millions of refugees were an especial cause of worry, the British and German authorities erroneously assuming that they would be prone to Communist blandishments. In fact, fear of Communism and of the Red Army was already widespread in Germany at the end of the war, and was reinforced by the experiences of those driven from their homes in the East. Nevertheless, the morale of the refugees was low, and they might prove vulnerable to nationalist appeals from politicians whose commitment to Western-style parliamentary democracy could not be taken for granted.[4] It would be wrong to depict the Western zones of Germany as being politically vulnerable to Communism in 1947, but the fears of the authorities were understandable, and there is no telling into what authoritarian courses German public opinion might have been channelled without the decisive commitment to the West which occurred in 1948.

Economically the situation was also discouraging, although some progress had been made to overcome the initial problems faced by Germany in 1945. Before the war, Germany had possessed the most powerful European industrial economy. As we have seen above,[5] that economy lay in ruins in 1945.

As with the Marshall Plan and the Western European recovery, Germany's re-entry into the world market as a major exporting nation has been the subject of fierce controversy. Enthusiasts for the Western orientation of the Federal Republic explained its happy economic development in terms of currency reform, Marshall Aid, and Ludwig Erhard's free-market economic policies. This was the famous 'economic miracle' beloved of journalists, even though Erhard and his supporters staunchly denied there was anything miraculous about it.

From the beginning, however, there was a different interpretation,

---

[4] See, e.g., I. Connor, 'The Bavarian Government and the Refugee Problem', *European History Quarterly*, 16/2 (Apr. 1986), 133 ff.

[5] See above, Ch. 5.

according to which West Germany's economic recovery had been well under way in 1948, thanks to wise planning by the Allies and especially the British, and that Erhard's policies were simply allowing precious resources to be squandered in non-essential luxury areas for the benefit of the better off.[6] A more sophisticated version of this interpretation stresses the extent to which recovery had preceded currency reform in June 1948, denies that the Marshall Plan made any decisive difference to Germany's economic development, and suggests that Erhard's free-market experiment lasted only a relatively short time in any case, because the crisis brought about by the Korean War in 1950 forced the West German government to accept a form of economic control, but one which was self-administered by industry and could therefore be graced with the title of 'corporatism'.[7]

The issues of the uses to which Marshall Aid were put and the impact of the Korean War on German policy will be tackled in later chapters. It is important, however, to examine the argument that at the beginning of 1948 West German recovery was already well under way, and that free-market policies were irrelevant—or even counter-productive—to its further development. It could certainly be argued that by the end of 1947 the major bottle-necks in transport and power production which had crippled German industry in 1945 had been largely overcome. The occupation authorities could point with pride to the rapid restoration of a devastated transport-system; by June 1946 93 per cent of railway tracks and 800 bridges were open again. In 1947 there was further concentration on improving transport, and by January 1948 Germany's railways and waterways were functioning so well that transport difficulties were no longer regarded as a hindrance to the economy.[8]

Coal production, which had been the object of strenuous encouragement by the British authorities, including a points system giving face-workers access to more rationed goods than other citizens, was showing considerable improvement. It has even been claimed that from October

---

[6] T. Balogh, *Germany: An Experiment in 'Planning' by the 'Free' Price Mechanism* (Oxford, 1950).

[7] W. Abelshauser, 'Korea, die Ruhr und Erhards Marktwirtschaft: Die Energiekrise von 1950/51', *Rheinische Vierteljahrsblätter*, 45 (1981), 316; id. 'The Economic Policy of Ludwig Erhard', *EUI Working Paper*, 80 (Florence, Jan. 1984); and id. 'Ansätze "Korporativer Marktwirtschaft" in der Koreakrise der frühen fünfziger Jahre: Ein Briefwechsel zwischen dem Hohen Kommissar John McCloy und Bundeskanzler Konrad Adenauer', *Vierteljahreshefte für Zeitgeschichte*, 30/4 (Oct. 1982), 734.

[8] Abelshauser, *Wirtschaft in Westdeutschland*, 155–6; W. Carlin, *The Development of Factor Distribution of Income and Profitability in West Germany, 1945–1973* (MS; D. Phil thesis; Oxford, 1987), 162.

1947 the coal industry had been fulfilling its role as the locomotive of German reconstruction.[9] Certainly more people were working in West Germany's coal-mines; by December 1947 the British were claiming that the work-force in the Ruhr coal-mines was substantially higher than it had been in 1936.[10]

If one draws a production curve from October 1946 to the summer of 1949, the rate of growth in the earlier years looks impressive, even if the actual figures for production are low. So the argument is that the month of June 1948, when the Allies introduced a new currency and Erhard abolished many controls, is not such an important watershed as the 'myth' of the Federal Republic would have us believe.

A further reinforcement of this argument is deployed as the result of the currency reform itself. By the end of 1947 it was evident that the old Reichsmark had had its day and would almost certainly be replaced by a new currency. It was only natural, therefore, the argument runs, for firms to hoard goods so that they could sell them later for currency with real value. This led them to report misleadingly low estimates of production in the period before currency reform, thereby making the upswing after the reform look more spectacular than it actually was. Investigations of the use of electric power before and after the currency reform seemed to show that there was less contrast between the pre- and post-reform periods than had previously been thought.[11] Delays in implementing the currency reform slowed up a growth pattern which had already developed in the post-war period, although the harsh winter of 1946–7 had been a set-back which would have affected any economic system.

The sceptics about West Germany's recovery also point to the undoubted underlying strength of the country's industrial base, its lavish provision of machine tools and other equipment, and its well-trained labour-force, which was continually supplemented by refugees.[12] Looked at from this viewpoint, the post-war recovery in Germany does

---

[9] W. Abelshauser, 'Probleme des Wiederaufbaus der westdeutschen Wirtschaft 1945–1953,' in H.-A. Winkler (ed.), *Politische Weichenstellungen im Nachkriegsdeutschland, 1945–1953* (Göttingen, 1979), 208–53; see also the table in Abelshauser, *Wirtschaft in Westdeutschland*, 43, and id., 'Economic Policy', 14.

[10] Abelshauser, *Wirtschaft in Westdeutschland*, 141.

[11] Ibid. 55–60. These calculations on the basis of electricity supply have been challenged by A. Ritschl in 'Die Währungsreform von 1948 und der Wiederaufstieg der westdeutschen Industrie: Zu den Thesen von Matthias Manz und Werner Abelshauser über die Produktionswirkungen der Währungsreform', *Vierteljahrshefte für Zeitgeschichte*, 33/1 (Jan. 1985), 136 ff. For a modification of Abelshauser's position, see W. Abelshauser, 'Schopenhauers Gesetz und die Währungsreform', ibid. 214–18.

[12] See above, Ch. 5.

not seem especially remarkable, nor does the choice of economic policy by the government seem to have been so vitally important.

This is an argument which is unlikely ever to be settled to everybody's satisfaction, but the more the author has looked at the period from 1945 to 1949, the more impressed he has become with the importance of reintroducing the free market and committing United States aid to Western Europe.

First of all, we should remember that, by the end of 1947, production had reached only about half the level attained in the same area of Germany in 1936. Nor was there any sign of business confidence, without which sustained growth could hardly be aspired to, let alone achieved. Most significant in this matter was investment, or rather the lack of it. Investment levels in German industry were actually negative in 1945–7, that is to say industrial plant was wearing out more quickly than it was being replaced.[13] Most businesses were simply vegetating, with no incentive to increase production, because money was less valuable to them than the piles of materials and half-finished goods they held in their extraordinarily well-stocked inventories. It was estimated that in 1947 about half of the business deals carried out in industry were barter transactions, despite Allied regulations which strictly prohibited such operations.[14]

Here again, the fundamentally unhealthy nature of the controlled economy, or *Zwangswirtschaft*, reveals itself. Contrary to normal commercial practice, firms in West Germany in 1947 and the first six months of 1948 held very large stocks of both labour and materials. A sample of factories surveyed in Hesse in February 1948 revealed that they held more than twice as much in their inventories than had been the case in 1936—a year of full production in Germany—and that they had enough supplies on hand to keep production going for twelve months.[15] The value of the inventories was nearly three times as high as it had been in 1936.[16] One observer described the attitude of industrial managers thus: '[the] motives of the businessman are to keep his business in being, to retain the goodwill of his customers and to maintain his stocks of raw materials in the hope that some day conditions may improve'.[17]

---

[13] See Carlin, *Factor Distribution*, 183; see also the table in Krengel, *Anlagevermögen*, 106. Measured in D-Marks, investments in industry were 171 million in 1947, 296 million in 1948, and 1.433 billion in 1949.

[14] Buchheim, *Die Wiedereingliederung Westdeutschlands*, 57.

[15] Id., 'Währungsreform 1948', 197.

[16] Id., *Die Wiedereingliederung Westdeutschlands*, 55–6.

[17] A. M. Stamp, 'Germany without Incentive', *Lloyds Bank Review*, 5 (July 1947), 21, cited in Carlin, *Factor Distribution*, 178.

This was at a time of drastic shortages and widespread privation. Fixed prices and high taxation were disincentives to produce goods for sale, quite apart from the worthless nature of the German currency.

Owing to the absence of a free-price mechanism, it was quite impossible to tell what real prices were, because their functions as indicators of scarcity had been destroyed by price-control regulations. Despite the removal of physical bottle-necks to production such as wrecked rail-bridges or damaged power-stations, the black market was still flourishing at the beginning of 1948. Allied attempts at repression were shrill but ineffective. In Hamburg an egg cost 8 marks on the black market. A skilled worker—whose wage was, of course, artificially pegged by law—received about 10 marks a day.[18] In many factories employees were induced to stay at work by payments in kind. This encouraged still further the uneconomic system of barter.

One American observer, Gustav Stolper, himself a former German liberal economist of great distinction, remarked early in 1948 that

To study a 'planned economy' and bureaucratic regulations gone mad, one merely had to visit the Anglo-American zones of Germany in 1947. Here, as an homunculus in the retort, we can study what happens to a bureaucratically directed economy once the regulating forces of money and the market are abandoned.[19]

Small wonder that market economists like Miksch, who was working within the British economics administration at Minden, railed against the social injustices of the control system. In June 1947 the planning and statistics department at Minden produced a memorandum on 'German Economic Need' describing the desperate condition of the German economy. Far from suggesting that a recovery was under way, it claimed that West Germany had been living off reserves and that a bad situation would soon become worse unless drastic measures were taken. The West Germans could not be controlled more rigorously without jettisoning democracy. Only improved nutrition, large-scale imports, a reformed currency, and a more reasonable taxation-system could enable the West German economy to recover. The memorandum referred to the 'vegetative' condition of German industry and illustrated this with reference to iron and steel. In 1936, before the main rearmament programme had started, the Reich had manufactured 20 million tons of steel; the Bizone would only produce 2.5 million tons in 1947. The longer nothing was done to improve matters, the more expensive it would be to put right. The memorandum cited a comment by Röpke

[18] Buchheim, 'Währungsreform 1948', 193.
[19] G. Stolper, *German Realities* (New York, 1948), 75.

to the effect that the costs of economic restoration in Germany would rise in geometric progression the longer the debilitating crisis went on and the longer comprehensive assistance was denied.[20] This was obviously aimed at the Allies, and it is as well to remember that the supporters of market freedom were also working to liberate German industry from foreign control and even foreign ownership. If the *Zwangswirtschaft* were to be abolished, the managerial expertise of pre-war owners and their staffs would be indispensable. Threats of internationalization or socialization would thus disappear.

Yet the Allied occupiers did not dare to relinquish control over the German economy, partly because they did not trust the Germans to run it for the benefit of Europe as a whole, and partly because they feared starvation if rationing was relaxed. The British, in particular, tried to plan German industrial expansion to fit in with their own conception of what was good for their zone. The results were not encouraging. In the coal-mines of the Ruhr, where there was every reason for the authorities to stimulate output, attempts to direct surplus labour into the mines generated resentment and confusion, but little else. By the summer of 1947 the amount of labour employed in the mines had risen to 127 per cent of the 1936 figure, but output stood at only 57 per cent, and per capita production at a mere 55.5 per cent.[21] After the abject failure of labour conscription, various stratagems were tried to attract labour into the mines and to improve productivity. In January 1947 a special-points allocation was announced for coal-miners, giving them coupons with which to buy goods otherwise almost unobtainable except on the black market. Not unnaturally this aroused jealousy outside the industry. It was estimated that in the spring of 1947 20 per cent of all the textiles available to the Germans in Bizone were going to the miners—a sixtieth of the population receiving one-fifth of the goods. Certainly the measure stimulated a rush of labour

---

[20] Leonhard Miksch was probably the author of this memorandum. See 'Die deutsche Wirtschaftsnot', Der Hauptabteilungsleiter Hauptabteilung B. Planung und Statistik, Minden, 18 June 1947, pp. 10–11. BA Z8 1326.

[21] Dr Ernst Deissmann, director of the *Arbeitsgemeinschaft Kohle*, pointed this out in Aug. 1947. British zonal administration press notice, 8 Aug. 1947, ibid. See also Carlin, *Factor Distribution*, 161. Müller-Armack was particularly critical of 'combing out' labour for coal-mines. In July 1946 he argued that the voluntary commitment to work which only market forces would liberate was far preferable to the direction of labour. A Müller-Armack, 'Die Anfänge der sozialen Marktwirtschaft', in Löwenthal and Schwarz (eds.), *Die zweite Republik*, 138. For extensive discussion of the coal industry in the British zone, see M. Roseman, *Recasting the Ruhr: Manpower, Economic Recovery and Labour Relations in the Ruhr Mines, 1945–58* (Oxford, 1991), and also his chapter on 'The Uncontrolled Economy: Ruhr Coal Production, 1945–8', in I. D. Turner (ed.), *Reconstruction in Post-war Germany*. In both these accounts he effectively documents the complete failure of compulsion to solve the labour problems of the coal-mines.

into the mines. But it did relatively little for per capita productivity. Underground workers were operating at only 60 per cent of 1936 efficiency levels.[22] One reason was that supplies of materials used in mining remained affected by controls and could not be ameliorated by special points for miners. It was not possible to treat one section of the economy in isolation. If incentives were to be introduced, they would have to operate across the board.

In the textile industry also, the control system was more noteworthy for its imposing bureaucratic structure than for its effectiveness in stimulating production. During the Third Reich each industrial sector had been marshalled under Nazi control, so that employers would comply with demands of the state, whilst at the same time dividing up the market between themselves. When the British took over responsibility for economic affairs in their zone, they simply adapted the Nazi system to their own needs. The director of the textile division at the British economic headquarters in Minden was a certain *Geheimrat* Hagemann who had been an official under the Wilhelmine Empire and then the Commissar for Clothing in the Third Reich. At Minden he carried on where he had left off, allocating raw materials to various sections of the industry and planning their production. The rules of distribution were set according to regulations issued in November 1939. Textile-manufacturers associations, which had reappeared rapidly after the war, were involved in this activity. Attempts by the British to prevent them exercising executive functions were explained away by Hagemann as an Anglo-Saxon quirk, which the associations could best deal with by quietly making themselves indispensable.

The only people who really suffered under this cosy arrangement were the consumers. In December 1946 it was estimated that a normal consumer in a Rhineland city would have to wait 200 years to obtain a winter coat if he were male, and 350 years if she were a female.[23] When the British Economics Administration was merged into the bizonal system at Frankfurt in 1947, the officials became even more ambitious and looked forward to establishing a comprehensive plan based on better statistical information than had so far been available to them. At this, even the producers' associations jibbed, pointing out they would be more strictly controlled than they had been during the war. It was not until the arrival of Erhard as director of bizonal economic affairs that such schemes were finally shelved.[24]

[22] Roseman, *Recasting the Ruhr*, 68 [Ch. 2, 'Bringing Home the Bacon'].
[23] A. Drexler, *Planwirtschaft in Westdeutschland, 1945–1948: Ein Fallstudie über die Textilbewirtschaftung in der britischen und Bizone* (Stuttgart, 1985), 112–13.
[24] Ibid. 105–11.

The example of textiles is indeed noteworthy, because it casts doubt on any simplistic suggestion that the alternatives open to Germany in the late 1940s were either a restoration of 'corporatist' capitalism or a benevolent, if slightly cumbersome, system of state planning. If 'corporatism' is taken to mean a system in which producers divide up markets at the expense of the consumer and with the benevolent connivance of the state, the *Zwangswirtschaft* was certainly more 'corporatist' than the liberal alternative. The fact was that corporatism and state controls went quite happily together, as the Nazis had proved. The one type of economic system which was not compatible with corporatism was the competitive market economy.

Apart from the economic irrationality of the *Zwangswirtschaft*, its critics could point to the fact that it was manifestly unjust. Controls were imposed in the name of social justice; their effects were anything but equitable. As the system broke down, so respect for the rule of law and the authority of the state collapsed with it. Gustav Stolper remarked. 'A planned economy of hunger requires a society of saints to whom mortification is a moral aim in itself.'[25]

Leonhard Miksch, who became one of Erhard's most enthusiastic lieutenants in the Frankfurt Economics Administration, reminded his readers in November 1948 just how irrational and how vicious the whole control apparatus had been. Having pointed out that state direction of the German economy had been a Nazi invention, he argued that after the collapse of the Third Reich 'the clever people in Germany' fell to blaming Bismarck, Otto the Great, or even the Nibelungs, but it never occurred to them that the Nazis' economic policy might have something to do with it. On the contrary, that mixture of war economy, deceit, and repression was accepted as socially necessary and worthy of preservation.

People would go on being tyrannized by the labour and accommodation offices, the economics and the food offices, as if these were a suitable breeding-ground for a new German democracy. As true liberals watched aghast at what was happening, 'the word social' (*die soziale Phrase*) excused everything. Nobody bothered about the fact that ration entitlements and prices existed mainly on paper. Soon nobody could live on the rations. Help given in a truly humane spirit by the victor powers could not ease the misery, because it reached the consumer only through the dirty filter of a corrupt rationing-system. Many people

developed an astonishing capacity to evade the powerless regulations and to live well, and indeed extremely well. They bought on the black market, traded

[25] G. Stolper, *German Realities*, 76.

on the black market, drove illegally, and worked illegally. They dodged taxes, bartered, and hoarded. They had good reason to do this, for it positively became an imperative of human existence and self-preservation to evade official regulations. And because that was so, the law fell into deep contempt. . . . The social injustice of this situation was indescribable. Whilst one person grew fat, another starved. As one built up property, another had to sell family souvenirs, household goods, and clothing [*Hausrat und Leibwäsche*]. And all that under the slogan of social justice.

In fact it was a completely unfair and arbitrary system.

For it was not possible to tell who was living well and who was starving by looking for the traditional categories of capitalists, Jews and nobles. The people who had gained everything had no distinguishing features. It was a pure matter of chance whether one person could live by honest work or whether he had to starve, and that it was just Lehmann who was able to enjoy cream cakes on a Sunday, while Schulze[26] could not even provide his children with dry bread.[27]

Miksch's vivid description may have overstated the case, but it reflected the widespread hatred of a control system which was demoralizing the labour-force rather than protecting it.

One other disaster area should be mentioned at this point: the German export market. If West Germany was going to establish a healthy and dynamic economy, it would need to expand its foreign trade. Quite apart from anything else, the very poor levels of nutrition in West Germany caused by food shortages could be overcome only if the Germans were able to import more food. In many urban areas calorific levels were so low that experts did not believe workers could be expected to produce effectively.[28] By 1948 the danger of starvation was over, but demonstrations and strikes over the unacceptably low rations showed that inadequate food-supplies were still a major political issue and were hampering production.[29]

To break the vicious circle, more supplies were needed. Yet the prospects for West Germany's export trade remained remarkably gloomy at the beginning of 1948. Under Allied rule Germany's commerce was rigidly controlled. The French and the Russians successfully milked their zones for vital raw materials or, in the Soviet case, manufactures and machinery. In the Anglo-Saxon zones exports were reduced to a

---

[26] Two very common German names.

[27] L. Miksch, 'Vom Zwang zur Freiheit', in *Wirtschaftsverwaltung* (issued by the Verwaltung für Wirtschaft des Vereinigten Wirtschaftsgebietes, Frankfurt-Hoechst) 11 (Nov. 1948), 3.

[28] J. Gimbel, *The American Occupation of Germany* (Stanford, Calif., 1968), 35, cited in Carlin, 'Economic Reconstruction in Western Germany', 10.

[29] See above, Ch. 5.

trickle, and all sorts of obstacles were put in the way of a successful resumption of German foreign trade.

According to Allied policy directives, the Germans could import only goods essential to maintain a frugal standard of living, and the cost of these imports was to be the first charge on any exports. All German exports had to be paid for in dollars (the 'dollar clause'). The aim of these measures was to ensure that reparations demands did not ruin the British and American zones, and that exports would fund essential imports in such a way that keeping the Germans alive did not become a charge on their occupiers. In this respect the policy did not succeed, since occupation undoubtedly *was* a heavy burden on the British and costly even for the Americans.[30]

The 'dollar clause' may indeed have protected West Germany from grave losses of goods and equipment in the early years of the occupation, but it was believed to be highly damaging by German exporters at the time. It meant that dollar-starved European countries would have little incentive to increase their imports from Germany. Nor was this the only problem in the way of commercial development. The conduct of trade had to go through the Allied Joint Export–Import Agency (JEIA), which inevitably involved bureaucratic delays. Each individual export-contract had to be approved by JEIA. The Allied authorities fixed the prices at which goods could be exported, often at an unattractively high dollar-level. The German exporters, on the other hand, received only the fixed domestic price for their products, paid to them in Reichsmarks, and so had no incentive to export.

The fact that before the summer of 1948 there was no formal dollar exchange-rate for the Reichsmark did not make matters easier. The physical problems facing exporters were also daunting. German businessmen were very limited in their opportunities to travel abroad, and were reliant on the embassies of the Allied occupiers for help, since West Germany had no foreign representation. Importers of German goods had to pay for them in advance. There were awkward problems in some belligerent countries over possible claims to German property, so that imported German products might be in danger of confiscation. It was hardly a situation to encourage dynamic exporters.[31]

This did not mean that the Allied authorities were necessarily opposed to German exports. Since 1946 the British had been eager to promote them in order to earn dollars to offset the high cost of feeding their zone with American wheat. Without flexibility and economic

[30] Buchheim, *Die Wiedereingliederung Westdeutschlands*, 9–14 and 24–30.
[31] Ibid. 22–31.

incentives, however, German industry was unlikely to achieve even the relatively modest British hopes for its export performance. In the autumn of 1947, the authorities in Bizone did admit that incentives for exporters were necessary, and took the extraordinary step of offering them a foreign-exchange premium of 5 per cent of the export price of their products. This could be used to pay for imported consumer goods—unobtainable under normal circumstances—which could be distributed amongst the firms' workers.[32] Such a measure was obviously unjust to workers in other industries, but it illustrated the problems of creating incentives in a society where money wages were so worthless they had to be supplemented by payments in kind from factory production.

In August 1947 one of the advisers to General Clay, the American military governor, wrote that 'the bizonal economy is being controlled to death'. He advised that, since no German administration existed with enough competence to take strong measures, the Anglo-American authorities should simply abolish price and wage controls and allow the free-price mechanism to operate.[33] Even Clay found this too radical a step to take. It needed a German administration to grasp the nettle of abolishing controls. It was the task of informing that administration and stiffening its resolve which fell to the neo-liberal economists in West Germany in the early months of 1948.

Whatever progress was being made by the neo-liberals in propagating their ideas, it is important to remember that the situation still looked very gloomy at the end of 1947. Indeed, the twelve months between the announcement of the Marshall Plan in June 1947 and the implementation of currency reform can hardly be described as a period of optimism in Germany. The Marshall Plan itself was not necessarily intended as a basis for West German independence. Only in the autumn of 1947 was it announced that Germany could receive Marshall Aid, and this concession was promptly nullified in German eyes by the Allied publication of a further list of industrial plants which were going to be dismantled. Allied ambivalence about Germany's economic future was also expressed in four-power negotiations which dragged on until December 1947, and which kept open the possibility of inter-Allied harmony being achieved at the expense of German interests.[34]

---

[32] Ibid. 58.

[33] Krieger, *General Lucius D. Clay*, 377–8.

[34] For the argument which has raged amongst historians ever since about the intentions of the occupying powers towards Germany and the part played in West Germany's rehabilitation by the Marshall Plan, see H.-J. Schröder (ed.), *Marshallplan und westdeutscher Wiederaufstieg: Positionen—Kontroversen* (Stuttgart, 1990). For a recent American view, see

Despite measures to strengthen the institutions of Bizone in a fashion which clearly implied moves towards economic independence, few German men and women had much cause to rejoice at New Year 1948. In January and February there were street demonstrations against food shortages, and when, in Bavaria, the trade unions called for a protest strike, a million workers downed tools.[35] In some ways the autumn and winter of 1947 saw morale in West Germany sag to its lowest point.

It was in this troubled climate of opinion that Wilhelm Röpke paid his first visit to Germany since his enforced exile in 1933. He was struck by the pessimism and lassitude which characterized his countrymen's attitude towards the economy, an aspect of post-war German life he evidently found as disturbing as the material destruction. Speaking to an audience in his former homeland in Lower Saxony, he tried to explain how German affairs looked to an observer in Switzerland. He took issue with the Germans for seeking salvation in socialism. Socialization, which many seemed to see as something modern and desirable, was simply a dangerous irrelevance: 'The striving for socialization appears today in Europe like an epidemic which flares up here and there, and then dies away again after the disillusionment which quickly sets in.'[36]

The real problem with modern industry was concentration of power. Yet socialization would increase that concentration and vest it in the state. It was hardly logical to solve problems of concentration by creating hyper-concentration.

Considering the economic plight of Germany, Röpke distinguished between the damage caused by the war and the fourteen years of plunder and 'vampire economy' of the totalitarian system under Hitler, and the damage caused by the fact that the remaining productive forces were not being deployed effectively. Germans did not clearly understand how badly they were impoverished, because of convenient fictions which they tended to accept. For example, people still behaved as though they had incomes. In reality they did not. They also behaved as if there were capital funds available in Germany, and low interest-rates seemed to imply a flourishing capital market. This fictional situ-

Hogan, *The Marshall Plan*. For British policy towards Germany, see A. Deighton, *The Impossible Peace: Britain, the Division of Germany, and the Origins of the Cold War* (Oxford, 1990), and the same author's 'Cold War Diplomacy: British Policy Towards Germany's Role in Europe, 1945–9', in I. D. Turner (ed.), *Reconstruction in Post-war Germany*, 15–34.

[35] Benz, *Besatzungsherrschaft*, 92–3.
[36] W. Röpke, 'Diagnose und Heilung der deutschen Wirtschaftslähmung', in *Wilhelm Röpke: Wort und Wirkung. 16 Reden aus den Jahren 1947–64*, ed. W. Hoch (Ludwigsburg, 1964), 158.

ation made it easy for people to overlook the true cause of their poverty, namely the collectivist experiments of the Nazi period and its aftermath. Röpke argued that one had to choose between socialist and free-market methods of economic organization, and that the worst thing of all was to have neither the one nor the other, when no real system (*Ordnung*) existed and they were left with chaos or anarchy.[37]

Many people believed this could all be put right by currency reform, although some said it would need large imports of raw materials to make it work. Röpke did not disagree with the latter assertion, but argued that much more was required, namely a recognition that Germany was suffering from suppressed inflation which had to be cured. Planning and 'cheap money' would have to be eliminated before Germany's economy could recover. The real problem here was not the currency itself but the fact that prices did not fulfil their proper function as indicators of scarcity. It would be possible to reintroduce market principles without reforming the currency. This would mean that prices would rise rapidly, but they would at least become real prices. This would restore the will to work that one could see, for example, in Italy, where an open inflation was not inhibiting diligent reconstruction.[38] Suppressed inflation, on the other hand, could lead to the destruction of the entire economy.

Röpke made it clear that, although he and those who thought like him inside and outside Germany had believed it necessary to combine currency reform with certain controls, he had come to the conclusion that the only solution lay in the liberation of economic life by the abolition of those controls. He even went so far as to demand the end of foreign-exchange restrictions, in order to eliminate what he called the 'rouble phenomenon' in Germany, by which he meant the impossibility of finding a real exchange-rate relationship between the German Reichsmark and foreign currency. A modern economy simply could not do without the steering mechanisms of competition and free prices. It was a great pity that the Germans always seemed to fall back on the outdated concept of socialization when trying to solve their problems.

He told his audience that with the Marshall Plan the Americans were fulfilling the role of blood-donors to a sick Europe, but they were not going to give blood if it did not lead to a constructive result. He foresaw three solutions: the Molotov solution, which simply meant giving a blank cheque to the recipients; the Bevin solution, which involved an international plan to tackle the problem but did not deal with

---

[37] Ibid. 167.   [38] Ibid. 172.

its domestic aspects; and Röpke's own conception that 'charity begins at home', meaning that each nation should cure its own economy. The cure would clearly involve a return to sound money and free prices. He ended the lecture with a reference to the Eastern part of Germany. The best they could do about that problem, he argued, was that they should:

create in Western Europe once again a core area of economic, moral, and political health and that we rely on the radiance and impact of this area, that we present an example which it will be difficult to withstand—an example of what the principles of the West, the Occident, are able to achieve; the principles of freedom of respect for the individual, of justice and reason.[39]

This was a view to be championed in subsequent years by Konrad Adenauer. It was often very unpopular. But events were to prove its wisdom.

Röpke's own influence was beneficial, but as an exile his effectiveness was necessarily limited. It was up to those German experts who had direct access to the decision-making processes in Frankfurt to ensure that rational economic theories were not only disseminated, but acted upon by those in power. In the next chapter we shall describe the major effort in that direction which occurred in the early months of 1948.

[39] Ibid. 176.

9

Theory into Practice:
The Struggle over Policy, 1948

BY the summer of 1947 the development of a unified administration for Bizone—the fusion of the British and American zones—was far advanced. As we have seen above, the southern German political leaders were able to prevent a Social Democrat being given the directorship of the bizonal economic administration, and they also demanded that its headquarters should be in Frankfurt. So its first chairman was a Liberal from Hesse, Rudolf Mueller. He was a moderate man who gained the confidence of the Minden staff, despite his scepticism about the value of state control.[1] In January 1947, however, pressures from Kurt Schumacher and the SPD led to his forced resignation and his replacement by Viktor Agartz, the chief Social Democratic economic specialist in the British zone, and an enthusiast for a planned economy. This affair left a bad impression among both officials and non-socialist politicians in Western Germany—even some of the SPD figures involved were ashamed of it.[2]

Later in the same year measures were taken to further the integration of the Anglo-American zones and establish an Economic Council at Frankfurt, which was itself the administrative centre of the American zone. The council would be a sort of administrative parliament for Bizone. The balance of power in this body was shaded against the Social Democrats, and their CDU/CSU and Liberal opponents were not inclined to show them any indulgence when it came to electing the new and more powerful heads of the administrations which were to operate in Frankfurt. After an acrimonious debate in the Economic Council on 22 July 1947, the Bavarian Christian Social politician Johannes Semler was elected to run the Economics Administration. He announced himself as a disciple of the free market, and since he was an accountant, whose father had been a Hamburg Reichstag deputy for Stresemann's

[1] Interview with Hans Möller in Munich, 14 Sept. 184. For Rudolf Mueller's appointment, see above, Ch. 7.

[2] See the account in Benz, *Besatzungsherrschaft*, 46–9. There is an interesting memorandum on this incident written by Mueller under the title 'Minden und die SPD' in the Strauß Papers, IfZG ED 94, vol. 59. The move to Frankfurt took longer than originally foreseen.

DVP, this seemed entirely probable.[3] He urged the dismantling of controls dating from the Nazi period and wanted the reduction of crippling bureaucratization for the benefit of 'an automatically functioning free economy'.[4]

However, Semler, a founder-member of the CSU, was more of a politician and a manager than a professional economist. He could not ignore the fact that most of his staff in the new Economics Administration to be established at Frankfurt would be drawn from the old Minden office, in the British zone, with its strongly *dirigiste* inclinations. In his report to the Economic Council on 5 September 1947, Semler paid tribute to the officials of the Minden headquarters with whom he had been working in preparation for the move to their new base at Frankfurt-Hoechst. Although he was unable to resist mentioning the fact that the Minden administration did not enjoy a good reputation with the public, there was no suggestion that any major change in policy would be associated with the move to Frankfurt. Indeed, he made it clear that the staff in Minden would form the backbone of the new administration, even if not all of them could be found employment in it.[5]

Semler's chief anxieties lay in the continuing Allied programme of industrial dismantling and the need to get West Germany through the coming winter without starvation. Allied views had been communicated to the Economic Council on 12 July 1947 in 'principles of economic policy'.[6]

These stressed the need for priority to be given to basic industries (*Grundstoffindustrien*) such as coal, transport, and energy, as well as food production. The Allies further demanded a steady rise in exports. Semler did point out that the German people could not be expected to meet these requirements without some small amelioration in their living conditions. Hunger and cold awaited the Germans in the winter. He certainly did not deny that: 'we must consciously give up the possibility of raising our people's living standards by increasing consumer-goods production'.[7]

He spoke of the need to reconstruct the system of economic control and to give it more elasticity. To do this, they would have to get rid of damaging encumbrances taken over from the Nazi war-economy. Yet

[3] Benz, *Besatzungsherrschaft*, 68.
[4] Ibid. 86, citing article, 'Vor einer tragischen Situation', *Süddeutscher Zeitung*, 16 Aug. 1947.
[5] 'Bericht des Direktors der Verwaltung für Wirtschaft Dr J. Semler, vorgetragen in der Sitzung des Wirtschaftsrates', 5. Sept. 1947, BA Z8 1325, pp. 24–6.
[6] Ibid., p. 5.
[7] Ibid., p. 6.

his words were cautious rather than optimistic. He spoke of the need to proceed step by step to avoid creating hardships in particular areas. Even when the goal was reached, it was not to be that of a free-market economy. Semler hoped only to give the economy 'a certain freedom and to accord the customer the opportunity of choosing in most cases his own supplier'.[8]

This was to be done through the complex mechanism known as 'final-consumer allocation' (*Endverbraucherkontingentierung*), the controversy surrounding which will be mentioned again later in this chapter. Lastly he commented on the problem of hoarding, which was a constant headache for the authorities. Once again, he denied the possibility of root-and-branch reform, but indicated that further measures would be prepared in the coming months in conjunction with the *Länder*—a clear indication that he was thinking in terms of punitive action rather than a change in economic policy.

, In the winter of 1947–8, therefore, the Economics Administration of the Bizone was working towards a system of improved planning and resource allocation, combined with the long-awaited currency reform. Although it was hoped that this would be more flexible and at the same time more consistently applied throughout West Germany, it certainly did not amount to the liberalization being demanded by neo-liberals such as Walter Eucken or Wilhelm Röpke.

Of course, the officials in the administration did not see themselves creating a centrally directed economy along the lines of that being established in the Soviet Union. Not even hard-line Social Democrats such as Agartz or Nölting favoured that, although the practical differences between their schemes and those of a *Zentralverwaltungswirtschaft* were not always easy to detect. Similarly, free-market enthusiasts were far from demanding a return to *laissez-faire*. The real conflict of opinion was between those who felt that the price mechanism must be reintroduced into Germany as quickly as possible as a means of distribution, and those who thought it must be severely limited in its applications so as to fulfil social and economic priorities which the market could not be expected to accomplish by itself.

Of crucial importance was the fact that, both inside and outside the administration, the supporters of liberalism could make their views known, and that the combination of academic pressure and administrative support proved enough to overcome opposition. The civil servant at the head of the administration, Walter Strauß, was a cautious liberalizer. He had worked in the Reich Economics Ministry in the

---

[8] Ibid., pp. 11–12.

Weimar Republic, where he had been involved in drawing up legislation on cartels. The anti-cartel aspect of neo-liberal theories certainly appealed to him, and he was acquainted with the work of Lampe and Böhm. A former member of the Berlin CDU, Strauß had shown an interest in theories of Christian Socialism after 1945. Although he was no friend of totalitarian planning, he was certainly not an adherent of *laissez-faire*.[9] Furthermore, Strauß himself was not a product of the Minden office, which contained the most zealous *dirigistes*.

One of the most enthusiastic and conscientious advocates of controls was Dr Günter Keiser, head of the planning department in Minden. In the 1920s he had evidently sympathized with those urging a compromise between socialism and the market economy. Later on, as we have seen, he was impressed by Nazi success in creating constant growth with apparently stable prices. An energetic and idealistic man, he nevertheless epitomized the type of official thinking to which liberal economists were opposed.[10] Keiser was not, however, a dogmatic person. He welcomed the cut and thrust of economic argument, and when the administration moved to Frankfurt, he suggested to Strauß that Hans Möller, an economist working for the government of Württemberg-Baden, should be brought in to strengthen the team. Keiser had worked with Möller before and knew that he was sympathetic to the liberal standpoint; it may even be that he thought Möller would be a useful foil upon which he could sharpen his own more *dirigiste* ideas before presenting them to the administration.[11]

Möller's appointment was to be of considerable importance because, before accepting Strauß's invitation to move from Stuttgart, he stipulated that he would be willing to work in the bizonal administration only if it were assisted by an advisory board (*Beirat*) of academic economists who could address themselves to the issues of the day unencumbered by administrative or political pressures. This suggestion was, as Möller well knew, attractive to Strauß. When the latter had been an official in the Reich Economics Ministry during the Weimar Republic, he had found the lack of contacts between administrators and academic economists a serious disadvantage.[12]

[9] Information on Strauß in the index to his papers, IfZG ED 94.

[10] See above, Ch. 7.

[11] This thought was expressed to me by Prof. Möller when I spoke to him on 14 Sept. 1984. Like all other contemporaries I met, he spoke of Dr Keiser with personal warmth.

[12] When Strauß met Möller by chance on a train to Berlin shortly after the end of the war, Strauß had lamented the lack of contact between officials in the Reich Economics Ministry and the academic world. Strauß himself had been purged by the Nazis for being 'racially' Jewish and had been forced to work in a munitions factory until Hitler's death. Möller interview, 14 Sept. 1984.

Möller may well have hoped to use such an advisory board as a means of pressing for a more liberal policy, but at the same time it could be attractive to the administration generally. Whatever course of action was followed, it was clear that some fairly drastic measures would be needed to rectify Germany's economic ills. The imprimatur of an 'objective' academic body would be very useful in this respect. Just as important was the need to impress the Allies and foreign opinion with the advisability of treating West Germany less harshly than had hitherto been the case. In particular, shortages of food and raw materials could be met only by generous foreign credits. Semler evidently hoped that weighty comments by a board of internationally respected academics would also help his administration on this front.[13]

Planning certainly seemed the leitmotiv of the administration in the autumn of 1947. On 13 October one senior official, Dr Meinhold, sent out a memorandum urging that a plan be drawn up for the year 1948.[14] He noted that, since February 1947, the bizonal authorities had refused to produce any such plan, and that this had perhaps been just as well in view of the catastrophic situation. Nevertheless, it was necessary to set objectives to be aimed at in various areas of production. There should be six individual plans: for coal, steel, agriculture, transport, energy, and exports. Once these had been worked out, they should be conflated into a comprehensive overall plan. A special planning committee was set up at which detailed schemes for bizonal economic activity were thrashed out. At the end of January 1948, for example, Meinhold told the committee that the offer of Marshall Aid funds made it an urgent necessity to draw up a recommended plan for the Bizone.[15]

The committee also considered the standardization of methods used when licensing industrial enterprises. Meinhold argued that they must make clear what economic considerations should govern licensing decisions. 'Here', he claimed, 'there is a serious task for planning at a regional and central level, and this must be systematically analysed and defined.'

Keiser also played a prominent part in the work of this committee. He told the same meeting that the system of virtually total economic control which had been developed during the war was experiencing a domestic crisis. 'On the other hand,' he went on, 'it is still a completely

---

[13] See Semler's comments and reported views at the first meeting of the *Wissenschaftlicher Beirat*, below, pp. 186–7.

[14] See 'Rundschreiben Hauptabteilung B, Planung und Statistik, Mai 1947–Juli 1948'. Economics Administration files, BA Z8 1326.

[15] Report on the meeting of the *Sonderausschuß Planung bei der VfW*, 29 and 30 Jan. 1948, ibid., fos. 38–40.

open question what economic system is best suited to the present economic and political circumstances, and there is also no decision about what tasks should be fulfilled by planning, either from the long-term viewpoint or in the concrete question of economic control.'

As reform of the currency approached, so it became more urgent to get the basic issues of principle sorted out. Remembering that Keiser had been an enthusiastic observer of the command economy in action in 1939, there was little doubt which sort of option he himself would favour. He was, in any case, personally responsible for the vital sector of coal planning. In a report to the committee on that issue he stated: 'Coal distribution is today the decisive instrument in the direction of the economy [*Wirtschaftslenkung*]. In order to fulfil this task it must be centrally organized by experts [*fachlich-zentral*].'[16]

Needless to say, this view did not command approval amongst the *Länder* governments, especially those in the American zone. Yet the type of agenda presented to the officials in Frankfurt presupposed that economic control of some sort would be likely for a long time to come. It was also true that the granting of Marshall Aid to West Germany would stimulate planning discussions, since it was evident that the Americans would require a clearly worked-out set of economic objectives before they would part with their money. The question of future planning also loomed large on the bureaucratic horizon early in 1948, for the legalistic reason that Nazi ordinances or economic controls which had been taken over by the Allies were due to run out at the end of June.[17]

As far as the planners were concerned, therefore, there was good reason to suppose that they could continue to exercise great influence over the economic policies of the country. So serious were the shortages and bottle-necks in production that a rapid return to a reliance on market forces seemed out of the question. It would, however, be necessary to present an acceptable alternative to the price mechanism. This had, indeed, been developed, albeit somewhat clumsily, by a number of economists who sought a form of planning suitable to an advanced, non-Communist Western Society. It was to be found in various schemes being considered for the division of the market into free and controlled areas—what was known as the *Marktspaltung* solution—and the concept of 'final-consumer allocation', which would preserve the administration's control over food and raw materials but allow the consumer to choose between competing producers who

---

[16] Ibid., fos. 39–40.
[17] Report on VfW, Hauptabteilungsleiterbesprechung, 20 Mar. 1948, BA Z8 95.

would process his allocation of the products required. Keiser was very interested in these possibilities, and he enjoyed support from academics like Wilhelm Kromphardt, the Professor of Economics in Hanover, as well as more clearly committed Social Democrats like Gerhard Weisser or Karl Schiller in Hamburg. As we have seen, even some convinced exponents of the free market, like Müller-Armack, accepted the need for a transition phase during which *Marktspaltung* could be operated.

On the other hand, there were those inside the administration who favoured a far more radical attitude to the regulated economy. Whilst accepting that controls could not be eliminated altogether, they favoured what became known as the 'leap into cold water' (*Sprung ins kalte Wasser*), whereby currency reform would have to be associated with drastic measures to decontrol industry and leave market forces to fix prices in as many areas as possible. The most powerful voice in this group belonged to the deputy director of the economics section of the Minden administration, who was, of course, Leonhard Miksch. He was by no means an isolated figure. Heinrich Rittershausen, a specialist in banking theory who later became Professor of Economics at Cologne, was also employed at this time in the Economics Administration and clearly disapproved of the directed economy.

Then there was the staff of the new body established on the German side to influence Allied thinking about currency reform. This was the *Sonderstelle Geld und Kredit* (Special Bureau for Monetary and Currency Matters) at Bad Homburg, which had been deliberating since October 1947 under the leadership of Ludwig Erhard.[18] Clearly Erhard's influence would be put on the side of market forces. Möller was one of his younger appointees, and a more senior expert, Curt Fischer, was a former pupil of Walter Eucken. When, in the spring of 1948, Fischer published the draft law for the reform of the German currency which had been drawn up in the *Sonderstelle*, he made the following comments about Germany's economic situation: 'As the result of inflation and frozen prices, our modern economy, with its division of labour, has regressed into that of a medieval society based on barter.' Even if, as all German economists devoutly hoped, the worthless German currency were to be reformed, that alone would not automatically cure the country's ills: 'One should resist the dangerous illusion that currency reform as an isolated measure can bring about economic miracles. The

---

[18] See the discussion of the *Sonderstelle* in the finance committee of the bizonal *Beirat*, 30 Sept. 1947, at which Pferdemenges expressed fears over Allied policy, BA Z4 9. For details of Erhard's leadership of the *Sonderstelle*, see Ch. 7.

currency reform may be seen only as the first step towards the solution of the central and multi-faceted task of giving our economy a new order.'[19]

When he spoke of a 'new order' Fischer was clearly hoping for the restoration of open competition and the free-price mechanism.

It should not be thought, however, that the conflict in 1948 was simply between convinced exponents of *laissez-faire* capitalism on the one hand, and determined socializers on the other. Both extremes had been so discredited by the events of the previous two decades that they commanded little support. As Walter Eucken wrote to Meinhold in 1950, looking back over the arguments of the previous three years:

The argument today is not at all that between *laissez-faire* and economic planning. It is not a matter of conflict about whether the state should interfere only a little or somewhat more. Actually the defenders of *laissez-faire* have completely disappeared. The conflict is a different one. One side, to which I belong, is of the opinion that the state must influence, or even directly establish, the forms and institutional framework within which the economy must work. It should, however, avoid the attempt to steer directly the everyday business of the economy. Others believe that the state must not just establish the framework, but must influence the day-to-day working of the economy on the basis of central planning.[20]

This conflict of views so ably summarized by Eucken did indeed come to a head during the early months of 1948. Perhaps the most important forum in which it was hammered out was the newly created academic advisory council (*Beirat*) of the Economics Administration.[21] As mentioned above, the intention of Semler in establishing such a body may have been to use the 'objective' views of internationally respected economists to reinforce his pleas for more generous treatment from the Allies. Nevertheless, there was bound to be a division amongst the experts chosen about the fundamental principles of a future German economic policy. It was therefore not unimportant that the task of drawing up the list of economists to be selected fell to Hans Möller, whose enthusiasm for the idea had chimed in so well with that of Dr Strauß. Möller chose most of the invitees himself, and jokingly put code letters against them: 'L' for liberal, 'LL' for extremely liberal,

[19] C. Fischer, *Entwurf eines Gesetzes*, 61. In Oct. 1948 Fischer sent a copy of this to Eucken, with a personal dedication, and Eucken refers to the book in his London lecture of 1950. WEI Eucken NL.

[20] Eucken to Meinhold, 15 Feb. 1950, discussing the historical introduction to the publication of the collected memoranda of the *Wissenschaftlicher Beirat* of the VfW, BA ZA B102 12560.

[21] *Wissenschaftlicher Beirat bei der Verwaltung für Wirtschaft*. The correct translation would be 'scientific advisory council', since in Germany, as in other civilized countries, 'science' describes all forms of scholarship.

and 'P' for planned economy. Dr Strauß suggested a few names, mostly from the Christian side, since he had close links with the Protestant Church. Möller and Strauß were careful to work for a balance between opposing views, but it is fair to say that, if anything, the scales in the first *Beirat* were weighted more heavily on the side of market economics than on that of planning.

The first list of those invited included Eucken himself, Franz Böhm, Adolf Lampe, and Erwin von Beckerath. On the side of the planners stood Gerhard Weisser and Karl Schiller, with men like Müller-Armack and Wilhelm Kromphardt occupying a middle position, although Kromphardt was certainly more inclined towards the maintenance of controls. A fourth tendency might be decribed as presenting market economics with a Christian conscience, its clearest representative being Oswald Nell-Breuning. It had been decided that the deliberations of the advisory council should also be attended by the professionally trained economists working for the Economics Administration, as well as the heads of departments which were directly responsible for organizing the business of the *Beirat*. The inaugural meeting was held in Königstein on 23 and 24 January 1948. As its first task the *Beirat* was asked to consider how far the direction of the economy (*Bewirtschaftung*) would be needed after currency reform.[22] The meeting was important, not because the deliberations of academics would necessarily be received with great deference by the officials in the administration, but because the *Beirat* proceedings were a forum within which the different views inside the administration itself could be formulated and subjected to critical scrutiny.

When the first meeting of the *Beirat* assembled in Königstein on 23 January, the administration was strongly represented at its deliberations: Strauß, Keiser, Miksch, Möller, Meinhold, and Rittershausen all took part.[23] Semler himself opened the proceedings by pointing out that both the preconditions for a currency reform and the policies to be adopted thereafter were under consideration.

We are all devoting ourselves to questions such as 'Where is our economy going?' To what extent can it work by itself and to what extent must it be provided for by state economic administration? To what extent can the economy operate alone in the interests of the population at large and to what extent is

[22] VfW, Strauß to Hauptabteilungsleiter, 6 Feb. 1948, BA Z8 95 18.
[23] 'Bericht über die erste Sitzung des Wiss. Beirates bei der Verwaltung für Wirtschaft', 23/24 Jan. 1948 (hereafter 'Beirat'), Möller Papers. I am indebted to Prof. Möller for letting me see this material. See also the collection of recommendations of the *Beirat* published with a historical introduction: Bundeswirtschaftsministerium (ed.), *Der Wissenschaftliche Beirat bei der Verwaltung des Vereinigten Wirtschaftsgebiets, Gutachten 1948 bis Mai 1950* (Göttingen, n.d.).

the state and administration forced, for its part, to undertake the direction of the economy? To what extent in the future will it be necessary, as the result of fundamental considerations of principle, to reform the relationship of the state to the individual . . . ?[24]

He stressed the importance of psychological factors in the future development of the economy. It was noteworthy that Semler himself offered no real guide-lines to the assembled company; his speech seemed to leave all options open. Later in the meeting, Semler asked what would happen if everything was left to the laws of supply and demand? If they decided that, what measures would be needed to keep the price structure under control? Rittershausen also reported at one point that Semler wanted answers about controls so that he could say rationing and other unpopular measures would have to be maintained, at least until after the currency reform, and that it would help him greatly to have the authoritative support of professional economists for such politically unpalatable decisions. It therefore seems not unreasonable to suppose that Semler's aim was to provide himself with a protective shield behind which he could continue some form of controlled economy, modified no doubt by the effects of the currency reform when it occurred.[25]

Whatever Semler's intentions may have been, they were of comparatively little importance, because he was about to lose his job. As he himself told the conference, he had aroused the ire of the Allied authorities with some comments which were sharply critical of the occupying powers. This was the famous 'chicken-feed' speech made in Erlangen on 4 January at a meeting of CSU leaders, including the Bavarian Prime Minister. Semler had evidently not expected his plain speaking would be reported. He was also perhaps unfortunate that a contemptuous reference to grain fodder from the USA was literally translated as 'chicken-feed'—a term unlikely to be appreciated in Washington. Nevertheless, his intemperate and insulting attacks on all the Allies for their supposed economic exploitation of Germany could not go unpunished. He was dismissed by the Allied military governors on 24 January, the day the first working meeting of the *Beirat* began.[26]

Semler's dismissal coincided with another reorganization of the bizonal institutions, designed to strengthen their representative character. This followed the breakdown of the London foreign ministers' conference earlier in the month and the recognition by the Western

[24] 'Beirat', pp. 5–6.
[25] Ibid., pp. 48–9.
[26] Cf. Gimbel, *The American Occupation of Germany*, 192, n. 11. See also Benz, *Besatzungsherrschaft*, 86.

powers that agreement with the Soviet Union was impossible. Owing to this major reorganization, it was not until the beginning of March that Ludwig Erhard was elected as Semler's successor.

In the meantime, the arguments about the fundamental principles of economic policy continued to rage within the administration. They were formulated with great precision at the meetings of the *Beirat*, and in particular at its inaugural gatherings on 23 and 24 January 1948. The first point, on which all participants seemed agreed, was that the existing system of controls was chaotic and in the process of breaking down. Möller began the discussion by pointing out that 'We have no coherent system of controls. There is no legal basis for such a system.'[27] Statistics were not uniform either, although the authorities were attempting to rectify that problem. Rittershausen, in a statement about pricing policy, claimed that: 'The pricing system we have has come down to us from 1936. Until 1945 it was adjusted (upwards) by about 40 or 50 per cent. Since 1945 it has been further adjusted by an amount which on average has been 20 per cent of the original price level'.[28]

In fact, it was impossible to tell what 'real' prices were. To take the case of wood, there had been a serious shortage of this for years, but the price had only once been increased—by 20 per cent in 1946. Nobody had any idea whether this was the right sort of increase or whether the price should have risen by 200 per cent, 250 per cent, or 600 per cent. The fact that everybody was expecting currency reform did not make matters easier, nor did the lack of a real exchange-rate for the Reichsmark. The justification for the pricing policy since the end of the war had been that it was a temporary measure to prevent social disturbances, general strikes, and similar dangers. Rittershausen made somewhat unflattering references to the New Deal in the United States, which he evidently saw as comparable with the totalitarian system in Germany, and pointed out that American officials in Frankfurt were often 'New Dealers'. In his view, any attempt to build the existing price-arrangements into the new parliamentary system at Frankfurt would be 'an almost unrealizable work of art' (*ein kaum zu leistendes Kunststück*). The British, for whose zonal officials he seemed to have considerable respect, would oppose such a solution with powerful arguments. He ended his remarks with a rhetorical flourish:

Only if it is possible in the future to be confident that there can in all circumstances be a method of controlling monopolies and overmighty economic forces [*wirtschaftliche Vormachtstellungen*], will we be able to find a basis upon which to unite all parties in Germany. With this basis, one could find a

---

[27] 'Beirat', pp. 8–9.   [28] Ibid., pp. 9–10.

common platform upon which the powers of democratic price-fixing agencies could be established.[29]

It will be noted that Rittershausen was not proposing the abolition of price-fixing, although he stressed the artificiality of contemporary prices. It is also significant that he saw limitations on the powers of monopolies or other economically powerful sections of society as the prerequisite for a return to the market economy. This was symptomatic of the atmosphere created by two decades of economic disaster and social tension. Professor Lampe, for example, argued that the old idea of an ideological contradiction between liberalism and socialism belonged on the scrap-heap. The question at issue was ultimately the form of society and economic order they were seeking to create, and the freedom of the individual (*Persönlichkeit*) within that society. Without personal freedom there could be no such economic order.[30]

It was then that Eucken entered the discussion, shifting the emphasis decisively in the direction of free prices. He evidently felt that too much was being expected from the *Beirat* at this stage. A new social order was too ambitious; the important thing was to return to a sensible form of market economy. The problem was that no effective steering mechanism (*Lenkungsmechanismus*) existed for economic activity, because the existing price-structure was senseless. As a result, barter transactions were taking place, and a regression to antiquated forms of small-scale production: 'These are all quite appallingly primitive phenomena due to the fact that the steering mechanism of the economy is not working'.[31]

There was no way of increasing production until this had been put right. If one took the case of timber, cited earlier by Rittershausen, one could understand how difficult the matter was. There were different sorts of timber. Beechwood, for example, was being used in an extraordinarily varied number of ways and it would be quite impossible to price this in relation to other types of timber. Experts agreed that such pricing would have to be left to the market.

The currency reform ought not just to reduce surplus purchasing-power and make the control system work a little better so that a new set of fixed prices could be promulgated. The real cure was the free-price mechanism. However, this could be achieved only if the Allies played their part by providing credits for imported goods. Otherwise, the shortages would be too great, despite the liberating effect of free prices, and the public would lose confidence in the new currency.

---

[29] Ibid., pp. 10–12.   [30] Ibid., p. 13.
[31] Ibid., pp. 16–17.

Germany must also have access to the import-export market. Despite all the difficulties that he foresaw, Eucken came down firmly in favour of reducing controls to the minimum possible and allowing the free-price system to operate. His views were echoed in varying degrees by other academics, like Hoffmann of Münster and Wessels of Cologne.

Yet the case for *dirigisme* did not go by default. Keiser himself produced a powerful counterblast against the liberalizing trend. The administration, he pointed out, had to deal with facts, not theories. One fact was that the occupying powers operated on the basis of plans and would expect the Germans to do likewise. The Marshall scheme would mean that even more planning was needed. Congress was not going to hand over $600 million, tell the Germans they could set up a free market, and let them use the money any way they liked: 'We will not get a single dollar from over there if we don't specify at the outset what we are going to do with it.'[32]

There could be no question of liberalizing foreign exchange, which was strictly controlled throughout Western Europe.

Keiser also stressed the dangers which might arise within Germany as the result of currency reform. This could lead to renewed inflation, or to deflation and unemployment. He reminded the *Beirat* that in 1923, at the end of the great inflation, there had been 5.5 million unemployed. The poor physical state of German workers and production levels, which were only half those of 1936, were also facts to be reckoned with: 'As long as we have to reckon with these circumstances, the market mechanism cannot function.'

Other economic bogies were enthusiastically paraded before the meeting. The shortage of housing was restricting the free movement of labour. Under a free-price system, prices for consumer goods would rise more immediately than others and it was precisely those goods which presented serious problems in regard to raw materials. Shoes and textiles were examples of such 'problem' products. The economy possessed many bottle-necks which would at once become acute the moment production rose: 'If there were free disposition over funds generated by a free-price mechanism,' argued Keiser, 'there would scarcely be any money available for investment except by means of increasing credit.'

No sooner had one voice spoken out from within the administration in favour of planning, however, than another, that of Leonhard Miksch, burst forth against it. Nobody could tell, he argued, how much importance to attach to undernourishment and problems like

---

[32] Ibid., pp. 22–3.

housing shortages until the market had reappeared: 'It is completely out of the question to present such immobility factors [*Starrheitsfaktoren*] as absolute limitations. It is precisely by reactivating the market that we shall once again be able to inject mobility into this stagnant situation.'[33]

Miksch claimed that the purpose of currency reform had changed since 1945. Then, it would simply have been a matter of soaking up excess purchasing-power. Now, the issue was the resuscitation of the West European economy: 'The currency reform will already be a total failure if the controlled economy has to be kept going after the reform has taken place.'

On this note the first session of the conference ended and the participants had a chance to consult informally. It was not without significance that on the resumption, Franz Böhm was elected chairman of the proceedings. A clearer signal could not have been given that the sense of the meeting was inclined towards free competition.[34] When the discussion was resumed, Müller-Armack weighed in to support Eucken's views on restoring the price mechanism. He also criticized Keiser's objections about bottle-necks which would inhibit the restoration of the market. Drawing on his own detailed knowledge of the textile industry, Müller-Armack was able to claim that many of the blockages and bottle-necks were caused by market distortions resulting from controls.[35] They could be eased by reasserting market forces and adapting to them. For example, there could be double-shift working and price adjustments which would increase production. The same was true of the coal industry, of which he had first-hand experience. He was engaged in a commission of inquiry into the pricing-system for energy supplies in the Ruhr, and there, too, it was clear that a return to the maximum possible price-elasticity should be carried out as soon as it could be done. Indeed, by reducing the burden of subventions to the coal industry, they could facilitate the success of currency reform.

Nevertheless, Müller-Armack remained cautious about the timing of the liberalization. There would have to be a period of transition and they ought really to be discussing what arrangements should be made for that. He suggested a system of divided markets, freeing some proportion of all production from restrictions rather than allowing particular sections of the economy to find their own price level.

Rittershausen then chipped in to say that statistics actually overestimated German production when they seemed to show it at 50 per cent of the 1936 level. Real wages could not be driven down further by returning to the free-price mechanism, since those wages were already

---

[33] Ibid., p. 24.   [34] Ibid., pp. 25–6.   [35] Ibid., p. 27.

at rock bottom. He claimed to have been told by an American that German wage levels were 'lower than those of coolies'.[36]

Keiser, however, was not without his defenders. The most determined among them was Gerhard Weisser. He began his remarks by referring to the informal discussions he had enjoyed before the war with liberal economists in Tübingen and Freiburg. Several of those who had dared to receive the social democratic Weisser in their seminars in those dangerous days—including Böhm and Eucken—were present at the conference. Weisser noted that press comment had referred to a line of economic thought in West Germany stretching from von Hayek through Eucken and Röpke to economists in the camp of freedom-loving socialism.[37] He found this all very nice, but he had to point out that such an attitude ran the risk of covering up differences which needed to be kept in mind.[38] There were given facts which they just could not circumvent. One was their dependence on the occupying powers for their foreign trade, and the limitations on their capacity to expand imports. This all meant that they needed an overall plan of production, and that in turn ruled out a return to the free play of market forces. Certainly he agreed with Miksch that one should try to get the system moving, but that depended on what he referred to as 'high politics' (*die hohe Politik*), which could not be discussed at that meeting.

He pointed to the situation of the labour market and dismissed the notion that this could simply be left to the free play of forces between plants and individual workers. 'Nobody', he said, 'has suggested that and indeed it really does not need to be considered.'[39] In discussions between the trade unions and the Anglo-American occupiers it was always accepted that in this area, an overall plan with some sort of controlling mechanism was indispensable. Industrial location and housing would also have to be planned, and investment could not be left to the forces of capitalism, but would have to be organized from a Keynesian standpoint. He concluded that there must be direction of the core of the economy (*Kernlenkung*) and a system of rationing which, nevertheless, provided for consumer choice. This was the 'final-consumer allo-

[36] Ibid., p. 32.
[37] *Freiheitlicher Sozialismus*. In Britain this would probably be termed 'democratic socialism' to differentiate it from Soviet socialism. However, the German term *freiheitlich* conveys a particular implication of individual freedom which may not be so clear in the word 'democratic'.
[38] 'Beirat', pp. 33–4. Unfortunately the word 'nicht' is in this sentence in a way which negates it. This seems clearly false. It seems probable that 'nicht' is a misprint. It should probably be 'recht'
[39] Ibid., p. 33.

cation' proposal which Kromphardt had already published and which he had put before the committee in a special memorandum.[40]

Here then, were the main lines of the division within, not just the *Beirat*, but the Economics Administration, and ultimately the whole of Bizone itself. The struggle was not between *laissez-faire* free enterprise and a totalitarian command-economy, but between a free-price mechanism operating within a set of rules laid down by the state, and a mixed economy in which private business produced according to a global plan and operated within a state-regulated system of rationing. The second of these alternatives may seem remote from the reality in the atmosphere of the 1990s. It was far more likely to be taken seriously in a country which was just emerging from a rather similar system under the Third Reich, and in which the 'leap into cold water' of market economics seemed little short of suicidal when the shortages of raw materials, food, and foreign exchange were taken into account.

The doubts about the latter course which existed amongst economists and officials were revealed as the conference at Königstein progressed. Eucken contributed to a sharpening of the debate by stressing the differences between himself and Weisser. He denied that the limitations on foreign trade made a controlled economy essential. The fact that the amount of imported goods would be small did not mean that their distribution should be centrally directed.[41] If 1,000 tons of iron went to South Baden, where Eucken lived, for the economy such an import would count as external trade. How was it to be distributed? Who would decide between the countless possibilities as between artisans, industrial concerns, communications, repair works, etc.? No system of priorities existed. What was needed was an exact means of guiding supplies into the most effective areas of use, and that could only be the free-price mechanism.

The same was true about investment. Planners did not necessarily know best as far as that was concerned, and in any case, how could an industrial enterprise operating in the market have its investment planned from outside? Stress on labour-saving devices favoured by enthusiasts for planning like Weisser was not necessarily the most sensible way of using resources in a country with excess labour. Only the discipline of the free market could ensure rational decisions about such matters.

When Böhm summed up Eucken's remarks, he noted that his senior colleague favoured currency reform as soon as possible, coupled with a

---

[40] See the discussion of Kromphardt's memorandum given later in this chapter.
[41] 'Beirat', pp. 44–6.

return to market prices in all areas, and was prepared to put up with the 'somewhat drastic transitional difficulties' which would be created by jumping directly from the existing economic system to the new one.[42] This was clearly too much even for many liberal-minded participants in the meeting, and aroused strong reactions from those still hankering after planning. Weisser himself had interrupted Eucken's remarks several times to deny that he favoured a totalitarian, centrally directed economy. What he wanted was macro-economic planning along Keynesian lines, with a commitment to full employment.

Similar views were put strongly by Karl Schiller, who argued that the introduction of the market economy was dependent on a whole catalogue of preconditions—relating to supplies of raw materials and availability of capital—without which it would not work: 'When I look at the situation as it actually is, I have to come to the conclusion that these necessary conditions cannot be met.'[43]

The result of trying to get to the free-price mechanism would be not equilibrium, but disequilibrium. It would have to be all or nothing. He was therefore forced to the conclusion that he had to accept the facts as they were and 'make the best of it'—an English phrase of which German economists seemed rather fond. This meant that even after the currency reform, there would have to be 'restrictions on consumption in such a way that the otherwise inevitable price-distortions can be avoided'.[44]

Schiller himself then proposed a new method of distribution in which the state should function as a monopolist dedicated to meeting national needs. It would distribute allocations of goods according to the lowest costing on offer. This would ensure competition amongst producers when vying for allocations, thereby creating a mixed system which would best meet the needs of West Germany's current economic position.

Fundamentally, Schiller's suggestion was similar to those of the other supporters of a planned economy at Königstein. It involved global planning from the centre and controlled prices, but envisaged more scope for private initiative through a more flexible rationing-system. The disadvantage which its exponents faced was that, however attractive such schemes might be when described in general terms, as concrete proposals for action they seemed most unlikely to work in practice. It was easier for Rittershausen, Möller, and Böhm to urge that the meeting should concern itself with the immediate problems of price fixing and the reform of the *Zwangswirtschaft*, which all those present

---

[42] Ibid., p. 47.   [43] Ibid., p. 53.   [44] Ibid., p. 53.

agreed was not functioning properly as things stood. This tended to lead automatically to conclusions favourable to those who wished to return to market economics, since that at least was a system which was known to work in the real world.

Running through these discussions there was, however, another major area of difference, relating to employment. The supporters of planning and controls were determined to avoid the massive unemployment of the inter-war years. They believed that this could be done only by an interventionist policy of government credits, which would in turn necessitate controls over consumption. The neo-liberals wanted above all to eliminate the excess purchasing-power in the economy and return to the disciplines of the market. That meant a severe and deflationary reduction in the money supply, bringing with it high levels of unemployment. The supporters of the market argued that hidden unemployment already existed, and that the best way to overcome this was to increase production in response to real consumer demand. But there was no doubt that an interim period of severe unemployment was likely to result from 'leaping into the cold water' of the free-price system. This was in itself unacceptable to social democrats. Many officials, and the more pragmatic economists, saw it was a dangerous risk in view of its likely social and political consequences.

Certainly, Eucken's enthusiasm for a bracing jump into the icy waters of the free-price mechanism aroused concern even among his own supporters. Lampe expressed reservations, and the middle group of academics like Hoffmann, Preiser, and Peter were nervous about the social consequences of an immediate return to the market economy. Weisser and others who pointed to the danger of the rich benefiting at the expense of the already poverty-stricken masses had found a vulnerable chink in the liberalizers' armour. One academic lawyer, Professor Raiser of Göttingen University, expressed concern about social justice, and feared the effects which jettisoning controls might have on 'our terribly fragile state structure and the rule of law'.[45] Müller-Armack answered this by pointing out that the system they would be giving up was not at all socially just, and reiterated his own commitment to the market principle. Nevertheless, he also repeated his preference for a divided market as a means of getting through the transitional period after currency reform.[46]

Möller and Rittershausen were both eager to oppose mixed arrangements allowing some proportion of goods to be rationed and the rest to go free. Rittershausen argued that the scheme of 'free surpluses' (*freie*

---

[45] Ibid., p. 63.   [46] Ibid., p. 64.

Spitze) had been tried in Berlin and had not worked well. It would always be difficult to get shopkeepers to sell goods at fixed prices when they might get 'free' prices for them.[47] The danger would exist that such an introduction to the market economy would seem farcical and would be denounced by public opinion as impractical. Both Möller and Rittershausen made it clear, however, that they would continue to ration certain essential foodstuffs to secure a minimum standard of nutrition for the population. Eucken also favoured a simple and limited food-rationing system.[48]

It was this solution, the free-price mechanism linked to continued controls over food and housing, which was to emerge from the first two conferences of the *Beirat*, and it was this which was to form the basis of Erhard's policy in the summer of 1948. There can be no doubt that the neo-liberal school was immensely influential in the decision-making process which created such a policy. Eucken and Böhm set the tone of the discussions at the first meeting, and although Eucken was able to attend only on the first day, his passionate and uncompromising assertion of free-market principles threw the opposition on to the defensive and set up the parameters of the debate in such a way that the possibility of a streamlined form of directed economy was effectively ruled out.

That this would be the result of the *Beirat's* deliberations was, however, by no means clear when the first conference dispersed, on 24 January. The *Beirat* agreed that at its next meeting it would examine schemes for divided markets and for core planning (*Kernplanung*) from Kromphardt and Weisser. Although the general principle of the free-price mechanism had been accepted by most participants in the meeting, the second day's discussions had witnessed considerable divergences over the extent and nature of the exceptions to this principle. For instance, how much food should be rationed? Should rationed goods have subsidized prices or should their prices be free to rise? Schiller and Kromphardt both pleaded for rationing, fixed prices, and subsidies. The influence of Roman Catholic social teaching was brought to bear by Nell-Breuning, who urged that, in order to prevent excessive pressure on consumer industries, to the neglect of production industry, workers should be encouraged to obtain a share of the investment capital. This was a popular suggestion, warmly received by Böhm. Weisser also felt closer to this Christian position than he did to the liberalizers of Eucken's stamp.[49] Though they had suffered what

[47] Ibid., p. 67–8.   [48] Ibid., p. 70.

[49] Ibid., p. 90. For Weisser's views on Nell-Breuning, I am grateful to Prof. Weisser for his personal comments: interview with Gerhard Weisser, 21 July 1984.

might be termed a points defeat in the *Beirat*'s first conference, the adherents of planning could hope for better things when discussions resumed.

Certainly Keiser does not seem to have felt that any revolution had taken place in the administration. He told his staff at the end of January that there would have to be an intensification of planning so far as the distribution of goods was concerned, and that they would need to expand the administrative apparatus to be able to cope with it. Furthermore, the licensing of new industries should be permitted only after consultation with the central planning authorities. Keiser and his colleagues evidently felt that the real opportunities for planning were only just beginning.[50]

For his part, Strauß had always been inclined to restore the free-market mechanism, although he accepted the need for controls to overcome bottle-necks and for long-term structural planning to achieve a properly balanced economy.[51] On 31 January 1948 he drew up a list of tasks for the administration which included abolishing price subsidies and adjusting price relationships.[52] This did not, of course, necessarily imply the abolition of the rationing system, although it would have been a major step in that direction. Certainly the conflicts within the administration about economic policy were causing Strauß embarrassment in the early months of 1948. On 21 February he complained at a meeting of departmental heads that members of the administration were making contradictory public statements and that matters were being reported in the press 'while they were still not officially digested' (*noch nicht aktenreif*).[53] Rittershausen was one culprit, having published an article on pricing policy in the *Neue Zeitung*.

If the struggle over planning and free markets was still raging within the administration, it was also about to flare up again in the *Beirat*. Despite the efforts of Eucken, Böhm, and Lampe at the first conference, the opponents of the free-price mechanism were girding their loins for a counter-attack. This was to take the form of Wilhelm Kromphardt's memorandum on market-splitting and core planning. His ideas

---

[50] See above, p. 182 and fns. 15 and 16. Also 'Kurzbericht über die Sitzung des Sonderausschusses Planung', 30 Jan. 1948, VfW, BA Z4 27.

[51] Memorandum by Strauß, 'Wirtschaftsprobleme 1949', undated but probably early 1948, IfZG, Strauß Papers, ED 94, vol. 57.

[52] Memorandum by Strauß: 'Arbeitsaufgaben im Anschluß an das Memorandum vom 7. Januar 1948'. The memorandum referred to was a report on the problems arising from the failure of the London foreign ministers' conference. Ibid.

[53] Report of Hauptabteilungsleiterbesprechung, 21 Feb. 1948. Report dated 23 Feb. 1948, VfW, BA Z8 95.

had already been published in the summer of 1947, when he had presented them to the finance committee of the British *Zonenbeirat*.[54]

Kromphardt's theses had been seen at that time as a counterblast to liberal demands for a return to market forces. He claimed that the latter course was quite impossible, for reasons familiar to those involved in the planning debate; Germany's economic future was bound to involve planning and material allocations because of the demands of the Allies. The Germans would have to have an industrial plan, as well as controls over their maritime commerce and foreign trade. Disarmament and the—as yet unknown—reparation requirements from current production would also necessitate central planning.

Kromphardt claimed that split markets already existed, in fact if not in name. Thus in Germany there was a rationed market, a black market, a grey market of barter, and a premium market enjoyed by those workers, such as coal-miners, who had special ration-allocations. In other areas—the education system or in health-insurance schemes, for example—private and public markets existed side by side.

He therefore proposed that market splitting be regularized and recognized as a basis for Germany's future economic administration. There should be a 'core' sector, which would function with ration cards, fixed prices, and production norms set by a comprehensive national plan. Output levels in this sector would be set at 80 per cent of calculated capacity, and that amount of goods would be strictly rationed. The surplus would be fed into the 'marginal' sector, in which there would be market prices and no controls. Apart from the limited surplus from the core sector to be granted to it, the free market would also be allowed those goods which it was not felt necessary to ration. Just how marginal Kromphardt's free-market sector would have been is illustrated by his selection of decorative ashtrays as the sort of products which might avoid controls. Even then, freedom would be limited by prohibitions on goods regarded as so obviously inessential that they could be banned altogether. Whipped cream was one item picked out by Kromphardt for proscription. However, he did allow that, if circumstances improved, more luxuries might be permitted in the marginal sector—even whipped cream itself.[55]

[54] This meeting was held on 8 July 1947 in Hamburg. For a commentary on Kromphardt's proposals delivered at the same meeting, see 'Koreferat Wilhelm Naegel, Mitglied des Wirtschaftsrates zum Referat Professor Wilhelm Kromphardt über Marktspaltung gehalten auf der Sitzung des Finanzausschußes des Zonenbeirates in Hamburg' (n.p., n.d.), copy in Bundesrat Library, Bonn. For Kromphardt's published plan, see W. Kromphardt, *Marktspaltung und Kernplanung in der Volkswirtschaft* (Dortmunder Schriften zur Sozialforschung, 3; Hamburg, 1947).

[55] Kromphardt, *Marktspaltung*, 12.

The system of rationing proposed by Kromphardt was also of interest, because it exemplified attempts by democratic socialists to overcome objections to the inflexibility of planned economies. The key to its success was to be the concept of allocation rights (*Bezugsrechte*) which would run through the entire economy, from the consumer to the first producer. This would create competition amongst producers and force them to respond to consumer needs. Another name for this process was the clumsy *Endkontingentierung*, or 'allocation according to the needs of the final consumer'. Hence each customer entering a shoe-shop would have a ration of leather which he could choose to spend on different types of footwear; his choice would be passed back to the wholesaler and to the factory, and it would be on the basis of these coupons registering demand for his products that the manufacturer would get allocations of raw materials. The same process would apply to food supplies, textiles, and all other consumer goods, so long as they were considered important enough to count as serious necessities.

The exact manner in which this scheme would work in practice was never satisfactorily explained. When Keiser expounded one version of it to the administrative staff, he had to admit that it would be very difficult to give each housewife an allocation of steel every time she wanted a knitting-needle. In practice the allocations would go mainly to industrial customers. Obviously the system was going to be difficult to operate. He called for officials to use courage and imagination in implementing it and in combating the moral decline visible throughout the economy. Only if the administration had the power and determination to deal with matters after currency reform could this desirable type of 'rough and ready control' (*Grobsteuerung*) operate effectively.[56] Certainly no reduction in the size of the bureaucracy seemed likely if Keiser's vision were to be realized.

Another objection to the scheme was that, with prices in the free or 'marginal' sector so much higher than those in the core sector, there would be a tendency for rationed goods to leak away on to the open market. Kromphardt claimed, however, that this would be impossible, because the allocations of raw materials would be made available only on the basis of what had been sold in the core sector. The baker, for example, would have to estimate his needs in the core sector to get his flour and his coal for the ovens. If he underestimated his 'core' sales, he would receive too little in the way of raw materials to meet his

[56] Memorandum by Keiser, 'Die Neuordnung des Bewirtschaftssystems: Bewirtschaftung und Wirtschaftssystem', *Mitteilungsblatt*, undated but evidently spring 1948. Copy in WEI Eucken NL.

needs. If he overestimated, however, he would have to return more coupons from his core customers and would not be able to benefit from the 20 per cent of surplus operations on the free market.[57]

Kromphardt was so taken with this project that he coined for it the term 'utilization socialism'. The beauty of it was that it would direct the way in which property was utilized without necessarily altering its ownership. Hence the system would be quite compatible with private capitalism, co-operative enterprises, or state ownership. It would be acceptable to those who felt the need merely for a period of transition from a war economy to a free market, but at the same time socialists could welcome it as a potentially permanent system, involving as it did a planned economy. The tenor of Kromphardt's proposals made it clear that for him the scheme was attractive as a long-term proposition. He argued that, after initial difficulties had been overcome, it would not be necessary to dragoon entrepreneurs into such a system; they would be falling over themselves to sign up for it. The core sector of the economy would offer them long-term contracts at fixed prices guaranteed by the government. 'That is something', he claimed, 'for which every producer yearns and which he will not voluntarily forgo.'[58] There was an aftertaste of the Third Reich in that remark. Producers who, under Hitler, had ceased to worry about the laws of supply and demand, might indeed prefer the cosy security of fixed-price government contracts to the hurly-burly of market competition.

Certainly the social democrats on the *Beirat* were, and remained, hopeful that Kromphardt's scheme would head off the dangerous possibility of a return to the free market. On 4 March 1948, Weisser wrote to Ollenhauer, deputy leader of the Social Democratic Party, that the arguments in the *Beirat* had turned out quite well for the socialist cause. In the first session, the neo-liberals had tried to bind them to accept the free market as the ultimate objective of German economic policy. Weisser claimed that, whilst rejecting the *Zwangswirtschaft*, he had insisted that they could not contemplate an uncontrolled market as the goal towards which they should be striving. He had demanded a 'loosened form of controlled economy into which market elements could be incorporated'.[59]

Weisser himself produced a memorandum on this for the *Beirat*, copies of which were sent to Ollenhauer and Schumacher. In it he urged above all the retention of controls over raw materials and the

[57] Kromphardt, *Marktspaltung*, 9.
[58] Ibid. 10.
[59] 'Eine gelockerte Verwaltungswirtschaft unter Einbau marktwirtschaftlicher Elemente', Weisser to Ollenhauer, 4 Mar. 1948, FES PV Bestand Wipo, L19 01612.

adoption of Kromphardt's market-splitting scheme. Wages should be 'political wages' and not set by the market. They should be accepted by firms as prescribed costs, in the same way as taxes.[60] Weisser accepted that the scheme was complicated, but argued that: 'there is no ideal of simplicity in the economic system; because the economic life which has to be regulated is not simple and is constantly in flux'. The aim should be to 'avoid social injustice and to put the economy at the service of those cultural values which make life worth living'.[61]

Weisser's comments illustrate the extent to which the supporters of a planned economy in West Germany hoped to avoid a return to the liberal market economy even after currency reform. Given the enormous difficulties facing the administration and the Allied occupiers, there is reason to suppose that these views—or at least some variant upon them—might have prevailed had not the neo-liberal academics and their supporters in the administration fought with such tenacity to ensure the return of a free-price mechanism.

When the *Beirat* met again, on 29 February 1948, the proceedings began in sombre fashion with the announcement of Professor Lampe's early death—a reminder that the effects of Nazi tyranny and post-war privations were taking their toll among the middle-aged.[62]

At the centre of the discussion was Kromphardt's core-planning project. The tactics of the planners, among whom could be numbered Keiser, Kromphardt, and Weisser, were to stress the impossibility of a rapid return to the free market and present the core-planning option as an interim solution, the details of which should then be discussed.

Their opponents, on the other hand, denied that circumstances were such as to render the free-price mechanism impossible. They in turn stressed that Kromphardt's proposals were really just a more flexible version of a planned economy which, apart from its own inherent weaknesses, would obstruct the path to liberalization and might rule it out altogether.

At an early stage in the discussion, Keiser urged that they should work on the assumption that the controlled economy would have to go on. In that case it was a question of deciding how it could be made to operate in a more elegant and flexible fashion.[63] This would clearly

---

[60] Weisser 'Thesen zur Ordnung der Wirtschaft nach der Sanierung der Währung', p. 40, ibid.

[61] Ibid., p. 46.

[62] Lampe was 51 years old. He had been arrested by the Nazis in the wake of the attempt to kill Hitler in the summer of 1944.

[63] '"Wie können wir sie auflockern, eleganter gestalten?" Bericht über die 2. Sitzung des Wissenschaftlichen Beirates bei der Verwaltung für Wirtschaft am 29 Feb. 1948', p. 15, Möller Papers.

have been against the interests of the free-market supporters, and they did not hesitate to express themselves forcibly against it. Leonhard Miksch reminded his listeners that a system of controls could not be defended with reference to social justice, because 'There is no more unsocial system than the one we have at present, in which, as a result of the black market, inequalities of supply have reached unprecedented proportions.'

Under these circumstances, Kromphardt's scheme, however morally admirable it might be, simply would not work. The allocation mechanism was not functioning properly as it was, and there would be no chance of such a complex set of allocation rights creating a clear distinction between the core sector and the free sector of the economy.[64]

These arguments were taken up by Böhm in his commentary on Kromphardt's proposals, presented towards the end of the second day of the conference. Böhm admitted that there were advantages in the Kromphardt scheme. It would give entrepreneurs an interest in fulfilling norms and avoiding waste in the public sector, because they could thereby gain access to the free sector. For this reason it would be possible to operate planning in an indirect way (*mit leichter Hand*) and the free sector of the economy would give planning officials some idea of the true value of commodities. Since Kromphardt's scheme left the options open in the future as between planning and the free market, and since it simply involved adapting and legalizing the existing situation, it was highly seductive. Apparently Kromphardt had squared the circle. But for that very reason his proposals deserved very detailed criticism.[65]

It had to be recognized that Kromphardt was not proposing a halfway house between two economic systems, nor was he clearing the path for a leap into the market economy. His scheme meant the continuation of planning. It would involve the artificial definition of a core sector with fixed prices, the existence of an overall plan, allocation of goods by a coupon system, and the likelihood of production norms being set by the state.[66] Böhm adopted a rigid approach to the problem, claiming that a planned economy and a market economy could not be mixed up, because then neither of them would be 'pure'. On the one hand, planning would be affected by the free-price sector, and on the other, entrepreneurs would not be entirely dependent on market forces. Hence what Kromphardt had produced was not a combination of systems but a 'technically differentiated directed economy'.[67] He

---

[64] Sitzung 29 Feb./1 März, Sonntag/Nachmittag, p. 1, Möller Papers.
[65] Ibid., pp. 5–6.   [66] Ibid., pp. 6–9.   [67] Ibid., p. 7.

compared Kromphardt's free-price sector to a wildlife park, in which the animals only *seemed* free to an uninitiated spectator. Real wild animals needed real freedom, and it was the same with the market economy.[68]

All this was doubtless logical enough in theory, but it was unlikely to convince those who felt agnostic towards free markets in the first place. Böhm was on stronger ground when he pointed out that Kromphardt's scheme would not eliminate excess purchasing-power in the German economy. The planned sector would always need financing, and the easy money there would push up prices in his free-market sector. Above all, Kromphardt's plan was complicated and would need numerous highly trained officials to run it. It would encourage 'the perpetuation of the planned economy with a large apparatus of control which will never disband itself'.[69]

The real weakness of the Kromphardt option lay in its impracticability. If the existing wartime control-system was breaking down, how could they hope to succeed with a more complicated version of it? This was, indeed, a major factor in winning over what might be termed the middle ground in the *Beirat* to the side of the free market. Müller-Armack himself was among those who had been very concerned about the social dangers of too abrupt a leap into the cold water of free prices. Yet he was one of the most persuasive speakers in the *Beirat* in favour of risking the experiment, provided that measures were taken to protect the economically weak from starvation. He doubted whether it would turn out to be possible to find an effective form of allocation in Kromphardt's core-planning sector, since how could one decide on allocations of material between, say, typewriter factories and sewing-machine plants? If such a scheme was viable, it would only be possible for a very restricted area of raw materials of foodstuffs. Therefore Müller-Armack urged instead that they should adopt a quite primitive form of rationing—based on their existing arrangements and limited to the most essential agricultural products.

Müller-Armack made short work of the objections to the introduction of the free-price mechanism. The fact that raw materials were scarce did not mean that prices had to be controlled. It would be possible to leave them to rise but to mop up excessive profits by means of import licences. The strict control of foreign-currency transactions might not last for ever; there were hopes of a loosening-up in other countries in the long run. As for the argument that reparations would require a planned economy, Müller-Armack turned this claim on its head and

[68] Ibid.   [69] Ibid.

pointed out that the rapid introduction of a free market might actually inhibit the imposition of an excessive reparations burden on West Germany.[70]

Müller-Armack concluded his remarks by saying that he thought the way was open for a return to market prices, and that no external obstacles were serious enough to prevent this step. It cannot be claimed that his intervention was decisive, but it was symptomatic of a trend towards accepting a radical move away from planning and controls. When the *Beirat* came to draw up its first memorandum for the Economics Administration, a substantial majority of its members opted for the return to the free-price mechanism.

The *Beirat* memorandum, dated 18 April 1948, mirrored the divisions within West Germany's economics profession, but the majority report was a clear victory for the neo-liberals and the Freiburg School. It stressed that the currency reform, when it came, could make sense only when combined with a fundamental reform of the existing system of economic controls: 'As an isolated measure it [the currency reform] would be worthless, if not actually dangerous.'[71]

The reintroduction of the price mechanism in the economy was the major recommendation of the report. Controls on industrial production and raw materials should be abolished, apart from import licences. The price freeze of 1936 should be ended. It was less clear what was to happen to wages; the report spoke of an 'ordered wage-structure' on the basis of recognized contracts, although flexibility in wage settlements was to be encouraged in the interest of maximizing employment. Foreign-exchange controls should be relaxed as far as was consistent with the prevention of a flight of capital from Germany.

All these recommendations might be seen as representing the *laissez-faire* side of neo-liberalism. The social side was not, however, ignored. First of all, the report recommended that rationing be retained for basic foodstuffs—grain, meat, and fat—and that rents should continue to be controlled. Special measures would have to be taken to overcome the housing shortage. The report assumed that capital flows out of the country would be prevented, and in its last recommendation it specifically stated that both the majority and the minority groups accepted the possibility of influencing the development of the national economy by the use of credit policy or counter-cyclical measures.[72] Perhaps the most significant of all was recommendation 12, which began: 'To

---

[70] 2. Sitzung, 29 Feb. vormittags, 16–18, 22, Möller Papers.
[71] Bundeswirtschaftsministerium (ed.), Der Wissenschaftliche Beirat, 26–7.
[72] Ibid. 29.

prevent the abuse of economic power the *Beirat* believes the immediate and effective control of monopolies and their pricing policy to be indispensable.'[73]

In the first instance this was meant to apply to coal, but its implications were obviously very far-reaching.

For their part the minority of 'planners' in the *Beirat* stuck to their guns, urging that controls be retained for many manufactured goods, since an immediate return to the free market was out of the question. In particular, they pointed to the difficulty of maintaining employment levels without extensive government credits and the consequential need to ration goods.[74] To this end the panaceas of core planning and market-splitting were put forward as the alternatives to the free-price mechanism. Nevertheless, the majority view was the one which carried most weight.

It would be overstating the case to suggest that this formed a blueprint for Erhard's actions in the summer of 1948. He had arrived at similar conclusions by himself, and there were officials in the administration, like Miksch and Rittershausen, who would support him. But the influence of the *Beirat* was an important reinforcement for their views at a time when the direction of West Germany's economic policy was by no means fixed.

---

[73] Ibid. 28.   [74] For the minority report, see ibid. 29–30.

10

Erhard as Economics Director in Bizone

THE recommendations of the *Wissenschaftlicher Beirat*[1] clearly supported a 'leap into cold water' restoring the free-price mechanism and the market economy. Ludwig Erhard, who took up his post as economics director on 6 April 1948, was entirely at one with this view. Yet he could not be sure that it would enjoy the support either of German political leaders or of the Anglo-Saxon occupying powers.

Erhard's experience in the *Sonderstelle Geld und Kredit* had not encouraged him to think that the Allies themselves would automatically couple currency reform with the liberalization of the economy. When he had discussed these matters with the American financial expert Edward A. Tenenbaum on 20 November 1947, the latter had not been very encouraging towards Erhard's view that a free market should rapidly reappear in Germany. 'Some time', of course, it should be restored, but it was not going to be easy. Tenenbaum seemed to imply that controls would be difficult to remove.[2]

Erhard therefore had to take urgent steps himself to prepare for the day when Allied measures to reform the currency would force decisions about the nature of Germany's economic policy on the Economic Council. He was aware that within his own administration there were powerful minds which were fully committed to planning. He had, for example, experienced the eloquence of Günter Keiser in this respect when both had been participants in the *Sonderstelle Geld und Kredit*. At the same time he could count on the support of Leonhard Miksch, who was responsible for the section of the administration dealing with prices and incomes policy, on the fiscal expert Rittershausen, and on the new deputy director of the administration, Edmund Kaufmann, a lawyer and Roman Catholic CDU politician from Baden, who had previously been active in the executive committee of

---

[1] Of 18 Apr. 1948, 'Maßnahmen der Verkehrsregelung, der Bewirtschaftung und der Preispolitik nach der Währungsreform', in Bundeswirtschaftsministerium (ed.), *Der Wissenschaftliche Beirat*, 25–30.

[2] Laitenberger, *Ludwig Erhard*, 58.

the *Länderrat* (the body representing the governments of the bizonal *Länder*).[3]

Even before Erhard took up office, he found himself facing difficult political decisions. Four days after his election as director he received a ringing plea from Blücher asking him to fight day and night to modify the price-control laws which were being passed through the Economic Council, and which seemed to cement the bureaucratic control-system even more firmly into the German economy. Blücher pointed out that only the Free Democrats and the maverick *Wirtschaftliche Aufbau-Vereinigung* (WAV) refugees' party would oppose the measures, thereby implying that the Christian Democrats were not much use as protectors of the market.[4] In fact there was little that Erhard could do about this. The price-control system was being handed over from the Allied Control Commission to German administration, but the Allies made it clear they expected rationing—implemented by a suitably large staff of officials—to continue.[5]

Erhard's own views on staffing were very different. When he went to talk to senior officials at the Economics Administration on 20 March 1948, he gave them the grim news that a reduction in their establishment was essential. The main way of achieving this must be by devolving responsibility to the *Länder*,[6] a conclusion at variance with the views expressed less than two months earlier in Keiser's special planning committee, which had adumbrated schemes for increased co-ordination of planning between the *Länder* and the central administration—with consequential increases in planning staffs.[7] There can be no doubt that Erhard's arrival heralded a complete change of attitude at the top of the administration towards its functions, since, however many sympathizers with market forces there had been amongst the staff, planning had seemed an inevitable priority, and the forthcoming Marshall Aid Programme seemed likely to intensify the need for it.

The way in which the European Recovery Programme's funds would be used was certainly a source of concern for Erhard. There were grounds for fearing that the planners—supported by the New Dealers and socialists amongst the Anglo-Saxon allies—would insist on the money being pumped into a relatively small number of grandiose

---

[3] Ibid. 64.

[4] Blücher to Erhard, 6 Mar. 1948, BA Blücher NL, no. 83.

[5] 'Die Bedeutung des neuen Preisgesetzes', *Handelsblatt*, 25 Mar. 1948, and 'Wirtschaftsrat übernimmt Preispolitik', *Neue Zeitung*, 4 Apr. 1948.

[6] Report on Hauptabteilungsleiterbesprechung, 20 Mar. 1948, VfW, BA Z8 95.

[7] See above, pp. 182–3.

industrial projects which would do nothing to meet consumer demand and thus stimulate production. When the academic *Beirat* met on 12–13 June to discuss investment policy after the currency reform, Erhard admitted that the problem of financing industry from 'an empty till' was a very daunting one.[8] He did not seem to have a very clear solution to it, and indeed there was at that point relatively little he could do about it.

What he does seem to have been clear about was that Germany's own resources should be allocated as much as possible by market forces, which would in practice mean that consumer-goods industries would benefit. In so far as imports of raw materials were needed, he looked to Marshall Aid to provide them. It was also his intention to press for a relaxation of Allied restrictions on Germany's export trade. He rapidly made himself unpopular with the Allies—especially the British—for his constant attacks on the JEIA bureaucracy, which he accused of smothering German trade. Indeed, his complaints about the 'dollar clause' angered the Americans as much as the British. Erhard was not backward in demanding that the Western Allies give West Germany the wherewithal to recover her economic strength. On the other hand, he did not waste time lamenting the obvious division of Germany, an issue which exercised many, less flexible, politicians, and which was to become more acute after the currency reform in June, when Soviet threats culminated in the Berlin blockade. Erhard was prepared to make the best of the economic resources available in the Western zones, but he wanted the Allies to face the consequences of opting for a Western commitment by helping West Germany to recover and supporting those free-market principles which anti-Communism would logically require. This was not a self-evident reaction from the occupiers. Even the Americans, 'New Dealers' or not, were uneasy when faced with the point that the free market meant liberating Germany from *Allied* controls as well as German ones.

He heralded his new policy with a rousing speech to the Economic Council on 21 April 1948. This was his first major statement as economics director, and he set out his programme in an uncompromising fashion. Erhard made no bones about the poverty of achievement so far:

it would be pious self-deception to regard the very small revival of production since 1945 as the beginning of a real recovery. It is true that, by a planned concentration of energy upon certain centres of gravity, individual basic in-

[8] Report on the meeting of the *Wissenschaftlicher Beirat bei der VfW*, 12/13 June 1948, Möller Papers.

dustries have been furthered and existing bottle-necks widened, but by this onesidedness in our economic work, the lack of balance in our economic structure has become more and more perceptible and disturbing.[9]

By contrast to his predecessor, Semler, who had favoured heavy industry in his planning, Erhard urged a higher priority for consumer production. As for liberalization, there too Erhard stood for a more radical policy. Rejecting Semler's step-by-step approach, Erhard announced that a currency reform which did not involve an immediate return to free-market principles would be senseless. Although he agreed that controls could not be jettisoned all at once, he claimed that only by giving up the discredited control-system would it be possible to restore the authority of the state amongst the German public. Even the most conscientious citizen was forced to rebel against the overpowering bureaucracy of the planning system, and Erhard could not forbear a reference to the 'termite state'. He urged that German trade should be freed from restrictions and that the West Germans should be allowed to export more manufactured products and fewer raw materials. He pressed for West Germany's trade and industry associations to be more involved in the economic process.

He also made the controversial comment that it would be folly to empty German warehouses and factories of goods just before the currency reform. Although he denied any lack of determination to stop hoarding, it was easy for critics to assert that he was encouraging it. Indeed, it obviously made sense for firms to keep back their goods until they could sell them for real money. In any case, Erhard's statement hardly altered commercial practice; he simply had the honesty to make public what industry knew already.

On a more elevated plane, Erhard shrewdly pointed out that federalism and decentralization—concepts popular with the Americans and the CDU—would be quite incompatible with planning. Decentralized planning was a contradiction in terms.[10]

Erhard's peroration was so striking that the political adviser to the British authorities in Frankfurt, Con O'Neill, saw fit to draw it particularly to the attention of his superiors in Berlin and London. His remarks on it are not without interest for the light they throw on the extent to which Erhard's policy was of his own making, and on what amount of support it would be likely to achieve from the Allies.

[9] The text of Erhard's speech is reproduced in *Ludwig Erhard, Gedanken*. This translation is taken from a text provided for the British military government. PRO/FO/1006/4. See also Laitenberger, *Ludwig Erhard*, 66, and Ambrosius, *Die Durchsetzung der sozialen Marktwirtschaft*, 160–1.

[10] *Ludwig Erhard, Gedanken*, 119.

O'Neill stated that Erhard's speech deserved careful study as a very important pronouncement by the German administration: 'It is in fact their programme in the economic field.'[11] To the British diplomat, Erhard's speech

is extremely verbose and somewhat academic and theoretic [*sic*] in structure, but he succeeds in making himself plain enough. He strikes me as a man of pretty clear intelligence and fairly considerable force, though hardly a sympathetic character. He is regarded as crafty rather than straightforward. His appearance is rather against him, since he bears some resemblance, facial at least, to Göring. His small eyes and diminutive nose are almost lost in a wide expanse of gently undulating rosy flesh.

Nevertheless, O'Neill had found the speech self-confident and welcomed its readiness to accept without repining the situation of divided Germany and to assert that Western Germany had got the part of the German economy which really mattered. It showed a readiness to 'get on with the job and a belief that it can be done'.

He noted among other points: the stress laid upon liberation from state controls; a shift from capital goods to consumer goods; and an easing of German trade. He pointed out that the demand for important functions to be given to trade and industry associations in Germany was very widely supported, even in some parts of the SPD. Nevertheless, it ran counter to Allied policy. So far as Erhard's general objective of decontrol was concerned, O'Neill was intrigued but unconvinced. While welcoming Erhard's optimism, he thought it overdone: 'So much insistence on the abolition of bureaucracy and the beneficent influence of the free play of economic forces strikes me as astonishing in Germany's present situation.' Despite the fact that the speech might be expected to please the Americans, he saw no reason to doubt that Erhard meant what he said and 'It may be that in this surprising country there is some real prospect that the methods he recommends will do the trick.'

This was hardly a ringing statement of confidence in Erhard, but it does show that his debut in Frankfurt had made a strong impression. It is as well to note, however, that the attitudes of the military government in Bizone were not necessarily friendly to Erhard's purposes. The Western Allies looked at matters from a strategic rather than an economic perspective. When Pat Dean of the British Foreign Office replied to O'Neill, he remarked that the swing to the right in West

---

[11] O'Neill to the political division of the British Control Office in Berlin, with a copy to Pat Dean in the Foreign Office, 30 Apr. 1948. O'Neill also enclosed lengthy excerpts from Erhard's speech in English translation. PRO/FO/1049/1432.

German politics was 'unfortunate from our point of view in spite of the evidence of anti-communist feeling which it provides'. The British aim must be to encourage moderates in the CDU and the SPD to work together to face the common danger.[12] Admirable an objective though that may have been, it was incompatible with Erhard's radical approach to economics.

In fighting the German planners, therefore, Erhard also had to work against the Allied—and especially the British—itch to control. This he did in an outspoken, often tactless, but very effective way. One of his favourite targets was the Joint Export–Import Agency (JEIA), through which the West Germans had to conduct their trade with the outside world. On 15 May 1948 a report on a meeting between the military governors and German bizonal administrators noted rather plaintively that 'Erhardt [sic] complained in usual terms about JEIA's export and import procedural requirements' and 'brought forward his familiar demands for freer travel for German and foreign business men in and out of Germany, for more latitude in the import of non-essential goods for currency other than dollars and for facilities for official German trade delegations ... Usual explanations were given in reply.'[13] The 'usual explanations' did not satisfy Erhard and he was regarded with disfavour for his truculence on the subject. At one meeting early in June he described JEIA with some hyperbole as 'the most detested institution in all Europe'. On 14 June he confronted both the military governors of Bizone, Lucius D. Clay and Brian Robertson, and gave them his views on the matter. He provoked an explosion from Clay by claiming that German businessmen regarded the 'dollar clause' as a means of shutting German competition out of world markets. Clay retorted that if the German bizonal authorities wanted to get along without dollar assistance they had only to say the word. He refused to discuss the matter further, and Robertson was obviously not displeased at Erhard's discomfiture at the hands of the American military governor.[14] The liberation of West German trade would be an uphill task, but Erhard stuck to it.

The Allied authorities were not the only ones to have doubts about Erhard. That he should have been regarded with hostility by social democrats was understandable, but by no means all liberal-minded observers welcomed his forthright statements on the economy. In the spring of 1948, Countess Dönhoff, who was beginning her illustrious career as a journalist with *Die Zeit*, noted her impressions of a press

---

[12] Dean to O'Neill, 12 May 1948, ibid.
[13] Cabled report BICO Frankfurt to Berlin, 15 May 1948, ibid.
[14] Robertson to the Foreign Office, 14 June 1948, ibid.

conference given by Erhard in Frankfurt: 'If Germany were not already ruined, this man, with his absurd plan to abolish all controls, would certainly bring that ruin about. God protect us from him ever becoming Economics Minister. That would be the third catastrophe after Hitler and the dismemberment of Germany.'[15]

Erhard was thick-skinned enough to ignore criticism, from whatever quarter it came. His next step was to prepare the necessary measures to abolish controls on the allocation of manufactured products—the laws under which he operated prevented him from liberating raw materials. Prices were a more difficult problem, owing to the price law mentioned above. Aided especially by Miksch, he drafted legislation which could give him the power to overthrow the control system once the abolition of the old currency was implemented. Miksch therefore drew up a Law Governing the Guiding Principles for Controls and Pricing Policy after Currency Reform. This changed the legal basis of the administration's operations and gave the director much wider powers of decision in matters of allocation and pricing, thereby enabling him to abolish price controls and allocations if he were minded to do so. This Guiding Principles Law was to be the key measure in Erhard's liberalization programme.

Erhard's struggles did not go unappreciated. By early summer Blücher was reacting with enthusiasm to the chance being offered to help restore a liberal economic system. On 5 June 1948 he opened a stirring message to the leaders of the FDP in the British zone of Germany with the assertion that: 'Only now is the actual political work beginning.' Erhard's new draft law was the 'decisive step' which would enable Germans to escape from the fetters of the controlled economy with one mighty bound. This was due to the efforts of 'our friend', Dr Ludwig Erhard, whose measures were to be supported at all levels. Blücher confided to his readers: 'You know from our occasional conversations how great my fear is that, although he [Erhard] is fully equal to the intellectual demands of his post, he may not be able to master the organizational and technical administrative aspects of the work.'[16]

The problem might, it was to be hoped, be alleviated by the reductions in the responsibilities of the Economics Administration following the abolition of the controlled economy. This was another reason for Free Democrats to support wholeheartedly the proposed liberalization

[15] D. Koerfer, *Kampf ums Kanzleramt: Erhard und Adenauer* (Stuttgart, 1987), 46–7, citing M. G. Dönhoff, *Von Gestern nach Übermorgen: Zur Geschichte der Bundesrepublik Deutschland* (Hamburg, 1981), 149 ff.
[16] Blücher to FDP leaders in the British Zone, 5 June 1948, BA Blücher NL, no. 378.

measures. Blücher went on to claim that German business organizations (*Verbände*) would soon take over the distribution functions being
relinquished by officialdom. Since the Allies would not tolerate direct
involvement by the *Verbände* in the distribution process, their members
would have to operate as individuals within new, informal agencies—a
pragmatic suggestion which nevertheless implied a cosily managed
market. Had he read this comment, Erhard might have found it more
worrying than the criticisms of his administrative competence. He was
to be discomfited in the future by claims that he had just replaced state
control with the power of vested interests. Since well before Hitler's
access to power, neo-liberal theorists like Rüstow and Böhm had been
railing against the influence of pressure groups within the German
economy. Now they were apparently to be endowed with powers
which ought properly to belong to the state. How did this chime in
with Erhard's views on free competition and the destruction of cartels?

The issue of these business associations arose from the moment
Erhard began his operations. It was made more delicate by the strong
opposition from trade unions to employers getting more power without equivalent gains for themselves. Erhard had no wish to see the
trade unions involved in the day-to-day running of the economy. On
19 March he was having to assure *Land* economics ministers that he
had no intention of vesting the *Verbände* with state powers. Yet it was
also clear that he did envisage these bodies playing a more active role
in the months to come.[17]

It is fair to say that Erhard was less of a purist in dealing with the
Verbände than some of his more academic colleagues might have been.
He certainly worked quite happily with industrial associations, having
an intimate knowledge of them since his early days in market research.
Furthermore, in 1948 his chief objective was to dismantle the edifice of
planning and controls which was the post-war *Zwangswirtschaft*. If he
could pass some allocation duties on to the *Verbände*, he could more
easily dispense with the bureaucratic apparatus of planning, giving
the Economics Administration the task of setting out the rules of the
economic game and leaving the players to get on with it. The *Verbände*
at least represented hard-headed, practical people, and their role in
any allocation procedures would be limited by their own dislike of red
tape. Nevertheless, as subsequent events were to demonstrate, it
was not his intention to replace the *Zwangswirtschaft* with a market
rigged for the benefit of producers. The ultimate aim was free com-

[17] Report of meeting with *Land* economics ministers, 19 Mar. 1948, BA Z4 569.

petition, liberated from cartels and monopolies as well as from state interference.

For the time being, however, he had other problems. The decisive actions to free the economy from a stifling blanket of controls had to be taken very rapidly. His Guiding Principles Law had to be passed before currency reform was introduced. In the teeth of fierce Social Democratic and Communist opposition, he piloted the bill through the Economic Council in the early hours of the morning of Friday, 18 June.

This was certainly one of the high points of Erhard's career. Officially the measure was presented to the Economic Council with the authority of the entire *Verwaltungsrat*, the 'Cabinet' of the Frankfurt system whose president was Hermann Pünder.[18] Yet nobody doubted the authorship of the 'Guiding Principles' and it fell to Erhard to defend them in the debate, during the course of which he spoke three times. His arguments reflected the principles which had been propagated by neo-liberal economists—including himself—throughout fifteen years of *dirigiste* experimentation, most of it disastrous.

His first concern was to assuage fears that the return to market forces at a time of scarcity would lead to galloping inflation. This was a major thrust of Social Democratic criticism, and fear of inflation was by no means confined to the ranks of the Left. Erhard had the courage to stake his reputation on his belief that his economic theory would prove valid in the real world. He told the members of the Frankfurt Economic Council that although there might be some particular areas of difficulty, such as shoes and textiles: 'In the price spectrum as a whole a general inflationary increase cannot take place—even after a total liberation of prices—unless something miraculous occurs. But in the economy there is no such thing as a miracle.'[19]

So long as money was controlled properly, supply and demand would adjust to one another. Erhard did not pretend this would be an entirely painless process. There had to be price discipline. The way to achieve this was not to employ officials to tell people what they could buy, but to use the external pressure of free competition to enforce a more rational use of resources and reductions in costs. Falling prices would then be the consequence, especially if strict restraints on money and credit encouraged individuals to stop rushing after goods, as they had done so far, and to start seeking after money.

Referring to SPD accusations that his measures favoured the capi-

[18] *Wörtliche Berichte und Drucksachen des Wirtschaftsrates des Vereinigten Wirtschaftsgebietes, 1947–1949*, ed. C. Weisz and H. Woller, ii (Munich, 1977), 634 (hereafter cited as *Wirtschaftsrat*).
[19] Ibid. 624.

talist classes and were naïve about human nature, he said it was precisely because people were not angels that the administration was furthering the principle of competition; whereas his opponents on the left wanted to abolish it: 'I can tell you from my own experience that there are many in entrepreneurial circles who felt very happy under the previous economic arrangements. They had become a species of state pensioners—not at the expense of the state, but at the cost of the people.'[20]

Erhard assured his listeners that he would take care of a minimum standard of living for the poorest, and other incomes would build up from that minimum standard. He struck a responsive chord when he argued that the chaotic situation created by economic controls was undermining the authority of the state by alienating the people from it. He was careful to deny that the Guiding Principles were an 'enabling law' giving him dictatorial powers. This was an important point, because the term 'enabling law' had sinister echoes of Hitler's measure in March 1933 which had helped to establish the Nazi dictatorship. Erhard, on the contrary, could sincerely claim that his intention was to *reduce* government intervention and limit its activities. The highest authorities in the country should no longer decide whether people got one or two kilograms of marrowbones each, but should restrict themselves to the broad issues of economic policy. He ended his major contribution to the debate with a peroration about his determination to achieve a 'social economic policy' using liberal methods.[21]

The opposition to Erhard was angry but confused. Nobody wanted to defend the existing control-system. The Communists simply argued that controls were useless unless the means of production were owned by the people. Social Democrats wanted planning, but of a different and more perfect kind than that which existed in 1948.[22] This was scarcely a convincing alternative to Erhard's simple but radical proposal. More telling was the Social Democratic claim that distribution was not being freed, but was being handed over to self-interested business organizations.[23] Erhard quickly rose to deny this, but his arguments were not entirely convincing, and the FDP's enthusiasm for a measure which would give new tasks to the *Verbände* has already been noted. It was to be some time before business interests realized that Erhard meant what he said about the state's role in protecting competition. When they did, their indignation was intense.

---

[20] Ibid. 626.
[21] Ibid. 627.
[22] See below, Ch. 12.
[23] See comments of SPD deputy Meyer, *Wirtschaftsrat*, 636.

Perhaps Erhard's most worrying opponent in June 1948 was the sense of pessimism and doubt which extended well into the ranks of those who actually supported him in the debate. He was aided to a certain extent by the existing example of Belgium, where dollar credits had been used to reactivate consumer demand within the economy— as he intended should be the case in Germany—at the same time as state interference had been substantially reduced. But Erhard's main weapon was his own optimism and sense of conviction—a conviction based on sound economic principles.

Less than two days after the bill was carried, the currency reform was implemented by the Allied authorities. The old Reichsmark ceased to be legal tender. Each German in the three Western zones received 40 new 'Deutsche Mark' (D-Marks or DM) in exchange for the old currency. Otherwise, old banknotes became worthless.[24] This obviously implied the loss of people's savings. Fortunately for Erhard, it was an Allied measure against which Germans had protested. Nevertheless, he approved of the drastic reduction in purchasing power, and was eager to complement it with his own measures.

In fact the legislative position was by no means satisfactory, for the Guiding Principles Law still had to pass through the *Länderrat* and receive Allied approval. Erhard, however, acted as if he had the powers already. He proclaimed the relaxation of allocation rules in the administration's official gazette, with effect from the day after currency reform. He also had his press secretary announce on the radio on the Sunday that the following day price controls on many articles would be abolished. This affected most consumer goods, with some exceptions like clothes and shoes, although even they were less rigorously controlled than before. Otherwise, only essential foodstuffs, and raw materials like coal and iron, remained strictly rationed. Rents were also controlled, so that the whole package was similar in form to the recommendations of the *Beirat* in the spring.

The result was the phenomenon known as the 'shop-window miracle', which occurred on Monday, 20 June 1948. Germans went to their local stores and markets to find goods which had long since disappeared 'under the counter' once again on open display. This was partly due to the fact that in the months before the D-Mark was established, expectations of a currency reform had encouraged producers and retailers to hoard stocks. As we have seen, Erhard himself had made no effort to discourage this, since he wanted as many goods available for the free market as possible.

[24] See, e.g., J. Weber, *Das Entscheidungsjahr 1948* (2nd edn.; Munich, 1981), 182–98. Bank savings were reduced to 6.5% of their face value.

The main reason for the transformation, however, was that producers and shopkeepers needed the new currency, and they knew that they could charge realistic prices—scarcity prices—for the items they had on offer. For the consumer the transformation was also profound. Whereas before 20 June money had been plentiful but in practice hardly worth earning, now goods were appearing in far greater quantities but money was very scarce. This gave the German people a tremendous incentive to work and was also a stimulus to investment, as we shall see below.[25]

As is well known, Erhard's boldness did not arouse universal enthusiasm, despite its popularity with consumers. The Allied authorities were not used to German initiatives of this kind, and were loath to weaken their own powers of control. Erhard later claimed that he was called to account by the military governor of Bizone who pointed out that he had no right to alter price controls without permission. 'I have not altered them. I have abolished them,' came the bold reply.

Whether this conversation actually occurred in quite the form Erhard later recollected it seems open to question. The Allied bizonal authorities in Frankfurt had been willing to speed up their procedures to approve Erhard's legislation, and the military governors had agreed. There evidently were raised eyebrows at Erhard's precipitate moves to reduce controls, but even the British seem to have felt that it was best to accept the German action. There were still plenty of controls left.[26]

Nevertheless, it was just as well for Erhard that the governor of Bizone at that point was the American, General Lucius D. Clay, who was temperamentally more inclined to accept the free market than his British counterpart might have been. Certainly Clay must have known that such ideas would be politically acceptable to many on Capitol Hill, whereas in Britain belief in the beneficial properties of austerity and planning still dominated the official mind. The British were also less happy than the Americans with the Economic Council as an institution. They regarded with suspicion its attempts to override the authority

---

[25] See below, p. 229.

[26] See cable from BICO Frankfurt to the military governors in Berlin, 17 June 1948, PRO/FO/1049/1432. On 24 June, O'Neill reported that 'A certain amount of surprise was expressed at the fact that the Germans possessed sufficient authority to take such comprehensive measures without reference to the Economic Council or the Occupying Powers, and there were even some indications that the German authorities themselves were slightly dubious about the legal justification for taking such steps. The question was examined, however, by the Bipartite authorities in Frankfurt and it is considered that the Germans are keeping within the limits of their existing powers . . .'. O'Neill, 'Review of Developments on the German Side of the Bizonal Economic Organisation' (hereafter 'O'Neill Review'), 17–24 June 1948. PRO/FO/1049/1432.

of the *Länderrat*, upon which 'moderate' politicians, and especially the
more pragmatic leaders of the SPD, were to be found. On 21 June the
Länderrat had refused to ratify the vital legislation unless Erhard was
willing to discuss his measures with the *Länderrat*'s own executive
council and a new supervisory committee to be made up of representatives from the Economic Council and the *Länderrat*. Erhard had to
promise to accept this cumbersome procedure, but in practice the
bureaucratic obstacles put in his path could be ignored. It was significant, however, that the British regarded Erhard's concession as a
victory for the SPD and seem to have approved of it.[27] Fortunately for
Erhard, the Americans, and not the British, could really call the tune in
Frankfurt.

As for the French, their military governor, General Koenig, would
allow none of Erhard's liberalization in his zone, despite the fact that
the currency reform had taken effect there at the same time as in
Bizone. This was to have interesting results, for it demonstrated that
the currency reform was not the sole reason for West Germany's
meteoric recovery after June 1948. Despite the introduction of the D-
Mark, conditions did not improve to nearly the same extent in the
French area of occupation, the inhabitants of which came to regard
Bizone as a sort of German Switzerland, running with milk and honey.
Controls in the French zone began to break down. Röpke, writing in
the *Neue Zürcher Zeitung* in October 1948, pointed out that the absence
of liberalization in the French zone meant that it could function as an
experimental control-factor to show how currency reform would have
worked without the introduction of market forces. 'The effect has
been', he claimed, 'that the French zone has been more or less forced
to follow the same path as the Bizone, with or without changes in the
law.'[28]

In the Anglo-Saxon zones the impact of Erhard's measures was so
great that to countermand them would have been to court disaster for
the whole currency reform. This was a factor which helped to get
Erhard's law accepted by the much less sympathetic *Länderrat*, on 21
June.[29] On the same evening, Erhard broadcast to the German people.
It was a typically aggressive and optimistic performance, although it
did not make many concessions to the economic illiteracy of a lay

[27] 'O'Neill Review', 24 June 1948.
[28] Cited in Buchheim, 'Währungsreform 1948', 226–7. See also Benz, 237.
[29] Laitenberger, *Ludwig Erhard*, 72. Strictly speaking, the *Länderrat* should have passed
the law before Erhard implemented it. The impotence of the *Land* representation at this
point was symptomatic of the shift which was occurring in West German politics.
Effective German administration in Bizone now lay in the hands of the *Wirtschaftsrat*.

audience. He began by pointing out that on that day the Germans had gone quietly to work, and claimed that few of them would not have felt relief at being liberated from the impudent financial swindle of inflation disguised by fixed prices. The decision to return to sound money and real prices had shown them just how near to disaster they had been taken by the previous policies. Erhard assured his listeners that he himself had no property and that his policy was not designed to protect the interests of the possessing classes. On the contrary, it was aimed exclusively at the welfare of the entire economy and especially the broad mass of the population. He repeated his claim to the Economic Council that the many businessmen in Germany had been happy to function as state pensioners in the controlled economy. He was speaking for the abler entrepreneurs, but above all for the mass of the people, when he claimed that the necessary purging of the economy could not take place according to some set of bureaucratic rules, but would have to be left to a competitive market, in which achievement would be the only criterion of success. As for inflation, Erhard assured his listeners that rising prices would soon give way to the pressures caused by rationalization of production and increased supplies. If that did not happen, it would indeed be a miracle, and in the economic sphere he refused to believe in such things. For that reason he had regarded it as a social duty to abolish price controls so as to allow competition free access to the market and thereby help to cut prices.[30]

The social market economy had been well and truly launched. But it was facing rough water, and Erhard knew that neither the military authorities nor his political colleagues would hesitate to jettison him if it proved a failure. The first few weeks were especially bumpy. More money was drawn into the economy as the result of concessions to bank-account holders made in the currency-reform regulations. At the same time the government was trying to reduce the very large burden of subsidies which affected many important items, including coal. Prices began to rise and there were shortages of some essential consumer-goods, such as shoes. The opponents of the new policy scented a chance to bring it down by stirring up popular hostility.

On 6 August Erhard resorted to the microphone again. In a broadcast he attacked those numerous people who, 'blinded by demagogy or motivated by bureaucratic obstinacy', believed it was their duty to resist the spirit of freedom which was growing stronger all the time. He pointed out that price rises caused by reductions in subsidies were not real rises at all. All subsidies—whether on coal or steel or imported

---

[30] L. Erhard, 'Der neue Kurs', in *Ludwig Erhard, Gedanken*, 120–6.

raw materials—did not fall from heaven but had to be paid for by the people as a whole. After twelve years of fixed prices it was surprising that the difficulties with the market had not been greater. It was possibly true that before the currency reform a piece of clothing might have cost 12 marks, whereas it had now risen to 15 or 18 marks. But he drew attention to one essential point: before the currency reform such an article would not have been available to normal consumers at all. His critics were evidently banking on people having very short memories. They were proposing the return of a system which had not even been able to provide the housewife with needles, darning-thread, and a few trouser-buttons. He ended by claiming that 'the demand for democratic freedom will remain an empty formula so long as the basic human rights of free choice of occupation and consumption are not recognized as being inalienable and untouchable'. That and nothing else was the point of the free-market system.[31]

Erhard's truculent attack on controls did not endear him to officialdom, whether in Frankfurt, Berlin, or London, particularly when he pointed out that it would be useless to break down the Hitlerite *Zwangswirtschaft* if a new set of plans and controls were to be imposed as the result of Allied policy. Erhard complained to the US financial expert Tenenbaum and a British colleague that the Allies had saddled West Germany with all sorts of plans for the reconstruction of bits of the economy in which various control offices had an interest—e.g. the building of a fisheries fleet, the provision of 30,000 railway trucks, or the refurbishment of coal-mines. These programmes would tie up huge amounts of raw materials and labour which ought to be flowing into markets to meet the immediate requirements of the German people. The plans would hinder the restoration of a functioning economy, which would itself either fulfil such projects or discard them in accordance with the real needs of the country. Erhard also pressed hard for decontrol of coal and an end to the coal subsidy, thereby saving DM400 million annually. The British official who reported this to London commented that 'I believe we must realise that currency reform, if it is to be a success, is incompatible with many controls and restrictions that have existed in the financial vacuum of the last three years.' His chief financial director, on the other hand, minuted bleakly: 'This man goes too far!'[32] Such distrust of Erhard's swashbuckling approach to economic problems was characteristic of the British authorities in particular. Yet

---

[31] L. Erhard, 'Zur Kritik an der neuen Ordnung', in *Ludwig Erhard, Gedanken*, 127–33.
[32] Report from Ingrams to Sir Eric Coates, 30 June 1948, PRO/FO/1046/100. Coates was head of the finance division of the British Control Commission.

Erhard had one powerful factor in his favour: the currency reform was a success. Even his British critics had to admit that. Reporting to London and Berlin after Erhard's 6 August radio broadcast, Con O'Neill wrote that:

If you read again his April speech[33] you will see that a very great deal of the programme he then announced has since been accomplished. Certainly an amazing transformation of the economic life of West Germany has taken place, thanks primarily of course to currency reform, but thanks also to a great extent to the policy of relaxing controls which Erhard has pursued with consistent support and encouragement from American Military Government...[34]

This policy led to results which were not altogether popular, and rising prices had made Erhard the target of opposition abuse. However, he was a 'tough character and this criticism seems to leave him pretty well unmoved'. O'Neill once more painted a picture of Erhard which was unflattering but grudgingly respectful. He was a man 'with a strong but remarkably narrow mind . . . utterly lacking in any political sense . . . completely devoid of tact or skill in negotiation, and frequently spoils even a good case by presenting it in a manner which is at once plaintive and aggressive . . . Like the Fat Boy, whom physically he so much resembles, he asks incessantly for more; and if he gets it he appears to regard the giver not with gratitude but with contempt.' Yet he was the strong man of the Frankfurt administration and his policy might yet succeed.

The central fact, which Erhard's critics tend to lose sight of, is that the purchasing power of wages remains enormously greater than in the days before Currency Reform. The true standard of comparison is not between official prices now and official prices (where there were any) two months ago, but between official prices today and Black Market prices then. So regarded, prices have indeed fallen . . .

The British official regarded Erhard's success with mixed feelings.

It would be ungenerous to hope that the experiment Western Germany has now decisively, and for the next few months at least irrevocably, embarked upon, should fail. But it is difficult to hope that Erhard personally should succeed. Success in a game for such high stakes would place him in a position of almost dangerous authority: for outside the field of economic theory he is a fundamentally foolish man, rather aggressively nationalist in outlook, and no friend to us or our ideals.

O'Neill's report was read with interest by higher authorities in Berlin and London. One remarked that the snag in Erhard's theory was that

[33] See above, pp. 208–9.
[34] O'Neill to political division, British HQ Berlin, with copy to Pat Dean in London, 18 Aug. 1948, PRO/FO/1049/1432.

'in an economy of scarcity you cannot do away with controls'. But Christopher Steel, who, as political adviser to General Robertson, was the senior British civilian official in Germany, took a different view:

On the other hand, this is in many ways his moment. Marshall Aid will soon be there, the ration should be out of all proportion better this year, and human productivity per head is said to be up by 25% already. This is just the situation where his experiment should succeed if it is going to. He is a nasty, fat, bullying German and I would like to see him crash, but not at the expense of Western recovery![35]

In the face of rising prices, Allied half-heartedness, and the shrill opposition of many German politicians, the success of the leap into the chilly waters of the market seemed by no means assured. Erhard needed all the help he could get in bolstering the courage of those who had accepted the new course. Neo-liberal voices were raised to support him. Röpke continued his journalistic activities in Switzerland and West Germany, but this was a distant voice, and Röpke himself had by now become a target of social democratic abuse.[36] Erhard needed help nearer home; not least within the Economics Administration itself, where, as we have seen, the attractions of state control remained strong. Leonhard Miksch and his colleagues were determined to set out the views of pro-market factions in an effective manner, and shortly after Erhard took over they began to issue a fortnightly journal called *Wirtschaftsverwaltung*, in which the policies of the Economics Administration were discussed and defended. Miksch himself was a prominent contributor to the journal, and Erhard also used it on occasion to air his views.[37]

The sort of threat to the new policy which had to be combated was illustrated in an article by the deputy director of the administration, Dr Edmund Kaufmann, who, in September 1948, drew attention to a circular issued by one *Oberregierungsrat* P. Bausch, the deputy chairman of the CDU in northern Württemberg. Bausch was also the head of the price-control office in the Württemberg Economics Ministry, and therefore a person of some consequence for an important *Land* in the

[35] See minutes on O'Neill's report of 18 Aug., ibid.

[36] On 18 June 1948, during the debate in the Economic Council on Erhard's Guiding Principles Law, one Social Democratic member referred to professors telling Germany what to do from Switzerland—an obvious sideswipe at Röpke. *Wirtschaftsrat*, 18 June 1948, 654–63.

[37] *Wirtschaftsverwaltung* (issued by the Verwaltung für Wirtschaft des Vereinigten Wirtschaftsgebietes, Frankfurt-Hoechst), 18 (Sept. 1949), 482–5. Erhard published, e.g., 'Für Freiheit der Wirtschaft' in Sept. 1949, an article used as the basis of a speech to the Lower Saxon co-operative movement on 11 Sept. 1949, in which he urged further extension of the free market and above all trade freedom.

American zone. Bausch had told his readers that the price rises were caused by the current economic policies of the Frankfurt authorities and that on moral, political, and economic grounds these policies would have to be altered at once. Needless to say, such a fundamental attack on Erhard's activities from a member of the coalition which was apparently supporting him in the Economic Council was highly disturbing. Kaufmann countered with a vigorous defence of the social market economy, the term he used as the title for his article.[38]

He began by stressing in the most emphatic manner that the Economics Administration did not represent the standpoint of the liberalistic epoch of the nineteenth century or the belief in *laissez-faire—laissez aller*. In a sentence echoing Röpke's earlier analogy between sound market-principles and the rules of the road, Kaufmann claimed that the free economy, in which everybody can do or omit to do what he likes, is just as impossible as free traffic on the streets, with everybody walking and driving exactly as he pleases. On the other hand, there could be no question of maintaining the Nazi form of controls, and so there remained only the alternative of a third way. One could describe this as indirect control, or one could declare that a re-established market economy would have to be fitted into a social order. 'We need a market economy steered from social points of view. The new order must be economically sensible and socially just. The task of our time consists of the search for this synthesis.' Kaufmann earnestly argued that this was the viewpoint of Professor Erhard.[39]

He went on to stress that the price rises following the currency reform had been inevitable and in any case not the fault of Erhard's administration. The large subsidies to coal production, which had totalled 1.5 billion marks a year, could not possibly have been maintained. A rise in the coal price promulgated on 1 April 1948 had been inadequate—it eliminated only two-thirds of the subsidy. It also meant that the price for steel or for other coal-dependent products remained unrealistic. An Allied decision to value the Reichsmark at 30 US cents had been very necessary to end uncertainty, but had caused price rises for imported raw materials, and finally the Allies had approved a wage increase of about 15 per cent shortly before the currency reform. The impact of this was felt only afterwards.

Nevertheless, only by decontrolling prices and goods was it possible to dismantle the black market and get a clear idea of real prices. This too would mean an end to hoarding. He pointed out that, however

[38] Bausch was also a member of the Württemberg Landtag. See E. Kaufmann, 'Soziale Marktwirtschaft', in *Wirtschaftsverwaltung*, 8 (Sept. 1948), 2–7.
[39] Ibid. 2.

rigorous control systems were, they could not stop hoarding and black-marketeering. Even in Württemberg, where special commissions had tried to hunt down hoarders, the shop windows had been full on the famous 'X day' of currency reform. To deal with the problem of profiteers, however, he promised that, once the market had given clear indicators of real prices, the administration would send out lists of 'appropriate prices' (*angemessene Preise*), according to which the housewife could orientate herself so that she might avoid retailers trading at unreasonable levels. This kind of pressure would be far more effective than bureaucratic compulsion through a large apparatus of officials. In answer to those who would argue that such measures would be a breach of market principles, he repeated his declaration that the Economics Administration did not share the liberalistic-individualistic attitudes of the nineteenth century, but believed that the market economy should fit into a social framework and be guided by social viewpoints.[40]

It is possible to believe that this rather laboured argument was simply a necessary method of sugaring the free-market pill at a time when many Germans found it unpalatable. That is certainly a fashionable interpretation in the 1990s.[41] Kaufmann himself was a former planner who may have been reluctant to admit that his energies had previously been wasted. But one should observe that the measures he mentions in the article, and the policies of Erhard he defended, were entirely compatible with neo-liberal theories as they had been developed since the 1930s. In 1949 Walter Eucken wrote 'Government planning of forms—yes; Government planning and direction of the economic process—no. To know the difference between forms and process and to act accordingly—this is essential.'[42] Erhard's policies reflected this view.

However correct this diagnosis was, it was small comfort to many who felt themselves threatened by rising prices. It was not surprising that working people began to get restless. The liberation of prices had not been accompanied by a freeing of wages. The wage freeze which had been—at least theoretically—imposed in 1936 remained in force until November 1948. Depite Erhard's optimism, numerous less well-off citizens felt their living standards to be threatened by the 'leap into

[40] Ibid. 6–7.
[41] See Prof. Kaltefleiter's contribution to a discussion on the social market economy in Leipzig, in 'Soziale Marktwirtschaft: Symposion von Ludwig-Erhard-Stiftung und FAZ in Leipzig', *Orientierungen zur Wirtschafts- und Gesellschaftspolitik*, 44 (June 1990), 75.
[42] In *ORDO: Jahrbuch für die Ordnung von Wirtschaft und Gesellschaft*, 2 (1949), 1–99. Cited and translated in W. F. Stolper and K. W. Roskamp, 'Planning a Free Economy: Germany 1945–1960', *Zeitschrift für die gesamte Staatswissenschaft*, 135/3 (1979), 377.

cold water' of market economics. Surplus labour started to be combed out of industrial plants, and those with large families found the price scramble very frightening.[43]

The SPD and the trade unions blew up a campaign of denunciation against Erhard. A motion of no confidence was brought into the Economic Council against him and Pünder. The trade unions called for a twenty-four-hour general strike to start on 12 November, and demanded that emergency regulations be brought in to deal with the economy, including the establishment of a price commissioner. The no-confidence motion was defeated by the votes of the CDU/CSU and FDP. The general strike, however, went ahead, despite a broadcast appeal by Erhard on 11 November in which he pointed out that the unions' demands would lead to the return of the *Zwangswirtschaft*, with its black and grey markets.

This did not mean that nothing was done, or that the pure waters of the free market were unsullied by intervention. Erhard's administration sponsored a programme of utility items—in particular clothing— which should be manufactured to simple specifications and sell at low prices. This was the 'everyman programme' (*Jedermannprogramm*) which served at least as a consolation at a time of shortage. He also persuaded the Allied authorities to allow industrial firms to fix the retail prices of their products, a measure completely at odds with neo-liberal theories.[44] Erhard boasted that if one took this into account, along with the fixed price of *Jedermann* products and the fact that imported goods also had to be sold at fixed prices, more than half of the goods on sale to the German public would be covered by price controls, even if many of these would be set by manufacturers rather than state authorities. Nevertheless, he coupled this reassuring comment with a fervent plea that the rest of the market had to be left completely free, so that prices could find their own level on the basis of supply and demand.[45]

Erhard made this statement at one of the most remarkable political events which had thus far occurred in post-war Germany, a confrontation between economic experts organized in Frankfurt by the Social Democratic Party. The meeting took place in a tense atmosphere two

---

[43] See, e.g., Wilhelm Nölling, 'Die fehlende soziale Absicherung', *Orientierungen*, 36 (June, 1988), 48–9. Nölling points out that child allowances did not begin until 1954, and that for large families on low incomes such items as fares and school fees were a serious burden after currency reform.

[44] Erhard made a point of mentioning this in his pre-strike broadcast on 11 Nov. See *Ludwig Erhard, Gedanken*, 164.

[45] L. Erhard 'Im Streitgespräch mit Erik Nölting: Kundgebung der SPD im Zirkus Althoff, Frankfurt/M., 14 Nov. 1948', in *Ludwig Erhard, Gedanken*, 180–1.

days after the trade unions had held their general strike. An audience of several thousand gathered in the Zirkus Althoff to witness a speaking-duel between Erhard and Professor Erik Nölting, who, as Minister of Economic Affairs in the large *Land* of North Rhine-Westphalia, could apparently speak with almost as much authority as the economics director of Bizone. Nölting was one of the main economic specialists in the SPD and a firm adherent of socialist planning. Like Erhard, he was a former pupil of the liberal socialist Franz Oppenheimer, a point which Erhard did not fail to mention in his speech.

It is an illustration of Erhard's style that he took the enormous risk of exposing himself to this gladiatorial contest. 'Expert' ministers of the pre-war stamp from the Wilhelmine Empire, or even the Weimar Republic, would have considered such populist methods beneath them, and would in any case have feared humiliation. Most academics would have shrunk from a rumbustious public meeting as a forum for serious economic discourse. Yet both Erhard and Nölting took their audience seriously enough to argue for the fundamental principles of the social market economy on the one hand, and democratic socialism on the other. The occasion was viewed as an example of democracy in practice. Neither speaker tried to talk down to his audience, though both were prepared to make emotional, as well as rational, appeals on behalf of their firmly held beliefs. It is a sobering thought that such a political assembly would be inconceivable in the 1990s. Public-relations agencies would never allow politicians to hazard themselves in that way. The public at large, sated on television, would lack both the attention-span and the basic education to follow the arguments put forward.

Erhard made few concessions to the layman when he told his audience that the price rises they had experienced were the result of the Allied currency reform, which had allowed too much purchasing power into the system and encouraged a scramble for goods. The DM10.7 billion which had descended on the market as the result of the currency reform—marks which their owners wanted to use for consumption as soon as possible—could not be completely soaked up by the goods available and this led to price rises. Erhard pointed out that he had favoured a 25 per cent tax on industrial inventories (*Warenlager*), which would have had the double effect of encouraging owners to sell as quickly and therefore as cheaply as possible, and at the same time would have provided funding for the needy.[46] No such measures had proved possible, but the important aim must be to

[46] Ibid. 168.

achieve a properly balanced market based on realistic prices. So long as the Bank deutscher Länder kept a tight grip on credit, and the government restricted public expenditure, there could be no danger of a renewed inflation. The great advantage of the free-price mechanism was that it would enable the truly efficient to do best in the market— irrespective of previous status or official contacts. In a planned economy there was always the danger that those with good relations to the planners would be favoured irrespective of their worth. Under market conditions the only criterion was achievement (*Leistung*).[47]

In an assembly with a social democratic flavour, Erhard was quick to reject any idea that his policy should be equated with that of 'freebooting' *laissez-faire*. In a healthy economy, production was determined by the people, which meant the consumers. But this did not imply a rejection of macro-economic social and political objectives for the nation as a whole.

I am very far from denying the validity of overall economic planning and direction. No, ladies and gentlemen, very far indeed! If that is what you mean by a planned economy, then you may describe me from tomorrow onwards as a planner. Because of course the state has the duty to lead the economy in the direction it ought to take. The fact, for example, that we are faced with so many social tasks: housing, the reconstruction of the power industry, finding jobs for millions of refugees who need new places of work and equipment— that these are tasks which need to be assessed and planned by the state is self-evident.[48]

The difference between him and his opponents was that his planning was designed to steer the economy as a whole in certain directions through a system of opportunities and disincentives to individual producers and consumers, leaving them the maximum freedom to pursue their own interests in a sensible manner. The other kind of planned economy involved binding the citizen from dawn till dusk and laying down what he could and could not do. The first of these systems was, claimed Erhard, an 'organic' system, the second an artificial one. It was a favourite image, the 'organic' free market proving its superiority over an impracticable bureaucratic construct.

It cannot be claimed that Erhard was triumphantly victorious over Nölting, who was speaking on friendly territory, but the debate was widely reported and helped to popularize Erhard's views. His message—that the free-price mechanism and market competition were the only true bases of a healthy economy—began to carry conviction with many people who previously would have unthinkingly accepted such

---

[47] Ibid. 176. The Bank deutscher Länder was established in March 1948.
[48] Ibid. 178–9.

propositions as the 'just price' and the need for the state to control the distribution of goods.

Of course, propaganda activity was by itself not nearly enough. The public had to experience an improvement in their living conditions if the social market economy was to succeed. Erhard was able to point out to his audience in Frankfurt that estimates of future production made before June 1948 had proved grossly pessimistic; economic growth had been truly staggering over the four months since currency reform.[49] The inflationary problem did begin to improve at this time also. As Erhard had predicted, once the excess purchasing-power had been used up, and with the Bank deutscher Länder keeping a tight control on the money supply, prices started to peak. Marshall Aid purchases—or at least investments predicated on Marshall Aid funds— began to ease the supply situation of some German industries, especially textiles.[50] Erhard was also fortunate in that from the summer of 1948 food rations in West Germany had improved, so that malnutrition was really no longer an obstacle to production.[51]

Erhard certainly did not achieve these results without help from other quarters. Above all, he was able to rely on the parsimony of the Bank deutscher Länder, which pursued a firmly deflationary policy when faced with the price rises in late summer and autumn 1948. In November the bank increased the reserve ratios required of banks in West Germany by 50 per cent and put an embargo on new credits. Cash-hungry firms were forced to try to sell their products as quickly as possible. Cosy price-fixing arrangements broke as market pressures started to squeeze producers into a more competitive attitude. The inflation rate started to drop. Between the end of 1948 and 1950 prices in West Germany actually declined—one of the rare instances in recent history of such an occurrence. Rationalization of labour—hitherto unnecessary—became more marked. The overmanning which had characterized German firms under the *Zwangswirtschaft* could no longer be sustained. Within months the economic problems facing the country changed in character. Inflation took second place to unemployment. In the first half of 1949 this rose by 500,000 to 1.25 million—a level

---

[49] Ibid. 170. He reported that in June 1948 only 45,000 bicycles were produced, as against 105,000 in Sept.; a June production figure of 850,000 pairs of shoes had risen to over 2 million in Sept. His figures were so rosy that some in his audience doubted them.

[50] Buchheim, *Die Wiedereingliederung Westdeutschlands*, 74–6.

[51] In July it had been announced that, from Sept., the rations should be based on a normal consumption of 1,800 calories. See 'O'Neill Review', 14–19 July 1948, PRO/FO/1049/1432.

TABLE 2. *Productivity, Wages, and Prices after the Currency Reform* (% change)

	30.6.1948– 31.12.1948	31.12.1948– 31.12.1949	31.12.1949– 30.6.1950
Labour productivity[a]	17.7	26.0	8.8
Nominal wages[b]	15.0	8.4	2.1
Consumer prices[c]	14.3	−6.3	−5.7
Producer prices[d]	3.5	−5.7	−2.0
Real wages[e]	0.6	15.6	8.3

[a] Index of output per man-hour in industry (1936 = 100).
[b] Index of gross hourly earnings per worker in industry.
[c] Consumer-price index for representative household (four persons; 1950 = 100).
[d] Index of producer prices in industry (1950 = 100); only available from 31.7.1948 on; figure in table is estimated, based on backward extrapolation to 30.6.1948.
[e] Nominal-wage index as defined in note b divided by consumer-price index as defined in note c.

Source: H. Giersch, K.-H. Paqué, and H. Schmieding, *The Fading Miracle: Four Decades of Market Economy in Germany* (Cambridge, 1992), 51.

regarded as horrifying in the late 1940s, although it would scarcely raise an eyebrow in the 1990s.[52]

Nevertheless, production and productivity were rising and consumers were enjoying possibilities undreamed of a few months earlier. The combination of currency reform and decontrol had stimulated workers to greater levels of production. In Nuremberg, for example, employers reported that absenteeism had fallen from 18–20 per cent before the currency reform to 2–3 per cent after it. In the second half of 1948, productivity rose to 59 per cent of the 1936 level (see Table 2). Investment in industry was also rising very sharply. Whereas it had been inadequate even to keep the capital stock at its existing level, fixed investment in 1948 was more than double that of 1947, and most of the increase occurred in the second half of the year.[53]

This was encouraged by shifts in taxation which benefited profits and property at the expense of the lower income groups. Tax cuts were strongly favoured by the Frankfurt administration—including, of course, by Erhard himself—but the Allies resisted them. Partly to avoid the occupiers' displeasure, the German tax concessions concentrated on tax exemptions which encouraged investment in industry. Reinvested profits were exempt from tax, depreciation allowances were

[52] See W. F. Stolper *et al.*, 'Planning a Free Economy,' 375–87. Also Carlin, *Factor Distribution*, 190–1.
[53] Carlin, *Factor Distribution*, 186–8.

very liberal, loans to special sectors of the economy, such as residential construction or ship-building, were either fully or partially deductible from taxable income. Tax privileges were granted to savings-bank accounts and interest on securities.[54] The new German currency became stronger as 1949 wore on. In December 1948 it was quoted at 23 Swiss francs per 100 D-Marks; in June 1949 100 D-Marks could buy 74 Swiss francs.[55]

All this did not mean, however, that Erhard was out of the wood. He still faced constant criticism and obstruction from many of the *Länder* and from the occupation authorities. From the early months of the new course, *Länder* such as Schleswig-Holstein, which had particularly severe refugee-problems, were desperately short of money and found the restrictive policies of the Bank deutscher Länder very irksome.[56] In the initial stages of the currency reform the Allied authorities supported the bank's tough line, but as an apparently deflationary tendency appeared in 1949, so the clamour for cheap money began to be taken up by the occupation officials. Erhard insisted, rightly as it turned out, that the danger of a deflation like that which had devastated Germany in the early 1930s did not exist. Demand was strong and would increase as production rose to meet it. But his critics expected instant success, and were prone to cry disaster if it did not appear.

Allied planners, and above all the British, decided that the only way of overcoming the problem of increasing funds for German industry was to insist on budget surpluses and forced savings through higher taxation. These were precisely the sorts of measures which Erhard had decisively and publicly rejected. Savings should be voluntary. Towards the end of March 1949, Allied financial officials in Frankfurt reported that there was 'a serious gap between capital formation needed to ensure success of the ERP and the resources available for the purpose'. They proposed emergency credits for housing and a forced investment of 10 per cent of *Land* revenues in the Reconstruction Loan Corporation. They claimed that it would be pointless to consult the Germans about this, since they had already had several meetings with the director of the German Finance Administration. 'It has been made obvious in these discussions that enforced savings through taxation and the creation of budget surpluses are inescapable methods of deal-

[54] W. F. Stolper *et al.*, 'Planning a Free Economy', 389.
[55] Germans could not, of course, buy Swiss francs freely. Foreign-exchange controls were very strict.
[56] See complaints from Senior British finance officer in Kiel to finance branch of HQCC for Germany, Berlin, 2 Sept. 1948, PRO/FO/1046/683.

ing with the problem.' The Germans, however, had other ideas. 'The response so far', complained the Anglo-Saxon officials, 'has been so negative as to lead the Finance Group to believe that there is little to be gained by discussing these proposals with the German authorities and attempting to get . . . them put through by voluntary German Action.' They recommended instead 'nothing less than Military Government directions' to achieve their ends. The authorities in Berlin were less inclined to be high-handed, and in particular the American side of the military government refused to bully the Germans in this way.[57] Nevertheless the chorus of Allied disapproval rumbled on.

Nor was the urge to plan and direct recovery confined to the British. Günter Keiser produced a paper in April 1949 listing the capital requirements for Bizone, 1949/50. These came to DM4.2 billion and it was not at all clear where this money was to come from—except that Keiser hoped for DM2.5 billion from counterpart funds generated through the Marshall Plan and DM300 million in credits from the *Länder*. These demands were received with some scepticism and were subjected to critical scrutiny by Hermann Abs, who would later become one of Adenauer's most trusted financial advisers.[58]

Erhard strongly opposed backsliding into bureaucratic planning and his plain speaking certainly played its part in blocking measures which might have undermined his policy. On 7 April he attended a dinner in Berlin given by senior Allied officials. Also present were Blücher, Abs, Vocke of the Bank deutscher Länder, and Hartmann, the Frankfurt finance director.[59] The Germans were unanimously opposed to forced savings by budget surpluses and increased taxes—which they thought should be reduced. They also opposed a suggestion that the Bank deutscher Länder might issue a billion DM for capital investment. Two days later the *Frankfurter Rundschau* published an interview with Erhard in which he stated that even if Western Germany could raise the billions for investment demanded in the long-term programme, he would be opposed to its doing so, since this would necessitate such a restricted standard of living for the Germans that it would not be justified. He was opposed to the familiar methods of telling the people that they must tighten their belts just for four years more, so that better times might follow. There were better ways of maintaining the will to

---

[57] Correspondence between chairman of the Bipartite Control Office and the Bipartite Board, Mar. 1949. Clay made it clear at a meeting on 31 Mar. that he was prepared to tolerate higher unemployment levels than the British, PRO/FO/1046/699.

[58] Macdonald, BICO Frankfurt, to Sir Eric Coates, Berlin, 6 Apr. 1949, ibid.

[59] Coates to the British military governor, 7 Apr. 1949. Hartmann's name is spelt Harzmann, but this is clearly an error. Ibid.

work, and these were needed by the Germans, who had been waiting ten years for signs of progress. He attacked the policy of building up cash surpluses in the *Länder*. 'It was in no way the task of the state to save instead of the population.'[60]

What Erhard and the other Germans certainly did want was the release of counterpart funds which were supposed to accrue from the Marshall Aid Programme. In this they were supported strongly by General Clay, who was furious with the ECA in Washington for delays in making this money available.[61]

Even in the summer of 1949, with West German elections approaching and a new German government in prospect, Erhard still had to fight tooth and nail against attempts to retain controls. When he decontrolled ferrous metals and raw textiles, he was accused of breaching the terms of an ordinance which forced him to control 'raw materials which form an essential basis of trade and industry'. In fact the Economic Council had passed an ordinance making such rules permissive, but the *Länderrat* vetoed it. Even after the Economic Council overrode the veto, the military authorities objected on the grounds that the new ordinance could not come into effect for a month.[62]

The whole issue caused a rift between the British and the Americans. The British general Macready wrote to General Robertson, the British governor, on 5 July 1949, claiming that Erhard's ordinance was 'in no way an urgently necessary measure'. It would enable Erhard to decontrol any article without reference to the Economic Council or the military government.

Any military government control will become a farce if an appropriate German control machine does not exist. I am not sure whether professor Erhard's policy is dictated only by his theories on economic liberalism, or whether the Germans are not deliberately using the present vogue of decontrolling to shake off military government control by this device.

He recommended that the military governors disapprove the ordinance. He recognized, however, that the Americans would probably not wish to do so; in which case the list of commodities to be covered by it should be reduced. Not the least of the considerations behind British hostility to this measure was the impact it might have on public opinion in Britain. Meat and fats should continue to be rationed in

---

[60] Translation provided by political adviser's department, Frankfurt, to the British authorities in Berlin, 9 Apr. 1949, ibid.

[61] On 16 Aug. 1949 BICO applied to the ECA for DM873 million in counterpart funds, stressing the concern of the occupation authorities over unemployment, ibid.

[62] Macready and Adcock to chairman of the Bizonal Executive Committee, 24 June 1949, PRO/FO/1049/2122.

view of 'the strong feeling which derationing of these items would raise in the U.K.' After some haggling in Berlin the ordinance was approved, but a daunting list of items—including most foodstuffs, coal, iron and steel, mineral oils, electric power, and gas could still not be decontrolled without Allied permission.[63]

None the less these were rearguard actions. As the British political adviser in Frankfurt, Con O'Neill, had to admit in June 1949

Erhard remains the most significant man in bizonal politics, however little we may like much of his policy. He has a remarkable capacity for doing what he declares he intends to do. He enjoys a good deal of personal popularity; his supporters admire him for his success and many of his opponents for his courage and energy.[64]

With productivity shooting up and investment flowing strongly, it was evident that the jump into the cold water of the market had succeeded. From the end of 1948 Erhard ceased to be a target of public opprobrium and began to be associated with what journalists insisted on calling the 'economic miracle' (*Wirtschaftswunder*). There was, however, a cloud on the horizon. On 14 August 1949 the first West German parliament, the Bundestag, would be elected. As O'Neill reported to his superiors, if Erhard's supporters won, he would probably be Economics Minister in the new government.[65] But what if they did not win? Then the planners and controllers might reappear in force. Erhard's policy did not only have to prove itself in the economic sphere. It had to be politically successful also.

[63] Macready to Robertson, 5 July 1949. Also BICO to the *Wirtschaftsrat*, 15 July 1949. Ibid.
[64] O'Neill to Berlin, 22 June 1949, ibid.
[65] Ibid.

11

Erhard and the CDU

THE success of the social market economy in its first baptism of fire had not gone unnoticed by party politicians. As we have seen, Erhard was not a party man and, in so far as he had party associations, they tended to be with the liberal Free Democrats. Certainly he was no friend of the Bavarian Christian Social Union, which had treated him so shabbily during and after his period as Bavarian Economics Minister. Nevertheless, Erhard was of interest to the leader of the Christian Democrats in the British zone, Konrad Adenauer. Adenauer was determined to link his party to the right of the German political spectrum and to avoid compromise or coalition with the Social Democrats. In this he faced two problems.

The first, relatively minor but tiresome, was the adoption by the CDU of the British zone in February 1947 of what was known as the Ahlen Programme, a socio-economic statement which was considerably influenced by Christian Socialist thinking and which included an apparent commitment to replace capitalist strivings for profit and power with devotion to the common good. Although the programme itself was vague and rather contradictory, it did include the demand that coal should be taken into public ownership.[1] Adenauer, who had no liking at all for socialism, was able to temporize over the amplification of this programme, but he needed finally to bury it before the CDU faced a major West German election.

The second danger, which Adenauer took very seriously, was the possibility that, when West Germany was allowed to govern itself, the prime ministers of the *Länder* would try to engineer a great coalition between CDU and SPD. This would be very convenient for the CDU premiers, because it would enable them to work with the SPD at *Land* level. Adenauer was determined to scotch this possibility and keep the SPD out of the federal government. Erhard's role as economics director of Bizone fitted very well into his scheme of things. The power constellation in the Frankfurt Economic Council conformed with Adenauer's ideal—it was a coalition of non-socialist parties, with the SPD in opposition. Furthermore, Erhard's aggressive championing of

[1] KAS/Pütz (ed.), *Adenauer und die CDU*, 280–1.

the free market made any compromise between himself and the Social Democrats out of the question.

Last but not least, if Erhard's policy worked, and Adenauer saw that it was practicable enough to do so, the party which was associated with him would win the elections. He therefore invited Erhard to speak at the CDU party conference in Recklinghausen at the end of August 1948. The economics director was a great success, delivering a speech on the subject of 'Market Economics of the Modern Stamp' (*moderner Prägung*). This was no dry academic lecture, but a ringing denunciation of planned economies and a passionate denial that his policies were taken from the 'lumber-room of liberalism'. The freedom he was offering was not freebooting or irresponsible; it always involved conscientious commitment to the common good.[2] It was not just a matter of the 'free play of forces'. The socially responsible market economy allowed the individual to fulfil himself and put his personality at the forefront of its scale of values, whilst nevertheless rewarding him according to his achievements. This was the market economy of a modern type. He boasted that, in the weeks since the currency reform and despite all the moaning about hardship, 'the normal German consumer, who had been virtually forgotten, was able to consume far more than in all the three years of the controlled economy put together'.[3] Lively applause greeted this comment. Further ovations followed his claim that the German people were grateful once again to be free human beings, 'finally torn free from the slavery of heart and brain', and that he was receiving about a thousand letters daily—not from businessmen but from simple wage and salary earners thanking him for liberating them from chaos and enabling them to enjoy a decent existence once again.[4]

The message of the speech was the one which Erhard and his supporters in the Economics Administration hammered home throughout 1948–9: the market economy, if allowed to function without distortions, was far more socially just than any system of planning. It was the consumer, the small man, who benefited from the free-price mechanism, not the wealthy entrepreneur.

Such arguments went down well with the CDU in the British zone. As we have seen, they were not immediately convincing to everybody else. Prices went on rising. Erhard blamed this on the fact that the Allies had not cut back the money supply as drastically as the German plan, drawn up by his former think tank,[5] had advised. However,

---

[2] Ibid. 657–8. [3] Ibid. 659. [4] Ibid. 663 and 669. [5] See above. Ch. 7.

not for the last time, Erhard was lucky. The Allied currency-reform measures may have put rather too much money into circulation, but they did at least encourage very strong investment in West German industry. The measures envisaged by the Germans would certainly have meant more unemployment—it was assumed that production would be only 40 per cent of the 1936 level. As it was, Erhard pointed out that after the currency reform DM10 billion had been created, and prices had to be adjusted to this amount of purchasing power, bearing in mind the limited number of goods available. Once this was done, there could be no further inflation.[6]

The CDU supported Erhard in the Economic Council against the bitter attacks of the SPD and the Communists. Nevertheless, there were those in the *Länder* governments and the Christian trade unions who, like the British, regarded him as intolerably right-wing, a *laissez-faire* reactionary. By the early months of 1949, however, the success of his policies was manifest. Inflation was being conquered and productivity was soaring. Just as Erhard had been the target for brickbats in the difficult months of adjustment following currency reform, so he now began to reap the rewards of popularity, especially amongst middle-class consumers. This made him even more attractive to the CDU.

The party was particularly concerned about its own economic policy, to be presented at the elections for a West German parliament which would clearly be held within a matter of months. In the spring of 1948 Adenauer had established a working party to draft an electoral programme on the economy, but he had not insisted that it should make rapid progress, for fear that the Christian socialist wing of the party might insist on retaining parts of the Ahlen Programme. At a meeting of the zonal committee of the CDU in Königswinter on 25 February 1949, the chairman of the working party, Franz Etzel, was due to present the results of its deliberations. Adenauer invited Erhard to address the meeting.

Erhard began by saying that, although he was formally there as a guest, he felt that he belonged with the Christian Democrats and would do all he could to help them win the elections. He urged them not to adopt a defensive attitude towards the economy, but to go over to the attack by hammering at the miseries of planning and stressing the advantages of a free economy. He vigorously defended his policies, and reiterated that 'It is a complete illusion to believe that the planned

---

[6] See Erhard's speech to the Economic Council, 30 Sept. 1948, in *Ludwig Erhard, Gedanken*, 153. See also Laitenberger, *Ludwig Erhard*, 73.

economy is based on social principles whereas the market economy does not deserve to be described as social.' Quite the opposite was true. 'The planned economy is the most unsocial thing there is, and only the market is social.'[7] He told his audience that they should not hide their light under a bushel now that the correctness of the free-market policy was becoming apparent. He was addressing public meetings about three times a week, and wherever he went, the crowds were so large that many had to be turned away. The response to his message was everywhere a positive one. He was willing to devote himself to the election campaign and to address public meetings to the limit of his physical capacity. What was needed was optimism and forthright commitment to market forces. Above all, they had to avoid confusion which might arise if some CDU speakers seemed to contradict others. He suggested that his views might be knocked into shape by a subcommittee for use as electoral material.

After Erhard had earned admiring applause, Adenauer said that his speech should be published and used as the basis for the CDU's electoral programme. Etzel then relinquished his right to speak, claiming that the economic policies of the CDU were now those of Erhard. The drafting subcommittee—a list of whose names had been thoughtfully prepared—was then presented to the meeting. Despite doubts from some interest groups, and above all from Jakob Kaiser, representing the party in Berlin, it was agreed that this committee should produce a clear and fairly simple set of guide-lines on economic policy. Adenauer stressed that this should be restricted to support for the free market against controls and should not try to be a comprehensive economic, let alone social, policy.

The Königswinter meeting was also significant for the light it threw on Erhard's own tactics, and even, though here we must be more speculative, on his deeper beliefs. First of all, it was necessary for Erhard to stress that the policy he was presenting was not 'antediluvian' *laissez-faire* liberalism. He was aware that in a party with a trade-union wing and a strong Roman Catholic membership, individualistic market theories were regarded with suspicion. Roman Catholic social teaching and trade-union anti-capitalism were obstacles to his enthusiastic reception by Christian Democrats.

So far as the former was concerned, there was and has remained a powerful school of Roman Catholic thought which has rejected free-market liberalism on the grounds that individual freedom cannot be regarded as the highest social good, endangering as it does both

---

[7] KAS/Pütz (ed.), *Adenauer und die CDU*, 846.

ecclesiastical authority and social harmony. It has even been suggested that neo-liberalism was another outgrowth of that sceptical, individualist mode of thought which had its origins in the works of William of Occam in the fourteenth century, and which foreshadowed the errors of the enlightenment period.[8] Although there were few in Erhard's audience who could have sustained a theological debate, he must have been aware of the mistrust harboured towards liberal theories by many Roman Catholic politicians.

In his presentation Erhard pointed out that a party like the CDU would obviously give the freedom and worth of the individual personality high priority, and that this would bring with it consequential requirements in the field of economic policy. He was then able to belabour the faults and moral iniquities of bureaucratic planning. Towards the end of his speech he remarked that economics was in any case a crude matter, which should be regarded only as a means to achieve other, and higher, ethical objectives.

In the discussion which followed, one speaker on the social wing of the CDU expressed his scepticism. Johannes Albers, from Cologne, pointed out that Erhard had presented 'in a brilliant fashion' what was more or less the principle of a liberal economy. This meant jettisoning the basic propositions of the Ahlen Programme, the formulation of which had taken over six months. Adenauer intervened to defuse this potential landmine by blandly asserting that they were discussing an immediate problem of economic policy for the elections, and that the choice there was 'planned economy or market economy'. This had nothing to do with the Ahlen Programme, 'to which I am committed without reservation'. When Albers professed himself satisfied with this, but interjected the word 'social' before market, Adenauer reduced the company to laughter by suggesting that they present the alternatives as 'bureaucratic planned economy versus social market economy', a remark which illustrated his own fairly cynical attitude towards such labels.[9]

This well-known exchange has somewhat obscured Erhard's reaction to Albers's remarks. Showing that theatrical gift so helpful for politicians and academics, Erhard made an emotional appeal to his new colleagues, assuring them that he accepted entirely their fundamental principles and ethical objectives.

---

[8] H. P. Becker, *Die soziale Frage im Neoliberalismus: Analyse und Kritik*, (Heidelberg, 1965) 81 and 123–7.
[9] For this discussion, see KAS/Pütz (ed.), *Adenauer und die CDU*, 854–8.

if you ask me how I stand in relation to Liberalism, of which you perhaps suspect me, I reject it! The economy will no longer operate in the form of a business cycle [*Konjunktur*] because that era is past. What other reason would I have for being a crypto-liberal [*verkappter Liberalist*]? I do not represent the interests of the entrepreneurs. I have no talents as a capitalist . . . I own no house, no land, no stocks or bonds and no movable property. I am as un-capitalist as it is possible to be.

He then excused his omission formally to join the Christian camp by reference to his Bavarian origin, implying that he was not willing to join the CDU's Bavarian sister-party, the CSU. Adenauer skilfully supported him by telling the assembled company that he had already discussed the CSU with Erhard, who had put the question to him: 'If you lived in Munich would you join the CSU?' 'What did you reply?' asked an intrepid female member of his audience. 'I pretended not to hear the question,' said Adenauer, amid further merriment.[10]

Erhard was therefore able to finesse the issue of liberalism and use the 'social' adjective as a sop to those who might otherwise have opposed him. Yet it is important to note that in the whole of this discussion he made no reference to any major social aspects of his economic policy. Despite rejecting a *laissez-faire* attitude to business cycles, he proffered no concrete methods of overcoming them. Rather he was at pains to argue that downward market pressures on prices would not lead to a slump, but to a further surge of expansion, a prophecy which turned out to be correct.[11] His speech centred on the argument that the market was *itself* social, and that to restore it would eliminate social injustice. In one sense this eased matters for the supporters of the Ahlen Programme, since they could regard Erhard's views as relating to a fairly narrow area of economic expertise, leaving the social question to be solved by other means. Erhard himself encouraged such a view by telling Albers that: 'I would never take it upon myself to draw up a social programme. Naturally I have my own ideas about it, but I am not enough of a specialist to be able to judge proposals about that.'[12]

He implied that the social question should be left to experts, thereby uncoupling it from the general sphere of economic policy in a fashion scarcely compatible with the views of men like Müller-Armack or Rüstow. This does not necessarily undermine the value of the word 'social' in Erhard's concept. We should remember that he, like Adenauer, had his mind fixed on the coming elections, and wanted to use the CDU to ensure that his economic policy would be continued

[10] Ibid. 863–4.   [11] Ibid. 843–4.   [12] Ibid. 863.

into the Federal Republic. But it is clear that, for Erhard, competition and access to the market were more important guarantees of social health than redistributive taxation or public measures to relieve poverty. It is a tribute to Erhard's powers of persuasion that his optimistic assessment of Germany's future under market conditions carried his hardbitten audience of professional politicians and union leaders along with him, and convinced them that by accepting his policies they were backing a winner.

Thus it was that the social market economy of Erhard became the policy of the major anti-socialist party in West Germany in time for the first Bundestag elections in the summer of 1949. No party conference had approved this decision. It was taken by a committee which represented only the CDU in the British zone, even though some token efforts were made to associate southern Germany and Berlin with the final outcome. In practice it made little difference. The party was happy to bask in Erhard's reflected glory.

On 15 July 1949 the British-zone CDU issued the so-called Düsseldorf Guide-lines (*Leitsätze*), which should serve as its economic electoral platform. Through the Christian Democratic liaison office in Frankfurt it was accepted by CDU organizations elsewhere in Germany, although the Bavarian CSU ignored it.[13] The Guide-lines encapsulated what some have unkindly described as the CDU myth of West Germany's economic recovery. All was gloom, the reader was assured, until June 1948, when the currency reform was accompanied by Erhard's liberalization, which in turn created a magnificent recovery. The CDU took full credit for Erhard's policy. It made clear its commitment to the free-price mechanism and its contempt for socialist planning. However, and here Erhard and his editors had gone farther than his Königswinter speech, it also made very clear that the social market economy meant rejection of cartels and private monopolies. Having contrasted their policy with that of the planned economy, the Guide-lines went on: 'The "social market economy" stands in contrast also to the so-called "free economy" of the liberalistic variety. In order to prevent a relapse into the "free economy" it is necessary to protect creative competition by independent control of monopolies.'[14]

The Guide-lines also made it clear that cartels would be banned, and that market transparency would be furthered in defence of fair competition. Other demands included a policy of sound money and falling prices. Trade should be encouraged. The only economic *dirigisme* which

[13] Laitenberger, *Ludwig Erhard*, 79.
[14] KAS/Pütz (ed.), *Adenauer und die CDU*, 869.

was contemplated was a market-orientated combination of fiscal and monetary measures to reduce the damage caused by the effects of cyclical fluctuations and, above all, to prevent another slump. The details of the Guide-lines probably had little impact on the electorate. Adenauer's cynicism about economic programmes was well merited. But the overwhelming impression it left on the reader, or upon those politicians who broadcast it in the election campaign, was of enthusiasm for free markets and free competition.

This was a very important development in Germany's post-war history for two reasons. First, it marked the point at which Germany's new conservative 'people's party', the CDU, committed itself without equivocation to the market economy and the free-price mechanism. This was of great significance because it contrasted with the situation before the war, when nationalist considerations had been allowed to override a commitment to free trade, and when vested interests, in both agriculture and industry, had regarded economic liberalism with suspicion. It should, of course, be remembered that economic liberalization at this time applied mainly to the non-agricultural sector of the economy. Adenauer joked at the Königswinter meeting that he looked forward to the time when all pigs would be free to run about as they wished, but in practice neo-liberal principles were never to be applied to agriculture.

Nevertheless, the fact that competition and consumer choice were established as the distinguishing features of Christian Democratic policy, as against the planned economy favoured by Social Democrats, meant that, in future, protectionism and economic nationalism were less easily able to establish themselves as politically respectable in West Germany. This was one of the respects in which the CDU differentiated itself from the old Centre Party, and it was by no means the least important. The Federal Republic would possess a political asset denied to the Hohenzollern emperors or the Weimar Republic: a popular, conservative, Christian party committed to competition and the free market.

Erhard and the neo-liberals were by no means the only causes of this development; American influence over West Germany—as well as the general weakness of the Germans *vis-à-vis* their neighbours— undoubtedly had something to do with it. But it was very important that this particular method of articulating liberal economic policies was chosen by the CDU in the formative stages of the West German state.

As for Erhard, his relationship with the CDU was vital to the success of the social market economy, and to his own career. As we have seen, his most intimate contacts had so far been with the liberal Free Democratic Party. He was well known to Thomas Dehler, a leader of the FDP from his own home province of Franconia, he had been elected to the directorship of the Economics Administration in Frankfurt on the initiative of Blücher and his FDP, and the Free Democrats had supported his economic policies most enthusiastically in the Economic Council. The apparent lack of concern for social issues which made Erhard suspect to some sections of the CDU did not worry Free Democrats, many of whom regarded the word 'social' with distaste. The aspects of the social market economy which might arouse uneasiness in the business community—in particular the hostility to cartels and the belief that competition was an essential aspect of the free-market system—were not of urgent interest in the period 1948–9. It could be assumed they were mainly cosmetic, and even designed to appeal to the Americans. Indeed, it was because Erhard had such good contacts to the world of business that he was attractive to the FDP in the first place.[15]

As the time drew near for the first Bundestag election, the FDP leadership naturally assumed that Erhard would cast in his lot with the liberals. He was offered at least one, and probably more than one, constituency to fight as FDP candidate, and he would have been high on the party list. On the other hand, finding him a safe seat for the CDU was rather more complicated, especially since he still neglected to take out membership of the party. Indeed, Erhard's attitude to party politics was rather curious. Although a highly political animal, whose genius rested at least as much in public relations as in day-to-day administration, he seems to have wanted to retain his political independence, and to have seen the forthcoming elections as a plebiscite on his own economic policy, in which political parties like the FDU and CDU should form a shield to defend the free market. Needless to say, this attitude was bound to cause some irritation to the various party managers.

Erhard would have preferred to stand in North Rhine-Westphalia, but the CDU there had difficulties about this, and he was offered first place on the party's list in Württemberg-Baden. This meant, however, that he would be standing for the CDU in one of the regional strongholds of liberalism, opposing such prominent FDP figures as Theodor Heuss. Erhard did his best to avoid confrontation with the FDP, partly no doubt from a feeling of embarrassment at his less-than-grateful behaviour, but also because he sincerely believed the election should be fought on the basis of a common front against socialism, and in favour of the free market. He tried to co-ordinate his speaking engage-

---

[15] See above, ch. 7.

ments with those of Heuss and Blücher, and avoided open confrontation with them in his speeches.[16] He even went so far as to claim, in a letter to Blücher, that it was only the influence of a strong personality like himself which could keep the CDU on the liberal path of the social market economy and give it the necessary backbone for that task. Faced with the choice between supporting a democratic liberal party and carrying through a liberal policy on a stable parliamentary basis, he had, after much soul-searching, decided upon the latter course.[17] Doubtless there was a mixture of honesty and self-justification in Erhard's letter. In choosing the CDU he had picked a winner. On the other hand, his contribution to the winning team was to be a very important one.

The 1949 election campaign was not, of course, simply a judgement on Erhard's economic policy. Other factors were important, such as fear of Communism, which worked in favour of openly anti-socialist parties, and the confessional issue, which had always been of great importance in German politics and was to remain so during the next two decades. The anti-clerical posture of Kurt Schumacher, the SPD leader, certainly did not help him win over doubting voters. Nevertheless, when these qualifications have been made, the importance of Erhard to the CDU victory in August 1949 cannot be gainsaid. Public-opinion polls taken during the election campaign showed that the two best known and most popular politicians in West Germany were Kurt Schumacher and Ludwig Erhard. Adenauer had a less prominent profile with the electorate.[18]

Both Schumacher and Erhard were, of course, controversial figures who aroused dislike as well as enthusiasm. Yet Erhard was less frightening than Schumacher, and he already had something to show his supporters for their loyalty. There was no doubt that the German economy had been transformed since the summer of 1948. Consumer needs were by no means satisfied, but the prospect of normalcy was now a real one. Prices were falling. Unemployment was certainly increasing, but the percentage of the population affected by it was relatively small, and the number of jobs was actually increasing, since returning prisoners of war and refugees from the Soviet zone were having to be accommodated. Above all, the majority of people distrusted the alternatives to Erhard's policy. Democratic socialism and

[16] Laitenberger, *Ludwig Erhard*, 79–82.
[17] Erhard to Blücher, 14 July 1949. Ludwig-Erhard-Stiftung, Bonn, LES Erhard Correspondence, I-3, 1948–9, vol. 27. See also BA Blücher NL, no. 93. Cf. Benz, *Besatzungsherrschaft*, 268.
[18] Koerfer, *Kampf ums Kanzleramt*, 58.

more refined planning-methods were difficult to differentiate from the detested *Zwangswirtschaft* of the pre-currency-reform era.

It has sometimes been suggested that the period of adjustment in Germany from controls to the free market was one of great hardship, and that it could be viewed as a sort of vale of tears through which an entire generation had to pass before reaching the sunnier uplands of the 1960s. This fitted in with some Germans' own perceptions of their heroic and Spartan struggle to achieve economic growth and export-led prosperity. It has also been a comforting thought in Britain, where over a decade of dogmatic commitment to *laissez-faire* has not produced anything like the economic change wrought by Erhard's liberalization policy within one year of its implementation. Of course, West Germany in the fifties was a harsher place to live than many neighbouring countries, although very soon indignant voices were to be heard in Britain and France asking why the Germans had to put up with less austerity than their erstwhile conquerors and victims.

In reality the 'vale of tears' had been the Third Reich and the devastation which followed it. This was recognized by Germans themselves when, in the later 1950s, they were asked what had been the worst period of their lives and most of them selected the time of the Allied occupation. As Con O'Neill had perceptively remarked to his superiors in August 1948, the Germans had suffered a drastic drop in their standard of living as the result of Hitler's economic policies and their defeat in the war. The free-price mechanism did not create that drop, it simply revealed it.[19] Once the market had been restored and profitable production was able to restart, German living standards, although low, began to rise. Not all of this, of course, was attributable to Erhard. Food production lay outside his authority, and he was highly critical of the controls imposed upon it. The fact remained, however, that the rations of food for Germans were never to be as low again as they had been in the period from 1945 to June 1948. Erhard and the CDU could benefit from the association of their regimes—first in Frankfurt and then in Bonn—with an increasingly respectable standard of living. It was small wonder that the housewife's shopping-basket featured in their propaganda.

In the election campaign Erhard was as enthusiastic a public speaker as in the weeks following currency reform. Of all the public figures in West Germany, Erhard spoke as vigorously as any and his meetings were very well attended. The message was always the same. The free market was the only socially just way of solving Germany's economic

---

[19] O'Neill to Berlin, 18 Aug. 1948, PRO/FO/1049/1432. See above, Ch. 10.

problems, and only a vote for the anti-socialist parties could ensure its survival. He liked to describe himself not as a party speaker, but as a representative of the Frankfurt free-market economics policy. This formulation can hardly have aroused great enthusiasm amongst the more committed members of the CDU, and Erhard felt constrained to send a cable to the CDU/CSU working group in Frankfurt in which he rather pompously stated: 'as the lead candidate for Württemberg-Baden I am a CDU man',[20] a claim which most candidates would have found it unnecessary to make.

This did not prevent the Christian Democrats making the most of Erhard in their appeal to the West German public. The election campaign was an undignified display of mutual recriminations between the major parties, with mud being liberally thrown on both sides. The one concrete area of discussion, however, was that of West Germany's economy. This was what most Germans were concerned about in their day-to-day lives, and it was what the Frankfurt authorities had actually been administering since the establishment of the Economic Council. Not only could Erhard point to his record of achievement, but his friendly, non-partisan attitude was well-tailored to public-relations presentation. The CDU/CSU electoral organization disseminated a view of Erhard which was designed at once to reassure and to enthuse the public.

Erhard is a man of action of the sort our people and our times demand. Men of action need healthy optimism. He possesses a fantastic capacity for work, but at the same time he retains his human characteristics of kindness and humour. He just shrugs off the attacks of his opponents in a carefree fashion.[21]

Erhard could feel that public opinion was more and more swinging behind him and that 'the social market economy and the CDU were being identified with one another'.[22] Not for the last time, Erhard was viewed by many as the electoral locomotive which pulled the Christian Democratic train to victory.

The election—on 14 August—was, of course, a win for the CDU/CSU, in that the Christian Democrats emerged clearly ahead of the SPD. Nevertheless, it was by no means a resounding triumph. The Christian

[20] Laitenberger, *Ludwig Erhard*, 82.
[21] Benz, *Besatzungsherrschaft*, 268, citing a circular of the CDU/CSU information service, July 1949.
[22] Ibid.; see fn. 86, citing Erhard's statement on 10 Dec. 1971. Erhard's view of his own importance in the election is shared by many historians. See, e.g., H.-P. Schwarz, *Die Ära Adenauer: Gründerjahre der Republik, 1949–1957* (vol. ii of K. D. Bracher, T. Eschenburg, J. C. Fest and E. Jäckel (eds.), *Geschichte der Bundesrepublik Deutschland*) (Stuttgart, 1981), 27; Koerfer, *Kampf ums Kanzleramt*, 58–9.

Democrats (CDU/CSU) had won 31 per cent of the votes. The Social
Democrats 29.2 per cent. This meant that in the Bundestag the Christians
would have eight more seats than the SPD. Neither party was anywhere
near to an absolute majority. Had the result been a few percentage-
points the other way, it would have been very difficult to insist that the
SPD should be excluded from power altogether. As it was, those in the
CDU who wanted a 'bourgeois' coalition, free from any association
with socialists, could argue that the public had given a mandate to
the economic policies of the Frankfurt administration. Those parties
supporting a planned economy, the Communists and SPD, had gained
only 35 per cent of the vote between them. Therefore it was right
that the CDU should lead a market-orientated government *against* the
'Marxist' parties.

That certainly had been the intention of both Adenauer and Erhard,
even if their preoccupations were rather different—Adenauer's being
diplomatic and political, Erhard's economic. What both wanted was
the continuation of the party grouping which had supported Erhard in
Frankfurt—a CDU-FDP coalition including smaller parties of the right
such as the German Party (*Deutsche Partei* or DP). This was most likely
to be opposed, not by Schumacher himself, for whom collaboration
with Adenauer was just as unattractive as it was for his elderly opponent, but by powerful Christian Democratic figures in the *Länder*
governments. Regional leaders such as Karl Arnold, the premier of
North Rhine-Westphalia, Gebhard Müller, the state President of
Württemberg-Baden, and Werner Hilpert, chairman of the CDU in
Hesse, favoured collaboration with the SPD on both *Land* and federal
levels. Adenauer was able to use Erhard's support as a weapon in his
campaign to smother such tendencies.

Shortly after the election, Adenauer made it clear that Erhard would
be Economics Minister in any CDU-led government—a move which
ruled out collaboration with the SPD. The importance which Adenauer
attached to Erhard's position can be seen by the fact that, before
embarking on the complex negotiations which would be needed to set
up the new government, he and his confidant, the banker Robert
Pferdemenges, met Erhard to discuss their strategy.[23] On the following
day, 20 August, Adenauer went to meet the CSU leaders and the Prime
Minister of Bavaria in Frankfurt to discuss the disposition of such posts
as Federal President and President of the Bundestag and Bundesrat
(the Federal German parliament's upper house, which represents the
Länder). Once again, Erhard was involved in the discussions, though

[23] Koerfer, *Kampf ums Kanzleramt*, 61–2.

he was not present throughout. The following day Adenauer invited selected Christian politicians to his home in Rhöndorf near Bonn to decide on the nature of the new coalition.

Despite his lack of a party-membership card, Erhard had no doubt, as he walked up the famously long flight of steps to Adenauer's beautiful villa on the slopes of the Rhine valley, that he was sure of his place as Economics Minister in the first West German government. He found a distinguished gathering of powerful CDU/CSU leaders being cosseted in a family atmosphere which included a lavish buffet-lunch and plenty of good coffee, served by Adenauer's daughter. Adenauer had been careful to ensure that possible supporters of a coalition with the SPD were in the minority. As was to be expected, Erhard was one of the most eloquent advocates of a 'small' coalition, without the Social Democrats. Adenauer himself repeatedly made the point that 'the electors have chosen the social market economy and we are bound by this decision'.[24] By the end of the meeting the future was clear. The first government of the Federal Republic would be led by Adenauer and would include only those parties which had supported Erhard's policies in Frankfurt. Its economic policy would be that of the social market.

On 20 September 1949, Adenauer, who had been elected Federal Chancellor five days earlier, presented his new government to the Bundestag. In his speech he told the assembled members of parliament that: 'The question "Planned economy or social market economy?" played a dominating role in the election campaign. The German people came down with a large majority against the planned economy.'[25]

Needless to say, the Economics Minister in the new cabinet was Ludwig Erhard.

[24] Ibid. 63.   [25] Ibid. 66.

12

The SPD and the Social Market Economy

IN the SPD, as in all great parties, there were differing shades of opinion, German Social Democrats, like German liberals and German Roman Catholics, had gone through a difficult learning-process since 30 January 1933. The experience of the Third Reich, whether spent in exile, in Nazi concentration camps, or—as was true for the majority of rank-and-file Social Democrats—in impotent 'inner emigration', unable to do anything except avoid Nazi attentions and hope for salvation from outside, was bound to make many party members reconsider the party's programme. A simple reassertion of the old policies of the 1920s scarcely seemed appropriate for the post-war era. Schumacher himself stressed that what was needed was a 'new beginning' rather than a 'reconstruction' and that Weimar was past history.[1]

During the Third Reich many social democrats had been forced into exile, where they had plenty of time to reconsider their ideological position. One feature of exile politics, whether in Prague, Paris, or London, had been the continuing hostility between Social Democrats and Communists. This conflict had, of course, existed right from the foundation of the German Communist Party in December 1918, and had been especially virulent in the years before Hitler assumed power. After 1933, despite the attempts of some individuals at grass-roots level to achieve working collaboration against Nazism, the ill feeling between the functionaries of both parties deepened. Even the decision of the Comintern in 1935 to work for a popular anti-Fascist front made little difference. The SPD rightly regarded this move as a cynical *volte-face*, designed to serve the tactical interests of Moscow. They feared that, with the German people denied the right of democratic self-expression, the Communists, who were better prepared for clandestine activity, might gain control of the labour movement for themselves. Social democrats also disliked the Communists because they were agents of a foreign power, whereas the SPD, despite the taunts of right-wing

---

[1] K. Klotzbach, *Der Weg zur Staatspartei: Programmatik, praktische Politik und Organisation der deutschen Sozialdemokratie 1945 bis 1965* (Berlin, 1982), 177.

extremists, was staunchly patriotic. This issue became important in the Second World War, when Communists seemed ready to accept the idea of collective German guilt, a concept which Social Democrats rejected. They pointed out that they, and other German democrats, had been victims of Fascist repression long before the Allied powers bestirred themselves to resist Hitler.[2]

Social Democrats in exile had also come into contact with different, and often more pragmatic, attitudes towards the reform of capitalist society. In Britain, for example, Social Democratic exiles, led by Ollenhauer and Vogel, witnessed the publication of the Beveridge Plan for social security, and in America Social Democrats could experience the achievements of the New Deal. In view of the brutalities of the Third Reich and the similarities which seemed to be emerging between dictatorships of a Fascist or a Communist complexion, some Social Democrats began to reconsider the fundamental principles upon which their political movement was based. They still wanted a more just and more humane society, in which the interests of working people would be given the highest priority. But they began to doubt whether the methods of class conflict were the best way of achieving this. The seizure of capitalists' property—never a strong priority of the SPD when in government during Weimar—seemed something of a dangerous irrelevance.

Nazi repression also left its mark on the SPD, whether in exile or at home. Far greater importance began to be given to more elementary objectives which Marxists had previously dismissed as self-evident or even secondary because they affected only the 'superstructure' of society. Thus individual freedom from the fear of arrest, democratic rights to elect one's governors, and freedom of speech and assembly were 'liberal' objectives which now became of central importance for Social Democrats—just as they were for Roman Catholic politicians, who had once preferred a strong state to political freedom. As one exiled Social Democrat put it in 1939: 'We feel ourselves to be part of the great movement of the spirit which has come down through the centuries; to which liberalism as well as socialism belongs, resting as they now both do on the fundamental principles of freedom and humanity.'[3]

During the war there were some attempts to reformulate Social Democratic policy in the light of the new situation. Gerhard Kreyssig,

---

[2] A. Glees, *Exile Politics in the Second World War: The German Social Democrats in Britain* (Oxford, 1982), e.g., 93.

[3] Klotzbach, *Der Weg zur Staatspartei*, 31, citing Curt Geyer, 'Die Partei der Freiheit' (1939), in K. Klotzbach, *Drei Schriften aus dem Exil* (Berlin, 1974), 355.

later to be an SPD economic expert in the bizonal Economic Council, produced in London a scheme for a mixed economy, but with key sectors under state control and with macro-economic planning designed to achieve full employment. 'Expropriation of the expropriators' was not a prominent aspect of this proposal; the influence of Keynes, on the other hand, was very clear.[4]

A striking paper on the same subject was also drawn up by a young SPD journalist, Richard Löwenthal. This was later developed into a book, *Beyond Capitalism*, published under a pseudonym in 1947. Purist Marxists might have been affronted by Löwenthal's modification of their theories, since he evidently saw the primary task of state intervention to be the maintenance of full employment and the destruction of monopoly power. Nevertheless, his general assessment of developed economies was not likely to enthuse classical liberal economists. He stressed that capitalism of the old liberal character was dead; monopolies, class conflict, and power struggles between interest groups had created a situation in which, during the economic crisis in 1929–32: 'the structure of the old capitalist market-system collapsed irrevocably'.[5]

Löwenthal claimed that the market economy had been replaced by a planned economic system—as Marx had predicted—but under circumstances different from those Marx had foreseen. It was up to socialists to ensure that the planned state economy which was replacing capitalism should be run for socialist purposes—'victory is not inevitable'.[6] He praised the victory of democratic Labour in Britain and was highly critical of the Soviet Union, which was 'semi-feudal', 'absolutist', and 'totalitarian'. True socialism could be established only in a democratic political system and its main aim must be to smash the power of monopolies. It did not necessitate public ownership so long as private ownership did not imply monopoly control. The aim of socialist planning must be to obtain equal chances for all. It was clear that Löwenthal's model for democratic socialism was Great Britain during and immediately after the Second World War. It was a model which Röpke or Eucken would have rejected, but it was a move away from fundamentalist Marxism.

Indeed, for many politicians and trade-union leaders of a practical turn of mind, Marxism seemed to have weakened German Social Democracy between the wars by its stress on historical processes which

---

[4] Held, *Sozialdemokratie und Keynesianismus*, 176–7, and W. Röder, *Die deutschen Exilgruppen in Großbritannien: Ein Beitrag zur Geschichte des Widerstandes gegen den Nationalsozialismus* (Hanover, 1968), 272–4.

[5] P. Sering (Löwenthal), *Jenseits des Kapitalismus* (Lauf bei Nürnberg, 1947), 28.

[6] Ibid. 84.

lessened the need for individual initiatives. Wilhelm Hoegner, who became Social Democratic Prime Minister of Bavaria for a period after the war, later pointed out that 'scientific socialism' was an excellent doctrine for those who preferred talk to action, because it enabled them to wait for history to do their work for them.[7] Unfortunately history did not often oblige. There were many in the SPD who were now determined to put effective action before phrase-mongering and ideological purity.

By 1945 many Social Democrats were ready to modify the comprehensive vision of a socialist economy in which man's needs would be met by a centralized allocation-system, and property would be held in common. Instead there was a willingness to contemplate a politically free market both controlled and stimulated by state intervention designed to create full employment and a just distribution of wealth. Reformist attitudes towards the capitalist economy were to be found most especially in Bavaria, where there existed a tradition of reformist socialism dating back to the 1890s. Hoegner himself was contemptuous of radical theorists and preferred a common-sense approach to the economy. Although he was forced to resign as premier in 1946, the new SPD party leader in Bavaria, von Knoeringen, was also on the pragmatic wing of the party, and was eager to stress the compatibility of socialism with Christian ethics—a prudent stance for a politician in the predominantly Roman Catholic province of Upper Bavaria.

In 1948 the SPD Economics Minister in the Bavarian government, Rudolf Zorn, told the party congress at Düsseldorf that the aim of Social Democratic policy should be to regulate the market economy so that workers got a just share of the profits. Consumer choice might also be a legitimate objective for Social Democrats, but it should be combined with full employment. This 'regulated market economy' involved encouraging entrepreneurial investment by assuring businessmen that economic expansion would be a permanent feature of the economic landscape.[8]

Amongst the trade-union leaders also, there was a desire above all to avoid reliving the frightening experiences of the Third Reich. The German trade-union movement was helped to revive in the British

---

[7] Klotzbach, *Der Weg zur Staatspartei*, 30–1, citing W. Hoegner, *Flucht vor Hitler: Erinnerungen an die Kapitulation der ersten Republik* (Munich, 1978), 23 ff.

[8] Held, *Sozialdemokratie und Keynesianismus*, 214–16. The discussions amongst Bavarian Social Democrats about economic policy are described in H. Kronawetter, *Wirtschaftskonzeptionen und Wirtschaftspolitik der Sozialdemokratie in Bayern, 1945–1949* (Munich, 1988), esp. 7–23 and 158–80. Waldemar von Knoeringen's commitment to Christian ethics is mentioned in H. Mehringer, *Waldemar von Knoeringen: Eine politische Biographie, Der Weg vom revolutionären Sozialismus zur sozialen Demokratie* (Munich, 1989), 276–8.

zone by the active patronage of the occupation authorities, assisted by the British Trades Union Congress (TUC). Ernest Bevin, otherwise not distinguished by his fondness for the Germans, approved of reconstructing German trade unions along democratic lines and on an industry-wide basis, which avoided demarcation disputes. In this way Germany gained a union movement which was better geared to the needs of modern industry than were the unions in Britain. In addition, the Weimar institution of the works council—or *Betriebsrat*—representing workers' interests, was revived, having languished under the Nazi Labour Front.

In heavy industry, workers' representatives, who were often union officials, were put on supervisory boards as part of a co-determination policy furthered by the Western Allies to reduce the influence of supposedly pro-Nazi industrialists. In the early days of the occupation, trade-union functionaries were among those who could most easily demonstrate their innocence of National Socialism, and they were therefore employed by the occupiers in a variety of administrative functions, especially in connection with industry or social welfare.

This combination of Nazi repression and post-war opportunity generated a cautious attitude amongst German trade-union leaders, for whom militancy in the class war was less important than making concrete gains for their members and building up their own organizations. After the currency reform of June 1948, they were certainly angry at price rises and the poor provision wage-earners received when the mark was revalued. Nevertheless, their own union funds suffered severely as the result of currency reform, and they could not afford to risk too fierce a confrontation, even if they had wished to do so.

Mention should also be made at this point of some more conventional economists who joined the SPD after the war because it seemed to offer an acceptable alternative to 'clerical' Christian Democrats and because in the British zone of occupation the SPD seemed more likely to wield power than other parties. As we have seen, Leonhard Miksch was a member of the party, but his own convictions never wavered from his commitment to market economics. He evidently joined the SPD in the hope that he could teach Social Democrats some sensible economics.

Another young economist who was to play a powerful role in changing SPD policies was Karl Schiller. As a student Schiller had been present at the meeting of the *Verein für Socialpolitik*, in Dresden on 28 September 1932, at which Rüstow had demanded a strong state to stand above pressure groups and protect the free market. It had made a powerful impression on him.[9] After spending part of the war as an economist in the traditionally liberal Institute of World Economics at Kiel, Schiller became Professor of Economics at Hamburg and a Social Democratic member of the city council. As we have seen, he was one of the academic economists who opposed the neo-liberals on the advisory council of the Economics Administration, 1948–9, but his arguments were always cool and pragmatic, and he certainly did not reject the price mechanism. In September 1948 he welcomed Zorn's contribution to the Düsseldorf conference, and his own views were more sympathetic to Keynes than to Marx. Like Weisser and Eichler, he was keen to move away from class-war rhetoric and the rigidities of Marxism. Unfortunately there was to be a long and agonizing struggle before the SPD was willing to change course.

It should here also be mentioned that the experience of the Third Reich had created a certain ambivalence amongst German economists on the left as well as the right. Distaste for politically repressive aspects of Hitler's regime might be somewhat tempered—at least for those who stayed in Germany—by admiration for the Nazis' success in revitalizing the German economy after the appalling experiences of the Great Depression. The French and the British economies were still looking decidedly unhealthy—unemployment in Britain stood at 1.8 million in August 1938, a figure which contrasted with virtual full employment in the Third Reich. Talk of a 'recovery' in the British economy at this time due to the natural workings of the market is not convincing. A minor building-boom did not create an expansion in industrial production—it was left to the war to do that. As for the New Deal in the USA, that had been politically successful, but by 1938 the US economy had yet to recover its pre-1929 levels of production.

Only in Germany did the government seem to have discovered the means of achieving sustained growth and full employment without inflation. This had been done by high levels of government spending, often concealed from public scrutiny—strict controls on foreign trade and capital movements, and fixed prices. In other words, and as Schacht himself remarked, the classical tradition of economic theory had been abandoned.[10]

Even for Social Democrats in exile or under threat of persecution in

---

[9] Conversation between the author and Prof. Schiller, 15 July 1983.

[10] Schacht, *My First 76 Years*, 329. Schacht's actual words are: 'What mattered to me, however, was not the classical tradition of my economic theory but that the German people should be provided with the necessities of life.' In fact, the necessities of life could easily have been provided by the free market. It was the equipment of Nazi armies which required more ingenious financial devices.

the Third Reich, the sharp move away from market economics and monetary orthodoxy in most developed countries during the Second World War seemed a welcome development. The era of Schacht and Göring in Germany was paralleled after 1940 by a 'Keynesian revolution' in Britain and the intensification of the New Deal in the United States. The ideas, therefore, of central planning, high levels of public expenditure, and state control of foreign trade were well established; it seemed to many Social Democrats that their main task was simply to ensure that the right people were operating the levers of power.

At the end of the Second World War there were good reasons for supposing that the political organization most likely to inherit power in Germany would be the Social Democratic Party. It was the only great party of the Weimar Republic which continued to exist as a credible political force. The liberal parties had disintegrated in the face of the Nazi movement and many of their supporters—not to mention their members—had eagerly collaborated in the Third Reich. The Roman Catholic Centre was a shadow of its former self and after 1945 it was quickly outstripped by Christian Democracy. The Communist Party (KPD) certainly looked as if it would revive in the immediate post-war period, especially since it accepted the Yalta and Potsdam decisions and was willing to participate in 'anti-Fascist' groupings. But its association with the Russian occupation authorities in the Soviet zone, and the creation of a bogus 'Socialist Unity Party' there in 1946, rapidly discredited the KPD in West Germany.

The Social Democrats, on the other hand, could boast that they had refused to bend the knee to Hitler, having courageously opposed his enabling act in the Reichstag in March 1933, when other parties truckled in the face of Nazi intimidation, that they had carried on the fight against totalitarianism inside and outside Germany—although circumstances had rendered both types of opposition extremely difficult— and that they had never succumbed to the blandishments of Soviet Communism.

Furthermore, they possessed a determined and fearless leader in Kurt Schumacher, who rapidly emerged as the dominant figure in the SPD in the British zone, where it was most strongly supported. Schumacher, who had lost his right arm in the First World War, had been an energetic socialist agitator in Stuttgart during the Weimar Republic. He had been elected chairman of the party organization there in 1930, when still only 34 years old. In September of the same year, he was elected to the Reichstag. During the twilight years of Weimar he was an outspoken and militant opponent of the Nazis, claiming that

National Socialism was just an appeal to the 'swine in man' (*ein Appell an den inneren Schweinehund*).[11]

When Hitler took power in Germany, Schumacher refused to go into exile, but did nothing to hide his unyielding hostility to the Nazis. It was therefore no surprise when he was arrested in July 1933. He spent nearly ten years in Nazi custody, mostly in the notorious concentration camp at Dachau. When he was released in 1943 he seemed a physical wreck, and the Nazis assumed he could do no more harm. He went to live with relatives in Hanover, and after the city fell to American troops on 7 April 1945, Schumacher set about reviving the local Social Democratic Party there.[12]

Despite his appalling privations, which would have been enough to break many a fit man, let alone a disabled war-veteran, Schumacher flung himself with almost frenetic energy into the cause of social democracy. It ought perhaps to be noted that, even before his incarceration, he had been bitterly opposed, not only to the Nazis, but also to the Communists. In addition, he felt that the conservative élites and capitalist classes in Germany, the Schleichers, the Papens, and their supporters, were little better than Hitler, whom they had indeed helped into power. His own ideological position was not very clearly defined, and he certainly did not regard himself as a doctrinaire Marxist. He was patriotic in his attitude to the German state, which he regarded as the proper instrument for the socialization of German society.

In his doctoral thesis, presented in 1920, he took a much more positive attitude to the state than was common amongst Marxists. He admired the works of the 'new Marxists', who at that time were seeking benefits to the working class from state intervention, rather as Lassalle had done some sixty years earlier. Schumacher was particularly taken with the Austrian socialist Karl Renner's concept of a state-controlled economy (*Durchstaatlichung der Ökonomie*) and saw it as an achievement of the 'new Marxists' that they had replaced the 1789 concept of freedom with one created in 1914—which meant 'the ideal of voluntarily yielding up [one's] individuality to a collective person'.[13] It might be noted that in this respect Schumacher had evidently accepted the same 'Germanic' critique of individualism as that which had been swallowed—albeit with very different results—by intellectuals supportive of Nazism, including Müller-Armack, in 1933.

---

[11] L. J. Edinger, *Kurt Schumacher: A Study in Personality and Political Behavior* (Stanford, Calif., 1965).

[12] Ibid. 71.

[13] W. Albrecht, *Kurt Schumacher: Ein Leben für den demokratischen Sozialismus* (Bonn, 1985), 11–12.

However critical Schumacher may have been of Marx, he certainly admired both Marx and Engels as prophets, whose teachings about the class war had not lost their relevance. In 1947, when he spoke at the formal reopening of the Karl Marx House in Trier, Schumacher referred to Marx as the great 'investigator and discoverer'. Although his teachings ought not to be monopolized as a 'state religion'—an obvious side-swipe at the Communists—Marxism remained 'an indispensable method in the struggle to liberate working people'.[14] This reinforced his statement to the first SPD congress in Hanover on 9 May 1946, when he told the assembly that:

As Social Democrats we have absolutely no reason to denounce Marxism root and branch and throw it overboard . . . If Marxism is no catechism for us, it is nevertheless the method of approach which has been of more help to us, especially from the analytical viewpoint, than any other scientific or sociological method in the world. The class war is over only when all human beings have the same rights and the same duties.[15]

To sum up, Schumacher was a nationalist, anti-Nazi, and anti-Communist Social Democrat who looked to a powerful state to organize the economy in a fashion beneficial to the working class. The concept of class war played a powerful role in his thought. He had no love lost for German capitalism and blamed it for the miseries which he and others had suffered under the Third Reich. A man of rigid, and perhaps even obsessive, views, Schumacher was unlikely to be attracted by the concepts of the social market economy. And so it proved.[16] This is an important observation, because in subsequent party debates it was often convenient for reformers to cite Schumacher as an authority for their pluralistic approach to socialism. In fact, it is unlikely that Schumacher would have been whole-heartedly in favour of any of the changes which compromised the fundamentally working-class, anti-clerical policies of his SPD.[17]

Whatever Schumacher's ideological preferences, there was no doubt about his effectiveness as a political leader. Setting himself up to co-ordinate Social Democratic activity in the Western zones, and to thwart

[14] Ibid. 89.
[15] Kurt Schumacher: Reden Schriften Korrespondenzen, 1945–1952, ed. W. Albrecht (Berlin, 1985), 390. Italics in the original.
[16] Edinger, Schumacher, 42–8, gives an interesting assessment of Schumacher's views in the Weimar period. See also Albrecht, Schumacher: Ein Leben, passim.
[17] In his excellent biographical sketch of Schumacher, Dr W. Albrecht suggests that after 1945 Schumacher was enthusiastic for socialization but not for nationalization (Verstaatlichung). Like other Social Democrats, Schumacher wanted to avoid bureaucratization, but state planning was an essential feature of his economic policy. Albrecht, Schumacher: Ein Leben, 5.

Soviet efforts to capture the party, he was elected party chairman by the first post-war SPD congress, held in Hanover itself. From then on until his death in August 1952, he was undisputed leader of German Social Democracy, and was seen by many Germans and their occupiers as a likely head of government when the country gained its independence.

The main lines of Social Democratic economic policy were laid down by Schumacher in consultation with men like Viktor Agartz and Erik Nölting. Agartz was a former economics lecturer at a trade-union seminary and an official in the co-operative movement who had survived the Third Reich working as an auditor. In 1946 he was appointed the director of the Central Office for Economic Affairs (*Zentralamt für Wirtschaft*) in the British zone. Professor Nölting had been a Social Democratic member of the Prussian *Landtag* during the Weimar Republic, and director of the economics administration in the province of Westphalia. After suffering persecution under the Nazis, he was reinstated as Westphalian economics director in September 1945. This was an important appointment, because in summer 1946 Westphalia ceased to be merely a province of Prussia, and became a major part of the new West German *Land* of North Rhine-Westphalia. In 1947 the CDU premier of this *Land*, Karl Arnold, appointed Nölting to be his Economics Minister.[18]

Agartz and Nölting were among Schumacher's closest advisers. Both were committed to a planned economy, and wide-ranging measures of socialization. Although they would have denied wanting to establish bureaucratic state control of the sort operating in Stalin's Russia, it was clear that they stood for precisely the sort of collectivism so repugnant to neo-liberals like Eucken or Röpke.

So far as the economic policies to be adopted by a future SPD-led administration in Germany were concerned, planning and controls were very high on the agenda. The concept of 'socialization', the exact definition of which caused a great deal of difficulty, loomed large in any discussion of SPD policy. In some of the *Länder* where Social Democrats were actually responsible for economic affairs, plans for socialization were drawn up and even approved. In Hesse, for example,

---

[18] Details on Agartz and Nölting are given in Klotzbach, *Der Weg zur Staatspartei*, 79 and 88 respectively. For an interesting discussion on the distinctions being made between *freiheitlicher Sozialismus* and *sozialistische Planwirtschaft* in discussions at this time, see G. Ambrosius 'Wirtschaftsordnung und Wirtschaftspolitik in den Konzeptionen von CDU und SPD, 1945–1949', in C. Scharf and H.-J. Schröder (eds.), *Die Deutschlandpolitik Großbritanniens und die britische Zone, 1945–1949* (Wiesbaden, 1979), 161 ff.

only the veto powers of the American occupying authorities prevented such schemes being implemented.

Any doubts about the commitment of the Social Democratic Party in Western Germany to the ideal of socialization can be dispelled by looking at the record of an economic conference held by the party on 19 and 20 June 1947 in Bad Wildungen. Apart from a rally in a sports stadium, addressed by, among others, Nölting, there was a discussion chaired by Kreidemann from the SPD's central executive in Hanover and a report by Petrick on the definition of socialism—a matter of urgency, he claimed, since 'the time for theoretical arguments is passed'.[19]

Nölting himself, in a lecture on 'Freedom and Restrictions in the Socialist Economy', said that there were two answers to the current economic crisis. The first was a capitalist answer, which advocated the free play of market forces and a return to private enterprise. The second was a socialist answer, which demanded a centrally directed economy with special bodies for planning and control.

We must be clear in our minds that to give up existing controls and to return to the so-called free market would mean the physical destruction of millions of livelihoods [*Existenzen*]. As a party with a sense of responsibility we ought therefore under no circumstances to allow the reins to be slackened. Nor should we permit even the smallest beginnings of economic independence and caprice [*Willkür*] . . . Germany's economy has totally collapsed; reconstruction must not be left to blind chance.[20]

Free competition was no alternative, because in highly developed societies competition had been supplanted by monopoly capitalism. In the place of free competition there now appeared a brutal struggle for power: 'Monopoly capitalism . . . is in practice economic anarchy. Under its auspices the economy is refeudalizing itself.' *Dirigism* existed already—but for the benefit of capitalists: 'The socialist economist must know: there can be no going back to the free market. A controlled economy will exist whatever happens. It is just a matter of deciding how that economy is to be steered.'[21] This was very clearly a rejection of all that neo-liberal economists stood for.

Nölting admitted that the people had come to associate planning with shortages. He claimed that such shortages actually had nothing to do with socialism. It was not the planners' fault that shortages existed.

[19] Report on the Wirtschaftspolitische Tagung der Sozialdemokratischen Partei Deutschlands am 19. und 20. 6. 1947 in Bad Wildungen. *Referat Everhard Esser, Köln, auf der Sitzung des Wirtschaftspolitischen Ausschusses der SPD Oberere Rheinprovinz am 31.7.47*, FES PV Bestand Wipo, L1 142, p. 1.
[20] Ibid., p. 9.　　[21] Ibid., p. 8.

They had been caused by Nazi economic policies, the effects of the war, and the disruption of world trade.[22] In order to make planning more attractive, Nölting and Petrick both disassociated it from state bureaucracy and talked of a system in which all kinds of personal initiatives would be possible. Co-operatives and municipal enterprises as well as, apparently, modest private businesses would be allowed to flourish, but all within the framework of an overall plan. The nature of the initiatives allowed was left vague but, at least on Nölting's part, the rigidity of the planning system was not. Although the state should not itself act as an entrepreneur, the *whole* of the economy must be subordinated to a state planning system. Nölting posed the question 'How shall this planning be carried out?' and provided the answer: 'All planning must originate from a central institution if it is to be effective.'[23]

To prevent the individual from feeling that his freedom was being compromised, state control should be indirect wherever possible, using taxation, credits, customs duties, etc. as a means of steering the economy. Yet this seems to have been more a matter of sugaring the pill than of actually altering the fundamentals of a system in which state planning and a centralized directorate would call the economic tune. Even economic democracy, a popular idea in the labour movement, would have to be subordinated to the overall planning-mechanism. Nölting warned that it could never be a substitute for a socialist planned economy. He seemed to imply that democracy on the shop floor might be a useful weapon in the war against monopoly capitalism, but could not be an integral part of a socialist economy.[24]

In the summer of 1947, therefore, the economic policies of the SPD seemed poles apart from those of the neo-liberals. Collectivism and planning were conceived in a way which made them incompatible with the market. Competition was pooh-poohed as old hat. Amelioration of the workers' lot by co-determination was seen only as a stage in the struggle to overthrow capitalism altogether.

The conflicts in the Frankfurt Economic Council which followed, and the controversy over Erhard's decision to opt for the free-price mechanism after currency reform in June 1948, exacerbated the differences between the SPD and the supporters of market economics. As we have seen, even the relatively pragmatic Social Democratic economists on the academic *Beirat* in the spring of 1948 had been strongly opposed to the 'leap into cold water' proposed by the neo-liberals.[25]

Once that decision had been taken, SPD anger was unrestrained and

---

[22] Ibid., p. 10.   [23] Ibid., p. 11.   [24] Ibid.   [25] See above, Ch. 9.

undoubtedly genuine. In the Economic Council's debate on Erhard's policy shortly after currency reform, one Social Democratic speaker stressed the dangers of a sudden return to market forces, dangers which did not menace the CDU members of the assembly, because they belonged to that section of the community which possessed life-jackets in the form of real property. This was a benefit not provided for 'all the others who have now been thrown into the cold water as the result of the currency reform'.[26] This indeed was the core of the argument used against Erhard and his supporters throughout the period from 1948 until 1953, when the CDU victory in the Bundestag elections was so clear-cut that predictions of gloom could scarcely be maintained.

Schumacher's own attitude towards neo-liberal theories was well illustrated by a speech given to the Social Democratic Party congress in Düsseldorf on 12 September 1948. Having blamed the possessing classes for the failure of Germany's first democracy and the rise of Nazism, he claimed that the reappearance of such people on the German political scene was a greater political threat to democracy than the machinations of the Communists. As for their free-market theories:

The peculiarly degenerate variation on the concept of personal freedom with which they are operating has no validity; it is a doctrine of the isolated and atomized individual which is singularly unsuited to our times. It is impossible to accept the sanctification of even the most robust personal interests at the expense of the common good, because that would make no impact on the realities of the very complex life in our society. Excess of individualism is the opposite of freedom.[27]

He went on to praise Spinoza for pointing out that there was more freedom in collective decisions than in isolation: 'The liberalistic and purely egotistical point of view is an attempt to revive the idea of the "night-watchman state". How that is to be made compatible with a sense of Christian responsibility cannot be objectively explained.'

The speech was doubtless designed to stress the ideological cleavage between the SPD and Adenauer's CDU. It suited Schumacher's book to describe the aims of the CDU as those of primitive capitalist greed, thereby dismissing the strongly Christian element in the party. Hence his reference to the incompatibility of Christian ethics with free-market theories. In other respects he was not known for the habit of invoking

---

[26] *Wörtliche Berichte und Drucksachen des Wirtschaftsrates des Vereinigten Wirtschaftsgebietes, 1947–1949*, ed. C. Weiz and H. Woller, ii (Munich, 1977), 662.

[27] *SPD Protokoll der Verhandlungen des Parteitages, Düsseldorf 1948* (Hamburg, n.d.), 32. The speech was later pubished under the title 'Die Sozialdemokratie im Kampf für Freiheit und Sozialismus'.

the Christian faith; on the contrary, his rhetoric was often characterized by strident anti-clericalism.

In 1949 Schumacher and his colleagues were still claiming that the liberalization of the economy was taking place at the expense of working-class interests. Those hit hardest by the currency reform were the poor, who were left with virtually no savings, whereas the rich could take advantage of the opportunities of the market and were able to enjoy luxury consumer-goods at a time when necessities were being denied to those who were worse off.

As we have seen, Erhard, Miksch, and their supporters in the neo-liberal camp reacted vigorously to these charges, but in the years immediately after currency reform it was by no means certain that the market experiment would succeed.[28] The fact that unemployment was higher than in neighbouring countries and rising was seized upon by the SPD in its campaigns against Erhard. Commenting on the situation in the autumn of 1949, Schumacher wrote that the newly elected, CDU-led administration was creating unemployment as the result of its obsession with the free market: 'By means of a demagogic smear-campaign against the directed economy [*Zwangswirtschaft*], which no-body wants and which is not even being put up for discussion, they [the government supporters] reject necessary measures of planning in the deployment of capital and the distribution of credits.'[29]

The discomfort felt by the SPD in waging an electoral battle against the principles of the social market economy can be illustrated by the Social Democratic claim, in the summer of 1949, that the Düsseldorf programme of the CDU had actually been copied from them—in other words, the Christian Democrats had stolen their ideas.[30]

As one economist who sympathized with the Social Democrats wrote in 1950, it is always unconvincing to have to conduct an argument with the words 'Yes . . . but': 'If one says "planned economy but no com-mand economy" [*Planwirtschaft aber keine Zwangswirtschaft*], this, like every "Yes . . . but", is psychologically ineffective.'[31] 'Yes . . . but' was implied in many of their arguments. Abolition of controls—Yes . . . but no free market. A planned economy—Yes . . . but no centrally directed economy, as in Stalin's empire. Personal choice and initiative—Yes . . . but the decisive role must be reserved for central planners.

The defeat in the Bundestag elections of August 1949 did not cause

---

[28] See above, Ch. 10.

[29] *Jahrbuch der Sozialdemokratischen Partei Deutschlands* (Hanover, n.d.), 6.

[30] A claim reported in *Der Spiegel*, 3/31 (28 July 1949), 3.

[31] A. Weber, 'Sozialistische Marktwirtschaft' in *Das sozialistische Jahrhundert* (Berlin, 1950), no. 1, p. 5.

Schumacher to change his tune. He blamed the SPD's failure on the hostility of the Churches and the effects of the Allies' dismantling programme.[32] But, whatever the reason, the electorate had been mistaken. It would soon learn the error of its ways. The social market economy would reveal itself to be a fraud. The narrowness of the Christian Democratic victory, and the economic difficulties which faced the Federal Republic, made such a calculation far from unreasonable.

The post-mortem discussions on the election confirmed this hardline attitude. In the first week of September 1949, the party executive approved the so-called Dürkheim Points—a programme which committed the SPD to supporting full employment, a planned economy, the socialization of key industries, and a redistribution of wealth. The sixteenth and last point demanded the prevention of clerical interference in political affairs—a symptom of Schumacher's resentment towards the Churches. The gulf between Social Democrats and Christian supporters of the market economy yawned wider than ever.[33]

Nor were subsequent deliberations on the state of the economy noteworthy for a softening attitude towards Erhard's policies. On 25 November 1949, leading economic experts of the Social Democratic Party gathered in the parliament building in Bonn to discuss their future economic strategy. Those attending included the economics subcommittee of the party executive, members of the relevant Bundestag committees, representatives of party delegations in *Länder* parliaments, and other Social Democrats distinguished by their expertise in economic or financial matters.

Hermann Veit, the party's main spokesman in the Bundestag on economic affairs and chairman of the economics subcommittee, began the proceedings by pointing out that the SPD could not just stand passively by, waiting for the government's policies to break down. They had to try to get the best out of proposed legislation before the Bundestag, but at the same time to make clear where they rejected government policy. The SPD was not attacking a theory. It opposed the social forces which stood behind the Adenauer Government and which had already revealed their objectives in Erhard's economic policy during the regime of the Economic Council, 1948–9. The real bone of contention between the government and the opposition was this: the government only wanted to fund social welfare out of the surplus created by its economic policies. In order to achieve their conception of a blooming economy, however, they would have to cut taxes, which would in turn cut the funds available for social needs. 'Against

[32] Albrecht, *Schumacher: Ein Leben*, 65.   [33] Ibid. 65–6.

that, the SPD represents the view that one should not be as social as possible, but as social as necessary, and the inducements of the capitalist economic system will have to take a back seat [*zurücktreten*] in order to fulfil this obligation.'[34]

Speaking of the social market economy, he said this just amounted to the old ideas of Adam Smith supplemented by the view that the state ought to protect competition. In practice this meant the ruthless exploitation of shortages for private gain. Although Erhard announced the establishment of free competition, nothing in the least had been undertaken to achieve this end. On the contrary, the draft anti-cartel law had been shelved. A really social economy could be achieved only by a market system which would be planned and steered so that it would achieve the highest possible production levels, full employment, a decent level of real wages, personal security, and social welfare. To this end there should be socialization of productive areas where there were monopolies or oligopolies, co-determination in the factories, and the use of tax policy to redistribute the social product and affect investment.

It is noticeable that Veit was apparently limiting the extent of 'socialization' to areas where neo-liberal economists might themselves have found that intervention would be justified. On the other hand, his concept of a 'social economy' was very far from that of Erhard, since the emphasis was to be on control rather than freedom.

In concluding his remarks Veit said that he felt it important to discuss what the SPD would do, either in a coalition government or if it were to find itself with sole power. This comment reflects the possibility, which must have seemed by no means unlikely in November 1949, that the Adenauer Government would not last very long. A coalition led by an aged ex-mayor of Cologne with a wafer-thin majority did not look impregnable. This was one reason why the SPD was not inclined to engage in an agonizing reappraisal of its economic policies. Another lay in the personalities of its economic spokesmen. Veit, Agartz, and Nölting were committed to a planned economy and regarded deviation from it as a betrayal of trust. Most determined of all to resist change was Schumacher himself, who attended the second day of the conference and told the delegates that the SPD should take the offensive against the excessive manifestations of capitalism in Germany. One could not rebuild the country on a socially just basis so

---

[34] *Protokoll der Tagung des wirtschaftspolitischen Ausschusses beim Vorstand der SPD am 25. und 26. 11. 1949* (hereafter *SPD Wipo Protokoll*), FES PV Bestand Wipo, L2 143, pp. 1–3.

long as either the old type of entrepreneur or the old type of manager was still predominant.[35]

Some shift of emphasis can be detected in the discussion about future policy. Massive socialization plans were less in evidence than before, although not specifically rejected. Co-determination, or industrial democracy, was widely supported, and Schumacher himself made a point of mentioning it. There was acceptance of the fact that freedom for the consumer needed to be protected. In his report on 'Problems of Economic Control',[36] Dr Wagner of Munich pointed out that a socialist economy would have fundamentally to be a market economy—even if a controlled and manipulated market economy. He cited a Social Democratic programme which stated that a socialist planned economy would largely retain market forms and that 'economic planning is never an end in itself'. In addition to direct orders and prohibitions, planners could use a battery of indirect steering-mechanisms: finance and credit policy, price policy, wage and taxation policy, among others. He argued that Erhard was actually having to regulate prices and investment in many parts of the economy. The difference between him and a Social Democratic Economics Minister was that he was being forced into action by circumstances, whereas a Social Democrat would act from conviction and carry his policies to their logical conclusion.[37]

Even this somewhat backhanded acceptance of the market did not find favour amongst all those present. Gisbert Rittig argued that there was an important difference between liberal views on freedom and order and those of socially minded people. The 'directed market economy' (*gelenkte Marktwirtschaft*) of the Social Democrats could achieve its goals only through planning, not by allowing market forces to operate by themselves. Veit supported this criticism, disliking the very term 'market economy'. Koch, the SPD Economics Minister in Hesse, suggested using the 'free communal economy' (*freie Gemeinwirtschaft*) instead.[38] Like most such suggestions, it carried little conviction.

If the free-price mechanism was still alien to many social democrats, their views on cartels were far from identical with those of neo-liberals, even though attacks on overmighty capitalist enterprises obviously attracted them.

Petrick, who was involved in the parliamentary discussion of the anti-cartel legislation, presented the possibility of controlling cartels,

---

[35] Ibid., p. 9.
[36] The German word is *Lenkung*, which could be translated as 'steering', but that is clumsy. The French *dirigisme* would be better.
[37] *SPD Wipo Protokoll*, p. 8.
[38] Ibid., p. 9.

which should be registered with the government, as 'a wide-ranging encroachment in the fabric of the capitalist economy'. In fact, of course, Böhm and Erhard just wanted to make cartels illegal so that they could not enforce their rules in the courts. Social Democrats evidently saw this campaign as a form of interference with industry. One contributor to the discussion defended cartels because they helped create large enterprises, and 'if one wants a state-directed economy, one needs large economic units'.[39] Another argued that any anti-cartel laws accepted by the Allied authorities would just be part of their dismantling programme—a view shared by many industrialists.[40]

In the last stage of the conference Koch and Petrick discussed the future of socialization—Koch with special reference to the state of Hesse, where plans had been developed for some time, but had been shelved at the insistence of the American authorities. The nature of these plans and the discussion of them illustrated how far removed even democratic or 'liberal' (*freiheitlich*) social democrats were from the theories of the social market.

Koch emphasized that there should be no state ownership, because taken literally this would imply bureaucratization, and would lead to a new form of centralism.[41] Like many other Social Democrats at this time, he stressed that the question of ownership was *not* the main issue in socialization. The most important aim was a 'directed socialist economy in which matters concerning control, prices, credits, and investments would be decided for the economy as a whole'. Such a policy would apply to socialized industries. It was clear, however, that 'socialization' would be extensive. It would cover entire branches of the economy, such as transport, chemicals, and banking. Profit-sharing or share-ownership by employees would not be allowed. The trade unions had ruled them out because they would create two classes of workers. There were to be no mixed concerns; after the entrepreneurial class had been eliminated it must not be allowed in through the back door. In order to facilitate socialization, new forms of legal corporation would have to be established.

In Hesse's socialization proposals these were called *Sozialgemeinschaften* or social communities, which should run socialist enterprises. They should be administered by boards made up of representatives of trade unions, local authorities, including co-operatives, and *Land* (state) communities (*Landesgemeinschaften*), including some tradespeople and employers. The *Landesgemeinschaften* would help to direct the economy

---

[39] Ibid., p. 5.   [40] See below, Chs. 13 and 15.
[41] *SPD Wipo Protokoll*, p. 11.

and fix prices in consultation with the *Sozialgemeinschaften*, the ministries, and the state parliament.[42] Prices were going to be fixed at a 'socially just' level, although it was noted in discussion that this was difficult to determine and would probably mean that subsidies would be needed.[43] The entire scheme was a market economist's nightmare, and it was perhaps fortunate for the reputation of the Social Democrats in Hesse that nothing ever came of it.

Nevertheless, it illustrated the extent to which Social Democratic economic policy was wedded to public—even if not 'state'—ownership, planning, controls, and fixed prices. The whole idea of the market as a self-operating mechanism, with prices being set by the laws of supply and demand, was foreign to this way of thinking.

These views were reiterated by Veit in attacks on the social market economy at the Hamburg party congress in May 1950. Veit described Erhard as an Economics Minister who drew his DM40,000 per annum salary for demonstrating how unnecessary his office was, and who tried to pretend that the alternative to his self-operating market mechanism was the 'bogey' of a command economy which would lead straight to serfdom. The inventors of this bogey were either totally ignorant of socialism or were those very same people who had marched in the ranks of the Nazis and were now parading their love of democracy under the banners of the government parties. 'Whether [they are] with Hitler or with Adenauer, in any case they are against socialism.'

Veit then tackled the theory of the social market head on, and in a fashion which left no doubt about his total rejection of it. He pointed out that to oppose monopoly capitalism and cartels would be to fly in the face of historical developments which could not simply be reversed. Illiberal cartels had been produced by the liberal system of freedom of contract. The large-scale enterprises which had grown from these cartel arrangements could not simply be broken up. Only if one were to agree with Röpke that large-scale property, mammoth enterprises, and even large cities should be destroyed could one hope to put the clock back, and how could one do that without massive state intervention? Röpke had admitted, in *Gesellschaftskrise der Gegenwart*, that competition was a method of organizing a market economy but not 'a principle upon which one could build an entire society'. From a 'social-moral' standpoint it was actually a dangerous principle, since it tended to divide rather than unite the community. Veit himself accepted that competition could have its uses, but 'It is an illusion to believe that one

---

[42] Ibid., pp. 11–12.   [43] Ibid., p. 14.

can make out of it the dominant principle underlying an economy, a principle which is even supposed to fulfil ethical functions.'[44]

He strongly denied that market economics could be linked to Christianity.

This market economy is not and never will be social. An economic system which is driven and directed only by the motive of profit cannot attain ethical objectives. This economic system is also incompatible with Christianity . . . He who attempts to follow the laws of Christ in this system will be condemned to economic extinction, whereas he who follows the laws of the market will often have to bruise his Christian conscience.[45]

Veit struck a deep emotional chord in his audience when he pointed out that socialism was not just an economic programme but an idealistic struggle to reform society. 'Even if there were no such thing as the science of economics, we should still be socialists.' It was not cool, scholarly calculation which had enabled their fathers to resist persecution under the anti-socialist laws or to withstand the hell of the Nazi concentration camps, but the fire of an idea. If that fire were once extinguished, humanity would no longer deserve its name: 'This idea springs from respect for mankind and its worth, from love for our fellow men, and from an unerring commitment to justice.'[46]

Veit also had something to say about the 'democracy of consumers'. A democracy which gave hundreds and thousands of votes to a small minority, he claimed, would make the old Prussian three-class franchise-system look democratic indeed. 'That is no democracy; it is pure plutocracy.' After denouncing the unfairness of Erhard's liberalization, he claimed that the uncertainty created by cyclical fluctuations and unemployment would endanger democracy, encouraging people to seek security in more authoritarian forms of state. What was needed was a commitment to full employment. The right to work had to be guaranteed. He shrewdly observed that the government in Bonn was showing no enthusiasm for job creation, despite having established a scheme for that purpose.

It would be far more consistent with the conceptions of the government and their theoreticians if they could tell the people that unemployment was an inevitable outcome of the working of economic laws and that it must be left to the recuperative powers of the market to decide whether, and to what extent, this can be overcome.[47]

---

[44] *Protokoll der Verhandlungen des Parteitages der SPD vom 21. bis 25. Mai 1950 in Hamburg* (hereafter cited as *SPD Protokoll 1950*) (Frankfurt/M., n.d.), pp. 181–2.
[45] Ibid. 183–4.   [46] Ibid. 185.   [47] Ibid. 187.

They lacked the courage to do this, however, because they knew that such views would arouse a public storm which would sweep them from office.

Veit stressed that there were overriding social tasks which could not be fulfilled if the economy was left to function by itself, driven only by the forces of private greed. It was necessary to intervene to order economic affairs so that society's maximum potential for productive capacity was realized. For this they would require not only planning—since the free-price mechanism itself never produced the desired result—but also the expropriation of key enterprises: 'If the bastions of the economy remain in private hands, the struggle for control will be bound to end with a situation in which, instead of the state steering the economy, a few powerful private interests will be steering the state.'[48] Anybody who believed that planning and controls would render the issue of ownership irrelevant was forgetting Lasalle's words, 'constitutional questions are questions about power', a dictum which applied to the economy as well as to politics. He also allowed himself another thrust at those who sought salvation in decartelization. The concentration of industrial activity, he claimed, could well be a prelude to rational planning, and in those circumstances decartelization would be a reactionary step. In Germany's case it would also weaken her international competitiveness.

Finally, he stressed that the aim of socialization should not be to maximize profit, but to produce enough to satisfy justifiable needs: 'Nobody shall enrich himself as the result of socialization—unless it be the people as a whole.'[49] The people should know where its interest lay. Certainly not with those who spoke of freedom but thereby understood one freedom to enrich themselves at others' expense—leaving the masses only the freedom to sleep under bridges. It was a powerful speech and it aroused enthusiastic applause from the conference. There was no sign that rank-and-file social democrats were in a mood to welcome the social market economy.[50]

Schiller did manage to suggest to the delegates that to achieve full employment the free market had to be combined with elements of regulation (*Ordnung*) and claimed that the SPD's task was to 'bring freedom and order into harmony with one another'. One method did exist for doing that. It was called Social Democracy.[51] Despite this fine

[48] Ibid. 196.

[49] Ibid. 191–2.

[50] For an equally unflattering description of the social market economy, see *SPD Jahrbuch 1950–1* (Hanover, n.d.), pp. 273–8.

[51] *SPD Protokoll 1950*, 200–2.

rhetorical flourish, Schiller's speech did not dispel the general impression of the SPD as a party committed to rigorous planning-procedures. He himself made great play with the need for an economic general staff, even though he denied that this had anything to do with five-year plans or Soviet-style planned economics.

For those seeking a more fundamental change of attitude, the only real crumbs of comfort came from a highflown speech by Carlo Schmid entitled 'The SPD Faces the Spiritual Situation of our Time'.[52] A long and learned discourse about Marx, Hegel, Darwin, Sorel, Weber, and other intellectual giants, including Leonhard Nelson, it aroused much enthusiasm from the delegates by describing the inherent nastiness of the capitalist system. Yet Schmid also insisted that historical inevitability was no longer a tenable belief and that relationships between classes were much more complicated than had hitherto been imagined. Social democracy neither needed nor wished to have any dogmas. He reminded his listeners that Wilhelm Liebknecht had once said that a programme should not be a paper pope. He rejected the need for any sort of dictatorship, stressed social democratic commitment to democracy, and denied any conflict with the Churches. There was, however, no mention of the market economy.

---

[52] Ibid., 236. For the background to Schmid's speech, see Klotzbach, *Der Weg zur Staatspartei*, 256 and fn.

13

Erhard and the Korean Crisis

ERHARD may have enjoyed prestige for his successes when he transformed the Economics Administration in Frankfurt into the Economics Ministry in Bonn, but the task of establishing the social market economy in West Germany was by no means over. In many ways it had only just begun. Erhard had gained credit for sloughing off most of the hated *Zwangswirtschaft* which had been associated with military occupation. He now had to try to inculcate the principles of a socially orientated, competition-based market economy into both the political élites and the public at large. This was to prove a much more difficult task.

Indeed, the change from Frankfurt to Bonn involved some awkward problems of adjustment for Erhard. Domestically the move posed difficulties. Bonn had not been designed as a regional centre, let alone the capital of a federated state. There was a desperate shortage of accommodation, and Erhard had no proper home for several months. Politically, too, his electoral triumph had the paradoxical effect of reducing his stature within the West German government. In Frankfurt he had not been officially the leading figure in the bizonal administration, but he was regarded by many as its star turn. In Bonn he found himself working under an austere and autocratic Chancellor whose political skills were greater than his own. There was also the consideration that his administration no longer had quite the authority it enjoyed in Frankfurt, where economic policy had been an overriding priority for the Economic Council. In the new Federal Republic, the Economics Ministry would have to assert itself against other ministries which did not consider it to be a very prestigious institution.

Furthermore, he was evidently going to have to fight to assert his own personal authority against the claims of other ambitious politicians. One of these was the Federal Finance Minister, Fritz Schäffer, a very experienced Bavarian politician who could count on the support of the CSU. His legal training and administrative background were more likely to arouse confidence in Adenauer than the academic qualifications of Erhard. Schäffer asserted his right to control the spheres of money and credit—areas which Erhard regarded as essential for the success of the social market economy. Even more menacing as a rival in the early days was Erhard's former patron, Franz Blücher. Blücher was, of course, the leader of the FDP—Adenauer's most powerful coalition partner. Finding him a suitable post had been difficult; he finally had to be content with the honorific title of Deputy Chancellor, and the ministerial job of supervising the Marshall Plan. Here, too, there would be scope for friction. Blücher seemed too closely associated with groups representing the interests of heavy industry for the good of the Federal Republic's economic policy. He also seemed suspiciously keen to push Erhard into prestigious but politically impotent posts.

Erhard was so worried about the apparent threats to his economic policy as the result of the new political situation that on 24 November 1949 he wrote an impassioned letter to Adenauer warning against the influence of powerful pressure-groups which wanted to impede the policy of the social market economy. This policy, he declared, with its constant striving for higher achievements and more just distribution of income, could not always reckon on the whole-hearted support of vested interests. Hardships would be unavoidable, however soft the hand on the economic tiller. Erhard was aware that his views were shocking to some comfortably settled people but he knew what he was about: 'This is particularly true in the case of such important problems as decartelization and the liberalization of foreign trade, problems which must be properly solved if our social market economy is not to become a farce and the policy of the CDU is not to fail'. This was typical of what was to be a lengthy and rather one-sided ministerial correspondence between the verbose Economics Minister and his laconic, not to say acerbic, Chancellor.[1]

On the face of it Erhard lacked what the Germans call a *Hausmacht*, a political base which could support him in factional conflict. As a popular politician who actually lacked a party card, and as a professor with strong views but no great administrative talent, he seemed unlikely to last too long in the hard world of coalition politics. Things were made more difficult by the fact that, in the move from Frankfurt to Bonn, only 40 per cent of the old Economics Administration officials were taken over, and Erhard had little control over the general staffing-

---

[1] Erhard to Adenauer, 24 Nov. 1949, LES, Erhard Correspondence. For Erhard's concern in Nov. 1949 that his rivals would weaken the Economics Ministry and usher in a form of entrepreneurial planning which would undermine the social market economy, see part of this correspondence with Adenauer quoted in *Adenauer: Briefe 1949–51*, ed. R. Morsey and H.-P. Schwarz (Berlin, 1985), 464–5. He claimed that Blücher had suggested that Erhard should become president of the Federal Bank. The Erhard Correspondence also contains a stream of complaints from Erhard to Adenauer about Schäffer's ministry, which he saw as wedded to protectionist, paternalist taxation policies of a pre-war type.

policy adopted in establishing the new ministry. Nevertheless, he did have some advantages. Key positions in the ministry could be filled only with his agreement. He showed his determination to keep the ministry on the straight and narrow path of the social market by appointing Alfred Müller-Armack to run its economics department, an appointment which provoked Adenauer to snort contemptuously 'Yet another professor!'

Apart from his public popularity, which could wane as well as wax with West Germany's economic fortunes, Erhard had the experience of piloting Germany through the difficult year after currency reform, and he also had a staunch source of support in the Bank deutscher Länder.[2] His distaste for cheap money was fully shared there, and under the West German Basic Law, the bank enjoyed considerable independence *vis-à-vis* even such an autocratic Chancellor as Konrad Adenauer. Lastly, Erhard could look to the West German economics profession, personified in the Academic Advisory Council to his former administration, which was now attached to his ministry. The social market economy would not lack well-informed defenders, even if it was now entering a period of severe difficulty.

So far as the economic scene was concerned, the summer and autumn of 1949 was a period of apparent deflation. The rise in production fell away and exports stagnated. Unemployment rose as companies were forced to rationalize. This had the happy effect of cutting prices, but it was seen as catastrophic by many German and Allied officials.[3] Erhard came under great pressure from his colleagues and the occupation authorities to loosen the purse-strings and embark on programmes of employment creation. He strongly resisted these pressures and was supported in his determination by Wilhelm Vocke, the president of the Bank deutscher Länder.

During the winter, unemployment rose more steeply and by February had topped the 2 million mark. This was indeed enough to cause serious uneasiness in politicians who remembered the demise of the Weimar Republic, when a slump accompanied by mass unemployment had destroyed German democracy. Anton Storch, the Minister of Labour, who represented the trade-union wing of the CDU, was pressing

---

[2] The Bank deutscher Länder became the Bundesbank in 1957.

[3] e.g., on 27 July 1949 Ministerialdirigent Dr Strickrodt of the Finance Ministry in Lower Saxony wrote to the British military authorities claiming that: 'The revival of economy induced at first after the reform of currency . . . came on the whole to a standstill about Spring 1949 and has in the following months become retrograde. In consequence a certain number of enterprises and especially those located in this region that are otherwise sound and necessary have got into difficulties. . . . It is therefore necessary to assist these undertakings by a financial aid . . .', PRO/FO/1046/683.

for measures to create work. The Allies, too, decided that enough was enough. A confidential report which found its way into the public domain showed that Allied 'experts' feared that structural unemployment in West Germany might weaken the whole of Western Europe. Erhard did not regard the situation as serious, but he was forced to yield to political pressure. The Economics Ministry and the Bank deutscher Länder agreed to work stimulation schemes amounting to DM2 billion. Most of this programme consisted of bundling together existing schemes for development in transport, communications, and building. They had little notable impact on the situation and, perhaps fortunately, the more ambitious of them were never implemented, because circumstances changed in the summer of 1950. They were, however, a further indication of how misguided it would be to trust officials with investment decisions. One positive result of the imbroglio was that Erhard's ministry was given responsibility for such work-creation policies, thereby limiting the potential damage which they might cause.[4]

Erhard tenaciously continued his efforts to reduce controls and to lower taxation. He knew that the downturn was a temporary phenomenon and that Germany would be able to earn her way in the world as long as she remained competitive and trade was liberalized. His detractors, who claimed that the economy was too flat, were soon to be holding up their hands in horror as the economy overheated. Nevertheless, the tensions in the early months of 1950 damaged Erhard's standing in the Cabinet, since his ministry seemed to have been slow to react in what was perceived as a crisis. Erhard was not at his best in the cut and thrust of Cabinet discussion; he tended to be woolly and long-winded. Adenauer began to doubt his competence and even commissioned Wilhelm Röpke, still in Geneva, to compose a memorandum assessing the quality of West Germany's economic policy. Once again, a neo-liberal economist had the opportunity to influence his country's economic development.

Adenauer's motives in calling on Röpke's expertise are not clear. He may have genuinely distrusted Erhard and hoped to trump him with another specialist opinion. Röpke's reputation was such, however, that Adenauer could hardly have expected anything but reinforcement of the government's free-market position. This may indeed have been his objective, because by early 1950 rumours were already circulating that

[4] Schwarz, *Gründerjahre der Republik*, 85–6; Laitenberger, *Ludwig Erhard*, 92; For an account from a different viewpoint, but which comes to much the same conclusion, see: V. Hentschel, 'Die Europäische Zahlungsunion und die deutschen Devisenkrisen, 1950/51', *Vierteljahrshefte für Zeitgeschichte*, 37/4 (Oct. 1989), 715–58.

the time had come to consider a great coalition, such as the one between CDU and SPD which was apparently functioning so well in North Rhine-Westphalia under Arnold's leadership. One advantage the Economics Minister did have was that his resignation might have thrown the future of the whole Cabinet, including that of Adenauer, into the melting-pot.

Röpke's memorandum, which was swiftly published, with an introduction by Adenauer himself, was a sturdy defence of the social market economy. He praised Erhard for his courageous liberalization-policy in 1948, and stressed that it was market freedom, not currency reform, which had rejuvenated the West German economy. Röpke noted that the West German government was being criticized for high levels of unemployment by various expert bodies at home and abroad. In particular, a survey by a UN Economic Commission for Europe urged expansion of credit to combat deflation, and price controls to prevent inflation. Röpke tartly pointed out that there could hardly be threats of deflation and inflation at the same time. What was being proposed was a recipe for suppressed inflation of the kind from which Germany had recently escaped.

German unemployment, he argued, was not cyclical but structural—resulting from production bottle-necks, low mobility of labour owing to housing shortages, and the overmanning created by the command economy during the Third Reich. To implied criticism that the West Germans were ignoring post-Keynesian economic wisdom, Röpke replied that Keynes's theories had already been exploded. In any case, the situation was quite different from that in the early 1930s, when Keynes was formulating his theories and when there was real underinvestment, underused savings, and excess capacity. The way forward in the 1950s lay in the perfection of the market, not in the creation of bogus credit. Capital should be generated by voluntary savings, which could be encouraged by reduced taxation and realistic interest-rates. Although foreign-exchange controls were a necessity at that point, they should be seen as only temporary. Free convertibility and the liberalization of foreign trade should be achieved as soon as possible.[5]

It was a most satisfactory reinforcement of Erhard's policies, since his major objective was to press ahead with liberalization, particularly

---

[5] W. Röpke, *Ist die deutsche Wirtschaftspolitik richtig? Analyse und Kritik* (Stuttgart, 1950). For praise of Erhard, see p. 17; for contrast with the 1930s, see pp. 36–46, and for commitment to free trade etc., see pp. 55–61 and pp. 78–9. This was not the last time Adenauer asked Röpke for advice. It was he who suggested Walter Hallstein as the leader of the FRG delegation to discuss the Schuman Plan. Cf. H.-P. Schwarz, *Adenauer: Der Aufstieg, 1876–1952* (3rd edn.; Stuttgart 1991), 664 and 725.

in the field of trade. In September 1949 an event had occurred which seemed likely to make Germany's export prospects even less rosy than they already were. The British had devalued the pound sterling by 30 per cent, and other currencies were following suit. Within the German government there were divided views. The Bank deutscher Länder and Erhard were happier with a smaller devaluation, since it would cheapen imports and force price discipline on exporters. Business interests wanted a sharper devaluation to help export sales and dampen competition from foreign imports. The government leaned in their direction and proposed a devaluation of 25 per cent, but the French and the British vetoed this. The West Germans were only allowed to devalue by 20 per cent. Erhard was quite satisfied with that level, regarding it as 'just about ideal'.[6]

This was really the beginning of a phenomenon which went on for several decades and does not yet seem to have stopped. The Germans were pressed to make their money more valuable in order to help the trade of others; all that resulted was a benefit for their own trade. German exports did not sell on their price, but on their quality, their advanced technical characteristics, reliability, and after-sales service. Under these circumstances an increase in the value of the mark simply cut the costs of imported materials and increased German profits. Small wonder that Erhard approved of it, despite choruses of woe from the industrial lobby.

So far as trade itself was concerned, Erhard had already been having success in his struggle with the occupying powers to loosen the bonds which swathed German exporters under JEIA rules. In December 1948 the authorities agreed that it was no longer necessary for every single export-contract to be approved by JEIA. Instead, exporters could obtain general permission to carry on their business, and had much more leeway in the negotiation of contracts.[7] In February 1949 the hopelessly bureaucratic system of import licences was overhauled so that allocations of foreign currency were given to the *Länder*, and different branches of business or individual traders could submit contracts for them.[8]

Nevertheless, German trade was still hamstrung by the 'dollar clause', according to which importers of West German goods had to pay for them in dollars. The Americans were reluctant to relax this if it simply meant that European countries would set up bilateral trading-treaties with West Germany, excluding multilateral trade. Erhard pressed them hard for a relaxation, and the authorities responsible for the Marshall

[6] Schwarz, *Gründerjahre der Republik*, 61.
[7] Buchheim, *Die Wiedereingliederung Westdeutschlands*, 34.
[8] Ibid. 54.

Plan administration in the USA realized that the dollar clause was restricting German trade in a fashion which was undermining the whole purpose of the European Recovery Programme. In the councils of the OEEC, the Americans pressed for moves towards the liberalization of trade. With the establishment of the Federal Repubic, West Germany joined the OEEC, and Erhard was able to support the Americans in their efforts to further multilateral trade. He became the most enthusiastic European advocate of the American position.

His first real breakthrough came when it was necessary to renegotiate a trade treaty with Switzerland. Obstacles put in the way of the Swiss by JEIA bureaucrats, who were trying to fit Swiss exports to Germany into the West German import plan, threatened to wreck the whole treaty. Erhard publicly demanded the most liberal possible trade-arrangements with Switzerland, and under political pressure from the American and German administrations, JEIA agreed to a much more flexible trade-treaty with that country in August 1949. This enabled West Germany to engage in trade with Switzerland on the basis of a monthly foreign-exchange quota for German importers. Although nominally a bilateral treaty, it did not have the objectionable features of bilateral trade-deals as they had manifested themselves since the 1930s under the auspices of Hjalmar Schacht. There were no barter arrangements, no quotas, and no blocked bank-accounts. In this respect it fitted in with Erhard's free-market views, as well as with American hopes for an expansion of multinational trade. The Swiss treaty signalled the beginning of the end of the 'dollar clause'. By the last quarter of 1949 the Federal Republic could make trade arrangements with other European countries without having to demand payment in dollars. This was of great importance, for it meant that the West Germans could reopen trade with their natural commercial partners in Europe.[9] In the autumn of 1949 further treaties followed with Austria, Belgium, Denmark, Holland, Norway, and Sweden.[10]

Germany's re-entry into West European trade was made more palatable by the fact that, initially, it was the West Germans who sucked in imports from their neighbours. Erhard was quite happy to tolerate this, knowing that, so long as money was tight and wages did not explode, equilibrium would eventually be restored. In the meantime, imports forced German manufacturers to be competitive and went some way to satisfying home demand. They also helped stimulate German businessmen to attack the export market, investing long-term in sales forces and service back-up in foreign countries. Even in the short term, there

[9] Ibid. 42–9.   [10] Ibid. 120.

were impressive achievements. The period between October 1949 and March 1950 saw a surge of almost 50 per cent in West German exports. The ground had been prepared for that export-led boom which was to form the basis of German prosperity in the second half of the twentieth century.

It should be said at once that, although the liberalization of trade was entirely consistent with the social market economy, the real credit for re-establishing a liberal trading-system in the Western world must go to the Americans. Within the OEEC, and in bilateral negotiations with their European allies, they pressed hard for the old strait-jacket of trade controls to be loosened. They were quite prepared to use the threat of a withdrawal of American aid to Europe if effective steps towards liberalization were not seen to be being taken in a manner convincing to the Congress in Washington.[11]

In Erhard's favour, however, it must be recorded that West Germany was in the vanguard of those countries trying to liberalize their trade, whereas the British, in particular, were still wedded to the concept of controls, personified by the austere figure of their Chancellor, Stafford Cripps. In response to recommendations from the Council of the OEEC in the summer of 1949, West Germany abolished import restrictions on 350 imported items from other Marshall Plan countries, including sugar, cotton, tobacco, bicycles, lorries, and various types of machinery. This measure, which came into effect on 3 November 1949, meant that West Germany had liberalized about 35 per cent of her imports from OEEC countries—which put her well above average so far as liberalization targets in other countries were concerned.[12]

In September 1950 the Americans gained a major victory with the establishment, in the face of marked British reluctance, of the European Payments Union (EPU), a grouping of the West European states in receipt of Marshall Aid which committed themselves to liberalize their trade with each other. This was to be done by agreeing that debts would be paid off within the union, so that trade would not be hampered by foreign-exchange restrictions. Each member country received a credit quota. Creditors would be paid through the union, and not as the result of cumbersome bilateral arrangements. The whole enterprise was launched with a generous injection of US dollars, and its accounting arrangements were backdated to 1 July 1950.[13] Its aim was to liberalize

---

[11] Ibid. 104–7. For US pressure to integrate Europe, see D. W. Ellwood, *Rebuilding Europe: Western Europe, America and Postwar Reconstruction* (London, 1992), 158–9.

[12] Buchheim, *Die Wiedereingliederung Westdeutschlands*, 123. The average for OEEC countries was estimated at about 30% trade liberalization.

[13] J. J. Kaplan and G. Schleiminger, *The European Payments Union: Financial Diplomacy in the 1950s* (Oxford, 1989), 91.

about 75 per cent of the members' trade with each other as quickly as possible. The Federal Republic was a member of this union from the beginning, even though, unlike some other countries, it did not receive a special dollar-credit to smooth its entry.

Unfortunately for the Western Allies, the negotiation of the EPU treaty coincided with the outbreak of the Korean War, on 25 June 1950. Not unnaturally, there followed a desperate scramble to obtain vital raw materials and semi-finished products which would be necessary to meet the requirements of accelerating Western armaments programmes. The relatively optimistic atmosphere which had characterized the previous two years was transformed into one of uncertainty and fear of war. The Americans, preparing themselves for a major conflict, passed legislation for controlling their economy reminiscent of measures taken during the Second World War.[14]

Erhard saw no reason to alter his course. He did nothing to discourage the flood of imports pouring into Germany, and continued to try to liberalize the economy as fast as possible. He had, for example, recently been able to abolish one of his particular bugbears, the rationing of coal. His position thereby became very vulnerable. As we have seen, the British had always regarded him as a 'right-wing' *laissez-faire* fanatic, and within his own party there were those who doubted his competence. Nevertheless, he had been secure in the support of the US military government, even if he suspected individual American officials of New Dealer leanings towards *dirigisme*. Now, however, with the Americans facing a real crisis, in which their soldiers were being killed, any suggestion that doctrinal German views about free markets were obstructing the war effort would be likely to arouse indignation. The US authorities wanted to relieve the pressure on raw materials needed by their own industry. They also assumed that vital exports to European countries would be directed into those areas most helpful to the rearmament drive. Naturally such ideas ran counter to Erhard's belief in free-market choice. They were also incompatible with his tendency to favour consumer-goods industries over heavy-production sectors.

There followed two periods of acute difficulty for Erhard. The first was in October 1950 and was caused by the deficit West Germany immediately ran up in its trade within the EPU. One problem was that the credit quotas in the EPU had been fixed on the basis of 1949 trade

---

[14] In Sept. 1950 Congress passed the Defense Production Act and in Dec. a state of national emergency was declared; see Ludwig-Erhard-Stiftung/H. F. Wünsche (eds.), *Die Korea-Krise als ordnungspolitische Herausforderung der deutschen Wirtschaftspolitik* (Stuttgart, 1986), 17.

figures, and these of course still gave the Federal Republic a relatively low share of European trade. Her net credit-allowance was only $192 million.[15] With the rush for imports, West Germany soon went into deficit. At the same time, strains began to appear in the domestic economy. Shortages began to make themselves apparent and for the first time for nearly two years inflationary pressures were exerted on the home market. Fuel supplies became very difficult and at the end of October Erhard was forced, much against his will, to reintroduce coal rationing. This episode angered Adenauer, who was strengthened in his suspicion that Erhard was administratively incompetent.

Urgent measures had to be taken to deal with the EPU deficit, especially since Marhall Aid funding was beginning to taper off. The response of the *dirigiste* lobby would be predictable—the reintroduction of controls. Neither Erhard nor the Bank deutscher Länder was prepared to accept that—the former because it would undermine the free market, and the latter because it would almost certainly be associated with financial laxity. There was a difference of emphasis between Erhard's ministry and the bank, despite their fundamental agreement in opposition to a relaxation of monetary discipline. Erhard was quite happy to see imports of raw materials sucked into Germany, since he believed the economy would balance itself in due course. The bank became very alarmed at the consequences of a balance-of-payments deficit in view of its legal obligation to protect the D-Mark. Whereas Erhard constantly tried to play down the crisis or give the impression that it was nearly over, the bank was concerned to clamp down on credit to protect the currency. This required measures unpalatable to business. Vocke and his colleagues were not at all amused when, after they announced on 20 September that the minimum reserves required from banks would be increased by 50 per cent, Erhard chose the following day to tell the Frankfurt Trade Fair that foreign-exchange controls would be abolished within six months—a wildly optimistic forecast.[16]

Nevertheless, if measures were to be taken to overcome the deficit, Erhard obviously preferred monetary instruments to physical controls. He therefore supported the bank when it started to restrict credit. In addition to the increases in minimum reserves mentioned above, acceptance of loans by banks was made much more difficult. Importers were forced to deposit 50 per cent of the cost of imports with *Länder* banks before getting import licences, and at the end of October the

---

[15] Ibid. 16; Hentschel, 'Die Europäische Zahlungsunion', 734.
[16] Hentschel, 'Europäische Zahlungsunion', 738–9.

bank rate was raised from 4 to 6 per cent and the lending (*Lombard*) rate from 5 to 7 per cent. This latter measure was bitterly opposed by Adenauer, who summoned the bank's governing board to Bonn on 26 October to confront him in the Federal Chancellery—at that time a somewhat bizarre meeting-place, since it was normally a natural history museum and was still adorned with a number of stuffed wild animals. The bank's governing board was itself divided about the decision to raise interest rates. Had this not been done, there is little doubt that the liberalization of trade would have been jettisoned. But Vocke held firm and demonstrated, not for the last time, the independence of the federal bank.

For their part, Adenauer and Schäffer opposed the increase in interest rates, the former because it would damage industry and employment, the latter because he feared it would increase the government's costs of borrowing. Much to Adenauer's displeasure, Erhard supported the bank's decision, realizing that it would be the best way of stabilizing the market and saving his liberal economic policy.[17] It was, of course, a measure entirely in tune with the economic theories he and the neo-liberals had been preaching since the 1930s.

Erhard and Vocke realized that the crisis could be blamed on the liberalization of trade, since this had undoubtedly increased imports of all sorts of articles from many different parts of the world. On the other hand, the section of the economy which was still controlled also demanded foreign exchange, even though it was often not utilized rapidly or efficiently.[18] Yet at a time of difficulty, government interference to stifle market forces was easy to justify. The American general Macready told Erhard that free-market principles were all very well, but they should not be applied 'in a doctrinaire fashion'.[19] In an article defending the free market which he published on 7 November, the economic journalist Jürgen Eick quoted Alexander Rüstow:

it is an undoubted and powerful advantage for the planned economy that its principles can be enthusiastically understood within ten minutes by the simple layman—and indeed they will particularly appeal to him. On the other hand, even a full university training in economics may not be enough to enable one to understand the invisible and complicated mechanisms of the market.[20]

---

[17] LES/Wünsche (eds.), *Die Korea-Krise*, 17–20.
[18] Vocke to Adenauer, 14 Oct. 1950, ibid. 193–4.
[19] Protocol of a meeting between Erhard and the economics subcommittee of the Allied High Commission, 19 Oct. 1950, ibid. 197.
[20] Article in the *Industrie-Anzeiger*, 7 Nov. 1950, repr. in LES/Wünsche (eds.), *Die Korea-Krise*, 202.

Fortunately, however, the credit squeeze imposed by the bank, with Erhard's support, was also regarded with favour by two independent experts appointed by the EPU to examine Germany's deficit. Per Jacobssen and Alec Cairncross supported the higher interest-rate and pointed to the damaging consequences of a rejection of trade liberalization. It would be interpreted as a propaganda victory for East Germany and a smack in the face for the Americans. Jacobssen, in particular, put backbone into Vocke, who was evidently wavering over the higher interest-rate.[21] The two foreign experts recommended that West Germany be granted exceptional assistance, and this was accepted by the EPU, which in early November extended an extra credit of $120 million.[22]

This bought West Germany some time. Despite Erhard's buoyant optimism, to which he gave voice frequently, the crisis did not go away. The pressure on raw materials as a result of the war led to rising prices. In the period from October 1950 to October 1951 prices rose by 12 per cent, the highest inflation in the history of the Federal Republic. Bottle-necks and hoarding reappeared. Nor did West German imports drop appreciably. Indeed, they were 22 per cent higher in the period November 1950 to February 1951 than they had been from July to October 1950.[23] Erhard was quite happy to accept this, but it seemed dangerous to many of his colleagues. Fierce conflicts broke out within the Cabinet. Schäfer blamed Erhard for the lack of foreign exchange, saying his weak refusal to control imports meant that money was being spent on dates and nuts from abroad when it should have been going on vital raw materials.[24] For his part, Erhard blamed the Finance Ministry for not shaping taxes to help exporters, and was very angry when Blücher agreed on a quota of compulsory coal-exports from the Ruhr which Erhard argued would be ruinous for German industry.[25]

The coal issue exposed Erhard on another flank, because it brought him into conflict with the Allies. His anger over the coal situation was aggravated by the fact that the International Authority for the Ruhr (IAR)—effectively an Allied control-mechanism—was preventing the Germans from exploiting their own coal-resources in a rational, but at

---

[21] A. K. Cairncross. Report on the visit to Germany on behalf of the EPU, 28 Oct.–3 Nov. 1950, in LES/Wünsche (eds.), *Die Korea-Krise*, 207–11.

[22] For a critical account of this episode, see Hentschel, 'Europäische Zahlungsunion', *passim*. Hentschel is particularly censorious of Erhard's ingratitude to the EPU. For a more favourable assessment, Giersch *et al.*, *The Fading Miracle*, 103.

[23] Hentschel, 'Europäische Zahlungsunion', 749.

[24] Schäffer to Niklas (Minister of Agriculture), 1 Dec. 1950, in LES/Wünsche (eds.), *Die Korea-Krise*, 242–3.

[25] Erhard to Adenauer, 6 Feb. 1951, ibid. 246.

the same time self-interested, manner. It should be remembered that Erhard was a patriot as well as a free-marketeer, and he wanted to loosen Allied controls on German industry. He was very critical of Allied schemes to break up the coal and steel industries and 'decon-centrate' the chemical conglomerate IG Farben. Taken together with his obstinate refusal to reintroduce controls on the German economy, his obstruction of Allied plans in the heavy-industry sector did not always endear him to the British and the Americans, to say nothing of the French.

In October the Allied High Commissioners requested from Adenauer an undertaking that scarce materials and services should be equitably distributed in the interests of the common defence. Erhard made a vague reply but said that he wished to limit 'directing measures' as far as possible. On 6 November, when the Allied representatives pressed for a more specific answer, they were told that 'the institution of con-trols would be a major step for the Federal Republic and a commitment to do so would require careful consideration . . . because of the political consequences'. The Federal government refused to commit itself to such measures.[26]

This was hardly very satisfactory from the Allied viewpoint. In December a furious row blew up over coal supplies, since the Germans had realized they were going to be seriously short of coal despite Erhard's blithe assurances that the problem was only temporary. Adenauer wrote to ask the High Commissioners that the amount to be exported should be reduced. Their economic advisers blamed the whole problem on the Germans and their lack of foresight—a clear criticism of Erhard, who for his part made no bones about his views on the incompetence of the IAR, comparing poor coal-production figures with the index of industrial production in West Germany as whole. Nor were the Allies exactly reassured in February 1951, when Erhard explained to them that he was derationing oil and petroleum products— even though he tried to claim that this was not the equivalent of decontrol. It certainly amounted to a more liberal scheme for the sale of oil products than existed in some Allied countries. The chairman of the Economics Committee of the Allied High Commission reminded Erhard of the 'psychological problem' raised by decontrol at a time when other countries were reinstituting controls in their defence efforts.

[26] Meetings of the High Commissioners' Economics Committee with the Federal Minister of Economics, 19 Oct. 1950 and 6 Nov. 1950, PRO/FO/1005/1920. On the second occasion Erhard was not actually present but his views were conveyed by a senior official.

Erhard replied that 'with the public opinion in Germany, the maintenance of rationing is even more disturbing than decontrol'.[27]

Erhard did not just rely on committee lobbying and backstairs Cabinet intrigue to secure the social market. He realized that he needed more political support, so his ministry encouraged the foundation of the *Niederbreisiger Arbeitskreis*, a pro-market ginger-group within the coalition parties which produced a draft programme on 28 November 1950. This committed itself to supporting an economy based on competitive achievement in which the 'plan' for economic development was drawn up by businessmen and judged by the consumer. Businessmen had no right to engage in price fixing or market distortions such as cartels. State intervention should be compatible with the market and should be restricted to macro-economic steering by means such as credit adjustments, interest rates, customs duties, and taxes. The programme stressed that there was a long way to go before the social market economy was achieved. Two hundred price controls still existed in West Germany, and some of those would be necessary for some time. But the aim must be to work for complete freedom.[28]

Unfortunately the deficit got worse before it got better. In February the financial situation was so serious that the Bank deutscher Länder withdrew a billion Deutschmarks of credits from the banks in the *Länder*. The liberalization of German trade within the EPU was suspended and Germany began to restrict imports from EPU countries, a measure which naturally aroused indignation. This time the Americans decided to intervene against their 'invention', Ludwig Erhard. Already in November 1950, McCloy, the American High Commissioner, had told Cairncross that if the East Germans could set up twenty-seven divisions, why not the West Germans? If it meant deficit financing, so be it.[29] On 6 March 1951 he wrote to Adenauer demanding that the free market in Germany effectively be suspended, to enable raw materials and other goods to be directed towards those industries essential for rearmament. This was reinforced on 13 April by a letter to

[27] Meeting with Economics Committee of High Commission 21 Feb. 1951, PRO/FO/1005/921. The clash over coal supplies occurred on 8 Dec. 1950, PRO/FO/1005/920.

[28] *Niederbreisiger Arbeitskreis*. Draft programme, 28 Nov. 1950, LES/Wünsche (eds.), *Die Korea-Krise*, 229–38.

[29] Cairncross's report, ibid. 211. J. J. McCloy is regarded by one distinguished American historian of the Marshall Plan as 'committed to the corporative neo-capitalism espoused by top policy makers in the ECA' (Economic Co-operation Administration—the US body responsible for administering Marshall Aid). I am not altogether clear what this means, but it evidently entails commitment to 'Keynesian strategies of fiscal and monetary management' and 'positive programmes of social insurance and full employment'. Erhard was not, of course, enamoured of the ECA. See Hogan, *The Marshall Plan*, 355–7.

the Bank deutscher Länder from the American official responsible for the Marshall Aid Programme in Europe, who urged the bank to control credit for the benefit of industry and in particular to aim capital at contracts which were of direct relevance to the rearmament programme.[30] This was coming very near to the sort of economic methods used in Hitler's Germany.

The events of March 1951 seemed indeed to presage the nemesis of the social market economy. Erhard himself appeared to be thrashing about, unsure of his direction in a crisis, the depth of which he had evidently underestimated. On 14 March he delivered a speech to the Bundestag which lacked his usual confidence and clarity. He stressed the difficulties created by the Korean War and the need to ask the German people to accept sacrifices—which would, he claimed, be imposed with a sense of social responsibility. When he stated that 'we want to retain the function of the market. But we are convinced that some liberties and some freedom will have to be replaced by planned and sensible regulation,' his words were greeted with jeering laughter from the SPD.[31] Nor were his proposals for dealing with the crisis particularly convincing. He repeated an earlier suggestion of a credit-stamp savings scheme for consumers and some form of 'baby bonds' to encourage small investors in industry. He also stressed that tax evasion would be rigorously pursued and profiteering combated. The exact measures which would be taken to achieve these ends were left vague.

It was certainly not one of Erhard's happiest moments in the Bundestag, and his old opponent, Erik Nölting of the SPD, was quick to exploit his discomfiture. What the house had heard, Nölting claimed, was a 'graveside encomium for the market economy'. Phrases in Erhard's speech touching on the problems of heavy industry, the need for priorities in distributing raw materials, and the redirection of purchasing power were sins against the spirit of Erhard's previous economic policy: 'Professor Erhard, what you have brought to this podium today is the mummified corpse of your market economy. When you look in the mirror, I should like to ask if you can actually recognize yourself?'[32]

He made the telling point that the actual control of economic policy no longer seemed to be in the hands of Erhard or his ministry, but that a confusion of cooks—including Schäffer, Blücher, and Niklas, the Agriculture Minister—seemed to be spoiling the broth. He argued that

---

[30] Jean Cattier to the bank directorate, 13 Apr. 1951, in LES/Wünsche (eds.), *Die Korea-Krise*, 367–8.
[31] Deutscher Bundestag, 1. Wahlperiode, 126. Sitzung. Stenographische Berichte, repr. ibid. 301.
[32] Ibid. 317.

the latitude given to consumer-goods industries since 1948 had created an unhealthy imbalance in the German economy which was now manifesting itself. Imports of nuts, dates, bananas, caviar, and lobster had exemplified an economic policy which had allowed a narrow class of wealthy people to enjoy conspicuous consumption, while the masses suffered privation, and the real needs of the economy were neglected. He pointed to the austerity programme in Britain, which Erhard and his supporters had denigrated in the past. Now the Germans were faced with austerity whilst the British reaped the benefits of a healthy economy.

Nölting ended his peroration by urging the Bundestag to strip the Economics Minister of his salary, a rhetorical challenge easily beaten off by the votes of the government parties. More difficult to withstand were the pressures from within the Cabinet. Despite the fact that Erhard had aggressively proclaimed to the Bundestag on 14 March that he alone controlled economic policy in West Germany, he was indeed faced with a number of rivals for authority in the crisis. Schäffer was keen to introduce a special sales-tax (*Sonderumsatzsteuer*) which would be levied on selected items regarded as less essential by the government. The aim would be to reduce consumer spending while protecting the needs of the poor. He also seemed willing to implement the so-called Abs Plan for using depreciation allowances from the consumer-goods industries to help finance investment in heavy industry.[33] Erhard reacted angrily, sending a sharp message to Schäffer accusing him of economic ignorance and claiming that he was misinterpreting Cabinet decisions. From this communication it is clear that Erhard was against any major measures which would restrict commerce and cripple consumer-goods industries. He thought far more in terms of cuts in government expenditure and inducements to private investment.[34] He did not discreetly hide his displeasure, but did all he could to rally support from friends in the press and the Bundestag.

At the same time, Vocke in the Bankdeutscher Länder was alarmed by reports that a foreign-exchange commissioner was to be appointed to liaise between the government and the bank in matters relating to the disposal of foreign currency. He wrote to Adenauer protesting against a possible usurpation of the bank's prerogatives.[35] There seemed a real danger that the rest of the Cabinet would be panicked by American pressure into restoring a repressive control and taxation

---

[33] Schiffer to Erhard, 14 Mar. 1951, repr. ibid. 330–4.
[34] Erhard to Schiffer, 15 Mar. 1951, repr. ibid. 335–7.
[35] Vocke to Adenauer, 19 Mar. 1951, repr. ibid. 338–40.

system. This would have limited West Germany's ability to exploit the Korean boom which was about to take off. It would also have restricted Western European trade, thus damaging the recovery of Germany's neighbours.

Adenauer himself was furious about the confused image his government was presenting to the world, and was particularly vexed by Erhard's outspoken disagreements with his colleagues, not all of which remained confidential. The Federal Chancellor himself was no lover of theoretical economists, and took a pragmatic view of economic policy. On 12 February he told the federal committee of the CDU that he was not in principle a devotee of the free market, but would only support it so long as it proved successful.[36] On 19 March he sent a typically brief and trenchant note to his Economics Minister, in which he wrote

> Your whole behaviour is impossible. I must tell you of my most serious displeasure. You misunderstand completely the nature of a federal government. No federal minister has the right to carry out policy in decisive questions off his own bat and to seek support from the political parties against the decisions of the cabinet or the policy of the *Bundeskanzler* . . .

In Cabinet Erhard had accepted many of the measures he railed against in public, and it was unfair to Schäffer to attack him for carrying out the wishes of the government. Adenauer then went on to make more menacing comments on Erhard's conduct of business. He accused him of being personally responsible for the economic difficulties they were facing because he had not foreseen problems early enough. He had been far too optimistic in his public utterances, particularly in the case of coal, the shortage of which he had repeatedly minimized, and had even declared in December that by January nobody would be worrying about a coal crisis. Adenauer also claimed that the Economics Ministry was very badly organized and told Erhard that he was appointing a new state secretary in the ministry, Ludger Westrick, with whom Erhard would be expected to put things in order. Westrick was, indeed, seen as Adenauer's man in the ministry, who was supposed to control his undisciplined professorial chief.

It was hardly surprising that, on receipt of this thunderbolt, Erhard should offer his resignation. He did so, however, in a letter which presented a sturdy defence of his policy, and made it clear that if he stayed in office he would expect his ministry to be given full control over the economy in a way that had not so far been vouchsafed to it. In particular he criticized the Finance Ministry for its policies and accused it of trying to establish a 'treasury dictatorship' (*Finanzdiktatur*) which

[36] Koerfer, *Kampf ums Kanzleramt*, 96.

went far beyond a 'dictatorship of empty tills', with which he would have some sympathy. He reiterated his demand—for which he claimed the support of Cabinet and coalition parties—that credit and money-supply policies should be left to him and the Bank deutscher Länder and not to the Finance Ministry.[37]

Adenauer was genuinely angry with Erhard and contemptuous of the Cabinet in general. He declared at one point during the crisis that there was only one minister he could trust, and that was the Foreign Minister. Since Adenauer himself was the Foreign Minister, this hardly reflected well on his subordinates.[38] He organized a small group of businessmen, under the chairmanship of Friedrich Ernst, a Berlin banker, to act as his own staff of economic advisers. It was rumoured that Ernst would become chairman of a special economic Cabinet which would outflank the Economics Ministry.[39]

Nevertheless, the Chancellor shrank from sacking Erhard. In his otherwise condemnatory letter of 19 March he ended by recognizing the Economics Minister's achievement in reforming the economy, and there is no doubt that Adenauer sympathized with Erhard's general approach, even if he criticized his day-to-day methods. He also knew that Erhard had strong support within the Bundestag CDU *Fraktion*, and that the FDP might well leave the Cabinet if Erhard was thrown overboard. Adenauer's position as government leader was not yet strong enough for him to risk jettisoning Erhard.

Despite his apparently desperate position, therefore, Erhard was left to fight his corner in his ministry, and he did so with great determination. One threat revealed itself to be a blessing in disguise. Ludger Westrick, an experienced businessman, quickly gained Erhard's confidence in his post as state secretary, proving a loyal and effective subordinate. He was able to use his influence to improve relations between his minister and the Federal Chancellor, even if they were never to be particularly warm.[40]

---

[37] Correspondence between Adenauer and Erhard, 19 Mar. 1951, reprinted in LES/ Wünsche (eds.), *Die Korea-Krise*, 341–6. For Adenauer's displeasure over Erhard's optimistic claims on the coal crisis, see *Adenauer: Briefe 1949–1951*, 351.

[38] Hans-Peter Schwarz, introd. to LES/Wünsche (eds.), *Die Korea-Krise*, 10.

[39] Koerfer, *Kampf ums Kanzleramt*, 97. On 20 Mar. Erhard was informed of the danger by Victor-Emanuel Preusker, an FDP Bundestag member, who feared that Adenauer was capitulating to trade-union pressure and argued that soon the FDP would have no place in his government, LES/Wünsche (eds.), *Die Korea-Krise*, 346. The FDP's hostility to the reintroduction of controls was made very clear in the weeks which followed. Cf. the record of the meeting of the FDP's economics committee, 18 June 1951, chaired by the neo-liberal economist Hans Ilau, ibid. 399–407.

[40] AJN interview with Ludger Westrick, 28 Sept. 1985.

One result of this domestic crisis was that Erhard did indeed manage to assert his right to control emergency measures from his own ministry. He also beat off the most pernicious suggestions for restoring controls. Instead he used methods which, however unorthodox and in some cases illiberal they might seem, were less damaging to the market economy in the long run than the prescriptions of Social Democrats like Nölting, or even Americans like McCloy and Jean Cattier, of the Marshall Plan administration. Throughout the early months of 1951 Erhard had to resist tremendous Allied pressure to give up his liberal economic policies. In February he had told the Allied representatives in Bonn that West Germany's balance-of-payments difficulties were a temporary phenomenon, which would be overcome by her export capacity if this was not crippled by a return to allocations and controls. He was completely confident in the export capacity of German industry so long as it was exposed to domestic and foreign competition. He begged his American, British, and French colleagues not to throw down their free-market weapons at the height of the crisis. 'Give me another six months,' he begged. They were not impressed, and the outcome was McCloy's threatening letter.[41]

Nor were all the doubting Thomases foreigners. At home a rising tide of public concern about inflation, unemployment, and the coal shortage was encouraging those who had always hankered after planning. These included Günter Keiser, who was still playing a leading role in the Economics Ministry, and Otto Friedrich, the commissioner for raw material distribution, whom Erhard appointed as a sop to Allied demands for more effective priorities in implementing the Western armaments programme.[42] Erhard managed, however, to block the demands for *dirigiste* measures or head them off with palliatives which did not jeopardize the future progress of liberalization. He was aided by the workings of the market itself, which was generating its own solution to West Germany's problems. Already on 19 March 1951, Vocke, in his letter to Adenauer protesting about the appointment of a foreign-currency commissar, had been able to point out that the balance-of-payments situation was showing signs of improvement.

There is no doubt that the Korean crisis was the most serious challenge to Erhard's economic policy. Historians have come to widely

---

[41] Evidence of Fritz Stedtfeld in LES/Wünsche (eds.), *Die Korea-Krise*, 101.

[42] Friedrich already knew Erhard well. Although he was evidently more *dirigiste* than Erhard, he shared the latter's concern that German policy should not fall back into the habits of the pre-war era. See V. R. Berghahn and P. J. Friedrich, *Otto A. Friedrich, ein politischer Unternehmer: Sein Leben und seine Zeit 1902–1975* (Frankfurt/M., 1993), 135–60. See also the evidence of Heinz Krekeler, in LES/Wünsche (eds.), *Die Korea Krise*, 102.

differing conclusions about his response to that challenge. All agree that personally he overcame the threats to his own position, and that politically the CDU emerged victorious over advocates of what would effectively have been socialist planning. But there the consensus ends. Some of his critics, of whom Werner Abelshauser has been the most eloquent, have claimed that the McCloy letter and its aftermath effectively wrote the death certificate of the social market economy, since thereafter West Germany reverted from free competition to a 'corporatist' form of economic organization in which business associations rather than the state controlled the distribution of raw materials and the allocation of capital.[43] 'Corporatism' in this context means a form of collusion between business pressure-groups and government agencies designed to negate competition or override market forces. Such a system would be clearly incompatible with the principles of the social market.

The case against Erhard is based on two measures which were forced upon him in conflict with his free-market principles. The first was a levy on consumer-goods industries to provide capital for improvements in other sectors which had not revived as rapidly after the changes in 1948—in particular coal and steel, which seemed in need of major investment to increase output. In April 1951 Germany's industrial associations arranged this levy, producing a subvention of DM1 billion for heavy industry.

The second and apparently more cogent reason for adducing failure for Erhard in 1951 lies in the decision to agree with US demands for allocation of raw materials to particularly 'vital' areas of the economy, but to leave this allocation in the hands of West German business associations. Here, of course, the accusation of corporatism seems to have some force, since it was the power of just these associations, the *Interessentenverbände*, against which neo-liberals like Alexander Rüstow and Franz Böhm had been fulminating since the 1930s. Indeed, Franz Böhm himself reacted with dismay to the situation created by McCloy's pressure and the measures which followed it. At the end of April 1951 he told the Academic Advisory Council of the Economics Ministry that the 'delegation of state responsibilities to administrative bodies of a purely private character . . . is incompatible with current law relating to the state and the economy, and is certainly not compatible with the fundamental principles of a democratic constitution'.[44]

Social Democrats like Agartz and Schiller were not slow to pounce

---

[43] Abelshauser, 'Korea, die Ruhr und Erhards Marktwirtschaft', 310–14.
[44] Meeting of the Academic Advisory Committee, 28/29 Apr. 1951, cited ibid. 313.

on the inconsistencies of opposing state planning whilst allowing business interests to plan the economy.[45]

Much is made in the case against Erhard of the appointment of an 'Adviser to the Federal Government for Raw Material Questions' in the person of Otto Friedrich, the general director of the Hamburg Phönix rubber company, who was suggested by the West German industrialists' association, the *Bundesverband der deutschen Industrie* (BDI). The appointment of Friedrich and other experts with special functions regarding different parts of industry seemed to demonstrate that Erhard's ministry was losing its grip on the economy to other sectors of government, to the Bank deutscher Länder or even to private pressure-groups.[46]

How far is this condemnation of Erhard's policy justified? First of all, we have to accept that the Korean crisis was, indeed, a serious test of nerve for Erhard, and that there were times when his optimistic public statements were ill-chosen, or at least ill-timed. If one lifts one's eyes even a few months from the trough of the crisis, however, one obtains a very different picture of Erhard's policy and can realize that his apparent inactivity was actually tenacious and ultimately effective opposition to the clamour for reintroduction of controls. By standing firm, even at the cost of a few, largely meaningless, concessions, Erhard prevented a relapse into planning which might have had ominous consequences, not only for West Germany but also for Western Europe.

To take the case of capital investment in heavy industry first, it is true that Erhard did not cut a very decisive figure when dealing with this problem. This is partly because the areas of production concerned were still bedevilled by controls, despite Erhard's attempts to liberalize them. In his Bundestag speech on 14 March Erhard had shown a flash of defiance by pointing out to his critics that in this industrial sector: 'We certainly have had no market economy, but rather the lack of clear ownership-rights and responsible leadership has led to the realization, gentlemen of the Left, of the ideal of your economic policy.'[47]

Coal was a particular bugbear. It was hamstrung by the Allied Ruhr authority, and its ownership was in question as the result of denazifi-

---

[45] See below, Ch. 14.

[46] Abelshauser, 'Korea, die Ruhr und Erhards Marktwirtschaft', 313. For a rather more sophisticated, but equally negative, assessment of Erhard's market economy at this time, see Kramer, *West German Economy*, 166–73. His findings should be contrasted with those in Giersch *et al.*, *The Fading Miracle*, 101–5. See also, fn. 42 above.

[47] Deutscher Bundestag, 1. Wahlperiode, 126. Sitzung. Stenographische Berichte, repr. in LES/Wünsche (eds.), *Die Korea-Krise*, 305. For a recent study of the problems of investment in coal and the deleterious effects of price-fixing, see Roseman, *Recasting the Ruhr*.

cation and deconcentration. As we have seen, Erhard's attempt to deregulate coal in 1950 had been torpedoed by the onset of the Korean crisis. The result was very low productivity and a black market in coal. Because prices were fixed, there was no incentive for German businessmen to risk the high levels of investment needed to renew pits or tunnel new shafts.

So far as the capital needs of heavy industry were concerned, various schemes were being bandied about to deal with the problem. The Social Democrats wanted direction of investment by the state and the end of market liberalization. The Finance Ministry wanted a general sales-tax to finance government investment in industry. Business circles wanted depreciation write-offs to benefit mining and heavy industry. None of these solutions would have pleased Erhard, since all but the latter would have involved bureaucratic decision-making about the future of industrial enterprises. He himself came up with a rather different, but it must be said, unconvincingly 'academic' scheme. This was the proposal, made in January 1951, that some consumer goods should have an extra charge imposed on them for which purchasers would receive points or bonus stamps which would be treated as a sort of savings account and would attract interest. The money thus raised would be channelled into an investment fund for industry. Theoretically this had the advantage of being a voluntary rather than a compulsory form of saving. It would also give the consumer a stake in industry through a form of mini-debenture. It must be said, however, that the whole scheme was hardly a practical solution to an urgent problem, and the alternative offered by the business associations was a much more effective one.

Nor should this solution be regarded as necessarily implying a failure for the social market economy. As we noted above, Erhard had always preferred using associations of businessmen who knew what they were doing to direction on the part of civil servants. Even his British critics admitted in the summer of 1948 that such business groups contained the most efficient and hard-headed elements in the West German economy.[48] The share of total investment taken up by heavy industry under these arrangements was certainly not large by comparison with what it would have been under the *dirigiste* plans of

---

[48] See above, Ch. 10. See O'Neill's report to the British Berlin HQ of 30 Apr. 1948, PRO/FO/1049/1432. Also the report of a British Treasury official to Frankfurt in Apr. 1949, who spoke very critically of the German authorities, including Erhard, whom he described as an 'unattractive person and also muddle-headed', and who thought a free economy run by businessmen was preferable to controls run by the Frankfurt administrators. PRO/FO/104/100.

the sort which existed when Erhard took up office in Frankfurt. Nor can it really be claimed that direction of economic activity by the *Verbände* became a permanent feature of the West German economic scene after 1951. With the liberalization of the capital market which was to crown Erhard's achievements in the 1950s, German entrepreneurs could look elsewhere for their funding. The fact that the business associations were used in 1960 to help finance aid to underdeveloped countries is hardly a convincing proof of their predominant authority.[49]

So far as McCloy's demands for state direction of the economy to aid the rearmament programme were concerned, there is no doubt that Erhard was bitterly disappointed with the Americans over this. He not unreasonably felt that Washington was backtracking on its free-market principles. Having overcome his first shock, however, he did everything he could to stiffen Adenauer's backbone against giving in to the Americans. This was difficult for Adenauer, who wanted nothing to cloud German–American relations, especially since he hoped to use the Korean crisis to obtain more sovereignty—and a defence capability—for the Federal Republic. Nevertheless, he too was no friend of state controls and he wanted to retain the clear distinction between his domestic policy and that of the Social Democrats. So his answer to McCloy was emollient, but avoided any dramatic concessions to the American viewpoint. He listed the measures already taken to ensure that defence production should be given priority in the distribution of scarce raw materials, and expressed willingness to consider firmer measures should these appear necessary. But he stressed the delicacy of an operation which had to take account of consumer needs if productivity was to be maintained.[50]

As for the appointment of Friedrich and the distribution of raw materials through the industrial associations, Friedrich was himself appointed by Erhard's Economics Ministry and the role of the *Verbände* was informal and obviously temporary. Even so, it left the consumer with a great deal more choice than would have been the case with state direction. The controls on distribution were relatively lightly exercised

---

[49] Abelshauser, 'Korea, die Ruhr und Erhards Marktwirtschaft', 314–15. The BDI persuaded its members voluntarily to donate DM1.2 billion to aid underdeveloped countries which the industrial associations' own bodies would distribute. Berg, the BDI president, was understandably proud of this, and said it showed that industry was capable of extraordinary achievements even without state direction. Abelshauser's comment is that 'the business associations had finally taken over state functions and were carrying them out on their own reponsibility and under their own direction'. This does, of course, depend on one's definition of what 'state functions' should be.

[50] Adenauer to McCloy, 27 Mar. 1951. See Abelshauser, 'Ansätze korporativer Marktwirtschaft', 739–45; the letter is repr. in LES/Wünsche (eds.), *Die Korea-Krise*, 347–53.

by the trade associations concerned.[51] It was important that Erhard's ministry had dismantled a lot of the bureaucratic machinery needed for a full-scale rationing–system. This was one of the achievements which stood him in good stead in 1951; restoration of the *Zwangswirtschaft* would hardly have been possible, even if it had been contemplated. Doubtless the policies adopted were not entirely in line with theories of perfect competition. Erhard, however, had never been a man to let the best be the enemy of the good.

Within weeks of the McCloy letter, West Germany's economic problems began to right themselves, not through state intervention or fine tuning, but because of the working of market forces. German firms had rationalized their production methods, improved labour productivity, and used their imported materials to increase production. They were now able to exploit a sellers' market in the high-quality products they produced. Germany's balance-of-payments deficit began to improve rapidly and the country was soon to become the largest creditor of the EPU rather than its leading debtor. The suspension of trade liberalization with EPU countries could be jettisoned, and once again West Germany could operate as the chief supplier of many European countries with industrial products.

Much of the credit for this achievement must go to Erhard. Many contemporary observers agreed that he was the rock upon which the collectivist clamour broke.[52] The more the Korea boom got under way, the higher his star rose. Adenauer's group of economic advisers in the Federal Chancellery shrank in significance.

If Erhard had won his political battle within the government, the crisis had shown that the West German public still had a lot to learn before it accepted the social market economy as the normal and optimal economic system in the Federal Republic. Whereas the liberation from the *Zwangswirtschaft* had aroused enthusiasm in 1948–9, by 1951 the reappearance of inflation, fuel shortages, and power cuts created a very different atmosphere, one in which the call for government action to 'correct' the failings of the economy aroused positive responses. Erhard had always kept a weather-eye open on public reaction to

---

[51] Abelshauser notes this in 'Korea, die Ruhr und Erhards Marktwirtschaft', 310–14, though without enthusiasm. For Friedrich's mildly bombastic description of his own activities, see his article in the *Frankfurter Allgemeine Zeitung*, 29 Sept. 1951, repr. in LES/Wünsche (eds.), *Die Korea-Krise*, 445–51. Although Friedrich praises his planning officials, it is clear that his activities were largely advisory.

[52] This was certainly the view of Westrick, with whom the author had a fascinating conversation on 28 Sept. 1985. See also the testimonies of contemporaries printed in LES/Wünsche (eds.), *Die Korea-Krise*, 101–9.

his liberalization policies. A specialist in market research himself since his period in Vershofen's institute, it was not surprising that he was an early user of public opinion polls. Eight days after the currency reform in 1948 he had commissioned investigations into public reaction to the new measures, and thereafter he was a good customer of public opinion surveys. Adenauer also paid careful attention to the polls, and regular surveys were made on behalf of the Federal government.[53]

Immediately after the currency reform in 1948 Erhard had been reassured to learn that the public was unlikely to splurge its new money in a reckless spending spree, but was inclined to await developments and hope that prices would go down.[54] Not all the results of opinion surveys, however, were reassuring. It very quickly became apparent that few people made a clear connection between the improvement in supplies in shops and the reduction in the amount of money available. Instead, the loss of savings sustained by less well-to-do people was regarded as unjust. A surprisingly high proportion of West Germans thought that the currency reform introduced in East Germany by the Soviet authorities was fairer than that carried out in the Western zones of occupation, although this did not mean that they thought life in the Soviet zone would be preferable to that in the West. In March 1949 more people claimed to prefer that eggs should be distributed at a fixed price than sold freely at a higher price. Such surveys are not always good indicators of respondents' reactions when faced with a choice of government, but they did illustrate the level of confusion about elementary economic principles which existed during the early years of the Federal Republic. The concept of the 'just price', which Erhard's mentor Rieger had so decisively rejected, was still very attractive to the Germans, and market prices were as likely to be associated with anarchy as with the natural order of things.[55]

In the second half of 1950 the combination of war threats and economic difficulties had a depressing effect on West German public opinion. At the end of every year a representative sample of the population of

[53] Rüdiger Schulz, 'Die Reaktionen der Bundesbürger auf die politischen und wirtschaftlichen Herausforderungen der Korea-Krise', ibid. 69.

[54] E. Noelle-Neumann, 'Disziplin, Hoffnung, Unsicherheit: Umfragen nach der Währungsreform', *Orientierungen zur Wirtschafts- und Gesellschaftspolitik*, 36 (June 1988), 35–7.

[55] Ibid. 35% thought the 'Erhard' method of currency reform better, whereas 32% preferred that in the Eastern zone. On eggs, 47% were for controlled prices and 41% for free prices. In view of the wording of the question, which spoke of 'higher' free prices, the latter result was not too discouraging. See also E. Noelle and E. P. Neumann, *Jahrbuch der öffentlichen Meinung, 1945–1955* (Allensbach/Bodensee, 1956), 233, and H. Wellmann, *Die soziale Marktwirtschaft im Spiegel von Meinungsumfragen* (Ph.D. thesis; Cologne, 1962), 90.

the Federal Republic was asked 'Are you looking forward to the new year in fear or in hope?' Between 1949 and 1984 there were only two occasions when the fearful outnumbered the hopeful, and one of them was December 1950. Then, only 27 per cent were optimistic about the future; 43 per cent were pessimistic and 17 per cent were sceptical. Despite the fears of war, concern over the economic situation loomed largest in the popular mind. Nor did this concern dissipate in the months which followed. The improving balance of payments in summer 1951 may have impressed professional economists and administrators, but the public impression of the economy was anything but positive by the autumn of that year. In October, 45 per cent of those polled thought that the most important task in Germany was 'the improvement of the economic situation', whereas 'securing peace' was in second place with only 20 per cent, and the restoration of German unity was chosen by 18 per cent.[56] At the height of the crisis, in March 1951, 46 per cent of those questioned blamed the economic policy of the government for rising prices, and only 37 per cent thought they were caused by a rise in world commodity-prices. There was little sign of faith in the healing properties of a self-operating market. When, in May 1951, people were asked whether the government could do something about rising prices if it wanted to, a massive 75 per cent answered 'Yes' and only 9 per cent rejected the suggestion.

Other polls in the spring of 1951 were even less encouraging. Given a choice between fixed prices and free prices based on supply and demand, 47 per cent of those asked favoured controlled prices, as against 37 per cent for the free market. On Erhard himself, a survey in May 1951 showed that a mere 14 per cent of those asked had a good opinion of Erhard, whereas 49 per cent had a low opinion of him. On the other hand, only 14 per cent professed to not knowing who Erhard was: a remarkably low proportion and an indicator of his prominence in German political life. Nevertheless, this demonstrated that the euphoria over derationing had now evaporated. One distinguished pioneer in German public opinion surveys has spoken of 'unpopularity hanging over Erhard like dark clouds' during the Korean crisis.[57]

It was evident that, from an ideological viewpoint, the theories of the social market economy were no more comprehensible to the man in the street than they were to Konrad Adenauer. In the early 1950s it was

[56] R. Schulz, 'Die Reaktionen der Bundesbürger', 72. The other gloomy year was 1973, but then only 34% were fearful as against 30% who were optimistic. In 1981 pessimists and optimists tied at 32% each.
[57] Noelle-Neumann, 'Disziplin, Hoffunung, Unsicherheit', 37. For the 1951 survey figures, R. Schulz, 'Die Reaktionen der Bundesbürger', 77–80.

discovered that most Germans regarded 'social' policies as being more important even than 'democratic' ones. When social issues were under consideration, the CDU tended to be regarded as less helpful than the SPD. This went so far that when, in March 1953, people were asked which party supported the social market economy, 12 per cent supposed it to be the SPD, as against only 5 per cent answering up for the CDU. The vast majority of those questioned (81 per cent) either did not know which party to choose or admitted they were not informed about the social market economy.[58]

It was one of Erhard's self-appointed tasks to propagate the ideal of the market and of state-protected competition, and his supporters in the neo-liberal economic camp were eager to help him. Erhard was always willing to enlist public support for his views, even if this might seem unorthodox or even disloyal behaviour to more conventional politicians like Adenauer. In September 1952 a group of sympathetic industrialists in Cologne set up an association for the furtherance of social compromise (*Gemeinschaft zur Förderung des sozialen Ausgleiches*) which also went under the title of *Die Waage*. It placed advertisements and cartoon features in the popular press extolling the benefits of free competition.[59]

Other educational activities involved the neo-liberal economists who had been the architects of the social market economy. Eucken had died unexpectedly in 1950, and Röpke remained in his Swiss exile, but Rüstow had come back to a chair in Heidelberg, and Böhm had been elected to the Bundestag for the CDU. Müller-Armack, of course, was at Erhard's side in his ministry, and remained an enthusiastic proselytizer for the policy whose name he had coined.

The neo-liberals' robust hostility to the monopolies and power concentrations which had characterized German heavy industry, in particular, since the late nineteenth century had the paradoxical consequence that they themselves were enthusiastically supported by pressure groups associated with consumer industries or medium-sized business enterprises. Müller-Armack's connections in this respect have already been noted.[60] Franz Böhm and Walter Eucken were involved in the activities of the Working Association of Independent Entrepreneurs (*Arbeitsgemeinschaft selbständiger Unternehmer*, or ASU), founded in September 1949. The driving force behind this body was evidently Dr C. A. Schleussner, the proprietor of a well-known but medium-sized

[58] Ibid. 76.
[59] Franz Greiss, 'Erhard's soziale Marktwirtschaft und DIE WAAGE' in G. Schröder *et al.* (eds.), *Ludwig Erhard: Beiträge*, 94–109.
[60] See above, Ch. 6.

photographic company, ADOX. At the second working conference of the ASU, Böhm and Eucken had explained why they did not believe that human freedom was possible without independent entrepreneurs. Writing in the ASU information sheet in February 1952 Schleussner approvingly cited Röpke's words from *Civitas Humana* to the effect that

At the moment when we have turned against monopoly, concentration, and colossus capitalism in the name of true market economics, and the moment we speak up for an economic policy directed by humanity and common sense, aimed at the reduction of hardship and friction and favouring the economically weak, at that moment we have already made our choice in favour of small and medium enterprises in all branches of the economy.[61]

This identification of the social market economy with the interests of small and medium-sized entrepreneurs was obviously crucial to Schleussner. He bent his energies towards re-educating businessmen to accept the anti-monopolist ideas of the neo-liberals. He saw these both as an intellectual weapon with which to combat Marxism and as a shield for the independent entrepreneur against combines or monopolies. For obvious reasons, he was less than enthusiastic about such concepts as equal opportunities or inheritance taxes.[62] Such men as Schleussner were of some importance, in that they helped to provide the institutional means to disseminate social-market theories amongst both the business communities and the public at large. In July 1953 Schleussner himself produced a book called a *Primer on the Social Market Economy*, designed to give businessmen easy access to the ideas of Röpke, Müller-Armack, and Rüstow.[63] The ASU's social committee was active in promoting measures which would protect independent businessmen from property taxes on the one hand and large-scale capitalism on the other.[64] The ASU was also eager to set up institutes and university courses designed to train budding businessmen in the theories of the social market economy—evidently as a weapon against less attractive points of view. They remarked on the existence of trade-union institutions for the propagation of socialist theories.

[61] See W. Röpke, *Civitas Humana: Grundlagen der Gesellschafts- und Wirtschaftsreform* (Erlenbach-Zurich, 1944), 80. For C. A. Schleussner's comments, Böhm NL, KAS I-200-017.

[62] For Schleussner's views, see a draft report to the *Grundsatzausschuß* of the ASU, 4 Sept. 1953, Böhm NL, KAS I-200-017/1.

[63] A. Schleussner, *Fibel der sozialen Marktwirtschaft: Zur Orientierung für Unternehmer und Unternehmensleiter* (Düsseldorf, 1953). Müller-Armack wrote a preface to this 'primer' in which he described the social market economy as a new conception of market economy which combined the principle of freedom, essential to man if he was to assert his own value as a human being, with the 'social needs of our time'.

[64] For the work of this committee, see Böhm NL, KAS I-200-018.

Schleussner himself was eager to extend this didactic activity beyond the confines of the ASU. He was also very active in the Action Group for the Realization of the Social Market Economy (*Aktionsgemeinschaft Soziale Marktwirtschaft*—ASM) which had been founded on 23 January 1953, under the leadership of Otto Lautenbach. This had its headquarters at Heidelberg, where Rüstow was a professor, and was bound by its statutes to strive for the realization of the social market economy, with the aim of achieving the highest possible rise in the standard of living, to protect private property, preserve for the entrepreneur the freedom of decision in his enterprise, and to secure free competition based on achievement (*Leistungswettbewerb*).[65] It did this by organizing conferences, lectures, and publications supporting the social market economy. In the autumn of 1957, for example, a competition was arranged—financed by private firms—for the best essay by a pupil in a vocational school on the theme 'What is the social market economy?' It was won by a sixteen-year-old apprentice in a wholesaling firm, who did indeed demonstrate a clear grasp of neo-liberal theories. So far as their social objectives were concerned, he picked out social housing policies and the aim of a career open to talent.[66] At the ninth working conference of the ASM, held in November the same year, Schleussner commented on the need for similar competitions in schools to help pupils distinguish between neo-liberal and socialist views. There should also be more teaching of the theories of the social market economy at universities and more economics chairs should be filled with enthusiasts for the system.[67]

It is, of course, very difficult to assess the impact of such activities. Certainly the public attitude towards the social market economy improved in the 1950s, although only slowly. A public-opinion poll in April 1950 indicated that over half those questioned had no idea what the social market economy was, and only 12 per cent were able to give correct answers to questions about it. In November 1952, 48 per cent of those questioned still admitted knowing nothing about the social market, 37 per cent gave wrong answers, and only 7 per cent seemed well informed. By 1960, however, public opinion polls showed 61 per cent expressing support for the social market economy, although

---

[65] Satzung der ASM, Böhm NL, KAS I-200-077/1.

[66] The essay was published by Stoyscheff Verlag, Darmstadt, which specialized in magazines for apprentices. Erhard wrote an introduction praising the German system of vocational training and denying that it needed reform. Böhm NL, KAS I-200-008.

[67] The conference attracted 484 registered participants, including Erhard and Adenauer's son. Nearly half seem to have come from commerce and industry.

whether they were so much better informed than earlier respondents is somewhat doubtful.[68]

More important, of course, was the changed atmosphere brought about by the success of Erhard's determination to trust market forces. In the second half of 1952 the economy grew very rapidly. Production was increasing by 9 per cent per annum. West Germany had established herself as a creditor nation in the EPU and her exports were booming. Inflation had dropped away and even the unemployment situation was improving. There were less than a million out of work, or 5.5 per cent of the labour force. This was actually a much better figure than it seemed, because new jobs were still being found for refugees from East Germany. It was certainly a better record than the Federal Republic could show in the 1980s. In 1952 the West Germans also built about 430,000 dwellings, of which about a fifth were constructed with public money.[69] A dynamic growth in housing enhanced the country's economic expansion, and reinforced the view that a combination of market forces and social responsibility could overcome West Germany's problems.

So far as public opinion was concerned, economic progress and Adenauer's diplomatic achievements ensured that, in September 1953, the CDU would achieve a stunning success in the Bundestag elections. Although not yet quite in possession of a majority of the popular vote, the Christian Democrats had a majority in the Bundestag, and their leadership in the government could not be challenged. Röpke referred to this victory as 'a bull's-eye after the long series of misses in Germany's recent history'. He claimed that it demonstrated that the German people was fundamentally middle-class, a judgement less on its sociological composition than on its mental attitude.[70]

Erhard now had much less to fear from left-wing cries for controls and socialization. West Germans had turned their faces against socialism, and the tragic events in the Soviet zone in July 1953 reinforced their aversion to it. On the other hand, the social market economy was far from being achieved. In future he would find his opponents coming from a different and more influential quarter. The struggle to achieve genuine competition through free trade and anti-cartel laws was only just about to begin.

[68] See note 55.
[69] Schwarz, *Die Ära Adenauer, 1949–1957*, 193–4.
[70] Ibid. 197.

14

The SPD and the Struggle
for Reform

By the early 1950s it was becoming clear that the SPD would find it difficult to go on supporting a planned economy if it wished to expand its support amongst the German electorate.

At the first SPD congress after the war, held in 1946 on Schumacher's home ground in Hanover, the party leader had told the assembly that the Social Democrats did not need a programme, and that it was too early to try to create one. Willi Eichler was brave enough to disagree with him, pointing out that it would be necessary for socialists to clarify their minds about concepts and problems which a few decades earlier seemed to have been solved and settled. The kind of questions he had in mind included the socialization of the means of production, the party's attitude towards small businesses and farmers, the historical assessment of the Bolshevik revolution, the relationship of social democracy to Christianity, and the significance of the Socialist International.[1] Eichler was putting down a marker for the revision of the SPD programme along the lines favoured by the ethical socialist reformers.

Schumacher himself was somewhat ambivalent in his position on this issue. Certainly he was at pains to deny a commitment to a monolithic state-directed economy, and to stress the humane aspects of social democracy. He claimed that one could as well become a socialist by studying ethical philosophy or even the Sermon on the Mount as from the results of economic analysis.[2] At the Hanover congress he claimed there could be no socialist society without the most varied forms of production and types of industrial enterprise.[3] Nevertheless, Schumacher avoided defining the nature of socialism too carefully, and in this he was being politically shrewd. A discussion on that matter in

---

[1] S. Miller, 'Zur Wirkungsgeschichte des Godesberger Programms', in B. Rebe, K. Lampe, and R. von Thadden (eds.), *Idee und Pragmatik in der politischen Entscheidung. Alfred Kubel zum 75, Geburtstag* (Bonn, 1984), 129–30.

[2] Cited in T. Meyer, *Grundwerte und Wissenschaft im demokratischen Sozialismus* (Berlin, 1978), 84.

[3] Cited by G. Weisser in 'Vielgestaltiges soziales Leben', in C. Schmid, K. Schiller, and E. Potthoff (eds.), *Grundfragen moderner Wirtschaftspolitik* (Frankfurt/M., 1958), 143.

the turbulent post-war years would have almost certainly created more strife than harmony.

Reformers within the party had to content themselves with trying to reassess the fundamental values upon which social democracy was based. Willi Eichler, who had become the editor of the *Rheinische Zeitung* after his return to Germany from British exile, was active in this enterprise. He played a leading part in a Social Democratic conference at Ziegenhain in August 1947, chaired by the deputy leader of the SPD, Erich Ollenhauer. Eichler and Ollenhauer had both been exiles in London during the war. Gerhard Weisser was also one of the main speakers, and the report produced by the conference was drafted mainly by another ethically minded socialist, Professor Carlo Schmid of Tübingen University, who was SPD Minister of Justice in the French-controlled *Land* of Württemberg-Hohenzollern.[4]

The report paid tribute to Marx and his followers, but pointed out that they were men of their time and that their views about economic determinism had been proved inadequate. Socialism must recognize individual responsibility and the need for spiritual freedom. This was a view which echoed the arguments of ethical socialists like Heimann and the Nelsonian group in the 1920s. It was also a response to developments within the Protestant church, where voices were being raised for a commitment to social responsibility after what was seen as a shameful collaboration with National Socialism in the Third Reich. Shortly after the Ziegenhain conference the *Bruderrat* of the Protestant church had enunciated what were known as the Darmstadt Theses, which accepted German guilt for the Second World War and sharply criticized German Churches for their association with reactionary pro-pertied classes and their apparent lack of concern for the poor.

Schumacher had actually taken part in discussions with Protestant Church leaders, and the Ziegenhain deliberations might have been seen as part of a bridge-building process between the SPD and sections of the Protestant Church. In practice, however, this development did not get far. Schumacher does not seem to have been very interested in it. At the end of November 1947 he explained to a meeting of SPD newspaper editors that the Ziegenhain declarations related only to the particular sub-area of cultural policy and thereby deprived them of any implications for the wider programme of the SPD.[5] Although discussions about cultural policy continued to be held, the generally

---

[4] For the Ziegenhain meeting, see Klotzbach, *Der Weg zur Staatspartei*, 182 ff.
[5] Ibid. 183–4.

anti-clerical tone of Schumacher's propaganda did not change, nor, of course, did his commitment to planning and controls.

During the next few years, the party was absorbed in the political struggle against Adenauer's government. It still entertained the hope that it could overthrow the Chancellor in the Bundestag elections due in September 1953. The hold of orthodoxy on the party's full-time officials was too great to allow of fundamental changes in their programme, especially while Schumacher was alive.

Furthermore, in the early 1950s there did not seem to be any reason to engage in divisive wrangling on matters of economic principle. Erhard's 'experiment' might fail. It seemed to be creaking under the strain of the Korean War. In 1951, as we saw above, allocation of raw materials had become a necessity, and this function had been given over to associations representing heavy industry. Karl Schiller was quick to point out that this step was entirely inconsistent with neo-liberal principles. Speaking to an academic audience in Munich in September 1951, he argued that it was no longer a question of freedom versus regulation (*Bewirtschaftung*), but of state regulation or regulation by private pressure-groups. The latter course, which Erhard had chosen, obviously brought with it moral dangers and was a threat to a genuinely free market. If the impersonal forces of supply and demand were going to be given up, state regulation was the only respectable alternative.[6] This was a shrewd thrust, since it coincided with arguments from some of Erhard's own supporters, including Franz Böhm.

In the economics field Schiller was indeed the most determined exponent of liberalizing the Social Democratic attitude towards competition and the market mechanism. Weisser was unambivalent in his rejection of centralized state direction and his support for competition, and nobody could doubt his genuine commitment to democratic socialism. But he clearly favoured a system which, if highly differentiated, was still firmly socialist, and he bluntly rejected neo-liberalism in his programmatic statements. As for other aspects of reform—the relationship to the Churches and the ethical foundations of socialism, including a commitment to personal liberty—these were the particular concern of Eichler and his circle of former adherents of Leonhard Nelson, especially Grete Henry-Hermann, Suzanne Miller, and Gerhard Weisser himself.

In April 1952 the SPD executive appointed Eichler chairman of a committee to draw up what was described as an 'action programme'

---

[6] K. Schiller, *Scheinprobleme und Existenzfragen: Vier wirtschaftspolitische Hauptaufgaben der deutschen Gegenwart* (Munich, 1951), 14–15.

for the party. Doubtless the approaching Bundestag elections were uppermost in the minds of the party executive at that point—the SPD had to have some clear alternative to government policies. Eichler did his best to shift the party in a reformist direction, but his situation was not made easier by Schumacher's insistence on class-war rhetoric and the reluctance of other functionaries to face up to the fact that Erhard's policies were becoming increasingly popular. When Eichler presented the 'action programme' to the SPD conference at Dortmund on 26 September 1952, he explained that the party could not be expected to produce a comprehensive theory of socialism, because in recent years developments in sociology, psychology, and economics—to say nothing of natural sciences—had been so rapid and complex that the time was not ripe for such a venture.[7]

He rather lamely excused the shortcomings of the document by telling his comrades that it was easy enough for a middle-class party to produce a programme, since all it had to do was to satisfy the bourgeoisie's need to protect its property, its monopoly of education, and the privileged set of power relationships which such advantages created. For those who believed in social justice, solidarity, and personal freedom, however, the means of attaining those objectives could not be stated simply. As an example he cited the old Marxist view that the socialization of the means of production was the proper way to free human beings from the fetters of capitalism. But it had not been foreseen that such measures might lead to an omnipotent state which could threaten individual freedom. Experience had taught socialists the need to safeguard liberty, and to accept the fact that planning must be combined with the protection of freedom.[8]

This did not, of course, mean the acceptance of the social market economy. Eichler specifically denied that it would be possible to achieve the objectives of German social democracy if Erhard's policy was retained. He spoke harshly of the 'capitalist law of the jungle'. Yet his formula for achieving social justice was less radical than his rhetoric might have implied. Democratization of economic life through co-determination, planning through direction of investment, support for heavy industry; these were relatively pragmatic demands compared with those of the immediate post-war period. Only coal and steel were to be nationalized, and then for political rather than economic reasons.[9] The programme was careful to make nice noises about small farmers and craftsmen, and it is worth noting that Eichler particularly

---

[7] *Protokoll der Verhandlungen des Parteitages der SPD vom 24. bis 28. September 1952 in Dortmund* (hereafter cited as *SPD Verhandlungsprotokoll 1952*) (Bonn, n.d.), 103.
[8] Ibid. 104–5.   [9] Ibid. 110.

stressed the SPD's commitment to religious tolerance. He claimed that there was much common ethical ground between Christianity and socialism, and that leading men in the Churches were beginning to show more understanding of what it was that socialists were striving for. The last assertion was almost certainly wishful thinking, but it clearly signalled a change of spirit from the anti-clerical attitudes of the past.

It was perhaps fortunate for Eichler that Schumacher was no longer looming over SPD policy discussions, the heroic but obstreperous leader having died in August 1952. His influence was certainly felt in the discussion, however, because he had written the preamble to the programme shortly before his death. The class-war tone of that section was markedly more strident than the tenor of the rest.[10] The 'action programme' hardly represented a dramatic change in the party's ideological position. Nevertheless, there were indications that the old certainties were beginning to crumble.

Voices were heard at the congress urging the SPD to tailor its economic policy to what could realistically be paid for rather than what was just socially desirable. The fear of inflation was a powerful factor in German politics. Furthermore, the changing economic climate was making planning less popular, even among SPD supporters. Karl Schiller told the conference that things had changed since the Weimar Republic, and Social Democrats had to be able to deal with a very complex economic system. This implied a more 'elastic' policy; one which favoured free trade, a stable currency, and genuine competition: 'Nobody has a greater interest in free competition between business firms', he declared, 'than the German worker in his capacity as a consumer.'[11]

The Social Democrats should demonstrate that they had not stood still economically, in contrast to their opponents, who were bogged down in the *laissez-faire* attitudes of the nineteenth century. An informed listener would have found it difficult to distinguish between much of Schiller's discourse and the views of those who supported the social market economy. Schiller himself was critical of the economic sections of the 'action programme'. He wrote indignantly to Ollenhauer, Schumacher's successor, that they were vague and amateurish.[12]

Even so, the programme's statements on the economy had included approving references to 'true competition based on achievement' (*echter Leistungswettbewerb*), which was presented as a proper principle upon

[10] Klotzbach, *Der Weg zur Staatspartei*, 262.
[11] *SPD Verhandlungsprotokoll 1952*, 150–1.
[12] Klotzbach, *Der Weg zur Staatspartei*, 261.

which those parts of economic life suited to it should be based.[13] Another young, university-trained politician from Hamburg, Helmut Schmidt, argued that there was not enough clarity in the programme about how all the social policies were going to be funded without inflationary deficit-financing. He urged reform of inheritance tax and a national budget. He was not the only delegate to press the benefits of competition and a stable currency. It was evident that a desire to maximize production and to raise the general standard of living was beginning to rival the traditional socialist goal of meeting proven needs (*Bedarfsdeckung*).[14]

Schiller was keen to develop this train of thought so that the advantages of competition and consumer choice would not simply flow towards the Christian Democrats. He saw that social democracy had to accept the market mechanism, however powerfully that might be complemented by state initiatives to stimulate employment or encourage economic growth.

Schiller himself was the most effective and persistent protagonist of the reform of the SPD's economic programme in the early 1950s. He did not, of course, present the reformist position as an acceptance of neo-liberalism. On the contrary, he was one of Erhard's more dangerous critics, since he argued from a position of common sense and realism, rather than a dogmatic commitment to a frighteningly radical ideology.

During the Korean crisis, as we have seen above, he was quick to point out the inconsistency between Erhard's claims to protect economic freedom and the government's decision to allow the industrial pressure-groups to allocate raw materials. On the other hand, he argued that concepts such as perfect competition and the rigorous exclusion of state influences from the economy were ideologically blinkered forms of utopian liberalism which would simply lead to economic distortions and social injustice.

In truth, Schiller was more a Keynesian than a Marxist. He favoured modest deficit-spending and demand-stimulation to generate employment and create a modest redistribution of wealth. This might have been a popular position in the early 1950s, but it lost its appeal halfway through the decade, as West Germany achieved full employment and began to outstrip her neighbours economically. Keynesian economic theories were more difficult to explain to the party faithful than the old certainties of the class war—or than the simple laws of supply

---

[13] *Handbuch sozialdemokratischer Politik* (Bonn, 1953), 255.
[14] *SPD Verhandlungsprotokoll 1952*, 140–2 and 167.

and demand propagated by Erhard's supporters. Nevertheless, Schiller did do his best to cajole his party towards a more sensible appreciation of economic realities.

In his Munich lecture of September 1951 mentioned above, he was at pains to pooh-pooh neo-liberalism as both dogmatic and irrelevant. He pointed out that Rüstow himself had admitted to disappointment over the fact that only those parts of the social market economy had been implemented which re-established the old-fashioned capitalist system, whereas the rest of the programme had been obstructed by vested interests. In fact, claimed Schiller, the abandonment of controls had just reinstated the *laissez-faire* conditions of the nineteenth century. He specifically rejected Hayek's assertion that all state interference would be bound in the end to lead to the command economy—the 'road to serfdom', as it was dramatically described. By rather unfairly associating Hayek's more *laissez-faire* brand of liberalism with the theory of the social market economy, Schiller was able to draw a comforting contrast between it and his own common-sense approach.

'We need a bit more pragmatism,' he claimed,[15] and this meant, not 'muddling through', but being prepared to use a variety of economic tools, including state regulation where it seemed appropriate. Although this lecture was presented as a critique of liberal economic theory, it also illustrated the extent to which there existed a middle ground common to both sides. In particular, the acceptance of the market mechanism as lying at the core of any future economic policy put Schiller very close to some of his neo-liberal opponents.

He broadcast a similar message when he addressed a conference of Christians and socialists held at Königswinter from 3 to 5 January 1952. Once again, his attitude to the social market economy was critical but somewhat ambivalent. On the one hand he argued that 'freedom-loving' socialism, which was only partly influenced by Marx, was much closer to Christianity in its readiness to shoulder moral commitments than was neo-liberalism.[16] There was some truth in this, since Roman Catholic theorists in particular found free-market economics ethically repugnant.[17] Even so, a willingness to stress the common values in Christianity and social democracy was in itself symptomatic of a certain flexibility of mind in the SPD on the early 1950s.

Other parts of Schiller's discourse were even more revealing. He

[15] Schiller, *Scheinprobleme und Existenzfragen*, 4.
[16] Id., *Thesen zur praktischen Gestaltung unserer Wirtschaftspolitik aus sozialistischer Sicht. Vortrag gehalten auf einer Tagung von Christen und Sozialisten in Königswinter vom 3. bis 5. Januar 1952* (Hamburg, n.d.), 20.
[17] See above, Ch. 11.

attacked liberal economic theorists because their solution demanded perfect competition in a perfect market, which required that all participants should be equally well informed and behave in an entirely rational way. This was just as extreme a position as that which supported centralized planning. Neither solution was compatible with social democracy: 'The freedom-loving socialist solution presents us instead with the attempt to prevent either of the other methods, the market economy and the centrally planned economy, from going to extremes; it tries to find the "solution of the Third Way".'[18]

The 'third way' had, of course, also been an objective of neo-liberal thinkers, even though they sought a rather different compromise between the two unpalatable extremes. Schiller went on to urge a synthesis between competition and planning so that each would complement the other 'like the right and the left shoe'.[19] Purists on both sides denied that such a possibility existed, but here he shrewdly cited Eucken's claim that a combination of planning and market economics would be like two orchestras playing against each other in the same room. Such arguments, he claimed, ignored the realities of the situation in which, at least since the First World War, numerous examples of combined systems had manifested themselves. It was essential to give competition as much opportunity as possible. Competition should be legally protected so that innovation and enterprise would benefit society as a whole. On the other hand, state intervention was needed where the market was unbalanced. Above all, there should be a national budget for the economy, allowing the state to encourage development in areas which were economically or socially desirable. This would require various kinds of steering mechanism, but the maximum possible freedom should be retained within the system. Therefore Social Democratic economic policy was fundamentally concerned with the minimum possible interference—what Schiller called 'minimal planning'.

He suggested a number of titles for this 'third way', including 'regulated market economy', 'socialist market economy', 'planned market economy', and even 'market economy of the left' (*Markwirtschaft von links*). Schiller ended the lecture by stressing the complete distinction between 'freedom-loving socialism' and totalitarian and Soviet doctrines, because the former recognized and defended consumer choice and rejected the centralized command economy.[20] He also stressed, and his message was well suited to his audience, that social democracy was no longer mainly interested in attacking property, and that in any

---

[18] Schiller, *Thesen zur praktischen Gestaltung*, 7–8.
[19] Ibid. 8.   [20] Ibid. 19.

case 'socialism only means state ownership in exceptional cases'.[21] On the other hand, neo-liberalism and freedom-loving socialism were fundamentally different, because the latter accepted that the state might interfere in the economic process itself, whereas the neo-liberals allowed for state activity only to protect the framework within which the market could operate.

In many ways Schiller's address to the conference illustrated very well the objectives of the reformist wing of the SPD. There was an emphasis on ethical values, a downgrading of Marxist atheism and class-war doctrines, and the acceptance of a market mechanism, albeit in a more restricted form than was the case among liberal economists. Hence it could attract consumer interests in Germany, whilst the retention of state intervention where necessary might have an appeal for those numerous people who had found themselves amongst the also-rans in the race for prosperity after 1948. The fact that such ideas were being seriously discussed in the SPD in the early 1950s was undoubtedly due to the challenge of Erhard's social market, and the redrawing of the economics agenda by neo-liberals like Eucken, Böhm, and Röpke. The capitalist free market was no longer a bogey, or a dinosaur destined for the scrap-heap of history, but a living organism which seemed to be growing stronger every year.

Nevertheless, Schiller's views were far from being accepted among his comrades. The full-time party officials were particularly reluctant to rock the boat by starting a new 'revisionist' controversy like the one which had split the SPD in 1905. In any case, the issue upon which the party somewhat unwisely but not surprisingly chose to fight in the 1950s was not economic, but foreign policy. The SPD saw itself as the true representative of the German nation, and attacked Adenauer over his indifference to reunification, his willingness to abandon the Saar, his decision to rearm Western Germany and commit her to NATO, and the acceptance of the supranational, capitalistic EEC. Since the economy was growing fast, the government did not seem so vulnerable on that front.

Even within the economic sphere old ideas died hard. Men like Agartz and Nölting still exercised much influence, and Veit, the chairman of the economic subcommittee of the party executive, hardly radiated enthusiasm for the free market. Socialization was certainly not a dead issue. 1953 saw the production of draft Social Democratic legislation for the public ownership of heavy industry, and this question continued to take up a lot of committees' time until the end of the

---

[21] Ibid. 16.

1950s. It was not until after Godesberg in 1959 that this tired old war-horse was put out to grass.[22]

Even if the old guard still held sway at the higher levels of the SPD, the successes of German economic policy in creating 'real' jobs and overcoming scarcity pushed even hard-line socialists into stressing those aspects of their policy which most clearly differentiated them from the Communists in the Eastern zone. Much greater emphasis was now put on macro-economic planning through a national budget, socially equitable taxation policies, and the establishment of co-determination in industry.[23] In this respect the objectives of the SPD began to converge with those of the more socially concerned adherents of the social market economy.

Three particular areas of convergence can usefully be isolated here. The first was the issue of co-determination (*Mitbestimmung*) mentioned above. The German trade-union movement was strongly committed to this idea, which promised them influence over decision-making in major plants in heavy industry. As we have seen, the neo-liberals were reluctant to limit the responsibility of the entrepreneur for his own business, but they conceded that employees should have a say in the way their work-place was organized in large-scale concerns (*soziales Mitgestaltungsrecht*), and they did admit that the quality of life for industrial workers was a serious problem which would not be solved by a *laissez-faire* attitude.[24] From the Social Democratic viewpoint, the struggles for industrial co-determination also had important ideological implications. If co-determination worked, it would mean that capitalist enterprises could be made more 'democratic'. There might therefore be an unspoken assumption that they would not have to be 'socialized'. Such a possibility did indeed cause some labour leaders to warn against the whole concept of industrial democracy.[25]

Trade-union movements are bound to have an ambivalent attitude towards the capitalist system, since if it were abolished, they would cease to exist. In a totally planned, centrally directed, economy, trade unions would either become redundant or be transformed into labour-mobilization agencies subservient to the state, a degradation which had already been implemented in Stalin's Russia. In West Germany

[22] In a television interview on 2 June 1965, Schiller was still having to deny wanting to nationalize the coal-mines. When asked whether, in a crisis, the 'old nag' (of socialization) would not be led out of the stable, he answered 'I think the nag is dead.' 'Gespräch zur Wirtschaftspolitik', in *Sopade Redner Dienst* (Bonn, n.d.), 3–5.

[23] See the SPD programme set out in *Jahrbuch der Sozialdemokratischen Partei Deutschlands 1952/53* (n.p., n.d.), 270.

[24] See above, Ch. 6.

[25] See above, Ch. 12.

Adenauer himself shrewdly appealed to union leaders by pointing out that co-determination was a better way of meeting the needs of their members than socialization, but it would render large state enterprises both unnecessary and inappropriate.[26] Co-determination would increase the trade unions' influence without undermining their independence.

Politically too, the struggle over co-determination weakened the more rigidly isolationist attitudes in the Social Democratic camp. At a time when the party was out of office in Bonn it could nevertheless join forces with the labour-orientated wing of the CDU in opposition to the industrialists' pressure groups which were resisting *Mitbestimmung*. By comparison with the total repression of trade unions practised under Hitler, the attitude of Adenauer's government seemed positively benevolent. A real stake in a 'mixed economy' would be worth more than a distant promise of socialist utopia. The trade-union movement had established itself on a federal basis in October 1949 with the foundation of the *Deutscher Gewerkschaftsbund* (DGB), and had agitated strongly for *Mitbestimmung* in the years which followed. In 1950/1 it was successful in persuading Adenauer's government to confirm the co-determination arrangements in the mining industry—in plants employing more than one thousand workers. Such arrangements had already been approved by the occupying powers but were very unpopular with employers. The trade unions pressed for the extension of these rights to other firms but were unsuccessful.[27] Nevertheless, the law passed in July 1952 consolidating works councils in most industrial enterprises (*Betriebsverfassungsgesetz*) did give workers consultative rights, even if it did not satisfy union demands. The parliamentary conflicts over this law—on which Christian and Social Democrats had sometimes had to stand fast against liberal (FDP) opposition—demonstrated that sympathy for the workers' rights was by no means confined to the ranks of the Social Democrats.[28]

Related to the issue of co-determination was that of worker participation in profits and the extension of share-ownership amongst a broader spectrum of the population than had traditionally been the case. This aspect of the social market began to be discussed intensively from 1953 onwards, and exercised Social Democrats a good deal, since

[26] P. Weymar, *Konrad Adenauer*, 397–8. See also Adenauer's speech to the Bundestag on co-determination, 14 Feb. 1951, in *Konrad Adenauer, Rede 1917–1967. Eine Auswahl*, ed. H.-P. Schwarz (Stuttgart, 1975), 220–4.
[27] H. K. Rupp, *Politische Geschichte der Bundesrepublik Deutschland: Entstehung und Entwicklung. Eine Einführung* (Stuttgart, 1978), 88.
[28] Ibid. 88.

on the one hand, they appreciated that it might appeal to their supporters, and on the other, they rejected it as an irrelevant alternative to serious policies of social reform.[29] Co-determination and co-ownership, however, were areas where the hard-line socializers were on weak ground, and where reformers might hope to make progress, using the CDU's social market economy as a useful pace-setter.

Secondly, there was the relationship of the SPD to the Christian Churches. The neo-liberals had a strong interest in Christian ethics and moral values in society. Schumacher's anti-clericalism had alienated many potential supporters in Germany. He, for his part, had accused the Roman Catholic Church, in particular, of bias in favour of the CDU. Changes were taking place, however, both within the Churches and the labour movement, which tended to blur the old animosities. Those in the SPD who wanted to stress the humane, warm, freedom-loving aspect of socialism saw good reason to work for a reconciliation with the Christian religion, and it is therefore no coincidence that it was in the apparently peripheral sphere of 'cultural policy' that the reformers did begin to make some headway.

As usual Willi Eichler and the 'Nelsonian' group were in the vanguard of this tendency. Just as the neo-liberals had found it necessary to rethink their attitude towards the social teaching of the Christian— and especially the Roman Catholic—Churches, so the social democratic reformers sought a community of interest with socially committed Christians.

One puff of wind which helped to incline the sails of the SPD in the direction of reform was felt at the refounding congress of the Socialist International, held at Frankfurt from 30 June to 3 July 1951. It issued a statement of fundamental principles, in the drafting of which Willi Eichler had participated. Under the title 'Objectives and Tasks of Democratic Socialism', this statement stressed the differences between Social Democracy and Communism, and stressed the International's commitment to freedom. It also presented socialism as an international movement stemming from a wide variety of intellectual, religious, and humanitarian antecedents.[30] In March 1953 the International organized a special conference on the relationship between socialism and religion. Held in the Dutch town of Bentveld, it was attended by delegations from eleven countries. It was perhaps not too surprising when the conference came to the conclusion that the principles underlying Christianity and socialism were entirely compatible, and that Christian

[29] See above, Ch. 12.
[30] Klotzbach, *Der Weg zur Staatspartei*, 259.

teachings were one of the ethical and spiritual sources of socialist thought.[31]

Thirdly, and perhaps most important from the view of the impact of neo-liberal thought on the policies of the SPD, there was the question of cartels and monopolies. Opinion on this was divided within the party.

As we have seen, reformist socialists, such as Heimann, had been opposed to cartels from the 1920s. Competition was regarded as healthy so long as it took place within the framework of a planned economy. On the other hand, many of the more orthodox SPD functionaries regarded economic concentration and price-fixing as good in themselves, since they were paving the way for socialist control. It is evident that some trade-union representatives and Social Democratic administrators shared the view of industrialists that cartels were essential to give Germany a trading advantage *vis-à-vis* her competitors and that, if matters were allowed to relapse into the 'chaos' of a competitive market, German workers as well as German entrepreneurs would suffer. In some ways the argument within the SPD in the early 1950s mirrored that which was raging among government supporters. Willy-nilly, the reformers were pushed into a position similar to that of Erhard, and their reasoning echoed that of neo-liberals like Böhm or Rüstow, even though they were loath to admit it.

This matter came to the fore in 1952, when the government's draft anti-cartel law was under discussion in the economics subcommittee of the SPD executive. In April Veit chaired a meeting of the committee at which Schiller and Weisser pressed for a complete ban on cartels along the lines envisaged by Franz Böhm. This view was hotly contested. Objections to the draft law, which was to be considered by the Bundesrat on 24 April 1952, were that it would introduce a 'foreign body' into a future socialist system and that cartel restrictions would be mere shadow-boxing (*Spiegelfechterei*), which could not alter the facts of capitalist economics. The most important cartels could not be dealt with anyway, and the whole idea of perfect competition was neither feasible nor a priori to be desired.[32] Hence the critics wobbled between damning the anti-cartel law as too weak to curb the powers of big business and expressing a sneaking preference for cartels as a way of taming the market.

The latter view came to the surface in a memorandum from the

---

[31] Ibid. 260.
[32] Wipoausschuß beim Vorstand der SPD (Wipo) Sitzungsprotokoll, 4 Apr. 1952, FES PV Bestand Wipo, L4 01602.

union of white-collar workers, the *Deutsche Angestellten-Gewerkschaft* (DAG). First, the union expressed distaste for the neo-liberal tone which pervaded the draft law. 'Ideology and economic dogmas', it commented unctiously, 'must be kept out of discussions of the cartel question.' It went on to express regret that once again the false alternative of the free market versus state direction was being presented—there was no such thing as a pure economic system and what was required was an optimal combination of market forces and planning.[33] After this relatively uncontroversial preamble, the memorandum went on to comment that cartels need not be damaging to consumers if they kept costs and prices down (!) and employment conditions could also make cartel arrangements 'thoroughly desirable'. The union recommended that a fundamental prohibition of cartels 'would be not only pointless but actually harmful'.[34]

Despite such preferences for cosy protectionism, the SPD's economics committee, encouraged by two of its most eloquent members, Weisser and Schiller, had in April 1952 issued a circular to *Land* Social Democratic parties urging them to vote for the principle of making cartels illegal (with one or two exceptions, like public transport). Delegations to the Bundesrat had followed this instruction, despite rumblings in various parts of the party. Meanwhile, Fritz Berg, the head of the West German industrialists' association, the BDI, launched a fierce attack on Erhard's proposals as impracticable and economically damaging. This was the 'Sermon on the Mount' (*Bergpredikt*), which signalled open and bitter resistance to the anti-cartel law from West German capitalists.[35]

In the SPD's economics subcommittee the reformers had their work cut out to keep the party in line behind the principle of prohibiting cartels. On 20 November 1952 Weisser and Gert von Eynern, an economist from Berlin, found themselves fighting hard to prevent the sceptics from watering down SPD policy. One speaker commented darkly that they should not regard the Allies as their partners, and that occupation policies of deconcentration had actually been aimed at dismantling the German economy. Whilst the German chemical industry was being unravelled, for example, the Americans built up giants like Dupont. The aim should be to get out from under Allied control and create a German economic policy, a nationalist sentiment which echoed the bellowings of the industrialists' association.[36]

---

[33] *Das deutsche Kartellgesetz* (Hamburg, May 1952), ibid.
[34] Ibid., p. 15.
[35] For details of Erhard's conflict with the BDI, see Ch. 15.
[36] Protocol of Wipo meeting, 20 Nov. 1952, pp. 5–6. FES PV Bestand Wipo, L4 01602.

Gisbert Rittig went further and claimed that 'support for legislation to prohibit cartels means committing ourselves to the views of Erhard and Böhm'. He wanted no part of that. It was best to stay out of the whole argument. Schiller's view, put at an earlier meeting, that there was a difference between monopoly capitalism and competitive capitalism (*Konkurrenzkapitalismus*) was 'charming but false'.[37] It would be foolish to line up with Erhard and Böhm at a time when the Berg pronouncement showed that Erhard was caught between two fires.

Weisser's answer to this was interesting as a statement of the reformist position which saw itself as an alternative to neo-liberalism rather than as simply accepting parts of the neo-liberal doctrine. He firmly denied that the anti-cartel policy was taken over from Böhm or Erhard. Pointing to the decisive change which had taken place in Social Democratic theory under the influence of such people as Heymann (*sic*) he stressed that they could not allow themselves to admire or approve of monopoly capitalism. The Social Democratic change of heart in that respect had taken place long before the appearance of neo-liberalism.[38]

Probably it was less the conviction of reformist arguments than the embarrassment of changing tack which held the SPD on course. The chairman, Veit, had never seemed entirely clear about the important difference between imposing a legal ban (*Verbot*) on cartels and putting them under controls to prevent 'abuse' (*Mißbrauch*). But he pointed out that they could not allow Erhard to say 'I was on the point of doing away with these nasty monopolies but the SPD opposed me.'[39] They should work for the postponement of the whole thing, but supply the party with economic arguments.

The discussion was certainly half-hearted enough to arouse Schiller's concern when he read about it. In a sharp letter to the secretary of the committee, Pass, he pointed out that they had agreed on prohibition in April and that some *Länder*, like his own (Hamburg), had already committed themselves to this in the Bundesrat. The action programme of the SPD had expressly demanded that the German economy should be reconstructed as a mixture of economic planning and competition between individual enterprises. But effective planning which confined itself to essentials ought not to be faced with an economic system tangled up with monopolies and oligopolies. Planning and competition could be combined according to the intentions of the programme. If planning was combined with economic monopoly, the result would be

[37] Ibid., p. 6.
[38] Ibid., p. 7. The misspelling is in the record. Weisser was well aware of Heimann's name.
[39] Ibid., pp. 9–10.

victory for monopoly capitalism.[40] Berg's 'sermon' had let the cat out of the bag and shown how right the SPD had been to back the ban on cartels. Everyone knew that a law against the abuse of cartels could easily be reduced to a dead letter. It meant nothing more than white-wash. As for the claim that support for the principle of prohibition would turn the SPD into followers of neo-liberalism, Schiller argued that, from a socialist standpoint, monopoly capitalism should be re-jected much more decisively than competitive capitalism. Nothing in such a general ban need affect state or communal enterprises.

Schiller actually felt that the problems the Erhard proposals were facing from Berg and his supporters in the CDU would work to the SPD's advantage. It would demonstrate the hollowness of the social market economy if its supporters could not defend their central prin-ciple—state protection for competition—on the first occasion they tried to put it into practice. The SPD would then stand out as the real friends of the consumer, just as it was the champion of the workers and the masses in general.

In another memorandum, of 2 December 1952, Schiller asserted that:

One is not more liberal than the Liberals, but more social, because at the decisive moment the Liberals do not have the courage of their convictions or do not act, because they do not have the *will* to act. It is, however, astonishing to see how precisely those circles which keep on praising the blessings of the 'free economy' are now suddenly talking and writing about 'unbridled, destructive competition', and thereby jettisoning their own fundamental principles.[41]

For the socialists, he claimed, true competition operating in the proper sphere was 'social'.

Despite Schiller's eloquence, and the respect his views clearly com-manded in the economics subcommittee, the SPD did not retain its firm resolve over the prohibition issue. On the whole, the political functionaries and the 'men of business' in the SPD, like Heinrich Deist, were less impressed by the possibility of appealing to the electorate as the true disciples of open competition, than they were by the distaste felt for 'American' free-market ideas among trade unionists and others in their own camp. Like the employers' organizations representing heavy industry, Social Democratic leaders were suspicious of American intentions, and tended to confuse anti-cartel laws with what they saw

---

[40] Copy of a letter from Schiller to Pass, secretary of the committee, 18 Nov. 1952. FES PV Bestand, L4 01602.

[41] Schiller, 'Stellungnahme zu den Fragen zum Gesetzentwurf gegen Wettberwerbs-beschränkungen'. 2 Dec. 1952, ibid.

as punitive Allied measures of deconcentration, or even dismantling.[42]

Erhard's draft law was killed by the Bundestag elections of September 1953, which meant that it had to be reintroduced from scratch in the new parliament. In December of that year Heinrich Deist was telling the subcommittee that the SPD should not get tied up in the legislation relating to a prohibition or state approval of cartels, but should use the issue to open up a general discussion, presumably of competition and socialism.[43]

Meanwhile the SPD parliamentary delegation in the Bundestag had been reconsidering the whole bill, which was making slow progress in any case, owing to conflicting views within the government parties. When Schoene reported on this to the economics subcommittee in May 1954, he described a cartel as 'a concept of capitalist economic theory', and commented rather ominously that in other forms of economic system different terminology would have to be found to describe the same or similar institutions.[44] That hardly suggested unswerving determination to resist cartels, and indeed the SPD's main concern seems to have been to protect public utilities and communal enterprises against interference by anti-cartel arrangements. Schoene urged the SPD to work for a general provision whereby cartels could be approved or disapproved by the Federal Economics Minister, and this suggestion was indeed incorporated in recommendations to the party executive on 10 May 1954.[45] This was, of course, precisely the sort of 'whitewash' suggestion against which Schiller had been inveighing more than a year earlier.

In the end, as we shall see, the anti-cartel legislation did go through, with the prohibition principle being accepted—i.e. that cartel arrangements were deemed fundamentally unlawful, even if there were numerous exceptions to the rule. Although the SPD did not go as far as Schiller would have liked, in that it did not take to the barricades against cartel arrangements, his campaign in favour of prohibition undoubtedly influenced the party's stance and may have affected the outcome of the legislative process. It can hardly have been a coincidence that when, in June 1954, the Bundesrat voted on the crucial issue of prohibition versus prevention of abuse, the scales were tipped in

---

[42] For an admirable survey of the German entrepreneurial resistance to decartelization, see Berghahn, *The Americanisation of West German Industry*, ch. 2.

[43] Protocol of the Wipo meeting on 4 and 5 Dec. 1953, p. 7, FES, PV Bestand Wipo, L5 01603.

[44] Protocol of the Wipo meeting on 7 and 8 May 1954, p. 3. FES PV Bestand Wipo, L6 01604. At this meeting Veit still referred to the issue of prohibition versus hindrance of abuse as the *Gretchenfrage*.

[45] Annex to Wipo meeting, 7/8 May 1954, ibid.

favour of prohibition by the delegation for the SPD-dominated *Land* of Hamburg, where Schiller was a senator.[46] The tendency, which was becoming more marked as the 1950s progressed, to stress compatibility between social democracy and competition in the economy hindered what might otherwise have been an embarrassing solidarity between trade unions and reactionary industrialists ranged against Erhard's proposals. It remained to be seen whether this tendency could lead to more substantial reforms in Social Democratic economic policy.

Amongst trade-union leaders and SPD ministers in *Länder* like Hamburg and West Berlin, Schiller's pragmatism was finding a sympathetic response. He followed up the minor gains which had been made at the Dortmund party congress by a more outspoken address to a Social Democratic conference on economic policy held at Bochum on 28 February 1953. A great deal of his discourse was an attack on Erhard's neo-liberal policies, with their dogmatic refusal to accept any combination of market economy and economic planning. In the speech he put a gloss on the SPD's Dortmund 'action programme', stressing the pragmatic and flexible nature of its economic policy. Having castigated the neo-liberals for their rigid refusal to consider a mixture of state intervention and market forces—detecting therein a tendency to take things to extremes which should be discarded in a democracy, he went on to claim that the SPD's 'action programme' presented a harmonious mixture of planning and competition.

Produced as the result of lengthy deliberations, this programme included a commitment to the 'economic liberation of the personality', rejected the command economy (*Zwangswirtschaft*), and 'approved of free consumer choice'.[47] Naturally enough, Schiller cited that passage in the programme which supported 'genuine competition in those branches of the economy which were suited for it'. All this he summed up in the neat but striking formula: 'As much competition as possible, as much planning as necessary' (*Wettbewerb soviel wie möglich, Planung soviel wie nötig*).

This slogan was to be hammered home by Schiller in economic arguments over the next six years. By December 1953 he was absent-mindedly telling colleagues in the SPD that it had been part of the 'action programme' itself, and in 1954 it was indeed placed at the head of the economics section of the policy statement approved by the party at its Berlin congress. As Schiller put it in an early draft of the speech,

---

[46] Berghahn, *The Americanisation of West German Industry*, 178.
[47] Karl Schiller, 'Produktivitätssteigerung und Vollbeschäftigung durch Planung und Wettbewerb', in SPD Vorstand (ed.), *Die Wirtschaftspolitik der Sozialdemokratie* (Bonn, n.d.), 38–9.

the aim was to have 'the best of both worlds'; whereas the neo-liberals, with their refusal to accept anything but the unattainable goal of perfect competition, would lose the benefits of state intervention to increase production and allocate resources to areas of need.[48]

It is perhaps worth noting at this point that up to 1948, when market economists were still on the defensive, they had themselves firmly denied that there was a simple choice between market economics on the one hand and state intervention on the other. By the time Schiller was getting into his stride in the 1950s, however, the boot was on the other foot. It was planning which had become discredited and market economics which held the upper hand. Now the Social Democrats had to fight for the notion that planning could be part of an effectively functioning market economy.

To this end Schiller and his supporters skilfully exploited the Bochum meeting to give the impression in subsequent years that it marked a great watershed in SPD thinking about the economy. The party had at last accepted the market economy and competition as the fundamental principles upon which Social Democratic economic policy should be based. In actual fact Schiller's speech sounded at the time more like a pragmatic critique of neo-liberalism than a revolutionary change in economic policy. His contribution to the discussion had been preceded by an address from Veit in which the usual fulminations against liberal economics and its bogus concept of freedom had been aired.[49]

Nevertheless, Schiller was highly adept at using the success of his speech, and in particular the skilful slogan 'As much competition as possible, as much planning as necessary', as a wedge to open up the debate on economic policy in the SPD, and force the planners on to the defensive. In this he was supported by his Hamburg SPD colleague Helmut Schmidt. A study of Schiller's own thinking, as it was revealed in his speeches and writings during the 1950s and early 1960s, makes it seem likely that he was in fact loyal to the fundamentally liberal economic views he had developed in the 1930s, when, as a student, he had heard Rüstow calling for a strong state to regulate the market and protect it from greedy special interests.[50]

Schiller appreciated that the cruder models of market economics did not satisfy the needs of complex modern societies. For example, he pointed out that the idea of 'consumer sovereignty' was highly dubious, partly because consumers were actually often at the mercy of

[48] Draft notes enclosed with letter from Schiller to Pass, 31 Jan. 1953, FES PV Bestand Wipo, L29 01618.
[49] *Die Wirtschaftspolitik der Sozialdemokratie*, esp. 19–21.
[50] See above, Ch. 2.

pressures generated by producers and their advertising agents, but mainly because the unequal distribution of wealth made it absurd to speak of truly free consumer choice. It will be noted that neither of these objections really militates against the principles of the social market economy. Indeed, Schiller seems to have regarded the chief aim of state activity to be to create a framework within which genuine competition could operate—a view compatible with the teachings of Eucken and Röpke. He once told a gathering of consumers' associations that his slogan 'As much competition as possible, as much planning as necessary' could just as well be 'As much competition as possible, as much market regulation as necessary', the idea being that market regulation should be necessary only where proper competition could not function.[51]

Schiller had the same attitude towards the discipline of economics as Eucken, in that he believed there were general principles governing economic activity which it was the duty of the economist to elucidate. In that sense he was not sympathetic to the old 'historicist' school of nationalist German economists. Nevertheless, he accepted that modern industrial society was far too complex for the simple model of perfectly balanced markets, achieved through free competition, to operate. Most markets were imperfect. What was needed was a synthesis of the Freiburg School's commitment to state protection for competition on the one hand, and the 'Keynsian prophecy' of full employment through government spending on the other. He was insistent that this should be a genuine synthesis leading to an economic policy shaped as a coherent whole (*aus einem Guß*) and not just an unprincipled eclecticism. He believed that

out of the conglomeration of contradictions and inconsistencies which have been handed down to us from the interventionist epoch we must achieve a new harmony of ordered economic systems [*Interdependenz der Ordnungen*]! The keynote of this new order cannot be that of an extreme solution, but must therefore be a synthesis.[52]

Schiller therefore believed that what was needed was a micro-economic policy which used state-protected competition to create a harmonious and self-regulated market, combined with a macro-economic system which used indirect methods of control to achieve maximum growth and stability. In the micro-economic sphere this could be described as

---

[51] K. Schiller, 'Verbraucher und Wettbewerb', in *Der Ökonom und die Gesellschaft: Das freiheitliche und das soziale Element in der modernen Wirtschaftspolitik. Vorträge und Aufsätze* (Stuttgart, 1964), 142. This was originally a lecture given to German consumer associations in Cologne, 28 Apr. 1954.

[52] Id., 'Die Extrememodelle der vollkommenen Marktwirtschaften', ibid. 54.

'minimal planning' to overcome the market distortions which would occur if overmighty subjects were not restrained by a powerful state. Monopolies might thus be run by public enterprises which could be induced to behave as if they were subject to the pressures of competition, and cartel arrangements would simply be unlawful.[53] On the macro-economic level, trade policies, tax rates, interest rates, and levels of public expenditure could be adjusted to steer the economy towards full employment and steady expansion, whilst avoiding slumps or periods of inflation. This was to be Schiller's own contribution to German economic policy—the 'global steering' (*Globalsteuerung*) with which he countered a minor recession in the mid-1960s. It was not to be a policy which recommended itself to social market economists, some of whom saw it as the beginning of a dangerous and woolly-minded retreat from the disciplines of the market.

Nevertheless, it should be stressed that it was very far from the type of planning envisaged in the immediate post-war era by men like Veit and Agartz. In his Bochum speech Schiller had certainly boasted that he would not shrink from necessary planning-measures, even if they did not conform to the market in a neo-liberal sense. State coordination of the economy was not 'taboo' for socialists; it fitted together with measures compatible with the market 'like the left and the right shoe'. He accused neo-liberals of wanting to stand only on one shoe, to the detriment of overall economic efficiency.[54] Yet an examination of his various suggestions for 'planning' reveals that he always preferred indirect pressures on the economic tiller to administrative interference, that he disliked price- or wage-fixing, and that the state interventions he foresaw were usually intended to remedy defects in the market rather than to usurp its functions. His views on agriculture, for example, were remarkably similar to those of Röpke, in that he disliked artificial pricing-arrangements and preferred subsidies to poor farmers if help had to be given.[55]

His general objectives were very similar to those of the neo-liberals, even if he did twit them with dogmatism and lack of flexibility. He strongly approved of equal opportunities created by social-welfare policies and education. This was, after all, entirely consistent with the furtherance of real competition in the economy. As he wrote in the German encyclopaedia of social sciences in 1962:

---

[53] Id., 'Verbraucher und Wettbewerb', ibid. 142–3.
[54] *Die Wirtschaftspolitik der Sozialdemokratie*, 40.
[55] K. Schiller, 'Wirtschaftspolitik', in *Der Ökonom und die Gesellschaft*, 71.

Without the underpinning of welfare-state policies . . . the free-market economic system might well have collapsed under the political and social strains of the world economic crisis and the Second World War. Welfare state and dynamic market economics are mutually indispensable to one another, whether one calls the end result a 'social' or 'socially responsible' market economy or a 'mixed economy'.[56]

Of course, the defenders of the social market economy also disliked the term 'welfare state' because they regarded the versions of it supported by socialists as incompatible with the maintenance of stable prices and sound money. Here again, Schiller's statements on these issues make it clear that his ideas about social policy were nearer to those of Rüstow than they were to the more traditional and class-war orientated members of his own party. Schiller always laid great stress on resisting inflationary pressures,[57] and when referring to pensions or other social expenditure he was careful to insist that they should not weaken the competitive market economy.

Such views were beginning to have an impact on the SPD. For the fact was that, although the going was hard, a combination of enthusiastic lobbying and persistently disappointing election results was pushing the party further along the road towards programmatic reform. In the economic sphere, but also in the sphere of ethical principles and social objectives, the yardstick against which Social Democratic policies were measured had come to be that of the social market economy.

[56] Id., 'Wirtschaftspolitik', in E. von Beckerath (ed.), *Handwörterbuch der Sozialwissenschaften*, xii (Stuttgart, 1962), 210.

[57] In his Bochum speech, for example, he very firmly denied that counter-cyclical policies aimed at overcoming recessions could involve any inflationary tendencies. On the contrary, his concept of an overall national budget would help to iron out those dangerous oscillations between deflationary and inflationary movements which were so damaging to the economy. SPD Vorstand (ed.), *Die Wirtschaftspolitik der Sozialdemokratie*, 44–5.

15

Erhard and the Realization of the Social Market Economy

IN the years between 1953 and 1957 the Federal Republic established itself fully as a sovereign state. It became a member of the NATO alliance, with its own armed forces, the Bundeswehr. It participated in the counsels of the Western nations and became a founder-member of the European Economic Community. Its political system was markedly more stable than that of some European neighbours; the French in particular. In 1957 the Saar was returned to Germany—a symbol of the end of the post-war occupation era.

Most remarkable of all, and the foundation upon which political successes rested, was the economic development of West Germany, which was now referred to by Western journalists with the misleading cliché 'the economic miracle'. Erhard pressed ahead with his support for the most rapid possible re-establishment of multilateral trade. As the crisis created by the Korean War receded and the post-war boom gripped the West, the old batteries of controls appeared more and more redundant. By 1959 a liberalized trading-system was operating in the Western world, with one glaring exception—agriculture. Even the capital and foreign-exchange markets, which had been the most difficult and sensitive areas to set free, had been substantially released from state captivity. From the beginning of May 1959 the D-Mark was fully convertible, and capital could be exported. It is important to remember, of course, that by the time these measures were taken, West Germany had already started its powerful economic expansion and was a net creditor in the EPU. It was therefore likely to be a magnet for investment rather than vice versa. Major German companies showed a readiness to invest long-term in their own futures rather than realize their assets and export them abroad.

Did this mean that Erhard had completed his task? With the triumph of the free-price mechanism and consumer choice, was there nothing more to achieve in the field of political economy? From the point of view of the 1990s, this might seem a plausible argument. *Laissez-faire* has once again become an acceptable—even preferred—answer to economic problems. But for the neo-liberals and social market economists the promised land had only been reached. It had yet to be conquered.

We should at this point reconsider the objectives of the social market economy, and the different strands of thinking which were woven into it. Opposition to direct governmental manipulation of the economic process was common to all its supporters. At the same time, however, it had committed itself to supporting the idea of *Startgleichheit*, or an equal chance for a career open to talent, irrespective of parental wealth; to the maximum possible extension of property ownership; to support for small and medium-sized businesses against mammoth concerns; and to the protection of rural environments against soulless urbanization. There was also to be a social net which would afford a minimum standard of living for those who, through illness or incapacity, were incapable of participating in the competitive market system.

If taken at face value, this was rather a radical programme, and some of its advocates, like Alexander Rüstow, were clearly prepared to interpret it in a radical fashion.

But in the 1950s the climate of opinion was moving decisively to the right. This was partly due to the Cold War and the understandable fear of Communism generated by Stalin's reign of terror in Eastern Europe. It was a tendency reinforced by hostility to the phenomenon of the 'welfare state' as it had appeared in Britain and Scandinavia. It was noticeable that, once the danger of socialization in West Germany had passed, the tone of neo-liberal deliberations became more socially conservative, and opposed to any state measures which might imply redistribution of wealth.

Wilhelm Röpke was an example of this shift to the right; as he became more pessimistically conservative, his position became less and less easy to distinguish from those 'paleo-liberals' about whom Rüstow had complained during the war. He spoke of his 'apprehension, bitterness, anger, and even contempt for the worst features of our age', and claimed that this was not the result of his growing gloom but of the 'progressive deterioration of the crisis in which we live'. He even flirted with the Moral Rearmament movement at Caux, defending this bizarre choice of allies by claiming that, despite their lack of sophistication, their hearts were in the right place when it came to fighting Communism. His writings, too, lost some of their earlier cutting edge, and became exercises in nostalgia for a romanticized small-town Germany of the past, in which peasants and tradespeople knew their place, and did not try to ape their betters in the educated middle class. He was bitterly hostile to British policies such as the National Health Service or the reformed, post-1944 education system.

The notion that university education should be provided free roused him to splenetic fury, and he raged against 'educational Jacobinism'. Yet such measures were surely justifiable if the theory of the social market economy was to have any meaning in real life.[1]

On the other hand, he was an early, and trenchant, critic of development economics, describing with great accuracy the follies to which bureaucratic 'aid' for 'underdeveloped' countries would lead in terms of waste and damage to established social patterns. He was also a warning voice amongst the chorus of approval for European protectionism, as presented in the Schuman Plan and the EEC.[2]

Walter Eucken, too, had been stressing the more conservative aspects of neo-liberalism before his untimely death on a visit to London in 1950. He claimed that the 'social question' had changed from that posed by the problems of the nineteenth century. These had been solved by the market, which had given workers a far greater choice of jobs and therefore a greater freedom. The new social question was that caused by 'enslavement to the state'.[3]

It should not be thought, however, that these developments heralded the demise of the social market, or that its advocates had simply been using the word 'social' to mask their innate desire to restore *laissez-faire* capitalism in its pre-war form. Even if one takes the issue of social welfare, it is clear that the social-market approach differed fundamentally from that which informed the supporters of the welfare state in Britain or Scandinavia. The neo-liberals accepted a certain level of state support for social purposes, but they wanted this to be self-limiting as far as possible. Therefore they thought in terms of remedial help rather than continuous—or, as they might have put it, chronic—aid to less successful areas of the economy or society. An ailing industry should not be propped up by subsidies, but money should be provided to retrain its labour-force in more economic activities. So far as personal welfare was concerned, the theory of the social market demanded that as much should be done by individuals as possible, which meant that pensions and health services should be funded on an insurance basis and should not just be a charge on public expenditure.

---

[1] W. Röpke, *A Humane Economy: The Social Framework of the Free Market* (trans. E. Henderson; London, 1960), p. viii and pp. 160–1. This is a translation of *Jenseits von Angebot und Nachfrage* (Erlenbach-Zurich, 1958).

[2] Some examples of such views: W. Röpke, 'Unentwickelte Länder', *ORDO: Jahrbuch für die Ordnung von Wirtschaft und Gesellschaft*, 5 (1953); 'Wirtschaftssystem und internationale Ordnung', *ORDO*, 4 (1952), and 'Zwischenbilanz der europäischen Wirtschaftsintegration: Kritische Nachlese', *ORDO*, 11 (1959), 69–94.

[3] W. Eucken, *Grundsätze der Wirtschaftspolitik*, ed. E. Eucken and K. P. Husel, (4th edn.; Tübingen, 1952), 193 and 314.

If people were very poor, state help could be provided, but it should take the form of targeted support for individuals or families over such matters as rent supplements, rather than blanket projects which might not discriminate between those who could pay and those who could not. Subsidized municipal housing of the kind very popular in Britain in the post-war period obviously did not fit in with this concept. On the other hand, a combination of state financing and private enterprise to provide low-cost housing to overcome the post-war emergency was a much more acceptable policy from the neo-liberal viewpoint.

Above all, however, there was the concept of state-protected competition. This was an indispensable component of the social-market system, accepted by Eucken, Rüstow, and Erhard alike. In his lectures on economic policy published after the Second World War, Eucken made it clear that his main answer to social problems lay in the support for competition, which would so increase the nation's wealth that it would render other forms of social welfare superfluous.[4] Like Röpke, he associated the rule of law and the commitment to freedom with the concept of 'ordered competition'. This meant state-protected competition in which the rules prevented unscrupulous individuals manipulating the market by abusing their economic strength.

For Erhard too, the main economic function of the state was to keep the ring for the competitive market, and ensure that nobody was shut out of it by price rings, monopolies, or unfair trading-practices. From the early days of his appointment as director of the bizonal Economics Administration, Erhard had ordered the preparation of legislation to prevent cartels from obstructing market forces. At that time, however, the picture was confused by Anglo-American demands for the deconcentration of German industry connected with the post-war occupation programme of denazification and demilitarization. Many in industrial circles thought Erhard's rhetoric against cartels was a form of protection against even more draconian Allied measures, and it is certainly true that, well into the early 1950s, Erhard was constantly complaining about Allied plans to break up the German coal and steel industry, or the chemical giant IG Farben. The Allies, for their part, complained about German obstruction of their deconcentration laws.[5]

Erhard certainly had some grounds for irritation over American attitudes towards German cartels. The Americans had, of course, a

---

[4] Ibid. 314.
[5] Records of meetings of the Economics Committee of the Allied High Commissioners in Germany with Erhard at the Petersberg, 1950–1, esp. the meetings on 19 Oct. 1950, 22 Nov. 1950, PRO/FO/1005/920; 31 May 1951, PRO/FO/1005/921. See also Berghahn, *The Americanisation of West German Industry*, 159.

powerful tradition of antitrust legislation, and they were eager to extend the blessings of rugged competition to Germany. There was also the security aspect of Allied policy towards German industry. The Potsdam declaration of 2 August 1945 had urged that German industry be decentralized as quickly as possible, and that the industrial syndicates and cartels be abolished. Nevertheless, problems were presented by the implementation of this policy. The Americans realized that to impose such measures by fiat would be to undermine their popularity; on the other hand, they did not trust the Germans to stop cartels themselves. It was assumed that the cartel habit was too deeply ingrained in the German businessman's psyche for him to give it up, and this assumption was not without foundation. So the Americans banned cartels by decree in February 1947 and hoped that this would help to condition the Germans 'to learn of the principles and advantages of free enterprise'.[6]

The Germans had no intention of being excluded from discussions about decartelization, since, as we have seen, there were many economists, and not a few businessmen, who regarded the old market-rigging habits of the pre-war era as one of the causes of Germany's economic problems before 1933. On the other hand, there were also many defenders of 'legitimate' cartels, even if their voices were somewhat muted in the menacing atmosphere of Allied occupation. The south Germans had established a decartelization committee, of which Erhard was a member, and in February 1947 it demanded a German law to regulate cartels, but not to ban them altogether. It did, however, pronounce in favour of 'a fundamental set of principles for the German economy based on achievement and the principles of competition'.[7]

In the summer of 1947 the Economic Council in Frankfurt started to take a closer interest in cartel legislation. A draft law was drawn up by a group of experts in Stuttgart chaired by Paul Josten, formerly head of the cartel department at the Reich Economics Ministry. Among the

---

[6] R. Robert, *Konzentrationspolitik in der Bundesrepublik: Das Beispiel der Entstehung des Gesetzes gegen Wettbewerbsbeschränkungen* (Berlin, 1976), 100–3, and P. Hüttenberger, 'Wirtschaftsordnung und Interessenpolitik in der Kartellgesetzgebung der Bundesrepublik, 1949–1957', *Vierteljahrshefte für Zeitgeschichte*, 24/3 (July 1976), 287 ff. See also, Berghahn, *The Americanisation of West German Industry*, 155. It has been argued that the 1947 law was less draconian than some American trust busters would have liked, and that from May 1947 the US decartelization policy stagnated, until it was revived by McCloy in late 1949. Be that as it may, German concern over Allied deconcentration measures remained acute. Cf. J. Gillingham. *Coal, Steel and the Rebirth of Europe, 1945–1955: The Germans and the French from Ruhr Conflict to Economic Community* (Cambridge, 1991), 111–15.

[7] See Robert, *Konzentrationspolitik*, 100. For Böhm's views on this issue, see letter of 15 May 1947 in Böhm NL, KAS I-200-004/6.

experts involved in drafting this proposal was Franz Böhm, but not all those involved were so rigorously liberal in their attitudes. Kromphardt, for instance, was not particularly committed to the freely competitive system. Erhard encouraged the group to refine its draft and on 5 July 1949 the final version was presented to him, his own officials in the Economics Administration having been at work on the same subject. One of them, Eberhard Günther, had been one of Walter Eucken's most brilliant pupils.

The 'Josten' draft included a flat prohibition of cartels. This was in line with the neo-liberal view, expressed most eloquently by Böhm, that the simplest and most effective way of dealing with cartels was to remove their legal status. Since cartel treaties would then be unenforceable at law, the cartel system would disintegrate. This would not require any complicated apparatus to enforce it. Previously, cartel laws had involved policing cartel arrangements to make sure they were not against the public interest, a cumbersome and usually fruitless operation which any skilled lobbyist could evade with ease. The prohibition of cartels was therefore the *sine que non* of serious reform.

However, the Josten draft also included strong measures to break up enterprises which dominated any particular market. The anti-monopolistic aspect of the draft was also in line with neo-liberal views about perfect competition and the need to destroy what were known as *Machtballungen*, or power concentrations, which were held to distort the market. However, such measures might be seen to be playing into the hands of the occupying powers, who were at that time pressing hard to 'deconcentrate' various sectors of German heavy industry, including coal, steel, and chemicals. Erhard himself felt the need to co-operate with the leaders of German business, many of whom were happy with cartels and most of whom disliked deconcentration. Some of his own officials seem to have thought that the Josten draft was too radical and ignored German business traditions. They could point to the fact that the Havanna Charter, adopted at American prompting in March 1948, had pressed for anti-cartel legislation but had not demanded deconcentration.[8] It has also been claimed that Erhard himself was not really bothered about deconcentration, having worked with large-scale industrial organizations before and during the war.[9] Certainly he regarded the elimination of the cartel mentality as more important than concern about oligopolies in some branches of produc-

---

[8] Berghahn, *The Americanisation of West German Industry*, 156–7.
[9] Id., 'Ideas into Politics: The Case of Ludwig Erhard', in R. J. Bullen, H. Pogge von Strandmann, and A. B. Polowsky (eds.), *Ideas into Politics: Aspects of European History, 1880–1950* (London, 1984), 182–5.

tion. So long as the market could work, competition would make itself felt.

The Josten draft was further compromised by the fact that it was mysteriously leaked in a relatively obscure economic publication called the *Wirtschaftskorrespondenz*. This aroused considerable anger in political circles and Erhard deemed it prudent not to press the proposal, using the perfectly reasonable excuse that the Economic Council in Frankfurt could hardly be responsible for controversial legislation when it was about to be replaced by the new Federal parliament shortly to be established in Bonn.[10]

None the less, Erhard remained committed to the notion of protecting competition through a legal framework which would discredit cartels even if it did not entirely eliminate them. In December 1949 an official German delegation was sent to America under the leadership of Franz Böhm to study American antitrust legislation. On their return they produced a sixty-page memorandum explaining the American system.[11] At a time when admiration for American business methods was growing in Germany, information about antitrust laws in the USA was ammunition for the German anti-cartel lobby.

Erhard himself published an article on 16 December 1949 in which he stated that:

interference with the free workings of competition, through planning and controls, is no less deplorable and harmful when it is exercised on the part of the entrepreneurs than when it is exercised by the state . . . all market agreements, and especially those concerned with prices, are in the last analysis directed towards imposing a limitation of some kind on the free operation of competition.[12]

He warned his readers that if entrepreneurs allowed the free market to be compromised, they would lose the ability to defend it against state direction.

On the other hand, Erhard was less concerned to oppose concentrations of economic power. He stressed that the struggle against cartels and oligopolies should not be allowed to weaken the productive capacity of the German economy. He told the Bundestag on 27 May 1950 that it was not his intention to throw the baby out with the bathwater and behave like a bull in a china shop. His metaphors may have been mixed but his meaning was clear.[13] He would not yield more than he

---

[10] Robert, *Konzentrationspolitik*, 106. In a letter to Günther dated 12 Apr. 1952, Böhm claimed that the draft had been deliberately leaked by officials in the ministry to block the anti-cartel law. Böhm NL, KAS I-200-004/I.

[11] Berghahn, *The Americanisation of West German Industry*, 169.

[12] Cited and trans. in Erhard, *The Economics of Success*, 65.

[13] Robert, *Konzentrationspolitik*, 189.

had to over Allied insistence on deconcentration. As we have seen, the Germans, including Erhard, were reluctant to do anything which would make such deconcentration effects easier.

In the case of steel, the Americans and the British were determined to break up the industry into smaller units, and had established twenty-four companies under Allied control. They also wished to eliminate the 'vertical' concentration of coal and steel interests which had been a feature of pre-war German heavy industry. The Allies agreed that the ultimate decision about ownership of the steel companies should be left to the Germans, but were determined that the shape of the industry should be decided by the occupying authorities. Apart from anything else, uncertainty was damaging for the industry. Erhard urged that responsibility for deconcentration should also be passed over to the Federal German authorities. However, when, in January 1950, Adenauer passed this proposal on to the Allies, they reacted with scepticism, regarding it as a means of circumventing Allied deconcentration restrictions.[14] Certainly Erhard's ministry was likely to be more favourably inclined towards the former owners of the steelworks than the Allies had been. This was an interesting example of overlapping and sometimes contradictory pressures at work within the free-market camp. Deconcentration could be regarded as a healthy measure to encourage competition. It might also be regarded as an attempt to weaken German heavy industry in line with post-war Allied policies. In 1950, the latter argument was very plausible.

Erhard went on criticizing Allied measures of deconcentration, and complained particularly bitterly that the Allies were not consulting the Germans about them. For their part, the Americans accused him of obstruction. In 1951 the Allies repeatedly asked Erhard when his own anti-cartel legislation would be ready, to be met with prevarication.[15] The Germans clearly hoped that the longer the whole issue could be put off, the weaker the Allied position would become. Eventually they accepted deconcentration arrangements in major German heavy industries which were much milder than had orginally been envisaged by the Americans.

'Deconcentration' was not, however, just an Allied objective designed to keep Germany weak after the war. It was also an aspect of competition policy within Germany. The small and medium-sized businesses to which Erhard was particularly appealing with his free-market philosophy were ambivalent in their attitudes to cartels. On the

---

[14] I. Warner, 'Allied–German Negotiations on the Deconcentration of the West German Steel Industry', in I. D. Turner (ed.), *Reconstruction in Post-war Germany*, 161.

[15] See reports of the Economics Committee of the Allied High Commissioners, 11 Apr. and 31 May 1951, PRO/FO/1005/921.

one hand, they welcomed freedom from artificially high prices for industrial materials and machinery forced upon them by cartels in heavy industry. On the other, they feared that, without their own defence mechanisms for price maintenance, they would be destroyed by the cutthroat competition of large-scale enterprises prepared to sell at a loss in order to wipe out small-scale rivals. Franz Böhm was concerned to reduce opposition to a ban on cartels from such smaller business-interests by stressing the need for state protection against abuses of power by 'market-dominating' firms. He accepted that rules should be established to ensure that large firms treated their customers equally and did not use their power to cripple competition. Unhealthy power concentrations should be avoided where possible. However, to define these power concentrations in a way which made it possible to combat them effectively by legislative or executive action was to prove very difficult.[16]

. If Erhard had back-pedalled over decartelization and deconcentration in order to save as much as possible of German heavy industry from what was regarded as Allied retribution, there were other reasons why an anti-cartel law, to which he was strongly committed, took a long time to emerge in the 1950s. There was a constant struggle within the ranks of the ministerial experts and within industry over the vexed question of 'prohibition' or 'supervision'. The true neo-liberals, like Böhm or Rüstow, remained wedded to the concept of an absolute legal prohibition on cartels; the 'men of business', and especially the newly formed BDI, wanted to continue the older principle of supervision, which in practice meant that cartels were legalized. Even within the Economics Ministry, there were divided counsels. State secretary Strauß, who had come back from the Ministry of Justice, favoured an American-type ban on cartels, but Müller-Armack was prepared to be pragmatic, as were departmental heads involved in the cartel issue, such as Günther and Roland Risse. 'Pragmatism' meant acceptance of the 'abuse' principle, which would have undermined the law. The attitude of officials was important, because Erhard did not leave his subordinates very precise instructions, and they were left to divine his real intentions from newspaper articles or lectures.

---

[16] F. Böhm, 'Stellungnahme zu den Änderungsvorschlägen der Arbeitsgemeinschaft selbstständiger Unternehmer zum Gesetzentwurf gegen Wettbewerbsbeschränkungen' (1952), and C. A. Schleussner, 'Ein Unternehmer zum Kartellgesetz', in Böhm NL, KAS I-200-38/2. Also Robert, *Konzentrationspolitik*, 37–50 *et passim*. For interesting details of the arguments between Erhard's ministry and the Allied authorities over steel deconcentration, see Warner, 'Allied–German Negotiations', 161–9. Also Robert, *Konzentrationspolitik*, 151–64; Berghahn, *The Americanisation of West German Industry*, 109–10.

Erhard undoubtedly supported the liberal theorists, but he had to tread carefully, especially since the CDU needed industrialists' financial help at election time. The West German *Länder*, vital for the fate of legislation because of their position in the Bundesrat, tended to be cool about the prohibition of cartels. In the early 1950s the political parties, too, were unhelpful. The CDU did support the law on the whole, but there were many individual exceptions. The supposedly liberal FDP thought that the government should not be too finicky about cartels, and until 1954 the SPD openly opposed any form of competitive economy. Thereafter the Social Democrats shifted their position, but by that time opposition was hardening from other quarters. In particular, the Bavarian CSU, never enthusiastic about Erhard, was obstructive towards the law, especially after Franz-Josef Strauß joined the government in 1953. Strauß was much happier working with industrial interest-groups than defending market freedom. Nationalistic politicians, like those in the refugees' party (*Bund der Heimatvertriebenen und Entrechteten—BHE*) and the German Party, consistently favoured cartels.

Erhard also had to face opposition from other ministries and from Cabinet colleagues. Whereas the justice and labour ministries were ready to see the law sharpened against monopolies, the ministries of transport, postal services, and finance wanted whole areas of the economy—such as railways, communications, banking, and insurance—excluded from the law altogether. Their opposition to Erhard's proposals slowed down their legislative progress, as did the growing clamour from industrial and business pressure-groups.[17]

This problem became more acute as time passed. Ironically, once the deconcentration question had been solved, and Allied pressure became less important, many German industrialists assumed that the struggle for a return to the good old days had been won and that they could forget about decartelization. Their indignation was all the more intense when they discovered that Erhard was intending to press ahead with the measure, and was denying that it was in any sense an American notion which was being transplanted into German soil.[18] A major struggle followed, in which Erhard found himself ranged against many leading industrialists, not a few economic 'experts', and—perhaps most important of all—the Federal Chancellor.

[17] For shades of opinion within the Economics Ministry and Erhard's administrative methods, see Robert, *Konzentrationspolitik*, 120–4; Also Hüttenberger, 'Wirtschaftsordnung und Interessenpolitik', 297. For problems with *Länder* and ministries, Robert, *Konzentrationspolitik*, 140–1.

[18] Berghahn, *The Americanisation of West German Industry*, 167, citing a report in the *Frankfurter Allgemeine Zeitung*, 17 Nov. 1953.

In June 1952 Erhard introduced a bill into the Bundestag which banned cartels but made provision for exceptions in special circumstances. This bill was obstructed by those interests ranged against it, and could not be enacted before the parliamentary session ended with new elections in 1953. In February 1954 the bill was reintroduced, but hopes that it would make speedy progress were doomed to disappointment. The major interest-groups of industry, the BDI and the German Industrial and Trade Association (DIHT—*Deutscher Industrie- und andelstag*), remained quite opposed to the ban on cartels and clearly hoped for a solution which would allow the same sort of proliferation of price-fixing arrangements that had existed in the 1920s.

At first they stressed that the time was not ripe for a cartel-free Germany, in view of the weakness of the economy after the war and the need to protect it from foreign competition. In the early 1950s, however, the BDI realized that a ban on cartels was firmly on the Economics Ministry's agenda, and started attacking the whole principle behind the measure, sneering at unworldly professors who had no idea of business. They commissioned their own economic experts to demonstrate that, far from being harmful, cartels brought stability and long-term employment. It was even claimed that a ban on cartels would be contrary to the Basic Law of the Republic, since it limited an individual's freedom of contract.

The most assiduous of the BDI's expert supporters was Professor Rudolf Isay, a long-standing advocate for cartels, who had crossed swords with Böhm in the past. In 1928 he had told the German Lawyers' Conference (*Juristentag*) in Salzburg that:

Today, after the economic disruptions caused by war and inflation have been largely overcome, employers' cartels are just as essential for the economy as co-operatives are for farmers, craftsmen, or consumers, and trade unions are for workers. For capital-intensive industry—especially industries producing raw materials or partially finished goods—they [cartels] provide an indispensable reduction of capital risk.

It was perhaps no coincidence that in 1954 he published a book commenting favourably on the Reichsgericht's decision in 1897 to uphold the legality of cartels. Erhard's own 'brains trust' responded robustly, spearheaded by Böhm.[19]

It should be emphasized that at this embryonic stage in the Federal Republic's development it would have been quite possible for industry to slip into its old protectionist habits. In June 1953 the annual report of

---

[19] Report on Isay's speech in Böhm NL, KAS I-200-002/4. For BDI policy, Robert, *Konzentrationspolitik*, 169–84; Berghahn, *The Americanisation of West German Industry*, 174.

the BDI attacked the 'dogmatists of a purist (*modellgetreu*) laissez-faire' in the 'ordo-liberal' camp.[20] This showed how little the industrialists cared to understand 'ordo-liberal' theory, because it was precisely in order to stop *laissez-faire* arrangements distorting the market that the ban on cartels was to be introduced.

Erhard battled on, supported by the ASM, by academic enonomists of the liberal school, and by a loyal group of CDU members of the Bundestag described somewhat satirically as the 'Erhard Brigade'.[21] Franz Böhm was an enthusiastic member of this group, and polemicized tirelessly against the pro-cartel lobby. The reintroduction of the 1952 bill was greeted by howls of rage from the BDI, and accusations of bad faith from Berg, its president. Threats of withdrawal of funds from government parties had less effect in 1954, since the next election was three years away. The industrial lobby sponsored a memorandum to the government by Isay, who, unsurprisingly, advocated the old solution of state supervision to avoid 'abuses'. More worrying was the activity of the Christian Democratic Economics Minister for North Rhine-Westphalia, Sträter, who tried to organize opposition to the bill in the Bundesrat. In June 1954 Erhard told the Bundesrat that the cartel legislation was the economic equivalent of the Basic Law—the Federal constitution. His determination paid off and, with the support of a Social Democratic *Land* like Hamburg, the Bundesrat accepted the measure.

The law was by no means home and dry. Erhard was being pressed by Adenauer to come to a compromise with Berg and the BDI. On 1 July 1954, he wrote to the Chancellor complaining bitterly that the BDI had shown complete intransigence, and that—far from giving ground—its negotiators had escalated their demands to a grotesque degree. It was clear to him that their cartel concept was still embedded in nationalist categories of thought and that international cartels were basically designed to seal off the national area and isolate it. 'All attempts at political and economic integration', he warned Adenauer, 'will therefore not only be endangered by cartels but will actually be

---

[20] Cited in Berghahn, *The Americanisation of West German Industry*, 175. For a more detailed account of the resistance by industry to Erhard's proposals, see Berghahn and Friedrich, *Otto A. Friedrich*, 117–33. Otto Friedrich tried to play a mediating role between Erhard and the BDI, and certainly Erhard was not so rigid in his attitudes as Franz Böhm, for example. But the rather disappointing results of the anti-cartel campaign were due more to Erhard's weak political position in Bonn on this issue than to his lack of enthusiasm for reform.

[21] The name was a pun on an earlier and much more sinister force in Germany's history, the *Brigade Ehrhardt*, which tried to overthrow German democracy in the Kapp Putsch of March 1920.

sabotaged by them.' Doubtless he hoped that this point might worry a Chancellor who was working hard for Western European integration. He told Adenauer that Berg and his allies did not speak for major parts of German industry. He ended his letter by stressing that he was not prepared to accept a compromise which would reduce the social market economy to 'a farce and a delusion [*Blendwerk*]'.[22]

Following up his claim that the BDI was not properly representative of German industry, Erhard and his allies were able to mobilize business groups which regarded the older cartel-methods favoured by heavy industry as outdated and actually damaging to their interests. In late July 1954 a number of prominent figures from various spheres of industry published an open letter supporting Erhard's principle of a ban on cartels. This helped push a sulky BDI towards more productive negotiations with Erhard, and by the end of the year he had yielded more exceptions to the ban in return for BDI acceptance of the major principle. The fact that in October 1954 the Federal Republic finally achieved sovereignty from the Allies over German industrial policy also clarified the position and gave reason to hope the issue could be swiftly resolved in Bonn.[23]

For his part, Erhard continued to agitate for his anti-cartel measure amongst sections of the population not otherwise noted for their commitment to rugged free enterprise. Speaking at a conference of the ASM held on 17 November 1955, Erhard praised the independent middle class, or *Mittelstand*, which, he claimed, was proving far more resilient than had been predicted in the gloomy forecasts of the Marxists. The *Mittelstand* would be able to adapt themselves to changing circumstances so long as they remained independent and responsible for their own actions. Free competition was essential and was being fought for at that time in the cartel discussions before the Bundestag: 'I could not comprehend how members of the *Mittelstand* could side with a policy supportive of cartels—for under all circumstances they would be the losers from such a policy.'[24]

This was typical of Erhard's resolute wooing of classes which, in the past, had tended to support protectionism. He skilfully combined attacks on cartels with a heartfelt horror of inflation, which he absolutely rejected as being likely to destroy people's security in old age and render them dependent on the good offices of the state.[25] Erhard's

[22] Erhard to Adenauer, 1 July 1954, LES Erhard Correspondence.
[23] Robert, *Konzentrationspolitik*, 114, and Berghahn, *The Americanisation of West German Industry*, 180.
[24] W. Hoch (ed.) *Ludwig Erhard: Wirken und Reden* (Ludwigsberg, 1966), 332.
[25] Ibid. 328.

prestige as an economist and a successful minister lent weight to these views with the German public.

Even then there were many alarms and excursions before the bill was finally passed into law in July 1957.[26] Adenauer gave his Economics Minister little support over the cartel issue, and there were rumours that he was going to replace Erhard with Berg. Jealousy over Erhard's popularity probably played no small part in Adenauer's tactics, especially since there was talk in the CDU of the need to find a successor to *Der Alte*, who was now 80 years old.

In 1956 the economy showed some signs of overheating, and industrial interests were pressing for tax concessions and more protective policies towards imports. Schäffer and Erhard got together and followed the opposite policy; tariffs were cut and the Bundesbank was supported in its decision to raise the bank rate, which it did on 19 May 1956. A few days later the BDI was holding its annual conference at the Gürzenich conference hall in Cologne, a conference which Adenauer attended. He listened without apparent demur to a ferocious attack on Erhard's policies from Berg. Then he himself got up to denounce the policy of the Bundesbank as harmful to the 'little man', and to assure his delighted listeners—very few of whom were 'little men'—that he would immediately demand an explanation for what was going on from Erhard and Schäfer. In Cabinet on 24 May he upbraided Erhard for offending potentially powerful supporters at a time when elections were appearing on the horizon.

Nevertheless, thanks to behind-the-scenes work by Westrick and Hans Globke, State Secretary in the Federal Chancellery, no irrevocable breach occurred and government policy remained committed to free-market principles.[27] So far as the anti-cartel law was concerned, however, Erhard owed more to allies in the Christian Democratic party group in the Bundestag, to friends in the press like Gerd Bucerius, the owner of *Die Zeit*, and to the support of pressure groups representing small business, than he did to Adenauer or the Cabinet. There also appeared a marked tendency for the SPD to support harsher measures against cartels—an unexpected development which enabled Erhard to appear as a moderating force and to keep a low profile in parliamentary debates.

In the end, Erhard did succeed in getting this key act of social-market legislation on the statute book. It was by no means an ideal measure for true believers in perfect competition. Political necessity

---

[26] It actually came into effect on 1 Jan. 1958. Robert, *Konzentrationspolitik*, 331.

[27] Koerfer, *Kampf ums Kanzleramt*, 117–8.

and the strength of the vested interests involved meant that the cartel ban which lay at the heart of the law was riddled with exceptions. Franz Böhm was so incensed at what he saw as backsliding by the Economics Ministry that he introduced his own, very much tougher, proposals to the Bundestag in March 1955. These may have had tactical value to Erhard in frightening the still-dangerous conservative opposition.

Nevertheless, a measure of the law's weakness was the fact that the parliamentary subcommittee considering the final draft reported with satisfaction that the prohibition of cartels was now acceptable because it had been so watered down that small businesses would not be exposed to price competition, and in all cases where it made 'economic sense', business could establish cartels. To describe the law as the Magna Carta of the social market economy, as some government supporters did, was an exaggeration. Erhard himself admitted to the Bundestag that too many cooks were spoiling the anti-cartel broth, but stoutly maintained that the principle of a ban on cartels was the only course compatible with an economic system based on free competition.[28]

Certainly it is now customary to minimize the anti-cartel law, and to point to its weaknesses rather than its strengths. The most authoritative German historian of this period suggests that a weak piece of legislation was the price paid to industrial interests for support at forthcoming elections.[29] Böhm, as we have seen, was dissatisfied with it. Yet thirteen years later Müller-Armack could congratulate Böhm himself on the law and claim that, although it had its faults, the law: 'bore, as a whole, the imprint of your hand [*Ihre Handschrift*]'.[30]

There is a lot to be said for that view. However unsatisfactory the law was, it still represented a breakthrough in German business practice. It clearly announced that cartels were an exceptional and unsatisfactory method of regulating markets, and that only competition should be seen as the respectable method of fixing prices. It also established a watchdog body, the Federal Cartel Office (*Bundeskartelamt*), which would not only police the workings of the act with regard to

---

[28] Erhard's speech was made to the Bundestag on 24 Mar. 1955; see Erhard, *Deutsche Wirtschaftspolitik*, 269–70. Also H.-U. Siebler, *Wirtschaftstheorie, Wirtschaftspolitik und das Gesetz gegen Wettbewerbsbeschränkungen: Begründung und Begründbarkeit neo-liberaler Wettbewerbspolitik* (Diss.; Frankfurt/M., 1966), 13, and Robert, *Konzentrationspolitik*, 328–9; On Bucerius, see Koerfer, *Kampf ums Kanzleramt*, 149–50. Bucerius was one of the 'Erhard Brigade' in the Bundestag.

[29] Schwarz, *Gründerjahre der Republik*, 335.

[30] Speech by Müller-Armack presenting Böhm with the Freiherr vom Stein Prize (Hamburg, 1970).

cartels, but could also act against unhealthy concentrations of economic power or tendencies towards monopoly. Here again, the powers may have been limited in practice, but the precedent created by the establishment of such as office was important. The fact that the first director of this office was Günther, a strong disciple of Eucken and one of Erhard's most effective lieutenants in the Economics Ministry, indicated the direction its policy was likely to take.

As one American observer wrote in May 1954, should Erhard's anti-cartel bill be rejected, 'West Germany may well slip back into the economic authoritarianism of the old days', but if the bill were accepted: 'even in a modified form, [this] would mean a major victory, perhaps the greatest victory ever won in Europe, for the principles of dynamic American-style capitalism'.[31]

This is certainly how Erhard would have liked to have seen the law. He was not so fanatical about economic concentrations as some of his colleagues, but he did want to ensure that the principles of competition and free trade were effectively established in West Germany. In the early 1950s this was by no means a foregone conclusion; Erhard himself spoke of his fear that cartels would burst forth like mushrooms once Allied restraint was removed.[32] Although, in the 1960s and 1970s, West German industry demonstrated the same tendency towards merger and concentration as that of other Western countries, the competitive, consumer-orientated characteristics of the post-war period were not lost.

For one thing, the influence of the old 'smoke-stack' industries of coal and steel was weakened by deconcentration, and although they had some success in coagulating again in the years which followed, they were never able to re-establish their former pre-eminence in the German economy. Erhard contributed to this process by enthusiastically encouraging the import of oil products through a policy of deregulation and relatively free trade, thus helping to bring about a decisive shift in German energy usage. By the end of the decade, coal had lost its status as the backbone of the economy and was becoming a declining industry.

Under these circumstances, and with the climate of legal and economic opinion created by neo-liberal campaigns, cartelization did not reappear as the chronic problem which had existed before the war. In

---

[31] Berghahn, *The Americanisation of West German Industry*, 175–6, citing Gilbert Burck in *Fortune* (May 1954).

[32] Already in early 1950, Erhard was warning that if nothing was done to curb cartels they would re-emerge 'Wie einst im Mai', Berghahn, *The Americanisation of West German Industry*, p. 167.

1930 it was estimated that there were between two and three thousand cartels operating in Germany. In 1978 there were 266 cartels registered with the Federal Cartel Office, and by 1985 the number had fallen to 241. Erhard's law was by no means the only factor in this development, but it played a part in shaping a climate of opinion less inclined towards protection than that of the pre-war period.[33]

Other factors which affected the shaping of the post-war West German economy were the system of co-determination, or *Mitbestimmung*, which was established in German industry, and the development of European economic institutions such as the Coal and Steel Community (Schuman Plan) and the European Common Market. None of these was particularly welcome to neo-liberal economists, and some of them were regarded with positive dislike.

Mitbestimmung in the coal and steel industries had been granted to the trade unions by the Allied occupation authorities in the British zone before 1949. It involved the election of worker representatives on to the supervisory boards of large firms. Social Democrats saw it as a form of workers' control or, more specifically, control by trade unions;[34] the British hoped trade-union influence would act as a counter-weight to predatory, militaristic tendencies amongst the firms' management. So far as German political parties were concerned, the SPD was firmly in favour of co-determination, and the labour wing of the CDU also supported it. Since the industries concerned were heavily controlled by the Allies and were the subject of denazification and deconcentration, the question of *Mitbestimmung* seemed a relatively minor issue. A certain amount of worker participation was apparently a small price to pay for the restoration of sovereignty over the German coal and steel industries and the abolition of restraints on their development.

For neo-liberals and for the FDP, as well as for the more conservative sections of the CDU/CSU, co-determination represented a dangerous erosion of entrepreneurial authority which would undermine managerial freedom. In the blueprint for the social market economy published by Müller-Armack in 1948, there had indeed been mention of the worker's right to a *Mitgestaltungsrecht*, or right to have a say, especially in the conditions of his work. Böhm and other neo-liberals regarded the sort of co-determination demanded by trade unions to be a form of 'cold socialization', seeing it as weakening the leadership of an economic enterprise. Liberal economic theory demanded that the entrepreneur—

[33] Grosser *et al.*, *Soziale Marktwirtschaft*, 44. For the tendency towards concentration, see Robert, *Konzentrationspolitik*, 37–50.

[34] See Hubsch, 'DGB Economic Policy', in I. D. Turner (ed.), *Reconstruction in Post-war Germany*, 74–83.

or perhaps more crudely, the capitalist—should take the responsibility for decisions about his enterprise, since its survival in the competitive market-place was his overriding concern. A worker's right to a say in the way a plant was operated was, however, a different matter. This was a recognition of the alienation created by conditions in many large factories.[35]

From the early days of Adenauer's coalition, Storch, the Minister of Labour, was eager to put a co-determination law on the statute book. Adenauer supported him, since he believed it would help to buy peace with the unions, whilst weakening their attachment to the SPD. Erhard, on the other hand, was able to use the threat of radical co-determination measures as a lever to obtain business support for his anti-cartel free-market policies. Only if the entrepreneurs showed themselves genuinely committed to competition could they protect their own freedom to manage their enterprises.[36]

In January 1951 Adenauer came to an agreement with Hans Böckler, the leader of the *Deutscher Gewerkschaftsbund* (DGB), the German trade union organization, in which he accepted equal worker-participation on the supervisory boards of companies in the mining industry. A law providing for this was passed on 21 May 1951. The trade unions and the SPD pressed hard for similar rights to be granted in other parts of the economy, but when the Works' Constitution Law (*Betriebsverfassungsgesetz*), covering industrial relations in large firms, was passed in July 1952, worker representatives filled only a third of the seats on the supervisory boards of companies. This meant that entrepreneurial responsibility was safeguarded, and could be regarded as compatible with the principles of the social market economy.

Co-determination in this limited and sensible form proved an important factor in securing labour peace in West Germany. The fact that neo-liberal economists were willing to accept that workers in large undertakings had rights as well as duties differentiated their attitude from that of 'paleo-liberal' thinkers from the pre-war era. Acceptance of limited co-determination also marked a move away from the traditional views of German industrial managers, who had liked to regard themselves as 'masters in their own house', treating trade unions as sub-

[35] See above, Ch. 6. For Böhm's critical view of co-determination, see his notes on the subject in Böhm NL, KAS I-200-047.

[36] Erhard to Berg, 10 July 1952. When criticizing Berg over his support for cartels, Erhard remarked that: 'it is to be expected with certainty in the light of such manipulation of the market that there will be a demand for equally balanced co-determination [*paritätische Mitbestimmung*] and that under such circumstances it will be difficult to resist such a logical demand'. LES Erhard Correspondence. This letter has been published in Erhard, *Deutsche Wirtschaftspolitik*, 201 ff.

versive agencies to be repressed. This softening of class conflict was entirely compatible with neo-liberal principles, and helped Erhard to persuade trade-union leaders to moderate wage demands in the boom years after 1953.

Another set of issues upon which Erhard and his neo-liberal supporters had different views from others in the anti-socialist camp was that of European integration. This arose in connection with the Marshall Plan, when the Americans had insisted that the Western European countries co-ordinate their projects for reconstruction with a view to moving towards some kind of European unity—at least in the economic sphere. Erhard had been all for the concept of multilateral free trade which underlay American policies towards Europe, but things looked rather different when actual proposals for integration began to emerge from within Europe itself.

Prime movers in this development were the French. They were deeply worried by the changed position of Germany as the result of the Cold War. They had hoped that the post-war arrangements would place firm economic restraints on the Germans to prevent them ever threatening French integrity again. By 1949 it was obvious that the British and the Americans—especially the latter—were determined to use German industrial power as a means of strengthening the West against Communism. This was especially significant so far as the Ruhr area was concerned. That region, which had been, and at that time remained, the industrial heartland of Germany, had been put under international control through the establishment of the International Authority for the Ruhr (IAR) on which the French were represented. Through this they hoped to restrict German heavy industry and prevent it regaining the dominant position it had held before the war. However, once the Americans had determined to rehabilitate the German economy for the benefit of Western defence, the French realized that the days of the IAR would be numbered. Somehow a way had to be found to recognize West Germany's sovereignty whilst keeping her industrial powerhouse from threatening the French economy.

It was at this point that the brilliant French administrator, Jean Monnet, concocted his ingenious plan to pool the coal and steel resources of Western Europe under one supranational authority. Announced by the French Foreign Minister, Robert Schuman, at the beginning of May 1950, this scheme offered something to everybody. It pleased the Americans as a step towards European unity, it gave the Germans the chance to play a role as equals in a new European enterprise, and it reassured the French that Germany's re-emergent industrial power would be under European control. Even the British, who stayed out of the scheme, were pleased that it might improve relations between Paris and Bonn.

However, it was not at all clear what form this 'pool' would take. Monnet himself was an admirer of American business methods who believed in the invigorating properties of competition and wanted to see French antitrust legislation tightened up.[37] He hoped for an open and transparent market in which efficiency would be the key to success. But the coal and steel interests in France and West Germany evidently had other ideas; for many of them the Schuman Plan looked like a heaven-sent opportunity to restore the price rings which had characterized European heavy industry before the war. In particular, the old international steel cartel, of which Germany had been such a powerful member, might well be resuscitated, especially since neither the French nor the British government seemed very rigid in its views about free competition. French industry was already strongly cartelized, and it seems that German businessmen hoped to influence the negotiations in a protectionist sense.[38]

For the neo-liberals this was a worrying development. The Schuman Plan seemed to some of them to be a dangerous form of customs union which would only serve to inhibit free trade. At one point Röpke claimed that either it would not work or it would become the biggest cartel in history.[39] Adenauer himself favoured employing a very conservative industrialist and warm supporter of cartels, Ludwig Kastl, as head of the German delegation to negotiate the details of the Schuman scheme. It seems fairly clear that if more traditional nationalist economists and politicians had dominated the Federal Economics Ministry, the German attitude towards the coal and steel pool would have been protectionist in character. As it was, the suggestion of Kastl was dropped, and Professor Walter Hallstein, a much more liberal figure recommended by Wilhelm Röpke, was chosen to head the German negotiating team. Erhard's ministry was certainly open to influence by industrial circles, but it asserted that government delegations and not pressure groups would take the lead in the negotiations.[40]

It is clear that the final constitution of the European Coal and Steel Community (ECSC) was very much more liberal than had been envisaged by German iron and steel interests in the summer of 1950.

[37] Berghahn, *The Americanisation of West German Industry*, 116–7. For an admiring view of Monnet's role, see Gillingham, *Coal, Steel and Europe*, 136–8; 228 ff.

[38] Gillingham, *Coal, Steel and Europe*, 273–4; Berghahn, *The Americanisation of West German Industry*, 120–4.

[39] Gerhard Curzon, 'International Economic Order: Contribution of the Neo-liberals', in Peacock and Willgerodt (eds.), *German Neoliberals*, 184.

[40] Berghahn, *The Americanisation of West German Industry*, 120–1.

They had expected and desired a 'large cartel-like organization'.[41] That this was not carried out to their satisfaction was largely due to Monnet and the support he received from the Americans, who were strongly opposed to cartels and who wanted to establish a new and competitive West German coal and steel industry on the basis of the deconcentration measures which German industrialists found so distasteful.[42] It is also of interest that Erhard's ministry did not support Monnet when he produced a firmly liberal draft plan in October 1950, in which the High Authority of the ECSC was to ban all agreements which would restrict competition or fix prices, limit production or divide up markets, customers, or raw materials. Instead the Germans presented a counter-proposal of a much milder character, supposedly based on the principles of the Havanna Charter. This protected competition in international trade, guaranteed access to markets, and blocked monopolistic tendencies, but it obviously left the door open to price-fixing arrangements within the member states of the ECSC. The Monnet scheme allowed no exceptions to the ban on cartels, whereas the Germans would have permitted exceptions, and they evidently received support from other negotiating countries for this view.[43]

The whole matter was intertwined with the issue of deconcentration of the German coal and steel industry, which was being negotiated between the West Germans and the Allies—mainly the Americans—at the same time. Adenauer was torn between his concern to work with the Americans to regain German sovereignty and his sympathy for 'pragmatic' industrialists. Erhard did not adopt a consistent liberal position over this issue. He resisted—with partial success—American demands that the vertical concentration of coal and steel production in the Ruhr should be broken up.[44]

In this respect it is worth remembering that the Korean crisis was well under way at this point and that Erhard was simultaneously lecturing McCloy, the American High Commissioner, on the virtues of decontrol, whilst trying to block measures designed to create greater competition in heavy industry. It is not surprising that the Allies sometimes suspected his motives to be as much nationalist as liberal. This was illustrated by his unwillingness to oppose a joint sales-organization for all Ruhr coal-mines to which, in December 1950, the

---

[41] Ibid. 126.
[42] Ibid. 132–40.
[43] Ibid. 142.
[44] For the terms of the deconcentration arrangement eventually accepted, and for the linkage between this and the Schuman Plan negotiations, which the Germans were able to exploit to their benefit, see Warner, 'Allied–German Negotiations', 166–85.

Americans were taking strong objection on the grounds that it would limit competition. Erhard was most adamant that a state-owned sales-organization had to be avoided because 'the socialisation of the sales [system] easily leads to complete socialisation', but privately controlled joint sales-organizations under state supervision would be acceptable.[45] This illustrates Erhard's relative lack of concern about private combines, and suggests that his main interest was the liberation of West German industry from Allied controls.

Be that as it may, the influence of neo-liberal, anti-cartel elements in the Ministry of Economics did at least make it easier to accept the final proposals for the ECSC constitution, which went most of the way towards the liberal antitrust ideal of Monnet and the Americans, whilst permitting horizontal agreements in certain circumstances and giving the High Authority interventionist powers to deal with serious crises.[46]

Perhaps the most important aspect of the ECSC from Erhard's viewpoint was that it would supersede the International Authority for the Ruhr, which was dissolved in September 1952. It was also significant, however, in that it heralded an era of greater Western European integration, and in particular the establishment of the European Economic Community or Common Market. This is not the place to recount the story of the establishment of the EEC. But it should be remembered that from the neo-liberal viewpoint, the Common Market had almost as many drawbacks as advantages. Adenauer wanted West Germany to take her place in the EEC as smoothly as possible, thus asserting her equal status with her European neighbours, and providing his government with another achievement before the 1957 Bundestag elections. For Erhard and his academic supporters in the Mont Pèlerin Society, however, the restricted nature of the Common Market was a grave disadvantage. They wanted the economic integration of the Western world as a whole, including Britain and the USA, and they wanted this to be achieved by lowering tariffs, establishing convertible currencies, and breaking down other commercial barriers.[47] In other words, they favoured the largest possible free-trade area, but were not enamoured of more complex institutional developments, especially if these might shut some nations out of the market thus created.

The whole issue of the EEC caused another rift between Erhard and Chancellor Adenauer. From the first, Erhard was sceptical about European integration based on supranational authorities. He also dis-

---

[45] Quoted in Berghahn, *The Americanisation of West German Industry*, 151.

[46] Ibid. 144–5.

[47] Koerfer, *Kampf ums Kanzleramt*, 136–7.

trusted the protectionism and *dirigisme* of the French. In November 1954 he attended a meeting of the General Agreement on Tariffs and Trade (GATT) in Geneva, where he had found many delegates worried about French protectionist policies and the prospect of Franco-German integration. Erhard had assured such people that, while Germany naturally wanted friendship with France:

It is, however, in no way intended to create a particular economic axis between Paris and Bonn . . . No agreement in the economic sphere will therefore be concluded between Germany and France which we will not be willing to enter into with all other countries. My assurances were received with great satisfaction . . .

It is not clear that Adenauer was so satisfied with his minister's performance when the latter triumphantly reported it to him.

Nevertheless, by the spring of 1955 it seemed that some agreement might be achieved between the Economics Ministry and the Federal Chancellery over West Germany's attitude towards EEC negotiations. Alfred Müller-Armack was considerably more flexible on the issue than Erhard himself, although he was also thoroughly committed to free-trade policies. In May 1955 Müller-Armack hosted a meeting at his country house in Eicherschied bei Münstereifel at which Erhard, Westrick, von Brentano of the German Foreign Office, and Franz Etzel, the vice-chairman of the ECSC, agreed that there could be an institutional framework for European integration based on a customs union of the six ECSC countries.[48] As the negotiations went ahead, most notably at the Messina conference in June 1955, Erhard began to have renewed doubts. He did not like the implied protectionist functions of the proposed system, nor was he pleased that Britain would not be part of it. Erhard's renewed criticism of the EEC looked like lack of principle to his colleagues, and especially his Chancellor. John Foster Dulles, an enthusiastic apostle of European integration, upbraided Erhard for his lack of support—another point of conflict with Adenauer, by whom Dulles was seen as a close diplomatic ally.

In January 1956 Adenauer issued a directive to his Cabinet making it clear that West Germany should support the decisions taken at the Messina conference, which had committed the states of the ECSC to create a European economic union. This would help German interests by forging European solidarity *vis-à-vis* the USSR, without which Soviet

---

[48] For Erhard's report on the meeting in Geneva, sent to Adenauer on 13 Nov. 1954, LES Erhard Correspondence. For Müller-Armack's views, A. S. Milward, *The European Rescue of the Nation-State* (London, 1992), 198. For the meeting at his house, Koerfer, *Kampf ums Kanzleramt*, 136–7.

concessions could hardly be expected. It would also further the *rapprochement* between Bonn and Paris. Such were the principles upon which West German policy was to be based and all ministers would be expected to act accordingly.[49] This was obviously aimed at Erhard, whose reservations about the EEC were well known. As often happened in the 'Chancellor's democracy' (*Kanzlerdemokratie*), in which the Federal Chancellor was supposed to exercise rigorous authority, his admonition was ignored. Erhard continued to object robustly to the concept and the terms of the European Community.

On 11 April 1956 he wrote to Adenauer saying that, although he would stand by him in East–West confrontations 'through thick and thin', he had quite a different view about European integration: 'That obsessive [*monoman*] attitude which welcomes anything so long as it can be got up to look as if it is "European" cannot lead to a result which is either truly European or satisfactory.'

He made no bones about his opposition to Adenauer's 'integration order', because he realized it would not lead to genuine integration but to a splitting and enfeeblement of the economy. What was on offer was only a partial solution, which would hinder rather than help genuine integration. 'Errors and sins against the economy are not made good by proclaiming them to be European.' In any case, the Germans could only gain their political objectives in the closest collaboration with Britain and the USA.[50]

This set the stage for a running battle between the Chancellor and the Economics Minister which Erhard lost all along the line. He objected to the concessions being made to the French in a protectionist sense, particularly those relating to agriculture. In fact, German farming interests had always been able to resist exposure to market forces fairly effectively even within the Federal Republic, but Erhard had hoped that in the future the social market economy could apply to be this sector also. It was clear that if French farmers were to be accommodated, this would not happen. Erhard, like other neo-liberals, was not enthusiastic about the French, whose economy seemed an uneasy combination of capitalism and state direction. Röpke referred to a 'perfumed planned economy on the French pattern'. He warned that 'the sick might contaminate the sound' in the European Community—in other words, the planned, cheap-money economies might weaken the robust, free-market economies.[51] Erhard likewise argued that France and other European countries should sort out their own econ-

---

[49] Milward, *The European Rescue*, 374; Koerfer, *Kampf ums Kanzleramt*, 137–8.
[50] Koerfer, *Kampf ums Kanzleramt*, 138–9.
[51] Ibid. 142.

omic mess before being integrated into Europe, for fear that they would infect the whole Common Market with *dirigiste* notions. With respect to agriculture, this fear proved all too justified, although German protectionism was no less damaging than French in that sector.

On 5 October 1956 Erhard delivered an address to the Federal Cabinet on the European issue, arguing that it had been inadequately discussed and that not only was France receiving concessions for her industry and her agriculture which were incompatible with the free market, but that Britain might be permanently excluded from the EEC, which was not in Germany's interests.[52] Erhard found little support, and the Treaty of Rome was signed on 25 March 1957. It is worth pointing out that, as the result of the Federal Republic regaining full sovereignty in 1955, the German Foreign Office had grown in status within the government. It was therefore the new Foreign Minister, Heinrich von Brentano, and not Erhard, who led the negotiations—fully protected by Adenauer.

This was not, of course, the end of the matter. Erhard continued to press for a free-trade policy within the EEC and for an agreement with the European Free Trade Area (EFTA), which the British had established as some sort of riposte to the Treaty of Rome. The constitution of EFTA was certainly much more in line with neo-liberal theory than that of the EEC in Brussels. It did not seek to interfere in detail with member states' economic policies, it did not develop a large and expensive bureaucracy, and it stood for free trade.

Röpke was particularly critical of the protectionist and *dirigiste* aspects of the EEC. He argued that it was not only economically retrograde but politically dangerous, since it would divide the West in the face of the Communist threat. At a meeting of the ASM in November 1957 he publically attacked the EEC, saying that German politicians should be ready to leave the Community if remaining in it meant a permanent breach with the free-trade-area countries. This provoked a typically intemperate riposte from Berg of the BDI. He sneered at Röpke as a Swiss professor with little knowledge of Germany who was always ready to interfere in German affairs. The quarrel was continued in a vitriolic correspondence, and in April 1958 Röpke wrote an article in *ORDO* claiming that if the EEC were not rapidly merged with the free-trade area it would become a force for the *disintegration* of Europe—'dynamite instead of cement'. He contrasted the benevolent integration carried through in OEEC and EPU with the

---

[52] Ibid. See also H. J. Küsters, 'Adenauers Europapolitik in der Gründungsphase der EWG', *Vierteljahrshefte für Zeitgeschichte*, 31/4 (Oct. 1983), 665.

bureaucratic 'collectivism' envisaged by the Treaty of Rome. He made slighting reference to 'Little Europe', and argued that 'social harmonization' would just mean 'harmonization of inflationary pressures'.

The ASM itself, representing as it did the cream of the neo-liberal intelligentsia, proclaimed its distaste for the *dirigiste* tendencies of the European Economic Community. In March 1958 it published an 'action programme' in which, amongst other things, it demanded that European economic integration should not be established through supranational interventionism, but only on the basis of free markets, free trade, and freely convertible currencies. In particular, the protectionist and inflationary tendencies of the EEC should be overcome by expanding it into a comprehensive free-trade area.[53]

Unfortunately EFTA was not a success politically. It could not satisfy the British urge to enjoy a place at the new 'top table' of Western Europe created in Brussels. Meanwhile the appearance of de Gaulle at the helm in France increased British isolation in Europe, more especially since Adenauer and the French President began to develop a special relationship which was popular in the Federal Republic. Erhard was openly critical of the French association. In October 1959 he even had published large newspaper-advertisements with the formula 6 + 7 + 5 = 1, a demand that all European states outside the socialist camp should be united in a common market. This was clearly not compatible with the aims of de Gaulle.[54]

Neo-liberal uneasiness about the EEC did not abate, although the financial policies of de Gaulle's government were more reassuring than the profligate methods of the discredited Fourth Republic. In 1959 Röpke could see no reason to change his unpopular attitude towards fashionable Europeanism. He argued that the proper way to integrate Europe was for all countries to adopt monetary discipline and convertible currencies. The achievement of international convertibility had been a tremendous advance and, if this was taken to its logical conclusion, the EEC would become superfluous. A supranational bureaucracy was bound to develop along 'collectivist-*dirigiste*' lines, especially if the tone was set in the Community by protectionist states

---

[53] For the correspondence between Berg and Röpke in Apr. 1958, see Böhm NL, KAS I-200-800/1, also W. Röpke 'Gemeinsamer Markt und Freihandelszone: 28 Thesen als Richtpunkte', *ORDO: Jahrbuch für die Ordnung von Wirtschaft und Gesellschaft*, 10 (1958), 31–62. See also Aktionsgemeinschaft Soziale Marktwirtschaft, e.v., *Aktionsprogramm* (Würzburg, 1958), 5.

[54] Koerfer, *Kampf ums Kanzleramt*, 395. Erhard's 18 European states were the 6 of the EEC plus the 7 of EFTA plus Greece, Iceland, Ireland, Spain, and Turkey. Yugoslavia, with its socialist economy, was excluded, even though it was not in the Soviet bloc.

like France and Italy. Bombastic phrases about the 'unstoppable progress' of the 'wheel of history' should not blind observers to the faults of a protectionist block.[55]

In 1962 Macmillan's government attempted to gain entry into the EEC. Erhard made no secret of his sympathy for the British position, and Müller-Armack, his main lieutenant on European affairs, actively supported British entry. This was due less to any particular Anglophilia than to a belief that broadening the EEC would help to incline it more towards a free-trade policy. Erhard was strongly opposed to a centrally directed economy steered from Brussels. On 20 November 1962 he addressed a session of the European Parliament and publicly attacked the proposals of the European Commission for medium and long-term planning of the economic development of the European Community. The fact that this scheme was sponsored by his former colleague Walter Hallstein did not inhibit Erhard from pouring scorn on it. Economic planning over a long period, he told the European parliamentarians, never worked. It only led to dangerous dependence on planning bureaucracies which were incapable of appreciating the human factor in the economy. Europeans did not need central direction from Brussels; they needed a common understanding of the ways in which the concept of free competition could be realized throughout the Community. The Commission ought to be more concerned about broadening the Community and speeding up the process of integration than with half-baked schemes for economic planning.[56]

Erhard's hopes that Britain would appear in the EEC as a counterweight to France were soon to be dashed. On 14 January 1963 President de Gaulle publicly and demonstratively vetoed British entry into the EEC. Erhard and others in the German government, including the Foreign Minister, Gerhard Schröder, wanted to put pressure on the French to alter their decision. They were furious when Adenauer supported de Gaulle. The Chancellor saw no reason to damage his new and fruitful relationship with the French leader for the benefit of the inconsistent British government, especially since he suspected Macmillan of being willing to strike an agreement with the Soviet Union over the heads of his European partners. On 22 January, therefore, Adenauer signed a Franco-German friendship treaty at an emotional ceremony in Paris. A week later Couve de Murville

---

[55] W. Röpke, 'Zwischenbilanz der europäischen Wirtschaftspolitik. Kritische Nachlese', *ORDO*, 11 (1959), 70–3 and 77–85.

[56] Koerfer, *Kampf ums Kanzleramt*, 708.

confirmed to the EEC Council of Ministers that the French veto against British entry was irrevocable.

Müller-Armack was so incensed by the French action and Adenauer's response to it that he publicly distanced himself from his government's position and offered Erhard his resignation. For his part, Erhard proclaimed his own bitter disappointment and then openly disagreed with the actions of his Chancellor. The row went on in the press and in parliament, despite a letter from Adenauer brusquely reproving Erhard for encroaching on matters of foreign policy which lay outside his competence and demanding that he accept Müller-Armack's resignation. The latter actually received a message of sympathy and thanks from Edward Heath, the chief British negotiator. It seemed a fitting close to Müller-Armack's political career, struck down in defence of the free-market principle against nationalist protectionism. In fact, however, West German politics were by this time so chaotic that Erhard ignored Adenauer's order, and Müller-Armack stayed on until the autumn.[57]

The row over the Franco-German treaty and Britain's exclusion from the EEC signalled the beginning of open conflict between Erhard and Adenauer over the chancellorship, a battle which ended in October 1963 with Adenauer's resignation. It did not, however, do anything to broaden the EEC or ameliorate its bureaucratic, protectionist tendencies. On the contrary, the Common Agricultural Policy (CAP), which took the lion's share of the Community's budget, developed into the most grotesque system of price-fixing, subsidies, and artificial purchasing-arrangements which had ever been created in a modern industrial economy. The 1930s Brazilian coffee-purchasing scheme, which Röpke and other neo-liberals had used as an awful example of interventionist folly, began to look positively benign by comparison with the CAP. When it came to overcoming the relatively small but politically powerful and ruthless agricultural lobbies in France and Germany, neo-liberal propagandists proved wanting.

There was one other area of policy in the Federal Republic over which the social market economists were to be disappointed. This was to be social policy, and in particular, pensions. By 1956 the first and most difficult period of West Germany's economic development was over. The real hardships and austerity which had characterized the

---

[57] Müller-Armack NL, KAS 030, letter from Heath to Müller-Armack, 5 Feb. 1963. After he finally did resign, Müller-Armack went back to teaching economics at the University of Cologne, where the institute he founded survives him. For the conflict between Erhard and Adenauer and the publication of their correspondence, including that relating to Müller-Armack, see Koerfer, *Kampf ums Kanzleramt*, 724–7.

post-war period were receding into the past. Full employment had effectively been achieved, especially if the continuing flow of refugees from East Germany was taken into account. Yet, as was inevitable, some sections of society had been less able to benefit from the economic resurgence than others. Erhard had never pretended that the social market economy would bring wealth equally to all the people; he had simply argued that all would benefit from an increase in the gross national product. Ostentatious wealth enjoyed by the economically successful had indeed been a feature of the Erhard era, and one upon which hostile critics and foreign observers alike tended to comment.[58]

Most obviously disadvantaged were pensioners, who had been unable to exploit the economic opportunities offered by the free market. They felt that the time had come for them to enjoy a share of West German prosperity. In this they were supported by the refugee organizations, the Social Democrats, and powerful elements in the labour and Roman Catholic 'social' wing of the CDU. Owing to the war, many Germans were in receipt of some form of pension—the elderly, those wounded in the war or injured in bombing, and war widows and orphans. In 1953 it was claimed that 20 per cent of the West German population received some sort of assistance and, according to another estimate, in 1955 every other German household received an element of state assistance. This does not imply, of course, that all of the millions of people involved were dependent on state pensions for their livelihood.[59] There was a very complex and inconsistent network of assistance for different categories of people who had suffered some form of deprivation or who were incapable of supporting themselves fully. The high level of public spending on welfare could, indeed, be seen as a vindication of the social market, since it did provide a safety net for those incapable of competing in the market-place. But social welfare was not systematically organized or co-ordinated in a manner compatible with neo-liberal principles, nor was it particularly just in its distribution arrangements.

Certainly there was no doubt that, as living standards rose for most of the population, the relative deprivation of the pensioners became very marked. Demands for a much more generous settlement for pensioners began to be widely voiced, and Adenauer, mindful of elections in September 1957, paid heed to them.

From the point of view of the social market economists, such claims

---

[58] See above Ch. 12, for the comments of social democratic critics on this point.

[59] Schwarz, *Gründerjahre der Republik*, 329, and H. G. Hockerts, *Sozialpolitische Entscheidungen im Nachkriegsdeutschland* (Stuttgart, 1980), 196.

were dangerous. Certainly they believed that the poorest in society should receive carefully targeted help to maintain a decent, if frugal, standard of living, but they were determined that this should be done without compromising a robust market-economy. Over-generous pension-schemes would be objectionable in a number of ways. First, they would involve large public expenditure which would reduce the amount of money available for private investment. Secondly, they would encourage a dependency on the state for welfare hand-outs which might undermine the self-reliance of the mass of the population.

Before the first Bundestag elections there had been controversy about the nature of pensions between the SPD and their opponents in Germany. The latter wanted to cleave to the traditional method of insurance payments which linked the level of pension to the individual's contribution. The SPD wanted a much more generous scheme, paid from taxes. The victory of the anti-socialist parties in the Economic Council and the 1949 Bundestag elections meant that the traditional method was retained and pensions did indeed remain very low.

Erhard and his colleagues could argue that the way round this was to encourage those who could afford to do so to make larger contributions for their future retirement, and perhaps make special arrangements for existing pensioners in a manner which would not mortgage the future. Unfortunately, the pensions issue was not one which fell directly under Erhard's purview at the Economics Ministry. He had always argued that social policy was a separate issue from economic policy, and implied that he was more flexible on the former than the latter. An improvement in pensions would demonstrate that the social aspect of the social market economy could bring benefits to the worse off. He sometimes supported Storch, the Labour Minister, in struggles over competence with other ministries which wanted to reduce spending on social welfare by insisting more rigorously on means-tested benefits.[60]

Erhard was, therefore, not in a particularly strong position to resist a generous pensions-policy. The politician who was in the firing-line in this respect was the Finance Minister, Schäffer, and he certainly put up vigorous opposition to lavish spending on pensions. There ensued a tug-of-war between the finance and labour ministries, with Erhard's Economics Ministry staying on the sidelines. The Finance Ministry

---

[60] See above for Erhard's speech to the CDU economics committee at Königswinter, [CDU] Feb. 1949, and see also his comments to Sir Stafford Cripps on a visit to London, 23–30 Nov. 1948, recorded in a report by Mr Killich, 10 Dec. 1948, PRO/FO 1049/1190. For the Finance Ministry's view, see Hockerts, *Sozialpolitische Entscheidungen*, 237–8, and for Erhard's attitude, ibid. 277.

wanted a comprehensive streamlining of social policy designed mainly to save money. Means-testing loomed large in its proposals. Storch, however, was determined to prevent Schäffer taking control of social welfare, and a statistical survey in 1955, which Schäffer's ministry had hoped to use as ammunition against wasteful welfare-expenditure, reinforced the point that pension provisions for many underprivileged people were inadequate. Storch proved effective in defending his authority over social policy, and Erhard does not seem to have intervened on Schäffer's behalf.

Schäffer's position was further undermined by his own frugality. During the early 1950s, bearing in mind the future requirements of the West German army, which had yet to be formed, Schäffer had built up a war chest from budget surpluses. This came to be known as the *Juliusturm*—'Julius Tower'—referring to a tower in Berlin where French indemnity payments had been stored after 1871. It was not unnaturally the target of greedy eyes in the spending departments. When it became clear that the Bundeswehr could not be built up as rapidly as had been expected, Schäffer found himself vulnerable to piratical raids on his treasure chest. The *Juliusturm* was stormed in an orgy of pre-election spending and poor Schäffer earned nothing but unpopularity when he tried to defend it.[61]

Storch and, far more important, Chancellor Adenauer himself were eager to present a major pension-reform. They were faced with social democratic critics who had been agitating over pensions since 1952 and who were only too willing to outbid the CDU with even more generous proposals. A report by a lecturer in Cologne, Wilfrid Schreiber, pointed out that the old Bismarckian system of pensions could hardly be sustained in view of the inflations of the early 1920s and the post-war era. Such experiences had rendered contributions-based pensions an absurdity. In future each working generation would have to accept responsibility for its own pensioners, in return for a promise that it would receive adequate pensions in its turn. The older system of contributions-based pensions was to be replaced by a scheme in which pensions would be related to the earnings of those still in work. This was what was known as the 'dynamic pension'. It seemed to protect the pensioner against inflation, since, as other wages rose, so would his pension. Once that principle had been publicly adumbrated in government circles, it was impossible to go back on it. The old form of contribution-linked pensions was dead.

Erhard and Schäffer were opposed to this proposal. They pointed to

[61] Schwarz, *Gründerjahre der Republik*, 325–6.

the dangers of inflation in such a scheme, the future effects of which would be impossible to calculate. Actuarial estimates for the new pensions came from the Labour Ministry. Its critics claimed it had only one qualified mathematician, and his calculations were doubted by experts in the insurance industry.[62] From the neo-liberal viewpoint the plans were highly objectionable because they took no account of market conditions. An attempt to replace wage rates with the level of national production as the yardstick for setting pensions was resisted by Storch and Adenauer, even though it would have been much more in line with the principles of the social market economy. The enthusiasm in the Bundestag for a generous pension-settlement, combined with Adenauer's determination to produce a domestic achievement for the elections, swept 'dynamic pensions' on to the statute book. They certainly achieved their short-term objective; many pensioners benefited from back-payments during the summer of 1957, and in September of that year the CDU/CSU gained an absolute majority in the Bundestag elections. On the other hand, Erhard was not alone in thinking that dynamic pensions were mortgaging the future for present advantage, and this view is shared by at least one historian of the Federal Republic.[63] For social market economists the pensions scheme marked a shift away from market-orientated policies towards the primrose path of the welfare state.

Erhard certainly felt unhappy about this development, and complained to Heuss and Adenauer early in 1957 that a spirit of primitive greed for material welfare was undermining other values. Röpke constantly inveighed against the welfare state, referring to it as an 'immediate danger' to freedom and human dignity.

The ginger-group ASM continued to be critical of the reforms, claiming that they actually worked to the disadvantage of the poorest pensioners. At a conference of the ASM held in January 1959 and attended by Erhard, Alexander Rüstow pointed out that social services were costing the Federal Republic DM33 billion per annum, even though the economy was booming. Yet many of the poorest citizens were still living in a fashion incompatible with human dignity. Social policy was a moral necessity, but it must be properly planned by the state and not allowed to proliferate like a jungle. It was paradoxical, but not inconsistent, that liberals should oppose a planned economy but insist that the framework within which the free market operated should be carefully planned. That applied to social policy. The distinction between the 'new liberals' and the 'old liberals' was that the

---

[62] Ibid. 333.   [63] Ibid. 336.

former accepted the need for this planned framework and the old liberals did not. Another speaker at the conference claimed that dynamic pensions had been 'a defensive measure designed to avoid a proper reform'.[64]

For the time being the still-rising production levels in the Federal Republic served to disguise negative aspects of the government's policies. Nevertheless, most liberal economists in Germany regard the dynamic-pensions law as a fateful deviation from the pure doctrine of the social market economy, and it has remained the object of constant criticism.

The dangerous principle of indexing social payments spread from pensions to other areas of the system, such as unemployment benefit. There was also a general laxity about monitoring the finances of the pension arrangements once the linkage between contributions and payments was removed. Thus no account was taken of those who retired early, even though they thereby reduced the amount of revenue coming into the state pension-funds. The percentage of their incomes that German workers had to pay in social-security contributions rose steadily, as did the tax burden. An increasingly unfavourable age-structure also meant that the prospects for future funding of such generous pensions were very bleak.[65] This was precisely the sort of inflexible encroachment of public debt on private incomes which liberal economists most detested. As the leading historian of this period in German history has pointed out, it was ironical that it was not Adenauer who paid the price for his profligacy, but Erhard, who had constantly warned of the dangers of a social-welfare system which could be maintained only at a time of boom and full employment. By the time these particular chickens came home to roost, Erhard was Chancellor.[66]

---

[64] See Koerfer, Kampf ums Kanzleramt, 133. On Röpke's views, see, e.g., W. Röpke, Welfare, Freedom and Inflation (London, 1957), 14–15; for Rüstow's speech and the comments by H. Neumeister about the dynamic pensions, see Aktionsgemeinschaft Soziale Marktwirtschaft, Tagungsprotokoll Nr. 12 (Ludwigsberg, 1959), 20 and 110–16 respectively.

[65] For critiques of the dynamic-pension policy see, e.g., Norbert Kloten, 'The Role of the Public Sector in the Social Market Economy', in Peacock and Willgerodt (eds.), German Neoliberals, 95–7. In 1961 the liberal Swiss economist Cario Mötteli claimed that social insurance contributions in West Germany could not go any higher. At that time old-age pension insurance stood at 14% of income. In 1971 contributions had risen beyond that level and it was estimated they would soon reach 18% of income. This excluded health insurance, which in 1961 had averaged 8.5% of income. See H. O. Lenel, 'Does Germany Still Have a Social Market Economy', in eid. (eds.), Germany's Social Market Economy, 263. This is a translation of Lenel's article in ORDO: Jahrbuch für die Ordnung von Wirtschaft und Gesellschaft, 22 (1971).

[66] H.-P. Schwarz, Die Ära Adenauer: Epochenwechsel, 1957–1963 (vol. iii of K. D. Bracher, T. Eschenburg, J. C. Fest, and E. Jäckel (eds.), Geschichte der Bundesrepublik Deutschland) (Stuttgart, 1983), 158.

TABLE 3. *Liberalization of West Germany's Private OEEC Imports*[a]

	30.6.1950	15.8.1952	31.12.1954	30.9.1956	30.6.1958
All goods	47 (56)[b]	80.9 (65)	90.1 (83.0)	91.5 (88.8)	94.0 (82.6)
Food and feeding stuffs		71.5	79.4 (79.3)	81.3 (82.7)	85.4 (78.8)
Raw materials		90.7	97.8 (91.6)	98.0 (97.6)	99.3 (88.7)
Manufactures		80.0	93.8 (78.2)	96.2 (84.8)	98.2 (79.3)

[a] Percentage share of imports without quantitative restrictions at the given date; weighted with 1949 import shares. State imports were exempted from the OEEC liberalization requirements.
[b] Bracketed figure is OEEC average, base year 1948.

Source: H. Giersch, K.-H. Paqué, and H. Schmieding, *The Fading Miracle: Four Decades of Market Economy in Germany* (Cambridge, 1992), 110.

It should not be thought, however, that the second half of the 1950s was just a period of defeat for the social market economy. Erhard himself was a living disproof of that. His popularity continued to be a feature of the political scene in the Federal Republic, so much so that he came to be regarded as Adenauer's natural successor as Chancellor. *Der Alte* did all he could to block this development, but without success.

Erhard's policies triumphed in so far as West Germany continued to stand for trade liberalization. A major step in this direction had been taken when the Federal Republic negotiated entry into GATT at the third round of the GATT negotiations held in Torquay, 1950–1. Although German tariffs were initially fairly high, Erhard used the success of Germany's export trade and the threat of imported inflation as reasons to cut import duties. Between 1955 and 1957 Erhard carried through five major rounds of unilateral tariff-reductions. The level of effective tariff-protection in the Federal Republic fell from 19.6 per cent to 10.6 per cent. So far as convertibility of currencies was concerned, Erhard gained some notoriety as a result of his enthusiastic support for this measure. Indeed, his energetic crusading was sometimes perceived by others as counter-productive.[67] Nevertheless, by 1959 all controls on foreign exchange and capital movements had gone, multilateral trade with other developed countries had been established, and German industry was exposed to competition from abroad in a way which it did not always appreciate (See Table 3).

[67] The British, in particular, were irritated by Erhard's uncompromising demands for complete liberalization, which, in May 1953, seemed to render their own attempts at a compromise reform of the EPU more difficult. See Kaplan and Schleiminger, *European Payments Union*, 196. On trade liberalization, see Giersch *et al.*, *The Fading Miracle*, 111.

This was particularly true in the field of heavy industry, where Erhard resolutely turned a deaf ear to protectionist pleas from self-interested pressure-groups, often supported by Adenauer. By the end of the decade there was overproduction of coal and it was clear that structural problems in the coal industry needed attention. Cheap oil imports were good for industry in general but bad news for coal. Adenauer expressed concern when pits were closed and jobs were lost, and Westrick—himself a former businessman—had to explain what a blessing it was that such developments were occurring at a time of booming expansion, when workers could be employed in other economic sectors.[68]

Berg and the BDI, in the councils of which smoke-stack production industries still had a disproportionately strong representation, were not impressed, and regarded oil imports as a form of treason. In December 1958 Erhard had been reluctantly forced to accept a voluntary cartel arrangement to limit oil imports into Germany and divide the domestic market between oil and coal interests. Like most such arrangements, this proved impractical because smaller oil firms ignored it and the larger ones were then forced to give it up. The Ruhr coal industry was faced with ruinously expensive overproduction. The irony of this cannot have been lost on Erhard, who, less than nine years previously, had nearly lost his post for playing down coal shortages. His ministry produced a very sound scheme, entirely compatible with the social market economy, according to which imported heating-oil should bear a tax, the proceeds of which could be used to aid restructuring in the coal industry, with a view to reducing the number of pits and retraining coal-miners.

Adenauer unexpectedly intervened at a Cabinet meeting on 28 August 1959, bitterly criticizing the Economics Ministry for lack of foresight and demanding a comprehensive energy policy for Germany. It is clear that his memories of the pre-war depression in the coalfields may have played a part in this, but a desire to humiliate Erhard was also probably a factor.[69] The BDI, supported in an unholy but not very surprising alliance by the coal-miners' unions and the SPD, entered the fray. Berg demanded a comprehensive *Zwangskartel*, or compulsory distribution arrangement, which would in effect have reintroduced the controlled economy in the field of energy. He justified this with the

---

[68] Author's interview with Ludger Westrick, 26 Sept. 1985. For an interesting example of Erhard's difficulties with the coal industry, see W. Abelshauser, 'Kohle und Marktwirtschaft: Ludwig Erhards Konflikt mit dem Unternehmensverband Ruhrbergbau 1957', *Vierteljahrshefte für Zeitgeschichte*, 33/3 (July 1985), 489–546.

[69] Koerfer, *Kampf ums Kanzleramt*, 382–3.

usual claim that West Germany had to be prepared to pay for self-sufficiency in fuel. This was an important moment in the post-war economic history of West Germany because, had Berg got his way, the bad old habit of propping up uneconomic industries with public money would have received a tremendous boost. As it was, Erhard's colleagues in the Cabinet and, above all, in the Bundestag, conducted a successful campaign to prevent this retrograde step. The heating-oil tax was accepted and the *Zwangskartel* dropped. German industry benefited from being able to use the fuel of its choice, but the coal-miners were compensated for loss of work and offered retraining. It was a classic example of self-liquidating state expenditure which met justified social needs.

Another area in which a success could be chalked up was that of distributing property amongst as large a section of the community as possible. One method of doing this was by giving tax concessions to small businesses, private insurance policies, small savers, and those building their own dwellings. The latter policy did lead to some extension of home ownership in Germany at this time, but the Germans were traditionally flat-dwellers rather than house-owners, and rented accommodation remained the norm.

More progress was made with the concept of 'people's shares' in industry. In the victorious Bundestag election campaign of 1957 Erhard had made great play with the notion of 'property for all'. Doubtless this was partly a defensive measure against Social Democratic calls for socialization and redistribution of wealth. But, thanks to the previous discussion of these issues in the ranks of social-market enthusiasts, the drive for a people's capitalism had a momentum of its own, and could even cause serious concern in the ranks of the SPD.[70]

Two major privatizations were carried through under Erhard's stewardship, that of the Preußag concern in 1959 and, far more spectacularly, that of the prestigious Volkswagenwerk in Wolfsburg in 1961. Volkswagen was a symbol of West German economic success, and its privatization marked a victory for the new Germany, since it had originally been set up under Hitler's auspices to produce a 'people's car'. The cars had become available to the people only after Hitler had been defeated and democracy restored. Now they could buy the plant as well, because shares were sold off in such a way that small investors received priority and those on low incomes could claim a discount on their purchases. So favourable was the situation at the time of flotation that the shares could quickly be resold at twice what

[70] See Ch. 14.

their purchasers had paid for them. It was perhaps no coincidence that this sale occurred shortly before the 1961 Bundestag elections. Already in the 1957 elections the attraction of 'people's shares' had been demonstrated. At that time the trade-union leaders in the Volkswagen works had refused Erhard a platform for an election speech, probably because they disliked the prospect of privatization. Thereupon Erhard's skilful political lieutenant, Karl Hohmann, arranged for every worker in the car-plant to be sent a letter pointing out that, under privatization, special arrangements would be made to ensure that the work-force were able to buy shares in the enterprise. When the votes were counted, Wolfsburg was gained for the CDU for the first time; hitherto it had been firmly social democratic.[71]

This certainly did Erhard's reputation no harm, and it was entirely in line with social-market theories. Apparently various policies to encourage savings had quite a powerful effect because in 1958 the state share in property accumulation fell from 38 per cent to 24.9 per cent, and it only rose slightly, to 26.9 per cent, in the following year. In 1961 it had risen again to 36.1 per cent but, given the overall rise in wealth in Germany, it was clear that private property ownership was growing. Unfortunately nemesis was looming in the shape of a recession in the mid-1960s which coincided with Erhard's own period in office as Chancellor. In 1965 he tried to repeat the Volkswagen success with the sale of another state concern, VEBA, but the fall in stock-market prices pulled the value of the stock down so far that purchasers would make a loss selling it. This put an end to 'people's shares'.[72] After Erhard's fall in 1966 the experiment was not repeated in Germany, though it was taken up with gusto in Mrs Thatcher's Britain and enjoyed a recrudescence of popularity outside Germany in the 1980s.

Another area in which progress was apparently being made was in the development of macro-economic advisory mechanism designed to instil responsibility into an already sophisticated German labour-force and prevent dangerous cyclical swings from rocking the socio-economic boat. In 1956 the *Wissenschaftlicher Beirat* of the Economics Ministry

---

[71] For the background to Volkswagen denationalization, see Reich, *Fruits of Fascism*, 189–201. Reich points out that Erhard faced resistance from the Finance Ministry, which controlled Volkswagen and did not want it privatized. He also claims that arrangements for the company's ownership did not entirely comply with Erhard's principles under the *Soziale Marktwirtschaft*: ibid. 194. I do not find Reich's suggestions of *dirigisme* towards Volkswagen by West German governments very convincing. He himself states that the company's management welcomed the lowering of tariff barriers because Volkswagen's superior product enabled it to benefit from free trade, ibid. 196. See also Koerfer, *Kampf ums Kanzleramt*, 158–9.

[72] For the sale of state enterprises, see Schwarz, *Epochenwechsel*, 158–60.

had recommended the establishment of an independent council of economic experts to give advice to the nation on economic policy. A law setting up this council of experts was passed by the Bundestag in 1963. The council was to evaluate the economic situation in the light of the four objectives considered most likely to guarantee prosperity. These were: price stability, a high level of employment, an external trade-balance, and steady economic growth.[73] Reports from this council were produced annually from November 1964 and reinforced calls for sensible economic policies—in addition to the admonitions of the Bundesbank and the Economics Ministry. On the other hand, the council was independent of the government, and its statements therefore had a greater ring of authority.

Nevertheless, the steam seemed to be going out of the social market economy by the end of the 1950s. For some, this was due to the feebleness of politicians who were too timid to implement it. In March 1958 the ASM published an 'action programme' designed to remind the political leadership of its duties. As we have seen, the ASM was sponsored or led by most of the leading figures in the neo-liberal camp, including Böhm, Röpke, and Rüstow. Erhard was an honorary member. Having pointed to the achievements of the social market since 1948, it asserted that, 'we are still very far from our goal. The social market economy has only been very imperfectly realized.' The ASM pointed in particular to sins against the holy ghost of the free market which had been committed by politicians in the Bundestag session of 1953–7. Despite material improvement, the development of the market-based competitive system had stumbled to a halt. The state was still interfering in too many aspects of the economy and favouring too many special interests. In place of this economic pluralism, the ASM demanded an independent policy formulated according to uniform principles (*aus einem Guß*). A democratic system with a social market economy could not be achieved by trying to correct the market with piecemeal planning-adjustments—what was later to be known as 'fine tuning'.

The ASM demanded a vigorous counter-offensive to answer the Communist threat—which, in the post-1956 atmosphere of intensified Cold War, was causing great concern on the right of the political spectrum in Germany. Such an offensive should stress the moral value of private property and emphasize the fact that state control of the means of production produced precisely that sort of exploitation and

---

[73] Giersch *et al.*, *The Fading Miracle*, 139.

oppression for which the Communists blamed private ownership.[74]

The ASM then issued concrete demands for the realization of the social market. Some of these were predictable enough—the value of the currency should be maintained as a matter of absolute priority and competition should be protected. To attain these ends there should be no privileged sections of society with inflation-proofed incomes or overmighty enterprises able to manipulate prices to the detriment of their weaker competitors. The anti-cartel law of 1957 allowed too many exceptions and was too weak to prevent unfair practices aimed at destroying competition. Just conditions of entry into the market should be protected by economic policy. The state was still not neutral in the way it regulated conditions of access to the market; any discrimination against medium and small enterprises must be rooted out. Public funds could be used to create a socially just education system, so long as the general level of wealth was not high enough to ensure that all citizens could finance their children's education in a way that was worthy of free human beings.

It warned against a wage–price spiral and criticized the privileged position of the trade unions under Article 9, paragraph 3 of the Basic Law, effectively the constitution of the Federal Republic. It approved of workers owning shares in their companies, but only suggested that the former be encouraged to save through tax incentives and vaguely defined improvements in the law relating to share transactions. Since no form of savings was to be given an advantage over any others, it is not easy to see how the objective of a share-owning working class was to be achieved.

The economic activities of the state should be restricted as far as possible. State enterprises should be privatized if their nature did not make it technically necessary for them to be run by the state. Atomic energy, which was arousing positive political interest at that time, should be carefully regulated, but run by private enterprise. The amount of the country's GNP taken up by the public sector was 'a very disturbing sickness' and should be curbed.

On the social front, the ASM demanded the rapid reduction of spending on public services, so that only those who could not afford to insure themselves against misfortune would be protected by the state. Any form of price controls should be dropped. The housing market should be liberated, with temporary help being given to needy tenants. A comprehensive social plan should be drawn up, with the evident aim of preventing individuals or families drawing double payment

---

[74] ASM, *Aktionsprogramm*. See fn. 53.

from different programmes. Pensions should be kept to a minimum and for anything above that, individuals should insure themselves. State benefits should not exceed the pay of those in work. Child allowances were not favoured, since a family should be responsible for its own children. Predictably, but illogically, income-tax concessions for parents were acceptable.

So far as the relationship between town and country was concerned, an even more bizarre concept of 'organic settlement policy' had found its way into the programme, together with the notion of semi-agricultural industrial communities. This echoed Gottfried Feder's fantasies in the early Nazi era. It was no surprise that the programme ended with an outburst of hostility against the welfare state. 'The best social policy is a good economic policy' was the motto. The state should be asked to help only when no other form of assistance was available—a principle described by the ASM as that of 'subsidiarity', by which it evidently understood a minimalist attitude to social welfare. The tone of the document is perhaps best captured in its final paragraph, which read: 'The Bolshevik East is drilling its underlings in Communism. We will only be able to overcome it if we learn to identify ourselves with, and to represent to others, the social order in the building of which we are engaged, and which can alone secure freedom and welfare.'[75] This programme was issued only a few months after the greatest Christian Democratic election victory in West Germany's history. Yet its tone was one of pessimism and frustration. It was markedly more conservative than the writings of neo-liberals in the 1930s and 1940s. With its stress on minimalist social welfare and complete 'neutrality' on the part of the state in economic affairs, it seemed to be heading towards a reassertion of those *laissez-faire* market principles which its protagonists had always strongly disowned. A number of factors may have been responsible for this; the Cold War atmosphere of the 1950s, the influence of business pressure-groups on the ASM, the weakness of social democratic opposition—which thus reduced the need for liberal economists to demonstrate social concern—and, perhaps more important but less easy to prove, the ageing process amongst an intellectual group which now tended towards a more pessimistic view of the future, even at a time when Germany was prospering as never before.

This tendency helped to limit the appeal of the social market economy to the younger generation. It became accepted that the word 'social' had been a cosmetic device to disguise the restoration of capitalism

[75] Ibid. 8.

T ABLE 4. *Economic Development of the Federal Republic, 1951–1963*

	Growth rate[a]	Price rises[b]	Unemployment[c]	Trade surplus[d]
1951	10.5	7.9	9.1	1.9
1952	8.9	2.0	8.5	2.5
1953	8.2	−1.7	7.6	3.8
1954	7.4	0.1	7.1	3.4
1955	12.0	1.6	5.2	2.4
1956	7.2	2.5	4.2	3.4
1957	5.7	2.3	3.5	4.1
1958	3.7	2.0	3.6	3.9
1959	7.3	1.1	2.5	3.4
1960	9.0	1.4	1.3	2.6
1961	4.4	2.3	0.9	2.2
1962	4.7	2.9	0.7	1.2
1963	2.8	3.0	0.9	1.5

[a] Percentage growth in GNP at 1980 prices.
[b] Annual adjustment of the price index for living costs of a four-person family in the wage-earning category.
[c] Percentage of those unemployed out of the total of employed and unemployed workers.
[d] Exports minus imports expressed as a percentage of GNP at current prices.

Source: D. Grosser, T. Lange, A. Müller-Armack, and B. Neuss, *Soziale Marktwirtschaft: Geschichte, Konzept, Leistung* (2nd edn.; Stuttgart, 1990), 229.

T ABLE 5. *Percentage Growth of GDP in Industrialized Countries, 1951–1965*

	1951–1955	1956–1960	1961–1965
Belgium	4.5[a]	2.6	5.0
FRG	9.5	6.5	5.0
Denmark	2.0	4.4	5.3
France	4.1	5.0	5.8
Britain	3.9[b]	2.6	3.1
Italy	5.5[c]	5.5	5.2
Netherlands	5.1	4.0	4.8
Austria	6.6	5.5	4.3
Sweden	3.4	4.3	5.2
Switzerland	5.0	4.3	5.3
Spain	5.2[d]	3.5	8.5
USA	4.1	2.3	4.6
Japan	7.2[b]	8.6	10.2
AVERAGE	5.1	4.5	5.6

[a] 1954/5
[b] 1953/4
[c] 1952/5
[d] 1955

Source: D. Grosser *et al.*, *Soziale Marktwirtschaft: Geschichte, Konzept, Leistung* (2nd edn.; Stuttgart, 1990), 232.

after the war. For a generation or more, the social market economy lost its hold, first on the young and then on the electorate.

However, in October 1963, when Erhard left the Economics Ministry to become only the second Federal Chancellor in the Federal Republic's history, he certainly did not look doomed to failure. On the contrary, his social market economy seemed to have achieved its final triumph. The economy was in fine shape, with unemployment below 1.5 per cent, and labour productivity in manufacturing growing by 5 per cent per annum. A current-account deficit in 1962, which had arisen as a result of revaluation of the mark the previous year, had reverted to a healthy surplus in 1963, and by 1964 the growth rate of real GDP was up to an annual average of 6.7 per cent, having been only 2.8 per cent in 1963.[76] Nevertheless, the growth rates in the 1960s were not to be as spectacular as those in the previous decade (see Tables 4 and 5).

Erhard also had his successes in the area of trade liberalization. In May 1963, he went to Geneva to participate in the GATT conference which set in train the process of world-wide tariff-reductions known as the Kennedy Round. Erhard's role in the conference was so important that the American ambassador in Bonn, George McGhee, enthusiastically declared it should more properly be called the Erhard Round. Certainly Erhard warmly supported GATT's free-trade policies.[77]

As an 'Atlanticist', Erhard showed less enthusiasm for the bilateral relationship with France which Adenauer had favoured. De Gaulle complained that the Franco-German treaty of January 1963 had not been consummated and that he was 'still a virgin'. Erhard's supporters felt that Germany was more likely to be the partner ravished in such a liaison. They wanted to improve relationships with the Anglo-Saxon powers. In June 1965 Müller-Armack drew up a memorandum as a basis for negotiations between the European Community and EFTA. He pointed to Germany's interest in developing trade with EFTA countries. French obstruction prevented progress on this front, however.[78]

The social side of the government's programme made respectable progress, with agreement between Bonn and the *Länder* in June 1964 to expand universities and improve scholarship facilities for needy students. *Startgleichheit* moved nearer to reality. In 1965 a law was passed 'for the creation of property', designed to encourage labour

---

[76] Giersch *et al.*, *The Fading Miracle*, 142.

[77] K. Hildebrand, *Von Erhard zur Großen Koalition, 1963–1969* (vol. iv of K. D. Bracher, T. Eschenburg, J. C. Fest, and E. Jäckel (eds.), *Geschichte der Bundesrepublik Deutschland*) (Stuttgart, 1984), 36.

[78] Ibid. 106–7.

contracts which included provisions for employees to own shares in their companies.

Yet Erhard was not a success as Chancellor. He was not able to control his ministerial colleagues, who felt themselves released from the iron grip of *Der Alte*. Public spending began to rise ominously. In 1965 the Federal budget rose by 8 per cent, whereas the gross national product grew by only 5 per cent. Spring 1965 saw inflation at 3.2 per cent—a figure which would be regarded as highly satisfactory in most countries, but which caused anxiety in West Germany.[79]

In the Bundestag elections of September 1965, Erhard's popularity seemed undimmed, and he was once again the electoral locomotive which pulled his party to victory. His commitment to the social market was somewhat overshadowed in the election campaign by a more grandiose slogan offering the public a 'formed society' (*formierte Gesellschaft*). This was a woolly concept which had evidently been invented for electoral purposes in imitation of Lyndon B. Johnson's 'great society' slogan in the 1964 American presidential contest. Despite Erhard's success in the election campaign, he did not win an overall majority, and his coalition partners, the FDP, fared comparatively badly at the polls.

Once the elections were over, it was clear that action had to be taken to cool the overheating economy. In November 1965 the council of economic experts produced a report entitled *Stabilization without Stagnation*, in which it urged a concerted effort by government, employers, and unions to take steady action against inflation by moderating wage demands and gradually tightening both monetary and fiscal policy. The aim was to calm the boom down without sudden deflationary measures or a profit squeeze.[80] Erhard's government, however, preferred more rapid and less co-ordinated action. The Bundestag passed a law to secure a balanced budget, and in May 1966 the Bundesbank raised interest rates to 5 per cent. Domestic demand was sharply reduced.

The result of this rather panicky response to a situation which was by no means near a crisis was a severe drop in private investment and a mild rise in unemployment, to a peak of 3.2 per cent in February 1967. Although in reality the country was still prosperous, German public opinion—looking back to the inter-war period—became nervous. A poll taken in summer 1966 showed that 20 per cent of those ques-

---

[79] Ibid. 124 ff.
[80] Giersch *et al.*, *The Fading Miracle*, 144.

tioned thought a 1929-type slump to be 'certain' and another 42 per cent thought it 'fairly probable'.[81]

Meanwhile Erhard's position as Chancellor was being sabotaged by his enemies within the CDU, ranging from Adenauer and Strauß to the Federal President, Heinrich Lübke. Even the Free Democrats, who had previously supported Erhard, became unreliable after the elections, influenced, no doubt, by the belief that, with Erhard as Chancellor, voters would not feel the need for an independent liberal party. The FDP was also unwilling to take the responsibility for tax increases which might upset its wealthier constituents. At the end of October 1966 matters came to a head and the FDP left the coalition. Their behaviour showed how wise Erhard had been to make his career in the CDU, but he had neglected to buttress his own support within that party, and Strauß's Bavarian CSU had never been reliable. By the end of November 1966 Erhard's position had become untenable and he resigned. On 1 December his ministry was replaced by a Christian-Social Democratic coalition led by Georg Kiesinger.

Kiesinger's Minister of Economic Affairs was Karl Schiller, the Hamburg professor who, as a student, had been so impressed by Rüstow's impassioned speech to the *Verein für Socialpolitik* in 1932.[82] Schiller attempted to put into effect an active economic policy designed to achieve Eucken's objectives of price stability, economic growth, and an 'enlightened market economy with social commitment'.[83] In fact it was a form of macro-economic planning—or 'global steering'—using public expenditure and taxation policy as a way of nudging the economy out of recession. It involved joint consultations with business and trade-union leaders in 'concerted action' to obtain socially beneficial economic growth. The whole scheme really owed as much to Keynes as to Eucken and was unpopular with most neo-liberal observers. Initially it seemed very successful: within a year there was a 'partly export-led upswing in which the incomes of the self-employed shot up by 18%'.[84]

In one sense Schiller's achievement was a tribute to the social market economy, since the social democrats demonstrated that they had jettisoned the command economy in favour of a market system. On the other hand, 'global steering' proved only temporarily effective. The disciplines of the market began to be ignored in the unwise belief that endless economic growth would soak up the growing costs of an

---

[81] Hildebrand, *Von Erhard zur Großen Koalition*, 207.
[82] See above, Ch. 2.
[83] Grosser *et al.*, *Soziale Marktwirtschaft*, 37.
[84] Berghahn, *The Americanisation of West German Industry*, 303.

ambitious public sector. The late 1960s and early 1970s were a period of post-Keynesian complacency—a complacency which was rudely shaken by the impact of the oil shock of 1973 and the debilitating effects of the Vietnam War on the American economy.

In the meantime, however, the warnings of the neo-liberals went unheeded. The social market economy seemed to have been overtaken by a more ambitious social agenda. There had also been an important change in the cultural climate of West Germany. The building of the Berlin Wall in 1961 and the apparent Western victory over Khrushchev in the Cuban missiles crisis had helped to create a new atmosphere. On the one hand, refugees from East Germany no longer kept on reinforcing the fear of Communism; on the other, the feeling of security established in the West encouraged the younger generation to rebel against its parents. Aspects of the Nazi past which West Germans had been eager to forget were now being investigated anew, and Cold War anti-Communism was supplanted by 'anti-Fascism' as the modish stance of the young intelligentsia. The supporters of the social market economy were attacked as Cold Warriors, which they may indeed have been, and Fascists, which they certainly were not.

To take one example, in 1972 the journal *Kyklos* published an article by Hajo Riese in which he accused Walter Eucken of being theoretically barren and simply concerned to defend the capitalist market economy. In a particularly offensive passage, he criticized Eucken for thinking that at one point people chose the market economy for all time. This, according to Riese, showed that Eucken was a victim of the *Zeitgeist* in the Third Reich, because the 'Fascist Leader state' had drawn its legitimation from a singular act of the popular will.[85] Similar outbursts of radical hysteria lumped all socially conservative Germans together as part of a reactionary élite who had supposedly benefited from the Third Reich. The fact that the younger generation of Germans was now asking awkward questions about the Nazi past made it easy for the supporters of the social market to be tarred with the brush of guilt-by-association, even if, as we have seen, most of them had opposed National Socialism, and their neo-liberal theories were quite incompatible with the type of nationalist *dirigisme* practised by Schacht, Funk, Goering, and Speer.

---

[85] H. Riese, 'Ordnungsidee und Ordnungspolitik: Kritik einer wirtschaftspolitischen Konzeption', *Kyklos: Internationale Zeitschrift für Sozialwissenschaften*, 25 (1972). Böhm was furious about this article but urged his colleagues to counter it with rational argument rather than personal invective. Böhm to Meyer, 17 Apr. 1972, Böhm NL, KAS I-200-007/2.

16

The SPD and the Triumph of Reform

FROM 13 to 15 November 1959, the Social Democratic Party of Germany (SPD) met at Bad Godesberg—only a short distance from the West German parliament on the outskirts of Bonn. The purpose of this specially summoned party congress was to deliberate over, and agree upon, a new fundamental programme for German social democracy, the first completely redrafted statement of objectives since that produced at the Heidelberg party congress in 1925.

In the first part of the Godesberg Programme one could read the following: 'Democratic socialism, which in Europe is rooted in Christian ethics, in humanism, and in classical philosophy, has no intention of proclaiming absolute truths . . . The SPD is the party of intellectual freedom [*Freiheit des Geistes*].'[1]

The section of the document which dealt with economic and social matters contained the following passage: 'The aim of social democratic economic policy is constantly growing prosperity and a just distribution of the fruits of the economy amongst all the population; a life in freedom without degrading dependence on others and free from exploitation.'

To achieve this happy condition the modern state would certainly have to influence the economy, particularly through decisions about taxes and finances, fiscal and credit policies, and related matters.

The state cannot evade this responsibility for the out-turn [*Ablauf*] of the economy. It is responsible for a forward-looking policy to control the business cycle, and should restrict itself mainly to indirect methods of influencing the economy. Free consumer-choice and free choice of work-place, free competition and free initiative on the part of the entrepreneur are important elements in it . . . The totalitarian directed economy destroys freedom.[2]

None of this seems particularly remarkable now. It resembles many other party programmes which promise much, deliver little, and are actually read by very few voters. Yet at that time, in 1959, the Godesberg Programme could be seen as a daring document. It con-

---

[1] *Grundsatzprogramm der Sozialdemokratischen Partei Deutschlands. Beschlossen vom außerordentlichen Parteitag der SPD in Bad Godesberg vom 13. bis 15. November 1959* (hereafter cited as *Godesberger Programme*) (Bonn, n.d.), 5–6.

[2] *Godesberger Programme*, 18–19.

tained no mention of the socialization of the means of production, distribution, and exchange. Instead of talk of class conflict, there was the demand for a more just distribution of the national product, a reformist rather than a revolutionary objective. Marx was not mentioned in the programme—unless he could be seen as part of the Christian and humanist tradition referred to in the section on fundamental principles.

Such moderation was not calculated to win the hearts and minds of dedicated traditionalists within German social democracy. SPD leaders were so uncertain about the reception which would be given to this policy statement that they even considered abandoning the special party conference and shelving the programme itself. In the event, they decided it was too late to draw back and the proceedings went ahead. The result was a chorus of public praise, even from sections of the press not usually sympathetic to the SPD. Doubters at once became enthusiasts, and the new, post-Marxist social democracy could present itself as a realistic choice for the German electors, who were beginning to tire of Adenauer's rule.[3]

As we have seen, the liberalization of the SPD's programme being demanded by men like Eichler and Schiller would have been scarcely credible when the party re-emerged into German politics after the tribulations of the Third Reich. The rejection of the class-war doctrine was not easy to achieve in a party historically associated with it, despite the changing climate of opinion created by the Cold War. Some distinguished Marxists remained influential in the party—prominent amongst whom was Wolfgang Abendroth.

Although East Germany was a poor advertisement for planning, the mid-1950s witnessed a great deal of interest in what was going on in Yugoslavia, where an independent Communist regime was apparently having some success with socialist production-methods involving a form of workers' control. Since the depressing results of this experiment had yet to reveal themselves, left-wing critics of the market economy could see the Yugoslav model as an attractive alternative.[4]

However, the position of those social democrats who wanted to jettison the old shibboleths of socialization seemed greatly strengthened by the victory of Adenauer's CDU/CSU government in the Bundestag elections of September 1953. The Christian parties increased their share of the poll from 31 per cent to 45.2 per cent, whereas the SPD, despite

---

[3] Schwarz, *Epochenwechsel*, 198.

[4] See, e.g., K. Schiller, 'Sozialismus und Wettbewerb', in C. Schmid *et al.* (eds.), *Grundfragen moderner Wirtschaftspolitik*, 249–50.

gaining a million votes, stagnated in percentage terms. In 1949 the party might have seemed within striking distance of its main opponents. Now, however, it looked a hopeless also-ran. In various ways this result reflected badly on the old-style methods and programme of the SPD. A new look, and perhaps new men, were needed.

Another factor shifting the balance of forces in the SPD towards a position more favourable to the social market economy was the growing importance of the party's parliamentary delegation in Bonn. Under Schumacher the party apparatus, housed in the forbidding 'barracks' building on the road from Bonn to Bad Godesberg, had been the decisive force in the party's decision-making process. But, as the Federal parliament began to legislate, and after Schumacher had died in 1952, the parliamentary politicians—organized in their *Fraktion*— came to exercise greater influence. Among them were many who had grown impatient with the old dogmas and who were eager to turn the SPD into a genuine 'people's party'. They included Heinrich Deist, Fritz Erler, Carlo Schmid, and Herbert Wehner.

The Bundestag delegation met regularly, four times a week. It had access to good sources of information about political events and it could also keep in touch with public opinion in the constituencies. In this respect it could claim to have an advantage over those working in the somewhat claustrophobic isolation of the party headquarters.[5]

It may perhaps be useful to look more closely at one member of the Bundestag delegation, since he was to play an important role in the economic counsels of the party. This was Heinrich Deist. Whereas men like Erler and Wehner concentrated mainly on improving the organization and general political appeal of the party, Heinrich Deist was one of the architects of a more pragmatic approach to economic matters. Deist's whole career had been shaped by the tragic history of the SPD in the Weimar Republic. His father had been a printer and an active member of the SPD under the less-than-benevolent regime of Kaiser Wilhelm II. After the revolution of 1918/19 he became Prime Minister of the tiny state of Anhalt. Meanwhile his son Heinrich studied law and entered the Prussian civil service, where his social-democratic allegiance made him an obvious candidate for a responsible post in the police administration. Having reached the rank of *Regierungsrat* in the Prussian Ministry of the Interior by the time Hitler came to power, he was rapidly dismissed, and had to keep himself going by working in his wife's stationery business. He trained as an auditor and worked freelance until the end of the Second World War, even managing

---

[5] Klotzbach, *Der Weg zur Staatspartei*, 276–7.

to find time to obtain a doctorate in political science at Cologne University. Shortly after Hitler was defeated, Deist resumed his activities in the labour movement and was appointed a trade-union representative on the supervisory board set up by the occupying powers to control the German iron and steel industry. He was also involved as a union representative on the boards of mining industries, and had therefore gained an appreciation of the practicalities of economic life before he was elected to the Bundestag in 1953.[6] Deist could be seen as a pragmatic man who was drawn into the process of reforming the SPD's economic programme by what he perceived to be the dictates of common sense.

He found himself collaborating with reformers whose own opinions were far from uniform. For Weisser and those who had worked with the party in the 1920s, the key was to get the message across to the electorate that democratic socialism accepted competition and consumer choice and was based on humane ideals, not Soviet ideology. This would still involve laying great stress on the difference between capitalism and the more pluralistic, market-orientated type of socialism they favoured. For Schiller and other, more pragmatic, newcomers in the party, including Helmut Schmidt, the object of the exercise was to educate the SPD in market economics and to present the electorate with a fundamentally liberal economic system modified by steering mechanisms and full-employment strategies of a Keynesian type. In the end the latter course proved the easier to implement—at least in the economic sphere. The contrast between the two approaches did not, however, make it easier to achieve consensus in the party in the barren decade after the 1949 elections, when the fruits of office seemed likely to be permanently denied to the SPD.

None the less, it was a sign of the times when Erich Ollenhauer, the party leader, for whom the election had been a personal defeat in a contest with Adenauer, made a conciliatory and moderate speech in the Bundestag at the beginning of the new parliament on 28 October. He specifically rejected the accusation that his party stood for a planned or command economy. Rather he stressed precisely those phrases in the action programme which accepted free consumer-choice, competition, and entrepreneurial initiative.[7] This comment was greeted with a mixture of *Schadenfreude* and disbelief in the conservative press.

Weisser was so incensed by this that he wrote to Ollenhauer complaining that the Dortmund action programme had placed too much stress on the acceptance of market forces and not enough on the

---

[6] Ibid. 375.   [7] Ibid. 288–91.

more radical aspects of reformist policies which, he insisted, had been gestating since the 1920s. In particular he referred to the redistribution of wealth and the encouragement of different forms of economic enterprise, by which he evidently meant co-operatives and municipal undertakings. Instead of appealing to the young in a positive way, the Dortmund action programme had sounded like an admission of guilt (*Sündenbekenntnis*). Skilful propaganda had created a situation in which those whom the SPD should be fighting with all its strength were able to breathe a sigh of relief and say 'Aha—at last they have become bourgeois'. Even Ollenhauer's Bundestag speech had been twisted in this sense.[8]

In an article he published to combat such notions, Weisser claimed that men like Böhm—whom he personally respected—knew perfectly well that the issue was not just a crude choice between state direction and 'freedom'. In any case, it was time the neo-liberals faced up to some socialist questions. What type of person was being favoured in their society? Did they just want a community in which the predominant motive was making money? How could they just shut their eyes to the lack of equality at the start of life which rendered 'competition' so unfair?[9]

Schiller, on the other hand, saw Ollenhauer's speech in a far more positive light. He told the economics subcommittee of the party executive in early December 1953 that the elections had been lost because in 1948/9 the SPD had mistakenly allowed itself to be identified with planning and controls. Of course, it should not now simply throw planning overboard; the liberalization of social-democratic economic policy ought not to be allowed just to degenerate into an acceptance of neo-liberalism. Nevertheless, they had to distance themselves more clearly than before from total planning, the command economy, or bureaucratic controls.[10] What people wanted was a clear-cut economic programme. A mish-mash of different solutions would compare badly with the dazzling consistency of earlier programmes—'from Marx to

---

[8] Copy of a letter from Weisser to Ollenhauer, 8 Nov. 1953, FES PV Bestand Wipo, 0018, 'Weisser Briefwechsel'.

[9] G. Weisser, *Für oder gegen Marktwirtschaft. Eine falsche Frage: Bemerkungen eines Sozialisten zu einem Artikel von Franz Böhm* (2nd edn.; Cologne, 1954), 4–6. The pamphlet refers to an article by Böhm in the *Frankfurter Allgemeiner Zeitung*, 24 Oct. 1953: 'Marktwirtschaft von links und rechts' [Market Economy from the Left and the Right]. Böhm welcomed the prospect that the SPD might embrace the market and claimed that a competition between market economies of the 'left' and 'right' would be far from the worst thing that could happen to Germany. See *Franz Böhm. Reden und Schriften*, ed. E. J. Mestmäcker (Karlsruhe, 1960), 149–57.

[10] Protocol of Wipo meeting, 4 and 5 Dec. 1953, p. 2, FES PV Bestand Wipo, L5 01603.

Murks', as Schiller put it. They needed a lively formula to encapsulate their position, and of all those suggested he preferred 'market economy of the left' (*Marktwirtschaft von links*). This, he claimed, had been the only slogan to take root during the election campaign.

The importance of the neo-liberal challenge to the SPD is illustrated by Schiller's comment that Franz Böhm himself was openly criticizing the failings of the 'market economy of the right' in the Federal Republic. The 'left' market economy should not involve a long list of objectives, but rather set the tone of an economic system in which justice, fair dealing, security against crises, and the highest possible level of employment should be the objectives. This meant tough anti-cartel laws and measures to create market transparency. Wealth should be more equitably distributed, but social policy should not be too ambitious, lest it weaken the economy.[11] There was nothing in that to which Rüstow or Müller-Armack could have taken objection. Even *Mitbestimmung* was not taken for granted by Schiller; it could, he said, be taken too far and might create confusion in the economy. The trade unions would do better to imitate their American colleagues and concentrate on the struggle in the labour market itself.

As for socialization, that had been discredited by what was happening in the Soviet zone of occupation. Rather than produce draft laws for the expropriation of industry, they should urge the Bundestag to start an inquiry into the ownership of, and working relationships within, German heavy industry. They could then consider reforms in the system of share ownership and the nature of corporate organization.

With pardonable enthusiasm for his own role in changing the image of his party, he referred back to the Bochum meeting in February 1953 as if it were a major watershed in the SPD's history.[12]

Although Schiller's views were supported by several academic members of the committee, the reaction of professional politicians and trade-union functionaries—like Heinrich Deist—was decidedly less enthusiastic. One trade unionist, Spathen, expressed anxiety lest people like himself should find themselves 'to the left of the SPD' and urged a slower tempo in the process of reorientation. The idea of an inquiry into heavy industries was seen by several present, including Veit, the chairman of the committee, as a means of burying socialism. Veit himself made it clear that he would be most unhappy about using cosmetic adjectives such as 'social' or 'left' to cover up the cloven hoof

---

[11] Ibid., p. 3.
[12] Ibid., p. 5. See above, pp. 317–18.

of the free market. He reminded his listeners that they were committed to introducing a draft law to socialize basic industries.[13]

The views of many moderate men were summed up by Heinrich Deist when he said that they could not reject all policies which had been compromised by events in East Germany—if they did that they might as well give up. The idea of a fully planned economy had been dead in the SPD since the early years of the Weimar Republic. On the other hand, they could not let the pendulum swing too radically in the other direction or they might lose the 8 million voters who had supported them at the recent elections. What was needed was more practical proposals for problem areas like heavy industry, energy, transport, and agriculture.

In his reply to the discussion Schiller assured the committee that market economics were an instrument and not a philosophy (*Weltanschauung*); nobody believed in the 'predestined harmony' of Leibniz. It was just a matter of influencing the form of the market by a state policy of protection for competition.[14] Socialization was not an immediate problem and he did not think the workers in the industries concerned were very enthusiastic about it. Fritz Baade, one of Schiller's supporters, pointed out that the CDU had broken through into the Protestant electorate of Germany and something had to be done if subsequent defeats were to be avoided. The social democrats needed to clear up their relationship with the Protestant church. Another delegate, von Eynern from Berlin, put the blame for defeat on theoreticians like himself for not having developed a clear economic concept to counter that of the neo-liberals. He saw the key issues as the distribution of wealth and equal opportunities (*Startgleichheit*). In this, as in other respects, the shadow of the social market economy loomed over the SPD's discussions.

The committee could not agree to Schiller's demands for an inquiry, but fell back on the time-honoured expedient of setting up subcommittees to discuss particular problems. By April the following year some of these had reported back and the committee was asked to make recommendations to the party executive. It submitted a memorandum in which the socialization issue was played down. The executive itself rejected this memorandum, much to Schiller's fury. He wrote an angry letter to Veit pointing out that the recommendations had in any case been a compromise and that Willi Eichler, who had been made responsible for considering the fundamental principles underlying social democracy, had participated in the discussion.[15]

---

[13] Ibid., pp. 13–14.   [14] Ibid., pp. 16–17.
[15] Schiller to Veit, 5 May, 1954, FES PV Bestand Wipo, L6 01604.

The whole issue was discussed again on 7–8 May and a new set of proposals produced which did reject 'capitalist' economic policies designed to squeeze the utmost amount of production out of working people—though it was careful to reject also 'Fascist' and 'Bolshevik' methods directed to the same end. It also favoured taking iron and steel and energy industries into public ownership, although this was justified by the argument that in these industries competition could not sensibly be expected to operate and concentrations of economic power were inevitable.[16]

Otherwise the recommendations stressed the need for a combination of market economics and planning, economic freedom and social security. There should be a coherent and dynamic policy of encouraging competition and ensuring proper distribution of wealth. Measures needed included laws to control monopolies and cartels, the reform of company law to ensure transparency of the market, free choice and protection for consumers, and co-determination for workers. With the possible exception of the still-extensive plans for public ownership, all this was compatible with the social market economy but that, needless to say, was not mentioned. The parameters of the debate were gradually being redrawn. The recommendations did also include the stipulation that there should be a national economic budget to help nudge the market in the right direction, but that was as much a matter of emphasis as a radical alternative to neo-liberalism—a 'market economy of the left'. In a final plea for more equitable distribution of wealth—which of course the neo-liberals also favoured—the recommendations accepted that the masses should have the chance to build up their own property, which, it was claimed, was 'a precondition for the free development of the independent personality'.[17] It was a long way from the Erfurt Programme, and it was far from pleasing everybody in the SPD.

The extent to which Schiller's 'market economy of the left' disturbed traditional social democrats—especially the middle ranks of the party and union apparatus—is illustrated by the reaction of Viktor Agartz, who was now a leading figure in the German trade-union federation (DGB). At the federation's conference, held in October 1954, Agartz infuriated Schiller, and upset even the more moderate members of the subcommittee, by delivering an aggressive speech in which he

---

[16] *nicht sinnvoll möglich* was the phrase used. See 'Empfehlungen zur Wirtschaftspolitik', 8 May 1954, ibid.
[17] Ibid.

roundly denounced market economics as being incompatible with socialism. Like Schiller in his remarks to the Wipo committee the previous December. Agartz harked back to 1948, but the lessons he drew from the experiences of that period were very different. He told his trade-union audience that currency reform had been carried through at the expense of small savers and pensioners, leaving those with access to real wealth untouched. There had never been such a blatant piece of capitalist expropriation. What had occurred was simply a 'restoration' of the old élites who had set the social tone in the Third Reich and were now justifying their reappearance by parading their anti-Communism. As Agartz darkly remarked, 'By no means everybody who demonstrates his hostility to the East is a good and reliable democrat.'[18]

Agartz pooh-poohed the idea of share ownership for workers, saying it would only affect a very small number of people and it might inhibit trade-union wage bargaining.

More provocative than this, however, was the peroration with which he ended his speech—a full-blooded attack on market economics. It was, he flatly stated, impossible to create a market based on free competition. Nor could the lame formula 'As much freedom as possible' disguise the true state of affairs in the economy. He shrewdly pointed out that well over half Germany's GNP was produced in areas, such as agriculture, transport, banking, and housing, which were not governed by market forces and, even in the other half, many products like motor cars, cigarettes, books, and pharmaceuticals were covered by price-fixing arrangements. He calculated that only about 30 per cent of GNP came from what could be described as a 'free' market. He also drew a sharp distinction between the 'freedom' which meant equal rights for all in a democratic society and the egoistical 'freedom' of the propertied middle-class citizen concerned only with personal enrichment.

'On the one hand we have democratic freedom, the legal equality of all, and the recognition of the value of human life, and on the other, the liberal freedom for competition, the war of all against all, and the exploitation of others.'[19]

At the end of the Second World War capitalism had been so discredited that its supporters had realized the need to distance it from

---

[18] Viktor Agartz, 'Wirtschafts- und Steuerpolitik: Grundsätze und Programme des DGB', p. 1–5, FES PV Bestand Wipo, L6 01610.
[19] Ibid., p. 20.

Fascism. At the same time they wanted to present it as the real alternative to the totalitarian system in the East. So they had gone back to the old liberal concept of freedom which declared itself to be freedom for the consumer and competition, but which was in fact freedom for the propertied, freedom for private profit, and freedom for capitalists to dispose of their property and their labour-force as they saw fit: 'Market economics is economic liberalism; it is the economic system of the *bourgeois*, not however the ideal of the citizen of a democratic state.'

It was clear that he saw planning and socialization measures as essential to combat such 'freedom', which, he also implied, was being exploited to restore Nazis to positions of power and influence in Germany. Once again, the social market economy was being denounced as a cosmetic device—a mixture of hypocrisy and greed. Agartz ended his speech with an emotional appeal to socialist solidarity—'Brothers, to the Sun! to Freedom!'[20]

Agartz's outspokenness aroused considerable dismay amongst the SPD's reformers, and even Veit was concerned that Agartz had not consulted with his colleagues in the Wipo committee, despite the fact that he was nominally a member of it. By late autumn, feelings were running so high that the subcommittee felt it would have to thrash matters out with Agartz, and his speech was circulated, together with some highly critical comments which bore the hallmarks of Schiller's views.

It was pointed out that demagogic attacks on the market would be perceived by the public as support for the command economy, the dreaded *Zwangswirtschaft*.

If Agartz, who—despite repeated invitations—has refused to participate in the work of the economics subcommittee or the preparation of the action programme, is now going publicly to attack the formulation of that programme 'As much competition as possible' . . . then he is acting as a bull in the china shop of German social democracy, because out there among the electorate they will only understand this as a polemic against the market economy.[21]

Agartz eventually agreed to meet the committee on 9 December and denied trying to suggest that the trade unions should take over the function of government—a syndicalist implication which Helmut Schmidt, in particular, had found objectionable in the speech. Nevertheless, the division of opinion about market economics remained

---

[20] Ibid., pp. 21–2.
[21] Comments circulated by Pass, 3 Nov. 1954, FES PV Bestand Wipo, L6 01604. See also discussion by Wipo, 3 Dec. 1954, FES PV Bestand Wipo, L6 01601.

unresolved, even though Agartz was clearly out of tune with most of those on the economics subcommittee over the matter.[22]

It was not only in trade-union circles that rumblings against the market and competition could be heard. At the SPD congress in Berlin in July 1954 free consumer-choice was attacked by one irate delegate as 'liberal ballast', which should be thrown overboard and replaced by a commitment to meeting proven needs. It was claimed that the workers in East Berlin who had rebelled against Ulbricht's dictatorship the previous year had not done so for the sake of Erhard's market economy. Veit himself answered this point by saying that simply meeting proven needs (*Bedarfsdeckung*) would involve giving up a lot of freedom, whereas the SPD's aim was to combine socialism with freedom. Competition should be employed where it fulfilled social functions. Cartels, for example, should be prohibited, since they sought to regulate the economy for the benefit of private interests.[23]

Schiller himself stressed that for social democrats competition was just one tool in their working equipment, to be used as required. It was not an end in itself as was the case for liberal economists: 'It is part of the liberal ideology that competition and planning are incompatible . . . but we socialists are of the opinion that competition and planning can be combined with one another.'[24] He went on to demand a law to ensure full employment, a proposal which most neo-liberals would have viewed with distaste.

Despite the fact that the economics section of the 1954 programme was headed with Schiller's formula 'As much competition as possible, as much planning as necessary', the 1954 congress did not mark as sweeping a change in the party's character as many reformers would have liked.

In the years which followed, the old distrust of competition and the market mechanism repeatedly showed itself, and the matter was not helped from the reformers' point of view by the fact that Veit, who remained chairman of the executive's economics subcommittee, was himself cool on the issue. Indeed, remarks made by him at the party congress held in Munich in July 1956 reopened old wounds.

Veit claimed that unscrupulous propaganda from the right, which had falsely accused the SPD of favouring the hated *Zwangswirtschaft*, had forced the SPD to go perhaps too far in the direction of the free market. There was, however, no further need for misunderstanding:

---

[22] Protocol of Wipo meeting, 9 Dec. 1954, FES PV Bestand Wipo, L6 01604.
[23] *Protokoll der Verhandlungen des Parteitages des Sozialdemokratischen Partei Deutschlands vom 20 bis 24 Juli 1954 in Berlin* (hereafter cited as *Berlin Protocol*) (n.p., n.d.), 185–6.
[24] Ibid. 326. See also Klotzbach, *Der Weg zur Staatspartei*, 321.

'Today everything is clear. We are not the last detachment of the Erhard Brigade. We are still worlds apart from him.'

The aims of the SPD's economic policy were full employment, just distribution of wealth, and the stability of the currency: 'It is an error to believe that these targets can be achieved by themselves through the free play of [market] forces.'[25]

These comments drew severe criticism from Helmut Schmidt and others, who feared that the party's commitment to competition was still not clear enough, and that the electorate might be persuaded to associate the SPD with rationing and controls.[26]

Generally speaking, however, these years saw a steady advance of those in the party who wanted to adopt a more flexible approach to economic matters and who were prepared to jettison the Marxist 'ballast' of class war and historical determinism. The reasoning and objectives of such people had many affinities with those of the supporters of the social market economy, even if Social Democrats were careful not to identify themselves with neo-liberals.

After the 1953 election débâcle a commission was set up to propose reforms in the non-organizational aspects of the party's functions. Schiller played a part in drafting its conclusions, along with Fritz Erler, a rising star in the party, and himself a force for moderation and common sense. So far as the theoretical position of the party was concerned, a minority wanted to include the blunt statement that: 'to the extent that the SPD ever was a Marxist party, it no longer is one in the dogmatic sense invented by its opponents'.[27]

The majority preferred a more involved formulation rejecting any similarity between social democracy and Soviet Communism and quoting the declaration of the refounded Socialist International in July 1951—a declaration of which Eichler had been a co-author and which included the following words: 'Irrespective of whether socialists draw their convictions from Marxist or other forms of social analysis or whether they base them on religious or humanitarian principles, they are all striving for the same objective: a community based on social justice, freedom, and peace.'

It pointed out that the Dortmund action programme was founded on those principles and that the forthcoming congress at Berlin would

---

[25] Protokoll der Verhandlungen des Parteitages der SPD 10–14 Juli 1956 in München (Bonn, n.d.) 194. For reference to the 'Erhard Brigade', see above, Ch. 15.

[26] Protocol of Wipo meeting, 6 Oct. 1956, FES PV Bestand Wipo, 01605.

[27] 'Beratungsergebnisse der Kommission zur Behandlung der nichtorganisatorischen Gegenstände der Partei-Diskussion', Entwurf des Redaktionsausscusses, 2 Feb. 1954, FES PV Bestand Programmatik 001599/K22.

confirm them—which it duly did. The report also urged co-operation with the Churches, and Schiller proposed that a special appeal should be made to the 'new' middle class, including managers and members of the free professions, as well as pensioners.

More difficult was the issue of party symbols—the Red Flag, for example, and traditional songs rallying the faithful in the class war. The commission felt it could not abolish these things by decree, but urged discretion in their use, so as not to offend the susceptibilities of non-members attending public meetings.[28]

In April 1954 a gathering of socialist academics was organized at Mehlem to discuss the fundamental principles upon which socialism should be based, a subject the importance of which Eichler had been tirelessly reiterating since before the foundation of the Federal Republic. The conference heard a strong critique of Marx delivered by Gerhard Weisser and a defence from Wolfgang Abendroth. The conclusion reached by those present was an uneasy compromise stitched up into the 'Mehlem Theses'—an indigestible package of socio-philosophical observations. These included approving references to Marx's scientific achievement in establishing the principle that changes in society could only occur if historical conditions were suitable, and a commitment to producing an analysis of the existing social situation in any new statement of the party's fundamental principles. On the other hand, such a statement was also to make clear the ethical and cultural principles upon which socialism was based. Some of the 'theses', however, were clearly influenced by the reformers. One stated that, in the circumstances of the twentieth century, socialists ought not to give the state the sole authority for the ordering of affairs. If freedom were to be preserved, there must be a pluralist system which would embrace different forces shaping society.[29]

An unfortunate result of these deliberations was that they saddled the reformers with the duty of producing a sociological/historical analysis (*Zeitanalyse*) of Western Germany in the 1950s—a thankless task, which wasted much time. It was eventually cast aside in 1959, by which time the rigidly Marxist element in the party had really lost all chance of influencing the new programme.

After the 1954 Berlin congress Eichler was entrusted with the chairmanship of yet another committee to hammer out the fundamental principles upon which social democracy was based. The 'Nelsonian' reformers were well represented, with Weisser and Henry-Hermann

<hr />

[28] Ibid.
[29] 'Ergebnis einer Tagung sozialdemokratischer Wissenschaftler in Mehlem,' 12–14 Apr. 1954, FES PV Bestand Wipo, K22 001599, pp. 3–5.

being members of the committee and Dr Suzanne Miller functioning as its secretary.[30] In the years which followed they wrestled with value systems, the nature of human freedom, social justice, and socialism itself. Progress was extremely slow, but despite some opposition from Abendroth, the committee moved steadily away from the certainties of class conflict into the fuzzier area of ethical socialism and social justice, to be achieved without giving up the market economy.

On 21 January 1956, Grete Henry-Hermann presented the committee with a long and intellectually demanding paper on the subject of fundamental values in politics. The committee evidently found this somewhat beyond its capacities, because it decided that it could not deal with purely philosophical issues. None the less, Henry-Hermann's contribution laid the basis for an important aspect of the future SPD programme—a commitment to the ethical principles of freedom, justice, and solidarity.[31] Although these things might seem self-evident to a pragmatic or a cynical observer, they were important in a movement with a history of ideological wrangling and a Marxist legacy to slough off.

The reformers were generally active in trying to create an intellectual atmosphere within the SPD sympathetic to change. The summer of 1954 saw the appearance of a new bimonthly journal, *Die neue Gesellschaft*. Willi Eichler was one of its directors, and the advisory editorial panel included Grete Henry-Hermann and Gerhard Weisser, as well as Wolfgang Abendroth, Heinrich Deist, Fritz Erler, Carlo Schmid, and Herbert Wehner. It was a social democratic organ set up in response to an initiative of the Dortmund congress, but it was deliberately intended to attract contributors and readers from outside the ranks of social democracy.[32]

The first article in the new journal was by Gerhard Weisser. He denied that socialism was an ersatz religion. Marx's teachings were less important for their scientific content than for their inspirational qualities—a view which would have been regarded as rank heresy in the Soviet bloc. In fact, Weisser continued, most socialist movements had been based on Christian foundations, and social democrats themselves might be Christians.[33]

In the same edition of *Die neue Gesellschaft* Gisbert Rittig, a man who could not be suspected of softness towards neo-liberals, argued that

[30] Miller, 'Zur Wirkungsgeschichte des Godesberger Programms', 131.
[31] Meeting of the Programmkommission, 21 Jan. 1956, FES Deist NL.
[32] Klotzbach, *Der Weg zur Staatspartei*, 318.
[33] G. Weisser, 'Krise der Bewegung oder Krise ihrer Lehre?', *Die Neue Gesellschaft*, 1 (1954), 1–12.

the objectives of neo-liberalism and social democracy were the same: to give the individual freedom and justice. The sovereignty of the consumer was something which nobody who took freedom seriously could deny. It was foolish to present the issue as a conflict between a perfect market—which could never exist—and a centralized, planned economy. In reality there were many forms of mixed economy. Where social democrats parted company from liberals was in their view that distortions created by the uneven distribution of purchasing power had to be ironed out by some form of intervention.[34] Rittig's approach was pragmatic and conciliatory, and was in marked contrast to the tone of his comments in discussions four years earlier. Like Weisser, he stressed that socialism should be regarded as a means to an end, not a *Weltanschauung*, a view which echoed those of the neo-liberals when describing the social market economy.

In January 1956 a two-day conference was held in Cologne on the subject of the 'Reform of Germany' (*Neuordnung Deutschlands*) attended by SPD leaders, members of the Bundestag, and leaders of *Land* governments and parliaments. This reflected a new interest in the problems of modern industrial society: automation and atomic power as well as the more urgent political issue of old-age pensions. Here again, and as we have seen above, the wily Konrad Adenauer moved swiftly to outbid his opponents with his adoption of the 'dynamic pension', automatically rising in line with employees' pay rises, which helped him to win another smashing election victory in 1957.

Nevertheless, the Cologne conference did start leading members of the SPD trying yet again to work out a new approach to economic policy. Frictions over tactics as well as ultimate strategy held back the process of reform. It is clear that some professional politicians, as well as trade-union leaders, in the party executive doubted the value of a new set of fundamental principles for social democracy of the kind which Eichler's commission had been instructed to draw up. They feared that such a programme might limit their freedom of action or arouse more hostility than enthusiasm. Weisser, who was chairman of the programme commission's subcommittee for economic and social issues, was especially indignant at the lack of support his committee was receiving, and at the extent to which the executive's own economics subcommittee—chaired by Veit—was ignoring its work, or even duplicating it. On 25 January 1958 he wrote to Ollenhauer complaining about the confusion between these two committees. Veit's group had

---

[34] G. Rittig, 'Sozialismus und Liberalismus.' Annäherung oder Distanz ihrer wirtschaftspolitischen Anschauungen?', *Die neue Gesellschaft*, 1 (1954), 42–9.

apparently just started hectic activity in an area on which Weisser and his colleagues had been working for months. There should, he argued, be a clear division of competence, and specific tasks should be allocated to each committee.

These suggestions will probably run up against the objection on the part of some comrades that they don't in any case want to have a programme of fundamental principles, because thereby the party will be restricted too much. This view was expressed at the last meeting of Veit's committee . . .[35]

This was probably not just a matter of departmental in-fighting. Weisser was a staunch opponent of neo-liberalism, despite his willingness to accept the market mechanism in a socialist economy. He disliked any suggestion that the SPD was sliding into an acceptance of Erhard's social market economy. On 2 August 1957 he wrote to a colleague that

It is indeed always the same old problem—those comrades who have grasped that we, as freedom-loving socialists, must support a strongly market-orientated economic system, uncritically accept in justifying [that course] the language of neo-liberalism, instead of explaining our own regard for autonomy in economic life, which stems from the intellectual history of our movement and from that movement's confrontation with the new demands of the twentieth century.[36]

He therefore wanted to stress the aspects of socialist policy which differed from those of Erhard or Böhm, basing his views on the reformist movements of the Weimar period. Above all, he wanted to emphasize the need for different kinds of economic enterprises other than conventional capitalist ones, and a commitment to effective forms of economic steering and the redistribution of wealth. The problem was that his proposals tended to be highly complicated—he himself always stressed the complexity of socio-economic phenomena. Yet for politicians seeking to sell their wares to a critical but economically unsophisticated electorate, the pragmatic approach of a man like Schiller might seem more attractive, while to conservative socialists, the class-war certainties of the Marxists were apparently safer.

Fortunately for the SPD, a middle way was found between these positions, embodied in the common-sense practicality of Heinrich Deist. As a trade unionist and administrator with business experience, Deist could not be accused of academic other-worldliness. His personal history was enough to ensure his acceptance as a dedicated social

---

[35] FES PV Bestand Wipo, 0017, 'Weisser: Reden, Aufsätze, Interviews'.
[36] Weisser to Henning, 2 Aug. 1957, FES PV Bestand Wipo, 0018, 'Weisser Schriftwechsel'.

democrat who had suffered for his allegiance during the Third Reich.[37]

In 1956 he published a number of articles on the economy in *Vorwärts*, the official organ of the SPD, stressing that automation and atomic power were two areas where state intervention was needed to protect human rights. Freedom was also the leitmotiv of a volume of essays on fundamental questions of modern economic policy edited by Carlo Schmid, Eric Potthoff, and Karl Schiller, and published the following year.[38] In this volume a number of neo-liberal principles came to the surface, albeit in rather altered form—examples being Schiller's commitment to *Startgleichheit* and Gerhard Weisser's stress on the need for 'personal autonomy'.

By the Stuttgart party congress of 1958 Deist, who was now the SPD's most authoritative economic spokesman, produced the formula *freiheitliche Ordnung der Wirtschaft* (freedom-loving organization of the economy), which was accepted by the overwhelming majority of the delegates. This involved a form of indirect controls by budgetary planning—a position not identical to, but not so very far removed from, that of the social market economists. Indeed, it could rightly be called 'a market economy of the left'.

Deist was determined to woo the SPD away from class-war attacks on private property or grandiose socialist shopping-lists.[39] In the keynote speech opening the economics debate at the Stuttgart congress, he stressed the importance of small businesses and independent undertakings—adopting a line on them which echoed the arguments of the famous revisionist Social Democrat Eduard Bernstein, who, well before the First World War, had argued that modern technical development would always create new opportunities for the middling and smaller firms. Therefore social democracy should be concerned to create the greatest amount of economic freedom and should firmly deny the intention of attacking private property.

On the other hand, public enterprises were necessary precisely to resist the threat to free competition posed by overmighty private concerns and private monopolies. Deist stressed the varied nature of the modern economy and pointed out to his listeners that there was no single panacea for economic problems.

---

[37] See above, p. 369.

[38] *Grundfragen moderner Wirtschaftspolitik* (Frankfurt/M., 1958).

[39] See Deist's speech to the Parteitag in May 1958, *Protokoll der Verhandlungen des Parteitages der SPD vom 18.–23. Mai 1958 in Stuttgart* (hereafter *Verhandlungsprotokoll 1958*) (Hanover, n.d.), 188. Cf. his draft for an article 'Wirtschaftspolitik von Morgen' for the Berlin Socialist student journal *Standpunkt*, 5 ff, FES Deist NL, no. 3.

The result of our deliberations is that we are not dealing with a unified economy with a monolithic structure, but with a mixed economy with countless small and medium-sized concerns, communal and public enterprises which can function as starting-points for more freedom of action in the economy and act as tools for the restriction of the power of large-scale businesses.[40]

He stressed that public enterprises should not be state-run but should be decentralized and autonomous, within the loose direction of the national budget. The aim should be 'no more state than necessary. And in the economy as much freedom as one can possibly have'.[41]

Deist himself thought of the energy industry—especially coal and atomic power—as the really essential candidate for public ownership, though he stressed that where private firms were taken over, compensation must be paid. He did not argue for a rejection of capitalism, but for a need to protect competition in areas where *laissez-faire* would lead to private monopoly.

After Deist's speech, which was well enough received, Veit delivered a balancing contribution which sounded like a gramophone record of all the old socialist themes—the injustice of the social market economy, the evils of 'late capitalism' to which the market economy was bound to lead, and the inherently false character of the 'freedom' which capitalist economists were offering. It aroused the enthusiasm of the faithful, but it was the swan-song of post-war social democracy rather than a stirring cry to radical action.[42]

The defeat in the 1957 elections had finally brought with it the eclipse of the old party-apparatus which had held sway in the SPD headquarters since the early days of the Federal Republic. The propaganda chief, Fritz Heine, lost his post on the executive. Two reformers, Wehner and von Knoeringen, were elected deputy leaders, and were joined on a newly created *Präsidium* by Deist and Erler. Brandt and Schmidt were both elected to the party executive.

Eichler's committee—or commission as it was more properly called—on fundamental principles was told to hurry on with its work, and in April 1958 Eichler hastily patched its findings together. They included the kind of sociological/historical picture of the age (*Zeitanalyse*) demanded in the Mehlem Theses. This overloaded the whole report and was eventually dropped. More important was the commitment to a series of fundamental values—freedom, justice, and solidarity. In the economics section, largely drawn up by Deist, free consumer-choice,

---

[40] *Verhandlungsprotokoll 1958*, 183.
[41] Ibid. 185.   [42] Ibid. 197–207.

free choice of work-place, and freedom for initiative on the part of employers were essential, and free competition very important.

Between spring 1958 and the autumn of 1959 Eichler and Deist spoke to several hundred SPD meetings about the programme. However, it was from the Austrian Socialist Party, not for the first time in the history of German social democracy, that the final push came. In 1958 the Austrians produced a fundamental programme, and in May the SPD executive asked one of its authors, Benedikt Kautsky, to get together with the editor of the *Deutsche Presse Agentur*, Fritz Sänger, to knock Eichler's draft into a publicly presentable shape. The result, less philosophical but more easily digested, was the Godesberg Programme.

The programme was regarded with some doubts by the party's professionals. Many of those who were keen to brighten up the SPD's image and present an attractive package to an ill-informed electorate feared that too much agonizing over basic principles would open the party up to external attack and invite internal division.

However, as the preparations for the special congress, which was due to open in Bad Godesberg on 13 November 1959, got under way, the party became aware that public reaction to the new programme was remarkably favourable. The Adenauer era in the Federal Republic was beginning to draw to its close. His government's relationship with the press was not as happy as it had been. For many intellectuals—and journalists in particular—the prospect of a credible left-wing alternative to the long-serving Christian Democratic regime was distinctly attractive. The new programme seemed to open up exciting possibilities for German politics. Even 'bourgeois' newspapers treated the SPD's proposals with respect.[43]

By the time the extraordinary congress convened, therefore, the new course was already assured of support, both from the party's rank-and-file and from the professional politicians, who were not slow to appreciate the change of climate.

In his opening address to the congress Ollenhauer paid tribute to those who had organized the fruitful discussions within the party which had gone on since 1954. He drew applause when he remarked that: 'the alliance between scholarship and research on the one hand and the socialist workers' movement on the other, which goes back to the beginnings of our history, must constantly be cemented by active co-operation'.[44] A sentiment rarely heard at British political gatherings,

[43] Schwarz, *Epochenwechsel*, 197–8.
[44] *Protokoll der Verhandlungen des Außerordentlichen Parteitages der Sozialdemokratischen Partei Deutschlands vom 13.–15. November 1959 in Bad Godesberg* (Hanover, n.d.) (hereafter cited as *Godesberg protocol*), 52.

it illustrated one source of SPD strength which was becoming more important in an age when support from the educated electorate was essential for the party's future success.

Ollenhauer urged the delegates at the congress not to allow arguments about Marxism to divide them. That would only play into the hands of their enemies. The demand that the programme of Marx and Engels should shape the contents of a fundamental policy statement by the SPD in 1959 was 'as un-Marxist as it possibly could be'. If they followed that line, they would, within measurable time, become a 'sect without influence on the political struggles of our age'.[45] He hastened to assure his listeners that the SPD's commitment to freedom had nothing to do with 'liberalistic' concepts which would, in the end, lead to anarchy and the war of all against all.

Ollenhauer admitted that the economic section of the programme was the most controversial. He rather defensively denied that the SPD was just committed to minor reforms, and in other respects differed only in nuances from the policies of Ludwig Erhard. He made it clear, however, that they had given up state ownership of industry as a serious objective and had dispensed with a 'shopping-list' for socialization. The overall control of the economy would be far more comprehensive and effective under the system they were proposing, a comment which drew applause, even if it remained somewhat imprecise in its meaning.[46] Later in the discussion, Deist made it clear that state control would be exercised by indirect means, exploiting the fact that 30–40 per cent of the national income passed through public exchequers.[47]

By this time it was clear that the wind was blowing strongly in the reformist direction. The professionals had accepted the need for change, and more academic figures like Schiller on the one side, or Abendroth on the other, played no public role in the congress. Eichler did defend his fundamental ethical principles of freedom, justice, and solidarity against the charge that they were simply bourgeois values inherited from the French Revolution,[48] but in these areas the battle had long been won.

It was time for the heavy guns of the party to commit themselves, sensing that the new programme would be effective electoral ammunition. Most striking was Herbert Wehner's eloquent appeal to the delegates. A former Communist, he spoke as one who had been 'burned' by the fires of false radicalism in the Weimar Republic and who had

---

[45] Ibid. 55.   [46] Ibid. 65.   [47] Ibid. 181–3.

[48] See Mildenberger's objections on this point and Eichler's reply, ibid. 85 and 120.

suffered under the Third Reich as a result. The new programme, he claimed, would help the SPD to power but would not stop them being social democrats.[49] It was a powerful appeal, which shrewdly associated Wehner with the new course whilst reassuring the old guard that they were not betraying their principles by accepting it.

Such rhetoric caught the headlines, but the real spadework for change had been done by others. It was a tribute to the preparatory labours of Eichler and Deist that only 16 out of the 340 delegates at the Godesberg congress voted against the programme.[50]

There is no doubt that the need to grapple with the challenge presented by neo-liberalism had a major impact on the SPD and forced it to rethink its intellectual position. The philosophical and theoretical arguments to which this gave rise may have seemed earnestly Teutonic to foreign observers, and many SPD leaders would have liked a more pragmatic—in reality a more opportunistic—approach. It is not surprising that the British Labour Party was often cited as an example of a socialist movement which did not concern itself with dogmas but dealt rather with practical, relevant issues.[51] Yet the British Labour Party never did work out its attitude to the market mechanism. Clause 4 of its constitution, committing members to work for the public ownership of the means of production, distribution, and exchange, was to be the object of an abortive challenge by Hugh Gaitskell at the Labour Party Conference in November 1959. This failed ignominiously and the clause has ever since been printed on party membership cards. It was perhaps not entirely surprising that Labour was the only major socialist party not to be represented by a delegation at the Godesberg congress.[52]

At least the SPD had worked out a convincing rationale for a mixed economy with 'as much competition as possible, as much planning as necessary'. It was to be the 'market economy of the left' which accepted enough common ground with its liberal opponents to make consensus politics work. Germany was spared the oscillations between *laissez-faire* and socialism which proved so disastrous for Britain in the years which followed.

Nevertheless, there were drawbacks about the way in which the Godesberg Programme was presented. The emphasis on slick public relations demanded by the party executive doubtless helped its impact

[49] Ibid. 99–101.
[50] Miller, 'Zur Wirkungsgeschichte', 132 ff.
[51] See, e.g., the comment of Troeger that the SPD executive should imitate the Labour Party and avoid ideological propaganda, tackling practical matters instead. Protocol of Wipo meeting, 6 Oct. 1956, FES PV Bestand Wipo, 01605.
[52] *Godesberg Protocol*, 68. Morgan Phillips, the Labour Party secretary, sent an apologetic message.

outside the party. But it encouraged a tendency to regard the whole discussion as a victory for pragmatism without much serious intellectual content. The implications of Godesberg for the philosophical development of socialism in Germany were not discussed after 1959 as much as the reformers would have liked. Weisser had already remarked rather bitterly to a colleague in August 1957 that social democrats who accepted the market economy 'uncritically employ the language of neo-liberalism'.[53]

It became all too easy for opponents to claim that the party had simply jettisoned its principles in a search for office. That, indeed, was the line of Ludwig Erhard himself when he described the new SPD policy as 'plagiarism' and saw in it an attempt to creep into power by adopting the ideas of others.[54] In the 1960s, when the SPD was able to create coalitions, firstly with the Christian Democrats and then with the Liberal FDP, such strictures did not seem worth worrying about. But by 1969 Young Socialists (*Jusos*) at the party's Munich congress were accusing their elders of giving up their socialist convictions in favour of a 'false pragmatism' which had left the party with a 'theoretical deficit'. This was far from fair on the reformers of the 1950s. As one of them later remarked: 'The authors of the Godesberg Programme had the intention of offering the party the basis for a policy orientated on ethical values. In no sense was it meant to legitimize a lack of political principle and an opportunistic willingness to follow the tides of circumstance.'[55]

Unfortunately the young were not inclined to listen, and primitive Marxism reappeared in the party, to its considerable detriment.

Nevertheless, the Godesberg Programme remained the basis of SPD policy and served it well electorally. The combination of ethical commitment and economic pragmatism helped the SPD to broaden its appeal and move out of the social ghetto in which it had apparently been imprisoned since the Weimar Republic. This broadening was not just a matter of class. Perhaps more important was the fact that

---

[53] See fn. 36.

[54] Erhard reacted very sourly to the SPD's 'conversion'. He was particularly angry at the use of the term 'welfare for all' (*Wohlstand für alle*) by the Social Democrats. On 4 June 1962 he told the CDU congress in Dortmund that 'a copy can never replace the original', and warned his receptive audience that the SPD conversion was probably not genuine. 'That spirit of Godesberg, which the SPD today is so keen to spread abroad, has—as I constantly observe—in no way infused the leading functionaries; they behave as they have always done, in the style of their Marxist doctrines.' Publ. in *Ludwig Erhard: Gedanken*, 758.

[55] Miller, 'Zur Wirkungsgeschichte', 135.

it included an appeal to Christians, for many of whom the SPD had previously seemed beyond the cultural pale. Symbolic of this emergence from ideological isolation was a formal visit paid by Fritz Erler and an SPD delegation to His Holiness Pope Paul VI on 5 March 1964. To mark this historic visit to the Vatican by German Social Democrats, Erler and his colleagues chose to present the Pope with a document of a suitably conciliatory nature. It was the Godesberg Programme.

Conclusion: The Social Market Economy in Retrospect

IN a lecture delivered in 1976 Alfred Müller-Armack made the following statement: 'All protagonists of the current theory of market economics have expressed themselves so decisively against the possible renewal of "*laissez-faire* liberalism" that there can no longer possibly be any doubts on that issue.'[1]

Citing Rüstow, he went on to claim that the old liberalism appeared 'neither worthy nor capable of being retained'. This view was, however, coupled with the knowledge that competition was an indispensable instrument of social organization. When speaking of the social market economy, he asserted, the word 'social' simultaneously combined a number of different insights and concepts which had to be borne in mind when approving in principle of the mechanism of competition. In contrast to the older form of liberalism, it was now realized that there were certain inadequacies in the competitive system: imperfect markets, oligopolies, and monopolies. The organization of credit and money could not in practice be set up as a self-operating mechanism. Therefore it had to be accepted that at most the market worked in a semi-automatic fashion, and required 'sensible management' (*sinnvolle Bedienung*).

Income generated by the market was not necessarily distributed in a fashion compatible with social justice or with social conditions acceptable to civilized people. A state's budget redistributed income, and it was important to establish the proper principles of social justice upon which to base such taxation measures, always assuming they were in conformity with the market.

Modern liberals also knew that the market itself could not meet particular requirements for just distribution and security. To overcome this problem, suitable stabilizing mechanisms, especially those designed to influence the business cycle (*Konjunkturpolitik*) were needed.

The competitive economy did not, in any case, offer people enough for a full life. It 'needs to be complemented by a social policy which does not just envisage man functionally as a producer and a consumer, but also takes into account his personal being'.[2] He developed this

[1] A. Müller-Armack 'Dreißig Jahre Soziale Marktwirtschaft: Rückblick und Vorschau', in *25 Jahre Seminar für Staatsbürgerkunde e.V. Olpe, 1951–1976, Heimvolkshochschule Haus Wildenstein* (Olpe, n.d.), 12–25.
[2] Ibid. 17.

rather high-flown concept by referring to the need to create a society in which human beings could live in freedom whilst being socially secure. 'This task requires the spiritual and social structure (*Ordnung*) to be set in a meaningful relationship with the economic system.' In the nineteenth century there had seemed to be two short-cuts to the achievement of this happy result. The first was to leave everything to the market (*laissez-faire*), and the second was to abolish the market altogether, replacing it with a centrally directed, collectivist economy. Neither worked.

Müller-Armack reiterated the view of all neo-liberals when he denied that there was anything fundamentally moral about any form of economic organization. The market was primarily just a means to an end (*instrumentales Mittel*). 'The social market economy cannot and should not be a *Weltanschauung*, in the sense of old-fashioned liberalism or socialism.' The concept of the social market in economics did not mean that the state abjured active responsibility for the economy. What was indisputable, however, was that, in order to reach the objectives for which they were striving, economic policy had to be adjusted to make it conform with market principles.[3] Hence one-sided policies to create full employment were unwise; instead there should be selected measures, in conformity with the market, to counteract slumps. The modern social state—and here, of course, Müller-Armack avoided the term 'welfare state'—could only fulfil its function of reconciling the various classes in society if it enabled the dynamics of the market to ease its task.

He indicated how he saw such policies in concrete terms by proposing that social alienation be combated through better education, encouragement for self-employment, industrial decentralization, and an improvement in the status of long-serving skilled industrial workers. He also added a controversial rider to the effect that, just as they had made the defence of competition a public duty, so they should establish counter-cyclical economic measures (*Konjunkturpolitik*) as an element in their social policy.[4]

This lecture has been treated at some length because it illustrates how one of the major architects of the social market economy still believed after thirty years that his policies were very different from those of *laissez-faire* liberalism. It is inconceivable that Müller-Armack was simply advancing his thoughts on social policy as a camouflage for a more primitive Darwinian capitalist system. His own contempt for the collectivist left was well known, and was constantly documented.

---

[3] Ibid. 19.   [4] Ibid. 24.

In June 1973 he had castigated those, from Mao Tse-Tung and Herbert Marcuse to Sicco Mansholt, who wrote off the social market economy as irrelevant and even tried to replace it with such dubious terms as 'late capitalism'.

The revival of Marxist theories in the 1960s had conveniently ignored the work of economists in the inter-war period—men of such differing standpoints as Mises and Schumpeter, Sombart and Lamprecht—who had demolished Marx's economic theories. Marx's forecasts concerning capital accumulation and the declining rate of profit had also proved woefully wrong.[5] During the era of the 'student rebellion' and the resurgence of collectivist politics amongst Germany's intelligentsia in the late 1960s, Müller-Armack sturdily defended the theories of the social market economy, pointing to their proven successes, and to their social validity.

In the 1990s the critique of the social market comes from a very different quarter. With the collapse of Communism, the discrediting of Marxism, and the eclipse of Keynesian, or perhaps more accurately neo-Keynesian, economics has come a resurgence of what Rüstow might have described as 'paleo-liberalism'. This denies any validity to the concept of social justice and rejects a role for the state in the economy other than the policing of property. Herbert Spencer's 'night-watchman' is back with us again. How far does this reflect the success of Ludwig Erhard's Germany?

The West German economy has been a tremendous advertisement for the blessings of market forces and competition. Yet any objective observers of the history of West Germany over the last four decades must agree that the Federal Republic has been anything but a night-watchman. The citizen is supported by his community (*Gemeinde*), his *Land*, or Federal state, and by the *Bund*, or federation. His education is free. School children and students are assisted in numerous ways, the latter with loans, grants, and subsidies of various kinds. Hundreds of thousands of apprenticeships are provided every year by German industry, supplemented by state-funded adult-education programmes. Although there is no national health service, there are subsidized health-schemes of a kind so lavish that there are more hospital beds than patients, and workers are regularly sent on expensive convalescent 'cures' at the expense of their insurance fund. In all but a few very large towns, there is no serious housing shortage, even though the reception of hundreds of thousands of Germans—from Russia,

---

[5] A. Müller-Armack, 'Die wissenschaftlichen Ursprünge und die künftige Verfassung der sozialen Marktwirtschaft', *Wirtschaftspolitische Chronik*, 22/3 (Cologne, 1973), 9–11.

Poland, Rumania, and the former German Democratic Republic—has recently put pressure on housing resources. The public purse played an important role in rehousing Germans after the war, and refugee problems are regarded as a problem for the state also. The Federation and the individual *Länder* have their own economics ministries, and the success of states like Baden-Württemberg and Bavaria in attracting thriving modern industries has not been due to a supine reliance on the effectiveness of the 'hidden hand'.

Yet how much of this, if anything, has been due to the social market economy? How much of it would have happened irrespective of the political colours adopted in Bonn or the theories of economics professors? Are not national traditions of industriousness, discipline, respect for education and training, and willingness to abjure short-term gains for the benefit of long-term success factors more easily explicable with reference to anthropology than to history, let alone the history of ideas?

In considering these questions we have to distinguish between the theory of the social market economy as it was propounded by its most ardent advocates—especially Müller-Armack and Rüstow—and the more limited approach to economic policy adopted by Erhard and his supporters after currency reform in June 1948. Once that has been done, we have to make another distinction: between the West German policies which were pursued by those holding social-market beliefs and those which were forced upon them against their will—or, as their supporters would put it, against their better judgement. Only by making such distinctions will we be able to assess the importance of the social market economy in West Germany, or estimate its impact on the newly united Germany, where social-market theories are having to be explained to a public unused to any form of market economics.

We should be very chary of attributing economic success to national characteristics, or even social traditions. Germany's neighbours have too often tended to take refuge in nationalist clichés when attempting to explain why the Federal Republic has outstripped them in its trading performance. Yet we should remember that for many years before 1989 it was widely believed that the German Democratic Republic possessed an effective industrial economy. There were even claims—ludicrous to those who knew both countries—that per capita income in the GDR was higher than that in the United Kingdom. It was assumed that the well-educated, well-organized, and highly motivated East German labour-force could make a success even of Marxism-Leninism. The collapse of the Iron Curtain and the unification of Germany have exploded this particular myth. The appalling state of the East German economy shows that nationality is far less important than a sound economic system.

Without a market-orientated economy the most determined workers cannot satisfy the needs of their fellow citizens effectively. In the First World War, and during the Third Reich, different types of command economy harnessed the industriousness and skill of the German population with apparent initial success; in both cases they led to economic disaster. Even during the Weimar Republic, protectionism in various forms hampered economic recovery. Nationalist delusions of grandeur and socialist commitment to class conflict prevented the development of that mutual respect for the rights and beliefs of others without which there can be no social harmony.

There is little doubt that Erhard himself was not very interested in the social-welfare aspects of neo-liberal theory. This does not necessarily mean that he rejected them. On a visit to Britain in November 1948, during which he was received by Sir Stafford Cripps, Erhard stressed that his own policies—regarded by the British as right-wing and doctrinaire—were *economic* rather than social, and that so far as social policy was concerned, he differed from right-wing parties—presumably a reference to the FDP and the German Party.[6] This fitted in with his statements to the CDU at Königswinter in February 1949, when he was persuading the party's economic policy committee to accept his programme as its own.[7]

Erhard's priority, however, was economic. He always showed more interest in increasing the gross national product through competition than in distributing it justly. Uneven distribution might or might not be regrettable but, so long as the cake was getting bigger, even the poor would be better off. Therefore the liberation of market forces, first from state controls and then from private cartel restrictions, was the central core of his policy. In this he was supported by traditional 'Ordo-liberals' such as Eucken, Böhm, and Röpke. In his *Grundsätze der Wirtschaftspolitik* Eucken defended competition against criticisms of its 'cut-throat' character, claiming that the most ruthless behaviour was usually associated with those trying to destroy competition by monopolistic practices. Social policy should really take the form of organizing an open competitive system rather than the redistribution of wealth. Private property should be sacrosanct.[8]

---

[6] Report by Killick on Erhard's visit to London, 23–30 Nov., 10 Dec. 1948, PRO/FO/1049/1190.

[7] See above, Ch. 11.

[8] W. Eucken, *Grundsätze der Wirtschaftspolitik*, 248 and 312. Eucken had thought hard about the property issue and was well aware of its opponents' views. He seems to have had a grudging respect for Proudhon, who was depicted in a sketch on the wall of Eucken's study in the act of smashing bourgeois property.

It was this aspect of the social market economy which Erhard, encouraged by his academic admirers, implemented in the 1940s and 1950s. He was spectacularly successful in liberalizing internal and external trade. Anti-cartel and anti-monopolistic policies were more weakly applied, but the propaganda campaign which accompanied them served to inculcate the idea of competition into the political culture of West Germany as something positive. Protectionism and price-fixing—hitherto traditional features of German industrial practice—were not abolished completely, but they did lose respectability.

What of the more obviously social side of government policies in the Federal Republic? Here it must be admitted that in many areas—especially housing, co-determination, and pensions—policies were pursued which were either irrelevant to, or actually incompatible with, the social market. The case of the dynamic-pensions law was the most glaring example of this. In dealing with agriculture, also, the support for German farmers from the Ministry of Agriculture, soon to be reinforced by the grotesquely protectionist policies of the Brussels CAP, had little to do with the theories propounded by Röpke and Rüstow for protecting a healthy class of small farmers.[9]

So far as agricultural policy was concerned, Erhard was unable to overcome its inherently protectionist character. He did not cease to attack the distortions created by this, but party politicians in Germany were never able to apply market economics to the farming community. The SPD could not overcome its traditional lack of an agricultural policy; the CDU/CSU and the FDP depended too much on regionally concentrated farmers' votes to dare the 'leap into cold water' which market principles would have implied. The result has been an increasingly serious agrarian crisis throughout Western Europe, a crisis staved off by larger and larger payments from the industrial sector in the form of artifical food-prices and direct subsidies. To this uneconomic character of agriculture has been added an anti-social dimension, since subsidized farming-methods seriously damage the environment.

When we turn to social-welfare policies, the picture is rather different. Although co-determination, subsidized housing, controlled rents, and higher pensions, did not fit into the social-market framework in the way purists would have liked, the concept that social spending could be assimilated with market economics so long as it was *marktgerecht* did enable parties like the Christian Democrats and then even the Social Democrats to accept the principles of market competition without surrendering their commitment to family security or social justice. As for the liberals, the Free Democrats themselves

[9] See above, Ch. 4.

began to adopt strong social programmes in the late 1960s, including extended forms of co-determination and improved public education. They were able to do this without compromising their commitment to individual enterprise and private property, since the principles of the social market clearly protected them.

Social-market theories have been criticized for their inconsistency. It is argued that the desire to protect competition by state action is incompatible with true market freedom, and that, in any case, it may conflict with the maximizing of production which is the ultimate aim of liberal economic policy.[10] Similarly, taxation to pay for social benefits is incompatible theoretically with the defence of private property. The social market economy has been attacked by the 'paleoliberals', whose star has risen in the 1980s, and by the protagonists of Roman Catholic social teachings. The former accuse it of not being a free enough market, and the latter see its individualist motivations as undermining the solidarity of a Christian society.[11] Yet, as Röpke remarked in the early 1940s, competition might be a *sine qua non* of a healthy economy, but there could be no question of 'chemical purity': 'Planning also has its clearly defined, positive tasks, particularly in the sector referred to as country planning [*Landesplanung*].'[12] A completely watertight theoretical system for a national economy would produce intolerable results—Stalin's Russia on the one hand, and some capitalist Latin American economies on the other, are illustrations of this. As one well-informed historian of the social market economy put it, 'A social market economy may be described as a permanent search for an economic and social framework designed to encourage both an efficient production of the means of material well-being and personal freedom in a socially balanced order.'[13]

In this respect it can be argued that the academics and politicians who supported the social market economy did have a lasting impact on the political economy of Germany. By reconciling social democrats and Roman Catholic populists to the market economy, and by teaching liberal middle-class citizens that social problems could be solved in ways which did not violate market principles, the neo-liberals created a

---

[10] Robert, *Konzentrationspolitik*, 86 *et passim*.

[11] e.g. E. E. Nawroth denies that neo-liberalism is really a new 'third way' theory, but claims it is just a 'warming up of old rationalism, as neoliberal idealization of the English [sic] enlightenment shows': id., *Die Sozial- und Wirtschaftsphilosophie des Neoliberalismus* 425. For similar views, see H. P. Becker, *Die soziale Frage im Neoliberalismus: Analyse und Kritik* (Heidelberg, 1965) and H. Schmid, *Neoliberalismus und Katholische Soziallehre: Eine Konfrontierung* (Cologne, 1954).

[12] Röpke, *Gesellschaftskrise der Gegenwart*, 292.

[13] Watrin, 'The Principles of the Social Market Economy', 419.

consensus in favour of the pragmatic yet principled search for material well-being, personal freedom, and social balance referred to above. This consensus has proved of great benefit to the German people. Perhaps one day it will also benefit their neighbours.

Bibliography

Primary Sources

1. UNPUBLISHED

Konrad-Adenauer-Stiftung, St. Augustin
Curt Becker Papers.
Franz Böhm Papers (cited as 'Böhm NL').
Müller-Armack Papers (cited as 'Müller-Armack NL').
Lampe Papers (cited as 'Lampe NL').

Budesarchiv, Koblenz
Blücher Papers (cited as 'Blücher NL').
Rüstow Papers (cited as 'Rüstow NL').
Files of the *Reichskanzlei*, 1944.
Documents relating to the Economics Administration in the Bizone, 1948–9, and to the Federal Ministry of Economics, as well as to the Wissenschaftlicher Beirat which advised both bodies.

Friedrich-Ebert-Stiftung, Bonn-Bad Godesberg
Parteivorstand records (cited as 'PV')
Deist Papers (cited as 'Deist NL').

Ludwig-Erhard-Stiftung, Bonn
Correspondence of Ludwig Erhard.

Walter-Eucken-Institut Archive, Freiburg im Breisgau
Eucken Papers (cited as 'Eucken NL').

Theodor-Heuss-Akademie, Gummersbach
Blücher Collection.

Institut für Zeitgeschichte, Munich
Strauß Papers.

Private Papers of Professor Hans Möller, University of Munich
Papers relating to the Wissenschaftlicher Beirat of the Verwaltung für Wirtschaft der Bizone.

Archives of the University of Münster
Documents relating to the Forschungsstelle für allgemeine und textile Marktwirtschaft an der Universität Münster and the Forschungsinstitut für Siedlungs- und Wohnungswesen der Westfälischen Universität zu Münster.

Public Record Office, Kew, London
Foreign Office documents relating to the British occupation of Germany.

2. PUBLISHED

Memoirs and Documentary Collections

Adenauer, K., *Adenauer, Rhöndorfer Ausgabe*, ed. R. Morsey and H.-P. Schwarz: *Briefe 1949–1951* (Berlin, 1985); *Briefe 1951–1953* (Berlin, 1987); *Teegespräche, 1950–1954* (Berlin, 1984).

Bundesregierung, *Die Kabinettsprotokolle der Bundesregierung*, ed. H. Booms (Boppard/Rhine 1982–).

Bundeswirtschaftsministerium (ed.), *Der Wissenschaftliche Beirat bei der Verwaltung des Vereinigten Wirtschaftsgebiets. Gutachten 1948 bis Mai 1950* (Göttingen, n.d.).

Colm, G., and Neisser, H. (eds.), *Kapitalbildung und Steuersystem. Verhandlungen und Gutachten der Konferenz von Eilsen vom 26. bis 28. Oktober 1929* (2 vols.; Berlin, 1930).

'Gutachten zur Arbeitslosenfrage. Erstattet von der Gutachterkommission zur Arbeitslosenfrage', *Sonderveröffentlichung des Reichsarbeitsblattes* (Berlin, 1931).

Hitler, A., *Hitler: Reden 1932 bis 1945*, ed. M. Domarus (4 vols.; Wiesbaden, 1973).

Konrad-Adenauer-Stiftung (ed. H. Pütz), *Konrad Adenauer und die CDU der britischen Besatzungszone, 1946–1949. Dokumente zur Gründungsgeschichte der CDU Deutschlands* (Bonn, 1975).

Ludwig-Erhard-Stiftung, Bonn, *Grundtexte zur sozialen Marktwirtschaft: Das Soziale in der sozialen Marktwirtschaft* (Stuttgart, 1981); trans. D. Rutter as *Standard Texts on the Social Market Economy: Two Centuries of Discussion* (Stuttgart, 1982).

—— (ed. H. F. Wünsche), *Die Korea-Krise als ordnungspolitische Herausforderung der deutschen Wirtschaftspolitik* (Stuttgart, 1986).

—— *Die Ethik der sozialen Marktwirtschaft: Thesen und Anfragen* (Stuttgart, 1988).

Michaelis, H., and Schraepler, E. (eds.), *Ursachen und Folgen vom deutschen Zusammenbruch 1918 und 1945 bis zur staatlichen Neuordnung Deutschlands in der Gegenwart* (26 vols.; Berlin, n.d.).

Noakes, J., and Pridham, G. (eds.), *Documents on Nazism* (London, 1974).

Schacht, Hjalmar, *My First 76 Years: The Autobiography of Hjalmar Schacht* (London, 1955).

Schumacher, K., *Kurt Schumacher: Reden, Schriften, Korrespondenzen, 1945–1952*, ed. W. Albrecht (Berlin, 1985).

Sozialdemokratische Partei Deutschlands, *SPD Protokoll der Verhandlungen des Parteitages Düsseldorf 1948* (Hamburg, n.d.).

—— *Jahrbuch der Sozialdemokratischen Partei Deutschlands 1952/53* (n.p., n.d.).

—— *Protokoll der Verhandlungen des Parteitages der SPD vom 21. bis 25. Mai 1950 in Hamburg* (Frankfurt/M., n.d.).

—— *SPD Jahrbuch, 1950–1* (Hanover, n.d.).

—— *Protokoll der Verhandlungen des Parteitages der SPD vom 24. bis 28. September 1952 in Dortmund* (Bonn, n.d.).

—— *Handbuch sozialdemokratischer Politik* (Bonn, 1953).

—— *Protokoll der Verhandlungen des Parteitages der Sozialdemokratischen Partei Deutschlands vom 20. bis 24. Juli 1954 in Berlin* (n.p., n.d.).

—— *Protokoll der Verhandlungen des Parteitages der SPD 10.–14. Juli 1956 in München* (Bonn, n.d.).

—— *Protokoll der Verhandlungen des Parteitages der SPD vom 18.–23. Mai 1958 in Stuttgart* (Hanover and Bonn, n.d.).

—— *Protokoll der Verhandlungen des Außerordentlichen Parteitages der Sozialdemokratischen Partei Deutschlands vom 13.–15. November 1959 in Bad Godesberg* (Hanover and Bonn, n.d.).

—— *Grundsatzprogramm der Sozialdemokratischen Partei Deutschlands. Beschlossen vom außerordentlichen Parteitag der SPD in Bad Godesberg vom 13. bis 15. November 1959* (Bonn, n.d.).

—— (Vorstand), *Die Wirtschaftspolitik der Sozialdemokratie* (Bonn, n.d.).

Weber, J., *Das Entscheidungsjahr 1948* (2nd edn.; Munich, 1981).

Wirtschaftsrat des Vereinigten Wirtschaftsgebietes, *Wörtliche Berichte und Drucksachen des Wirtschaftsrates des Vereinigten Wirtschaftsgebietes, 1947–1949*, ed. C. Weisz and H. Woller (Munich, 1977).

Books and articles written by neo-liberal authors or others discussed in the text, and biographical accounts of individuals in symposia or contemporary obituaries. Biographies are listed in the main bibliography

Böhm, Franz, *Wettbewerb und Monopolkampf: Eine Untersuchung zur Frage des wirtschaftlichen Kampfrechts und zur Frage der rechtlichen Struktur der geltenden Wirtschaftsordnung* (Berlin, 1933; facsimile repr. with preface by Böhm, 1964).

—— 'Das Reichsgericht und die Kartelle', *ORDO: Jahrbuch für die Ordnung von Wirtschaft und Gesellschaft*, 1 (1948), 197–213.

—— 'Wettbewerbsfreiheit und Kartellfreiheit', *ORDO: Jahrbuch für die Ordnung von Wirtschaft und Gesellschaft*, 10 (1958), 167–203.

—— *Franz Böhm. Reden und Schriften über die Ordnung einer freien Marktwirtschaft und über Wiedergutmachung*, ed. E. J. Mestmäcker (Karlsruhe, 1990).

Coing, H., Kronstein, H., and Mestmäcker, E.-J. (eds.), *Wirtschaftsordnung und Rechtsordnung. Festschrift zum 70. Geburtstag von Franz Böhm am 16. Februar 1965* (Karlsruhe, 1965).

Eisermann, G. (ed.), *Wirtschaft und Kultursystem. Festschrift für Alexander Rüstow* (Elben-Zurich, 1955).

Erhard, Ludwig, *Deutsche Wirtschaftspolitik: Der Weg der sozialen Marktwirtschaft* (Düsseldorf, 1962).

—— *The Economics of Success* (London, 1963).

—— *Kriegsfinanzierung und Schuldenkonsolidierung. Faksimiledruck der Denkschrift von 1943/44* (Frankfurt/M., 1977).

—— *Ludwig Erhard, Gedanken aus fünf Jahrzehnten: Reden und Schriften*, ed. K. Hohmann (Düsseldorf, 1988).

Eucken, Rudolf, *Der Sinn und Wert des Lebens* (Leipzig, 1908).

—— *Socialism: An Analysis* (trans. J. McCabe; London, 1921).

—— *Rudolf Eucken: His Life, Work and Travels—by Himself* (trans. J. McCabe; London, 1921).

Eucken, Walter, *Verbandsbildung in der Schiffahrt* (Munich, 1914).

—— *Kritische Betrachtungen zum deutschen Geldproblem* (Jena, 1923).

—— 'Das Übertragungsproblem: Ein Beitrag zur Theorie des internationalen Handels', *Jahrbücher für Nationalökonomie und Statistik*, 3rd ser., 68 (1925), 145–64.

—— 'Das internationale Währungsproblem: Ein Überblick', *Schriften der Vereinigung für staatswissenschaftliche Fortbildung*, 1 (1925).

—— 'Auslandsleihen', *Magazin der Wirtschaft*, 4/4 (26 Jan. 1928), 120–3.

—— 'Staatliche Strukturwandlungen und die Krisis des Kapitalismus', *Welwirtschaftliches Archiv*, 36/2 (Oct. 1932), 297–321.

Eucken, Walter, *Nationalökonomie: Wozu?* (Leipzig, 1938).
—— 'Die Überwindung des Historismus', *Schmollers Jahrbuch*, 62/2 (Munich, 1938), 63–86.
—— 'Das ordnungspolitische Problem', *ORDO: Jahrbuch für die Ordnung von Wirtschaft und Gesellschaft*, 1 (1948), 56–90.
—— *This Unsuccessful Age (or the Pains of Economic Progress)* (trans. W. Hodge; London, 1951).
—— *Kapitaltheoretische Untersuchungen* (2nd edn.; Tübingen, 1954).
—— *Die Grundlagen der Nationalökonomie* (8th edn.; New York, 1965).
—— and Husel, K. P. (eds.), *Grundsätze der Wirtschaftspolitik* (4th edn.; Tübingen, 1952).
Greiss, F., and Meyer, F. W. (eds.), *Wirtschaft, Gesellschaft und Kultur. Festgabe für Müller-Armack* (Berlin, 1961).
Hoch, W. (ed.), *Ludwig Erhard: Wirken und Reden* (Ludwigsberg, 1966).
Miksch, L., 'Zur Theorie des Gleichgewichts', *ORDO: Jahrbuch für die Ordnung von Wirtschaft und Gesellschaft*, 1 (1948), 175–96.
—— 'Walter Eucken', *Kyklos: Internationale Zeitschrift für Sozialwissenschaft*, 4/fasc. 4 (1950).
Mises, Ludwig von, *Theorie des Geldes und der Umlaufsmittel* (2nd edn.; Munich, 1924); trans. H. E. Bateson as *The Theory of Money and Credit* (Yale, 1953).
—— *Liberalismus* (Jena, 1927).
—— *Die Ursachen der Wirtschaftskrise* (Tübingen, 1931).
Müller-Armack, Alfred, *Entwicklungsgesetze des Kapitalismus: Ökonomische geschichtstheoretische und soziologische Studien zur modernen Wirtschaftsverfassung* (Berlin, 1932).
—— *Staatsidee und Wirtschaftsordnung im neuen Reich* (Berlin, 1933).
—— 'Die Marktforschung in der gelenkten Wirtschaft', *Forschungsstelle für allgemeine und textile Marktwirtschaft. Arbeitsberichte zur Marktforschung*, 1 (Münster, 1941).
—— 'Wissenschaft und Wirtschaftspraxis', *Forschungsstelle für allgemeine und textile Marktwirtschaft. Arbeitsberichte zur Marktforschung* (Münster, 1941), no. 3.
—— 'Zur volkswirtschaftlichen Problematik des Textilmarktes', *Forschungsstelle für allgemeine und textile Marktwirtschaft, Arbeitsberichte zur Marktforschung* (Münster, 1943), no. 6.
—— *Genealogie der Wirtschaftsstile: Die geistesgeschichtlichen Ursprünge der Staats- und Wirtschaftsformen bis zum Anfang des 18. Jahrhunderts* (3rd edn.; Münster, 1944).
—— *Wirtschaftsordnung und Marktwirtschaft* (Hamburg, 1946: 2nd edn. 1948).
—— *Das Jahrhundert ohne Gott: Zur Kultursoziologie unserer Zeit* (Regensburg, 1948).
—— *Vorschläge zur Verwirklichung der sozialen Marktwirtschaft*, ed. and publ. Volkswirtschaftliche Gesellschaft e. V. (Hamburg, 1948).
—— 'Die Wirtschaftsordnung sozial gesehen', *ORDO: Jahrbuch für die Ordnung von Wirtschaft und Gesellschaft*, 1 (1948), 125–54.
—— 'Wirtschaftspolitik in der sozialen Marktwirtschaft', in P. M. Boarmann (ed.), *Der Christ und die soziale Marktwirtschaft* (Stuttgart, 1955).
—— 'Wirtschaftspolitik als Beruf', *Wirtschaftspolitische Chronik*, 19/1 (Cologne, 1969).
—— *Auf dem Weg nach Europa: Erinnerungen und Ausblicke* (Tübingen, 1971).

—— 'Die wissenschaftlichen Ursprünge und die künftige Verfassung der sozialen Marktwirtschaft', in *Wirtschaftspolitische Chronik*, 22/3 (Cologne, 1973).

—— 'Dreißig Jahre soziale Marktwirtschaft: Rückblick und Vorschau', in *25 Jahre Seminar für Staatsbürgerkunde e. V. Olpe, 1951–1976, Heimvolkshochschule Haus Wildenstein* (Olpe, n.d.), 12–25.

—— *Alfred Müller-Armack: Ausgewählte Werke*, ed. E. Dürr, H. Hoffmann, E. Tuchtfeldt, and C. Watrin: *Genealogie der sozialen Marktwirtschaft: Frühschriften und weiterführende Konzepte* (2nd edn.; Bern, 1981); *Religion und Wirtschaft: Geistesgeschichtliche Hintergründe unserer europäischen Lebensform* (3rd edn.; Bern, 1981); *Diagnose unserer Gegenwart: Zur Bestimmung unseres geistesgeschichtlichen Standorts* (2nd edn.; Bern, 1981).

—— *Wirtschaftsordnung und Wirtschaftspolitik: Studien und Konzepte zur sozialen Marktwirtschaft und zur europäischen Integration* (2nd edn.; Bern, 1976).

—— and Schmidt, H. B. (eds.), *Wirtschafts- und Finanzpolitik im Zeichen der sozialen Marktwirtschaft. Festgabe für Franz Etzel* (Stuttgart-Degerloch, 1967).

Neumark, F., 'Erinnerung an Wilhelm Röpke', in Ludwig-Erhard-Stiftung, Bonn (ed.), *Wilhelm Röpke: Beiträge zu seinem Leben und Werk* (Stuttgart, 1980).

Nelson, Leonhard, *Politics and Education* (trans. W. Lonsdale; London, 1928).

Oppenheimer, Franz, *Die soziale Frage und der Sozialismus: Eine kritische Auseinandersetzung mit der marxistischen Theorie* (Jena, 1925).

—— *Erlebtes, Erstrebtes, Erreichtes: Lebenserinnerungen* (Düsseldorf, 1964).

Rieger, Wilhelm, 'Die Wiederherstellung einer stabilen Rechnungseinheit', in *Wilhelm Rieger: Erinnerungen und Dokumente aus 50 Jahren seines Wirkens*, ed. J. Fettel (Nuremberg, 1968).

Röpke, Wilhelm, *Die Arbeitsleistung im deutschen Kalibergbau unter besonderer Berücksichtigung des hannoverschen Kalibergbaus* (Berlin, 1922).

—— *Die Konjunktur: Ein systematischer Versuch als Beitrag zur Morphologie der Verkehrswirtschaft* (Jena, 1922).

—— *Geld und Außenhandel* (Jena, 1925).

—— 'Auslandskredite und Konjunktur' in K. Diehl (ed.), *Schriften des Vereins für Socialpolitik*, clxxiii: *Beiträge zur Wirtschaftstheorie, Konjunkturforschung und Konjunkturtheorie* (Munich, 1928).

—— 'Praktische Konjunkturpolitik: Die Arbeit der Braunskommission', *Weltwirtschaftliches Archiv*, 34/2 (1931), 423–64.

—— 'Trends in German Business Cycle Policy', *Economic Journal*, 43 (1933), 427–41.

—— *German Commercial Policy* (London, 1934).

—— *Die Lehre von der Wirtschaft* (Vienna, 1937).

—— *Die Gesellschaftskrise der Gegenwart* (4th rev. edn.; Zurich, 1942), trans. A. and P. S. Jacobsohn as *The Social Crisis of Our Time* (London, 1950).

—— *International Economic Disintegration* (London, 1942).

—— *Civitas Humana: Grundlagen der Gesellschafts- und Wirtschaftsreform* (Erlenbach-Zurich, 1944); trans. C. S. Fox as *Civitas Humana: A Humane Order of Society* (London, 1948).

—— *Die deutsche Frage* (Erlenbach-Zurich, 1945); trans. E. W. Dickes as *The German Question* (London, 1946).

—— *Ist die deutsche Wirtschaftspolitik richtig? Analyse und Kritik* (Stuttgart, 1950).

—— *Maß und Mitte* (Erlenbach-Zurich, 1950).

—— 'Wirtschaftssystem und internationale Ordnung', *ORDO: Jahrbuch für die Ordnung von Wirtschaft und Gesellschaft*, 4 (1952).

Röpke, Wilhelm, 'Unentwickelte Länder', *ORDO: Jahrbuch für die Ordnung von Wirtschaft und Gesellschaft*, 5 (1953).

—— *Welfare, Freedom and Inflation* (London, 1957).

—— *Jenseits von Angebot und Nachfrage* (Erlenbach-Zurich, 1958); trans. E. Henderson as *A Humane Economy: The Social Framework of the Free Market* (London, 1960).

—— 'Gemeinsamer Markt und Freihandelszone: 28 Thesen als Richtpunkte', *ORDO: Jahrbuch für die Ordnung von Wirtschaft und Gesellschaft*, 10 (1958), 31–62.

—— 'Zwischenbilanz der europäischen Wirtschaftspolitik. Kritische Nachlese', *ORDO: Jahrbuch für die Ordnung von Wirtschaft und Gesellschaft*, 11 (1959), 69–94.

—— *Wilhelm Röpke, Briefe 1934–1936: Der innere Kompaß*, ed. E. Röpke (Erlenbach-Zurich, 1976).

Rüstow, Alexander, *Das Versagen des Wirtschaftsliberalismus* (2nd edn.; n.p., 1950).

—— 'Die staatspolitischen Voraussetzungen des wirtschaftspolitischen Liberalismus', in *Alexander Rüstow, Rede und Antwort: 21 Reden und viele Diskussionsbeiträge aus den Jahren 1932–62*, ed. W. Hoch (Ludwigsberg, 1963).

—— *Freedom and Domination: A Historical Critique of Civilization* (abr. and trans. S. A. Attansio, ed. and introd. D. A. Rustow; Princeton, NJ, 1980).

Sauermann, H., and Mestmäcker, E.-J., *Wirtschaftsordnung und Staatsverfassung. Festschrift für Franz Böhm zum 80. Geburtstag* (Tübingen, 1975).

Schröder, G., Müller-Armack, A., Hohmann, K., Gross, J., and Altmann, R. (eds.), *Ludwig Erhard: Beiträge zu seiner politischen Biographie. Festschrift zum fünfundsiebzigsten Geburtstag* (Frankfurt/M., 1971).

Schröder P. (ed.), *Vernunft, Erkenntnis, Sittlichkeit: Internationales philosophisches Symposion Göttingen vom 27.–29. Oktober 1977 aus Anlaß des 50. Todestages von Leonhard Nelson* (Hamburg, 1979).

Spencer, Herbert, *The Man Versus the State* (London, 1884).

Secondary Sources

Abelshauser, W., 'Die Ordnungspolitische Epochenbedeutung der Weltwirtschaftskrise in Deutschland: Ein Beitrag zur Entstehungsgeschichte der sozialen Marktwirtschaft', in D. Petzina (ed.), *Ordnungspolitische Weichenstellungen nach dem zweiten Weltkrieg* (Berlin, 1991).

—— *Wirtschaft in Westdeutschland 1945–1948: Rekonstruktion und Wachstumsbedingungen in der amerikanischen und britischen Zone* (Stuttgart, 1975).

—— 'Freiheitlicher Sozialismus oder soziale Marktwirtschaft? Die Gutachtertagung über Grundfragen der Wirtschaftsplanung und Wirtschaftslenkung am 21. und 22. Juni 1946', *Vierteljahreshefte für Zeitgeschichte*, 24/4 (Oct. 1976), 415–49.

—— 'Probleme des Wiederaufbaus der westdeutschen Wirtschaft, 1945–1953', in H.-A. Winkler (ed.), *Politische Weichenstellungen im Nachkriegsdeutschland, 1945–1953* (Göttingen, 1979).

—— 'Korea, die Ruhr und Erhards Marktwirtschaft: Die Energiekrise von 1950/51', *Rheinische Vierteljahrsblätter*, 45/3 (1981), 287–316.

—— 'Ansätze "Korporativer Marktwirtschaft" in der Koreakrise der frühen fünfziger Jahre: Ein Briefwechsel zwischen dem Hohen Kommissar John McCloy und Bundeskanzler Konrad Adenauer', *Vierteljahrshefte für Zeitgeschichte*, 30/4 (Oct. 1982), 715–56.

—— 'The Economic Policy of Ludwig Erhard', *EUI Working Paper*, 80 (Florence, Jan. 1984).

—— 'The First Post-liberal Nation: Stages in the Development of Modern Corporatism in Germany', *European History Quarterly*, 14/3 (July 1984), 285–317.

—— 'Kohle und Marktwirtschaft: Ludwig Erhards Konflikt mit dem Unternehmensverband Ruhrbergbau 1957', *Vierteljahrshefte für Zeitgeschichte* 33/3 (July 1985), 489–546.

—— *Die Weimarer Republik als Wohlfahrtsstaat: Zum Verhältnis von Wirtschafts- und Sozialpolitik in der Industriegesellschaft* (Stuttgart, 1987).

Aktionsgemeinschaft Soziale Marktwirtschaft, e.v., *Aktionsprogramm* (Würzburg, 1958).

Albertin, L., *Liberalismus und Demokratie am Anfang der Weimarer Republik: Eine vergleichende Analyse der Deutschen Demokratischen Partei und der Deutschen Volkspartei* (Düsseldorf, 1972).

Albrecht, W., *Kurt Schumacher: Ein Leben für den demokratischen Sozialismus* (Bonn, 1985).

Ambrosius, G., *Die Durchsetzung der sozialen Marktwirtschaft in Westdeutschland 1945–49* (Stuttgart, 1977).

Becker, H. P., *Die soziale Frage im Neoliberalismus: Analyse und Kritik* (Heidelberg, 1965).

Beckerath, P. G., and Groppler, A., 'Der Begriff der sozialen Verantwortung bei Friedrich Naumann', *Preisschriften und Abhandlungen der Friedrich-Naumann-Stiftung*, 1 (Bonn, 1962).

Bentin, L. A., *Johannes Popitz und Karl Schmitt: Zur wirtschaftlichen Theorie des totalen Staates in Deutschland* (Munich, 1972).

Benz, W., *Von der Besatzungsherrschaft zur Bundesrepublik: Stationen einer Staatsgründung, 1946–1949* (Frankfurt/M., 1984).

Berghahn, V. R., *The Americanisation of West German Industry 1945–1973* (Leamington Spa, 1986).

—— 'Ideas into Politics: The Case of Ludwig Erhard', in R. J. Bullen, H. Pogge von Strandmann, and A. B. Polonsky (eds.), *Ideas into Politics: Aspects of European History, 1880–1950* (London, 1984).

—— and Friedrich, P. J., *Otto A. Friedrich, ein politischer Unternehmer: Sein Leben und seine Zeit, 1902–1975* (Frankfurt/M., 1993).

Besson, W., 'Zur Frage der Staatsführung in der Weimarer Republik', *Vierteljahrshefte für Zeitgeschichte*, 7/1 (Jan. 1959), 84–111.

Bilger, F., *La Pensée économique libérale dans l'Allemagne contemporaine* (Paris, 1964).

Blaich, F., *Kartel- und Monopolpolitik im kaiserlichen Deutschland: Das Problem der Marktmacht im deutschen Reichstag zwischen 1879 und 1914* (Düsseldorf, 1973).

—— ' "Garantierter Kapitalismus": Subventionspolitik und Wirtschaftsordnung in Deutschland zwischen 1925 und 1932', *Zeitschrift für Unternehmensgeschichte*, 22/1 (Wiesbaden, 1977), 50–70.

Blum, R., *Soziale Marktwirtschaft: Wirtschaftspolitik zwischen Neoliberalismus und Ordoliberalismus* (Tübingen, 1969).

Blumenberg-Lampe, C., *Das wirtschaftspolitische Programm der 'Freiburger Kreise':*

Entwurf einer freiheitlich-sozialen Nachkriegswirtschaft. Nationalökonomen gegen den Nationalsozialismus (Berlin, 1973).

Böhme, H., *Deutschlands Weg zur Großmacht* (Cologne, 1966).

Borchardt, K., *Perspectives on Modern German Economic History and Policy* (trans. P. Lambert; Cambridge, 1991).

—— 'Wirtschaftspolitische Beratung in der Krise: Die Rolle der Wissenschaft', in H.-A. Winkler (ed.), *Die deutsche Staatskrise 1930–1933: Handlungsspielräume und Alternativen* (Munich, 1992).

—— and Schötz, H. O. (eds.), *Wirtschaftspolitik in der Krise: Die (Geheim-) Konferenz der Friedrich-List-Gesellschaft im September 1931 über die Möglichkeiten und Folgen einer Kreditausweitung* (Baden-Baden, 1991).

Braun, H.-J., *The German Economy in the Twentieth Century* (London, 1990).

Bresciani-Turroni, C., *The Economics of Inflation: A Study of Currency Depreciation in Post-war Germany, 1914–1923* (London, 1968; 1st edn. 1937).

Buchheim, C., 'Die Währungsreform 1948 in Westdeutschland', *Vierteljahrshefte für Zeitgeschichte*, 36/2 (Apr. 1988), 189–231.

—— *Die Wiedereingliederung Westdeutschlands in die Weltwirtschaft, 1945–1958* (Munich, 1990).

Bullen, R. J., Pogge von Strandmann, H., and Polonsky, A. B. (eds.), *Ideas into Politics: Aspects of European History, 1880–1950* (London, 1984).

Burbach, W., 'Friedrich Mittelhauve', in W. Först (ed.), *Beiderseits der Grenzen* (Cologne, 1987).

Büttner, U., 'Politische Alternativen zum Brüningschen Deflationskurs: Ein Beitrag zur Diskussion über "Ökonomische Zwangslagen" in der Endphase von Weimar', *Vierteljahrshefte für Zeitgeschichte*, 36/2 (Apr. 1989), 209–51.

Cairncross, A., *The Price of War: British Policy on German Reparations, 1941–1949* (Oxford, 1986).

Carlin, W., *The Development of Factor Distribution of Income and Profitability in West Germany, 1945–1973* (MS; D. Phil. thesis; Oxford, 1987).

—— 'Economic Reconstruction in Western Germany, 1945–55: The Displacement of "Vegetative Control"', in I. D. Turner (ed.), *Reconstruction in Post-war Germany: British Occupation Policy and the Western Zones, 1945–1955* (Oxford, 1989).

Connor, I., 'The Bavarian Government and the Refugee Problem', *European History Quarterly*, 16/2 (Apr. 1986), 131–53.

—— 'The Refugees and Currency Reform', in I. D. Turner (ed.), *Reconstruction in Post-war Germany: British Occupation Policy and the Western Zones, 1945–1955* (Oxford, 1989).

Curzon, G., 'International Economic Order: The Contribution of the Neo-liberals', in A. Peacock and H. Willgerodt (eds.), *German Neoliberals and the Social Market Economy* (London, 1989).

Dohn, L., 'Wirtschafts- und Sozialpolitik der Deutschen Demokratischen Partei und Deutschen Volkspartei', in K. Holl, G. Trautmann, and H. Vorländer (eds.), *Sozialer Liberalismus* (Göttingen, 1986).

Drexler, A., *Planwirtschaft in Westdeutschland, 1945–1948: Eine Fallstudie über die Textilbewirtschaftung in der britischen und Bizone* (Stuttgart, 1985).

Dürr, E.-W., *Wesen und Ziele des Ordoliberalismus* (Winthertur, 1954).

Edinger, L. J., *Kurt Schumacher: A Study in Personality and Political Behavior* (Stanford, Calif., 1965).

Ellwood, D. W., *Rebuilding Europe: Western Europe, America and Postwar Reconstruction* (London, 1992).

Eschenburg, T. *Jahre der Besatzung, 1945–1949* (Vol i of K. D. Bracher, T. Eschenburg, J. C. Fest, and E. Jäckel (eds.), *Geschichte der Bundesrepublik Deutschland*) (Stuttgart 1983).

Farquharson, J. E., *The Western Allies and the Politics of Food: Agrarian Management in Postwar Germany* (Leamington Spa, 1985).

Feldman, G. D., *Iron and Steel in the German Inflation, 1916–1923* (Princeton, NJ, 1977).

—— *The Experience of Inflation: International and Comparative Studies* (Berlin, 1985).

—— 'Industrialists, Bankers, and the Problem of Unemployment in the Weimar Republic', *Central European History*, 25/1 (1992) (Atlantic Highlands, NJ, 1993), 76–96.

—— (ed.), *Die Nachwirkungen der Inflation auf die deutsche Geschichte 1924–1933* (Munich, 1985).

—— Holtfrerich, C.-L., Ritter, G. A., and Witt, P. C. (eds.), *Die deutsche Inflation. Eine Zwischenbilanz: Beiträge zu Inflation und Wiederaufbau in Deutschland und Europa 1914–1924* (Berlin, 1982).

Fischer, C., *Entwurf eines Gesetzes zur Neuordnung des Geldwesens (Homburg Plan)* (Heidelberg, 1948).

Fischer, C. E., 'Die Geschichte der deutschen Versuche zur Lösung des Kartell- und Monopol-Problems', *Zeitschrift für die gesamte Staatswissenschaft*, 110 (1954), 431–2.

Folz, W. J., *Das geldtheoretische und geldpolitische Werk Walter Euckens* (Berlin, 1970).

Giersch, H., Paqué, K.-H., and Schmieding, H., *The Fading Miracle: Four Decades of Market Economy in Germany* (Cambridge, 1992).

Giles, J., *Students and National Socialism in Germany* (Princeton, NJ, 1985).

Gillingham, J., *Coal, Steel and the Rebirth of Europe, 1945–1955: The Germans and the French from Ruhr Conflict to Economic Community* (Cambridge, 1991).

Gimbel, J., *The American Occupation of Germany: Politics and the Military, 1945–49* (Stanford, Calif., 1968).

Glees, A., *Exile Politics in the Second World War: The German Social Democrats in Britain* (Oxford, 1982).

Grosser, D., Lange, T., Müller-Armack, A., and Neuss, B., *Soziale Marktwirtschaft: Geschichte, Konzept, Leistung* (2nd edn.; Stuttgart, 1990).

Hamerow, T. S., *The Social Foundations of German Unification: Struggles and Accomplishments* (Princeton, NJ, 1972).

Hayek, F. A. von, *The Road to Serfdom* (Chicago, 1944).

—— *Law, Legislation and Liberty*, ii: *The Mirage of Social Justice* (Chicago, 1976).

Held, M., *Sozialdemokratie und Keynesianismus: Von der Weltwirtschaftskrise bis zum Godesberger Programm* (Frankfurt/M., 1982).

Hentschel, V., 'Die Europäische Zahlungsunion und die deutschen Devisenkrisen, 1950/51', *Vierteljahrshefte für Zeitgeschichte*, 37/4 (Oct. 1989), 715–58.

—— *Ludwig Erhard: Ein Politikerleben* (Munich, 1996)

Herbst, L., 'Krisenüberwindung und Wirtschaftsneuordnung: Ludwig Erhards Beteiligung an den Nachkriegsplanungen am Ende des zweiten Weltkrieges', *Vierteljahrshefte für Zeitgeschichte*, 25/3 (July 1977), 305–40.

—— *Der totale Krieg und die Ordnung der Wirtschaft: Die Kriegswirtschaft im Spannungsfeld von Politik, Ideologie und Propaganda, 1939–1945* (Stuttgart, 1982).

—— Bührer, W., and Sowade, H. (eds.), *Vom Marshallplan zur EWG: Die Eingliederung der Bundesrepublik Deutschland in die westliche Welt* (Munich, 1990).

Hertz-Eichenrode, D., *Wirtschaftskrise und Arbeitsbeschaffung: Konjunturpolitik 1925/26 und die Grundlagen der Krisenpolitik Brünings* (Frankfurt/M., 1982).
Heusgen, C., *Ludwig Erhards Lehre von der sozialen Marktwirtschaft: Ursprünge, Kerngehalt, Wandlungen* (Bern, 1981).
Hildebrand, K., *Von Erhard zur Großen Koalition, 1963–1969* (vol. iv of K. D. Bracher, T. Eschenburg, J. C. Fest, E. Jäckel (eds.), *Geschichte der Bundesrepublik Deutschland*) (Stuttgart, 1984).
Hockerts, H. G., *Sozialpolitische Entscheidungen im Nachkriegsdeutschland* (Stuttgart, 1980).
Hogan, M. J., *The Marshall Plan: America, Britain and the Reconstruction of Western Europe, 1947–1952* (Cambridge, 1987).
Hohmann, K. *Fränkische Lebensbilder,* ii: *Ludwig Erhard (1897–1977)* (Neustadt-Aisch, 1984).
Holl, K. (ed.), *Wirtschaftskrise und Liberale Demokratie: Das Ende der Weimarer Republik und die gegenwärtige Situation* (Göttingen, 1978).
Holtfrerich, C.-L., *Die deutsche Inflation 1914–1923: Ursachen und Folgen in internationaler Perspektive* (Berlin, 1980).
Hubsch, P., 'DGB Economic Policy with Particular Reference to the British Zone, 1945–49', in I. D. Turner (ed.), *Reconstruction in Post-war Germany: British Occupation Policy and the Western Zones, 1945–1955* (Oxford, 1989).
Hunold, A. (ed.), *Vollbeschäftigung, Inflation, und Planwirtschaft* (Erlenbach-Zurich, 1951).
—— (ed.), *Wirtschaft ohne Wunder* (Erlenbach-Zurich, 1953).
Hüttenberger, P., 'Wirtschaftsordnung und Interessenpolitik in der Kartellgesetzgebung der Bundesrepublik, 1949–1957', *Vierteljahrshefte für Zeitgeschichte,* 24/3 (July 1976), 287–307.
James, H., *The German Slump: Politics and Economics, 1924–1936* (Oxford, 1986).
Jens, W., 'The Classical Tradition in Germany: Grandeur and Decay', in E. J. Feuchtwanger (ed.), *Upheaval and Continuity: A Century of German History* (London, 1973).
Jones, L. B., *German Liberalism and the Dissolution of the Weimar Party System, 1919–1933* (Chapel Hill, 1990).
Kaplan, J. J., and Schleiminger, G., *The European Payments Union: Financial Diplomacy in the 1980s* (Oxford, 1989).
Kershaw, I. (ed.), *Weimar: Why Did German Democracy Fail?* (London, 1990).
Kloten, N., 'The Role of the Public Sector in the Social Market Economy', in A. Peacock and H. Willgerodt (eds.), *German Neoliberals and the Social Market Economy* (London, 1989).
Klotzbach, K., *Der Weg zur Staatspartei: Programmatik, praktische Politik und Organisation der deutschen Sozialdemokratie 1945 bis 1965* (Berlin, 1982).
Koerfer, D., *Kampf ums Kanzleramt: Erhard und Adenauer* (Stuttgart, 1987).
Könke, G., 'Planwirtschaft oder Marktwirtschaft? Ordnungspolitische Vorstellungen sozialdemokratischer Nationalökonomen in der Weimarer Republik', *Vierteljahrsschrift für Sozial- und Wirtschaftsgeschichte,* 77/4 (1990), 457–87.
Kramer, A., *The West German Economy, 1945–1955* (New York, 1991).
Krengel, R., *Anlagevermögen, Produktion und Beschäftigung der Industrie im Gebiet der BRD von 1924–56* (Berlin, 1958).
Krieger, W., *General Lucius D. Clay und die amerikansiche Deutschlandpolitik, 1945–1949* (Stuttgart, 1987).
Krohn, C. D., *Wirtschaftstheorie als politische Interessen: Die akademische Nation-*

alökonomie in Deutschland 1918–1933 (Frankfurt/M., 1981).

Kromphardt, W., *Marktspaltung und Kernplanung in der Volkswirtschaft* (Dortmunder Schriften zur Sozialforschung, 3; Hamburg, 1947).

Kronawetter, H., *Wirtschaftskonzeptionen und Wirtschaftspolitik der Sozialdemokratie in Bayern, 1945–1949* (Munich, 1988).

Kruedener, J. von (ed.), *Economic Crisis and Political Collapse: The Weimar Republic, 1924–1933* (Oxford, 1990).

Küsters, H. J., 'Adenauers Europapolitik in der Gründungsphase der EWG', *Vierteljahrshefte für Zeitgeschichte*, 31/4 (Oct. 1983), 646–73.

Laitenberger, V., 'Zur Programmatik und zur Politik Ludwig Erhards in der Vor- und Frühgeschichte des Bundesrepublik Deutschland', *Orientierungen zur Wirtschafts- und Gesellschaftspolitik*, 3 (1980), 19–24.

—— *Ludwig Erhard: Der Nationalökonom als Politiker* (Göttingen, 1986).

Lange, M.-G., 'Die FDP: Versuch einer Erneuerung des Liberalismus', *Studien zur Entwicklung der deutschen Parteien bis zur Bundestagswahl 1953*, Schriften des Instituts für Politische Wissenschaft (Stuttgart, 1955).

Leaman, J., *The Political Economy of West Germany, 1945–85, An Introduction* (London, 1988).

Lee, J., 'Policy and Performance in the German Economy, 1925–1935. A Comment on the Borchardt Thesis', in M. Laffan (ed.), *The Burden of German History, 1939–1945* (London, 1988).

Lenel, H. O., 'Does Germany Still Have a Social Market Economy?' in A. Peacock and H. Willgerodt (eds.), *Germany's Social Market Economy: Origins and Evolution* (London, 1989).

—— 'Zum Historikerstreit über die Produktionskapazitäten 1948', *Orientierungen zur Wirtschafts- und Gesellschaftspolitik*, 54 (Dec. 1992), 72–7.

Löwenthal, R., and Schwarz, H.-P. (eds.), *Die zweite Republik: 25 Jahre Bundesrepublik Deutschland—eine Bilanz* (Stuttgart-Degerloch, 1974).

Lukomski, J. M., *Ludwig Erhard, der Mensch und der Politiker* (2nd edn.; Düsseldorf, 1965).

Maier, C. S., *Recasting Bourgeois Europe: Stabilization in France, Germany and Italy in the Decade after World War I* (Princeton, NJ, 1975; repr. 1988).

Mandt, T., '25 Jahre textilwirtschaftliche Forschung in Münster', *Textildienst*, 10/9 (Münster, 1965).

—— *25 Jahre Forschungsstelle für allgemeine und textile Marktwirtschaft an der Universität Münster, 1946–1966* (n.p., n.d.).

Mehringer, H., *Waldemar von Knoeringen: Eine politische Biographie. Der Weg vom revolutionärem Sozialismus zur sozialen Demokratie* (Munich, 1989).

Meier-Rust, K., 'Der neue Liberalismus nach Alexander Rüstow', *Orientierungen zur Wirtschafts- und Gesellschaftspolitik*, 56 (Junes 1993), 10–14.

Meyer, T., *Grundwerte und Wissenschaft im demokratischen Sozialismus* (Berlin, 1978).

Miller, S., 'Zur Wirkungsgeschichte des Godesberger Programms', in B. Rebe, K. Lampe, and R. von Thadden (eds.), *Idee und Pragmatik in der politischen Entscheidung. Alfred Kubel zum 75. Geburtstag* (Bonn, 1984).

Milward, A. S., *The Reconstruction of Western Europe, 1945–1951* (London, 1984).

—— *The European Rescue of the Nation-State* (London, 1992).

Möller, H., 'Die westdeutsche Währungsreform von 1948', in Deutsche Bundesbank (ed.), *Währung und Wirtschaft in Westdeutschland, 1876–1975* (Frankfurt/M., 1976).

Möller, H., 'The Reconstruction of the International Economic Order After the Second World War and the Integration of the Federal Republic of Germany into the World Economy', *Zeitschrift für die gesamte Staatswissenschaft*, 137/3 (Sept. 1981), 344–66.

Nawroth, E. E., *Die Sozial- und Wirtschaftsphilosophie des Neoliberalismus* (Heidelberg, 1962).

Nicholls, A. J., 'Ludwig Erhard and German Liberalism—An Ambivalent Relationship?', in K. H. Jarausch and L. E. Jones (eds.), *In Search of Liberal Germany, Studies in the History of German Liberalism from 1798 to the Present* (Providence, RI, 1990), pp. 389–416

Noelle, E., and Neumann, E. P., *Jahrbuch der öffentlichen Meinung, 1945–1955* (Allensbach/Bodensee, 1956).

Noelle-Neumann, E., 'Disziplin, Hoffnung, Unsicherheit: Umfragen nach der Währungsreform', *Orientierungen zur Wirtschafts- und Gesellschaftspolitik*, 36 (June 1988).

Ortlieb, H.-D. (ed.), *Eduard Heimann: Sozialismus im Wandel der modernen Gesellschaft. Aufsätze zur Theorie und Praxis. Ein Erinnerungsband* (Berlin, 1975).

Peacock, A., and Willgerodt, H. (eds.), *German Neoliberals and the Social Market Economy* (London, 1989).

—— (eds.), *Germany's Social Market Economy: Origins and Evolution* (London, 1989).

Petzina, D., and Euchner, W. (eds.), *Wirtschaftspolitik im britischen Besatzungsgebiet, 1945–49* (Düsseldorf, 1984).

Pogge von Strandmann, H., 'Widersprüche im Modernisierungsprozeß Deutschlands: Der Kampf der verarbeitenden Industrie gegen die Schwerindustrie', in D. Stegmann, B.-J. Wendt, and P. C. Witt (eds.), *Industrielle Gesellschaft und politisches System: Beiträge zur politischen Sozialgeschichte. Festschrift für Fritz Fischer* (Bonn, 1978).

Pörtner, E., *Die Verfassungspolitik der Liberalen—1919—Ein Beitrag zur Deutung der Weimarer Verfassung* (Bonn, 1973).

Pridham, G., *Christian Democracy in Western Germany: The CDU in Government and Opposition, 1945–1976* (London, 1977).

Reich, S., *The Fruits of Fascism: Postwar Prosperity in Historical Perspective* (Ithaca, NY, 1990).

Riese, H., 'Ordnungsidee und Ordnungspolitik: Kritik einer wirtschaftspolitischen Konzeption', *Kyklos: Internationale Zeitschrift für Sozialwissenschaften*, 25 (1972), 24–48.

Ritschl, A., 'Die Währungsreform von 1948 und der Wiederaufstieg der westdeutschen Industrie: Zu den Thesen von Matthias Manz und Werner Abelshauser über die Produktionswirkungen der westdeutschen Industrie', *Vierteljahrshefte für Zeitgeschichte*, 33/1 (Jan. 1985), 136–65.

Rittig, G., 'Sozialismus und Liberalismus: Annäherung oder Distanz ihrer wirtschaftspolitischen Anschauungen', *Die neue Gesellschaft*, 1 (1954).

Robert, R., *Konzentrationspolitik in der Bundesrepublik: Das Beispiel der Entstehung des Gesetzes gegen Wettbewerbsbeschränkungen* (Berlin, 1976).

Röder, W., *Die deutschen Exilgruppen in Großbritannien: Ein Beitrag zur Geschichte des Widerstandes gegen den Nationalsozialismus* (Hanover, 1968).

Roesler, J., 'The Rise and Fall of the Planned Economy', *German History*, 9/1 (Oxford, 1991), 46–61.

Roseman, M., 'The Uncontrolled Economy: Ruhr Coal Production, 1945–8', in

I. D. Turner (ed.), *Reconstruction in Post-war Germany: British Occupation Policy and the Western Zones, 1945–1955* (Oxford, 1989).

—— *Recasting the Ruhr: Manpower, Economic Recovery and Labour Relations in the Ruhr Mines, 1945–58* (Oxford, 1991).

Rupp, H. K., *Politische Geschichte der Bundesrepublik Deutschland: Entstehung und Entwicklung. Eine Einführung* (Stuttgart, 1978).

Scharf, C., and Schröder, H.-J., (eds.), *Die Deutschlandpolitik Großbritanniens und die britische Zone 1945–1949* (Wiesbaden, 1979).

Schiller, K., *Scheinprobleme und Existenzfragen: Vierwirtschaftspolitische Hauptaufgaben der deutschen Gegenwart* (Munich, 1951).

—— *Thesen zur praktischen Gestaltung unserer Wirtschaftspolitik aus sozialistischer Sicht. Vortrag gehalten auf einer Tagung von Christen und Sozialisten in Königswinter von 3, bis 5. January 1952* (Hamburg, n.d.).

—— 'Produktivitätssteigerung und Vollbeschäftigung durch Planung und Wettbewerb', in SPD (Vorstand), *Die Wirtschaftspolitik der SPD* (Bonn, n.d.).

—— 'Sozialismus und Wettbewerb', in C. Schmid, K. Schiller, and E. Potthoff (eds.), *Grundfragen moderner Wirtschaftspolitik* (Frankfurt/M., 1958).

—— 'Wirtschaftspolitik', in E. von Beckerath (ed.), *Handwörterbuch der Sozialwissenschaften*, 12 (Stuttgart, 1962).

—— *Der Ökonom und die Gesellschaft: Das freiheitliche und das soziale Element in der modernen Wirtschaftspolitik, Vorträge und Aufsätze* (Stuttgart, 1964).

Schmid, C., Schiller, K., and Potthoff, E. (eds.), *Grundfragen moderner Wirtschaftspolitik* (Frankfurt/M., 1958).

Schmid, H., *Neoliberalismus und Katholische Soziallehre: Eine Konfrontierung* (Cologne, 1954).

Schmitter, P. C., 'Still the Century of Corporatism?', *Review of Politics*, 36/1 (Notre Dame, Ind., Jan. 1974).

Schmölders, G., *Der Wetterbewer als Mittel volkswirtschaftlicher Leistungssteigerung und Leistungsauslese* (Berlin, 1942).

Schmoller, G. von, *Grundriß der allgemeinen Volkslehre* (Leipzig, 1900).

Schneider, W., *Die Deutsche Demokratische Partei in der Weimarer Republik 1924–1930* (Munich, 1978).

Schröder, K., *Die FDP in der britischen Besatzungszone, 1946–1948: Ein Beitrag zur Organisationsstruktur der Liberalen im Nachkriegsdeutschland* (Düsseldorf, 1984).

Schulz, G., 'Inflationstrauma, Finanzpolitik und Krisenbekämpfung in den Jahren der Wirtschaftskrise, 1930–1933', in G. Feldman (ed.), *Die Nachwirkungen der Inflation auf die deutsche Geschichte, 1924–1933* (Munich, 1985).

Schwarz, H.-P., *Vom Reich zur Bundesrepublik: Deutschland im Widerstreit der außenpolitischen Konzeptionen in den Jahren der Besatzungsherrschaft, 1945–1949* (2nd edn.; Neuwied/Berlin, 1980).

—— *Die Ära Adenauer: Gründerjahre der Republik, 1949–1957* (vol. ii of K. D. Bracher, T. Eschenburg, J. C. Fest, and E. Jäckel (eds.), *Geschichte der Bundesrepublik Deutschland*) (Stuttgart, 1981).

—— *Die Ära Adenauer: Epochenwechsel, 1957–1963* (vol. iii of K. D. Bracher, T. Eschenburg, J. C. Fest, and E. Jäckel (eds.), *Geschichte der Bundesrepublik Deutschland*) (Stuttgart, 1983).

—— *Adenauer: Der Aufstieg, 1876–1952* (3rd edn.; Stuttgart, 1991).

—— *Adenauer: Der Staatsmann: 1952–1967* (Stuttgart, 1991).

Seraphim, H. J., *25 Jahre Institut für Siedlungs- und Wohnungswesen der westfälischen Wilhelm-Universität zu Münster* (Münster, 1964).

Sering, P., *Jenseits des Kapitalismus* (Lauf bei Nürnberg, 1947).

Sheehan, J. J., *German Liberalism in the Nineteenth Century* (Chicago, 1978).

Siebler, H.-U., *Wirtschaftstheorie, Wirtschaftspolitik und das Gesetz gegen Wettbewerbsbeschränkungen: Begründung und Begründbarkeit neo-liberaler Wettbewerbspolitik* (Diss.; Frankfurt/M., 1966).

Smyser, W. R., *The Economy of United Germany: Colossus at the Crossroads* (London, 1992).

Stamp, A. M., 'Germany without Incentive', *Lloyds Bank Review*, 5 (July 1947), 14–28.

Stephan, W., *Aufstieg und Verfall des Linksliberalismus 1918–1933: Geschichte der Deutschen Demokratischen Partei* (Göttingen, 1973).

Stolper, G., *German Realities* (New York, 1948).

Stolper, T., *Ein Leben in Brennpunkten unserer Zeit: Gustav Stolper 1888–1947* (Stuttgart, 1979).

Stolper, W. F., and Roskamp, K. W., 'Planning a Free Economy: Germany 1945–1960', *Zeitschrift für die gesamte Staatswissenschaft*, 135/3 (1979), 374–404.

Theiner, P., *Sozialer Liberalismus und deutsche Weltpolitik: Friedrich Naumann im Wilhelminischen Deutschland* (Baden-Baden, 1983).

Treue, W., *Deutsche Parteiprogramme, 1861–1954* (Göttingen, Frankfurt/M., 1954).

Turner, H. A., *German Big Business and the Rise of Hitler* (Oxford, 1985).

Turner, I. D., 'Great Britain and the Post-war Currency Reform', *Historical Journal*, 30/3 (1987), 685–708.

—— (ed.), *Reconstruction in Post-war Germany: British Occupation Policy and the Western Zones, 1945–1955* (Oxford, 1989).

Ungeheuer, H.-J., *Die Wirtschaftsprogrammatik und Wirtschaftspolitik der Liberalen Parteien Deutschlands unter besonderer Berücksichtigung der Entwicklung in der SBZ und in der britischen Zone* (MA thesis; Bonn, 1982).

Vorländer, H., 'Der soziale Liberalismus der FDP', in K. Holl, G. Trautmann, and H. Vorländer (eds.), *Sozialer Liberalismus* (Göttingen, 1986).

Warner, I., 'Allied–German Negotiations on the Deconcentration of the West German Steel Industry' in I. D. Turner (ed.), *Reconstruction in Post-war Germany: British Occupation Policy and the Western Zones, 1945–1955* (Oxford, 1989).

Watrin, C., 'The Principles of the Social Market Economy: Its Origins and Early History', in R. Richter (ed.), *A Symposium: Currency and Economic Reform. West Germany after World War II, Zeitschrift für die gesamte Staatswissenschaft*, Sonderheft, 135 (Tübingen, 1979), 405–25.

Watrin, C., *Alfred Müller-Armack* (Krefeld, 1980).

—— 'The Social Market Economy: Its Significance for the Economic Development of the Federal Republic of Germany in the Early Years of the Konrad Adenauer Administration', in A. J. Nicholls (ed.), *Adenauer at Oxford: The Konrad Adenauer Memorial Lectures* (Oxford, 1983).

Weber, A., 'Sozialistische Marktwirtschaft', in *Das sozialistische Jahrhundert* (Berlin, 1950), no. 1.

Weissbrod, B., *Schwerindustrie in der Weimarer Republik: Interessenpolitik zwischen Stabilisierung und Krise* (Wuppertal, 1978).

Weisser, G., *Sozialisierung bei freisozialistischer Wirtschaftsverfassung* (Hamburg, 1947).

—— 'Vielgestaltiges soziales Leben', in Schmid, C., Schiller, K., and Potthoff, K., (eds.), *Grundfragen moderner Wirtschaftspolitik* (Frankfurt/M., 1958).

Wellman, H., *Die soziale Marktwirtschaft im Spiegel von Meinungsumfragen* (Ph.D. thesis; Cologne, 1962).

Weymar, P., *Konrad Adenauer: The Authorized Biography* (London, 1957).

Wheeler-Bennett, J. W., and Nicholls, A. J., *The Semblance of Peace: The International Settlement after the Second World War* (London, 1972).

Winkler, H.-A., *Von der Revolution zur Stabilisierung: Arbeiter und Arbeiterbewegung in der Weimarer Republik, 1918 bis 1924* (Berlin, 1984).

—— *Der Schein der Normalität: Arbeiter und Arbeiterbewegung in der Weimarer Republik, 1924 bis 1930* (Berlin, 1985).

Woodham-Smith, C. B., *The Great Hunger: Ireland 1845–1849* (London, 1962; revised edn. 1980).

Wünsche, H. F., *Ludwig Erhards Gesellschafts- und Wirtschaftskonzeption: Soziale Marktwirtschaft als politische Ökonomie* (Stuttgart, 1986).

Zundel, R., *Die Erben des Liberalismus* (Freudenstadt, 1971).

Index